THE
SHAPING
OF
SOUTHERN
CULTURE

· · · · · · · · ·

THE
SHAPING
OF
SOUTHERN
CULTURE

Honor, Grace, and War, 1760s–1890s

BERTRAM WYATT-BROWN

The University of North Carolina Press

Chapel Hill and London

Designed by Jackie Johnson
Set in New Baskerville by
Tseng Informations Systems, Inc.

P. iii: Photograph by William G. Rose

Manufactured in the
United States of America

The paper in this book meets the
guidelines for permanence and durability
of the Committee on Production Guidelines
for Book Longevity of the Council
on Library Resources.

Library of Congress
Cataloging-in-Publication Data
Wyatt-Brown, Bertram, 1932–
The shaping of Southern culture:
honor, grace, and war, 1760s–1880s /
Bertram Wyatt-Brown.
p. cm.
Includes bibliographical references (p.)
and index.
ISBN 0-8078-2596-4 (alk. paper) —
ISBN 0-8078-4912-x (pbk.: alk. paper)
1. Southern states—Civilization—1775–1865.
2. Southern States—Moral conditions.
3. Honor—Southern States—History.
4. Southern States—Social life and customs—
1775–1865. 5. Rhetoric—Social aspects—
Southern States—History. 6. United States
—History—Civil War, 1861–1865—Influence.
I. Title.
F213 .W957 2001
975.03—dc21 00-069952

05 04 03 02 01 5 4 3 2 1

The following chapters have been previously
published and were revised for this volume.
They appear here by permission.

Chapter 2, as "Honour and American
Republicanism: A Neglected Corollary," in
Ideology and the Historians, Historical Studies 17
(Dublin: Lilliput Press, 1991), 49–65.

Chapter 3, as "Andrew Jackson's Honor,"
Journal of the Early Republic 17 (Spring 1997):
1–36. Copyright © 1997 Society for Historians
of the Early American Republic.

Chapter 4, as "Religion and the Civilizing
Process in the Early American South,
1600–1860," in *Evangelicalism: Comparative
Studies of Popular Protestantism in North America,
the British Isles, and Beyond,
1700–1900*, edited by Mark A. Noll et al. (New
York: Oxford University Press, 1994). Used by
permission of Oxford University Press, Inc.

Chapter 6, as "Modernizing Southern Slavery:
The Proslavery Argument Reinterpreted," in
*Region, Race, and Reconstruction: Essays in Honor
of C. Vann Woodward*, edited by James M.
McPherson and J. Morgan Kousser (New York:
Oxford University Press, 1982). Used by
permission of Oxford University Press, Inc.

Chapter 7, as "Church, Honor, and Secession,"
in *Religion and the American Civil War*, edited by
Randall Miller, Harry Stout, and Charles Wilson
(New York: Oxford University Press, 1998).
Used by permission of Oxford
University Press, Inc.

For my sister,

Laura Serena James,

and in memory of my mother,

Laura Little Wyatt-Brown,

and my daughter,

Laura Mathews Wyatt-Brown

CONTENTS

Preface, *ix*

Part I. Race and Politics

ONE
Dignity, Deception, and Identity in the Male Slave Experience, *3*

TWO
Honor, Dread of Enslavement, and Revolutionary Rhetoric, *31*

THREE
Andrew Jackson's Honor, *56*

Part II. Grace: Southern Religion in Transition

FOUR
Religion and the Unchurched in the Old South, *83*

FIVE
Paradox, Shame, and Grace in the Backcountry, *106*

SIX
Modernizing Slave-Owning Rhetoric, *136*

SEVEN
Church, Honor, and Disunionism, *154*

Part III. War and Aftermath

EIGHT
Shameful Submission and Honorable Secession, *177*

NINE
Innocence, War, and Horror, *203*

TEN
Death of a Nation, *230*

ELEVEN
Honor Chastened, *255*

TWELVE
Honor Redeemed in Blood, *270*

APPENDIX
Recent Historiography on Honor, *296*

Notes, *305*

Acknowledgments, *397*

Index, *401*

PREFACE

On 12 April 1865 the task of receiving the surrender of Major General John B. Gordon's Confederate troops fell to Major General Joshua L. Chamberlain, serving under Ulysses S. Grant. The commander of the Union armies had ordered that there be no untoward demonstration of victory that might embarrass the defeated foe. Rather, Grant had in mind as solemn a show of respect as seemed fitting. The youthful Chamberlain was eager to comply. The dramatic scene that followed, beginning at nine o'clock in the morning, epitomized many of the concerns of this book.

From the hilltop where the Rebel soldiers stood, they could see the Appomattox Courthouse below. Without stirring drums, blaring trumpets or any music whatsoever, the defeated soldiers—lice-ridden, gaunt, emotionally drained—fell into line. The surrendering units moved forward "with practiced ease in the old route step," according to one description. Chamberlain ordered his subordinates, as he later recounted, to have their men reach "the position of 'salute' in the manual of arms as each body of the Confederates passed us." He did not command the officers to bark: "present arms." Inappropriately, that order would have signified "the highest possible honor to be paid even to a president."[1] Instead, it was the "carry arms" command, with the weapon "held by the right hand and perpendicular to the shoulder." Chamberlain signaled the bugler as Gordon, Robert E. Lee's subordinate, arrived opposite himself. While the martial notes filled the air, the Union ranks came to " 'attention,' " Chamberlain recalled. There rang out the crisp, chunky noise of the soldiers' hands as they grasped musket stocks in unison.

According to Chamberlain, General Gordon, young, slim, and chivalric, rode at the head of his troops. "His chin drooped to his breast, downhearted and dejected in appearance almost beyond description." But responding to the bugle and the "snap of arms" echoing down the lines, the Rebel commander touched "his horse gently with his spur, so that the animal slightly reared, and as he wheeled, horse and rider made one motion, the horse's head swung down with a graceful bow and General Gordon dropped his sword point to his toe in salutation." Chamberlain ordered all the Federals to follow the procedure of the first ranks as the men in homespun gray began their sad work. "Bayonets were affixed to muskets, arms stacked, and cartridge boxes unslung and hung upon the stacks." The war-weary Rebels ceremoniously draped their old and tattered battle flags on the piles of weapons or spread them reverently on the ground. "Some of the men who had carried and followed those ragged standards through the four long years of strife," Chamberlain remarked, "rushed, regardless of all discipline from the ranks, bent about their old flags, and pressed them to their lips with burning tears."[2]

The ritual of surrender and sober celebration of victory that the ceremony expressed was deeply embedded in martial honor—what the soldiers of both sides considered to be the code's highest form of sanctification. Chamberlain understood perfectly. In a Boston newspaper in 1878, he explained, "Whatever was surrendered and laid down, it was not manhood, and not honor. Manhood arose, and honor was plighted and received." The allusion to a marital love pledged and ratified by formal tie was appropriate to the reuniting of the temporarily separated sections. General Lee's men, Chamberlain asserted, knew that their simple ethic required them not to betray the rules of their parole. Never again were they to take up arms against the United States. "They are men of honor, and they meant it, and their word of honor is good," the Union general had then affirmed. In laying down their arms and pledging themselves loyal citizens once more, the Union general claimed, the men had also surrendered the ideal as well as the institutional existence of slavery. "God, in His providence, in His justice, in His mercy, in His great covenant with our fathers, set slavery in the forefront, and it was swept aside as with a whirlwind, when the mighty pageant of the people passed on to its triumph."[3]

Chamberlain's introduction of divinity into his recollection was most fitting even if he identified God's divine plan with emancipation, a proposition that few white Southerners would have countenanced. Despite the military foundation of the rites near the Virginia courthouse, the religious component must always figure in determining the course of regional identity and history, particularly in a work of this nature. Ironically, indeed tragically, the same honor which the general from Maine and the general from Georgia had so elegantly acknowledged in their liturgy of capitulation also sustained the cause of white superiority and the imperative of black submission. Chamberlain overlooked that vital point in his postwar expression of sectional reconciliation, a popular undertaking in the 1870s and 1880s. For at least half a century, the Old South has been largely defined almost exclusively by the adherence of its white loyalists to slavery and racial sanction. In all other respects it was merely a replication of the North. The historian James Oakes has gone so far as to maintain that in the South, "except for its defense of bondage, the slaveholders' ideology was strikingly similar to the Republican party ideology of the 1850's."[4] John C. Calhoun and most others would have heartily denounced such a claim.

The preeminence of race domination in Southern life—whether in the form of bondage or the postemancipation forms of race proscriptions—cannot be gainsaid. For that reason, the book begins with aspects of African American bondage. Yet, as a cultural determinant, two other factors apart from white hegemony contributed to that preeminence. These were, first, an adherence to the code of honor; and second, a commitment to evangelical faith. This book proposes honor as the ethic which white Southerners believed supported the other two pillars of their society: white supremacy and Christian faith.

In *Southern Honor: Ethics and Behavior in the Old South* (1982), I offered a lengthy definition of that elusive topic, not to be repeated here. At the time that volume appeared, the concept of honor required close investigation. The venerable ethic was not then part of contemporary academic or popular conventions. Since 1982 *manliness* and *masculinity* have assumed historiographical prominence. The reader might wonder why these terms are not employed here, particularly since honorableness remains more elusive, complicated, and easily misconstrued. Indeed, according to one scholar, manliness had already become the preferred designation by the end of the nineteenth century. Then the word *masculinity*, practically unheard-of before, dominated the discourse and became the fashionable term. Meantime *honor* all but disappeared linguistically, except in military circles, the monitoring of college examinations, and the accepting of checks. That shift, it has been argued, symbolized the *embourgeoisement* of the concept.[5] But scholars who currently use the term *masculinity* are most often referring to Northern, possibly New England, usages. The distinction between Northern and Southern versions will become clearer in this work. Despite the prevailing mode, I still prefer the term *honor*. It stresses the division of the sexes and the expectations of not just brave but right behavior as perceived by the community involved, regardless of the standards we might nowadays apply to the past.

Anyhow, from 1760 to 1890 (and even beyond), Southern honor embraced hierarchy—especially about race—which the word *manliness* or *masculinity* cannot convey. Oddly, as we will see, slavery was sustained by notions of honor. Lynch law carried similar messages of honor and shame, purity and degradation just as *Blut und Ehre*, the Nazi slogan of blood and honor served to justify the enslavement and even annihilation of a European race. At the same time, honorableness concerned reputation for integrity and also responsibility for meeting conventional expectations. In conforming to the language of the era under discussion, however, I am by no means advocating an uncritical approach to the ways that the ethic of white, male, hierarchical honor was applied or even understood.

With concern for the second element, grace, that appears in the subtitle, scholars of Mediterranean concepts of honor—Julian Pitt-Rivers in particular—have come to realize that honor and spiritual benediction are more closely linked than they had imagined when first embarking in the 1960s on explorations of the ethic in Mediterranean societies.[6] Playing on the irony of their juxtaposition, Shakespeare recognized such a connection in his play *Love's Labour's Lost*, as the opening epigraph reveals. Grace and honor are conjoined in his difficult but significant rendering. They are distinguishable but finally cannot be separated altogether. In its most essential meaning, of course, grace is the gift of mercy and forgiveness that God affords his sinful, wretched human creatures. As used in these pages, grace must be treated in this light but also as the sacred element in the concept of honor—God's conferment upon those who claim to honor Him and yet pursue matters of war, community, governance, and daily routine certain of their state of grace.

Surprisingly, honor, when coupled with grace, may even amalgamate with the passion of Christian love. That is a strong statement. It might seem to defy the previous definitions of honor. Do we not know this form of honor when we see it? Honor may stimulate self-sacrifice even to the point of death. In American wars, we signify respect by the conferring of the highest medal that a republic can confer. A classmate at St. James School near Sharpsburg, Maryland, won the Congressional Medal of Honor posthumously for valorous conduct in the Korean War. He had saved his squad from being overrun by Chinese soldiers, but a mortar shell killed him before he could carry a wounded comrade to safety. To die for one's friends should be so rewarded with the nation's most distinguished medal.

There are also unwarlike expressions of honor as well—the decision to defy conventional prejudice of one sort or another and stoically undergo the stigma of shame, however long it may last. Some element of grace or striving for a higher goal must be present, it seems to me, in acts of justice or mercy that include honor but go beyond its secular meanings of status, fame and reputation. In our own day some Southern judges—Frank Johnson of Alabama, for instance—underwent such an ordeal during the backlash of the civil rights era. In crises of great magnitude or in decisions that transcend the ordinary, grace and honor may become one. Such courage was also present in the life and death of the Reverend Martin Luther King Jr.

Regrettably, however, both honor and grace or, more accurately religious preconceptions, can harmonize in a most tragic way. Throughout the era of slavery, Christians, reading the Book of Genesis, were certain that God had placed through Noah a "curse" upon his obnoxious son Ham and Ham's descendants, a malediction against those of Negro blood. Justifications for slavery flowed from that source. As Stephen R. Haynes sees the issue, we have generally failed to recognize the religious component in American white racism. Because they take a secular approach, most historians have ignored that element, just as they have often missed its connection with the ethic of honor. All mankind, traditional Calvinists maintained, were marked by Adam's Original Sin. It therefore followed that the curse against Ham imposed "Original Dishonor," to use Haynes's phrase, upon the black race and consigned all of such color to perpetual bondage. Looking upon the nakedness of his father, the patriarch, Ham had violated God's laws and shamed the old man, for which indiscretion punishment had to be exacted. The honor of God, the honor of the patriarchal order, which Noah represented, required stern vindication. In this light, honor and grace—as opposed to shame and dis-grace—were linked in advancing the religious proslavery argument and in the bedrock of Southern white folk tradition about race as well.[7]

At the same time, honor and grace may wear different and equally tragic masks. Grace can descend from the empyrean heights and be mistaken for the will of a misguided but determined community. The words of a presiding clergyman or the prayers of rioters often invoked the grace of God as the fires of an earthly hell licked at the quivering flesh of a black victim in a post–Civil War lynching. The witnesses to such traumatic scenes were certain that the act they performed was sanctioned by Holy Writ and had the blessing of a righteous God. In Morganton, North Carolina, in 1889, prayers of the mob executioners went heavenward, one might say, as two blacks met their doom in the rising flames.[8]

The spiritual aspect of honor is not easily described in historical terms. Yet we must acknowledge that a domain quite outside modern experience does exist. In this situation, logic and consistency have to surrender to utter bafflement and disgust. Can we truly understand how anyone, past or present, could seek a vindication of ideals by sacrificing some vulnerable creature, allegedly inferior?—And do so in the name of honor and grace? Yet, as if the relationship of those concepts were not already complex enough, the two principles can be poles apart. Christian orthodoxy has always related honor to a guiltless conscience—purity of soul. For the Church Fathers, only in worship of God could the believer find true honor. In this sense honor and grace become separable. Southern white Christians did not always recognize that polarity.

Few words are needed to explain the centrality of war in the Southern mentalité. By war is meant the American Revolution, the second war with England, in which Andrew Jackson played his famous role, and, above all, the Civil War. The role of honor in that last encounter has been almost overlooked. To be sure, historians when quoting contemporary fire-eaters often choose those passages referring to the Southerners' sense of insult over Charles Sumner's notorious speech in May 1856, John Brown's raid or Abraham Lincoln's election. The South went to war to vindicate its collective notion of honor because its Northern critics had so maligned, as they saw it, the holding of slaves and intended still greater aggressions against it. In the fighting of the war, honor more than "duty," or duty construed as honor, prompted Confederate enlistments and even death in battle. In the almost unimaginable disaster of Lee's surrender both grace and honor were the victims. God had clearly withdrawn divine favor and at the same time, the vulgar, godless Yankees had tossed Confederate aspirations in the dust. The result was a common phenomenon, the development of a myth of heroism and glory in the very midst of defeat and humiliation.

Former Confederates were suddenly a "lost people." They were not to blame. Instead, like the Old Testament Israelites, they deemed themselves to be victims of forces beyond their control. The ancients had felt the wrath of a God who loved them but had momentarily deserted them because of their sins. Yet Jehovah's mercy and justice would return to save His Chosen People. The same reaction can be seen in the recent Serbian response to Kosovar resurgence and the Serbian glorification of the ancient battlefield on the field of blackbirds, which the Christians lost to the Muslim Turks in 1389. But similarly observable in the former Yugoslavia was the scapegoating of vulnerable minorities. The bitter desire to blame a weaker element for defeat could become a rationale for atrocities of unspeakable proportions.[9]

Predictably, in the American South the targets of such a lashing out were the freed people. As beneficiaries of Union occupation during and just after the war, they seized the opportunity for freedom to their owners' astonishment and despair. Such a turn of events shifted the center of honor's gravity. In a crude sense, it moved from the duel to the democratic mob of lynchers. The vows to protect white womanhood and to cleanse the body politic of black men's corruption and supposedly outrageous presumptions of equality took on a sacred and honorable mien. That transition did not occur immediately after Appomattox but developed in the so-called Redeemer period with the overthrow of Republican Reconstruction.[10]

Thus if honor often presented two faces—magnanimity and vengeance —so too did grace. It could sustain a people's faith in a forgiving Lord. Yet it also might be invoked to promote hatred and punishment with the intention of allegedly purifying a fragile and suspicious community. By such means, horrifying evils were supposed to be eliminated. That, I contend, was the legacy of Confederate defeat in the violence of racism that followed that humiliation. What could have been more appropriate than the incantation of the word "Redemption" to identify the restoration of white hegemony over the supposed evils of a black presence in politics? It must have seemed to that generation and to several that followed as if Jesus Christ had come down from the Cross to applaud their delayed but glorious and honorable victory of white supremacy.

In light of my stress on the connection of honor with grace, and also with regard to the addition of war as a major component of Southern white memory and pride, this study might well be considered a sequel to *Southern Honor: Ethics and Behavior in the Old South*, published by Oxford University Press in 1982. Some important themes were missing from that volume, most especially the political features of the ethic as well as the role of religion in Southern life. Moreover, in *Southern Honor* I had sought only to explore the ethical rules of the slave South, with few references to later developments. The Civil War with its enormous and almost permanent effect on the Southern white psyche during and even long after that conflict found no place in an already lengthy volume. This work seeks to rectify those omissions.

Under the title of "Race and Politics," the first section consists of three chapters. In Chapter 1, "Dignity, Deception, and Identity in the Male Slave Experience," I reexamine Stanley Elkins's provocative comparison of African American enslavement and the Nazi concentration camps. By no means, though, should it be read as an endorsement of his overly simplified typologies. In contrast to the rest of the text, this reconsideration of the Elkinsian thesis deviates from the almost exclusive study of white Southern patterns and conventions from the Revolution to the close of the nineteenth century. Yet it does suggest how whites continued to retain hegemony over black destiny from the era of the Middle Passage to the inhuman racism of Jim Crow and the rule of the lynch mob. Simultaneously the chapter seeks to illuminate the place of dignity and honor in African American life. Nobility of character and sturdy self-identification were possible even under the direst forms of slavery. Nonetheless, I propose, the psychological costs of oppression must be confronted as well. That result should never be seen as a stigmatizing mark on any race whatsoever. Rather, oppression may function in some but not all cases to distort the ethical and psychological sensibilities of slave owners and their subordinates.

The second chapter, "Honor, Dread of Enslavement, and Revolutionary Rhetoric," demonstrates the salience of honor in the American Revolutionary South. This topic has been almost totally neglected in historical scholarship. The third, "Andrew Jackson's Honor," discusses through the role of the Tennessee hero the imprint of a violent and hierarchical notion of honor on the political life of the region throughout the years of the Early Republic. Partisan politics then had an almost military cast. So many politicians were either veterans of the Revolution and the War of 1812 or militia officers. Patron-client connections structured political factions, especially in the South.

Chapters 4, 5, 6, and 7 form a natural coherence regarding the role of the church in Southern life before the Civil War under the second sub-heading of "Grace: Southern Religion in Transition." Chapter 4, "Religion and the Unchurched in the Old South," addresses the relationship of honor to the Old and New Testaments. In addition, it reveals the tensions between the pious elements of a community and the truculent non-churchgoers. An adoption of recent theological interpretations, which link honor to the Scriptures, sheds fresh light on how the white South accepted the moral prescriptions of Christianity while adhering to the sometimes contrary impulses of the ancient ethic. The Primitive Baptist phenomenon in Chapter 5, "Paradox, Shame, and Grace in the Backcountry," discloses how even in that very plain-spoken sect—a Southern version, one might say, of Quakerism—the imposition of shame on community and church dissidents was played out in the ethical scheme of things. In Chapter 6, "Modernizing Slave-Owning Rhetoric," I argue that at the core of the proslavery argument was its basis in biblical literalism but not without gradual modifications from secular influences. Chapter 7, "Church, Honor, and Disunion," relates church leadership to the crisis of secessionism, with some urbane and highly influential authorities very doubtful about and even hostile to the prospect of separation and inevitable bloodshed.

Placed under the final subheading of "War and Aftermath," Chapters 8, 9, 10, 11, and 12 examine the effect of disunion, war, defeat, and slave liberation on the mentality of those engaged and on the lives of those who inherited the legacy of the Confederate generation. Chapter 8, "Shameful Submission and Honorable Secession," explains how the secession movement was a culmination of political concepts of honor. In the sectional conflict, both sides defined that ethic according to separate understandings. Yet in the South vindicating an intense if not fanatical sense of honor was uppermost in the minds of disunionists. They argued that failure to answer the insult of Northern moral criticism and especially the election of an antislavery president meant a loss of collective manhood and a feminization of the Southern spirit. In Chapter 9, "Innocence, War, and Horror," the issue of just how hard did Johnny Reb fight reaches the conclusion that he performed for the most part in a most exemplary fashion under unimaginably trying circumstances. There were, however, high psychic prices for sustaining that level of valor, which not all Rebels were willing to pay. The immediate aftermath of the failed struggle resulted in a profound sense of anguish and humiliation, as recounted in Chapter 10, "Death of a Nation." "Honor Chastened," which is Chapter 11, proposes that the depressive character of so many former Rebels, penurious and sometimes maimed in mind and body, partially made hollow the boosterism and sense of progress that Southerners, especially middle-class city dwellers, liked to imagine. Finally, Chapter 12, "Honor Redeemed in Blood," connects the shame of defeat in war and economic stagnation in peace with the scapegoating of the liberated race in ways sometimes beyond rational comprehension. The last four chapters have not appeared in print before. With only one exception, all the others, previously in print, were thoroughly recast with the inclusion of additional data. In most instances, expanded interpretations have been provided. All of the older material has been brought up to date in recognition of the progress made over the last twenty years or more in understanding Southern history.

Finally, it should be pointed out that this book is mostly about men. The almost exclusive preoccupation with issues in which the male sex was the principal force is most evident in Chapter 1, "Dignity, Deception, and Identity in Male Slave Psychology." To have included female slave responses to their plight would have overburdened an already lengthy investigation. Moreover, slave women faced dilemmas and impositions peculiar to their sex, rape and even lesser forms of sexual coercion being obvious concerns. The psychological effects of overlordship upon African American women need to be more thoroughly examined than they have been so far, but that is a task not appropriate for this enterprise. In any event, physical vulnerability placed women at a great disadvantage whereas male slaves had to be carefully watched for signals of rebellion, flight, or disruptive conduct and compelled to act in appearances of unmanliness and compliance. Furthermore, in the first chapter this approach conforms to the general character of the book, which privileges men engaged in action and expression.

I make no apology for choosing this course. A full half of *Southern Honor* was devoted to the role of women, children, and family households. These subjects were once overlooked in Southern historical scholarship. Instead, *The Shaping of Southern Culture* is almost exclusively concerned with the world of public performance, where men took the dominant roles. We deal with them in matters of governance, religious leadership, and war.

In many respects the people of the nineteenth-century South shared a common appreciation for the ancient ethic with other contemporary social orders in other parts of the world. The historian Thomas W. Gallant, for instance, has noted that in nineteenth-century Greek society "for a man, honor equated to public, collective recognition that he was in con-

trol of those things that mattered most: women, property, and prowess."[11]
Add ownership over slaves and post–Civil War dominion over free African
Americans to the equation, and the statement well applies to the white
male South with which this work is almost wholly concerned.

In sum, *The Shaping of Southern Culture* is intended to illuminate matters of ethics that require further investigation.[12] The study of honor, past
and present, along with that grand, ambivalent, and mysterious theme of
grace, offers promising harvests of meaning for the future.

PART ONE
RACE AND POLITICS

CHAPTER ONE

DIGNITY, DECEPTION, AND IDENTITY
IN THE MALE SLAVE EXPERIENCE

Slavery, in the form of prejudice, is as fatal, yea, more
fatal than the pestilence. It possesses imperial dominion
over its votaries and victims.
—*Hosea Easton, 1837*

When the great lord passes the wise peasant bows deeply
and silently farts.
—*Ethiopian proverb, quoted in James C. Scott,*
Domination and the Arts of Resistance

In 1829 Abd al-Rahman Ibrahima, a lowly slave from Adams County, Mississippi, returned to his African homeland, perhaps the only slave ever do so from the soil of the American republic.[1] He will serve as a symbol of African American honor and the status of shame that the slave condition imposed. Paradoxically, even in the subordination of bondage, dignity can arise when the circumstances indicate that the gestures of the slave will be reciprocated by an equally fitting recognition on the part of the master. In light of this proposition, slaves, like their masters, did have a sense of honor that applied to their sphere, constricted though their autonomy was. The subject of male slave identity and psychology involves issues of honor and shame not only in the presence of masters but also among the slaves themselves.

Ibrahima's history in African freedom and American bondage bears resemblance to the mythic journeys of classic heroes who endure exile and travail but finally return to the land they had striven so long to reach. Ibrahima was the son of Sori, the *almaami*, or theocratic ruler, of the Fulbe country, a major figure in Guinean history. Timbo, Sori's capital, had ties to distant Timbucktu, where Abd al-Rahman had earlier received Islamic training. At the head of a cavalry detachment, Ibrahima had been ambushed by rebels and captured. Fearful of Sori's revenge if his son were executed, they sold him to African slave traders near the Gambia River.[2] In August 1788, Thomas Foster, an American settler in Spanish Natchez, bought Ibrahima along with a slave bearing a less elegant name — "Samba." Both shared the Fullah tongue of their native Futa Jallon.

Abd al-Rahman's experience in bondage offers clues about the nature of honor in the slave quarters. Spurning Ibrahima's gestures to indicate that his freedom could bring Foster riches in cattle from Futa Jallon, Foster dubbed his new prize "Prince." He intended mockery. The American settler ordered Abd al-Rahman's long plaits of hair cut. He sought to demonstrate his power and compel his new purchase to recognize it. Outraged, "Prince" resisted, and Foster promptly had him shackled. In Abd al-Rahman's eyes, he, a Fulani warrior, had sunk to the level of a Pullo youngster.[3] (Pullo is the singular of Fulbe.) Despite the barked commands, Abd al-Rahman refused to join the field hands. As pastoralists, Fulani males disdained manual labor. That was the work of women and underlings, the Jalunke, many of whom the Fulbe had conquered and enslaved. Whipped for repeated disobedience, Abd al-Rahman ran off to the woods after dark. After some weeks, he realized the hopelessness of his situation. Suicide violated the Qur'an and a Muslim's sense of honor. Clearly Allah had chosen his fate. The ensuing event was long remembered in the Foster clan. He appeared one morning in the doorway of the ramshackle cabin when Foster was absent. Sarah, Foster's wife, abruptly looked up from her sewing. She made out the figure of a tall, ragged frame with eyes fierce and staring. Rather than recoil in terror, though, Sarah offered her hand in greeting. He took it, then knelt on the floor and placed her foot on his neck.[4]

Few stories explain how newly arrived Africans reacted to their fate. Seldom do the rituals of African aristocracy reappear on American shores. The anonymity that shrouded Samba's first days in America was more typical.[5] And yet there was a connection between Abd al-Rahman's misfortune and the issue of "Samboism," the expression of complete servility, the sign of abject moral and social dehumanization. In fact, Abd al-Rahman's gesture can serve as a trope for the process of learning the demands of servitude. All the millions of slaves in the Western Hemisphere over the centuries had to adopt the outward appearance of abject subservience. Yet against the forces of oppression, Abd al-Rahman and countless other blacks retained independent judgment, a sense of their inner manliness and separate identity. As Erik Erikson has pointed out, "it takes a well established identity to tolerate radical change."[6]

. . . .

The nature of male slave psychology that Ibrahima displayed poses vexing problems. Scholars have not fully recognized its complications and contradictions and instead have generally interpreted the issue in simple terms. The subject divides itself into three categories: first, a reflection on the intriguing but flawed analysis by which Stanley Elkins pioneered the topic some years ago;[7] second, an examination of the parallels between African and American slave systems and their effect on the male personality and means of coping; and finally, a necessarily brief exposition of how slave honor, shame, shamelessness, and identity developed.

With regard to the first of these matters, Stanley Elkins's *Slavery*, published in 1959, proposed that the stereotypical slave, Sambo—docile, deceitful, fawning, and childish—was a social reality, not a myth. He drew comparisons between American slavery and German concentration camps. His purpose was to show that the exertion of raw power, unfettered by any institutional restraint, created emotional disorder among victims of both forms of tyranny. African American slaves exhibited childlike docility and prevarication not because of some racial inadequacy but because absolute power, Elkins contended, permanently corrupts both the oppressor and the oppressed. This depiction of Sambo-like behavior, however, no long seems psychologically plausible. Such conduct might become habitual through rituals and strategies of subordination. Nonetheless, a change in status from slavery to autonomy could quickly erase all vestiges of subservience. During the civil rights era of the 1960s, white liberal and African American intellectuals denounced the whole idea from start to finish. Even today feelings can run high against using analogies between Nazi atrocities and American slaveholding practices.[8]

Then, in a famous report on the black family prepared for the Lyndon Johnson administration, Daniel Patrick Moynihan argued that Elkins was essentially right. To justify remedies for family disintegration, the bureaucrat argued that African Americans were heirs of the oppressions suffered under slavery, a system that undercut a sense of black manhood and responsibility. Infuriated, the lately deceased labor historian Herbert Gutman challenged the Elkins-Moynihan thesis and raced to the other extreme. He championed the enduring integrity of the black family in both slavery and freedom and denounced modern welfare rules regarding male cohabitation.[9] Neither position can explain the very conflicted relationship between master and slave. The basis for the continuing controversy had thus begun.

Elkins based much of his theorizing on contemporary Holocaust scholarship, then in its infancy. The first studies of oppressive dehumanization reached the public at a time when so many victims were still understandably reticent about the traumatic events that they had undergone. Cold War preoccupations superseded much West European and American interest in the recent, particularly Jewish, past. His comparison of slavery with Nazi concentration camps met additional challenges. Critics pointed out the obvious fact that total genocide was the objective of the Nazi regime, whereas slave masters sought labor and profits, not annihilation.[10]

Nor, in making his case, did Elkins have the benefit of recent advances in the psychology of trauma and cultural alienation. He had no access to the literature on what was later called post-traumatic stress disorder. That was the term used during the Vietnam War for what earlier had been called battle fatigue or, in World War I, shell shock. Victims of various forms of calamities—war, accident, epidemic, kidnaping, hostage-taking, massacre, torture—we have learned, cannot wholly escape the desensitizing effects of their experience. Unfortunately, little advanced scholarship was available to Elkins to use in his analysis. Moreover, he failed to account for the brave if ultimately hopeless attempts at uprising and sabotage in the Jewish ghettoes and Nazi camps. The photographic exhibits and sites at Birkenau (where Jewish women, at great personal sacrifice, destroyed Crematorium number 4) and Auschwitz in Poland and Theresien and Theresienstadt in the Czech Republic, for example, will convince any observer of the actuality of prisoner disobedience and resistance when slivers of opportunity infrequently arose.[11] Nor did he appreciate the Nazi preoccupation with hierarchical honor and how it functioned in the camps. Nazi honor identified Germans as the master race, whereas Jews, Poles, Russians, Gypsies, members of the dark races, homosexuals, the disabled, the mentally retarded or ill were all stigmatized as degenerate species.

Why resurrect Elkins's vulnerable analysis so many years later? The reasons lie in the incompleteness, not the irrelevance of his innovative approach to comparative history and to the application of interdisciplinary techniques on historical issues. He correctly proposed that the slave and the Nazi victim's experiences were similar in important respects (which we must carefully delineate). Yet Elkins did offer far too limited a vision of what total subjection can produce. Three factors are absent. The Columbia University scholar failed to examine the reactions of suicide, depression, and post-traumatic stress disorder. With regard to the first of these, German Jewish refugees in France talked of greeting the invading Nazis in 1940 with "*Selbstmord.*" Paul Louis Landsberg argues in *The Moral Problem of Suicide* that it was "the best door left open, if life in such a society has lost all meaning." The novelist Arthur Koestler remarked that in 1941 he and his friends in Paris "all carried some stuff in our pocket."[12]

Many Nazi victims died at their own hands to escape the inevitable tortures under the SS. Others took their own lives rather than carry out Nazi orders against their fellow sufferers. Adam Czerniakov, chairman of the Warsaw Jewish Council, received a directive to increase the supply for the death camps to nine thousand per day. The ghetto leader recorded in his diary, "There is nothing left for me but to die." He killed himself that day. At Bialystok, Poland, Zvi Wider, a member of the town's Jewish Council, refused to meet similar demands and killed himself. Once in the camps it was sometimes harder than in the ghettos to find the means to carry out a self-imposed death sentence. At Birkenau, Poland, many, however, found the means. A Dutch physician, for instance, hanged himself on the electrified barbed wire.[13]

Regarding the issue of life-threatening despair in European camp or African barracoon, hardly any autobiographical account from either location failed to note the desperation of the victims.[14] While Jews did resist their fate to a much greater degree than Elkins claimed, despair often had a deadening effect. After all, we hear nothing much about resistance among the 1.4 million Russians in German work camps. Similarly Russian POWs offered little resistance. The death rates in both groups were incredibly high. The SS guard cared little more for these victims than for the Jews. No disgrace or cowardice should be ascribed to any of these for a failure of nerve. Conditions scarcely permitted rebelliousness.[15]

Moreover, such paralysis of will was a natural reaction under the horrible circumstances for all these subjects of horrendous tyranny, no matter when or where they met their fate. When that inanition occurs, writes Lawrence L. Langer about the Holocaust victims, it "flows from a profound despair."[16] Likewise, the trauma and the melancholy of African slaves were so deeply felt that even before arrival in America, captured Africans frequently willed themselves into a physical and emotional decline. Isaac Wilson, a surgeon on an English slaver, reported that two-thirds of the 155

who died in the course of an Atlantic crossing were victims of "melancholy." When taken on board, he had noticed that "a gloomy pensive-
ness overcast their countenances and continued in a great many." Women
fell into wailing loudly; the men into bitter sullenness. Sometimes sailors
forced the despairing to dance "to our bag-pipes, harp, and fiddle," as
one ship captain explained. Making them sing did not produce a happier
frame of mind, another observer recalled. The songs were usually "melancholy lamentations of their exile from their native country."[17]

Depression not only diminished life-supporting appetites but also exposed the captured slaves to diseases that a more optimistic disposition
would have helped to overcome. One slaver reported that on a voyage to
the Barbadoes, "We had about 12 negroes did willfully drown themselves,
and others starved themselves to death." Age also played a role. Newly arrived Africans were more likely to kill themselves than those whose ties
to the homeland had gradually receded from memory. Also, the younger
the slave the more quickly did he or she recover, whereas older Africans
were more prone to suicide and despondency. Those with noble birth
equivalent to Ibrahima's sometimes took the Roman option. By that term
is meant a preference for death to lifelong humiliation. They could not
fall on a sword but found other means. Before the House of Commons,
a Dr. Harrison reported that a Jamaican slave of rank in his home country had refused to work. His master ordered him to be moved to another
plantation. On the way, however, the slave preserved his dignity by leap-
ing from a bridge to his death.[18] No doubt, many of those who died on
their way to the death camps in Eastern Europe suffered from trauma so
severe that it weakened their will to survive.

Was the Holocaust really so very different from the slave experience?
The analogy was not as close as Elkins portrayed it but not so dissimilar
as his critics claimed. In terms of time they certainly were unalike. The
Shoah concentrated massive death and horror for six millions into the
space of six years, a brief but calamitous era. Slavery in America lasted
two and a half centuries. But surely as many died appalling, stricken ends
in the course of that epoch as in the shorter horror of the mid-twentieth
century, even if the purpose of the trade and enslavement was not death
but profit and work.

Regardless of the differences in purpose, German oppression and the
Atlantic trade were strikingly similar in their processes of dehumanization by shaming, indifference, and neglect. In 1958 Primo Levi, a former
inmate at Auschwitz, explained that the victims were treated as *unter-
menschen*—"vile creatures."[19] "Nothing belongs to us any more; they have

taken away our clothes, our shoes, even our hair; if we speak, they will not listen to us, and if they listen, they will not understand. They will even take away our name" and supply numbers tattooed on the arm in their place. Even male Jews still living in or outside the camps had to add Israel to their names, and female Jews had to adopt Sara. These were meant to humiliate those whose names did not otherwise signify their so-called "race." Gizella Abramson, a survivor of the concentration camp at Majdanek, Poland, explains that captives like her had felt these humiliations along with the incessant verbal abuse as painfully as if such blows had been applied with the brutal force of a whip. Abramson calls herself as much a slave as those who had endured the Middle Passage.[20]

Like these European victims, the Africans, arriving in the New World and equally committed to their homeland, families, and communities, must have reacted with similar dismay, confusion, and despair. They, too, lost their names or soon would under a new master whether the owner was English, French, or Spanish. Abd al-Rahman—and many others—had been shaved to deprive them of a sense of themselves just as concentration camp inmates were. In the Nazi camps privacy was impermissible, and abrupt commands for all to disrobe were frequent. Likewise, when the slave-drivers in Africa emptied the barracoons and loaded the ships they were, as a rule, "entirely stripped, so that women as well as men go out of Africa as they came into it—naked." As the historian Michael Gomez observes, the purpose was to instill a sense of "profound humiliation and disintegration of identity."[21] In the slave trade, sharp-eyed buyers required full exposure of their prospective purchases in order to check their health and strength. Slaves could hold no mementos of their former life. Traders not only coveted their small possessions but appropriated them to signify the impotence of the slave.

The same situation prevailed in the Nazi Holocaust. "Clothes, valuables, hair: these were among the spoils of the German war against the Jews," writes Martin Gilbert.[22] In *The Last Days*, a documentary film about the Hungarian Jews, one of the survivors reported that she managed to keep possession of diamonds which her mother had given her just before their arrest. She swallowed them to avoid detection and then picked through the feces to recover and hide them. She did so time and again, not because of their value but because they were the last objects linking her to her beloved parent. They symbolized her own determination not to become the automaton that the Nazis demanded. One can imagine that slaves in similar circumstances were often deprived of that connection with their domestic life and cultural past. Perhaps a few were as lucky and as resourceful as the Hungarian survivor in holding on to some small signifier of special meaning.

In light of such analogies between the Nazi and the slave trade pasts, something of Elkins's basic claims do not seem so far-fetched as his critics once insisted. Not knowing exactly what their ultimate fate would be, the captives suffering under Nazi hands and the Africans seized for the slave trade bear legitimate comparison. Trauma batters and sometimes dominates a victim's personality, in whatever age or culture it may occur. As Orlando Patterson, the Harvard sociologist, observes, "To the Greeks, the slave had been 'two-footed stock'; to the Romans, 'a vocal instrument'; and to the Southerners, a black beast, the archetypal *bête noire*, a Sambo devoid of manhood."[23]

The critic may consider Patterson's observation simple hyperbole. Yet in the antebellum period, Hosea Easton, a free African American clergyman and astute observer, gave strong evidence for Patterson's proposition. In 1837, Easton declared slavery to be a monstrous and "withering influence" that tore at "the very vitals of the colored people—withering every incentive to improvement—rendering passive all the faculties of the intellect—subjecting the soul to a morbid state of insensibility." In every sphere, Easton protested, the slave was reminded of his condition. Pointing to the demeaning linguistic messages of prejudice, Easton argued that calling the underrace "niggers" was to suggest a "deformity of person." Whites roundly mocked African American speech patterns as well. Nor did white youngsters learn respect for dark skins and idiomatic discourse, Easton continued. On tucking them into bed, parents warned, "Go to sleep, if you don't the old nigger will carry you off . . . how ugly you are, you are worse than a little *nigger*." Easton died before he could elaborate on his probing of prejudice and its effects on both white and black, master and slave. Yet in his surviving sermons, he was remarkably accurate in seeing slavery as a form of "social death," to borrow Patterson's terminology.[24] Legal codes, even when strictly enforced, and masters' exercise of a benevolent paternalism, he maintained, were insufficient to ameliorate the psychological damage that was possible under the conditions of slavery and white contempt. These oppressions, he insisted, worked together "to justify the expenditures of . . . soul-and-body destroying energies." Easton grieved that he could record the names of scores whose "dissolution can be traced to a cloud of obstructions thrown in their way to prevent enterprise."[25]

The means of reducing human beings to animals in the eyes of others—the linguistic, color, and mental stereotyping of the alien "other"—which

Easton depicted in his anger—was similar in both the slave and the Holocaust situations. According to Ahron Appelfeld, the children of Jewish victims underwent similar forms of vile treatment—denunciations of their appearance, ways of speaking, looks, and moral inferiority.[26] American slave children were the most vulnerable and often the most sorely treated in the slave population. The historian Wilma King comments that when black youths felt the lash or witnessed the punishments of friends and family members, the experience "chipped away at their own self-esteem, thus leaving the way open for feelings of frustration and resentment."[27]

. . . .

Analogies with the Jewish plight in Central Europe are not only appropriate but lend an immediacy to the American slave experience which occurred in the far distant past. Even so, it is almost impossible for modern readers to grasp just how captives of any sort coped with their plight and resisted it—or, understandably, succumbed to monstrous circumstances that could destroy or maim them physically or emotionally. Fortunately, we have access to the fugitive slave narratives and the large collection of WPA reminiscences of former Southern slaves about their childhood. Both sources are indispensable tools for historical retrieval. Yet another source for comparison and insight is available in the study of slavery in the American slaves' original homeland, Africa itself.

For one thing, the African homelands of the transported were honor-shame societies, too. Like most others shipped to America, Ibrahima was already familiar with the dehumanizing bondage of Sori's territory. Under happier circumstances he would have been an heir through his father to slaveholding himself. He was a prince, but Samba, his colleague in wretchedness, was a commoner and perhaps an animist and not a Muslim.

Honor, shame, and distinctions of social rank were no less a part of the order of things than they were in the management of plantation slavery in the Southern states. In Pular-speaking areas, the condition of slavery was one which the late anthropologist Paul Riesman says "most clearly expressed everything that is the opposite of Fulani." As if to fulfill Elkins's own description of the Sambo image, slaves and captives belonging to that people were labeled "black, fat, coarse, naive, irresponsible, uncultivated, shameless, dominated by their needs and their emotions."[28] Slavery was a status given to strangers who were captured or bought. They remained kinless and subordinate, a humiliating experience in societies based on lineage and kinship networks.

More to the point was the lowly position of slaves born in another Fulbe corner of West Africa today. The anthropologist Bernd Baldus has studied the slave systems of Fulbe herdspeople in the Borgou region of northern Benin. The Batomba, agriculturalists, and the Fulbe (Abd al-Rahman's language group) had lived side by side since the Fulbe's small, peaceful migrations began in the eighteenth century. Like other West Africans, the Batomba had long believed that if a child's teeth appeared first in the upper jaw, fearful disaster would afflict the kinspeople and tribe. Parents underwent rites of purification. The babies, however, were killed. After the Fulanis' settlement, the Batomba gave or sold the infants as slaves to their new pastoral neighbors whose Islamic beliefs did not include the dental taboo.

Called *machube*, the stigmatized slaves and their descendants thereafter have stood lower than those subject to other less permanent forms of servitude in the area. As a result, when slaves of Bourgou were freed under French colonial rule ninety-odd years ago, the machube continued in bondage more or less by force of custom alone. (Except briefly and ineffectively at the time of official abolition, they have never risen up against their masters.) The Fulbe seldom had to resort to violence to enforce their will. When the anthropologist interviewed the slaves, he found that they had internalized their lowly status, ranking themselves below the Fulbe and Batomba. Baldus found that the machube blamed themselves, not their superiors, for their plight. Their sense of humiliation was so powerful that, much abashed, they hesitated to account for their bondage until the anthropologist explained that he already knew. Being humiliated signified complete rejection as a living being, the most important element of conscious existence. Yet just how much was hidden of inner thoughts out of deference to greater authorities and how much was absorbed as part of their personalities could not be detected then or now. One may presume that much was an external, impermanent show.[29]

Somehow the machube were convinced that the Fulbe provided them with special status. Whereas the Pullo master assumed authority as a right, the machudo (the word for the single individual) accepts slavery out of a mixture of awe for Fulbe magic and a sense of gratitude. Said one: "I work for the Pullo because he has taken me as a child from the Batomba. He has raised me, washed me, he has given me milk. . . . For this reason, as a sign of recognition, one carries out all his commands."[30] This mode of adaptation to an oppressive system very much resembled what Anna Freud called "identification with the aggressor" as a means for surviving danger.[31] Those who adopted the strategy were by no means irrational or childish in some pejorative sense. Nor were their actions altogether selfish, because the whole group may have benefited. Cosmic ideas also reinforced machudo docility. The slaves of the Fulbe adopted a fatalism similar to Abd al-Rahman's Islamic faith of centuries ago, but it was more intense. They found safety, protection, and even ultimate salvation by doing exactly as their forefathers had done and Allah commanded. Asked why they obeyed so unquestioningly, the machube replied with such aphorisms as " 'If you have a cock, then you do with the cock what you want, don't you?' "[32]

This identification with the owner's perspective rather than with their own suggests the mimetic feature of dependence: the desire to imitate the master's ways. By this means, something of the status of the Fulbe was supposed to be accessible to the slaves. They wanted "to look like a Pullo," dress like him, talk like him, swagger like him. In error-ridden and inappropriate ways they took on some of his exclusive customs despite the mockeries and derision of the Batomba and Fulbe. The point was not to win favor from the masters but to raise their own low self-esteem and create a distance between themselves and others who did not share the social standing or the Islamic faith of their masters. One is reminded that when American slaves belonged to "quality folks" they often disdained the so-called po' white trash.

The African pattern had its American parallel. As the historian Ariela Gross points out, Southern whites argued that slaves were essentially imitative even with regard to moral behavior. She observes that John Belton O'Neal, an ornament to the South Carolina antebellum bench, contended that "prudent masters" set an example before their slaves, but bad ones sometimes reaped an unwelcome reward. "*Like master, like man*," wrote Judge O'Neal, "was too often the case, in drunkenness, impudence, and idleness." The judge was much shrewder than Dr. Samuel Cartwright and other scientific racists who argued that dependency was structured into the very essence of an African.[33] They were even alleged to breathe differently at night, to the ill-effect of their blood and brains. By enforcing rules of slave conduct with a lash or with material incentives, masters did help to shape an imitative response.

The kind of behavior that prompted slaves to follow a pattern laid down by a master, for good or ill, is part of the cultural order itself. Conventions of subservience are elements in the group's accepted wisdom. Just as whites in the Old South assumed their status over blacks and the sanctions and alleged superior worth that their whiteness conferred, so slaves, as a means of getting along day by day, generally accepted their position. They had lives to live, children to raise, holidays to anticipate. It took too much energy to be constantly in turmoil. Ordinarily the human condition restrains perpetual remorse, guilt, and sorrow as well as unremitting indignation and unremitting rebelliousness. American slaves were, however, by no means passive. When some unjust act or demeaning situation arose, some were reminded of their status and resented it. Sometimes, albeit rarely, when conditions seemed opportune, they reacted in anger.

We would like to find some ennoblement in the midst of tyranny, and examples of strength and bravery are numberless. Yet evil is not easily mastered. Why men under absolute rule act selfishly and sometimes fail to resist heroically is a painful but unavoidable problem. A partial answer comes from an anthropological approach. The African specialist Bernd Baldus argues that our Western notions of corrective conflict, whereby the oppressed inevitably rise up in moral indignation, may simply not apply in certain situations, particularly if the constraints on self-dependence have become part of an underling's social heritage as well as immediate experience.[34] Indeed, evidence from various parts of Africa supports his generalization. Observing "a prescribed code of conduct," T. J. Allridge, an English trader, recounted how Mende slaves were accustomed to "cringe up and place their two hands one on each side of their master's hand and draw them back slowly . . . while the head is bowed." His language suggests his bias, but cringing was undoubtedly part of the expected ritual. Similarly, on one occasion a recently imported African from Futa Jallon, possibly an enslaved Jalunke (a non-Fullah black), met and recognized Abd al-Rahman in Natchez. "Abduhl Rahahman [Ibrahima]!" he cried in wonder and fear of so miraculous a sight. At once he prostrated himself on the ground before him.[35] The ritual, we must remember, is most likely a matter of psychological habit and not a permanent form of action persisting long after freedom has been acquired.

At the same time, a deference that included efforts to imitate the white masters' ways must be seen as a subtle, subversive device. Henry Louis Gates has found that, as early as the eighteenth century, observers noticed how slaves "frequently 'enounce' their sense of difference by repetition with a signal difference." Nicolas Cresswell, Gates reports, wrote in his journal of the 1770s: "In [the blacks'] songs they generally relate the usage they have received from their Masters or Mistresses in a very satirical stile [*sic*] and manner."[36] Gates argues persuasively that African and African American rhetoric encompassed a complexity of forms that functioned as a kind of writing. The speakers delighted in the "undecidability," that is, their recognition of double entendres that owners did not catch. The tradition did not, as white Southerners thought, signify mere repetitive and imitative speech and gesture but a subtle multiplicity of meanings.[37]

Undoubtedly, the American slave had more access to liberating values than did the machube in Africa today. Even masters knew that their unguarded discussions of "liberty" and "rights" easily and often reached the wrong ears—from their point of view. As Sylvia Frey points out, during the American Revolution, some slaves overcame the inhibitions prohibiting rebellion that they had known in Africa itself as well as their fears of reprisal in an effort to resist the slave-owning Whigs and join the British liberators.[38] Philip Morgan also reminds us that every sort of emotion—good and bad, helpful and excessive—existed in the slave quarters: "antagonism, hostility and mistrust" on the one hand, and "a sense of common identity" and "racial camaraderie" on the other.[39] Wearing colorful and elegant clothes—at least when the ordinary working garb could be put aside on holidays, Sundays, and times away from the field—was one way to demonstrate self-possession. In the American South, slaves were issued the coarsest sorts of materials for everyday attire. Field hands did not always dress, however, in the rags and shabby hand-me-downs that abolitionist engravings portrayed. Women were especially imaginative. Men as well liked to be seen in respectable, sometimes flamboyant clothes. Yet a master could justly suspect that too much fanciness violated rules of subordination. In all societies where honor is a significant force, sumptuary custom and even strict laws have required inferiors not to wear apparel beyond their status for that very reason—the assumption of a role that threatened ranked order.

Colonial scholars Shane White and Graham White recount the story of one Daniel belonging to George Swain, a North Carolina planter. Daniel broke a plantation rule and had a long-planned holiday cut short on Swain's orders. Daniel, his master thought, had "deranged his mind" by making himself "a perfect fool" in hopes of impressing the black community with his grand outfit. When denied the full opportunity to walk about in his best clothes, it was "more than his tiny soul could bear," fumed Swain. Daniel ran off without a pass. As far as Swain was concerned, the absconding slave "had entirely forgotten who he was, or what grade and station he ought to fill." But the significance of the incident was Daniel's self-assertion and pride, despite the punishment that might ensue. As early as the eighteenth century, runaways were sometimes described in advertisements as wearing new European-style breeches and waistcoats. In defiance of white prohibitions, others wore clothing of African fashion.

In one case, male slaves were seen dressed in the early eighteenth century in "long frocks of white Plaines" to be found only in Africa itself.[40]

That sort of freedom was not to last long, however. Although good clothing might be permitted in the quarters for special occasions, owners were wary about letting down the barriers of appearance to separate the races. In Africa, in contrast, there were forms of slavery that provided for the slaves' secure incorporation into the local society. Sometimes descendants were allowed to marry into the nonslave community. When told later that African and American slavery were much alike, Abd al-Rahman disagreed: "No, no, I tell you, [a] man own slaves [at Timbo]—he join the religion—he very good. He [master] make he slaves work till noon, go to church, then till he sun go down, they work for themselves." Alas, Abd al-Rahman exaggerated the benignity of his homeland institution, just as white masters did in America. Slavery made it possible for the Fulani and other slaveholding tribes to procure "basic needs."[41] Nonetheless, the West African experience of bondage involved only the issue of caste or status but not race—as in the Western Hemisphere. That distinction made an enormous difference.

. . . .

Although death camp analogies and African patterns of slavery help to broaden our appreciation of the North American slave, the latter's sense of identity and honor was sui generis. Long acculturated American slaves held concepts of liberty far more sophisticated than those of slaves serving the Fulani (or Fulbe). Nonetheless, their outlook incorporated a peasant caution with its own sanctions and rituals of allegiance as part of their understanding of master-slave relations. Frederick Douglass recognized that the country slaves among whom he grew up were ignorant of alternatives to servitude: "Life, to them, had been rough and thorny, as well as dark."[42] Even after emancipation some country blacks found it hard to break old habits of deference. Henry William Ravenel of South Carolina was pleased to note in his diary in 1866, "The negroes have all behaved well, & seem to wish to get along." Doffed caps and respectful greetings continued.[43]

The first two forms of servility, the ceremonial type that Abd al-Rahman epitomized and the more common pattern of cultural response to subordination, are somewhat different in character. The first involved less habitual response than the second. Both, however, entailed outward demonstrations of fidelity beyond simply work faithfully performed. (Masters, for instance, liked to hear their slaves singing in the fields, even if the songs meant something different and more autonomous to the singers. Silence, though, was certain to denote a threatening sullenness.) In keeping with that expectation, Abd al-Rahman became what one of the Fosters' Pine Ridge neighbors described as "'a faithful, loyal servant.'" To please his American-born wife and Sarah Foster, his mistress, he even attended Baptist services on a regular basis after 1818. Nonetheless, he did not entirely forgo his Muslim religious practices. From recent studies of eighteenth-century religious history, we now understand how significant the Muslim faith was in the development of slave culture. Moreover, the role of his wife in his semiconversion to Christianity had many contemporary parallels. Slave women exercised a leadership in spiritual matters in the quarters no less than did their white mistresses.[44] Ibrahima's combining of the new and old religions was therefore not as unique as one might have guessed.[45]

Drab and demeaning though the role was, servility and its rituals were for Ibrahima raiment to cover nakedness and vulnerability, a posture that most slaves adopted as occasion demanded. The prince had transformed himself into a peasant, but one with dignity and self-assurance. By such means, one suspects, as his master's driver he remained an autocrat, never forgetting *pulaaku*, the quality of character that identified the Fulbe as virtuous and honor-proud. He expressed his feelings by never smiling, or so one white acquaintance who had observed him for years reported.[46] Was his demeanor idiosyncratic? I doubt it. Too many instances in the records appear that show a male slave's defense of his honor. Insulted by whites who declared him unfit for their company, Frank, a slave of York County, Virginia, for instance, in 1681 stripped to his underclothes and challenged the offender, swearing "he would fight Macarty soe long as hee could stand."[47]

The second was a pattern that formed part of conventional wisdom among slaves themselves and involved a willingness to lower one's own self-esteem to gain advantage in the struggle against the master. Such a Sambo figure in the American context was not so habitually deferential as the machudo example. Nor was he so reserved and dignified as Abd al-Rahman. Sambo was not by any means the Elkinsian and minstrel show comic but a clever and more complex personality. When a slave took up the role—some more often than others—he generally was making use of the third proposition in the system of honor and shame: that is, shamelessness. Repudiation of ordinary and mediated ethics on the master's part could have induced an excessive servility on the part of the slave. The performance of the Sambo tactic could be understood as a form of ritual behavior. A reminder of how real this model of servility was appears in the diary of that remarkable South Carolinian Mary Chesnut, at the close of the war: "We had a wonderful scene here last Sunday—an old African—who heard he was free & did not at his helpless old age relish the idea. So he wept & prayed, kissed hands, rolled over on the floor until the boards of the piazza were drenched with his tears. He seemed to worship his master & evidently regarded the white race as some superior order of beings, he prostrated himself so humbly." The whites rewarded the gratifying performance with frayed blankets and other throwaways for the supplicant.[48]

The Samboism of the roguish, coarse, and deceitful slave describes only one role slaves might play. Yet in all honor-shame societies where slavery is a key institution, one finds the same ritualized and highly expressive phenomenon: in Muscovite Russia, Greece and Rome, Brazil, the West Indies, in fact, nearly everywhere save parts of Asia. In all such societies, even though many, perhaps most, individuals scarcely meet the stereotype, slaves were perceived by their owners as child- and womanlike in character, only more so—violent (when spoiled) but usually passive, even affectionate—and always devious and untrustworthy.[49]

In large measure, the source of shamelessness lay in the unpredictability of the master's behavior. The slaveholder could be shameless in rule, and the slave could be forced to behave in a demeaning, passive way to appease and cajole his superior. Both owner and servant could act with a lack of decorous inhibition and yet not be mentally "damaged" or neurotic.[50] As Orlando Patterson's study points out, those outside the circle of honor "aspire to no honor" and therefore "cannot be [made to feel] humiliated."[51] The point is only mildly exaggerated.

In that freedom from the restraints and rules of dignity the slave exercised a mean autonomy in response to the willful power of his owner. Slaves struggled to win space of their own, but it required "a perpetual balancing act," notes James Sidbury. The effort demanded close attention to the whims of owners and overseers. To show the universal character of such strategies a German concentration camp incident can illustrate. Sometimes tricksters, as clever victims found themselves obliged to become, heroically risked their lives in deceptions of the Gestapo authorities. To save himself as well as others in Block 21 at Auschwitz, the youthful Stanislaw Taubenschlag had to appease an oberkapo named Kerlin, who, though Jewish, served his own selfish needs by collaboration. Some slave drivers, too, took up that part. One day Kerlin killed ten workers with a cudgel and on the next suffocated sixty others by herding them into a room that soon became airless—simply for pleasure. Taubenschlag was compelled to agree with the self-congratulatory kapo that his jokes of death were "a stroke of genius." The inmate then promised the psychopath to entertain him with a surprise. To prevent further murders, the prisoner enlisted an old Parisian furrier to climb a tree and pretend to sing like a nightingale. When brought to the scene, Kerlin roared with laughter as the "Sambo" as we might poignantly call him, performed. Passing out some coveted rations for the actors, Kerlin demanded another surprise. Thus, on the following day, by prearrangement, the furrier barked like a dog. Luckily Taubenschlag was transferred elsewhere before further demands. Sadly he recalled, "The Frenchman paid with his human dignity, whereas I played the role of the king's jester." But, he continued, "Since our lives were at stake, no price was too high." Such brutalities to shame and even destroy the integrity of man may tragically occur whenever men feel no restraint of law or conscience to gratify a lust to appear manly, unyielding, godlike. Elkins discerned that peril but did not see how it actually functioned without necessarily jeopardizing the inner core of being.[52]

As a device for self-protection and enhancement, the most eloquent form of shamelessness was the wildly articulate lie. It was hardly a wonder, then, that black manhood was connected with the capacity to think, talk, and act quickly. More significant than the moral lessons of folk tales, acting out—"playing the dozens" as it is now called—taught by doing. In this children's game, one player insulted another's family so that the second party felt obliged "to defend his honor" (and that of his family). There are further escalating challenges and replies while the group eggs on the participants with laughter and groans. The game served a variety of functions—as group fun; as an outlet for aggression that could not be directed toward whites; as a way to pick leaders for verbal agility. An African American psychologist explains it as the participants' experiment in keeping "cool and think[ing] fast under pressure, without saying what was really on their minds." Even if only half-believed, the elaborate alibi could reduce the chance of white revenge. Yet such activity was amoral—shameless—defiantly so since the honor-shame nexus left no room for individual expression except in the form of the dramatically deceptive self.[53]

Gaming insult was an adaptation of a West African practice. In Abd al-Rahman's homeland, for instance, calculated mockery was a way for elders—mothers, fathers, older siblings—to insist on children's deference by reminding them of improper childhood defecation and so on. Needless to say, blunt references to family illegitimacies and unnatural sex habits were subjects of general mirth. The strategy complemented the routines of formal politeness. Yet the objective was really to show restraint under provocation. Fear paralyzes the tongue, so worthiness to belong among peers can be achieved through the exchanged tauntings. Also, it tested membership in the male circle. One Africanist calls it "familiarity with a vengeance."[54]

An early and very instructive example of how the slave hid personal feelings and articulated in almost parodic fashion the opposite of insult can be found in recorded testimony before the Governor's Council in South Carolina in 1749. A group of slaves, belonging to one James Akin, a Cooper River planter, had to testify before the council about an insurrectionary plot hatched by a former overseer on one of Akin's plantations a year or two earlier. The slaves' confessions before the dignitaries not only identified black conspirators on their own and other plantations but also named some white transients as guilty of complicity. The whole group, they claimed, were preparing to canoe downriver to Charleston, burn the city, blow up the magazine, and seize a ship to sail for Spanish St. Augustine.[55]

Other planters, including Akin's brother Thomas, eventually informed the council members that no such plot ever existed. Upon reexamination before the royal governor himself, one imprisoned slave named Cyrus recanted. He explained that before their first appearance before the council, Agrippa, another alleged conspirator, had told him and Scipio to leave the talking to him. Agrippa "knew how to go before Gentlemen . . . had waited before on his Master in the Council Chamber, and was used to it." But, Agrippa had warned, keep Kent quiet. He "was a Fool and did not know how to Talk before White People." Indeed, Cyrus continued, if Agrippa had not "stood by and Pinched him, he would have told all & blown them." Scipio also said that Kent had been deeply afraid. So Scipio confessed that he had "hunched him to make him speak as he ought to" before the governor. Some slaves could "jive," as the testimony shows, especially those who had frequent contact with the master class. Others were unable to do so and were thought in the slave quarters to be "fools."

When it became obvious during the hearings at Charleston that truth would prove more advantageous than falsehood, again it was the shameless Sambo-like slaves who seemed the most articulate and credible. George, another slave, began his confession by saying: "Sir I am in your presence, my Master tells me that you are head of the Country. It is true I am not a white Man but I have a soul as well as others, and I believe there is a Heaven and a Devil." He claimed to be afraid that "God Almighty" would punish him if he continued to lie. He was "glad he was sent for, that he might tell all."[56] The ease with which the stories changed to fit the exigencies of the situation, the care with which the slaves shielded themselves from blaming any white, especially their master, the contrast between the articulate Sambos and the frightened mutes like Kent, and the unreliability that coercion had forced all of them to exhibit showed how smoothly slaves could function in the honor-shame context.

Despite the many signals of slave inventiveness and individuality that can be located on every side, the system of Southern oppression was bound to have unhappy consequences for the African American community and personal well-being. Black personality under bondage was very dependent on the social climate that masters provided. For black honor under bondage, the true psychological limitation of slavery lay not in acceptance of honor-shame strictures. Rather, it resided in the absence of rules and structure—anarchy, sometimes legalized anarchy. Plantation chaos and cruelty could place an emotional strain on the slave that is hard for us even to imagine.[57] In other words, Abd al-Rahman's maintenance of high character depended in part on the steady reliability of his master. Had Thomas Foster been monstrous (as his prodigal sons were), his princely driver's actions might have been quite different indeed.

Thus there was a wide range of deferential modes and a range of inner acceptances within slavery. A bondsman adopted or rejected servility as plantation environment, personal temperament, mood, constraints that slavery had helped to make habitual, and even unconscious motive allowed. A small number may well have fit Elkins's unhappy description and lived lives of self-deprecation and deception. At the other, more inspired, extreme of Samboism, some slaves took positive delight in the jesting, roguish performance. In between were some who gave out contradictory or ambivalent signals. Such, for instance, was "Runaway Dennis," a slave belonging to Katharine Du Pre Lumpkin's grandfather in middle Georgia. Dennis constantly quarreled with fellow slaves. As a result, they " 'fought shy' of him." Yet the other slaves treated him as a protected outcast, she recalled from family retellings. When called to account by the black driver, overseer, or owner, Dennis would vanish. Yet he was never betrayed. Dennis "shamefacedly" reappeared only when word reached him through the quarters that he had been promised amnesty. Lumpkin's grandmother, whom he revered, usually served as intercessor. For a short time he was once more a model of conscientiousness and servile compliance. Even after freedom, the unreconstructed former slave showed loyalty to her by voting Democratic. He remained, though, "friendless" in the black community as he had been during slavery.[58] The incident demonstrated that slaves could at times prove their honor by not betraying even an unpopular slave. Dennis, however, ironically identified his status with the whites, although clearly conflicted in his behavior toward slavery and their rule over him.

Constantin Stanislavski, the great theatrical instructor, would have appreciated such attention to proper slavish behavior—the shuffling feet, hunched shoulders, downcast eyes, aimless gesturings of hand and body, along with shrewd or self-deprecating remarks to entertain overseer or master. As Stanislavski noted, "An actor lives, weeps, laughs on stage, but as he weeps and laughs he observes his own tears and mirth." This "double existence" could make "art" out of Samboism. Unfortunately, the black, unlike the actor, had few roles to play before whites, although most did not play the Sambo. No doubt the limitation of options had much to do with the rejection of shame that was part of the Sambo trickster role itself. "He who is ashamed," says Erikson, "would like to force the world not to look at him, not to notice his exposure." But, he continues, "too much shaming does not lead to genuine propriety but to a secret determination to try to get away with things, unseen—if, indeed it does not result in defiant shamelessness." Caught like a child in the grip of a demanding, arbitrary father, the slave might react in open shamelessness. Richard Wright in *Black Boy* describes firsthand how an elevator operator named Shorty, playing the slavish clown, maneuvered a Memphis white man into giving him a quarter in exchange for a kick in the rear. Wright was disgusted with the triumphant Shorty. " 'But a quarter can't pay you for what he did to you.' 'Listen, nigger,' he said to me, 'my ass is tough and quarters is scarce.' " Anything goes, so long as it means survival, as Elkins asserts, or at least advantage. Ethically, however, the Southern black lived in two worlds, each with different moral expectations. To please those in one sphere could well mean loss of respect in the other. Since ultimate power lay with the master, the temptation to rely on his largesse and good favor was understandable but by no means required a permanent commitment to servility.[59]

. . . .

The psychological costs of servility for some slaves were very high. To escape the dictates of shame and humiliation, male slaves largely had to repress emotions and exhibit nerveless behavior. The unpredictability of masters, the difficulty of avoiding white surveillance, the powerlessness of any slave in jeopardy could result in self-despisement and doubt, "the brother," Erikson says, "of shame." Charles Ball, a fugitive, explained these feelings in the case of his own family. Helpless to prevent the sale of his wife, Ball's father, once a man "of gay social temper," became "gloomy and morose . . . and spent nearly all his leisure time with my grandfather, who claimed kindred with some royal family in Africa." To avoid sale, Ball's father had to run away and only the grandfather remained to raise the boy. We find these emotions of rage, depression, and stony resentment—often inwardly directed—constantly emphasized in modern black literature: Ralph Ellison, Richard Wright, Ernest J. Gaines, James Baldwin, Eldridge Cleaver, and Alice Walker.[60] All of them deal with the *alienation of the self*—the threat of annihilation of mind as well as body that black males most especially feel. Some, we can speculate, respond in sexually aggressive self-assertions that fall far short of affection, intimacy, and permanent attachment with the women in their lives.[61]

The situation was the classic issue of neurotic conflict, as Karen Horney portrayed it in *Neurosis and Human Growth.*[62] Though justly condemned for his unrealistic portrait of the historical Nat Turner, William Styron depicted the cruelty that slaves had to adopt to protect selfhood. The very pecking order of the plantation—mirror image in the quarters of the patriarchal, male-dominated, honor-obsessed rankings of the white society—encouraged shamelessness, disesteem of others, and self-abnegation. House servants were contemptuous of field hands, drivers of their underlings, lowly male slaves of their women, and women of the inferior members of their own kind. Accepting white standards of physical beauty, slaves often expressed a preference for light skin. These circumstances should not surprise us. Despite the resilience and liveliness of their cultural life, these people in thralldom, no less than others more fortunate, had their own preferences, hatreds, diverse expectations.

Frederick Marryat, the English novelist, noted that "a quadroon looks down upon a Sambo, that is half mulatto half negro, while Sambo looks in his turn down upon a nigger."[63] Edward Wilmot Blyden, an early nationalist and advocate for Liberian settlement, declared, "We have been taught a cringing servility. We have been drilled into contentment with the most undignified circumstances." White oppressions stirred both compliance *and* fierce resentment, as Eugene Genovese explains. According to Frederick Douglass, a consequence was an awe of white power that rendered the slave almost inarticulate. Field slaves chosen to deliver a message to the master's mansion "make the dense old woods, for miles around, reverberate with their wild songs, revealing at once the highest joy and deepest

sadness," a poignant mingling of emotions as they chanted "most exul-
tantly" these words: " 'I am going away to the Great House Farm! O, yea!
O, yea! O!' " [64]

To make matters still worse, deep mistrust and rivalry rent the harmony
of the slave quarters. Such problems had potentially tragic consequences.
The darker side of "shamelessness," for instance, was that Sambos of that
character made untrustworthy companions. Doubtlessly they remained
rational even if they showed a callous disregard of others and sought only
their own advantage. The position of shamelessness or an impervious-
ness to moral controls made the effective trickster dangerous to the stability of the slave community.[65] Suspicion of the white overlord was bound
to lead to mistrust of those associated with him. Indeed, we must recall
how much effort, time, and emotional stress had to be directed toward
self-protection alone, leaving less energy for more creative pursuits and
self-development. What saved the situation from complete demoraliza-
tion was the strength of family ties in a wide kinship network characteristic
of both black American and African culture. David Brion Davis justly contends that, for all the problems of a family environment under slavery, the
bondspeople still drew strength from their "African tribal traditions." [66]
Though circumstances differed in both countries, sources of security outside the immediate family were not available. It did not pay to trust others
in the quarters.[67] Furthermore, escape from white scrutiny was impossible.
Frederick Douglass recalled that Covey, an overseer, "had the faculty of
making us feel that he was ever present with us." Under such circumstances, W. E. B. Du Bois observed how blacks responded with a "double-
consciousness," that is, a "sense of always looking at one's self through the
eyes of others, of measuring one's soul by the tape of a world that looks on
in amused contempt and pity." How different that was from the studied
and voluntary doubleness of which the stage director Stanislavski spoke.[68]

Equally serious was the sheer physical punishment that masters could
inflict. The point is so obvious that one hesitates to belabor it.[69] The prospect of 150 lashes would make almost anyone a cringing coward. What is
remarkable is the control that slaves *did* exercise. Many displays of such
fortitude also had African roots. In some tribal ceremonies in northern
Nigeria, the Sheriya tested men's manliness by sustaining floggings without flinching. In any event, the physical effects of lashings could be very
severe whether administered under law or the arbitrary passion of an irate
master. Sadly, even the most Christian members of the master class were
capable of unbelievable cruelties.[70]

From the psychological point of view, whippings had three major effects. They degraded the victim, shut down more normal communications, but, most of all, compelled the victim to repress the inevitable anger felt toward those responsible for the pain and disgrace. As a result even the merest hint of violence compelled the victim to retreat into as compliant a pose as possible. Young Frederick Douglass told an English audience in 1846, "I feel the scourge of slavery piercing into my heart, crushing my feelings, and sinking me into the depths of moral and intellectual degradation." Yet, far from slavery's reach though he was, he could not help at times feeling that he should "cower before white men."[71] Anyone who has experienced the trauma of powerlessness and threat to life, as victim of hijackers, kidnappers, concentration camp, prison, or police abuse, can readily appreciate Elkins's point about the way that fear can reduce anyone to mindless sycophancy or deep, inarticulate abasement.

In addition, there were less physically injurious brutalities. We scarcely need to mention the threat of sale and separation from family and community. The historian Peter Kolchin comments that the process of "atomization" began with the African slavery and relentlessly continued to the dispersal of families and individuals to the Southwest and West. Charles Ball, a remarkable narrator of his life as slave and fugitive, lost his mother by sale at age four and belonged to five different masters in the Chesapeake area. He then had four more in South Carolina and Georgia.[72] Such sudden and often unpredictable events prompted sorrows hard to imagine but also inevitably loosened the strings of familial affection. After the Civil War, thousands of freed people set out to find loved ones, sometimes great distances away. But many must have considered the task of retrieving long-absent loved ones a fruitless undertaking.

In addition, shaming rites sometimes enlisted the other slaves in enjoying the spectacle and thus doubling the misery while keeping the slaves disunited by mocking each other, a practice well documented also in the Nazi camps. Bennet Barrow, a Louisiana planter, once threatened to put an offending slave on a scaffold in the yard, wearing a red cap. In another example, a slave with an insatiable craving had stolen an enormous pumpkin from his master's patch. The other slaves told on him, and the master easily recovered the unconcealable object. So he made the slave eat "a big bowl of pumpkin sauce." The old slave who recalled the incident declared that "it am funny to see that colored gentleman with pumpkin smear on he face and tears running down he face. After that us children call him Master Pumpkin, and Master have no more trouble with stealing he seed pumpkins."[73]

Despite these harsh conditions, an essential self remained inviolable in the slave's mentality. Behind the mask of docility the slave was still himself and gave the lie to Southern claims for "knowing" their blacks. As W. J. Cash pointed out, "Even the most unreflecting must sometimes feel suddenly, in dealing with him, that they were looking at a blank wall, that behind that grinning face a veil was drawn which no white man might certainly know he had penetrated."[74] And yet the cost was high, less in playing the Sambo than in assertions for respect to counter the necessity of appearing servile.

Male honor was richly prized in the quarters, and defense of it established rank among fellow slaves. Only recently have we come to recognize just how violent slaves were toward each other, especially over sexual competitions. But black chivalry had its uglier side just as it did in Southern white society, a violence less related to female purity than to male possessiveness and fear of ridicule. With regard to white offenses against black women, though, the slave's honor had no recourse, short of murder with inevitable consequences.

Another sign of self-despisement can be located in the examples of sabotage or apparent plantation "accidents" that historians have largely attributed to motives of subversion rather than to racist ideas of black "laziness" and irresponsibility. To be sure, they could be antislavery expressions in some broad but probably unarticulated way. More important, however, they were symptoms of self-despisement. Taking out frustrations on a hoe or horse was not so much a politically calculated act than an impulsive expression of impotent rage, the source of which was seldom fully articulated or understood. We are unlikely ever to know what was strictly personal and what represented a self-conscious act of resistance. The two elements sprang from the same source of demeaning bondage. As we know from recent studies, male slaves also chose to abuse their own kin—wives and children—in brutal fashion. "The slave quarters," the historian Brenda Stevenson writes, often was a "place of smoldering emotions and anger. . . . Spousal abuse was not uncommon, prompting one slave woman, for example to comment that 'some good masters would punish slaves who mistreated womenfolk and some didn't.' Child abuse and neglect were also well-documented phenomena."[75] The problem, one might easily conclude, was even greater than plantation and court records show.[76]

If repression was one of the chief emotional problems of enslavement, another was the related problem of communal mistrust and its effect on the social personality of the slave. Possibly betrayal in the slave quarters did almost as much as the lash to keep the oppressed in fear. As the fugitive slave Henry Bibb recalled: "Domestic slaves are often found to be traitors to their own people, for the purpose of gaining favor with their masters; and they are encouraged and trained up by them to report every plot they know of being formed about stealing any thing, or running away, or any thing of the kind; and for which they are paid. This is one of the principal causes of the slaves being divided among themselves, and without which they could not be held in bondage one year, and perhaps not half that time." To illustrate from Bibb's list of treacheries, consider the issue of runaways. Often the best-laid plans went awry. Frederick Douglass, for instance, described how he and others on a plantation with a kind master tried to escape and failed. Someone had betrayed them.[77]

In the Gabriel Prosser revolt of 1800, Pharoah and Tom Sheppard revealed the conspirators' plans to their master Mosby Sheppard. They feared its almost certain failure, not its success, and sought to save themselves. Black Virginians ostracized the pair for their shameful betrayal, but they did not seek murderous vengeance. Denmark Vesey's plot ended in a similar fashion. An old domestic slave, fearful of the insurrectionary talk he had heard from a minor and indiscreet recruit, informed Peter, who, after some days' delay, gave the secret to his master, John Prioleau. The authorities acted swiftly. We are reminded that in the Nazi camps and Soviet gulags of the same era, as Primo Levi has recounted, there were similar tricksters. As in the betrayal of American slave plots, they were drawn into treachery not necessarily out of enjoyment of the role but out of fear of the apparent omniscience of the oppressor. The Russian inmates called an untrustworthy prisoner a "zek," Levi remarks. A zek exploited "the lack of solidarity" among the prisoners and won favors from the authorities by snitching on fellow prisoners. Did the zek do so with a pure conscience? Perhaps or maybe no.[78]

· · · · · · · ·

Despite misery and grief, the human spirit somehow renews itself. Even under servitude personal development was possible. Some slaves gained confidence in their manhood from possession of a special ancestry, status in the plantation hierarchy, or, more important, a craft or special skill. As early as the 1730s every sixth slave in South Carolina toiled beyond the fields. According to Philip Morgan, by the end of the eighteenth century, one of every four Carolina slaves had developed an occupation requiring experience and particular talents.[79] Preparing a fine cuisine was an early means of self-enhancement. That competence along with carpentering, boatbuilding, and blacksmithing, to name a few others, was sometimes passed down generation to generation in well-ordered plantation households.[80] An unusual talent also helped to create individuality. Abe Davis, a Florida slave who dove for fish, earned a fame that long outlasted his life.[81] Among the insurrectionists—Nat Turner, Denmark Vesey, Gabriel Prosser, and others—who could doubt their commitment or their sense of themselves? Perhaps they lived in a strange fantasy world to imagine that they could achieve their aim of freedom by challenging so powerful, ubiquitous, and vigilant a foe. Nevertheless, like Rosa Robato and the other women who blew up Crematorium number 4 at Birkenau, they showed unusual valor and self-possession and went to their death with spirits unbroken. The same was true of John Gell, Peter Poyas, and Jack Pritchard (Gullah Jack), who followed Vesey in his aborted Charleston plot.[82]

A certain stateliness, like Abd al-Rahman's, proved not as rare as antebellum racist theoreticians would have their contemporaries believe. The Hairston clan of North Carolina owned a slave with the Faulknerian name of Sam Lion, a figure as extraordinary as Sam Fathers in "The Bear" or Lucas Beauchamps in *Intruder in the Dust*.[83] Ambitious, he performed extra labor in field and forest to benefit his wife and ten children. He owned his own tools and lent them to the Hairstons' decent-minded overseer whenever asked. On one occasion in 1842, however, another, brutal overseer, whom Lion's master had recently hired, peremptorily demanded that he turn over an auger Sam Lion possessed. With the work crew observing, the slave had the "impudence" to refuse Beverly Brown's order. Furious, Brown ordered Lion to remove his shirt for a whipping. Again he said no. Quietly Sam Lion returned to chopping timber with his ax. Brown rushed him with a loaded whip handle; Lion turned to face his assailant just in time. Reflexively he swung his implement straight into the overseer's chest. The blow was fatal. Escaping from immediate capture, Sam Lion hid in the woods for a time but finally returned to the plantation. Family loyalty drew him home, a decision that he must have known would end in death. Inevitably he was sentenced to hang. An attempt to escape failed; a guard shot him dead. Nevertheless, he had fulfilled the tenets of the honor code with uncommon courage.[84]

Another source of personal identity lay in the religious realm. As historians have long confirmed, Christianity could mean one thing to masters and another to slaves. The elements that gave strength to the slave appeared in both the Old and New Testaments. Christ had promised the eternal joy of the weak and the damnation of the overbearing to those who followed him. Though African in many of their religious beliefs, converted slaves found comfort in the Bible, which some could read and all could hear from slave exhorters. Jesus, the slaves learned from Isaiah's prophecy, was "despised and rejected of men," a Savior who was "a man of sorrows, and acquainted with grief." The prophet himself declares, "I hid not my face from shame and spitting." Who could better identify with a crucified Christ by whose "stripes we are healed," the lacerated slave or that slave's Christian master? (Isai. 53:3–6, 50:6.) The famous spiritual declared, "They crucified my Lord; / an' he never said a mumbalin' word." The slaves easily identified with that situation; they knew the ideal of stoic silence under provocation.

Moreover, the Bible taught them to withstand the words of white preachers. The clergy pompously warned them not to steal and always to obey their masters. The black listeners might well have echoed the sentiments of Nancy Williams, a former slave. She explained, "Dat ole white preachin' wasn't nothin'. Ole white preachers used to talk wid dey tongues widdout sayin' nothin' but Jesus told us slaves to talk wid our hearts."[85] Moreover, according to the historian Mechal Sobel, by the 1850s in Virginia, all the black congregations were worshiping apart from the whites. African American preachers seemed to be everywhere in the slave states urging their flocks to live cleaner lives and pray for the return of the Savior. A handful even succeeded in earning their freedom from pious white owners, thanks to their charismatic preaching. Some exhorters were enabled to purchase their loved ones and set them free.[86]

As Leon Litwack has pointed out, liberation might mean different things to each slave, but all cherished that dream, even the machube, if ever released from the shackles of cultural deprivation. Upon reaching the end of his life, Abd al-Rahman dreamed of a return to his homeland. After a lifetime of building the estate of his master into one of the great (though transient) fortunes of Mississippi, Abd al-Rahman hoped to die in Futa Jallon. Aged like his slave, Thomas Foster at last was willing to release him. But a final irony was that Abd al-Rahman died at Monrovia on the coast, far from Timbo.[87] Abd al-Rahman was denied his hopes for a triumphal return. In fact, the American slave before the Civil War and the freedman afterward could find full-fledged freedom neither in distant Africa nor in this country. Yet for all the problems of betrayal and personal anguish that bondage created, strength and hope could yet be found in the building of a folk culture that has enriched the American experience and in the advances that the slaves' descendants have made against odds.

During the same period as Ibrahima's process of enslavement in Spanish West Florida, white Americans were engaged in freeing themselves from bondage—the threat, as they deemed it, of liberty denied them by a distant monarch. Honor and dread of shameful subjection demanded a truculent assertion of independence.

CHAPTER TWO

HONOR, DREAD OF ENSLAVEMENT, AND REVOLUTIONARY RHETORIC

Let us treat our rulers with all that honor and respect
which the dignity of their station requires; but let it be such an
honor and respect as is worthy of the sons of freedom to give.
—*Samuel West, 1776*

In 1767, nearly a decade before the outbreak of the American Revolution, Josiah Quincy, a young attorney, warned the readers of the *Boston Gazette* that ministerial powers in England were about to snuff out the lantern of liberty and enslave the white population of America. In graphic terms he depicted the scenes that would quickly ensue: how the "rank adulterer [the Tory neighbor] riots in thy incestuous bed, a brutal ravisher deflowers thy only daughter, a barbarous villain now lifts his murtherous hand and stabs the tender infant to the heart." On the basis of such popular notions of danger, despotism, and ministerial conspiracy, American Revolutionaries hoped to unite the colonies against the degradation of tyranny.[1]

Historians of the American Revolution have been uncomfortable with the bloodthirsty rhetoric to be found in the hundreds of Revolutionary pamphlets, reports of political rallies and riots, and correspondence of the Founding Fathers. As Gordon Wood noted some years ago, scholars have been preoccupied with the Revolution as a purely intellectual movement to the exclusion of other factors.[2] We know much about the evolution of republican theory but little about the ardor that gripped the revolutionary soul. Wood has observed, "The objective social reality scarcely seemed capable of explaining a revolution."[3] The missing element in the historians' grasp of events was an appreciation for the ethic of honor. That ancient code of conduct and social perception helps to explain the intensity of American colonial resentments. The Age of Reason was also an Age of Honor.

In his perceptive study *The Passions and the Interests*, Albert Hirschman examines the curious sea change of ideas that undermined the old order in the eighteenth-century Western world. He notes the gradual demolition of an ancient code whereby man's drive for ambition, power, and glory, largely through an exercise of martial prescriptions, came under attack but was not immediately replaced with one extolling the virtues of bourgeois, individualistic acquisition. Instead, he argues, the new ethos evolved from a new theory of the nation-state.[4] Yet the process did not totally remove the earlier modes. Instead, they were transformed. Even Adam Smith, as Hirschman points out, still believed, as Thomas Hobbes had before him, that "the craving for honor, dignity, respect, and recognition" remained "a basic preoccupation of man." Yet that desire, he proposed in *The Wealth of Nations*, could be harnessed to promote a better order of government and society.[5]

Thus the American Revolution erupted as the old values still obtained but as a new order of self-discipline, republican principle, and faith in human rationality was emerging. Not surprisingly, the old and the new themes of right conduct were not seen as antithetical. Rather, they often merged.

In viewing the American Revolution through the prism of honor, one cannot dispute the relevance of republicanism, about which so much has been written. Rather, the purpose is to offer another perspective that may be divided into three major components: first, the function of persuasion—what the political theorist Melvin Richter calls "the linguistic aspects of politics."[6] As Pierre Bourdieu observes, "The constitutive power which is granted ordinary language lies not in the language itself, but in the group which authorizes it and invests it with authority."[7] In reaction to specific, unpopular imperial measures, that kind of plain discourse moved men, high and low, to reject any sense of obligation to an unreliable mother country. Honor expressed itself best in actions—florid oratory or bursts of violence—rather than in cool terms of rational discourse. The second was the psychology and motives that drove men to take up their roles in the drama of revolt and military action. The third was the colonists' sense of liberty, as sectionally understood, and its negation, slavery. American Whigs thought that so despised a condition involved dependency, passivity, and moral degradation. Rejection of bondage to England, as it was presumed to be, was a matter of considerable weight in a nation half-slave and half-free at the conclusion of the Revolutionary era.

With regard to the rhetorical aspect, the American Patriots, of course, had no monopoly on the concept of honor. Instead, it was the lingua franca of all factions and groups in the transatlantic world, the common speech in which issues of political power were discussed. The importance of language in the enunciation of basic beliefs cannot be exaggerated. The words used were not empty gestures. As Murray Edelman has observed, "Language forms [serve] a crucial function [in politics] by creating shared meanings, perceptions, and reassurances among mass publics."[8] Nonetheless, the meaning of words changes over time and in altered environments so that we may find how earlier generations employed words at odds with current usage. Even within the same era, diverse or inimical groups attached different meanings to words in ordinary discourse. Honor was certainly one of these. For Tories, the code required submission to established authority. In 1762, for instance, in an election day sermon before the Massachusetts General Court in Boston on the eve of the Stamp Act Crisis, the Reverend Abraham Williams reiterated a familiar, old-fashioned sentiment: "A society without different Orders and Offices, like a Body without Eyes, Hands and other Members, would be incapable of acting, either to secure its internal Order and Well-being, or defend itself from external Injuries."[9]

Defiance signified a presumption to honor and power totally undeserved, unearned, and childish. When Henry Mowat of the Royal Navy, in October 1776, warned the Patriots of Falmouth, Maine, of his intention to raze their port, he justified the bombardment as "a rod of correction." The people had too long defied "the legal prerogatives of the best of Sovereigns."[10] Thomas Chandler, a New York Loyalist, in 1775 urged men to defy the insurrectionary Continental Congress because "You must know, that singularity in right conduct will be an honour to you, and a shame only to them that act otherwise." In once more appealing "decently" and "humbly" to "King, Lords, and Commons of Great-Britain," we must assure them, the Tory continued, "that we dread the very thoughts of an absolute independency; and that we see no prospect of security or happiness but under the powerful protection and mild superintendency of the mother country." Ambrose Serle, secretary to Admiral Richard Howe, voiced a common English sentiment when he wrote, "True & Regular Liberty requires such a Refinement of Laws & Institutions . . . such a Sentiment of Honor, such a Spirit of Obedience, & such a Sacrifice of private Interest & Connections to public Order, as can only be the Result of great Reflection & experience, and must grow to Perfection during several ages of a settled & established Government." That order of things, he insisted by quoting "a celebrated historian," was impossible in so young, anarchic, and untried a country as America.[11] Another Tory denounced the rebels as ungrateful children and worse—"detestable parracides [*sic*]."[12] Yet, such language only drove home the Patriots' case: that the Royalists at home and overseas haughtily denied the Americans—whatever their place in society might be—the honor due them as morally responsible adults.

In broader and more intellectual terms, the doctrine of a filial submissiveness to patriarchal authority had already come under attack on the European continent. For the French Encyclopedists, for instance, honor of this kind was identified with the corruptions of the Bourbon court and offered spurious warrant for noble privilege. In rebuttal, Montesquieu, a monarchist, argued that the pursuit of honor "brings to life all parts of the body politic" to the end that "everyone contributes to the general welfare while thinking that he works for his own interests." He is best remembered for his claim, which the Founding Fathers appropriated, that republics were founded on civic virtue. They challenged his notion, however, that such a form of government was suited only to small and homogeneous populations. Despite his conservatism, Montesquieu provided a definition of the ethic that was curiously applicable to the Patriots' understanding of its role even if that was neither the philosopher's intention nor an idea that had intellectual appeal to the American Whigs. "Foremost" among honor's "supreme laws," Montesquieu argued, "are the requirements that we may set a value upon our fortunes, but are forbidden absolutely to set any upon our lives."[13] What Patriot would not be stirred by that sentiment?

Montesquieu's second proposition submitted that "once we have been raised to a position, we should never do or permit anything that might seem to suggest that we regard ourselves as inferior to that position." Again, having achieved nearly complete self-government long before, the Patriots' duty, as they saw it, required them to relinquish nothing that jeopardized that degree of independence. Finally, Montesquieu proposed that "those things prohibited by honour are most rigorously forbidden when the laws do not make similar provision; and that those things demanded by honour are most insisted upon when the laws are silent."[14] His third category was perhaps the most pertinent of the three. It conforms with the modern anthropological understanding of the social, reputational character of honor and shame, its binary opposite. The realm of contumely and vengeance fell outside the law. By no means could the colonists, unrepresented abroad, have carried into court or Parliament their case against the British regime.

No doubt, Montesquieu would have been horrified that the honor which he so carefully defined could animate rebellion against a monarch and be adapted to a republican setting. Yet so it was. Whereas we tend to think of honor as either a purely military or aristocratic code, it is by no means confined to the barracks or courts but functions as the ethical basis of whole societies, as the anthropologist Julian Pitt-Rivers has demonstrated so comprehensively. According to his explanation, honor requires a sense of self-mastery and independence. Shame implies an inability to exercise will and power, a failure that involves deep opprobrium. Under these conditions, honor is a personal or, it may be, collective claim for public approval. When favorably rendered, that signal of respect and moral standing is incorporated into one's sense of selfhood or group identity. The opposite, however, is also true. To be shamed diminishes one's own self-image. Basically, the honor-shame ethos is deeply conservative and defensive. It relies on familial connections and attitudes so that the individual identifies with his lineage and his posterity. Kinlessness and solitude are the twin dangers to be avoided at all costs. Such a posture was well suited to a people certain that liberties practiced for over a hundred years were being assaulted and eroded by forces alien to the corporate body in which the individual finds protection. In the pursuit of self-determination, Americans looked forward to a new order, but they also glanced backward toward the kind of self-governance they had known of old.

The heritage of liberty required them to offer only a nominal submissiveness to royal authority. In the 1770s, they thought themselves reduced to powerlessness. That condition, argued the Patriot Aedanus Burke, degrades "men in their own opinion" of themselves. Unless quickly redressed, he continued, they soon manifest "timid, cringing habits" and become "fit tools for the ambitious designs, and arbitrary dispositions of haughty aspiring superiors."[15]

American Revolutionary pamphlets employed the grammar, vocabulary, and style of honor with a regularity that suggests its salience in everyday colonial life and habit. Sentiments regarding Christian faith, republicanism, and liberty were also evident, as historians have long recognized.[16] But self-expression in terms of the ethic must be taken into account as well. As linguists would say, the style employed was "conative" or "performative."[17] The foundation of Patriot polemics was simple, indeed primitive. Tract writers sought to animate manly instincts by portrayals of Tory or neutral citizens as gutless cowards. Charlestonian John McKenzie raged that Britain had "insulted—bullied—" and generally treated Americans as "emasculated eunuchs."[18] Like Josiah Quincy, Thomas Paine in *Common Sense* stressed manhood in defense of family dependents: "Are your wife and children destitute. . . ? Have you lost a parent or a child by their hand . . . if you have, and can still shake hands with the murderers, then you are unworthy of the name of husband, father, friend or lover, and whatever may be your rank or title in life, you have the heart of a coward, and the spirit of a sycophant."[19]

As one might expect, pious New Englanders, more than Southern Patriots, tended to couple honor with scriptural reference. They found the Old Testament especially appropriate, as well they might. The ancient Hebrew nation, like the modern Middle East, was well versed in the dictates of honor.[20] The irascible John Allen, a Baptist minister of Boston in 1773, took Micah 7:3 for his text. He expounded on the right of a chosen people to protest and even overthrow the tyranny of evil rulers. Allen thundered: "Have you not heard the voice of blood in your streets, louder than that which reached to Heaven, that cry'd for vengeance, that was, said the Lord to Cain, the voice of thy brother's blood?"[21] Peter Thacher of Malden, Massachusetts, however, became so overwrought that he forgot the customary biblical text for explication. At once he plunged into the heart of the matter. The preacher urged his flock to "spring to action, let us gird on the sword of the Lord and of Gideon, and determine to conquer or die! . . . Do not let us hear of any of you who behave like cowards." Only in the summation did he remember to insert the requisite scriptural passage: 2 Samuel 10:12. Yet it was quite appropriate: "Be of good courage, and let us play the men for our people."[22] Likewise, New England laymen rhapsodized on God's pleasure in righteous display of manly feelings. John Hancock of Boston declared, "I conjure you by all that is dear, by all that is honourable, by all that is sacred, not only that you pray, but that you act. . . . Break in sunder, with noble disdain, the bonds with which the Philistines have bound you." Dishonor entailed an unmanly spirit. As a result, he continued, Americans should reject "the soft arts of luxury and effeminacy" and sacrifice the pursuit of wealth to the cause of liberty. Those who admire wealth alone, he advised, "almost deserve to be enslaved."[23]

Such biblical phraseology and appeals to spartan righteousness were relatively mild. Thomas Paine, Moses Mather, Samuel Adams, and many others in the Northern states employed a rhetoric designed to rouse the passions by posing the direst calamities imaginable as the outcome of continued British rule: towns sacked, friends slaughtered, estates forfeited, houses burned, wives and children made destitute, and daughters raped.

As early as 1770, Dr. Joseph Warren, for instance, defied verisimilitude in conjuring up the image of the "murdered husband gasping on the ground," whose "infant babes" had to step on slippery stones "bespattered with your father's brains." Such scenes, he concluded, were the handiwork of "Britain that inflicts the wound." Throughout the period, terms like *infamy, villainy, fiendish,* and *shameless* filled the printed pages and the ears of listeners at political assemblies.[24]

References to a familial paradigm suggest the conservative character of American republicanism. Separation from the "mother country" was as necessary, the Patriots believed, as the departure of youth from the parental hearthside. In drawing upon this common metaphor, Richard Wells declared, in separating from England, "we look to manhood." But the departure was by no means amicable in light of the mother country's alleged betrayal and unnatural feelings of hostility toward her subjects abroad. As Samuel Langdon put it, the colonists were no longer satisfied to be the dependents of a parent ready to "wage cruel war with its own children in these colonies, only to gratify the lust of power, and the demands of extravagance!" In his study of this rhetorical construction, Melvin Yazawa observes: "The logic of the parent-child analogy thus had a compelling simplicity for the Revolutionaries: 'if they are not considered as children, their Treatment is that of Slaves, and therefore, if oppressed, they must unite,' as Nicholas Ray put it."[25] The benign domestic image contrasts sharply with the extreme hyperbole of the language employed. What royal governor Thomas Hutchinson called "mob-high eloquence" suggested that the English nation was literally bent on mass abuse and butchery of its colonial offspring.[26] The heightened rhetorical stakes frequently went far beyond the exigencies of the case.

Behind these outbursts, of course, there were just complaints. The list is familiar: unfair taxes; official corruption; and unjust parliamentary reprisals against the restive colonies. As Julian Pitt-Rivers observes, taxation and honor have always been incompatible. Coerced payment signifies abject disgrace. From the dawn of history, defeated enemies and inferior people had to forfeit property as tribute or tax. Free peoples, however, contributed to the king's treasury through subsidy, rendered out of affection for the ruler. In earliest times, revenues for the head of state was more or less a matter of gift exchange, albeit an unequal reciprocation. The revenues furnished were traded for the benefits of leadership and responsibility vested in the king. So it had been understood by the Parliament, for instance, at the time of the Ship Money crisis in the reign of Charles I. The outcry against British taxation without American representation and voice in the process arose from this concept. It was based on the honor of grant or subsidy versus mortification of taxation. Ofttimes polemicists turned to ancient history for precedent in developing this argument. James Otis, for instance, pointed out that in Periclean Greece, colonists were obliged only "to pay a kind of deference and dutiful submission to the mother commonwealth." But, he insisted, nothing more demeaning than that was required of them.[27]

As historians have long known, the parliamentary exactions on Americans to help reduce British indebtedness for the Seven Years' War were rather light by contemporary standards.[28] Yet colonists smarted under the affront of taxation with no means to bargain, modify, or persuade the parliamentary parties through colonial representation. In the Virginia Resolutions to Lord North in 1775, Thomas Jefferson argued, "Whereas, we have right to give our money, as the Parliament does theirs, without coercion, from time to time, as public exigencies may require, we conceive that we are alone the judges. . . . *Because* at the very time of requiring from us grants of Money they are" planning war against us, "which is a stile of asking gifts not reconcileable [*sic*] to our freedom." Likewise, the Congress's Resolutions of 31 July 1775 spoke of taxes as "gifts" not to be "wasted among the venal and corrupt for the purpose of undermining the civil rights of the givers." The resolution further demonstrated the significance of the ancient prescriptions: "We consider ourselves as bound in Honor as well as Interest to share our general Fate with our Sister Colonies . . . and having in vain appealed to the native honour and justice of the British nation," a new course of action is necessary.[29]

The category of involuntary taxpayer entailed reduced social and political status. Such exactions lessened one's own and one's family's independence—freedom from the control of or obligation to another. Machiavelli had long before warned that unwise rulers overtaxed their subjects at great peril, "for men forget more easily the death of their father than the loss of their patrimony."[30] In fact, by custom those who gained the most glory and authority from either military victories or officeholding were expected to pay for such honorifics. They should not burden marginal folk. Taxing Americans, however, had become popular in the home country, argued one pamphleteer, because the British had drained themselves while Ireland had been "impoverished to almost the last farthing."[31] Even Ireland, which, in James Otis's opinion, had fallen into English hands as "a *conquered* country," deserved "the same right to be free under a conqueror as the rest of his [majesty's] subjects." How much more worthy then, he asked, should America be when at no time was it a defeated province but one created by "*emigrant* subjects."[32]

The second grievance, bureaucratic malfeasance and venality, stimulated almost equal fury. Such vices violated the code in two specific ways. Nepotism and favoritism in officeseeking put Americans at more disadvantage than before when competing for titles and posts against placemen with contacts at Whitehall unavailable to the distant colonists. Second, corruption of this kind reinforced the sense of impotence that men of honor felt in the handling of political affairs. Their anger stemmed from the implied dependency and alienation from authority that the indignity of open corruption flaunted in their faces. After all, the British were masters in the art of condescension and arrogance; no wonder Americans were vexed. The Reverend William Gordon of Roxbury, Massachusetts, summed up American reaction with a quotation from Proverbs: "*a brother offended is harder to be won than a strong city, and their contentions are like the bars of a castle.*"[33] In thunderous response to the Stamp Act crisis, the Reverend Enoch Huntington of Massachusetts preached: "Already do the avaricious courtiers of *Great-Britain*, with the numerous train of their . . . hangers-on, with the whole tribe of dissolute spend-thrifts, and idle deboshee's, feast themselves" upon "the spoils of our future earnings." John Adams echoed the sentiment: "When luxury, effeminacy, and venality" have reached "a shocking pitch in England, when both electors and elected are become one mass of corruption; when the nation is oppressed to death with debts and taxes . . . what will be your condition under such a parliament? You would not only be slaves, but the most abject sort of slaves, to the worst sort of masters!"[34]

The third objection intimately connected with honor was the outcry against standing armies. Not only were they potential instruments of lawless tyranny, but their presence also signified mistrust of the local elite and the general populace. The use of professional forces set at conflict the members of a locale against military inquisitors into their exclusive affairs. Such an opposition has been traced to the late seventeenth-century Commonwealthman John Trenchard and earlier to James Harrington.[35] Suspicions of occupying armies, however, long predate that era. Clearly they violated the sense of local independence, the honor of the community. To the American colonists, the imposition of permanent forces, especially when quartered in civilian billets instead of barracks, signified humiliation and naked despotism.[36]

In sum, the language of protest and the source of the anger emanated from and in turn fed the perceived imperative for vengeance and self-vindication. British indifference to the Americans' welfare reflected a sense of hauteur and disrespect that had to be challenged with violent words, violent deeds. Sometimes the form of protest was pacific, for example, the movement against imported British goods. Yet the rationale was still linked to honor and its opposite. A Philadelphia editorial warned the city that "[There is] no Benefit in Wearing English wollens [*sic*], but dishonor."[37] More grimly, the Patriots' activities involved mobs and mass rallies. The various charivari or tarring and feathering to mock and enfeeble the Loyalists signified the adoption of old popular European shaming rituals.[38] Like their cousins overseas, colonial Americans believed in a corporate ideal whereby a community in its self-protective aim of consensus "might join together and riot to purge itself of deviants or to protect itself from outside intrusions," as the historian Paul Gilje has noted. In New York City, for instance, a lowly Tory shoemaker named Tweedy fell victim to a mob, endured an application of tar and feathers for denouncing the Patriot cause, and had to beg mercy on his knees by ritualistically " 'praying for Success to General Washington, and the American Arms, and Destruction to General Gage and his Crew of Traitors.' "[39] Claiming "Motives of Honour and Virtue," the magistrates of Westmoreland County, Virginia, refused to collect the Stamp Act revenues—after mobs had forced them to reconsider their plans.[40] Along with the destruction of statues of George III and other symbols of the hated regime, these protests weakened the sense of legitimacy that the English Crown had previously enjoyed in America. At Huntington, Long Island, in 1776 a crowd adopted a venerable shaming ritual. The leaders took an old liberty pole, made it into an effigy of King George with a black face, and added a wooden broadsword. Then they hanged and set it afire. The cross-Atlantic tie was no longer based on the idea of submission in exchange for "that protection which the King affords his subjects," as the Whig William Blackstone had defined allegiance in his *Commentaries*.[41] The king had lost his royal mystique.

Vestiges of royal custom and English law remained: the first being the duty of oath-taking, which, as students of honor recognize, was a particularly important aspect of the ethic. Honor, of course, involves the sacred—the sense that persons, nations, tribes, or communities honored bear a preferential tie to the deity, Christian or otherwise. The curse of shame and the oath of honor reflect that intimate connection. Even today, courts require an oath-taking before examination as witness before the bar, and armies require ritual words to signify allegiance to God and country. In the reign of Charles II, the House of Lords at the beginning of sittings insisted that all peers take the Oath of Allegiance and Supremacy in order to expose the Catholic lords as suspected traitors to the Crown.[42] At the time of the American Revolution, European monarchs, including George III, insisted upon oath-taking to assure loyalty of subjects at risk of forfeiting the oath-taker's honor and reputation.[43]

What were dissident colonists to do under such circumstances? In a thoughtful essay Michael Kammen offers a different interpretation of the ritual oath. He perceives it as purely a matter of conscience. But conscience and honor are really inseparable at this juncture. Both swearer and oath-giver are joined by invoking the third party in the covenant —God Himself. In fact, one of the Patriots whom Kammen quotes announced his refusal to swear loyalty to the king as being "contrary to my Conscience, my Honor, & my love to the Country," a trinity that resembles, of course, the famous "Honor, God and Country" at West Point.[44] Whereas rules of honor were assumed to apply in family relations without need of formulation, the oath surmounted the perils inherent in nonfamilial connections by beseeching God as arbiter. An English writer in 1614 declared it "the safest knot of civil society, and the firmest bond to tie men to the performance of their several duties."[45] In contrast, the Quakers considered any oath a signifying of worldly honor. To acknowledge the primacy of a king or judge's honor by taking an oath was a profanation of God's infinite superiority over men. Not surprisingly, swearing fidelity to the Crown could lead to an uncomfortable coating of hot tar, garnished with chicken feathers, the traditional shaming ritual. Kammen cites harsh coercion by various means. The spirit that guided such conduct belies his stress on "conscience" as the sole criterion of oath-taking for or against the Patriot cause.[46]

In overlooking so salient an ethic, Kammen is by no means unique among colonial scholars. Scarcely a one seems to have the slightest idea what the term meant in the colonial and Revolutionary periods.[47] Yet English law also played a major role in sustaining old customs, especially in Virginia, even though the most important economic, political, and social pillar of aristocracy was abolished. The way that properties were conveyed according to ancient English precedence upheld the aristocratic order of things. Entail—that is, the prohibition against the alienation of property in land and slaves except according to the rule of primogeniture—was strictly enforced in the Virginia courts throughout the seventeenth and eighteenth centuries. Even when the House of Burgesses passed exceptions, the royal governor might well nullify the action. As a member of the House of Burgesses in 1776, Thomas Jefferson set about to abolish the legal system because its spirit and its implementation hindered the growth of republican sentiment and held Americans captive to an indefensible form of feudalism. In 1848, Robert R. Howison, a legal scholar, remarked that under English common law "the father was lord in his lifetime, and the son was lord in expectancy and legal right. Nothing can convey a more vivid idea of the strong aristocratic feeling pervading Virginia, than her course as to [entail.]"[48] Yet, once entail was abolished, the enormous estates that continued to sustain the nobility and upper gentry in England could no longer serve in Virginia as the foundation of unwonted pride and monopolized power. Serving on the committee to revise the laws of Virginia, conservative leader Edmund Pendleton proposed to modify but not abolish entail by doubling the inheritance of the eldest son, following Hebraic custom. In *The Autobiography*, Jefferson recalled that he had rejoined, "if the eldest son could eat twice as much, or do double work, it might be a natural evidence of his right to a double portion; but being on a par in his powers & wants, with his brothers and sisters, he should be on a par also in the partition of the patrimony." His colleagues on the committee agreed.[49]

Even though the offending statutes were abolished by a narrow margin, the climate of honor was not erased by legislative mandate. The historian Holly Brewer persuasively contends that historians have long belittled the legal changes governing the transfer of property from father to eldest son and failed to recognize just how honor-bound, as it were, the ruling class of Virginia had been throughout so much of its early history. Not nearly as much free land, as historians persist in asserting, was actually available for settlement, Brewer reminds us. Thanks to the rigidities of colonial courts, the reason was the inability of large landholders to sell their holdings as needs arose. Instead, landlords leased land to tenant farmers. Yet even owners of large estates, who profited from the leases, chafed under the system because it permitted so little freedom in the disposition of their property to personal and familial advantage. Jefferson himself was once unable to secure the right to sell land held under entail; Governor Dunmore vetoed the necessary legislative measure. Conservatives, however, worried that the old values would be lost if property holders alienated lands and slaves to suit themselves and not the aristocratic hierarchy, upon which, Tories and conservative Whigs thought, civilization rested. Landon Carter had been outraged when Jefferson introduced his "cursed bill" and characterized its author as a "midday drunkard" for even contemplating so drastic an assault on principles of honor and ordered life.[50]

. . . .

With reference to the second issue—the motives for action in which self-regard in a worthy cause was uppermost—one can discern the significance of another and more elaborate form of honor: the stoic mode of gentility. Of course, English radical Whiggery—Gordon, Hoadly, Bolingbroke, and others—supplied Revolutionary pamphleteers with ideas, precedents, and useful citations. But Americans were also influenced by such writers as Joseph Addison, who extolled the virtues of stoicism and dignified forbearance in the exercise of power. His essays and especially his sententious play, *Cato*, in dramatic form sketched the struggle between tyranny and liberty.[51] As Forrest McDonald points out, the eighteenth-century gentleman cherished his "character" or public reputation above all else. Addison's *Cato* was largely designed to demonstrate illustrious reputation. The playwright had not sought to serve partisan purposes. The tragedy's American popularity, however, arose from its current pertinence: the role that heroes could play in the war against despotism.[52]

Defense of reputation became a matter of acute significance in the pre-Revolutionary years because of a growing awareness of British culture. Americans had become increasingly "anglicized" and sophisticated as a result of increased contact with the English during the Seven Years' War. As a result, they grew more self-conscious of their own status in the eyes of the Old World, and they harbored a fear of social and intellectual inferiority. Adopting the fashions of the enemy was one way to make a claim for parity. One manifestation was the adoption of the duel as a signal of gentlemanly status and values. Being a martial code, the ethic helped to regularize personal violence in the upper classes during the war with England. The convention of dueling, which those styling themselves gentlemen adopted from French and English military example, replaced the older and more haphazard modes—fistfights, cartwhippings, and tavern battles. Thereafter gentlemen, especially Southerners, were more likely to meet on the field of honor than to brawl as they formerly had. Penalties were light enough to serve as no deterrent.[53] In adopting the foreign custom, American duelists thought that they were proving how modern and civilized they were, but the practice would never have caught on had it not resonated, particularly in the South. Challenge and response set apart the worthy and allegedly well-born from the allegedly unworthy and vulgar. In a society based on slave coercion, contests of honor gave sanction to violence as a necessary part of society, but at least duels brought some order and restrictiveness in male rivalries.[54]

Although the system was based on a social, political, and economic hierarchy, by no means was honor a monopoly of the rich and powerful. Ordinary young men who entered military service used appropriately martial language for inspiration. In writing home on the first Fourth of July, a young Revolutionary recruit declared, "Our own and our country's honor all calls upon us for a vigorous and manly exertion, & if we now shamefully fail, we shall become infamous to the whole world."[55] Common soldiers were not immune to such blandishments. At the same time, class prejudices separated commoner from gentleman, so much so that foot soldiers suffered in the snows of Valley Forge not only because of an inefficient commissary but also because of the indifference of those on the home front. One historian has concluded that "the general populace did not care (befitting social attitudes of the times) since so many of those who suffered were from the laboring and indigent classes."[56] The soldiers either deserted or resigned themselves to their lowly rung on the social ladder.

In contrast, the officer corps was greatly inspired by the prospect of public respect and glory. General Robert Howe, hoping to assume command of American forces in South Carolina, wrote to Patriot Henry Laurens, "I have been long on the Brigadiers list and pant to get higher."[57] When given a staff instead of a line appointment as major general, Nathanael Greene ruefully remarked, "I am taken out of the Line of splendor."[58] One disgruntled colonel, who lost a seniority dispute with another, wrote to Washington: "It is impossible for a soldier, who is tenacious of his honor (the only jewel worth contending for) to suffer himself to be degraded by being superseded."[59]

Perhaps the most extreme example of ambition for glory and honor run awry was the case of General Benedict Arnold. Brave to the point of incautiousness, Arnold demanded that other generals respect him for his achievements and help him to repress gossip of his financial improprieties. Ethan Allen and Horatio Gates, however, belittled him instead. His most recent, sympathetic biographer, James Kirby Martin, observes that Arnold "would smite the enemy before him for his own glory and the restoration of his family name." Charles Royster summarized his character in a way reminiscent of Shakespeare's representation of Harry Hotspur. Arnold, writes Royster, "sought extremes: the highest rank, the hardest march, the hottest combat, the most luxurious social display, the coolest secret calculation, the most decisive act of war, the highest possible price." Congress refused him the rank of major general that he as well as General George Washington thought he deserved for his valorous services. After he proved himself in battle once again, Arnold finally gained the rank from the legislature but was pointedly denied the seniority that ordinarily went with promotion. Impulsively he protested directly to Congress. Arnold wrote the politicians, "Honor is a sacrifice no man ought to make, as I received so I wish to transmit [it] inviolate to Posterity." At that point members of Congress thought his implied defiance of civilian authority affected that body's honor, as it were, and stupidly refused to right the wrong. After Arnold's betrayal of his flag and country, an astonished public was outraged. If he were caught, Patriots swore to send him to the gallows and bury his leg wounded in the Revolutionary cause with complete military ritual but vowed to put the rest of him on the gibbet. (He escaped to England.) Needless to say, the traitor's former reputation for valor had vanished, and he was stigmatized as a coward in disguise. Arnold's famous recklessness in the face of danger became merely signals of an underlying mental instability and drunkenness.[60]

Congress was also affronted when Generals Henry Knox, Nathanael Greene, and John Sullivan threatened to resign if a French aristocrat, an artillerist, were given seniority over them. Fearful that such insubordination would lead to an overbearing standing army and the submission of civilian government to the military, the delegates were very alarmed. One of them complained that the trio were challenging "the authority, Esteem, or dignity of Congress."[61]

Many other members of the army elite were also completely devoted to what the colonial scholar Robert Calhoon describes as "sacred honor."[62] In a country in which there was relatively little distance in wealth between high and low and in which advanced education was rare, the task of fashioning a gentlemanly officer class was only partially successful. Charles Royster has recorded the uncertainties of status not only between company officers and their sometimes disrespectful men but also between senior officers of good family and juniors largely drawn from inferior homes. As he observes, "honor not only required a man to uphold his rank, keep his word, and demand the same of others; it also required that he resent any insult."[63] As a result, struggles for place were often intense. So acceptable was the language of honor that one could even risk sounding vainglorious in its pursuit. "To sink under the command of men whose superior in rank I had been acknowledged," wrote Adjutant General John Trumbull of Connecticut in 1777, "tasted indeed too loathsome of degradation."[64] Feeling injured by an order from the Continental Congress,

General Nathanael Greene wrote Washington in 1776 that he feared an attempt "to degrade me in Publick estimation. ⟨A measure⟩ of that sort would sink me in my own estimation and render me spiritless and uneasy in my situation and consequently unfit for the service."[65]

By the rubrics of the code, a desire for fame was virtuous so long as ambition was limited by deference to the judgment of those whose good opinion warranted respect.[66] Uncontrolled yearnings for power, like avarice, led directly to corruption under the honor-shame code of gentlemen. Nonetheless, self-restraint in this regard was hard to achieve. Democratic ideals were emerging. A Connecticut cobbler named William Brewster, for instance, claimed in the *Hartford Courant* that he and other artisans were unjustly excluded from political decision making and were roundly dismissed as "ignorant, vulgar, and partial." Intimidated, such common craftsmen as himself felt constrained by fear of ridicule. Indeed, a reply to "A Mechanick" pronounced the author "absolutely *insane.*"[67] Clearly, the European and colonial code of honor which dignified leaders with appropriate marks of distinction and gave them the bulk of power still applied.

The second trait was ambition, an outgrowth of the first, and one also that had inherent contradictions. The gentleman was distinguishable from ordinary mankind because he somehow combined self-sacrifice with self-regard, laudable ambition. Of course, the code of the gentleman required that he should disdain the call of purely worldly cravings for power and claim instead satisfaction in doing good at home. Often reprinted were Washington's statements, announcing a preference for the privacy of family and friends rather the honors of the world. On the eve of his election to the presidency, he wrote Alexander Hamilton that "my great and sole desire to live and die in peace and retirement on my own farm" still applied and he worried that "the world and posterity might possibly accuse me of inconsistency and ambition."[68]

Yet Washington was, of course, ambitious. The ethical way to handle the conflict between respectable modesty and political ambition was to take a passive role, at least outwardly, in one's advancement. Patrons of great power like Washington attracted clients like Alexander Hamilton, young men with ambitions that they could best promote, not by self-aggrandizement but by assisting the climb of their leaders. If successful, they in turn could reward their retainers with fitting offices and opportunities. They could then present themselves as figures of perfect self-sacrifice—the role of reluctant leaders who are called from the pleasantries of domesticity to the struggles of politics. Or else they could be selfless followers who served their patrons only for the sake of public good. This was the political style and structure of the day, based on the rules of gentility.

Those principles required that reciprocity should govern relations between the ruler and the public. The language of honor is very evident in the exchanges between these two forces in the early American republic. However hesitantly he may have presented himself before the people, the office seeker claims a worthiness even as he deprecates his own readiness for lofty duties. The reason for such ritual expressions is that the words disarm fears of tyranny—the speaker or writer says, in effect, I respect the judgment of the populace and honor the citizens for their honoring of me.

Stately deference to the populace was evident in the famous Farewell Address. The duties of the presidency, Washington said, "have been a uniform sacrifice of inclination to the opinion of duty, and to a deference for what appeared to be your desire. I constantly hoped that it would have been much earlier in my power, consistently with motives, which I was not at liberty to disregard, to return to that retirement, from which I had been reluctantly drawn." [69] He represented an entire social ethic. By this is meant the role of gentility, that rank-conscious form of the honor code. The reason why Americans so applauded Washington's character and demeanor was that he combined the best, as they saw it, of two political and cultural styles: the American republican and the English gentleman. The first category is probably well understood, but the latter term—gentleman—has fallen on hard times and deaf ears. Moreover, the word itself is elusive. But that opacity and outdatedness do not mean that gentlemanliness had no substance. Just as a people may speak a language without knowing its grammatical rules and structure, so too can societies form patterns of behavior and responses without fully appreciating the contradictions and vaguenesses in the social code. With that thought in mind, it is worthwhile to examine briefly the nature of gentility. At the beginning of the eighteenth century, Daniel Defoe proposed that "our modern Acceptation of a gentleman is this, A Person Born . . . of some known or Ancient family; whose Ancestors have at least for some time been rais'd above the class of mechanicks." Samuel Johnson gave first place in his five-part definition to the idea that he was "a man of birth; a man of extraction though not noble." Thus ever since the term *gentleman* developed a legal meaning as well as a popular one (about 1413), it had no linkage to nobility—that is, blood proximity to royalty. Instead, gentility was centered, however gingerly, on respectability of ancestry. Even that, though, was problematic, given the flux of fortunes and the ease with which some families like the Boleyns moved from the status of a London hatter to that of the Earls of Wiltshire in three generations.

In the early nineteenth century, Madame de Staël was amazed, she said, that "the son of a common shopkeeper," if talented at the bar, could rise to great rank and wealth and his sister could "marry a descendant of the Howards or the Percies, and become related to all the great nobility celebrated in the history of England."[70] Instead of rank being the chief determinant of English gentility, almost from the start, character, not the right to bear arms, as some think, was the popular criterion. Sir Thomas Elyot acknowledged the moral criterion in his treatise of advice, *The Boke Called the Governour* (1531). In it the prerequisite of "ancient lineage or great possessions" is mentioned but also the notion that the gentleman was "he in whom 'vertuous and gentle deedes did first appear.' " Later in the next century, another writer on manners and civil conduct advised his readers in Restoration England that the ambitious soul should "begin at the Mind" and "cast out thence all base and degenerous Inclinations, and make himself a Gentleman without help of Heraldry." Finally, Sir Richard Steele in the *Tatler* (1710) argued that "the appellation of a Gentleman is never to be affixed to a Man's circumstances but to his Behaviour in them."[71] Right conduct strengthened hopes of recognition.

Douglass Adair, historian of the Revolution, once remarked that he had discovered in the Founding Fathers "a sort of pathology of the 'love of fame' " that accompanied the pursuit of liberty.[72] One might expect that so secular an ideal would animate men in the deistical South more than in the evangelical North. Yet even in New England, the classical view of honor had such strong advocates that one is tempted to say that the ethic was itself a factor that helped to bind North and South at this time. With Addison's drama in mind, at the funeral for General Enoch Poor, military chaplain Israel Evans of New Hampshire, in 1781, likened the dead hero to Cato. Like the ancient Roman, he said, General Poor "*chose* to be virtuous rather than appear so; he preferred that self-approbation which arises from meritorious actions, to the changeable and tumultuous acclamations of the fickle multitude."[73] New England clergymen could preach the virtues of manliness as well as any host of army colonels. Samuel Sherwood rejoiced that the "main body" of Americans "know they are men, and have the spirits of men; and not an inferior species of animals, made to be beasts of burden to a lawless, corrupt administration."[74]

Whether Northern or Southern, Revolutionary leaders entertained hopes for eternal remembrance for their deeds during the crisis. From their classical reading, especially Plutarch and Machiavelli, Patriots knew that builders of empires and republics stood next highest to the founders of religion in the annals of history.[75] Alexander Hamilton, for instance, espoused "that love of fame which is the ruling passion of the noblest minds."[76] What they sought was "*the esteem of wise and good men.*" That aim might be called the political side of stoic, Christian gentility, a refined, class-based concept.[77] To be true to others first and thereby earn the respect and deference of the virtuous was the means for reinforcing one's own sense of identity and self-worth. Such pursuers of honor, Forrest McDonald argues, reversed the advice that Shakespeare put in the mouth of Polonius. Truth to others came first; after that one could be true to oneself.[78] So phrased, the maxim fits the nature of honor. The ethic relies on external appearances of bravery, magnanimity, self-regard, and other stalwart virtues but not on the inner life, an area usually unexamined.

Yet Washington practiced all the licit male vices—gambling, wenching, money-grubbing—and he was "a most horrid swearer and blasphemer."[79] Such vices took nothing from his status. Ordinarily such displays were greeted as welcome, ritualistic signs of virility. Under these conditions, to press forward for the sake of glory offered two advantages to the Patriot-hero—honor for himself and the creation of a nation prepared to revere him in gratitude for generations to come.

These feelings were not simply personal in character but were considered a necessary part of the social order itself. The desirability of fashioning a corps of leaders for the republic included the notion that honor was an indispensable element in republican education. It found its way into the curriculum of the new nation. As John Adams pointed out approvingly some years after the Revolution, "knowledge will forever be a natural cause of aristocracy."[80] The classics were culled for examples of honorable behavior, for heroes exemplifying the appropriate marks of Ciceronian patriotism, judgment, tough-mindedness, and proper ambition for glorious popular remembrance. One Revolutionary preacher declaimed over the bier of Brigadier General Richard Montgomery in early 1776 that, "according to the ancient Romans, in pedagogy, '*honour* is a more powerful incentive than *fear*.'" Men were seldom punished severely for "cowardice or neglect of duty but by what was accounted worse, a life decreed to ignominious expulsion and degradation from Roman privileges."[81]

In keeping with frequent reference to pagan forms of virtue, John Adams and most of the other Founding Fathers believed that mankind was forever governed by the same motives, both good and bad. Therefore, by reading ancient history the best precepts of government could be ascertained as well as the surest means of restraint against perfidy and disorder.[82] Americans did not study the ancients in the original or through English literature of the "Augustan Age" *only* to ponder the nature of republics, their pristine origins, and their subsequent degeneracy and fall. In addition, they sought to inculcate the essentials of pagan morality.[83] At late eighteenth-century Dickinson College in Pennsylvania, for instance, Latin professor Robert Davidson taught grammar by demonstrating the relation of ambition to slavery in this fashion: " 'Rome was enslaved. Caesar was ambitious. Connect them by the conjunction *because* and then it will be Rome was enslaved *because* Caesar was ambitious.' "[84] The purpose of such exercises was not merely to instill a love of liberty but to quicken awareness of an exemplary honor by imitating the excellencies of superiors and peers and rejecting the vices and disgrace of inferiors.[85]

. . . .

Finally, how honor was a factor in the relationship between liberty and what the Reverend James Emerson of New England called "vile ignominious slavery" has long puzzled American historians.[86] "How is it that we hear the loudest yelps for liberty among the drivers of negroes?" asked Dr. Samuel Johnson.[87] The Founding Fathers seemed blind to the contradiction between ownership of slaves and the insistence on universal freedom, as expressed in the Declaration of Independence. Among other meanings attributable to the phrase "all men are created equal" is the notion that claims to honor are open to all members of the white fraternity on an equal footing. So it was later understood in the antebellum South. According to the hierarchy which the ethic upheld, slavery, however, represented the most disgraceful, humiliating, and pitiable condition known to man. As Orlando Patterson has observed, human bondage is a state of non-being." The victims are rendered nameless, kinless, penniless, defenseless, and hopeless, except by the mercy, convenience, or whim of the master. In the eighteenth century, slavery was the most extreme form of social alienation. Yet other types of involuntary subordination— indentured servants, redemptioners, apprentices, landless laborers—were well-entrenched parts of the social structure. As a result, the notion of freedom implied some minimal social standing. The freeman was one capable of self-provision or enjoyed an immunity from political subordination under another. Hence the constant message of Revolutionary propaganda was to protest all marks of what Josiah Quincy called "the chains of vassalage."[88] Moreover, for centuries in political thought, slavery and liberty were by no means considered contradictory. Machiavelli and Algernon Sidney, John Locke's contemporary, both believed that love of liberty so animated the warrior spirit that their countrymen had the moral right to enslave those without such a heritage.[89] By such reasoning, liberty took the form of a hegemonic right to rule rather than a universal principle. The concept that enslavement in the presence of liberty was corrupting to both master and servant was a relatively new one that few besides such thinkers as Montesquieu and Jefferson took seriously.

Even had there been no slaves in the colonies, the white Patriots would have referred to slavery as the opposite of liberty. The presence of black bondspeople, however, added a note of immediacy and example. The American Whigs took for granted black isolation and political impotence. Slaves simply did not belong except as dependents. Thus, when criticized for hypocrisy, American polemicists argued not on grounds of universal rights but on matters of treatment as if asked about the way planters handled their horses. When challenged, most of the American spokesmen considered slaveholders men of honorable intention and high deportment. Pride and interest combined, it was thought, to assure kindness and forbearance of their black menials.[90]

The rhetoric involved should be understood within the context of an assumed connection between liberty and honor, slavery and shame. Said Thomas Gordon in *Cato's Letters*, "Oh Liberty! Oh Servitude! how amiable, how detestable, are the different Sounds! Liberty is Salvation in Politicks, as Slavery is Reprobation."[91] The conflation made possible the seeming paradox of slaveholders demanding freedom for themselves even as they implicitly denied it to a whole race. By the ethic of honor, such a discrepancy involved no paradox. It simply reflected a proper division of labor. The fitting analogy was the assurance, by usage and common law, that men held proprietary rights in their wives and children on the basis of natural, God-given ascriptive hierarchy.[92] As if to underline the point, the Reverend Jonathan Mayhew of Boston observed that colonial slaves shared their masters' opinions about British tyranny. They knew, he said, that "it would be more ignominious and wretched to be the *servant* of *servants*, than of freemen." Needless to say, slaves took a different approach. When given the chance, thousands of slaves, both in the North and the South, fled to British lines.[93]

Yet there was already a difference between North and South regarding the relative position of honor in relation to other favored attributes of a man's character. John Hancock, Samuel Adams, Paul Revere, and other radically committed Patriots in the North cherished the principles of honor. Still, some with more secular, progressive ideals, would have placed that principle below others. John Adams argued that while "honor is truly sacred," it "holds a lower rank in the scale of moral excellence than virtue." Too violent, too savage, honor could not "support a frame of government productive of human happiness."[94] For Southerners, however, the word had very intense meanings and might even be thought synonymous with virtue. Even as late as the mid-nineteenth century, honor held a special place in the Southern white breast. In 1866, Sarah Dorsey, a Louisiana novelist and wealthy landowner, observed that "virtue" always came in sundry guises: "With the Christian martyr, it is faith; with the savage, it is honor; with the republican, it is liberty."[95]

Moreover, in the slave states the connection between the honor of whites and the presumed dishonor of blacks was naturally more firmly held than it was in the North, where the institution of bondage was much weaker and was destined gradually to disappear. The white populace was well aware of the dangers that emancipation or insurrection might visit upon the social order. Furthermore, racial leveling would threaten community and personal honor. In the low country of South Carolina, for instance, the attorney Timothy Ford declared, "The instant a citizen is oppressed *below par* . . . in point of freedom, he approaches to the condition of his own slave, his spirit is at once aroused, and he necessarily recoils to his former standing."[96] On that basis, the classes of the South were united. No one could countenance slave uprisings. Among other things, insurrections threatened the status of honor of all whites. For that reason, gruesome punishment for slave rebellion had universal approval. In ancient Rome, a mass execution of all slaves was authorized by law if one among them had murdered their master. No doubt Southern planters considered themselves enlightened not to take so drastic and economically obtuse a step. But they did not shrink from putting heads of suspected rebels on poles as warning to other potential conspirators. A slave in 1740 was burned alive for having set fire to a white man's house in South Carolina. A nineteenth-century state historian justified the penalty "as a kind of *lex talionis* under the statute of Edward I."[97] Such barbarisms suggest just how insecure and fearful the whites were in contemplating a racial and social leveling. The brutality was based on the notion that slaves were nonhuman in some aspects of their nature.

Whether the danger came from below or from English authorities abroad, the revolutionary response was quick and potentially violent. Christopher Gadsden of Charleston urged that citizens be prepared "to avert by every means in our Power the abject Slavery intended for us and our Posterity; for my part I would rather see my own family reduced to the utmost Extremity and half cut to pieces than to submit to their damned Machinations."[98] To show any sign of weakness was to lose face entirely. As George Washington put it, "We must assert our rights, or submit to every imposition . . . till custom and use shall make us as tame and abject slaves, as the blacks we rule over with such arbitrary sway."[99] He intended no irony.

In asserting the claims of freedom, Patriots constantly spoke in polarities: glory and purity against villainy and disgrace, pure-minded liberty and craven slavery.[100] A committee of the Continental Congress resolved: "We are reduced to the alternative of chusing an unconditional submission to the tyranny of irritated ministers, or resistance by force. Honour, justice, and humanity forbid us tamely to surrender that freedom which we received from our gallant ancestors, and which our innocent posterity have a right to receive from us. We cannot endure the infamy and guilt of resigning future generations to that wretchedness which inevitably awaits them, if we basely entail hereditary bondage upon them."[101] A communication from the Massachusetts legislature neatly condensed the major themes of the Revolution in its declaration that Patriots should enlist for military service in response to "the dread of slavery, the sensations of honour and humanity, and the dictates of religion." The New England Baptist minister John Allen had concluded his sermon on the verses from Micah with particularly grim words: "Has not the voice of your father's blood cry'd yet loud enough in your ears, in your hearts? 'ye sons of America scorn to be slaves.' "[102]

Honor may be interpreted to help identify how the Patriots perceived their role. The old ethic, whether seen through the eyes of Montesquieu or the anthropological mode, underlay sectional self-justifications. This approach to the American Revolution by no means denigrates basic economic and political conflicts at the heart of the matter. Nonetheless, anger, a sense of insult, and outrage against arbitrary and arrogant behavior had to play a major role in the first great revolution of modern times. Other scholars who have stressed the role of reasoned republican idealism have sought to explain why those ideals were accompanied by a language and set of actions of a deeply conservative but inspiring character.

During the Revolutionary era, love of honor and fear of shame drew the North and South together in common antipathy toward British overlords. For a time, honor helped to cement the sections of the nation in a two-party system throughout the dire crises of the 1790s. At that juncture, revolutions and war were fiercely raging in Europe, and the new nation was embarking uncertainly on the largely untried course of constitutional republicanism. As the historian Joanne Freeman observes, "personal honor was the ultimate bond of party when all else failed," a notion that she finds crucial to making sense of the political culture of the first party system. Sectional mistrust threatened to split the Federalist camp in 1800. Presidential candidate John Adams of Massachusetts and vice-presidential nominee Charles Pinckney of South Carolina represented two states that would square off in 1861 as the most antagonistic of all those in the Union. In 1800, however, leaders in both states swore upon their honor to meet partisan obligations and not betray mutual trust. Republicans, too, faced the same problem of sectional suspicions—as well they might in view of Aaron Burr's later betrayal. "*Can we, may we* rely on the integrity of Virginia & the southern states?" wrote a New York Jeffersonian to James Madison. "[We] depend on the integrity of Virginia & the southern states as we shall be faithful & honest in New York." Madison replied that it would a "sacrilege" to repudiate commitments already pledged.[103]

In his ambition, though, Burr tried to seize the moment and the presidency for himself. The electoral tie between Thomas Jefferson and his New York running mate created a crisis that might have erupted into civil war. The Republican governors of Pennsylvania and Virginia came close to calling up the state militias. Thanks to a weakening of Federalist resolve, however, the stalemate was broken in favor of the Republicans. That and other threatening episodes in which honor played a part in resolving occurred throughout the subsequent years. Yet eventually the meaning of honor as Southerners and Northerners understood it so drastically changed over the next sixty years that the ethic became a source of acrimony, not harmony. That once unified paradigm of ethical and political values—faith in a rational republicanism and a continued devotion to honor for the defense of selfhood and vindication of community and personal repute—was not to last beyond the middle years of the next century. Northerners were to develop a different, secular ethic in which honor was institutionalized and made impersonal, abstract. It no longer signified personal bonds of friendship but was based on evangelical and commercial principles of individualistic redemption and material advance.

In contrast, Southerners continued to admire the Revolutionary rhetoric with its primal overtones that glorified ascriptions of power and race. That legacy of honor, including its most personally violent aspect, the ritual of paired combat, continued well into the Jacksonian era. In political terms, the most significant exemplar of gentlemanly honor was Andrew Jackson himself, who ironically but not inconsistently identified himself as white, honorable, and egalitarian. In those respects he was a true heir of the Revolution. For the most part, that upheaval did not obliterate the principles of honor but broadened the basis of the ethic far beyond the limits of aristocracy and monarchy, most especially and most enduringly in the slave South. Although a national leader and founder of a bisectional party, the sixth president personified the ideals—and failings—of a circumscribed slave culture. Jackson's South was doomed to fight a final and disastrous duel for survival.

CHAPTER THREE

ANDREW JACKSON'S HONOR

*Greater love hath no man than this, that a man
lay down his life for his friends.*

—John 15:13

*Behaviour that's admired
Is the path to power among people everywhere.*
—Beowulf *(Seamus Heaney translation)*

No one in American history and certainly no other president can be more closely identified than Andrew Jackson with the dictates of honor and the reward of power, as the epic poet declares, that accompanied admired behavior in his day. For Jackson, it was a matter of religious faith as deep as his melancholy wife, Rachel's, devotion to Presbyterian Christianity. He had almost no religious sensibility, but his devotion to honor and his ambition for public recognition had no limits. Better "death than dishonor!" expressed his grand ideal. For him, and many others of his generation in the South, honor adhered to a warrior on the battlefield as well as to a woman in her boudoir.[1] "Blessed are the open-handed, for they shall have friends and fame. Blessed are they who wreak vengeance, for they shall have . . . honor and glory all the days of their life and eternal fame in ages to come."[2] That religious mandate has always competed in Western civilization with the more familiar Beatitudes, but it was grounded in earthly public remembrance.

Certainly as soldier, politician, planter, and husband, Jackson represented these sentiments almost to perfection, particularly with regard to that lethal instrument of honorable vindication, the code duello, and—inseparably linked to it—what may be called protective or instrumental friendships. The principles of honor were the means to create and bind together a privileged group and to classify the ranks of its members for the purposes of establishing order and group cohesion. Under those circumstances, both strong friendships and duels, or sometimes less ritualized forms of personal combat, were significant in the organizing of leadership in political circles, particularly Southern ones.[3]

To identify Jackson as the very model of early American concepts of honor, however, is not meant as an unreserved compliment.[4] After all, the code to which he subscribed has always possessed such dark, brutal, even gothic aspects that its failings have been central to epics and dramas throughout the centuries of Western civilization. In *The Painter of Dishonour*, a play from the Golden Age of Spanish tragedy, Pedro Calderón's distracted aristocrat, Juan Rocca, feels compelled to avenge himself against an allegedly unfaithful wife. He laments in anguish, "Damn honour and its tyranny! . . . What madness dreamt up laws like these, these shameful rites the world accepts?"[5] Rocca's own capture in the entanglements of deception did not permit him broader contemplation of the code's defects. But had it been otherwise among the distortions that the protagonist might have justly perceived in honor were a heartless, overbearing male passion to rule untrammeled, especially over women and menials. In addition, a repression of self-exposing, seemingly effeminate feelings could prompt ill-recognized anger and melancholy. Finally, a lust for fame and immortality in men's memory was inevitably to appear. The latter risked the moral integrity of the seeker of honor itself. It was an overreaching that could become self-defeating. All three extremities required a Manichaean approach that allowed no shades of gray between honor and shame, right and wrong. That sharp differentiation helps to explain why the conferring of honor or a denial of it becomes a form of dramatization—a staging before a responsive audience.[6] Jackson's appeal to large aggregations of the male populace lay exactly in his ability to dramatize his manly uprightness and high sense of honor. A historian recently referred to Jackson as "the Caudillo," a fitting title.[7] Yet the excesses of his public displays of conviction shed light on his deepest flaws. How Jackson united the ethic to his personal identity in a lifetime comes finally out of the story as almost a tragic ending.

It is today all too easy to assail Jackson for his faults and for prejudices about gender, race, and most other opinions that our more enlightened era discountenances. In truth, Jackson's demands during the War of 1812 for fourteen million acres of Creek lands, as he sought to punish the pro-British Red Sticks, nudged even authorities in Washington to protest. Having decisively won the battle of Horseshoe Bend in March 1814, he reprimanded his critics, both white and dark-skinned. "Listen," he warned ominously, "the creek chiefs and warriors did not respect" our strength. They thought the British would be victorious, for which sentiment "they wanted flogging," he argued. "We bleed our enemies to give them their senses." Likewise, in the Seminole War of 1818 his actions were a study in flagrant disobedience, gross inequity, and premeditated ruthlessness. The late historian John William Ward noted, "He swept through Florida, crushed the Indians, executed the Englishmen, Arbuthnot and Ambrister, and . . . violated nearly every standard of justice." He claimed powerlessness only when, as president, he obligingly surrendered federal authority to the Southern doctrine of states' rights in the handling of Indian relations.[8]

Jackson's approach to free speech and assembly was equally mean-spirited. After the abolitionists' great national publicity drive in 1835, President Jackson, that alleged champion of liberty, showed his constitutional scruples by recommending that Congress prohibit by law the delivery of antislavery materials through the United States mails.[9] The two examples scarcely exhaust the list of public acts that seem reprehensible now. Like other men of honor, Jackson was also capable of decisions that even contemporaries would not have regarded as honorable. So long as they were not visibly committed by his dramatized or public self but took place behind the scenes (such as plotting to bring down a rival like John C. Calhoun without showing his hand), he lost in his own time no appearance of honor—and only appearance in a sense mattered.[10] In spite of these problems, the Hero of New Orleans possessed a charismatic greatness and complexity of character that were truly astonishing. Moreover, his activities early in his career in Nashville can serve to illustrate the nature of politics and patronage and their connection with dueling not only on the frontier but in the South, if not the nation, at that time. In other words, Jackson's sense of honor can be treated as a metaphor signifying a particular Southern distinctiveness. Above all, Jackson was as deeply committed to white Southern customs, convictions, and prejudices as any observer could imagine.

. . . .

As the epitome of honorable conduct and principle, Andrew Jackson was the only American president to have fought duels and, on one notable occasion, to have killed his adversary. Jackson's fight against Charles Henry Dickinson should be seen from two perspectives—first, for the light it sheds on the political culture of the early republic and second, for the duel's sources in Jackson's own personal history, an angle that reveals how his tragic past and reaction to it led him to the dueling ground. Such a mingling of political and community life with the purely psychological and biographical has become more acceptable in recent years. A dissatisfaction with the limitations of old-fashioned institutional approaches to politics and an appreciation of how personal, ethnic, gender, and racial factors affect the political realm has happily developed.

To set the stage for the first of the two considerations—Jackson's political expression of honor—an account of his most famous duel is worth telling. The trouble between the Tennessee leader and Charles Dickinson arose from a dispute over a horse race. Racing was more than an entertainment in that society.[11] It offered the wealthy a chance to display their power: Andrew Jackson took great pride in his fine stable of Arabians. His five-year-old Truxton was renowned even beyond the state borders.[12] Against Truxton, Captain Joseph Ervin posted his champion, Ploughboy. The stakes totaled $2,000, a considerable sum for the early nineteenth century. On the day before the race, Ploughboy went lame and had to be scratched. As a result, Ervin had to forfeit $800 in notes that Jackson had the right to approve or reject.[13]

Rumors circulated that the general was dissatisfied with the way Ervin and his son-in-law Charles Dickinson were handling the debt. The principals in the dispute had their cliques of hangers-on, militia cronies, and personal aides. One of them was Thomas Swann, a young lawyer from Powhatan County, Virginia, who served the Ervin-Dickinson leaders as a general factotum, gathering news, running errands, and canvassing during elections. Jackson had no respect for him. On one occasion during the growing rounds of charges and innuendoes, the general called Swann's patron, Charles Dickinson, a "*base poltroon and cowardly tale-bearer who will always act in the background.*"[14] The young lawyer Swann took the remarks as an affront to himself and his leader—as well Swann might.

At their next encounter in a tavern, Jackson knocked Swann down with a cane. Predictably, the youthful Swann demanded a duel.[15] Jackson refused. The challenger, he concluded, was no gentleman. Conforming to the rules of pistol etiquette, Jackson "would not degrade himself by accepting his challenge."[16] Jackson did aver, though, that if Swann could find a friend of appropriate moral rank, he would, as he put it, pledge "my word and my honor" to "meet him on any gentlemanly ground."[17] Duels, of course, were fought only between gentlemen of proximate age and reputation.

The squabble grew more complicated. Other members of the Nashville elite plunged into the spreading rivulet of male intrigue. Two of them —Jackson's best friend, General John Coffee, and Nathaniel McNairy, a Dickinson supporter—dueled over their superiors' dispute.[18] McNairy fired prematurely and shot Coffee through the fleshy part of the leg. After exchanging some hot words, the young men ended their showdown, both claiming "satisfaction" that their courage and self-esteem remained untarnished. In Irish duels, the leg was known to be the most popular part of the male anatomy.[19]

Meantime, Charles Dickinson felt obliged to offer himself as replacement for the rejected Swann. Dickinson himself had already insulted Jackson. Early in the dispute, Dickinson had questioned in public Rachel Jackson's honor, tarnished by a messy marital history. Jackson heard about the insult. His biographer James Parton claimed that Jackson "kept pistols in perfect condition for thirty-seven years" to use whenever someone "dared breathe her name except in honor." Jackson demanded explanation from the offender, who at once apologized and attributed his lapse of discretion to overdrinking. Jackson accepted the excuse, but he never forgot a slight. As he later declared, if Dickinson wished "to blow the coal, I am ready to light it to a blaze that it may be consumed at once, and finally extinguished."[20] The climax came when Dickinson posted a card in the local paper saying, among other things, "I declare" Jackson "'a poltroon and a coward', a man who, by frivolous and evasive pretexts, avoided giving the satisfaction, which was due to a gentleman whom he had injured."[21] Jackson's close friends advised that he had little choice. In the appropriate language of the code duello, the general replied to Dickinson, "Insults may be given by men, and of such a kind that they must be noticed and treated with the respect due a gentleman, altho (as in the present instance) you do not merit it. You have, to disturb my quiet, industriously excited Tho's Swann to quarrel with me," with the result that the "peace and harmony of society" had been outrageously disturbed. Jackson accepted the challenge.[22]

The fateful event took place on 30 May 1806, at a hostelry in Logan County, Kentucky. Dickinson was already well known as a superb marksman, but Jackson was no sharpshooter. He intended to hold fire, a dangerous but strategic decision. At the signal, at once Dickinson aimed and fired. A puff of dust was visible as the shot struck Jackson's bulky coat. The general swayed only a little. In utter amazement, Dickinson staggered back from his position, crying out "'Great God! Have I missed him?'" "'Back to the MARK, Sir,'" Jackson's second, Major John Overton, commanded as he pulled out his own pistol menacingly. By the code, Overton had every right to kill Dickinson on the spot for violating the rules. Dickinson obeyed. Meanwhile, Jackson aimed his gun carefully and slowly. He pulled the trigger. Click—that was all that could be heard. The hammer had stopped, half-cocked.[23] A conference took place, and the seconds apparently agreed that a mechanical failure should not deny Jackson the choice to proceed.[24] As Dickinson waited for what must have seemed an eternity, Jackson coolly recocked the pistol, drew down his pistol, and fired.

This time, Dickinson was struck in the upper part of his stomach, and the ball pierced through his back, leaving an enormous hole. Within hours, he was dead. "My God! General Jackson, are you hit?" exclaimed Major Overton. "Oh! I believe that he has pinked me a little," the hero replied. "Let's look at it. But say nothing about it there," nodding toward his prostrate victim whom Jackson intended never to learn whether he had struck him.[25] The ball had broken two ribs and rested in the chest cavity within millimeters of Jackson's heart so that it could never be safely removed.[26]

Dickinson's friends were dismayed. They complained that Jackson had deliberately worn a coat that was so ill-fitting that the marksman aimed amiss. But officially they had no grounds for protest: the time to register the matter was before, not after the event. Dickinson should have aimed at his head not heart. Even so, if the general was to be believed, the outcome would still have been the same. Jackson once muttered in his all-consuming, unholy hatred, "I should have hit him if he had shot me through the brain."[27] Dickinson's father-in-law, Captain Ervin, questioned Jackson's right to shoot after the first fire had failed. He admitted that the seconds had decided the issue on the field. Ervin, however, argued, "A snap not to be considered as a fire was never committed to writing" among the stipulations drawn up by the parties beforehand. Even Ervin had acknowledged that Jackson had not cheated. His cold-blooded decision to shoot a defenseless opponent certainly looked dishonorable in retrospect. Given the risk Jackson had already taken in waiting to fire, because of the inequality in their marksmanship, who would have done otherwise if placed in his boots? Despite the complaints, all that Dickinson's friends could do was prepare a memorial for publication, lamenting the loss. When word spread that Jackson was eager to scrutinize the document very closely, some twenty-five of the signers returned to have themselves removed from the page. These erstwhile friends of Dickinson agreed with Sir John Falstaff about the proportion of discretion that valor commands.[28]

From the perspective of early American political culture, the drama and the issue were not as pointless and trivial as they might seem. Duels separated respectable gentlemen from the rest of society. They engaged the larger public in a personal affair. By that means judgments could be made about the manliness and qualities of leadership that the antagonists exhibited. Seldom truly private in a climate of a democratic public, duels sometimes involved scores of observers and intriguers, most of whom belonged to a tight circle of males, usually politicians. (Most of them would not appear on the field of honor but would have participated in the preliminaries.) For instance, the congressional duel between Jonathan Cilley of Maine and William J. Graves of Kentucky in 1838 drew thirty-four people into the controversy. At least a dozen rumor-mongers elbowed themselves into the Jackson-Dickinson affair, in addition to the principals, seconds, physicians, and others at the duel itself.

By ritualizing violence in a punctilious grammar of honor, as it were, duels were supposed to prevent chaos. That scourge of public and familial order, the blood feud, could be avoided under the problematic idea that a man's sullied reputation would thereby be restored. As often happened, the Dickinson affair did not give the satisfaction sought. For a few months the controversy isolated Jackson both socially and politically, just as Aaron Burr's killing of Alexander Hamilton had damaged the vice-president's career. According to James Parton, after consulting some Nashville old-timers, "at no time between the years 1806 and 1812 could General Jackson have been elected to any office in Tennessee that required a majority of voters of the whole State." Robert Remini, Jackson's most recent biographer, agrees that the duel made him "virtually a social outcast in western Tennessee."[29] Jackson's later military successes erased much of the opprobrium, but certainly in national politics the incident at the Kentucky tavern still reverberated during the 1828 campaign in Northern sectors. President Adams's supporters disseminated a pamphlet that counted fourteen separate incidents when Jackson had "killed, slashed, and clawed various American citizens."[30] Northeasterners considered his dueling the most serious and barbaric of these offenses. Despite a temporary loss of local popularity and even opprobrium in larger circles, Southern duelists had their own rationale for their behavior. Above all, like Jackson, they were expressing their firm ties of loyalty in the patron-client relationships that political factions then required.

The last point needs elaboration since the relationship of patron and client has been regrettably understudied in this country, in contrast to the work done abroad.[31] The transaction is a noncontractual arrangement whereby two individuals of unequal power—"lop-sided friendship" as Julian Pitt-Rivers calls it—agree on the basis of mutual interest and cordiality to do favors for each other.[32] "Most clients," writes a historical expert on the topic, "rendered faithful service to their patrons and most patrons reciprocated by looking after the clients' interests."[33] The lesser party gained particular rewards, for instance, access through the patron to someone higher up the ladder of power. Friendships between gentlemen of the same status might be similarly instrumental, but the parties recognized each other as equals rather than as leader and subordinate.

In these exercises, the friend or client must not, however, become an obvious sycophant, out of fear of losing respect. Jackson felt uncomfortable in seeking offices. Once, while in Washington, Jackson claimed to have refused to act the "courteor [sic]." Yet he was hoping for appointment under President Thomas Jefferson for the post of governor of Louisiana in 1804 just after the acquisition of the territory. "Let me declare to you that before I would violate my own ideas of propriety," he informed his friend Congressman George W. Campbell, "I would yield up any office in the government was I in possession of the most honourable and lucrative." He added in the same paragraph how much he appreciated the "friendly attention of my friends" in his quest for appointment and commended Campbell's growing popularity that was based "on your own merit."[34] These sentiments were designed to show that he could appreciate the delicacy of friendly alliance as well as any office seeker. In a similar vein, as a presidential candidate in 1824, he explained to a Northern friend, "I have seen & enjoyed much of the honor . . . and regard of my country . . . without any covert solicitation on my part; . . . in nothing in which I have been engaged did I ever look to myself."[35] He probably believed every Cincinnatian word, but the remarks were typical and, by convention, designed to assert independence and disdain self-seeking.

The systems of patronage and instrumental or protective friendships, as they might be called, had defects. Any arrangement based on intense expressions of mutual affection, between equals or unequals, is bound to be brittle. Both parties demand complete loyalty, complete trustworthiness. When ambitions diverge or the status and power of the parties substantially change, frustration, jealousy, and hurt feelings quickly arise, as the sociologist Eric Wolf points out.[36] Another difficulty in friendly and patron-client structures is a lack of differentiation between public policy and private interest. A polite fiction of assistance heartily given masked the obligatory character of such exchanges of services. Honor demanded a show of manly autonomy. Any brisk trading of offices, emoluments, privileges, and special treatment for the performance of useful favors smacked of demeaning commercialism, greed, and corruption. "Office," Jackson charged in an address at the beginning of his presidency, "is considered as a species of property."[37] Indeed, factional opponents or losers in the grab for advantages almost invariably claimed that the winners had betrayed the public good, neglected principle, and exposed their villainy and lust for power before the world. In response, victors in such arrangements quite naturally denounced their rivals as scoundrels while claiming to be pure of heart, self-sacrificing, and noble in word and deed. The Manichaean approach in these usages of honor almost assured a volatile political landscape. The public air in the early years of national history was constantly filled with cries of treachery and rascality on the one hand and soothing voices of loyal commitment to statesmen of lofty mien on the other. In reference to early American political structure, Joanne Freeman concludes, "Politicians considered their own fighting unit a band of friends, all men of honor who promoted the common good." In an age when partisanship was thought an enemy of sound government, their adversaries labeled them as grasping self-seekers.[38] Members of neither one side nor the other perceived themselves in the light they attributed to their enemies. The certainties of their adversaries' evil and their own good were so embedded in their mode of thinking that the Christian admonition about the mote and beam very much applied.

A scholar of modern Italy, where thousands of duels took place from 1870 to 1930, would not be surprised to find a close connection between duels and early partisan politics. In that country, as in the antebellum South, members of the political elite set themselves apart from the lower social ranks not only by establishing close connections with the military but also by the fighting of duels. Steven Hughes argues that after the Risorgimento, the Italian leadership class was introduced for the first time to the hazards of a free press and the functioning of open parliamentary debate—along with a continuing tradition of the gentleman's status and role. The free press permitted libelous assaults. The party systems in both the pre–Civil War South and the unified, constitutional monarchy of Italy were still crude mechanisms. The notion of a "loyal opposition" was only slowly adopted into the political culture in either country. Heroic leadership was thought essential, and the duel helped to promote that ideal.[39]

In both instances, too, dependence on clientage also encouraged ritual combat. As political scientists and sociologists have examined patronage in a worldwide context, the patron, for his part, obtains the fidelity and the legwork that the junior can provide and also the prestige of having a stable of young followers with promise and increasing standing. Both parties, in fact, benefit from public notice of their association. Hospitality, for which the Old South was famous, was a way to advertise a renewal of old cordialities or announce new ones. To use Jackson's own words for exalting that male bond, "the sacred hand of friendship" between gentlemen could be advertised by means of dances, banquets, hunts, and barbecues. Often enough, such entertainments, as well as the choice of speakers and toast-givers to grace a formal occasion, could also flaunt the power of one patron's faction against that of another. Planter and politician James Henry Hammond of South Carolina was very conscious of the significance of staging elaborate diversions. With reference to a rival leader, he boasted in his diary, "Manning could not conceal it. He built his fine house in Clarendon to beat me," but, Hammond fumed, "I beat them *in their own line*—furniture, balls and dinner parties."[40] Hammond was unusually cynical about the primacy of palpable gains over ties of cordiality. Hope of reciprocated advantage *and* desire for friendship mattered in both relations between equal partners and those between patrons and clients.[41]

The world in which these practices flourished throughout the slave states differed from the gradually changing moral climate of the Northern states, especially in the era of the Second Great Awakening and the economic upsurge of the 1820s and 1830s. In the new language of the middle class, Yankees who deplored violence, formal or not, valued reliability, calculation, restraint, and deferred gratification. Increasingly, Northerners, driven by the so-called market revolution, made contracts, obtained loans, and settled debts by institutional means (chiefly local banks) rather than by personal arrangements with a local slaveholder of means. As late as the 1850s in the South, the yeomanry often sought help, in cash or in kind, from wealthy landowners with an unspoken understanding about who should receive the farmer's vote when the squire's name appeared on the ballot.[42]

To a large extent, Jackson's 1828 presidential campaign conformed to these differences in political values and practices because they were deeply embedded in sectional mores. The historian J. Mills Thornton comments that "Alabamians were preaching the substance of the Jacksonian faith long before Jackson had become its symbol."[43] The litany of that faith, as Thornton explains, included the fiercest possible defense of slavery as a prerequisite for white liberty, states' rights, individual autonomy, low taxes, and small government—all of which Jacksonians, especially Southern ones, believed sustained their collective honor and individual liberty. Nor were Alabamians alone in giving their Tennessee neighbor an enormous majority in 1828. Although highly popular throughout the nation, Jackson fell short of a majority in the Northern states' electoral count (49 percent) whereas from the South's electoral college representation he garnered 92 percent.[44] To be sure, Jackson had no monopoly on the rules governing the sectional ethic, but he epitomized it to perfection.

Armed with convictions that their political spokesmen shared—whether Democrat, National Republican, or states' rights Whig—Southern friends, patrons, clients, and gentlemen with a keen sense of military bearing cherished those manly virtues that required frequent affirmation before the public. They sought to display courage, coolness under fire, and unreflective, quick reactions to changes in the social temperature or to personal and collective danger.[45] Given these conditions of immediacy in handling personal confrontations, political duels readily emerged from minor disagreements and rebuffs. In effect, they were proclamations of a factional leader's weight in the community, something that had to be confirmed in the public eye. The credentials and potentialities of the client really mattered. Patrons like General Jackson did not feel obliged to move any numbskull ahead. For instance, John C. Calhoun adopted as his client the brilliant but unconnected George McDuffie, once an apprentice clerk in the store of Calhoun's father. Over the years the senior promoted his young friend as opportunities arose. In gratitude for past favors and future expectations McDuffie fought a duel with a Calhoun adversary, Colonel William Cumming. For the sake of Calhoun's honor as well as his own, McDuffie received a ball that nearly struck his spine. For years afterward, he suffered from the wound.[46] His survival, though, assured him of his patron's undying fidelity. Jackson, too, had in his loyal band such highly intelligent but not particularly well-born political professionals as John Overton, William B. Lewis, John Coffee, and John H. Eaton, all of whom aided his career while he assisted theirs.

Thus politics was a major avenue for the poor but educated young man to get ahead—that is, *if* he could qualify as an active member of the male elite. At a time when political parties were at best unsteady collections of factions led by local worthies, the ambitious young politician had to rely less on institutional allegiances than on patrons, friends, and kinspeople for support. Like a convenient marriage into money, a political office in those times opened doors to power and riches when opportunities were so limited for those primed to enter the ranks of the upper class. The chance to fight and perhaps kill the leader of a rival political faction as renowned as the middle-aged General Jackson indicated twenty-seven-year-old Dickinson's own rising status. Ironically, Jackson himself, when a young lawyer, challenged Waightsill Avery, an older attorney, who had refused to take him on as an apprentice and had mocked his courtroom blunders. Luckily, the subsequent volley of shots struck neither human target.[47]

Dickinson's role had another dimension. In addition to the natural anxieties of the young about manhood, employment, and place in the community, the potential duelist often belonged to the overcrowded profession of the law. Dickinson and his opponent were both members of the Nashville bar. There simply were not enough cases to go around. Hence the desperate hunger for political positions—attorney general, bailiff, judge, congressman, or whatever. One estimate suggests that 90 percent of Southern duels were fought by lawyers, an exaggeration perhaps, but not by much.[48] Lawyers became involved in the political arena as local editors, office seekers, or commissioned officers in the militia—sometimes taking on all three occupations. The title of major, colonel, or best of all, general did wonders for reputation in that very hierarchical society. Unlike modern America, the distance between the warrior culture of the armed services and civilian life was not very pronounced in Jackson's day. Valor at arms that nowadays attracts little cachet then was treated with solemn respect, most especially in the South. "We have here Colonel Tom and Colonel Dick and Major Billy," wrote the architect Benjamin Latrobe when traveling in the South. "You are right in wishing to get rid of the infernal and eternal title of *Captain*," confided an Alabama planter to his brother. "Col[onel] is the prettiest title belonging to the military profession in my opinion." His conviction was scarcely unique in a region where, a contemporary estimated, about one in every three members of the possessing class sported a militia rank of some sort.[49]

Whether graced with an official title or not, politicians had much need of distinctive reputation. To gain a place in the political domain the assistance of friends and the wealth of family members were necessary adjuncts to repute. Little else could make aspiring gentlemen eligible for public acclaim—no party apparatus worth mentioning, no source of funds from interest groups, apart from the often scandal-ridden, speculative land companies, no abundance of government offices to be filled but just a few that thus became the object of desperate rivalries. Unlike the free states, the underpopulated South lacked a sufficiency of towns and ocean ports that required ever-expanding federal postal and customs positions.[50] Under these circumstances of strong political hopes, high competitiveness, and military designations, coupled with an inadequate institutional structure, the chance to display manly reputation and vent career frustrations on the field of honor was very appealing. Dickinson had left his wife that Thursday morning with high hopes and promised to return a victor in the quarrel.

Both Dickinson and Jackson were aware that their followings required their appearance on the field. So long as the public affirmed the idea of a leadership based on an almost sacralized strength of will and heroic self-sacrifice rather than more secular virtues, politicians like them felt obliged to meet all affronts to their dignity and honor. Otherwise they risked losing the support of their clients and advisers and would soon become a neighborhood byword. For General Jackson, the duel was mandatory as well. Gentlemen like Jackson and Dickinson perfunctorily expressed regret over the necessity to reach to so drastic a step. Upon learning of the Earl of Clarendon's denunciation of dueling in England, President Jackson in 1837 declared, "The views of the Earle [sic] are those of a Christian, but unless some mode is adopted to frown down by society the slanderer, who is worse than a murderer, all attempts to put down dueling will be in vain."[51]

In addition to defending his own honor, however, Jackson had other commitments no less salient. He had to stand by his friend General Coffee, who had not fought McNairy just to avenge a slight against himself. Rather, Coffee had hazarded his life because of the ties of both affection and interest that bound him to General Jackson. To borrow from anthropology, a gift exchange, it might be said, was involved, an obligation on Jackson's part to duel, in part, on Coffee's behalf. Jackson and Coffee were sometime business associates and fast friends. In those days male comrades signed each other's promissory notes, complimented successes, lamented misfortunes, toasted undying cordiality, served as seconds on the dueling ground, and sometimes fought on the field of honor as surrogates if some reason prevented the principal from doing so.

John Overton's close relationship with Jackson as his second, business partner, and most admiring supporter from their earliest days in Nashville was another case in point.[52] Overton showed his fealty even after Jackson's death. He had his servants burn all his intimate correspondence with his patron, friend, and lord, as he probably perceived him. Overton was protecting Jackson's good name even after death. In sum, to repeat the epigraph, "Greater love hath no man than this, that a man lay down his life for his friends."[53] In that statement merges the sacrificial notion of the

Cross and the ethic of the sword wielded in behalf of warrior comrades. Once in giving advice to a young relative about his reading, Jackson recommended "the history of the Scottish chiefs." In particular he singled out Sir William Wallace because "we find in him the truly undaunted courage, always ready to brave any dangers, for the relief of his country or his friend."[54] That was also Jackson's personal credo, one that ended on the precise point of loyalty to companions. Those closest to the Nashville controversy were acting as blood brothers, an exclusive and sacred tie to which Jackson himself devoted his very life.

Finally, the duel served as a means to vent repressed feelings and hide material ambitions that could be articulated only in an act of aggression, not words of explanation or self-reflection. The rationale for dueling, however, was usually couched in opposite terms—that it made men civilized by that very repression. It is true that those seeking to avoid offense were therefore especially careful to conceal their resentments and consuming jealousies with courtesies and shows of magnanimity. Elegant toasts, bows and flourishes, stately language of address—all were ritual ways to assure listeners that intentions were innocent of malice.[55] In contrast, the duel supplied stylized words that required no personal invention. In Renaissance Italy such an epithet as "poltroon," "liar," or "coward" was called the *mentita*—giving the lie.[56] Yet even as coolness, silence, tight-lipped stoicism in the face of death marked the dueling heroes, their inarticulateness hid deep emotions that could return to haunt the survivor, sometimes with the force that shell-shock victims experience in war.

The duel with Dickinson as well as his famous political battles—most particularly his war against Nicholas Biddle and his allegedly corrupt, enslaving bank in Philadelphia—mirrored those precepts. The encounter at the Kentucky tavern demonstrated the patron-client character of early American politics, with its stress on honorable friendships and implacable enmities. That style of action must be seen as a factor in Jackson's most famous disputes, only two of which can be mentioned in so brief a sketch. The first was the general's explosive reaction to his loss of the presidency in 1825. A divided electoral college threw the decision into the hands of the House of Representatives. There, candidates John Quincy Adams and Henry Clay, reaching a tacit understanding, allied themselves with the result being Adams's elevation to the highest national post and Clay's swift accession to the status of presidential heir-apparent. Within days of his election in the House of Representatives Adams appointed Clay secretary of state, the traditional spot for a president's successor. Having outpolled

Clay, Adams might be seen as patron and Clay as client with obvious advantages to both. Having won in 1824 the highest number of votes of all candidates in both the election and the electoral college, Jackson was outraged. He and his camp charged duplicity, the thwarting of popular will, and the ruin of sound government. The general fumed, "So you see the *Judas* of the West [Clay] has closed the contract and will receive the thirty pieces of silver" from the puritanical high priest of Massachusetts. Needless to say, as the rules of the game provided, Adams claimed to have made the appointment on the basis of Clay's "talents and services" to the country. Meantime, Clay accepted the assignment because it made no sense, he argued rather pointlessly, not to serve under the candidate for whom he had voted in the House of Representatives.[57]

John Quincy Adams, no partisan leader, let his opponent set the election issues, including the "Corrupt Bargain" question, but Clay had blundered as well. The gift exchange of one high office and a subordinate one was too overt, too subject to charges of malfeasance, the abuse of public funds and perquisites of power for private gain. The charges of a "Corrupt Bargain" sparked a four-year Jackson campaign against the beleaguered incumbents. Ordinarily reciprocation for services rendered was not meant to be as immediate as Adams's nomination of Clay had been. So clumsy and hasty a return of an obligation could never be interpreted as something freely and generously given. Even among friends, gambling debts were to be paid at once because no personal tie could be permitted to blur the almost sacred distinction between winner and loser. Jackson's insistence that Major Ervin hand over notes as good as gold coin in paying off Ervin's racing debt was very much a case in point. Political debts, in which arrangement monetary exchange was forbidden, were to be regarded neither as games of chance with strangers nor as business contracts, signed and sealed. Instead, all patronage transactions were supposed to be voluntary, with merit and affection, not material gain, the basis. Such a fiction (as it sometimes was) was deemed necessary because politicians had to assert their autonomy at all times, albeit with expectation of a preferment, appropriately delayed. Clay should have thanked Adams for the offer but declined with hints that a later appointment or the advancement of a friend to the cabinet post would be welcome. If deftly arranged, no scandal would most likely have ensued. Instead, an inside deal, grossly mishandled as this matter was, suggested a dependency in the relation between patron and client that a majority of voters were likely to judge shameless and venal. Jackson had every right to protest, storm, and rage, even though as a conventional man of affairs he might himself have acted similarly—though probably more prudently under comparable circumstances.

With regard to a second example, the intricacies of patronage and clientelism bear reference to Jackson's outrage over John Calhoun's failure to serve his leader in the manner expected of him. As Eric Wolf has observed, instrumental or protective friendships like that of Jackson and Calhoun were fragile. In part, these sometime equals in the court of honor had fallen out because of a change in status—with Jackson in the presidential seat and Calhoun, his former chief when secretary of war, becoming second in command. These shifts of position eroded mutual trust and stimulated jealousy.[58] In addition, influenced perhaps by his aristocratic wife, Floride, Vice-President Calhoun crossed the general during the quarrel over Peggy Eaton's controversial social standing. She was the former mistress but current wife of John H. Eaton, the secretary of war.[59] With Rachel Jackson's honor stained for comparable reasons, Jackson, sensitive on the point, had embraced Peggy Eaton's cause as his own. In Jackson's opinion, Calhoun and his friends were busily plotting "to put Major Eaton out of the Cabinet, & disgrace me . . . [and] lessen my standing with the people" so that Calhoun could run in his place at the next election.[60]

In 1830, while president, Jackson learned from Calhoun's own publication of correspondence that, as secretary of war in Monroe's cabinet, Calhoun had not unequivocally stood by the general in his difficulties during the Seminole War in Florida. "I had a right to believe you were my sincere friend," Jackson admonished him, and explained that he had no expectation ever to exclaim "*Et tu Brute.* In all your letters as War Secretary you approved *entirely* my conduct in relation to the Seminole campaign. Understanding you now, no further communication with you on this subject is necessary."[61] To another correspondent Jackson wrote that Calhoun in cabinet council certainly possessed the right to act by his own lights, "but as long as a single spark of honor animates my own bosom I cannot concede to him the right of acting diametrically opposite to his professions." It was always all or nothing in Jackson's relationships. Also, in a pamphlet carefully prepared, Calhoun vindicated himself, as he thought, by disclosures of some of Jackson's letters. It was his "sacred obligation," Calhoun announced, to "vindicate my character, impeached as it has been," and show "myself not unworthy" of public trust.[62] The vice-president, though, had neither sought nor received the general's permission to reproduce his words. Worse, Calhoun disclosed the feud between himself and his cabinet rival, Martin Van Buren, to a degree that embarrassed the president and the Democratic Party. In a truly patriarchal sense, the cabinet officers were, after all, the president's official family whose business was bared for all the world to notice.

The age appreciated reticence about private matters but, of course relished the gossip when secrets were unveiled. Meantime, Calhoun could not challenge a sitting president to a duel. Universally the rules of the code duello permitted neither monarch, prime minister, nor elected ruler to risk life when entrusted with authority. Calhoun could only plot against his superior. The subordinate could not fire a treasonous shot at him because he would then succeed to the office himself. But apart from that consideration, as the Irish rules for dueling insisted, "equality" of rank was "indispensable" for all parties on the field.[63] Calhoun's quickened role in the Nullification crisis was perhaps partly a reaction to his powerlessness and utter humiliation in this struggle.

Given his insistence on unqualified loyalty, touched by bonds of genuine friendship, Jackson's shift of preference from his former running mate to Martin Van Buren was understandable. Shrewdly, Van Buren, who knew how to play the general's favorite tunes of courtesy and deference, resigned in the midst of the turmoil to smooth the president's path for remaking his cabinet and purging Calhoun's allies in it. As a result, Van Buren became heir to "Old Hickory's" presidency.[64] The two incidents, the "Corrupt Bargain" affair and the initial break with Calhoun, illustrate the role that the proprieties, rituals, and discourse of both patron-client relations and the ethic of honor played in national affairs.

. . . .

In turning to the second point—the relation of Jackson's personal life to the tenets behind the code duello—it is not implied that battle or duel traumatized him. Nevertheless, he had every reason to feel insecure and aware of life's brevity, to understand how quickly the world forgot the dead and how hellish the length of personal suffering could be. As a creature nurtured in hardship, Jackson felt a powerful urge to survive and to achieve high political, military, and financial aims. Ambition, intense and sometimes overbearing, propelled him forward to his remarkable destiny. Yet a subtext of a survivor's guilt and a repression of what would otherwise have been a debilitating grief marked his career as well. Jackson's father, a Scots-Irish settler in western North Carolina, died in a timber-cutting accident about the time that Jackson was born. Naturally the son idolized the missing parent.

During the American Revolution, his brother Hugh, age sixteen, became fatally ill from heat exhaustion after the Battle of Stono Ferry in 1780.[65] To avenge his death, young Andrew and his older brother Robert joined American forces hastily gathered in their neighborhood. They were captured, and in the course of brave refusal to blacken an officer's boots, both were struck with a sword. Though sorely wounded, Andrew survived the assault, but the blow to Robert's head was more serious.[66] The boys were released in an exchange of prisoners that their mother's entreaties helped to arrange. She and Andrew, shoeless, bleeding, and feverish, walked the forty miles home while Robert, barely alive, rode the horse. Elizabeth Jackson nursed her sons' injuries and attacks of smallpox and malaria, but Robert soon died. Then she herself abruptly fell fatally ill while treating some cousins in distant Charleston even as her only living son still lay delirious at home in the Waxhaws District. Four deaths to be mourned when the orphan Andrew Jackson was himself only fifteen! As Robert Remini has succinctly put it, "The scars remained with him through life."[67]

The memories of his mother that Jackson most often repeated were her words of warning about survival in a harsh, unfeeling world: "If ever you have to vindicate your feelings or defend your honor, do it calmly." In another phrasing of the sentiment, Jackson recalled her commanding him never to sue at law for "insult or battery or defamation. The law affords no remedy for such outrage that can satisfy a gentleman. Fight." These were lessons that she had learned from the Scots of Northern Ireland, having herself descended from Robert the Bruce. The Scots-Irish were more prone to personal violence and more conscious of honor than any other group then settled in the country.[68]

The miracle was that Jackson did not suffer more emotional damage than he did. According to psychologists, there is a pattern of reaction that separates the "invulnerable child" from other victims of early disruption and loss. Such an individual "develops," declares one analyst, "a kind of self-immunizing capacity against harsh and threatening environments." Often children of this character learn early to conceptualize perils as possibly arising from a variety of sources. They hone skills by which to survive, a precociousness that goes beyond courage and boldness to something more creative than the ordinary individual can muster. From a psychological perspective, such a resource is much harder to explain than a succumbing to narcissistic or alienating defensiveness. Nevertheless, there is usually some price to pay—a touchiness, an intolerance of disagreement or criticism, and other signs of hostility or affront, intended or not.[69] Moreover, the desperate road to a sense of self-possession may still require trials and errors of conduct and end up with a rigid and punctilious obedience to the bylaws and conventions of the orphan's culture.

In Jackson's case, a fatherless childhood was evident in his wild behavior. But after losing his mother and brothers, the youth became even more uncontrollable as if these losses had in a sense "detribalized" him. Defensive, often angry, given to cruel pranks, and aimless of purpose, he was clearly troubled.[70] At the same time, his health was highly problematic. Because of a neurological disorder, in his youth he had the unfortunate habit of drooling uncontrollably—an infantilizing condition that compelled him to fight anyone who made fun of him. A dermatological problem called the "Big Itch" covered his body in those early years of his life, and malarial fevers often returned. He had an almost laughable beanpole of a frame for which he compensated by habits of "frenetic bellicosity."[71] When a kinsman left him nearly four hundred pounds sterling in 1783, young Jackson spent the fortune on pleasures with abandon, a reaction that his biographer James Curtis identifies as "a kind of mourning." Unable to find his mother's grave in a Charleston cemetery, he hid his sense of anguish beneath laughter, drink, gambling, and wenching. How could he not conclude that his mother had abandoned him when he was so ill and then left this earth before he could even say good-bye? "When tidings of her death reached me I at first could not believe it, when I finally realized it I felt utterly alone," Jackson later recalled in a rare moment of self-revelation.[72] Yet fervently he romanticized Elizabeth Jackson's patriotism and high-minded honor. No wonder Jackson learned to conform himself to the moral world of honor in which he lived. Structure of some kind was necessary. Obeying all the rules of the code, including the duel, not only channeled his emotions in conventional, conservative rituals but also offered him the chance to win the public acclaim that confirmed his ambitions and completed his sense of identity.[73]

Yet the nagging sense of grief and injury unresolved was not entirely stilled. A further source of insecurity and anger, banked though it was, grew out of his marriage to Rachel Donelson. She was the daughter of his politically powerful and widowed landlady outside Nashville. Jackson's love for the winsome and attractive Rachel was deep and abiding. In truth, she became his anchor, not for herself alone but also for his earnest need of feminine companionship and succor in the absence of a mother and sisters. For instance, in 1796 he wrote her, "I mean to retire from the Buss of publick life, and Spend My Time with you alone in Sweet Retirement, which is My only ambition and ultimate wish."[74] The sentiment was sincerely felt at that moment but not at all what he had in mind for his future.

The story of their courtship and marriage can be summarized only briefly here. Rachel Donelson's marriage to Jackson took place before she was properly divorced from the despicable Lewis Robards. Much in love, Rachel Donelson and Jackson, although a practicing attorney who must have known better, conveniently presumed that she was free of the prior encumbrance. The result was embarrassing gossip that included both adultery and divorce—the two greatest blemishes on a lady's honor that could then be imagined. They were wise to clear up the legal muddle by a second ceremony in Nashville in 1794.[75] If Jackson had not already attached himself to the well-born and well-connected territorial governor William Blount, he might not have survived the uproar. Under Blount's patronage, however, he gained reappointment as attorney general and then as judge advocate of the local county militia.[76] Young Rachel, however, had to suffer from the sneers and contempt of Jackson's enemies. In 1803, following a successful campaign for governor, John Sevier charged that Jackson, once his fierce rival for the post of major general of the militia, "had run off with another man's wife."[77] After an undignified scuffle, Jackson and Sevier arranged to duel over the insult. In the ensuing encounter, Sevier ended up hiding behind a tree while Jackson ineffectually waved his sword about. No one was hurt.[78]

Over the subsequent years, affairs of honor, engagements in war, and other dramatic events did not dispel the insecurities in the Jackson household. For one thing, Jackson's health was so bad and the physical pain he endured so excruciating that, as Robert Remini notes, it was a miracle that he lived as long as he did.[79] Three bullets, one from Dickinson's pistol and the other two from Thomas Hart Benton's in another rencontre, had entered his chest, shoulder, and arm.[80] They caused all sorts of complications, particularly the ball in his left lung. He also suffered from rheumatism in his right arm, periodic hemorrhaging, amyloidosis, an inflammatory ailment, dysentery, and other stomach troubles for which he took great quantities of mercury and sugar of lead—then mistakenly thought to be efficacious. He fought the Creek War in 1812 when barely able to ride a horse. He had to hang himself between two poles because he could neither sit up nor lie down. In his declining years the former president's health was so poor that his will to survive, about which all his biographers marvel, resists credibility. If heroism were defined by a defiance of pain alone, Jackson was by far the most heroic of all the American presidents.[81]

But the Jackson family had problems of the mind as well. Jackson was subject to periodic bouts of depression. As Remini puts it, with special reference to the public uproar following his invasion of Spanish Florida, the general experienced in 1819 "extreme fluctuations of mood . . . from rage over the censure of 'conspiracy' to delirious exultation occasioned by the frenzied receptions of the American people repeatedly accorded him."[82] Abysmal health contributed to such swings, but deeper emotional troubles that had their origins earlier in his life contributed to his volatility.

Rachel Jackson was also not spared from a gloomy outlook. Early in the marriage Rachel became convinced that the disapproving gaze of the Almighty had fallen upon her. Barren at a time when childlessness was regarded as an unnatural offense, she became ever more religious, convinced that it was God's punishment for her sexual sins, a curse that Jackson, rather indifferent to religion, vainly tried to dispel. They adopted a child, Andrew Jackson Jr., in 1810. Even before that, the Jackson household was filled with baby nieces and nephews and neighborhood toddlers to cover the couple's frustration for having no offspring of their own. And death conspired against the pair as well. Having rescued after a battle a Creek child named Lyncoya, Jackson sent the orphan to Rachel in Nashville. Recalling his own baptism of horror in the Revolution, the general declared, "When I reflect that he as to his relations is so much like myself I feel an unusual sympathy for him." Although treated as a full member of the house, Lyncoya ran away more than once to rejoin the Creeks. Then, in his seventeenth year, he died of tuberculosis.[83]

Jackson's loss of his wife just before his inauguration exacerbated his underlying sense of life's impermanence. He had somehow managed to hold his temper when the Adams press named his mother as a British prostitute whose fornication with a black man produced Jackson himself.[84] Raking up the old issue, opponents called his wife a bigamist and adulteress. After the victory in the 1828 campaign, Rachel had discovered in a pamphlet the slanders circulating about her alleged sins, and she became hysterical. Robert Remini suggests that she gave up on life, and so it would seem. In any event, shortly thereafter she suffered a severe heart attack and died at the Hermitage on 22 December. Her death, so sudden and unpredictable, reinforced the dread of abandonment that had overwhelmed him with the death of both parents and all his siblings so many years before. Often, a second time of great loss reignites the grief of the first instance.

As if suddenly he was reentering the hell of those earlier deaths in the Revolution, Jackson was inconsolable, refusing to eat or drink for days. Over her grave in the Hermitage garden he placed a memorial tablet that included the words: "A being so gentle and so virtuous, slander might wound but could not dishonor."[85] Menachim Begin, the Israeli leader, was so despondent at his wife's death that he turned his face to the wall and died. Old Hickory might have done the same. He had been very dependent on her, almost as if she was not merely his wife but his mother. But with a presidential term yet to fulfill, Jackson stifled his despair, so long held in check, and summoned the old resource, a propulsive dread of extinction, to master any doubts and insecurities. To serve as a national leader, chosen by the people, was one way to give the lie to the calumnies that she had endured.

Apart from the childless Rachel and her relations, Jackson had no immediate family. In the rural, clan-bound culture in which he was immersed that loss was considered a special burden. Under these circumstances it was no wonder that General Jackson's reliance on friends and allies had an unusual intensity. For instance, early in the Seminole War in 1818, Captain Obed Wright of the Georgia militia obliterated a village of Chehaw Indians. Jackson was outraged and declared to Georgia governor William Rabun that Wright and his men were guilty of an "inhuman attack, on the old woman [*sic*] and men of the Chehaw village, whilst the warriors of that village was with me fighting the battles of our *country* against the common enemy. . . . This act," he thundered, "will to the last age fix a Stain upon the character of Georgia."[86] Fidelity to friends and allies—whether light or dark-skinned—was central to Jackson's notion of honor.

The fight with Dickinson in 1806 to a substantial degree underlined the importance of fidelity in Jackson's thinking and conduct but also illuminated how he translated a sense of doom and meaninglessness into an empowering anger and determination to outlive opponents. He need not have killed his helpless adversary on the Logan County meadow. When assailed for the deed, he argued that, had he known that he would himself survive, he would have dropped his weapon unfired. I doubt it. The man could hate with a passion. So far as Jackson was concerned, Dickinson, arrogant and contemptuous, got exactly what he deserved, particularly for his assault on Rachel's character.

Jackson drove away his own dread of anonymity and emptiness by embracing both love of friends and undying vengeance against enemies. Even as president he could act under the same impulses that directed his conduct in the confrontation with Dickinson. In 1833, for instance, Robert Beverly Randolph, a naval purser charged with rendering a false financial account, lost his commission on Jackson's orders. The president believed that the young man was "*an unfit associate for those sons of chivalry, integrity, and honor, who adorn our Navy.*" At a reception in Alexandria, Virginia, the disgraced officer approached Jackson and tried to pull his nose, an act to violate the honor of the president in the most insolent way then conceivable. Jackson immediately seized a cane and was preparing to thrash "the villain," as he shouted. Although "an old man," he declared himself quite capable of "punishing a dozen cowardly assassins." Those present restrained him, and Randolph fled. Years later, when Martin Van Buren was president, the offender was arrested for the assault. Jackson requested his successor in the White House to pardon the former naval officer because, Jackson insisted, his mother had warned him never "to indict" anyone for "assault and battery or sue him for slander." Physical reprisal was the only proper response to insult.[87] As always, Jackson was true to the rubrics of masculine honor.

. . . .

For a final reflection on Jackson's concept of honor, a return to the notion of the "Hero of New Orleans" as a metaphor for the mentalité of the slave South is appropriate. His preparations before the famous battle certainly qualify him as a general with a strong sense of honor—and political acumen. Through Edward Livingston's translation, Jackson addressed the fractious, French-speaking citizens of New Orleans on the eve of the encounter. He urged them to "rally around me in this emergency, cease all difference and division, and unite with me in patriotic resolve to save this city from dishonor."[88]

Such an exercise demonstrates that, on a personal level of honorable conduct, the duel in 1806 that occupied much attention here was a small-scale representation of a larger issue. It bore relationship to a more significant matter. Just as personal insults could lead to duels, so could Northern assaults on Southern reputation for honesty and Christian bearing result in civil conflict. John Brown's raid and Lincoln's election seemed a culmination of Northern contempt, hostility, and determination to destroy Southern wealth and power, all of which republicans considered dependent upon that corrupting national canker, slavery. Despite long-standing warnings of disunion, the Lower South secessionists were convinced that the North had had the effrontery to give the South "the lie direct," to use the dueling term. Translating personal fury into corporate resentment was not an illogical or novel step by the standards of the Southern ethic. Soon enough at the Battle of Franklin, not far from Jackson's Hermitage and other fields of honor, thousands of Americans, white and black, would die to uphold or eliminate the Southerners' interpretation of that ancient constitution for male conduct. Even the Southern women fully appreciated the manly cult. They warned their men, as Elizabeth Jackson had counseled her son, never to lose their sense of honor, die fighting, disdain retreat, and, as Peter Gay has put it, emulate "the fabled Spartan mother who enjoined her sons never to be caught with wounds on their backs."[89]

To revert to Jackson's career, whether fighting Biddle's bank or outmaneuvering the Nullifiers under Calhoun's leadership, the president used the principles of honor, as he defined them, as his guide. That set of rules governed all relations, but especially political friendships, in Jackson's estimation, and in its rubrics he found his identity and his inspiration. By the guidelines of honor he appealed to a public that could affirm his integrity and status. In his political contests, Jackson sought the approval of the populace not because of a modern and liberal concept of democracy in which all conditions of people were equal but because he reckoned the popular will to be an instrument of self-vindication.

For Jackson, *Vox Populi* was a fitting receptacle not merely for his own honor. Rather, in the egalitarian spirit he saw the opportunity for others, too, to display and command a right to honor—to achieve what I have called elsewhere a "people's timocracy."[90] By that term is meant a society in which the criteria of honor and the debasement of shame were the polarities for assessing everyone, especially community leaders. Membership was open to all who shared Jackson's convictions and belonged in that nationwide but still restricted fraternity of white, adult males. They need only swear unwavering allegiance to the American slaveholding Union. As early as 1810, Jackson had addressed the Tennessee militia, "*Who are we?* Are we the titled Slaves of George the third? the military conscripts of Napoleon the great? or the frozen peasants of the Russian Czar? No—we are the free born sons of america; the citizens of the only republick now existing in the world; and the only people on earth who possess rights, liberties, and property which they dare call their own."[91] How ironic that the founder of the world's first and oldest continuing party should have been so primitive, so biased and narrow, even merciless at times, and yet no less complicated and engaging than a protagonist in a Spanish tragedy from the Golden Age of drama.

If Jackson represented the common man as well as the principles of heroic honor, he was scarcely alone in his early lack of piety, which however he somewhat rectified in his later years. In this respect he represented in the antebellum period the gradual transformation of a religiously unheeding majority of white Southerners into the orbit of Protestant faith. That transition toward grace developed without fully altering in many respects the old commitment to honor.

PART TWO

GRACE: SOUTHERN RELIGION IN TRANSITION

CHAPTER FOUR
· · · · · · · · · ·

RELIGION AND THE UNCHURCHED
IN THE OLD SOUTH

But you, brethren, are not in darkness, that day
should overtake you as a thief; for you are all
children of the light and children of the day.
We are not of night, nor of darkness.
—*1 Thessalonians 5:4–6*

The meek may inherit the earth, but they won't keep it long.
—*Barbara Vine,* The Chimney Sweeper's Boy

The Southern mind has always been divided between pride and piety.
Only lately has much attention been paid to that dichotomy. Scholars have
recently helped to advance a better appreciation of the struggle between
what the devout called the godless and themselves.[1] The ethic of honor,
as we have learned, was instrumental in the forming of the religious as
well as the secular mind of the South—the ideology and mode of discourse that contended with Christianity for mastery of the regional soul.
Preachers had to fight "sin"—that is, those basic faults to which all mankind is subject—but also a system of rigid and sacralized customs that
stressed manhood over effeminacy, patriarchal over companionate marital life, and other formulations that drew lines between Christian modernity and ancient male privilege. A proper understanding of that conflict
helps to reveal the distinctiveness of Southern politics, as distinctive as
the region's religious system—rationalistic in the eighteenth century but
thereafter evangelical and revivalistic. The rhetoric and even the goals of
Southern politics—defense of white supremacy, conservative economics,
and limited government—rested, Southerners thought, on Christian con-

cepts of order and conduct, but also on honor, a martial ethic originating in pre-Christian Europe. An examination of these often competing forces, though not a narrowly political or narrowly religious exercise in itself, is a necessary precondition for understanding the singular unfolding of both religion and politics in Southern history.

Although dedicated to the higher criteria of Christian conduct, clergy and pious laymen were part of the social regime that upheld the regional conventions and mores. The divergences between the Old Testament, Acts, the letters of Paul, and the teachings of Jesus could be reconciled at times to the mandates of honor. Codification of the ethic could be located in these holy texts. Middle Eastern cultures, then and now, as well as that of imperial Rome, whose citizens Paul addressed, have been partly based on a rigid code of honor and a heightened fear of shame. The worship of God was itself an act conceptualized in terms of that code. The Book of Ezra, which the Right Reverend Stephen Elliott took as a text in the midst of the Civil War, demonstrated the point. The prophet declared, "Then I proclaimed a fast there . . . that we might afflict ourselves before our God. . . . For I was ashamed to require of the King a band of soldiers and horsemen to help us against the enemy" (Ezra 8:21–22). Faced with the decline in Confederate military fortunes, the Episcopal bishop warned that it was a forfeiture of honor to demand what the Lord Himself would not supply. "We cannot therefore require of any foreign agency— we should be ashamed to do it—'bands of soldiers and horsemen' to help us against the enemy." No doubt he had in mind the vain hope that so many entertained that England and France would compel the North to negotiate a peace for the sake of humanity and to resupply cotton to world markets.[2]

Prophets like Ezra and Micah issued jeremiads that denounced the wayward Israelites for the dishonoring offense of impugning the blamelessness of God. They took from God due honor and glory—two interconnected modes of praise rendered in the one Hebrew word *kavod* or kabod. According to the *Encyclopaedia Judaica*, it "is the most significant word in the Talmud to express the most desirable of relations of mutual respect for the dignity of one's fellow." Obviously, kavod applies to the honoring of parents, the fifth commandment, and other hierarchical orders of deference and condescension—from monarch to scholar, from priest to slave.[3] With equals, "Let the honor of thy colleague be as dear to thee as thine own honor," enjoined Hyrcanus (Avot. 2:10). Southern Protestants had no difficulty adopting such an approach to divine understanding.[4] "Riches and honor are with me; yea, durable riches and righteousness"

(Prov. 8:18). With regard to the seductions of a wanton woman, warns the scriptural author, "Remove thy way far from her . . . lest thou give thine honor unto others, and thy years unto the cruel" (Prov. 5:8–9).

Biblical scholars have lately discovered just how profoundly immersed in an honor-shame culture the Jews and the early Christians were. The reliance on family and tribe, the relative lack of privacy and individuality (by modern standards), the oral character of human transactions, and the smallness of communities were among the factors that influenced the writers of the Old and New Testaments. The result was the prominence of the "dyadic personality," that is, a blending of an individual identity with that of the larger social and kinship whole into which all members of society fit.[5] Southern Christians, of course, were more aware than the ancient Hebrews could be of individualistic and introspective forces in the human psyche. Yet they were nevertheless closer to that world of personalities embedded in a public framework than were their Northern brethren. For instance, they could understand Paul in 1 Thessalonians, when the apostle addressed a sadly common situation for early Christians. A church in Thessalonica had lost its sense of self-identity under persecution. Neighbors and former friends in the Macedonian capital considered them disgraced by their attachment to the new faith in Christ Crucified. Of course, death by crucifixion was meant to be the most disgracing form of capital punishment that Roman authority could impose on offenders.[6] Paul urged the congregants to see themselves not as pariahs of a shamed prophet but as "the children of the light, and the children of the day: we are not of the night, nor of darkness" (1 Thess. 5:5).[7] The unbelievers were the shameless, the evil ones—a concept easily translated by Southern anti-abolitionists to apply to their enemies. Be proud of your convictions, "and the very God of peace [will] sanctify you wholly" (1 Thess. 5:23).

At the same time, the Southern evangelicals, as Donald Mathews persuasively argues, stressed the importance of self-discipline, self-denial, and self-repression. "The holy life," Mathews observes, "was a constant and relentless struggle which, in Evangelical theory at least, consumed all available energy in restraining the dangerous passions of frail, unsteady 'flesh.'"[8] To sin was also to be shamed in the sight of God and to be denied access to His honor and the benefits of His blessing.

The interconnection of honor and moral conscience, along with shame and its relation to a sense of guilt, encouraged the Southern Christian to balance the two ethical systems or even make them one. Paul's letter to the Hebrews, for instance, helped to create that merger. The receivers of the message were to despise shame, to reject the worldliness of man, to stand humbly in the presence of God. Mankind, preached the saint, had but two choices: to seek worldly honor, that is, social approval, or to give honor and praise to God. To pursue the first course would inevitably bring down the wrath of the Almighty, Paul insists. To reject honor among men was the true way. Yet it was a path that the proud white Southerner found particularly difficult to follow—for all the earnest preaching from the evangelical pulpit. The Philippians were also enjoined to honor the Christ who had "made himself of no reputation, and took upon him the form of a servant . . . he humbled himself, and became obedient unto death, even the death of the cross" (1 Phil. 2:7–8).[9]

In 1849 Thomas Miles Garrett heard a sermon on the uncomfortable injunction to be found in Matthew 6:12: "Forgive us our debts, as we forgive our debtors."[10] In his diary, Garrett rejoined, "However much it may serve to make up a fine theory of human conduct [it] is neither consistent with notions of man, nor with the formation of society. For on the one hand a man who does not resent an injury done him will sink beneath the standard of honor." In Garrett's opinion, "there must always be a show of resentment sufficient to keep men from transgressing others." Southern preachers did their best to present themselves as men of honor worthy of male respect. Yet it took some time for planters and yeomen to recognize that honor and Christianity offered the same message. Only during the Southern crusade against the alleged threat of Yankee despotism— the Civil War—did the amalgamation of Christ's teachings and the valor of killing the enemy seem not only compatible but mandatory.[11]

In antebellum times it may have been particularly hard to comprehend any conjoining of honor and Christianity when one owned the lives of human creatures. In this respect, though, white Southerners felt they were no worse than the rest of mankind for falling far, far short. Were not the self-righteous, money-grubbing abolitionists and Yankees equally guilty of such deviation from God's stern instructions? Besides, there was always hope. The letter to the Hebrews makes clear that there was great honor for men in glorifying the honor of Christ. As the son of God, Christ of the Resurrection is himself exalted over Moses and ranks only "a little lower than the angels for the suffering of death, crowned with glory and honor; that he by the grace of God should taste death for every man" (Heb. 2: 9).

By such texts, Southerners could claim that they were honorable in the most Christian sense. Like the Thessalonians, they pictured themselves as a people ready to defend themselves from insult. They persuaded themselves to be faithful agents of Christ against the godless infidels—the abolitionists as well as the unbelievers in their own midst. As the sectional crisis deepened, the latter foe seemed a more serious threat than the unbelievers in the South itself. Benjamin Palmer, the influential Presbyterian leader in New Orleans, was certain of God's favor on the South. "To the South the highest position is assigned, of defending, before all nations, the cause of all religion and all truth. In this trust, we are resisting the power which wars against constitutions, and laws and compacts, against Sabbaths and sanctuaries, against the family, the State and the church; which blasphemously invades the prerogatives of God and rebukes the Most High for the errors of his administration."[12] The rhetoric was scriptural, the meaning honorable. God in heaven and Southern folk on earth had been traduced, insulted, thrown into contempt, Palmer implied.

For the preacher, to move from ancient texts to modern circumstance required no change of voice or sense. In 1844, at the time of the Methodist sectional schism, in Russell County, Alabama, the inhabitants complained that the Northern members of the Methodist General Conference were engaged in systematic "insult and outrage to the people of an entire section of the Union" by questioning the God-sanctioned legitimacy of slaveholding. The Republicans and abolitionists had "dishonored the very temple of God," declaimed the Presbyterian clergyman R. K. Porter of Savannah, Georgia. There was no difference in his mind between "the great principles of eternal justice, righteousness, and truth" and the code of honor that strengthened the courage and commitment of the Southern whites.[13]

That ease of transition from Holy Bible to sectional pride had much to do with the origins of the honor code itself. The ethic that had prevailed throughout the ancient world, as the classicist Paul Friedrich observes, could " 'look back' at what it presupposes and 'look ahead' to what it enjoins." Thus magnanimity, a prime virtue in the code of honor in which the power to give was displayed, resembled Christian charity in appearance if not entirely in motive. Southern hospitality sometimes involved both ethical modes. The primary threat to a Christian's notion of honor is the hazard of slighting the blessings that God had conferred by sacrificing his Son for the sins of the world. Covenants had to be maintained or punishment would inevitably follow. "Distrusting the Benefactor," explains the biblicist David Arthur deSilva, threatens one's honor because it deprives the suppliant "of the dignity conferred by God and privileges yet to be awarded." Moreover, "it reveals the base character of the one who distrusts so honorable a Being." The suppliant of God's favor must fear

Him, a bending of the heart that offers the promise of honor in God's esteem—though perhaps not man's. But to sin against His Will bears the burden of disgrace and punishment.[14]

In sum, the biblical rendering of honor endured among Southerners accustomed to the agrarian way of life. Their kin-based customs bore analogy with those of the pastoral societies from which setting came the Holy Word. The intellectual and even emotional links between the ancient and the modern world were deep. The classical texts of Aristotle, Quintilian, Cicero, and many others were still taught in the colleges of the antebellum South. The Old and New Testaments were more important than we might imagine in shaping the Southern mind. Further examination of the rituals, the thought, and the beliefs of white and indeed black Southern Christians disclose the ties that held honor and conscience, shame and guilt in some degree of strained balance.[15]

Other aspects of honor, however, were clearly anti-Christian, though stubbornly adhered to, even by Christians themselves. These factors involved issues of precedence—race, blood lineage, appearance, inherited wealth—matters that underlined inequalities in the social order. Old Testament vengeance against those dishonoring Jehovah certainly gave scriptural justification to acts of violence and feuding. But on a more secular, even pagan, level, an insistence on the equality of all Southern white men to strive for honor was itself an invitation to aggression. As Edward Ayers puts it, "Honor was the catalyst necessary to ignite the South's volatile mixture of slavery, scattered settlement, heavy drinking, and ubiquitous weaponry."[16]

The topic is broad and the concepts involved are elusive. Words like *honor, shame, conscience,* and *guilt* are merely glosses for much more discrete actions and attitudes that may contradict, overlap, or reinforce each other. For instance, such terms as *righteousness, truth, grace, faithfulness,* and *duty* were intimately related to the concept of honor, as Halvor Moxnes and other biblical scholars explain.[17] Yet a shorthand is necessary as well as a division of the topic into chronologically manageable parts. To that end the ethical/social development of the white South may be separated into three eras of relative dominance over the popular mind. The first is labeled the Age of Custom (roughly 1600–1760), a time marked by a continuation of English tradition along with a fragile but growing social and moral consolidation toward an American synthesis. During this period, the ascriptive character of Southern or more precisely Chesapeake and Carolinian life was much more evident than any religious set of prescriptions governing behavior, a contrast with the Puritan settlements of New

England and the Quaker province of Pennsylvania. The second era, to be called the Age of Fervor (1760–1840), represented a sharp break with the past. During this interval a Christian consensus gradually emerged to challenge or at least coexist with the older tradition. As the church in the slave South grew more self-confident, the region entered what is designated here as the Age of Ambivalence, a short span of still greater change that ended in 1861 with the establishment of a Confederacy based on a paradoxically dissonant union of honor and the cause of God.

．．．．．．．．．

In the first stage in social and religious development, early Southern society was crude, hierarchic, racialist, and communally mistrustful. Only gradually was a sense of helplessness and pagan fatalism shed. The unpredictability of life and fortune in the malarial semitropical climate of the South was responsible. In addition, ancient notions of magic persisted in all sections of early America, but most especially in the Southern colonies. For substantial numbers of Southern Christians, institutional religion and white magic were so intermingled that "the prayers of the common people were more like spells and charms than devotions," observed Sir Benjamin Rudyerd in 1628 with regard to his English contemporaries. Such incantations, argues the late historian Darrett Rutman, gratified "the thirst to systemize the unknown." Early Virginia planters placed books on the occult next to bound sermons and weighty political treatises.[18] "Witchmasters" and cunningmen, that is, individuals paid to mediate between unseen forces and their victims, served public needs as readily as did the Anglican clergy. Indeed, witchcraft and pagan divinations were as popular in Virginia as they were in the rural districts of Old England. By such means men sought control over their environment and prospects with the same hope of success as they might beseech divine favor in a more institutional setting. Such patterns of thought encouraged the old belief that a person's honor was more valuable than his life and that to place survival above honor was to be degraded.[19]

The church was not in the best position to alter supernatural belief and practice or to challenge the salience of honor and shame. One colonial historian argues that the settlers in America worshiped regularly. Southern churchmanship, however, did not match the national standard, which was itself low enough.[20] In addition, Southern church attendance was often spotty. On the one hand, in Middlesex, Virginia, in 1724, roughly a third of the white, adult citizenry were communicants, a total of 230. On the other hand, in that same year, Baltimore's St. Paul's, the "mother church" of Maryland, counted only 25 communicants in a settlement of nearly four hundred families.[21] Moreover, Sabbatarian enforcements by law guaranteed only physical presence, not mental attentiveness. As late as 1859, in Virginia, a relatively sedate region in the South, a newspaper editor denounced the "rowdyism"—some sort of fistfight and disturbance—at the Baptist church in Staunton. To the chagrin of the editor, a stranger from the western frontier voiced his astonishment at the apparent complacency of the witnesses to the affray. The observer wondered how well such a melee spoke for the morals of the community as a whole. In another editorial, the rival *Staunton Spectator* deplored the unpleasant tendencies of the younger churchgoers and even their seniors. Habitually they defiled "the floors of churches" by soiling "the skirts of ladies' dresses" with their expectorations of tobacco juice.[22]

The effort to refine the manners of the settlers had begun in colonial times. The program for Southern evangelization that the Society for the Propagation of the Christian Gospel initiated at the close of the seventeenth century made remarkable strides during the next half-century. Yet it still left pulpits unfilled, churches unbuilt, and white settlers—as well as vast numbers of Southern slaves—unchurched. All too often the church functioned in ways that combined secular needs with spiritual ones in a traditional English fashion that enhanced social life but not necessarily religious aims. Families gathered at church to gossip, display power and wealth, or make plans for business or entertainment.[23] Furthermore, the Anglican Church in the South upheld the system of honor, particularly with regard to political power. Parishioners elected gentlemen of standing to the vestry or vestrymen themselves filled vacancies with friends. Yet by one means or another the same end was reached: the confirming of the new vestryman's prestige in the community at large.[24]

Most important of all, the established church served as the guardian of social order in a coarse, undereducated, and rather institutionless society that recognized moral claims largely on the basis of assertions of power. Clerical leaders urged the maintenance of law, but the law was weakly enforced because household or patriarchal autonomy—freedom from outside control and from dependency—was the essence of all men's honor, regardless of individual social standing. Ceremony, draconian penalties, and clerical admonition could not master a people still living by an ethic of honor. In 1676, the Reverend John Yeo lamented that in his part of southern Maryland "the lords day is prophaned, Religion despised, and all notorious vices committed soe th[a]t it is become a Sodom of uncleanness and a Pest house of iniquity." Just or not, his complaint indicated that the church's mission almost had to be the upholding of public order rather than the saving of souls. After all, 1676 was the year of Bacon's Rebellion, one of several outbreaks that the traditional code had long encouraged in England as well as in early America.[25] Nor had the moral climate greatly improved some fifty years later. Governor William Gooch in 1735 confided to Edmund Gibson, bishop of London, that "gross Ignorance, an heathenish Rudeness, and an utter unconcernedness for the Things of God" were so prevalent that "many Parishes are even at this day, like churches newly Planted, but not well formed." Commenting on life in the mid-eighteenth-century Shenandoah Valley, Samuel Kercheval declared that "neither law nor gospel" domesticated a population both "illiterate" and "rough and tumble."[26]

Bearing these circumstances in mind, we can appreciate the insights of the German sociologist Norbert Elias, who sees a close connection between the way people in the past behaved and the material circumstances and social structures to which they were accustomed. According to Elias, central to the "civilizing process" was the development of an ever greater complexity of forms. Advances in the goods people owned and the specializations of work produced required an ever higher "threshold of shame" and tended toward the repression of sheer natural, childlike impulse. Yet as long as material circumstances provided little sense of privacy and self-differentiation, more primitive habits could not easily be reformed.[27]

In early modern times, men, women, and children—even stranger-guests—customarily slept in the same bed or at least the same room. Elias argues that people so disposed "stood in a different relationship with each other" from that to which we are accustomed. Men and women were much less conscious of the proprieties that create and express the notion of individual privacy and autonomy. They lacked the uncalculated social trust in the self-restraint of others that is the hallmark of the notion of individual privacy. That development was slow to arrive in the early South, owing in part to the harshness of material life and the impulsive character of its settlers.[28]

Living conditions in Virginia resembled the largely untamed state of life in southern England from which, according to linguistic evidence, the Chesapeake inhabitants had migrated.[29] As in the southern districts of England, seventeenth-century Southern houses were public, cramped, and uncomfortable. "Crowding people into a single room—sometimes as small as ten by twelve feet—made for a communal style of life," observes a colonial historian. "With so little specialization of space there could be only minimum differentiation of functions. Persons growing up in such an environment would not develop a sense of segregated self with a need for privacy."[30]

By the mid-eighteenth century, housing, furnishings, and amenities (such as tea and coffee) had improved considerably. Both taste and means had improved throughout the Chesapeake, argue two noted economic historians, but possibly as many as the entire bottom third of whites escaped their calculations, which are drawn from tax lists and will inventories. In any event, if Middlesex County, Virginia, was representative, most habitations were not much larger than they had been eighty or more years before. They were still, say the Rutmans, " 'Virginia common built' houses, more often than not one or two rooms and a loft, of weathering wood and inevitably in some degree of disrepair."[31] Crowding was unavoidable, even with blankets (though needed for warmth) to partition rooms. As late as 1776, Francis Asbury complained about living in a house in Virginia only "twenty feet by sixteen," with "seven beds and sixteen persons therein, and some noisy children."[32] Given these conditions, a sense of individuality, privacy, and introspection could not always overcome the tendency to merge oneself within the group. The world one inhabited was very much like the world that all others in the public sphere perceived.[33]

The concept of private shame that could undermine the psychology of public honor grew fitfully in the South partly, too, because of the rapid growth of slavery. Bondage permitted a raw, institutionless society to reproduce the untrammeled power that once had been the sole prerogative of the medieval nobility. Slavery encouraged vanity, one might even say vulgarity. Just as social hierarchy permitted a medieval lord's shamelessness in front of his valet or housemaid, such immodesty was accepted in the slave South. It also encouraged the most egregious forms of brutality. Although clergymen sometimes sought sometimes to inculcate habits of humanity and sensibility, their efforts often fell on indifferent ears. The Reverend Francis LeJau deplored the castration of runaways under eighteenth-century South Carolina law. Cropping the ears of runaway slave women also seemed to him excessive. He reported to the authorities of the Anglicans' Society for the Propagation of the Gospel in London that such penalties were a violation of God's law, particularly Exodus 21:26–27. That text, he noted, "setts a slave at libertty if he should loose an Eye or a tooth when he is Corrected."[34] South Carolina Baptists sought to excommunicate a master for castrating a runaway slave. Seeking judgment from Baptists in Devon, England, they were informed that since the "gelding" had the backing of South Carolina law, no violation against God's justice had been done. The punishment might even have combined "Some mercy" with "this Brother's Cruelty."[35]

Churchly silence and acceptance of so conventional a system helped to promote a diffidence toward slave humanness. It sometimes took casual, all but unnoticed forms. As late as the 1820s Frances Trollope, the caustic English observer of the American scene, reported how a young lady, so modest that she went out of her way to avoid touching the elbow of a male dinner partner on one occasion, laced her corset stays sometime later "with the most perfect composure before a negro footman." Even later still—in the 1850s—a Northern woman, newly married to a North Carolina planter, remarked that maid servants came and went through boltless bedroom doors as if it scarcely mattered what scene they might come upon.[36] The reverse order of immodesty also applied: black nakedness apparently violated no white propriety. In 1781, William Feltman, a Pennsylvania Revolutionary officer, reported in his diary that young slave boys waited on plantation dining guests in clothing that left nothing to the imagination. "I am surprized," he said, "this does not hurt the feelings of this fair Sex to see these young boys of about Fourteen and Fifteen years Old to Attend them. these [sic] whole nakedness Expos'd and I can Assure you It would Surprize a person to see these d——d black boys how well they are hung."[37] Slaves were almost universally whipped unclothed and were customarily forced to disrobe for buyers' inspection. Slaves, argued Dr. Benjamin West, often showed "courage, resolution and genious" far above the ordinary, but "a [white] man will shoot a Negro with as little emotion as he shoots a hare."[38]

Such a bestial view of slaves encouraged a coarseness of sensibility. In some instances even ministers treated slaves with unconscionable brutality. After supervising the fatal beating of his slave for running away, an Anglican divine of seventeenth-century Virginia remarked, "Accidents will happen now and then."[39] Planters of that period were hardly convinced that slaves deserved, needed, or were prepared for the gift of faith and redemption. As the historian Jon Butler notes, "Christianized slaves," some whites grumbled, "not only became 'proud' but 'irascible,' 'uppity,' and 'saucy'—words whose recitation assumed an almost ritual lilt among slave planters and farmers even before 1720." Anglican minister Charles Martyn remarked in 1762 that masters complained that converted Africans neglected their duties and held "too high an opinion of themselves."[40]

To be sure, revival and missionary work gradually softened that opinion as early as mid-century. Yet not all masters took kindly to the Christian-izing of their bondspeople. The Reverend Francis LeJau proposed that slaves attending church swear two oaths—first, to admit that their conversion did not lift their yoke of obedience to their masters and second, that they would give up the practice of polygamy and accept Anglican ideas of matrimony. The planters ridiculed these guarantees as being worthless while encouraging pride and rebellion. Indeed, one convert did inform a fellow slave that "an Angel came and spake" to him and a "hand" had given him "a Book, he had heard Voices"—all of which confirmed the masters' worst fears.[41] Of course, no slaves were freed simply because they had converted and were baptized in the faith. Even the relatively egali-tarian and pacifistic German Moravians of North Carolina refused to see any incompatibility between enslavement and Christ's holy teachings.[42]

Behind the clergyman's uncontrolled passions there lay a style of acting that betrayed the sense of helplessness, even hopelessness, which adher-ents to the code of honor sought to hide from themselves and others. Ma-lignity was a function of an unrecognized sense of impotence—an empti-ness that religious faith was supposed to fill. But under the hierarchies of race and class, honor, not the ideals of Christianity, provided the psycho-logical framework in an unreliable world.[43] Thus the purpose of the code was to unite the internal man and the external realities of his existence in such a way that the aspirant to its claims knew no other good or evil except that which the community designated.[44]

The white Southern colonist's lack of self-restraint was a way of asserting power to be publicly admired and to cast off any doubt of cowardice or weakness. Brutal fights in which a man might lose an eye, ear, lip, or nose erupted over the pettiest of quarrels. Rivalry for public esteem lay behind most of them.[45] Sometimes these passions spilled into the religious arena. In the 1770s a Virginia planter was furious with his son-in-law for bring-ing Baptist clergy on Christmas Day to preach to the hands. He "roused perhaps twenty rugged fellows," armed with weapons, "to drive all before them." The invited preachers hastily fled, and the ruffians transformed the service "into a great Christmas frolic."[46]

. . . .

During the second era in the "civilizing process," the Age of Fervor, cir-cumstances improved dramatically. Church membership began to climb. Christine Heyrman notes that "by a generous estimate" less than 20 per-cent of whites by 1810 had joined the three largest denominations—Bap-tist, Methodist, and Presbyterian. During the 1830s, however, perhaps a half of all Southerners, white and black, were churched in those denominations.[47] The hard code of family-based honor gradually softened as piety became a prerequisite for the determination of respectability (and yet found a home in the biblical ideology in which that code had dominated the cultures of the ancient Middle East). Living conditions for slaves—and for whites—also improved under the reign of King Cotton, whose profits financed improved shelter, diet, and clothing, as Robert Fogel and Stanley Engerman persuasively argue.[48] Greater privacy and self-respect for slaves not only benefited life in the quarters but gave whites a greater sense of order. Acculturated and Christian African Americans were unlikely to rebel; masters would have less occasion to be disorderly in slave management; and the white children would not witness and emulate displays of white adult ill temper and arrogance.[49]

Religious advances also aided a quickening pace of social amelioration, largely through the development of the dissenting faiths. Bitter for both social and religious reasons, leaders of the Baptist yeomanry in Virginia and elsewhere during the First Great Awakening sought to counter the example that the gentry class had set before the public. Declared David Thomas, a Virginia Baptist, "Riches and honor and carnal wisdom are no badges of the Christian Religion."[50] As Philip Fithian, the Yankee tutor in Virginia, noted, they were "quite destroying pleasure in the country" with their fervent prayer and "an entire Banishment of *Gaming, Dancing,* and Sabbath-Day Diversions."[51] On such grounds, Baptists as well as early Methodists did effect a major social revolution in the late eighteenth and early nineteenth centuries as their numbers grew. Yet, as Christine Heyrman points out, the Methodists in particular grew slowly in the eighteenth century because of the leaders' opposition to slavery. Only as their convictions waned did the church win converts in larger numbers.[52] Although opposed to the blood sports, races, and other games because of their long association with gambling, drinking, and similar male vices, the regenerates used physicality in what they called Christian ways. Thus the pleasures of motion in dancing and sports found expression in the movements and touching of converts that characterized the revival experience. Both Baptists and Methodists created new emotional ties among their members with rituals of embrace that made use of the older, uninhibited impulsive habits.[53] By giving them a more instrumental, democratic purpose, they not only changed men's habits, they also reshaped the meaning of respectability. Honor's value had depended on its exclusivity; the Christian gospel, as the dissenters interpreted it, in effect devalued honor by making salvation available to all regardless of their place in the social order.[54] In

addition, the dissenters replaced the ineffective Anglican reliance on public law for policing local morals with inner church discipline. As early as
the mid-eighteenth century and throughout the greater part of the nineteenth century, expulsion or even reprimand by one's brethren in church
often shamed culprits into conformity, sporadic or permanent.[55]

In the antebellum period, members of the Baptist and Methodist faiths
grew wealthier and more sophisticated with each generation. Despite
former convictions about the sins of Mammon and love of ease, Baptists
were more likely than any others to own slaves, a form of property that
encouraged luxury, license, and other violations of God's law. At the same
time, they established by means of ritual the practice of total baptismal im-
mersion, for instance, that gave special identity to those so converted. In
the eighteenth century most especially, non-Baptists had been amused or
horrified by the innovations in worship that they witnessed. The ceremony
of "being dipped" backward in the water, symbol of death, and resurfac-
ing as a sign of a new birth in Christ was a vulgar and unbecoming sight to
behold, they thought. Yet the rite had great meaning to the participants,
and the ceremony remained a part of the Baptist liturgy. Extending the
"right hand of fellowship" or the washing of feet also provided ways to
signify the oneness of the group, the ties that bound men, women, and
children—often of both races.[56]

At the same time, the evangelicals' religious life became more sedate
than it had been in the more emotional days of the late eighteenth century. Yet their adherence to the newly acquired honor of slaveholding
respectability increased. The sensibilities of antique honor and shame—
polarities of the old faith in the world of the unprivate self—began to
weaken and merge into the new individualized order of conscience and
guilt.

Other aspects of the older ethic underwent change, too. Because ine-
briation was a chief offense in church courts, sobriety became a more
widely approved personal virtue (although alcoholic consumption actually increased until 1835, when a slow decline began).[57] Earlier, in eighteenth-century South Carolina, for instance, diners at hunt-club feasts
would allow no member "to go home sober," an affront, recalled William J.
Grayson, "to good manners."[58] Piecemeal or in whole, antebellum Southerners were adopting the restrictive proprieties that the more economically advanced parts of the Western world had already established as conventions.

The story of the Second Great Awakening and its successes needs no
retelling here; the focus must be on factors inhibiting its impact.[59] First,

an eroding, but still lively sentiment thrived that male participation in church life was unmanly.[60] Part of the problem was men's growing wariness about women's intrusions and tacit or overt disapproval, of their associations outside the home. Stimulated by revivals and clerical admonitions to guard the house from sin, women exploited the changing ethical landscape to grasp for domestic power with claims of high religious motives in the eternal battle between the sexes. Quarrels and smoldering enmities sometimes arose from the struggles between pious women and husbands accustomed to "dissipating at the Races and Theatres; every day dining out," as one antebellum Southern matron complained.[61]

In Southern society the parallels between the church system that developed and the precepts of the old ethic were rather remarkable. The pagan fatalism of honor had its counterpart in the Predestinarianism of the Southern denominations. The Manichaean distinction of Good and Evil, hero and coward, resembled the Christian doctrines of heavenly reward and hellfire punishment. The camaraderie of the militia muster had its echo in the right hand of fellowship of the Wesleyan and Baptist faithful. As the historian Johann Huizinga noted many years ago, sports like cockfighting and horse racing often involved a oneness of man and beast in a "sacred identity . . . a mystic unity. The one has *become* the other."[62] The dejection of the gambler at loss and his ecstasy on winning mocked, in a sense, the Christian experience of alienation and conviction, for the polarities of victory and loss at games had their popular appeal. Rather than trust God's providence, the gambler and sportsman venerated a pagan fate in whose hands the bettor surrendered his hopes for the sake of virile self-regard rather than for a Christian humility and a pride in hard work.[63] "Those who participated in the emotional fervor of the revival meetings," the historian Ted Ownby declares, "were rarely the same people enjoying the hot-blooded competitions of male gatherings." The tension, he argues, between "the extremes of masculine aggressiveness and homecentered evangelicalism" endowed "white Southern culture" with its paradoxical and passionate character.[64]

By no means did the Christianization of the South in the nineteenth century, either before or after the Civil War, bring an end to the impulsive habits of Southern violence. The church leaders only imperfectly channeled aggression into revival ecstasies. Sometimes they even provided a subtext of hatred against nonbelievers and perceived community enemies. One Southern church historian has observed that in the absence of other institutions, the churches were "practically the only agency for the improvement of the people."[65] But so solitary a force could not meet the challenge of secular influences and declining use of church discipline that had depended on intensely familial social relations.

Northern missionaries who tried to evangelize the Southern backcountry met a resistance that led them almost inevitably to react with contempt and frustration. Sometimes the earnest young clergymen from the East hoped to win support by giving instruction on ways to improve agricultural practices. A Presbyterian in 1851 wrote contemptuously in a missionary magazine that "they go to hear the 'larned' preacher, and to see the new-fashioned plow . . . and then they return home, and . . . cling tighter to the old rickety plow, and to the see-saw, hum and spit preacher, feeling, that improvements are for others." [66] As a result, in future years, particularly after the Civil War, missionaries to Appalachia would bring "some limited succor through education and health care to mountain people," as Deborah McCauley phrases it, but otherwise would bang "on their doors like traveling salesmen with 'real' religion to sell." [67]

In a Tennessee-Kentucky border district in the late nineteenth century, the six local churches "were unsuccessful as agents of social change" and sometimes had to face the taunts of invading bullies during services. A mountaineer, arrested in 1905, interrupted worship by accusing the church folk of "stealing stove caps from women's cook-stoves, fornications, stealing hog heads and hog faces, laundered shirts etc." Such scenes had marked the experiences of missionaries and preachers in the Southern wilderness as early as the days of Rev. Charles Woodmason in colonial North and South Carolina. With only a few exceptions, church leaders, even in sophisticated areas, seldom treated violence as a regional or even local social problem.[68]

To control passions effectively, a transformation of the whole social and ethical order would have had to emerge. The church was not strong enough to accelerate the trend. Prohibitions against gaming, drink, and dueling, for instance, were all but unenforceable given the restrictive technicalities of the court system and the reluctance of juries to convict when communities and states attempted such approaches.[69] Overdrinking vexed nearly all those concerned with church discipline in antebellum America, but especially in the South. Although very strict in holding worshipers to accounts for inappropriate behavior, including fighting and verbal abuse, the Primitive Baptists of south Georgia and Florida, for instance, seldom expelled members for such offenses if they repented— over and over. Recalling the frontier past, a minister in Georgia described how "almost everybody was in the habit of drinking; young and old, rich and poor, saint and sinner, all would drink, and many of them get drunk into the bargain." Sometimes the "Hardshells" were called "Whiskey Baptists" or "Forty Gallon Baptists." One of their ministers ran a tavern. Often bearing the brunt of their husbands' binges, women occasionally acted independently. When a notorious lush asked once again for forgiveness from his fellow church people, all the men stood to signify their mercy. The women remained seated. When the numbers were counted, the women had the majority and expelled the sinner forthwith.[70]

Reasons for the problems of wayward social behavior in the Southern churches were several. First there was the institutional inadequacy of the denominations. Ministers continued to be in short supply throughout the antebellum period.[71] Suspicion of new ways, defense of noblesse oblige, and dread of outside encroachment on male and family prerogative continued to prevail. A deep-seated pessimism about the reformability of man conspired against participation in voluntary associations for moral purposes. In the 1820s and 1830s, missionaries from Northern benevolent societies met stiff resistance and sometimes ridicule. Voluntarism, declared suspicious Antimission Baptists—and others as well—was merely a "Money Making Scheme of less Public utility than common Lotteries."[72] One Pennsylvania missionary found Arkansas, his newly assigned district, so hostile that he called the new district "*heathen country*," compared with his itinerancy in Indiana, a truly "*Christian land.*"[73] As for the consumption of alcohol, good drinking water was not always available, and brandy or some other form of alcohol was often the most palliative medicine in the antebellum physician's black bag.

Among the many problems was the difficulty of finding male lay leaders to sponsor the new measures of voluntarism and clerical professionalism. Helping a pious itinerant stranger brought local laymen no particular community prestige. He might disseminate dangerous notions.[74] Moreover, for reaching the young with the Christian message, the lack of common schools ill-prepared both pupils and local teachers for Christian study. Old attitudes about child rearing worked against efforts to reach the young through the innovation of Sunday schools. Sheldon Norton, Northern missionary, discovered in Alabama that parents wished their offspring to be "unrestrained" because childhood was thought to be "a season which should be left run to waste."[75] (For church folk as well as the unchurched, aggressiveness in male children was not to be discouraged for fear of effeminacy.)

Finally, most evangelical clergy, even Methodist bishops, were, in a sense, part-time ministers. By necessity of low salaries—and for some no salary at all—they devoted most weekdays to farming or business, not to church activities or pastoral visits. In contrast, Northern and Western churchmen, whose stipends largely permitted full-time work, adopted modes of "associationism" and voluntary action with remarkable results both for religion and for "the civilizing process." Don Doyle, the urban historian, has pointed out that in antebellum Jacksonville, Illinois, a typical midwestern town, the voluntary association offered participants social and ethical advantages. Active members were likely to appear in the local paper, no mean advantage in "a young community of newcomers." Furthermore, benevolent societies served to "integrate sectional, religious, or political factions within the middle class." For ambitious young mechanics and craftsmen who found "card tables and billiard saloons" distasteful, the voluntary society was a more agreeable organization to join than the militia, the Southern ladder to social and political success.[76] Evidence indicates that the urban South lagged only slightly behind the advance of benevolent agencies in the free states. Yet most Southerners lived in tiny hamlets and rural districts where civic or charitable activity was bound to be less welcome, less organized, less sustainable.[77] In those locations, especially, the kinship bond was the chief foundation of church life, just as it was for most other social events in the South.[78]

The maintenance of Southern familial and community honor had traditionally involved the use of informal, extralegal modes of surveillance and control. To attack crime or wrongdoing required neither the forming of a moral reform society nor Whiggish calls for laws to be strictly enforced but rather the assembling of a community-based charivari. In Mississippi, a woman who conspired with her lover to kill her husband received a severe whipping at the hands of irate citizens. On the basis of a coerced confession, she was tried at the bar and convicted as an accessory to murder. Petitioners to Governor Hiram G. Runnels urged clemency, not because her rights had been violated but because the community penalty abrogated the need for any further punishment.[79] In the North such Federalist church leaders as those whom Harry Stout has portrayed promptly denounced the "people in the streets" when riots or vigilantism arose. In the antebellum South their clerical counterparts were mute. Churchmen rationalized their silence as a worthy insusceptibility to the clamors of political warfare. For Methodists, especially, the "family" of the faithful was to be kept separate from the world or else become contaminated by it.[80]

Yet Southern ministers were not altogether consistent about the handling of political agitations. During the Nullification crisis, some South

Carolinian clergymen spoke out pro and con. At Pendleton Village, Richard P. Cater invested the Nullifiers' case with biblical significance, likening South Carolina to the king of Israel in dealing with the "Princes of Ammon." Such outspokenness threatened congregational schisms. By and large, clergymen preferred a more tranquil gaze on the political scene, reserving their anger for such uncontroversial targets as the abolition menace.[81] Otherwise, the antebellum Southern divines guarded their reputations with care.[82] Their position, the church historian Samuel S. Hill explains, was that religion should be largely "a matter of the individual's standing before God, who would grant or withhold the pardon of sins and the reward of everlasting life, and of the sinner's relationship with the Lord, emanating in assurance and consolation." As a result, he concludes, "responsibility for the public order or for prophetic scrutiny into society's ways" played little role in the life of the Southern church.[83]

. . . .

Between 1840 and 1861, the Age of Ambivalence, church power had developed to a point that the rule of honor was jeopardized. Churches and church wealth were growing at the rate of 20 to 50 percent from 1850 to 1860 in Virginia. Other states showed similar advances. Colleges and seminaries sprouted even in denominations formerly opposed to advanced secular and even theological learning. By the end of the revival era, the Christian ethos had won official preeminence as the arbiter of "civil religion" for the South. In the upper reaches of society the "infidel" stood outside the charmed circle of gentility.[84] In less refined sectors of the region, Christian men professed their faith in Jesus Christ without the fear of ridicule that in colonial Virginia, for instance, had dismayed the faithful.[85] Strengthened by the successful planter-led mission to the slaves, the proslavery argument gave "divine sanction" to the region's economic and social foundation. A few churchmen openly advocated sanctified marriages and instruction to enable slaves to read the Bible. The intellectual rigor of the proslavery defense and mission efforts benefited enormously from the participation of Northern clergy in Southern parishes and Southern clergy trained at Northern seminaries.[86]

Nonetheless, the legacy of the past held back advances in the "civilizing process." First, the concepts of privacy and individuality were still underdeveloped as periodic mob actions continued to suppress deviancies. In the North, families retreated into what Mary Ryan calls "a narrowing social universe, one even more solitary than privacy—the domain of the self, the individual, of 'manly independence.'"[87] The latter term had a different meaning from that held by the white Southerner. For Northern church people, it meant a relative indifference to public conventions because virtue was self-generated, self-induced, not dependent on fears of public disapproval and shame. In the North, privacy implied a yearning for immunity from the influences of the street, a segregation from lower-class vices and crudeness. Such contaminations were thought especially harmful in the upbringing of children.

In the rural South, however, segregation of rich from poor was impossible. Plantation whites were in constant contact with slaves. Towns were too small and familial to permit the isolation available in the anonymity of city life. The same enraged impotence that sometimes led to cruelty toward slaves could affect the recipients as well, leading to a general mean-spiritedness. While acknowledging the universal piety of Huntsville, Alabama, the writer Anne Royall was nonetheless horrified at the churlishness of both whites and blacks. "I never have looked into the streets," she wrote, "but I see those brutal negroes torturing and wounding poor innocent cats, dogs, hogs, or oxen, and no one interferes." She concluded, "A curse must fall on a land so lost to feeling."[88]

Furthermore, a sanctioned virility remained so powerful a force in Southern culture that the church remained circumspect and ambivalent in dealing with conventions that still had important social functions. Only one of the leading moral issues can be touched upon here: the dram. In the antebellum period, Southern teetotalers tried to persuade churches to expel liquor dealers, excommunicate habitual drinkers, and press for total statutory prohibition, at home and in the tavern. Yet the movement failed, largely for four reasons. First, in areas where transportation was poor, it was more economical and efficient to distill grain than to ship in bulk. As a result, farmers were not eager to relinquish the option. Reflecting their constituency, politicians and publicans had little reason to encourage sobriety when a thirsty public still demanded the old custom of largesse at election time. Second, churchmen were themselves divided. In some quarters, both Baptist and Methodist congregations split over the issue of antialcohol and the expulsion of intemperates.[89] For some Christians the question also raised issues of class. Most alarmed were the "hard-rined" Anti-Mission Baptists, who saw in temperance the intrusions of educated snobs whose moral societies were themselves unsanctified in their use of rationalistic, noncommunal methods.[90]

Third, there was the outside pressure of ridicule from the mouths of the unchurched, particularly in the Southern river and coastal ports. For instance, no clergyman, not even Benjamin M. Palmer, the prominent Presbyterian divine, could puritanize the New Orleanians. Their bibulous tendencies, shuddered a pious Yankee businessman, were "perfectly chilling." On a single Sabbath, one New Englander counted some twenty profane events in the city, including two circuses, a French opera, duel, boxing match, cockfight, masquerade ball, waxwork exhibition, and countless dinner parties.[91] Ted Ownby records that whites and blacks in the post–Civil War South often congregated to trade horses, swap stories, bet on a cockfight, play cards, drink—and quarrel and riot. In 1880 at Collinsburg, Louisiana, for instance, a pious Baptist reported to a friend, "A Saturday hardly ever comes but the negroes and white men too will go to the stores and drink and gambol and then they will all have a general fight."[92]

Finally, traditions of both church and state upheld local autonomy of congregation, county, and family to oppose any scheme that implied a central authority, especially one with a Yankee odor about it. A stern temperance leader, General John Hartwell Cocke lamented that his fellow Virginians would discountenance any law that barred "a man [from] furnishing himself and getting drunk in his own House. This would be invading a privilege held sacred with us at present."[93] Likewise, not until 1886 did the Southern Baptist Convention officially commit itself to total abstinence, leaving such matters to local churches and state assemblies. Even so there were doubts about the efficacy of intruding into the dangerous waters of politics and personal decision making on questions of a public character. Sophisticated churchmen like James Henley Thornwell, the South Carolina Presbyterian leader, worried, as did the Primitive Baptists, that reliance on human instrumentalities of enforced prohibition endangered personal piety and family responsibility.[94] Reluctance to speak out on matters of general reform did not mean that religion played no role in politics but only that the clergy had to restrict themselves to those issues about which there was no disagreement at all.

The struggle against the traditional ethic of the South had always been piecemeal and ambivalent. As a codification of rules whereby Southerners justified the use of force, honor could not be wholly relinquished unless they were ready to accept women and blacks, most particularly, on a level of equality. Since that proposition was beyond imagining, the hard code of masculinity pervaded all the social classes. White supremacy, the centrality of family loyalty, the hierarchy of ascriptions, the primacy of public reputation over individual conscience, and the retributive nature of justice were presuppositions and enjoinings that the churched and un-churched shared and gave political voice to in one form or another. Dissent on these matters was not to be countenanced at any time or place. For instance, as late as June, 1865, both slavery and Southern independence lay in ruins, but the Methodist minister John H. Caldwell outraged his Newnan, Georgia, congregation when he argued from the pulpit that God had punished the South for its sins against the slave. "If our practice had conformed to the law of God, he would not have suffered the institution to be overthrown," he argued. Caldwell lost his church and was reassigned to a rough district, a position he declined out of fear for his life.[95]

. . . .

Despite the heavy hand of white conformity, the definition of the Southern ethic was itself undergoing transformation along Christian lines. Self-restraint had become part of the way men strove to behave, not always with success, as Northern and English visitors to the South were often quick to notice.[96] However slow the advance, overdrinking, male sexual license, and other sins of the flesh did arouse public criticism that eventually hardened into Victorian repressiveness. In the meantime, the two ethical systems coexisted in uncertain balance.[97] For all their vexation over selected aspects of male liberties of behavior which the code of honor permitted, the Southern evangelicals were as loyal to the cause of sectional vindication as the political "fire-eaters." By such means the clergy pledged loyalty to community values. In urging the cause of secession, preachers sometimes employed the same language as the politicians. Samuel Henderson, an Alabama Baptist editor, for instance, argued that his state "owes it to her own honor . . . to secede from the Union."[98] How easy it was to merge sentiments of honorable retribution with righteous indignation against abolitionist and Black Republican malevolence. They became one.

Under such circumstances, neither honor nor evangelicalism wholly triumphed. Instead, the South would have to live thereafter with a divided soul, a dissonance seldom acknowledged. The dichotomy that endured to affect the politics and history of the region well into the present century recognized no need to make choices between honor and Christianity, between Athens and Jerusalem. The white Southerners' deity could be worshiped not only as the Christ of Salvation but as the Ruler of Honor, Pride, and Race. At one time such a God was Gail Hightower's object of reverence, but by the end of Faulkner's *Light in August*, Hightower realizes that the churches' steeples as representations of that divinity were "empty, symbolical, bleak, sky-pointed not with ecstasy or with passion but in adjuration, threat, and doom."[99] Yet for all the tragedy that came from the fusion of honor and piety in early Southern culture, the result was a lightening of the load of human care in peace and an inspiration for many to nobility in war, albeit in a cause that thankfully came to naught.

CHAPTER FIVE

PARADOX, SHAME, AND GRACE
IN THE BACKCOUNTRY

Now to him that worketh is the reward not reckoned
of grace, but of debt. But to him that worketh not,
but believeth on him that justifieth the ungodly,
his faith is counted for righteousness.
—Romans 4:4–5

If I then, your Lord and Master, have washed your feet,
ye also ought to wash one another's feet.
—John 13:14

While the struggle against godlessness and the license that honor conferred upon men remained a persistent theme in Southern religious life, churches were riven by theological quarrels. The disputes reflected the changing social, economic, and political order of the early republic. During the Jacksonian years, the fast-growing Baptist denomination grappled with an issue similar to the old general's war against the Bank of the United States, eastern Whiggery, and federal encroachments on the rights of states. For them, as for President Jackson, sturdy reaction against their respective foes was a matter of honor. To be sure, the religious warfare was quieter than the political struggle. Redemption in the Lord was the prize to be sought—not office, wealth, or the world's esteem. When partisan issues arose, though, the traditionalists found the Jacksonian party the most compatible. In contrast, their opponents in the Baptist sphere tended toward centralizing Whiggery in outlook and method. One traditional-minded preacher declared, "Some persons may think it strange that nearly all Old School Baptists are State Rights Republicans. But if their form of government and *strict* construction principles were duly considered, it would appear strange that any of them should be otherwise."[1]

Just as Jacksonianism was itself paradoxical in its adherence to both status honor and egalitarianism, the antimission effort posed a challenge to the antique code, most especially among the sectarian traditionalists who came to be called Primitive Baptists. They viewed theological change and innovation—as evangelical Christians appeared to embody it—with grave suspicion. Under the influence of the evangelical revivalist Charles Grandison Finney in the 1830s, revivals became ever more a matter of human agency and less a gift from the Holy Spirit, as the Primitive Baptists saw the situation. The Old School Baptists received much ridicule for their position, but it was backed by a strong Calvinist tradition. This was a case of honor welling up from the bottom of the social order instead of descending from above.[2]

Though they were conservative theologically, their almost Quaker-like mistrust of institutional religion led them toward an equality within the plain walls of their churches that defied the common understanding of honor as a function of orderly hierarchy. Yet the dismissal of honor as a criterion of personal and collective worth was not altogether absent from the sect. The result was paradox. They defied the worldliness of the planter class. Yet in their own worship, disciplinary procedures, and social attitudes, they could not escape the encumbrances that a sense of honor and shame engendered.

We are inclined to think that honor belongs exclusively to the upper ranks of the social order—a status that practically none of these Christian traditionalists held. That view would be an error, not only in the American antebellum South but also in the other parts of the world which adhered to that ethic (often with, of course, strikingly different emphases and priorities). For instance, after studying the Bedouin clans of the Mount Sinai desert region, the anthropologist Frank Stewart concludes that egalitarianism and honor need not be thought antagonistic. Despite wide variations in property holding from a value of a few dollars to thousands, Bedouin honor "was in essence equally distributed among all adult men, and to the extent that one can talk about differences in honor, they were not based on wealth."[3] Thus it was possible to combine honor with equality. Certainly that was true in the South, where the yeomanry nearly everywhere and mountain folk in particular had very decided views about the superior protectiveness of male over female, white skin over dark—especially Native American and African colorations—and other aspects of the code.[4]

Nonetheless, in America and in much of the Western world, substantial holdings were certainly a component of social measure. By and large, Southern churchmen were not immune to the pull of profit and marketplace commerce from the use of and the traffic in slaves. It was a force that the Primitives resisted as best they could.[5] Undeniably but not unambiguously, honor in the South flourished throughout the Age of Jackson, the so-called Era of the Common Man.

It might be said that the Baptists in the South owed their earliest inspiration to a sense of egalitarianism that Jackson was later to exploit in politics. In colonial times, according to Rhys Isaac, all Baptists had protested the haughtiness, social monopolizing, and demands for deference of the Anglican Virginia gentry elite.[6] That tradition continued among some Baptists even though many others of their persuasion were climbing the social ladder to respectability—as early nineteenth-century inhabitants defined it.

The Southern ethic and the concept of innovation—the notion that reform and progress were unmitigated blessings—were not compatible even for the most egalitarian of Primitive Baptists in the period after the War of 1812. In the eyes of the traditionally minded Christians, the professional and urban clergy had strayed from the true way.[7] Along with the more forward-looking lay people, they were adopting the new techniques for evangelization—the use of modern steam presses, voluntary associations, centralized and metropolitan headquarters, and other innovations. This was an effort not perceived as a democratization of Christianity but the very opposite, the imposition of grades and ranks of Christians. Conservatives, most particularly in the Baptist denomination (but also some Methodists), rejected what seemed to them to be revolutionary methods that disturbed the old ways. The innovations, the dissenters argued, changed the nature of appropriate hierarchies, differentiating the lower elements of society from the middle-class, urbanized Christians and from the planter elite above them. The antimission sectarians claimed that such unbiblical means jeopardized the integrity of the old forms for worshiping God and protested what seemed to be moneymaking schemes designed to separate the pious agrarian from his meager pennies.

No less important was their fear that Baptist changes in ecclesiastical policy would destroy the creed of fundamental Calvinism to which they zealously adhered. In 1836, the Antioch Primitive Baptist elders set forth the doctrine of the tradition-bound. Appropriately they proclaimed the inerrancy of the Bible and then proceeded with a creed that set forth "the fall of Adam, the degeneracy of his posterity, the corruption of human nature, and the inability of fallen man to do that which is spiritually good, the everlasting love of God to his people, a covenant of grace with Jesus Christ . . . the joys of the righteous and the punishment of the wicked."[8] John Calvin had fashioned the doctrine that men are "metaphysically deranged, naturally inclined to reverse the order of things."[9] Since the adoption of the Westminster Covenant in 1647, the doctrines of "particular election" and predestination have been the foundations of the Primitive Baptist faith.

In the ecclesiology of these believers, the gift of homiletics was thought a blessing from God and not a profession. Seminaries or formal training of any kind were deemed unnecessary. Preachers were required to support themselves as best they could. Yet, contrary to what one might expect of a denomination that disapproved of higher learning, the Primitive Baptists have had to this day a strong sense of historical continuity and knowledge of their doctrinal past.[10] References to the London Confession of 1689, the events of the Reformation, and the apostolic succession, as it were, to earlier Christian times have been kept alive as much by oral as by written means.

For the Baptist of traditionalist views, modernity in the ways of worship and faith had to be stoutly resisted or they would disgrace their perception of God Himself. Sunday schools and revivals were never permitted in their churches. The Primitive Baptists (also called Regular Baptists, Old Regulars, and, derisively, Hard Shells) objected to the heightened emotionalism of revival preaching. They thought the practice degraded the spiritual experience of conversion. John Taylor of Kentucky, one of the leaders of the antimission movement, admitted that as a young man he had been attracted to the way "people hallooed, cried out, trembled, fell down, and went into strange exercises." But eventually he rejected revival passion as a passing novelty.[11] Taking his text from Paul's letter to the Romans, Taylor argued that works, including the stirring of revivals, were insufficient. Faith alone was favored by God. " 'Blessed is the man to whom the Lord imputeth righteousness without works.' Therefore those mercies are unmerited."[12] Most other Southern as well as many Northern Protestants who lived in the era of the Second Great Awakening felt otherwise about the utility, dynamism, and redemptive power of the camp meeting and preaching itinerancy.[13]

In contrast, the Primitives worried about the tendency in revivals to dilute the Calvinistic doctrines of election, human inability, and predestination. The adoption of a hopeful gospel was more appealing to American Protestants partly because it conformed with their more secular hopes in this life. The Old Regular Baptists worshiped quietistically in the venerable forms of prayer, sermon, and hymn-singing. Their ceremonies were simple: weddings, burials, ordinations, and the Lord's Supper (always closed). Nonetheless, non-Baptists disapproved and even mocked their other rituals because of their tactile—and allegedly sensual—nature: the washing of feet (separated, however, by the sexes), extending "the hand of fellowship," exchanging the "kiss of charity," and the "laying on of hands." The Primitives' singing was (and still is) "ocupella," that is, unaccompanied. As with the Disciples of Christ, organs and other musical instruments were forbidden. The hymns drew chiefly from words in the King James Bible. As the patriarchal underpinning of Regular Baptist prescriptions required, the designated leader of song had to be—and still is—male. He named the hymn, established the pitch, and began the verse. The other singers then joined in the sometimes dissonant harmonics and sang without vibrato and with almost no eye contact with others. The stylized and sedate nature of the singing with little overt affect nonetheless stirred deep emotion in the singers.[14]

The attitude of mind that prompted the antimission Baptists stood in the forefront of a reaction that seemed to parallel Jackson's hostility toward a centralized institution that allegedly profiteered at the expense of the common people. Power was to be vested as closely as possible in the family household and community of neighboring believers. In church government as in the Jacksonian ideal of political democracy, the males in the congregation had equal votes and voices. The more dynamic souls preached and served as elders. Sectarians of the restorationist persuasion believed that this arrangement, along with the autonomous congregation, mirrored the original churches that Paul and the Apostles had founded. The assembled worshipers—that is, the male members—were "to receive in and cast out," choose their own preachers, exhorters, and officers, and "exercise every part of gospel discipline and church government, independent of any other church or assembly whatever," as the Philadelphia Association had resolved in 1749.[15] Congregational liberties, patriarchal honor, and states' rights were certainly compatible ideals.

A hearty disapproval of female participation on a level with their male partners was also an important element in a defense of the Primitive Baptists' traditional values. They discovered perils of gender confusion in women's activities for foreign and domestic missions and other causes that Missionary Baptists espoused. Religious conversion of women without a father or husband's prior consent could be very disturbing to men, jealous of their authority. (In 1858 one angry husband in Mississippi shot and nearly killed the Reverend P. E. Green, a preacher who had won his wife for Christ.) Few Southern husbands went that far to assert patriarchal rights, but Christine Heyrman provides evidence of considerable anti-clerical hostility among Southern husbands jealous of any authority governing their wives apart from their own. Still, women in the Primitive faith were very restricted in what they could do within the church structure. In Mississippi, the Sarepta Baptist Church covenant in 1815 resolved that the sisters in fellowship follow Paul's advice "not to speak in the church nor usurp authority." Under the tidal wave of evangelical influence and power, however, the church dropped the prohibitionist edict. In 1834 the church members granted women "all the privileges of the male members of the church." Yet those faithful to the old ways provided two doors for entry into the church, with women on the left side and men on the right. Even today women are neither to preach nor to speak when church business is discussed.[16]

Deborah McCauley has found that mountain Baptists react solemnly to the communion part of a service, but the sacrament of foot washing (as it is usually called, instead of feet washing) is given the title "sacramental meeting."[17] At a service in the Appalachian foothills, one worshiper embraced and kissed a foot he had washed, while another sang softly as his own feet were sponged in the basin. Emotions flowed freely, even more so than during the preaching or in the administering of the Lord's Supper. The rite of foot washing is important because it signifies the very opposite of honor. The ritual is not a symbolic act of abject obeisance but rather sanctified humility in the presence of God and fellow worshipers. Faithful to the ancient sacrament, a twentieth-century antimission elder declared, "It's a great thing that you honor yourself down [and] . . . get down on your knees and skirt yourself with a towel and wash your sister's feet."[18] In this case, to "honor," as he put it, means to humble oneself in a manner that reveals the close tie between this form of the ethic and spiritual grace.

Set against the evil ways of the world in which honor plays so important a role, the Primitive Baptist figuratively turned away from "the great mass of corrupted wickedness." The rite has always served to express love of God and the brethren gathered in equality under the rule of a common meekness. Therefore, only those pure in fellowship should be admitted to the reenactment of the Lord's gathering during Passover. A scholar has appropriately entitled his study of the traditionalists' theology " 'Can Two Walk Together Unless They Be Agreed?' "[19] In the foot-washing rites, there is an implied defiance of worldly honor. Yet that repudiation does not deny the ethic its power. Paradoxically, the Primitive Baptists knew what respect, honor, and upright living demanded—a view held by most common people of the South.[20]

Not surprisingly the foot-washing dissidents who opposed the ways of the modern religious world were to be found in the remote hinterlands rather than in the more densely populated parts of the South. For instance, Roanoke, Danville, Richmond, and parts of the Tidewater in Virginia became strongholds of mission activity. Baptist associations of the Blue Ridge and of the sparsely settled sections on the North Carolina line, however, withdrew from fellowship with the advocates of missions. The same geographic placing applied in the piney regions and hills of Alabama, Arkansas, and Missouri.[21] The mountain people of Kentucky and Tennessee also seemed to be particularly affected. The mission and revival sectarians also gathered strength in the less remote and prosperous parts of these states. The Delmarva Peninsula of Delaware, Maryland, and Virginia was another hotbed of antimissionism. Bleak stretches on the southern Atlantic coastline, from Delaware to Florida, were dominated by the antimissionists. In the fastnesses of southern Georgia and Florida "the Missionary tide arrived weak and late." In 1838 an elder of the "always Primitive Ochloknee Association" happily announced that "we have had no difficulties with the missionaries."[22] In low-country and black-belt districts, where plantations flecked the landscape, antimissionists were usually found among the nonslaveholding farmers. Where the antimissionists thrived, the evangelicals found slim religious pickings. The Reverend Noah Baldwin in southwestern Virginia, for instance, had a "feeble band, numbering in the aggregate 14."[23]

One may surmise that antimissionist churches in the towns of the Deep South served almost exclusively migrants from outlying sectors, just as they did in such border-state centers as Cincinnati, Baltimore, and Wilmington, Delaware. With some exceptions here and there, African Americans, free and slave, were not much attracted to the antimissionist cause with its suppression of spontaneous emotion in worship.[24] Many of the northwestern antimissionists were probably transplanted Southerners from the hills of Kentucky and Tennessee, where antimission leaders John Taylor and Daniel Parker had practically eliminated all mission support by 1830. For instance, the Baptist church in Pigeon Creek, Indiana, where the parents of Abraham Lincoln lived, was the center for antimissionist sentiment in the state. The area was settled by Virginians and Kentuckians—yeomen like Thomas Lincoln, father of Abraham Lincoln, and the Hanks kinsfolk.[25]

During the Civil War the geographical heart of the future Confederacy—stretching from western Virginia to East Texas—was a stronghold of traditionalist sentiment. That large area, not much smaller than the territories of western Europe, scarcely furnished the most loyal and devoted enthusiasts for secession. In fact, nearly as many young men from what William W. Freehling aptly calls the "White Belt" fought for the Union as joined the Rebel armies. Desertion rates of Appalachian soldiers in Confederate forces were high, especially in the latter part of the war.[26]

Fiercely jealous of their independence, Primitive Baptists of the agrarian and mountain areas applied their own definition to the words *honor* and *shame*. Their intensely felt conviction of inner worth has been often been called frontier "individualism." But that spirit was less individualistic in our modern sense of the term than it was an expression of manliness and familial loyalty. The individual was part of a kinship unit, and so his honor involved more than himself. It concerned a man's whole lineage as well.

Because this sense of familial unity was very much a part of the social order, church discipline required the imposition of shame, loss of reputation, and often expulsion. From the eighteenth century on, the Old Regulars insisted on the prerogative of making "straight the crooked." They took their injunction from Paul's first letter to the Corinthians: "Do you know that the saints shall judge the world? And if the world shall be judged by you, are you unworthy to judge the smallest matters? . . . I speak to your shame. Is it so, that there is not a wise man among you?" And in Matthew, the scorning and unbelieving shall be exposed—"tell it to the church: but if he neglect to hear the church, let him be unto thee as an heathen man and a publican." These were figures of special degradation.[27]

The imposition of church discipline on those found guilty of moral violations was not the rule only for Primitive Baptists. In fact, most antebellum Southern Protestant churches scrutinized the morals of offenders by one means or another. In the governance of Baptist churchgoers at least, congregations, antimission or missionary, had to take into account issues of honor when deciding matters of personal conduct. Both branches of the church made considerable use of disciplinary committees to expel members found guilty of offenses deemed harmful to the purity of the church, to resolve disputes among the brethren, or to investigate and rule on domestic problems. In fact, Gregory Wills has noted that for Baptists of all stripes "the preaching of the gospel and the exercise of church discipline served the vision of the pure church by separating the righteous from the unrighteous." And indeed they did so with some relish. "When churches encountered troubles, ecclesiastical detectives could be counted on to round up the usual suspects—first among them being neglect of church discipline. Defectors from the straight and narrow found themselves admonished, denounced, expelled, excommunicated—and restored when they showed sufficient penitence. To be shamed in such ritualized fashion was sure to be a moment of real anguish, especially for the female worshipers, who were more likely than their men to stand in disgrace before the church fathers. As Wills further explains, social position counted, however, and the more powerful members of the church seldom received full measures of disapprobation or removal.[28]

Stephanie McCurry offers a telling example of how the dictates of honor affected the worshipers at the Gum Branch Baptist Church in Darlington County, South Carolina, in 1854. As the wealthiest member of the church, John Kelly exercised considerable power in the community and in the church. When his wife, Lenore, brought accusations of maltreatment before the elders, they recognized the solidity of her case but expelled both husband and wife. They hoped the verdict would lessen the impact of Kelly's loss of reputation. The Kellys were outraged, nonetheless. John's brother Willey Kelly forced a review of the decision. On the second round, the evidence against Lenore's husband was overwhelming, and John Kelly was removed from fellowship and his wife readmitted. Of course, that result only made matters even more contentious. "The threat to Kelly's honor as a man and, by extension to the honor of the entire Kelly family," McCurry writes, led to "radical measures" in opposition.[29] The minister, Reverend Culpepper, caught John Kelly in the act of forging an entry in the church records that would have indicated a withdrawal of Lenore Kelly's fellowship in the church and his own standing tacitly restored by a letter of dismissal. Outraged by the Kelly clan's whispering campaigns against the long-suffering Lenore and even himself, Culpepper publicly promised to resign unless his "character as a man and a Christian minister" was supported by church vote. The Kellys came out in force while Lenore Kelly's defenders, perhaps from fear of reprisals, could not carry their cause. As he had vowed, Culpepper resigned. Such was the power of the Kellys that Lenore Kelly finally gave up her membership in the church, moved to another part of the county, and worked as a servant in another farmer's household. She had no property and was apparently kinless. Finally, the church drew up the courage to expel all the Kellys and some of their associates—a total of twenty-four members.[30] In this instance, the force of masculine honor was potent enough to prevent vindication for a wife sorely dishonored by her husband in his physical cruelties. At the same time, the Gum Branch Church had expelled the most prominent figure in the community, casting the shadow of shame upon him and all his kin, and restored order by disgracing the fractious group as a whole.

Aside from what he regarded as an affront to his self-esteem, John Kelly may not have cared very much if he could no longer attend worship with his neighbors and "connexions." For most Baptists, regardless of sect, spiritual fellowship, however, was highly prized. To be excluded from it was for many a plunge into a sea of wretchedness. That was especially so in the small enclaves where the antimissionist movement flourished then and later. According to one keen observer of the modern Primitive Baptists, heirs of that tradition, "the power of this corporate experience and identity is a stay against the darkness of the hard doctrine" of a limited Calvinist election. That dogma "also accounts for the terror of exclusion." In addition, separation from others also prompts a feeling of isolation and mortification. In a conversation with S. T. Hawkins, of the Mt. Herman Primitive Baptist Church in Calhoun County, Mississippi, a friend belonging to another denomination asked, "What would you be if you weren't a Primitive Baptist?" Brother Hawkins replied, "I'd be ashamed."[31]

As recently as 1982, a small church in the Blue Ridge Mountains expelled a male member for having committed a fraud. In contrast to the Kellys so long before, his family was not very powerful in community affairs. He had claimed workers' compensation when he was not physically disabled. The whole clan moved out of the district. But the church was not satisfied with that outcome. The members voted to exclude those associated with the disgraced churchgoer as well. Some thirty-seven were eventually removed merely because, among other petty examples, they may have sat in the same pew with the departed offender or ridden in his pickup truck. Elders from other churches in the loosely organized neighborhood association of Primitive Baptists visited the church during worship to offer mediation and advice. Rejecting any outside authority, the preachers reviled them as "fools and wolves." These were "scriptural terms of abuse," as ethnographers James Peacock and Ruel Tyson explain. The mediators were thought ill-deserving of fellowship and had to be expelled.[32] (Following the fine example of Deborah McCauley, I occasionally use ethnographic sources because the Primitive tradition is primarily oral, with few and laconic records, and also because in theological, liturgical, and church governance, there has been little change over time.)

Whether the terms *honor* and *shame* are applied or some other designation is chosen, the issues of belonging and exclusion, grace and disgrace were evident in the mentality of the tradition-minded Baptists. In their Manichaean divisions, they believed in the ancient values of family and community governance, kept entirely free from outside intrusions. Any compromise with presumed evils posed grave perils. A deep sense of community loyalty, an adherence to the virile prerogatives of the patriarchal style and structure of church leadership, the primacy of faith over learning, and tradition over change were all part of their concept of divinely inspired rules of conduct. Grace—the gift of mercy from God—has always been at the center of the Primitive Baptists' faith. Herman B. Yates of Dingess, West Virginia, preached: "God is the God of grace, and by grace we are saved, and it is by grace from beginning to end, grace-planned salvation, grace-provided salvation, and grace works within His elect to overcome the hardness of their hearts, the obstinacy of their wills, and the enmity of their minds."[33]

On some level, the antimission Baptists—though at first sometimes antislavery—understood that the evangelizing they opposed could become the camel's nose under the tent of the "domestic institution." The same missionary impulse that animated so many church people of the Second Great Awakening also evolved in Northern religious circles. The Christian assault on slaveholding as sin and white Southerners, as the abolitionist William Lloyd Garrison might have phrased it, grew from that revival seed. In fact, out of fear of Yankee contamination, some missionary Baptists formed Sunday schools, for instance, without connection with the Philadelphia-based American Sunday School Union. As one agent of that organization reported, devout Southerners entertained the fantasy of "a rupture of our civil compact—dissolution of all social order—an armed host of incendiary *abolitionists*—blood and murder—and a thousand other hydra-headed gorgons dire, with the establishment of a Sunday school."[34]

. . . .

The movement that prompted the antimission Baptist reaction to antislavery agency had its origins well back into the early eighteenth century. The first sign of an "anti" spirit appeared when the "New Lights" or early missionary-minded, New England–based evangelicals began their labors in Virginia and the Carolinas in the 1750s and 1760s. Regular Baptists of British origins had already settled in small numbers below the Potomac and did not always welcome the newcomers from the Northeast. The Regulars, who also included church people under the auspices of the Philadelphia Association, disapproved of the full-throated revival preachings, the indecorous jerkings, and the noisy glossolalia of the New Lights, or Separates, as they were often called. Moreover, the Separates refused to accept the Calvinistic confession of faith adopted by the Philadelphia Association in 1742. This adaptation of the Westminster Covenant of 1647 uncompromisingly affirmed the doctrines of human inability, predestination, and election.

The Separate Baptists were notorious in pre-Revolutionary Virginia owing to the austerity of their manner, including simplicity of dress and short hair. Such plainness contrasted with the cocked hats, lace cuffs, brocaded vests—and lusty temperaments—of the planter aristocracy. The better sort thought the religious newcomers "the most melancholy people." It was said that their fervor drove them never "to meet a man upon the road, but they must ram a text of Scripture down his throat." Despite or perhaps because they were persecuted by the Anglican elite, the Separates appealed to the lower orders of society. According to Rhys Isaac, their Christian message offered spiritual and psychological relief from the hard life of toil, debt, meager diet, and mean shelter that was the fate of the poor.[35]

Meantime, the Regulars were unswayed by the revival enthusiasms of the Separates. Stoutly they swore themselves to the legalistic Philadelphia creed. Some, though, went further by accepting John Gill's interpretations of the original Westminster document. Gill, a learned English Baptist of Southwark, reacted against both the rationalism of the Augustan age and the enthusiasm, evangelism, and latitudinarian tendencies in English church life. Along with Joseph Hussey and John Brine, Gill believed that true, scriptural Calvinism prohibited all human efforts to win men for Christ. He had offered himself as a sacrifice only for those whom God had predetermined to save.[36] The Separates, in contrast, adhered to the more hopeful preachments of Jonathan Edwards and Isaac Backus.

The descendants of the Separates, who made up the dominant, evangelical wing of the Baptist persuasion, received further sustenance from Robert Hall and Andrew Fuller. These theologians rebelled against what they considered to be Gill's unrelieved negativism, introspectiveness, and baneful formality, and they urged a bold crusade to evangelize the world. There were many points of dispute between the Separates and Regulars, but the chief debate concerned Christ's atonement. If, as the Regulars maintained, Christ died only for the elect, then missionary labor seemed less needful than if His sacrifice was for all those who could be reached and converted. God honored only those who came to Him without the agency of human mechanisms. The Lord Almighty was prepared to condemn all others who insulted His mighty power by offering their own devices and not his.

In spite of these contentions, Separates and Regulars throughout the South dropped their distinguishing names between 1787 and 1801, but a division within the church remained hidden. By the close of the eighteenth century frugal living and sober habit had won the families and descendants of the first Separate converts a place on the social and economic ladder that made their struggle against the Anglican squirarchy a fading memory. The Separates' former antislavery convictions fell away, and many joined the slaveholding ranks. During the American Revolution, some Anglican planters and small farmers also became Baptists, disheartened by their church's political tie to the British Crown.

Some church historians have surmised that the controversies between the Regulars and Separates had been cheerfully interred beneath the sod that covered the church's early patriarchs. Indeed, competition with the rapidly expanding Methodists (most of whom adhered to the popular doctrine of human free will), periodic religious awakenings, and the outbreak of war against the British, the Baptists' colonial persecutors, had healed old wounds, at least momentarily. Yet the New Light latitudinarian view of dogma, stress on puritan decorum (the Separates had discarded their earlier revival extravagances), and willingness to bend all things to the needs of conversion were to reappear in the missionary or evangelical movement that developed most energetically after the War of 1812. The concern of the Regulars for doctrinal consistency, their easier accommodation to prevailing customs, and their narrow fear of innovation received new strength in the antimissionist insurgency. Moreover, there were in some instances traceable historical links that reveal the factional continuities within the Baptist associations. In other words, antimissionism did not lack an inner logic and historical integrity of its own. They had owed nothing to the New England mission effort of the 1750s and 1760s. The Regulars had been there in the South all along.[37]

By the end of the War of 1812 a general movement for missionary advance was well under way not only in the Baptist church but also among most of the major denominations. So powerful was the patriotic impulse that it even affected the loosely organized Baptists. The American Revolution had stimulated a democratization of religion as well as a leveling process in the political order.[38] In imitation of more centralized denominations, Northern Baptist congregations by 1814 had founded sixty-five small but ambitious societies to distribute elevating materials and to support missions. Later they gathered themselves into national benevolent associations. Meanwhile, other denominations pursued the missionary plan with still greater vigor. By 1830 the Methodists likewise had supplemented their regionally supported circuit-rider system with national agencies. Orthodox Congregationalists, Dutch Reformed, and Presbyterians collaborated in forming the American Bible Society, the American Tract Society, and other organizations, all of which enjoyed enough support from other denominations to give the appearance of a genuine Protestant ecumenicism.[39]

None of these agencies—large or small, interdenominational or sectarian—could avoid the taint of Northern parochialism. First, most of the mission leaders were themselves Northerners. In the Baptist Church Luther Rice and Adoniram Judson, proponents of foreign missions, and Francis Wayland and Jonathan Going, advocates for domestic expansion, were all New Englanders by birth or adoption. John Taylor, antimission leader in Kentucky, charged Luther Rice of having too great a "love of money" as well as a "prodigious appetite at table." His attack on the supposed greed of the missionary advocates was scarcely well founded, but it clearly indicated a division along lines of wealth within the Baptist faith. Given the Baptists' former antipathy toward the haughty Virginia squires, such a development was ironic. Moreover, those Regulars who were most imbued with the spirit of honor almost invariably accused their evangelical opponents of dishonorable, materialistic, and selfish villainy—much as Andrew Jackson did in his contemporary assaults on enemies. Class and sectional suspicions were inextricably woven together in the minds of the antimissionists.[40]

In other faiths, the pious Yankee was altogether too visible at evangelical functions, even though an occasional Southerner graced the roster of officers to lend a national flavor to a cause.[41] Second, most of these bodies had to depend on the wealthier parts of the country for support. Most funds came from the middle-class districts of big eastern cities and the more prosperous hinterlands of the North. The Baptist Tract Society of Philadelphia admitted, for instance, that its treasury received only one dollar in 1831 from the forty thousand Baptists of Kentucky. The Philadelphia headquarters noted that most of the contributions came from the Atlantic states north of Virginia.[42]

A further sign of a sectional orientation could be seen in the allocation of resources. Disproportionate sums were spent in regions of Northern settlement. For instance, between 1832 and 1841 the Baptist Home Missionary Society sent 605 missionaries into four northwestern states. Meanwhile, only 127 were active in the five Southern states along the Mississippi River. A Southern preacher estimated that there was one Baptist missionary for every 4,000 people in Michigan and one for every 428,581 in the states of the Deep South and Kentucky. The same discrepancy appeared in the work of the American Home Missionary Society, an interdenominational venture.[43]

Pressures of circumstance more than an overt policy of religious colonialism led to sectional imbalance. Churchmen in the Northwest clamored for special consideration from their former eastern neighbors and kinspeople. Many pious easterners had resettled in the West expressly to escape liberal, hedonistic trends, only to discover that "infidelity" and other temptations had not been left behind. It was unimaginable to frontier Presbyterians, Congregationalists, Baptists, and Methodists formerly from the Northern states that they should be permanently served by the unpredictable visits of circuit riders or by part-time preacher-farmers. By their lights, such casual arrangements could not promote a stable community life and provide settled pastors who could bind congregations to uniform social ideals and methods of worship. Eager to go where they were welcome and preferring familiar social conditions, young missionaries (mostly easterners) responded to the cries of western pietists to help save them from rationalism, Catholicism, "Lotteries, Strong Drink, and an almost universal rage for Politics," as one editor declared.[44] Meantime, proportionately few itinerants requested Southern assignments. Besides, in the fastnesses of the South, irregularity of worship was accepted as a condition of life.[45]

Finally, the missionary plan was sectionally inclined in its advertising policies. The largesse of Northern benefactors, the tradition of federalistic alliance of the missions with the Congregationalists of New England and the traditional churches of the Middle States, the tendency to pay homage to the patricians with ties to the benevolent agencies' metropolitan headquarters, and the relative lack of participating Southern gentlemen of prominence combined to make the movement appear to be solely the work of Northern men of property. Even the widely circulated newspaper testimonials of Chief Justice John Marshall (in behalf of Sunday schools), Francis Scott Key, and a small group of drawing-room luminaries, chiefly from the upper or coastal South, could not wholly alter the impression of a Yankee bias and an unpleasant snobbery. Withal, the evangelicals' effort was strictly middle class, despite extravagant boasting about the distinguished patrons in their midst. Smug dogmatism about "doing good," compulsion to obtain an immediate, almost commercial return on ecclesiastical investment, and elitist advertising combined to make the missionary plan objectionable to anyone who did not share the dream of a world of Sunday schools.[46]

Yet the evangelical movement should not be seen in a wholly negative light. Quite apart from the religious advances that the revival crusade generated, it laid the groundwork for the philanthropy of modern times—the bases for the endowments of universities and the establishment of foundations for the improvement of secular society. It is true that the evangelicals were thoroughly tied to the commercial world that the antimissionists suspected was fast destroying old values. The managers of the American Tract Society and other benevolent organizations championed the acquisition of wealth but only for its prompt distribution into charitable and religious enterprises. New York City merchant Lewis Tappan, for instance, wrote a tract entitled *Is It Right to be Rich?* The answer was a resounding no. Money to rent a pew in order to display wealth, for instance, was wholly unchristian, Tappan argued. The outrageous sums spent on such trivialities should instead be used to aid "the sick, the imprisoned, the ignorant, the vicious, and the unconcerned." One should work no more than six hours a day, Tappan proposed, and spend the rest of it in uplifting the fallen. Nevertheless, antimissionists and other critics of the evangelical movement claimed that power, not the spreading of Gospel truth, was the underlying motive. They were not, however, entirely justified in their complaints.[47]

Southern reaction to the evangelical cause began with the postwar depression of 1819. Backwoods opinion was running strongly against the Bank of the United States, the eastern establishment, and local Southern and western creditors in the towns and cities. When John Taylor, a Baptist preacher of Clear Creek, Kentucky, published his *Thoughts on Missions* in 1820, it produced a widespread response. Taylor had been a Regular Baptist when that designation still meant distrust of the Yankee New Light evangelists of the Great Awakening. He was proud that in his long career he had never sought outside assistance for the many little missions he had begun.[48] Like most Southern Baptist preachers, he ran his small plantation for a living, being a strong advocate of scriptural preaching without remuneration.[49] According to his pamphlet, missionaries like Luther Rice, Samuel J. Mills, and John F. Schermerhorn, who had traversed Kentucky in behalf of missions some years before, were modern Tetzels. They sold Protestant indulgences to gullible, sorely overburdened churchgoers. As far as Taylor was concerned, the "Female Societies, Cent Societies, Mite Societies, Children Societies, and even Negro Societies" that these religious dandies tried to found smelled too much of what he called "the *New England Rat.*"[50]

Taylor also worried that these specialized agencies would destroy the republican spirit of the Baptist Church by appealing directly to individual churchgoers for aid. They could, he feared, intervene between the part-time preacher and his congregation. Local church and community control would diminish. Meanwhile, alien, unreachable powers in distant cities would impose a regime of religious and political tyranny. Taylor had deep forebodings that a new aristocracy was emerging in America, one that subverted religious action to a spirit of commercial, Northern imperialism. He would never have approved the aims of the contemporary Christian Coalition.[51] His theme echoed the objections of Old Republicans like John Taylor of Carolina. With the rise of Andrew Jackson, the two Taylors in their separate spheres voiced suspicions of the new economic and social climate created by the possessing classes in both church and state life.

Antimissionist preachers also leveled charges of hypocrisy, self-righteousness, and mendacity against the missionaries' temperance campaigns. In a clapboard Baptist church in Georgia, Isham Peacock, a preacher more than ninety years old, damned the cold-water crusade while swigging whiskey from his hollowed-out cane to prove its health-giving qualities. His listeners probably needed little convincing. Christ drank wine, but men are supposed to refrain. "What sophistry of priests!" declared a North Carolina Baptist. For the Southern upper classes to imitate Connecticut bluenoses by trying to snatch away the convivial glass— one of the few cheap pleasures available to the dirt farmer—was a state of affairs not to be taken lightly. As a result, antimissionists, evincing a certain rude justice, expelled from church membership anyone who took the teetotal pledge, and they broke off relations with churches and associations that boasted of temperance society chapters. That does not mean, however, that antimissionary preachers and congregations rejoiced in drunkenness, saloon obscenities, and other offenses that their evangelical compatriots—both Southern and Northern—so highly deplored.[52]

Yet opposition to temperance or state-mandated prohibition of alcohol was prompted by fears of interference with the bedrock of virtue: familial governance, the honor of the patriarchal household. Imposed conformity rather than a more tolerant dismissal of temperance aims revealed the anxieties of the antimissionists. They believed that only through unanimous agreement could the community withstand the invasion of alien principles. Perhaps the Reverend A. Keaton of Green County, Alabama, had more than just rhetorical fire on his breath when he harangued a Baptist gathering: "Do not forget the enemy (missionaries), bear them in mind, the howling destructive wolves, the ravenous dogs, and the filthy, and their numerous whelps."[53] The choice of words was a reminder of how antimissionists used the biblical language of abuse, as James Peacock and Ruel Tyson have observed in more recent times. Could not the churches themselves handle such problems, asked the Primitive Baptist brethren and sisters? Indeed, Ted Ownby notes that, next to the sanctions against dancing and other recreations, the issue of overdrinking was the leading transgression adjudicated in some ninety-seven post–Civil War churches.[54]

Much more significant than the temperance issue was the reaction to religious instruction of slaves, a matter of concern, as later explained, to those seeking to improve, even perfect slavery to give the lie to abolitionist critics. Northern missionaries discovered that fear of black advance was a chief objection to their efforts. Richard Hooker, a Presbyterian Sunday school agent, wrote in 1830 from South Carolina that his foremost problems were prejudice against him as a Yankee, the antipathy of the Baptists, and most of all, the political and racial situation. He visited several Sunday schools managed by benevolent planters, where slaves were being taught simple lessons in reading and writing as part of their Christian training. The white participants were obviously exceptional, for the classes were racially mixed. "Suspicion that Sunday-schools tend to this result," wrote Hooker, "and their northern origin, together with the most flagrant party and sectional animosities kindle opposition." Gradually, he reported, the African Americans were being excluded. Yet to his own surprise, he found some masters who "were ready to weep" at the thought that the blacks would be forced out altogether.[55] Indeed, planters were becoming increasingly concerned with the Christianizing of their slaves. It seemed not only godly but also a practical way to build morale.[56] The devout among the master class, though, simply wanted the slaves to enjoy the blessings of redemption. For instance, missionary Baptist James Mallory, a plain farmer of Alabama, wrote in his diary that after a regular service in 1843 "six or seven of Mr Rice[']s servants came forward to the church & were received, truly do I hope they may be sincere."[57]

Pious antimissionists objected as vigorously to Sunday schools as they did to any other aspect of the benevolent program. It interfered, they believed, with the proper role of fathers in the instruction and guidance of their children. Moreover, the common people of Virginia, reported the experienced missionary James E. Welch, "think . . . that a Sunday school is too much like teaching blacks on Sunday while some of the poor are offended at it as too much like singling them out from their richer neighbors." W. A. N. Campbell wrote about the Sunday School Union in Knox County, Tennessee, that he was having difficulty locating and engaging "persons properly qualified and of suitable character to embark as teachers," owing to intense "sectarian and political prejudices." Southern Presbyterians were far in advance of other churchgoers in support of Sunday schools. Yet since they were a rather high-toned, traditional, and socially self-conscious group, their endorsement only heightened distrust among less fortunate people.

Whatever the sectarian, theological, or class origins of this antipathy to the Sunday school might have been, it was indeed regrettable. Graduates of Sunday schools may not have achieved the high expectations for morality that evangelicals promised. Certainly, there was reason to doubt the East Tennessee Presbyterian editor who claimed in 1829 that, in the words of a friendly observer, they "would yet revolutionize the world."[58] Religious instruction stimulated public demands for better secular education in other parts of the Union, but antimission hostility deprived the Southern educational movement of this source of public pressure. In 1837, the New Bethel congregation of the Choctaw Association in Mississippi protested ungrammatically "against all money mishionary supportion as they tend greatly to brake the peace of the church without a president in the word of god and will not suffer them preach it in our meting days."[59] "Brother" Scott, a Baptist of Cow Marsh, Delaware, summarized similar sentiments when he noted: "We are but a feeble body and much exposed to the innovations of the learned gentry of the day, who swarm out of the theological institutions like locusts, and are ready to devour the land." Methodists also felt the sting of missionary haughtiness. When a gathering of churchmen in East Tennessee considered the support of benevolent goals, a preacher described how one of "these pompous 'sons of Levi'" had paraded through "the Forked-Deer district," avoided "the poorer and more destitute parts of my circuit," and lived like "the fine gentleman . . . on the very fat of the land." After returning "eastwardly" he had "tried to justify his 'forty dollars a month' by '*falsely*' proclaiming that the whole region was 'in a state of moral degradation.'"[60]

Despite the ambiguities of the Jacksonian movement, it expressed the fears and yearnings of lower-class farmers and workers and of the small planters and landholders who dreaded and found it hard to adapt temperamentally to the increasingly mercantile world arising about them.[61] Buffeted by rising costs, economic dislocations, and new government-subsidized patterns of transportation and credit; perplexed by the steady arrival of young, alert competitors; bewildered by the talk of reform—antiliquor, antigambling, antislavery—these citizens, most of them loyal Democrats, jealously held on to familiar ways. David T. Bailey points out that the antimission Baptists rejected any "violation of their lifestyles, and antislavery, as much as missions or education societies, stood as a particular threat."[62] There was much truth to the comment of a Rhode Island missionary Baptist that John Taylor of Kentucky and his band were "old travelers," intimidated by the face of "new men and new measures" and "disturbed at being left behind." Their belief in the existence of an eastern conspiracy intent on bleeding the frontier South and West of their few financial resources was an adaptable formula.[63] It so lucidly explained the cause of turmoil and doubt around them that President Andrew Jackson himself did not scruple to exploit it in his war on the Bank of the United States.

Theological objections to the mission scheme were also important. They served as more than merely convenient screens to hide economic misgivings. Taylor and those who later took up the cry were mostly "Hyper-Calvinists," as the mission advocates phrased it. They were more Calvinistic, as it were, than Calvin himself. For the framers of the Westminster Covenant the doctrine of the illimitable sovereignty of God was never intended to encourage fatalistic resignation. The antimissionists claimed to reject a policy of inaction, but they did not wholly succeed. The sole issue, they felt, was scriptural regularity, the maintenance of the old ways. Only those means for conversion and regeneration that conformed to the simple evangelistic methods of Paul and the early Church Fathers were blessed by the Holy Spirit. All other inventions were profane. "Little tracts of four pages" were not moral instruments. Plainly they usurped the function of the Bible. According to the "Black Rock Address" of Maryland antimissionists, the Sunday school was based on the heresy "that conversion, or regeneration, is produced by impressions made upon the natural mind by means of religious sentiments instilled into it, and if the Holy Ghost is allowed to be at all concerned" in the process, it concedes only that He is "somehow blended with the instruction." With regard to seminaries, how many of Jesus' disciples, they asked, had attended a school of higher learning? Furthermore, to place "the revelation of God on a footing with mathematics, philosophy, law" and other "human sciences" was to dishonor the Holy Word. Even "protracted meetings" or revival services of an unemotional nature were condemned. The authors of the "Black Rock" declaration announced, "Regeneration we believe is exclusively the work of the Holy Ghost, performed by His divine power at His own sovereign pleasure according to the provisions of the everlasting covenant."[64]

At the center of these charges was the stricture that works alone cannot save. The benevolent agencies, critics complained, praised the widow's mite, but the large sums donated by gentlemen of property, whatever their daily business ethics might be, were almost guaranteed by the evangelical authorities to be recorded in the heavenly ledger. The partisans for evangelization did stress the conversion experience, sealed by revival commitment. Yet the new life in Christ was supposed to stimulate converts to participate as fully as possible in spreading the glorious word. In reaction, antimission Calvinists heartily condemned the earthly contrivances used by "well dressed *beggars*" to gather in the financial sheaves.[65] In Florida Hardy Brooks of Nassau County explained that an itinerant missionary had reported the death of his horse and asked for contributions and was rewarded with enough funds to buy two horses. The "pious scoundrel" pocketed the money, Brooks alleged, and then "had the impudence to mount his dead horse, and ride him around to preach" to those generous, deluded souls who had opened their purses and wallets for him.[66]

For antimissionists, this arrogation of divine providence in behalf of missions amounted to blasphemy. John Gill had thundered the same warning some years earlier in his sermon *The Doctrine of Imputed Righteousness without Works Asserted and Proved*.[67] As a people accustomed to the whims of nature, the sudden death of children, the accident while timber-cutting that deprived a wife of husband and offspring of a father—these experiences enforced an acute awareness of human finitude. Embracing a highly pessimistic form of Calvinism, the antimissionists offered less hope for redemption from a jealous God than Jonathan Edwards, Samuel Hopkins, or any of their successors in the New Light tradition. Opposed to the insidious poison of Arminianism, as they saw the doctrine of free will, the traditional Baptists emphasized divine grace—the blessing of God's honor on sinful man. His almighty power was thought to determine "the eternal conditions of their souls," as the historian Melanie Sovine points out. As a result, they "declined to accept the relationship of great eternal rewards for great religious efforts on earth."[68] It might be said that the Primitive Baptists placed justice before love in their understanding of Christianity.

In reply, the "effort brethren," as the evangelicals sometimes called themselves, accused their detractors of "*thick-skinned Antinomianism*," Robert Hall's epithet to describe Gill's disciples. Actually, American pietists had begun to drift away from even the qualified Calvinism of the late New Light theologians. General rather than particular atonement, practical over mystical piety, common sense over doctrinal speculations seemed better justifications for evangelizing with modern means than the notions of late eighteenth-century divines like Samuel Hopkins, Timothy Dwight, and their followers.

Daniel Parker assumed the mantle of leadership from John Taylor. Flamboyant about his rough country manners and his mediocre schooling, Parker adopted what he called the "God-honouring" doctrine of the two seeds. By this Manichean formulation, the Devil enjoyed almost as much authority in his sphere as God in His. In fact, all but a handful of men were born of Satan's seed, while Christ was the original source of the godly seed, whose current descendants were mostly to be found among opponents of missions. This theological division between good and evil had appeared as early as the Donatists of St. Augustine's era and found favor among such dissenters as the Paulicians, Novationists, Paternines, Cathars, Lollards, and Waldensians, the last of whom influenced the theology of John Calvin.[69] Antimission Baptists were proud of their apostolic lineage to such stubborn and intractable heresiarchs. As James Peacock and Ruel Tyson note, they were indeed "Pilgrims of Paradox" with a strong sense of history as well as a mistrust of higher learning.[70]

It is rather striking that at a time when Northern utopians and spiritual seekers were stressing man's perfectibility, these religious deviants in the South asserted a peculiar sense of doom that was derived from antique sources. The early and medieval heretics had never known the possibility or even the concept of human progress on this earth. The Primitives interpreted church history, declares one scholar, "as a story of corruption and decline from the Primitive model they found in the New Testament, a common theme among Restorationist groups in the early nineteenth century." The antimissionists claimed, however, not to be restoring what had been lost. Instead, they believed that they were simply preserving what had always existed by means of the succession of the faithful through the ages.[71]

Antimission Baptists knew well the perils of inner loneliness which their convictions wrought. An elderly Primitive Baptist woman (of our own day) reported a dream that reflected the old notion of acedia—the sin of religious indifference and despair. "Now you know a lot of people say there's no hell, but I've seen that," she said in a nightmare. "I seen my soul and it looked like just a black . . . crow. . . . Just flyin' around."[72] The spiritual narratives of antebellum Primitives, some of them published, almost invariably began in a similar vein. Jacob Bower of Kentucky, for instance, explained that at nineteen years of age, he felt "Lost, lost, forever lost

. . . I could see no way of escaping eternal judgment."[73] A modern Primitive declared, "I have been made to hate my own life." Even today, in the Primitive Baptists' vocabulary, shame seems to be a more common expression than guilt. The former concerns a loss of reputation that leaves the ill-doer diminished in his own eyes. A sense of guilt is a function of a more internalized remorse—a violation in God's sight not the public's. A contemporary antimission Baptist, Elder William R. Wellborn, explains, "But all my expectations were cut short by the hand of Omnipotence. . . . O, how wretched I felt! I was ashamed of myself."[74]

Shame could operate in a contrary way, too. In his narrative published in 1841, Elder Joshua Lawrence of Tar River, North Carolina, editor of the *Primitive Baptist*, recalled that he used to leave services only to rush off to greet his old mates at the tavern. "I was so shamed, and hated they should think that I had any notion of religion, that I tried to throw away all thoughts thereof out of my mind." Pleasure turned quickly to remorse. The ancient sin of acedia or *tristitia* was at the heart of his emotions. Human sloth and inattention to God's commands and to His offer of forgiveness, as acedia was identified in the Middle Ages, had seized the soul. To fall into such a state of mind was an offense against the Holy Spirit. The veil of despair lifted, however, when in a field Lawrence saw Christ himself about "thirty feet from the earth." Although his conversion was not immediate, the next day, upon waking, he threw off his sense of being, as he put it, "dead to myself" and felt God's blessing upon him. Lawrence shattered his fiddle with a hammer, gave up dancing and gambling, and began his preaching.[75]

These experiences, often elaborately told, gave spiritual meaning to the faithful, and their recounting followed along lines that evangelical Christians would also have recognized. Still, the traditionalists were somehow more exclusive, more inward-drawn, more suspicious of the larger world than their more expansive Christian opponents. John C. Vaughan, who edited an antislavery paper called the *Louisville Examiner* in the late 1840s, discovered some of the social and economic factors behind the rural antipathy of the antimissionists. He visited the "sand-hillers," as he called them, in company with the evangelical Charleston aristocrat Thomas S. Grimké sometime in the early 1830s. Attributing the "sand-hillers'" poverty to the planters' hunger for bottomlands, Vaughan and Grimké admired their "sort of wild wood liberty" but deplored their "hatred of labour," an aversion resulting from "the conviction that it degraded them, because it put them on an equality with the slaves." Efforts to introduce them to Sunday schools or even vocational training failed because, they believed, such human instruments were unscriptural. Hostility toward prosperous slaveholders, wrote Vaughan, was so great that proffers of charity met instant rebuff, even in times of starvation. Speaking for this class of people, Elder Lawrence preached, "I dread the tyranny of an unconverted, men-made, money-making . . . factoried priesthood; I had rather be under the government of a deist, an atheist, or a Turk." Unless the do-gooders were quickly stopped, he warned, "our fields and high roads, and decks of ships will soon be washed in the blood of our citizens."[76] Pride held the antimissionists aloof from the gentry's condescension.

The somewhat clumsy—and, indeed, condescending—policies of the missionaries only served to augment the rancor of the hard-handed elements in Southern society. The inexperienced young missionaries who toured the region could not hide their contempt for the ignorance, provincialism, backwardness, and presumed irreligion of the native whites. Besides, as John M. Peck, a missionary Baptist of Illinois, warned the secretary of the American Sunday School Union of Philadelphia, the "young men who come from the eastern schools" were unable to talk to "our backwoods folks." Fear of these literate upstarts and the moral improvements for which they struggled prompted an Illinois antimission preacher to announce, "We don't care any thing about them missionaries that's gone amongst them heathens 'way off yonder.' " Yet, he added, at home "these missionaries will be all great men, and the people will all go to hear them preach, and we shall be all put down."[77]

Eastern agencies tried valiantly to recruit older ministers, particularly those with regional ties of kinship to the people to whom they were assigned. Such men, said a clerical observer, could not, however, be spared from regular pastorates simply "to humour the prejudices against eastern men." It was only natural for the typical itinerant to gravitate toward the wealthier locations and seek the company of town ministers, militia colonels, and other dignitaries who were eager to promote religious enlightenment among their surly compatriots in the outlying countryside.[78]

The tour of John Endith of the Sunday School Union in 1828 may serve as an unhappy example. Endith had enjoyed success in founding Sabbath schools in Augusta, Georgia, where merchants and planters and their wives and daughters had assisted his easy labors. When he reached the isolated parts of neighboring South Carolina, however, he discovered that respectability, as he would define it, simply did not exist. There were few towns, he wrote headquarters in dismay. The dusty courthouse hamlets he visited were "filled up with lawyers (most of whom are almost destitute of every moral principle), and with michanics [*sic*] of the very lowest cast and with little petty shop keepers." Methodists and Baptists "of talent, character, and wealth" could be found in the vicinity of towns like Savannah or Augusta and in wealthy plantation neighborhoods. Otherwise, he observed, members of the two predominant faiths opposed the Sunday school scheme.[79] His analysis may have been accurate, but his lofty attitude probably accounted for the suspicions he aroused.

Although the antimissionists were unduly suspicious of their evangelical opponents' motives and policies, they did have reason to feel undervalued and even despised. Eastern missionaries tried to lift the folk to a higher level of civilization. The approach put them in a poor frame of mind for converting the Southern sinner. On a tour in 1824 Jeremiah Evarts, secretary of the American Board of Commissioners for Foreign Missions, deplored the "want of enterprise" of the East Tennesseans. Unlike his fellow Northerners, observed the New England visitor, they "seldom associate or confer together for any common purpose; and they get into such habits of living alone, that it seems almost impossible to impart to them the same principles of social conduct as exist among people in different circumstances." A consequence was that "small municipal legislation and government" languished. In contrast, people "at the north" became "acquainted with each other" through civic activities and thus patriotically helped to strengthen "our republican institutions." The ecclesiastical effect of such crabbed isolation, parochialism, and social irresponsibility, as Evarts characterized it, was that ministers could not expect a regular salary. What was given, Evarts reported almost incredulously, was done purely "from friendship." It was not thought of as "compensation for valuable services." That was not the way a New England Puritan divine or merchant would manage his life. Other complaints that missionaries registered against the rural sectors of the South were the lack of common schools and competent teachers, fear of any religious or cultural change, indolence, the unchecked liberty of youth, and drunkenness, all of which were in dismaying contrast to the ideals if not always the habits of their own people.[80] As Deborah McCauley observes, the evangelical brethren, both native Southern and Yankee, considered the antimission Baptists as almost a weird set of malcontents who deviated from the "national religion of the United States."[81]

What the stranger-missionaries failed to see was the form of order that did exist. Even Southern missionary Baptists showed a scarcely hidden contempt for their backcountry brethren. The well-educated and urbane Basil Manly declared in 1844, "I know that it is now 30 years since the subject was first generally agitated in this country," and at this juncture it should be a dead issue. But, he confided to Basil Manly Jr., his son, he had heard a young man from remote Pickens County harangue a Baptist convention about how "the missionaries harrass [*sic*] us with the cry of nations perishing without the Gospel" when, the speaker insisted, "God is everywhere, Jesus everywhere, and where Jesus is the gospel is preached in its purity and men can be saved." The Baptist divine claimed to question his own sense and marveled "that a man 21 years old c[oul]d live in this good year of 1844, in the white settlements, & know no better. Such was the fact." [82]

Yet the backwoods Baptists were faithful to a style that was certainly closer to the simple life of early Christians than was that of Manly and other members of the Alabama elite. The antimissionists' conventions rested even more firmly on family and neighborhood than those of their wealthier brethren, and Primitive Baptist and Methodist churches functioned less as a socially binding force than as an expression of familial transactions. "Family life," observes Beverly Bush Patterson, an expert on Primitive Baptist church music and culture, "is not necessarily limited to one's kinship group." The modern choral forms differ little from those adopted in the 1830s. The women most especially experience the church "as a family." She cites a convert who declared, "I just felt like I was one of them . . . I just felt like they was one of my family." [83]

Under such circumstances, the antimission Baptist churchgoers' notions of ethical behavior and organization did not require government policing any more than a family's governance would. [84] If men got drunk or disturbed the peace in obnoxious ways, the community expected nothing from the state. Instead, the church to which the members of the neighborhood belonged guarded the duty to expel them from fellowship. In procedures that the backlands churches established, kinspeople and neighbors were supposed to set egregious sinners apart by a rite of communal ostracism and expulsion. The object of removal was to purify the members from the contamination of the vicious but also to shame the offenders— if it was decided that punishments were necessary.

In the South, in both the antimission and the evangelical churches, discipline by congregational decision lasted much longer than in Northern Christendom. So long as a community remained cohesive and whites held slaves and freed people under full control, the traditions of church self-government over morals remained vigorous before the Civil War. The rise of railroading, larger cities, and increasingly strong action on all levels of the county and municipal court systems made shaming rituals in church settings less and less acceptable in the North. In the backcountry South, however, the old customs prevailed. If nonchurchgoers grossly violated local custom and expectations, the law might be invoked. Such community action as public whippings, tar and featherings, or some other devices, however, would visit sufficient disgrace upon the transgressors to hurry them out of the neighborhood.[85]

The ethic by which these Christians lived anticipated few but precious joys that a believer could expect in this world of unrelenting woe. Controlling the natural environment was problematic at best in a region in which, it was universally assumed, natural disasters were common, and death from diseases, childbirth, or farming, hunting, or lumbering accidents sad but all too familiar events. Furthermore, Indians still posed a threat in parts of the lower South. Like Andrew Jackson, the antimissionists resented the evangelical effort to Christianize the tribes and applauded Indian removal—as most of the unchurched did as well.[86] By contrast, the Methodists in Georgia strongly supported their denomination's highly successful missions to the Cherokees before their tragic removal in the 1830s.[87]

Time and social conditions favored the benevolent cause. Even the wealthiest Southern nabobs often needed more than mere economic affluence to attest to their success. To be sure, setting a fine table, breeding stallions, or collecting leather-bound compilations of *Blackwood's* and English novels were satisfactory means of displaying one's place at the top. But, for some, religion had an honored place by the plantation hearth. Only an estimated one-twelfth of the Southern people were devout churchgoers in 1829. Yet the increasing popularity of church membership before the Civil War indicates that in this particular instance religious activities were not merely gratifying in themselves. They also functioned as a sign of a man's value to his community. Moreover, they helped to give the lie to Northern impressions of Southern backwardness.

A section that prided itself on its scorn of material greed could do no better than stress its otherworldliness. Thus Senator Wilson Lumpkin, a latecomer to the ranks of Georgia's aristocracy, compensated for his rustic background by thrusting himself wholeheartedly into mission enterprises for the Baptists even as he defended the state from the conspiratorial machinations of Yankee missionaries to the Cherokees. Likewise, Richard Mentor Johnson, a Kentucky slaveholder and vice-president under Martin Van Buren, sought government relief for a mortgaged Baptist college in the Federal District. He fumed, however, about Northern

Presbyterian schemes to unite church and state by demanding the closing of post offices on the Sabbath. Such politicians as Lumpkin and Johnson knew that it was politically unwise to appear antireligious. Yet their fulminations against Northern fanaticism and the alleged attempts of a central power to interfere in the lives of families could strike responsive chords among backwoods folk and pious conservatives alike.[88]

The deep impressions that evangelicals made on Southern life, with their temperance and Sabbatarian principles, their revivals, and their institutions to instruct the young in Bible practice and belief, have remained an overwhelming force throughout Southern history. The point cannot be too greatly stressed. By the 1850s the older spirit of antireligion began, as Ted Ownby has pointed out, to succumb "to the softening impulses of evangelical religion." Various forms of male behavior were in competition, notable among them the hyper-masculine and the sanctified styles of the churchgoer. Between honor, genteel or primordial, and grace, there was always the possibility of a great moral and social chasm. Yet even the most principled of men in either camp recognized the sacred character of both honor and Christian devotion. The two faiths, if that term is permitted, could mingle in ways both subtle and obvious. That was particularly so because Holy Scripture furnished examples of every variety of human and holy condition: divine humility and godly vengeance; the glory of God and the innate sinfulness of mankind; the Golden Rule and the necessity to punish the wicked; despair in the face of God's withdrawal; joy and love in the bosom of the family; and redemption from sin in the promise of the New Testament.

It was the task of the Primitive Baptists to make the strongest case in the South against both the worldliness of honor and those artificialities that allegedly blemished evangelical claims of purity. In fact, the contempt with which the missionary newspapers, preachers, and contemporary historians greeted the antimission movement revealed that it had touched a raw nerve. Certainly, the backwoods critics were theologically and morally logical. To educate blacks and Indians, to eliminate John Barleycorn, to encourage ladies' aid societies, and to raise children on saccharine moral tracts and Elsie Dinsmore novels weakened the fiber of Southern resistance to Yankee encroachments. These plain folk cared little about the slave's lot in general although granting the few among them entrance into their services and into Christian fellowship. The traditionalists believed that nearly all mankind was fated to endure God's predestined wrath. However lacking in comfort this circumstance of general suffering might be, it was more consistent than a philosophy that too often promised spiritual bliss to the plucky and the rich and identified holiness with a material success that the black and white poor could not possess.

Of course, sophisticated churchmen were equal to the task of combining benevolence with complete mastery of the slave's life and of reconciling the old assumptions about feminine delicacy in a patriarchal system with women's church work. Northern evangelicalism was itself often defined in restrictive terms, although its tendencies promoted democratic and humanitarian impulses. Religious optimism and sentimental empathy may have lightened the slave's burden while leaving his shackles as firmly riveted as ever. Yet the missionary plan sustained an uncomfortable logic. Thus Hosea Holcombe, a native Alabama missionary, unconsciously stumbled into the ambivalence inherent in the Southern evangelical position when he denounced laws forbidding masters to teach slaves to read and then asked, "Is there no other way to make obedient servants, but to keep them in abject ignorance?" It was no wonder that pious Southerners cried out in alarm against tainting of the mission cause when antimissionists lumped "abolition societies" with the other agencies they condemned. Yet there was justification for the antimissionist rubric.[89]

The secession of antimissionists from fellowship with Southern Baptists of a more exalted status in society signified the extent of their failure to control the denomination. In statistical terms, however, the departing brethren constituted a sizable body. By 1844 a total of 900 antimissionist preachers, 1,622 churches, and at least 68,000 members (probably underestimated by pro-mission chroniclers) had completed the exodus. The notion that religious benevolence was another word for aristocratic pretentiousness and Yankee greed had its clear appeal. Distrust of Northern religious liberalism, philanthropy, and their evil partner, colonial exploitation, has too venerable a history from the time of John Taylor to recent times, with regard to the issues of abortion and citizens' rights to arms. There was also a positive aspect. Primitive Baptists opposed secret secular organizations, not only Freemasons and Odd Fellows but also secret antebellum vigilante and xenophobic societies. Whether that tradition included rejection of the Ku Klux Klan after the Civil War and after the First World War is not clear. Yet, while conforming to Southern racial mores, throughout their history they have been far less racist than one might have expected.[90]

Despite such adherence to a rather egalitarian Christianity, it could be argued that antimissionism represented the persistent Southern struggle to preserve old values in an alien, changing, and often self-righteous world. Pride was at stake in this battle as in so many conflicts that divided the nation sectionally. Whatever failings of heart and mind it also demonstrated along with its strengths of conviction, antimissionism was a part of the Southern ethic that still abides. As McCauley argues, it "has played an extremely significant role in American religious history, from the continuing traditions of Calvinist theological heritage to the Holiness-Pentecostal movements." In addition, it "has consciously continued the doctrinal traditions of *grace* and the *Holy Spirit*, especially by maintaining the centrality of *religious experience*."[91]

In summary, the Primitives represented the most dismissive expression of antihonor along with antimissionism that the South produced. In continuing the sort of resistance against "aristocracy," clerical and planter, that their progenitors had undertaken before and during the American Revolution, they stoutly remained true to their Calvinistic heritage. That theology had left little room for the conventions of a hierarchical scheme of honor. Yet, ironically, they could not entirely escape the Southern world's sanctions. Their patriarchal family life, their antipathy toward organized antislavery, their reliance on family and community against a chronically unreliable world, and their suspicion of progress as outsiders defined it kept them well within the orbit of Southern cultural and religious life.

CHAPTER SIX

MODERNIZING SLAVE-OWNING RHETORIC

What God sanctioned in the Old Testament,
and permitted in the New, cannot be sin.
—*Rev. Richard Fuller*

Both [peoples, North and South] read the same Bible,
and pray to the same God; and each invokes His aid against
the other. It may seem strange that any men should
dare to ask a just God's assistance in wringing their bread
from the sweat of other men's faces; but let us judge not that
we be not judged. The prayers of both could not be answered;
that of neither has been fully answered.
The Almighty has His own purposes.
—*Abraham Lincoln, Second Inaugural*

Recent studies of the proslavery argument have revealed complexities
that an earlier generation of scholars scarcely apprehended.[1] Not surprisingly, in the face of outside pressures and changes in perceptions of
the South in the free states, Southern churchmen were no less ambivalent about the role of slavery than about the function of honor in the
Old South. Both were thought indispensable for the maintenance of the
Southern way. But there were aspects of these pillars of Southern culture
that the clergy found hard to reconcile with their faith. Some, it is true,
claimed that slavery was the means by which God intended the African to
become Christian. Bishop Stephen Elliott of South Carolina, for instance,
replied to an inquiry from one of Queen Victoria's ladies-in-waiting, in
this vein: "It is well for Christians and Philanthropists to consider whether,
by interfering with this institution they may not be checking and imped-

ing a work which is manifestly providential. For nearly one hundred years the English and the American Churches have been striving to civilize and Christianize Western Africa, and with what results?" The bishop pointed to the sad state of African morals and English and American missionary efforts among the so-called heathen in Sierra Leone and Cape Palmas. In the latter locale Maryland colonizationists had established a free colony of former slaves. Compare those feeble efforts, the diocesan advised, to "the thousands, nay, I may say millions, who have learned the way to Heaven, and who have been made to know their Savior through the means of African slavery [in America]!"[2]

Bishop Elliott demonstrated a point that the religious historian Samuel S. Hill considers a major characteristic of Southern religion: "the peculiar relation which exists between the southern church and its surrounding culture. . . . The southern church is comfortable in its homeland, and the culture sits comfortably with its church." Since the white residents of the South came chiefly from the same British culture, they knew no other "alternative belief-systems," which as Hill puts it, "rarely penetrated the regional framework of thought."[3] It took little trouble to defend the Southern way of life, which in the opinion of the proslavery clergy, was firmly rooted in both Christianity and slaveholding.

So powerful was the intermixture of evangelicalism and the institution of slavery that it had wiped out whatever feelings of guilt Christian possessors of human property might have entertained. In fact, as the historian Beth Schweiger observes, some clergy found the conjoining of Christianity and slaveholding positively "exhilarating."[4] In the Revolutionary generation, enlightened thought and Protestant commitment had cast doubts on the legitimacy of bondage when the nation had just fought and won freedom for whites. But seldom did anyone propose that hell was reserved especially for anyone holding slaves. Rather, it was a moral evil that might lead to sinful temptation. That was a hazard the truly pious could ordinarily avoid.

By the time Jackson had settled in the White House, few churchgoers had any doubts, no matter how casually advanced. In a further passage of his letter to England, Elliott explained, "So far from the institution being guilty of degrading the Negro, and keeping him in degradation, it has elevated him in the scale being much above his nature and race, and it is continuing to do so." The clergy supporting Bible slavery were not intellectual simpletons. They knew their scriptural sources well and exercised as great a degree of self-confidence as any cluster of intellectuals.[5] South Carolinian Richard Fuller and the New England divine Francis Wayland published a work entitled *Domestic Slavery Considered as a Scriptural Institution*.[6] The proslavery preachers were aware of Southern vulnerability. Yet they were convinced that time would not betray them. The future for bondage could be bright. However distasteful their arguments, Southern theologians and thinkers did more than jab episodically at free-labor hypocrisies. They were no more alienated from their surroundings than such writers as Nathaniel Hawthorne, Henry Thoreau, and Herman Melville. Whether Northern or Southern, American intellectuals condemned the vulgarities of a heedless and hedonistic public.

Although self-serving, proslavery vindications had more vigor than one might expect in the defense of an institution which nearly all white Southerners accepted as a social, cultural, and racial given. The rationale for slavery's perpetuation was designed not solely to rally nonslaveholders to planter leadership or to calm the morally perplexed and fearful in slaveholding ranks themselves. These factors all played a part.[7] The first aim was to convince the Christian and conservative elite of both Great Britain and the free states that the Southern way was honorable, God-sanctioned, and stable. The second objective, with which this essay is chiefly concerned, was hortatory and instructional, as most appeals to one form of "right thinking" or another usually are. In the words of Henry Hughes of Mississippi, "The young men must be taught to reason the matter. They must learn why our home system is not wrong: why it is right: and be able to give the reasons for it."[8] That might involve some deeper thoughts on exactly what was being defended—not the behavior of the cruel and unchristian master and not every law or proscription that politicians ratified.

Intermingled with the declamations of regional glories was an important corollary: the desire to modernize, to improve the "home system." By that means its foundations would become no less secure, no less progressive than those on which free labor rested. In this context, modernization scarcely implies a wholehearted Southern democratic and urban tendency.[9] Believing that there was nothing inevitable or even desirable in marching to Yankee or British drums, the Southern intelligentsia repudiated middle-class mammonism and lamented the decline of gallantry. Nostalgia for lost virtues and hatred of modern cant and grubbiness were not themselves peculiar to plantation dreamers. British self-criticism, as the late Marcus Cunliffe pointed out, supplied them with ample means to catalog the wrongs of industrialization. Thomas Carlyle, Charles Kingsley, Sir Walter Scott, and other luminaries whom Southern literati admired offered the same kinds of ambivalent responses to modernity and the overthrow of ancient custom that they themselves felt. In fact, as noted later, Scott's popularity extended far beyond his romantic Waverley novels with their sentimentality and derring-do in battle regalia. For Scott, as for most of his Southern readers, there existed side by side a revulsion against the primitivism of warrior honor (duels were constantly, if ineffectively, deplored on every hand) and an antipathy to the impersonality of modern trends. Yet Scott's "elegy on the passing of the old Highland order comes not from a sitter-on-the-fence," as one recent critic has noted. Instead it arises "from the fair-minded man who knows that history cannot stand still, that there can be no change, even for the better without loss, suffering, and waste."[10] Since so many Southerners were themselves of Celtic ancestry, they found in him the spokesman for the world that they were losing even as they gloried in its alleged strengths of intense family life, intimacy with wild nature, and simple if bloody principles and passions.

However much defiance of Yankeedom may have masked inner doubts, Southern intellectuals sought to combine the best of two worlds. They did not wish to storm windmills in the ineffectual manner of Don Quixote. Without relinquishing the supposed virtues of their forefathers, whether Celtic, English, or Revolutionary American, they were determined to move forward. "Twenty years ago," declared George Fitzhugh in 1857, "the South had no thought, no opinion of her own." At that time, the region "stood behind all christendom, admitted her social structure, her habits, her economy, and her industrial pursuits to be wrong, deplored them as a necessity, and begged pardon for their existence." But, he boasted, a new order of things prevailed. Other nations had found "wage slavery" a system with grave defects, and they looked enviously upon the Southern mode. "This, of itself, would put the South at the lead of modern civilization," Fitzhugh insisted.[11] Thus literary justifications of slavery were not just hymns of praise for a changeless, primordial society. They offered a stirring call to place the South in the forefront of modern life. The effort required not only a new regional self-consciousness but also concrete demonstrations of just, humane, and morally uplifting techniques of patriarchal management.[12]

The basis of this enterprise lay in the evolutionary nature of the institution itself. Slavery changed as society changed. In a crude way, the historian may trace a progression from the beginning to the end of slavery. Three ways existed whereby masters could perceive the system: first, as crude chattel bondage, wherein slaves were more or less beasts of burden to meet the possessors' needs and whims; second, as familial proprietorship, in which reciprocal, parent-child obligations and affections

gave meaning to those involved. That system required a deeper appreciation of the psychology and wants of the dependent class, yet it still man-
dated that those beneath were obliged to give more in love and service
than those who ruled. Finally, the institution could be characterized as
state racial regulation, an interposition of government between white and
black. Under that relationship limits could be set on proprietary powers
and there could be a strictly defined set of racial boundaries.[13] None
of these perspectives was ever exclusive to one era or another. Roughly
speaking, however, "chattel bondage" was rather characteristic of colonial thralldom. Slaves were part of the household and its possessions,
but they were not often regarded as intimate family members, even if
the number extended no farther than the kitchen and parlor of the big
house and seldom included the ordinary slaves in the quarters. Stage two,
the familial concept, became more prominent in early national years. It
was largely an outgrowth of Christian evangelicalism.[14] Contrary to the
claims of slavery's apologists, slaveholding benevolence never achieved
more than spotty success. The ideal of Christian stewardship over bondspeople was established as a way to distinguish respectability from churlishness.[15] Stage three, state racial interposition, based on the growing use of
civil bureaucracies and legal professionalization, had made only limited
progress by 1861.

Sketchy though this description is, it helps to explain the point from
which proslavery vindicators departed and points in the direction to
which they were heading. Some years ago Willie Lee Rose observed a
"common tendency" among historians to treat slavery—250 years old in
America—"as though it were the same institution from start to finish."[16]
Proslavery authors did not make that mistake. They repudiated chattel
bondage but extolled the merits of patriarchal or "Bible slavery," as one
apologist called it.[17] James L. Petigru, a lawyer and planter of South Carolina, for instance, recognized the distinction. In 1835 he boasted, "The
only thing to flatter my vanity as a proprietor is the evident and striking
improvement in the moral and physical conditions of the negroes since
they have been under my administration. When I took them, they were
naked and destitute, now, there is hardly one that has not a pig at least."
His Christian bounty may have left something to be desired. Yet, like most
planters of the benevolent persuasion, Petigru judged his performance
against the grim squalor of forefathers and unenlightened neighbors.[18]
Stanley Engerman and Robert Fogel may have exaggerated the univer-
sality of Squire Allworthys like Petigru, but it stands to reason that advances in wealth and human sensibilities ameliorated plantation condi-

tions, if only because whites were becoming mindful of the comforts of general tidiness.[19]

The proslavery argument was largely based on the familial solicitudes that Petigru represented, but a complementary development, stage three, was also emerging. State legislators passed laws that intervened in the personal relationships of master and subject. To safeguard the public against insurrection, masters lost the discretionary right to train slaves in literacy, to permit autonomous black assembly, even to use their property as clerks in stores.[20] Setting boundaries around various work specialties, excluding blacks, bond and free, from public places, and other forms of racial discrimination were already appearing on statute books long before the days of Jim Crow.[21] At the same time, some slave states were enacting protective laws for the slave criminal and the slave victim of white crime as well.[22] These efforts at rationalizing the racial system not only conferred protections upon slaves and took privileges away from them; they also infringed on the traditional options that chattel bondage had granted masters.

Likewise, in jurisprudence, judges and lawyers sought to formalize the standards of admissible evidence, procedures, and resorts to appeal. Moreover, the penalties assigned to both white and black criminals were becoming more uniform and penitential rather than corporal in nature.[23] This transition may have influenced plantation justice, though hardly enough to mean much. The Reverend Charles C. Jones, an earnestly Christian master, was not a typical planter, but in 1859 he turned over to Georgia authorities a case of plantation thievery, an offense usually handled at an owner's discretion. For lack of sufficient evidence, the case was dismissed. Jones was delighted. "It is my impression," he said, "that if owners would more frequently refer criminal acts of their servants to the decision of the courts, they would aid in establishing different kinds of crimes committed by Negroes, give better support to Negroes themselves." His son, a forward-looking lawyer, naturally agreed with pleasure.[24]

The point of stressing the evolutionary character of slave culture is not to argue that the system would have died peacefully in a gush of Victorian sentiment but for Yankee intervention and war. Far from it. Establishing the ideal of Christian masterhood and strengthening state controls fell short of genuine black autonomy of any kind. The evolutionary process was not toward freedom but rather toward more refined means of perpetuating black dependency, either through acts of personal benefaction or through state regulations that also ensured white rule.[25] One could argue that in fact patriarchal slavery was more psychically damaging in fashioning the subservient personality than was chattel bondage. Under the latter formula, there was no reason to penetrate the slave's soul in order to save it, only to extract his labor. In any case, the evolution of slavery—"the domestication of domestic slavery," as Willie Rose calls it—was the chief point of departure for Southern antebellum polemics.[26]

There is little need to explain the attractiveness of the domestic analogy. Not only was it an obvious contrast to the chattel servitude associated with the squalid foreign slave trade, outlawed since 1808, but it also was intimately connected with evangelical and indeed scriptural reverence for familial government.[27] The historian Frank Vandiver once bluntly observed, "God counted in Dixie," especially when it came to defending Southern arrangements.[28] The ordinary slaveholder, seldom a reading man, appreciated the domestic imagery and paternal authoritarianism that he heard from the pulpit. According to Southern church fathers, slavery was a condition, not a moral evil. As such it resembled the family, civil government, hierarchies, all elements of social organization with which God had forever equipped his fallen, self-seeking creatures.[29] The institution did not involve personal sin. "Whether slavery was right or wrong, was a question which I did not consider," confessed the Reverend Jeremiah Jeter, a Virginia churchman.[30] Social guilt for a vast and complex institution simply failed to apply. Personal guilt for ordinary sins of omission and commission—drunkenness, unneighborliness, impure thoughts, greed, and the like—was quite another matter in the Southern evangelical view of the world. Many years later James McBride Dabney observed, "the more guilt" that a Southern Christian felt for private transgressions "the less he [or she] felt for his public" offenses.[31]

To be sure, some advocates of slavery, mostly politicians, called the institution a "positive good." Yet Southern preachers generally claimed that it was only potentially so, according to the moral fiber of those involved. Like the Southern lawyers, the professional clergy admired uniformity, rational objectives, in the evangelical assumption that what was truly practical and profitable was also divinely blessed. Therefore, they championed a form of slaveholding that extended the protective authority of a loving father over the entire household of whites and blacks.[32] Self-disciplined reciprocations of loyalty and duty bound the organic plantation community. Thus, in a vigorous attack on abolition, Lucy Kenny, a Virginia churchwoman, declared that "it is in the interest of the master to observe to his slave that kind of love which makes" the slave rejoice "to serve and obey his master; not with eye-service, but with heartfelt, Christian 'willingness.'"[33] Certainly there were biblical precedents to justify the Southern churchmen's faith in God's prescriptions for an orderly society. "Servants," the Apostle Peter advised early Christians, "be submissive to your masters with all respect, not only to the kind and gentle but to the overbearing." (1 Pet. 2:18.)

However false to the reality of slave attitudes it seems to us, this appeal, with its familiar overtones of the Golden Rule, made better sense to the planter than did the esoteric examinations of George Fitzhugh or the Bible-challenging scientific racism of Josiah Nott. As Eugene Genovese has often observed, the agnosticism of these early Southern Darwinians for the survival of the fittest affronted the clergy because the advocates of evolutionary science ran counter to Adamic origins for mankind.[34] To live up to the Christian proposition, however, was quite another matter, and the clergy, aware of human depravity, knew it.[35]

Religious simplicities not only established Abrahamic ideals of slaveholding fatherhood, they also implicitly defined what was ungodly, disreputable. They, too, gave the lie to the Northern abolitionists who claimed that the slave trade and slavery destroyed the family bond.[36] Without the domestic feature, declared one pious writer, "Negroes are herded on the plantation and propagate as mere animals." That was probably rare, though pious slaveholders admitted the practice of breeding for profit was sinful and a danger to the slaveholding community.[37] In contrast to unfeeling masterhood, Christopher Memminger, a Charleston layman, offered the ideal, which steadily became the most popular rendering of regional self-congratulation: "The Slave Institution at the South increases her tendency to dignify the family. Each planter in fact is a Patriarch—his position compels him to be a ruler in his household," guiding children, female dependents, and slaves alike with steady hand and loving voice. Like the image of the Southern lady, gracious and ethereal, the model of the Christian slaveholder was a stereotype that served a cultural function. It celebrated the alleged disappearance of old barbarisms and offered a standard of behavior to which respectable folk were to aspire.[38] The lines between what was and what ought to be were sadly blurred, but the instructional function remained.

Just as there was an outpouring of advice literature to parents and young people, so too advice on Christian masterhood flowed from busy Southern pens.[39] The duty of religious instruction to slaves was a chief concern, but particularly revealing was an emphasis on the need for moving slaves in moral paths by internal mechanisms of control.[40] Godly writers urged owners to reach for the Bible, not the lash. "Punishments," lectured the Reverend Charles C. Jones of Liberty County, Georgia, "should

be inflicted upon those proven guilty neither in anger, nor out of proportion to the offence, with as little resort to corporal chastisement as
possible."[41] Like Northern reformers, Southern thinkers had begun to
question old-fashioned corporal penalties in the handling of prisoners,
schoolchildren, and youngsters in the home. Application to slave management was not surprising.[42] The transition symbolized a growing awareness
of new psychological techniques that encouraged self-discipline, inner
moral consciousness, and a sense of individual dignity. Thomas Clay of
Bryan County, Georgia, and Calvin Wiley, a noted advocate of white common schools in North Carolina, both advised masters to apply rational
systems of rewards and nonphysical punishments to uplift slave morality.
They and others also stressed that every proprietor should know his hands
as individuals and select those disciplinary means suited to the abilities
and characters of each. As Eugene Genovese observes, "Principal church
leaders—Calvinist and Arminian, theologically orthodox and theologically liberal—agreed that God, in sanctioning slavery, commanded masters to follow the example of Abraham and treat their slaves as members of
their household and as brothers and sisters in the eyes of the Lord." Moreover, the Christian planter was supposed to follow scriptural injunctions
about the material wants of his people, provisions for decent housing,
clothing, food, and a sense of privacy that would promote the moral welfare of the whole plantation.[43]

According to some historians, the proslavery leaders in the church had
the better of the biblical argument. Forrest G. Wood, for instance, argues
that "English North Americans embraced slavery *because* they were Christians, not in spite of it."[44] That is a very doubtful proposition because the
nature of the Bible provides ample support for two approaches to ethics.
Honor, shame, and hierarchy, which includes slavery, are everywhere in
evidence both in the Old and the New Testaments, thus supporting, it
would seem, anyone then or now of a conservative persuasion. But the
Bible also contains much that opposes the premises for those ethical constructions. Some antebellum proslavery authorities and even a few of their
later admirers suggest that Christ failed to assault slavery as a monstrous
evil presumably because he was committed to the institution. That interpretation of Scriptures borders on the ludicrous. It suggests that Jesus
would have countenanced the return of fugitive slaves, the separation of
wives from husbands, mothers from children, or the buying and selling
of human flesh.[45]

To such Christian abolitionists as George Bourne, Beriah Green, and
Theodore Weld, for instance, the way that masters demeaned and op-

pressed bondspeople rendered them guilty of sin and corruption. As early as 1816 George Bourne, a Presbyterian minister in Virginia, cited Exodus: 21:16: "He that stealeth a man, and selleth him, or if he be found in his hand, he shall surely be put to death."[46]

Slaves, too, had a different and equally plausible reading of the Gospels. They fashioned a gratifying religious context from the same Bible that supposedly upheld the slaveholding system. "Antebellum black southerners," writes John Boles, "clearly recognized a parallel between the Israelites' bondage in Egypt and their own servitude." God was not a master holding them to field labor and perpetual submission. Instead, he was the Great Liberator. Jesus, continues Boles, was perceived as "both eschatological king and deliverer on one hand and as comforter, friend, and brother in the kinship of suffering on the other."[47] Was their reading of the ancient text as deficient as the abolitionists' or did it have its own integrity?

The problem lies within Christianity itself—a double tradition—in which the precepts of honor have prominence along with the familiar doctrines of love and God-centeredness. The proslavery clergy pointed to the Apostle Paul's injunction, "Slaves, obey in all things your masters according to the flesh, not serving to the eyes as pleasers of men, but in singleness of heart from fear of the Lord" (Col. 4:22–23). But Paul's letters, it must be remembered, were written to the upstanding, gentile members of the classical world in which the honor ethic had long reigned supreme. Therefore, the apostle, himself a Roman citizen, delivered a message shaped to win converts and make sense to those still comfortable with the current conventions and ideals. Faced with the obvious defects and offenses that slavery inescapably produced, Southern clergy had to argue the case for the primacy of orderliness, authority, and personal wrestling with sin and salvation as opposed to any meddling with the worldly order God had divinely created.

Of course, biblical passages were certainly available to meet their theological needs. In a widely read tract consisting of letters exchanged with Francis Wayland, a fellow Baptist theologian at Brown University, Richard Fuller explained that Abraham was a slaveholder and also "a friend of God," walking with him "in the closest and most endearing intercourse."[48] Albert Barnes, one of the most knowledgeable theologians of abolitionism, pointed out that the slaveholding of the Hebrew patriarchs Abraham, Isaac, and Jacob, for instance, did not have God's explicit approval. With the exception of a passage in Genesis (17:12, 13) regarding the circumcision of household menials who were bought with money, nowhere in the

Old Testament were the ancients commended by God for buying or sell-ing slaves for cash or credit.[49] The antislavery argument did not rest so much on direct reference to slavery itself than on the spirit of the whole. In larger terms, the Psalms and the Gospels of Matthew and Luke offered ample injunctions for the rich and powerful to show mercy and oppose any form of oppression. Psalm 12:5, Albert Barnes pointed out, declared, "He shall judge the poor of the people, he shall save the children of the needy, and shall break in pieces the oppressor." Throughout the New Tes-tament, Barnes insisted, the withholding of wages for work performed was denounced as a sin. Luke 10:7 affirmed that "the laborer is worthy of his hire." The clergyman also cited the Epistle of James: " 'And I will be a swift witness against . . . those that oppress the hireling in his wages, the widow, and the fatherless.' "[50]

Nonetheless, Southern whites assumed that the Bible itself overtly ap-proved the existence and even rightness of both slavery and honor. What authority was greater than the Bible itself? asked Southern whites. God approved of slavery, they insisted in rejoinders to their abolitionist critics. The Apostle Paul had returned Onesimus to his master Philemon, who was himself a Christian as well as a slaveholder. Albert Taylor Bledsoe, a learned professor of mathematics at the University of Virginia, demon-strated that Barnes was quibbling about meanings of words and ignoring the apostle's obvious acceptance of the institution.[51]

Increasingly antebellum Southern whites found solace and redemp-tion through Holy Scriptures that reflected the intermixture of honor and shame, conscience, and guilt.[52] Moreover, the earnest minister could pursue a humanitarian course. He could enjoin his slaveholding flock to embrace the attributes of Victorian modernity: self-control, rationality, practical consistency. Richard Fuller claimed to oppose state statutes for-bidding instruction in reading and writing and the legal recognition of slave marriages. Moreover, he admitted that "the power of the master" led to "frequent and shameful abuse," and he condemned mistreatment "as heinous sin."[53] But others were less liberal-minded. The South Con-cord Baptist Association of Kentucky in 1810, for instance, spelled out the duties of slaves in scriptural language: "Servants then are to be in sub-jection to their own masters according to the flesh, not only to the good and gentle; but also to the forward—they are not to render eye-service nor answer again . . . nor purloin . . . but to shew all good fidelity." Bad masters had to be obeyed no less faithfully than good ones.[54]

Secure in the conviction that racial order mattered most, proslavery thinkers grandly pronounced for the benefit of their doubting Northern brethren that slaveholding was modern in essence. It was as up to date as any organic system, true to nature and to God. Yet in preaching at home, there was room for more cautionary evaluations. More candid and indignant than Fuller, Calvin Wiley, the North Carolina educator, for instance, directed his fury at those masters who treated slaves as mere "chattel for profit and comfort" without considering their welfare. Yet such conscienceless slaveholders avoided their responsibilities by denouncing the institution as "an evil, a curse," in the manner of Thomas Jefferson. "This is not merely unchristian philosophy," he said; "it is supreme selfishness."[55] Sophisticated deism, such as Jefferson represented, was ungodly; likewise, attacks on God's natural order of master over slave were impious and dangerous. Attacks on planter misbehavior were rare, but some clergy who lamented the imperfections of the "domestic" slavery they cherished were sometimes outspoken.[56] A few even called for state interposition in behalf of slave rights. The Reverend W. T. Hamilton of Mobile, Alabama, denounced the failure to recognize slave matrimony in law—"an outrage to humanity . . . an insult to God!" The Reverend James Lyon intoned, "There is a natural repugnance in the breast of civilized men against tyranny; but there is none against the domestic relations. Let us, therefore, make slavery, by law, the patriarchal institution that is recognized and sanctioned in the Bible, and it will appear in entirely a different light to the eyes of the civilized world than that which it now appears."[57] Yet his call went unheeded. Perplexity over the principle of church-state separation, fear, complacency, religious and political conservatism—all prevented the use of political means.[58] Moral suasion was supposedly more Christian anyway. How much more, though, could be done to ameliorate the slaves' lot, lamented James Henry Hammond. The sole reason for any reluctance was not the slaveholder's fault but the Yankee critic's. "We have been compelled," he wrote, "to curtail some privileges; we have been debarred from granting new ones." Because of the agitation from abroad, "we have to rely more and more on the power of fear," a "painful" necessity, he claimed.[59] There was some truth in the matter, but whether planters would ever have welcomed change in their habits of management and racial assumptions seems very dubious.

In any event, proslavery writers relied on the drift of events, whose charitable direction was assumed to be in God's hands. George F. Simmons, another minister of Mobile, believed, for instance, that the progress of Christian refinement was sufficiently powerful to "eat the heart of slavery even as slavery continues." In his opinion, "the servitude" of the future "will not be grinding bondage, but a mutual and fraternal dependence."[60]

The words of Simmons, a Unitarian and a Yankee, were misapprehended. Under threat of a lynching, he fled to Boston. Nevertheless, his message, had it come from a familiar, native source, would have passed without comment, so unexceptional were such pulpit counselings. The Reverend James Henley Thornwell, leader of South Carolina's wealthy Presbyterians, for instance, proclaimed the immediacy of Christian triumph, calling the Southern system "regulated liberty," a discipline that opposed both "the despotism of the masses on the one hand and the supremacy of a single will on the other." Likewise, Woodrow Wilson's father, the Reverend Joseph Wilson, presented ameliorative slavery as a topic in a pulpit series on "family government." God, the North Carolina Presbyterian exclaimed in 1859, "included slavery as an organizing element in that family order which lies at the Foundation of Church and State." What other way, he argued, could blacks advance? The institution of bondage was "that scheme of politics and morals, which by saving a lower race from the destruction of heathenism, has under divine management, contributed to refine, exalt, and enrich its superior race!"[61]

Moving in religious and respectable circles, the clerical ideologues romanticized what they saw and ignored the unpleasant. Thousands of newcomers to slaveholding ranks were pushing their way up the social ladder with little regard for the niceties of Christian slaveholding, a chiefly upper-class posture. The advice literature aimed at the new additions as well as at those whose experience with ownership entitled them to set community standards. Yet the slavery advocate seldom acknowledged that his idealizations soothed more than they uplifted the savage heart. Compared with Yankee evangelical zeal, the fires of Southern missionary fervor flickered rather unevenly.[62] Nevertheless, Southern evangelicals, especially the Missionary Baptists, grew ever more confident in advocating what Matthew 28:19–20 proposed: "Go therefore and make disciples of all nations, baptizing them in the name of the Father and of the Son and of the Holy Spirit, teaching them to observe all that I have commanded you."

For all its manifold weaknesses, Christian patriarchalism remained the keystone of proslavery thought. In the last prewar decade, however, a new doctrine made an appearance. Though too exotic and academic to gain popularity, the approach was based on an idealization of actual changes in civil and legal conventions. Henry Hughes, a lawyer from Port Gibson, Mississippi, proposed a rationale in which the state replaced the familial arrangement as the foundation of overlordship. At ten o'clock P.M. on 1 January 1848, the eighteen-year-old Henry Hughes began to keep a diary. He would make weekly entries for over five years. His first remarks covered his personal life history up to that night, but he reveals little about his family and his relations with its members. Nor did he say much about his own life—why for instance, he decided to study law in New Orleans. Yet his father's early death and his legacy of bad debts had to have altered his prospects and his outlook on life considerably.[63]

"Of my Father who died when I was old enough only to love but not appreciate him," Hughes mourned, "the more I hear, the more I venerate him. He attempted to reform the dishonesties of cotton factorage; he would have succeed[ed] but death came. He was 'of the early breed of Athens.'" Hughes attributed his "veneration" to what he heard, rather than to what he felt. His image of his father came largely from without, and his respect came from his public, professional activities, not his role in his household. This may have been a result of Benjamin's financial troubles and Henry's need to "hear" that his father was an honest man who sought to reform corrupt practices. But it remained the public persona, not the parental figure, in which Henry expressed interest. He received love and affection from his sister and mother; he looked to his dead father to provide him someone to venerate and respect, someone who had achieved in his life public acclaim and recognition. Henry Hughes placed his father in a noble, but distant, historical dimension. One senses that the father-son relation—its distance and yet its reverential character—had something to do with the form of master-slave idealization that he was to promote in his philosophical studies.[64]

As romantically antinomian as any Yankee prophet, Hughes was only twenty-five when he published his *Treatise on Sociology* in 1854.[65] Intrigued with European positivism and learned in both ancient and modern literature, he was an unusually gifted thinker. Yet to judge from his diary, the young visionary suffered acutely in handling inmost feelings: "Let me shuffle of[f] this mortal coil, and burst forth into unpenetrated regions of space where God dwells in solitude and rush around the Circuit infinety [*sic*]," an extraordinary reference to his occupation of following the state judge from one county seat to another. "Am I a man, an angel, God, Devil. Is there a God or Devil. Why then do I not fear to shrink from. O, I feel like I could drive Satan from Hell. Down, down, thoughts, I am weary, O God let me die."[66] Aspiring to ambitions greater than those of Calhoun, Caesar, and Napoleon, the trinity he worshiped, Hughes set before himself the task of planning what he grandly called "A Universal Republic, Ultimum Organum, Longitude, Slavery Perfect Society; Myself the God-beloved, the human supreme of Earth's Politics,

Society, Philosophy, Economics, Religion & Aesthetics."[67] Such exuberant self-fascination matched similar introspections of such youthful romantics as Stephen Pearl Andrews, John Humphrey Noyes, and Henry C. Wright, among many other Yankee idealists.[68] In the Southern locale, among the trees and spacious houses of Port Gibson on the cliffs above the Mississippi, the intellectual ruminations of Henry Hughes led to different plans for human improvement from the dreams of reform that a Transcendental New Englander might entertain.

If, as one suspects, there is a relation between even the most antinomian prophecy and actual tendencies and social values in a society, then Hughes's writings deserve a serious reading.[69] They help to point the direction in which slave culture was heading. Certainly Hughes saw matters in an evolutionary context. "We know that our peculiar establishment is with a rapidity unparalled [sic] and marvelous perfecting itself; and hastening to set before civilized nations . . . a labor system . . . they must copy to prevent pestilence, starvation and countless crimes."[70] A believer in earthly perfection that any good Calvinist like Thornwell would consider blasphemous, Hughes announced the total withering away of a savage bondage just as the Unitarian Simmons did. That form of slavery, "a system of inhumanity and injustice," he confessed, had once existed, at the time of the Revolution.[71] Its horrors had moved the Northern Founding Fathers to emancipate Northern slaves, even as Southern heroes, like Washington and Jefferson, despaired that the system could ever be reformed. Knowing only the polarities of free and slave arrangements, they failed to see, Hughes claimed, the potentiality for another mode of labor discipline. But, he continued, this third form had evolved in the nineteenth-century South, a system that Hughes called "liberty labor" or "warranteeism."[72] By these terms, Hughes meant a labor-capital association, ruled by "moral duty, civilly enforced."[73] The young American positivist made no direct attack on Christian patriarchalism, but, like many other Victorian intellectuals, he entertained severe doubts about revealed religion. Yet, out of duty, he held religious classes for blacks in Port Gibson and later for Confederate soldiers under his command in Virginia. For himself, however, he reserved a faith in the absolutes of morality, not enjoined by divinity but by the state.[74] Thus "moral duty, civilly enforced" became the instrument of his slave millennium. Strangely enough, his disposition, his search for a utopia divorced from church institutions, resembled some features of William Lloyd Garrison's theology of moral absolutism. Hughes, an ardent secessionist, raised the figurative banner: "No Union with Non-Slaveholders."

Unlike most Southerners, Hughes admired the power and uses of the state, which he defined as "the economic sovereign. It is the supreme orderer. The capitalist (or slave master) is its deputy orderer." Thus, he maintained, slavery was an agency of the state, though management was delegated to owners. In this reading, the planter was a state functionary, a lay magistrate, exercising powers for the benefit of the commonwealth. To be sure, Hughes granted the familial concept a place in the scheme, describing the laborer and capitalist as members of "the same family," with the head of the household warranting "subsistence to all." Yet the planter's motives were neither personal profit nor paternal solicitude; instead, he undertook slaveholding responsibilities out of a sense of "civil duty."[75]

Whereas the proslavery clergy generally offered specific biblical texts, practical plans for Christian masters to administer, and comparative statistics and illustrations to contrast labor conditions at home and abroad, Hughes operated in the realm of pure abstraction.[76] As a result, he was able to insist that his "warrantees" or "simple-laborers" enjoyed the "judicial rights" of trials by jury, petition, habeas corpus, appeal, free counsel, and even freedom from some white felonies such as bigamy.[77] Also, they had material support for life, backed by law, whereas free laborers possessed the liberty to starve. Hughes thought that slave-protective legislation had already reached near perfection. He ridiculed those legislators— "the good, the wise, and the wealthy"—who persistently offered "some minor betterment" for the benefit of Mississippi's blacks.[78]

However eccentric and blind to realities Hughes was, his dreams illustrated the tendencies of the age. For example, slave ownership was still commonplace, but the trend seemed to be toward some concentration of slaves into fewer hands.[79] Hughes was no egalitarian. Yet he sought to bring slave mastership into every home, a program requiring the reopening of trade with Africa. The advantages, he thought, were compelling: "a lessening of white class antagonisms; the reorientation of the Upper South toward slaveholding neighbors; increased regional prosperity; greater congressional representation."[80] Other zealots were making similar expansionary pleas in the 1850s, but Hughes had something more in mind than simply alleviating the problems of the labor shortage.[81]

In speeches and newspaper columns, Hughes championed what he called African contract labor, whereby imported blacks would serve fifteen-year apprenticeships. The numbers, he believed, should be so massive that their presence would alter existing slave arrangements. Gradually the contract form would apply universally, perhaps within twenty years. Careful not to appear subversive of perpetual bondage, Hughes left unclear whether the African coolies (as they might be called) would subsequently become permanent slaves or whether resident slaves would merge into semiautonomous peonage.[82] As long as whites retained control of black destiny, it probably mattered very little to him. Intrigued with the possibilities of civil bureaucracy as a source for progress and internal security, Hughes envisioned new regulations under state auspices. Through the taxing power, for instance, the state could ensure a safe proportion of whites to blacks, native or otherwise, in any region. Furthermore, even before the reintroduction of African workers, there had to be new laws restricting the subservient race to noncompetitive, unskilled employments, thereby enabling poor whites to fill the positions that an expanding, diversified economy created.[83] At the same time, Hughes told a commercial convention at Vicksburg in 1859, the state must regulate "the negroes' hours of service, holidays, and food, raiment, habitation and peculium, and the other elements of their wages."[84] Satisfied though he was that slave criminals had already gained sufficient protections, he offered a few "minor betterments" of his own. The state, he suggested, ought to pay full, not partial, compensation to owners of convicted slaves in order to encourage masters to surrender suspects instead of running them off to another state for sale. Also, he urged Mississippi legislators to provide penitentiary sentences for slave convicts to replace some capital and corporal mandates. All these plans required an expanded public service to rationalize race controls.[85]

Like T. R. Dew and other proslavery thinkers, Hughes believed that the expansion of Southern population, newspaper networks, education, and transportation systems had made it easier, not harder, to control the underclass.[86] In October 1862 Henry Hughes, a colonel at the head of the Twelfth Mississippi Regiment, died from a war-related illness at his home in Port Gibson. He lived to see neither the defeat of the nation of which he had dreamed as the "Ultimum Organum" nor the enactment of the Black Codes of 1865. These fiercely suppressive laws to subvert Yankee-imposed emancipation came closer to what Hughes had in mind than any arrangement in the slave regime for which his schemes were designed. An earnest advocate of Christian masterhood preached the funeral oration at the Methodist church of Port Gibson. The Reverend W. D. Moore could scarcely conceal his distress that Hughes had lived a life of religious doubt.[87] Though disturbed at Hughes's admiration for the "socialistic writers" of Paris, Moore took solace in his friend's search for truth. As a Christian, Moore was proud of his opposition to Hughes's plan for contract African labor, given the dismal record of the old trade and the continued imperfections of men.[88] For those who believed in the more familiar, domestic vision of servitude, Henry Hughes had pushed too far ahead, toward the bureaucratic impersonality of an industrial apartheid.[89] By the time that system of exploitation was adopted, and not just in the Southern states, the proslavery argument was thoroughly repudiated and Hughes long since consigned to oblivion. Fortunately, Yankees had intervened before the modernizing of slavery was complete. At least, in a manner of speaking, Jim Crow at the turn of the nineteenth century was not literally a ward of the state, as Hughes had planned, or a possession of a condescending, Bible-toting patrician, as the clergy and pious laymen had sought to fashion. If Hughes, the most forward-looking of the proslavery zealots, had had his way, corporate servitude would have developed out of chattel bondage, a new system conferring some nominal liberties as modern means of ultimate control fed Southern self-confidence.[90] Yet the suffocation of the black soul would have continued as inexorably as ever. In the latter part of the Victorian age, as evangelical enthusiasms declined and the tenets of racial Darwinism, industrial boosterism, and imperial destiny arose, what room would there have been for the flowering of sentimental Christian mastery in the Southern states? The speculation that the country, spared both war and emancipation, might well have become a richer, more powerful version of South Africa may be fanciful. The late C. Vann Woodward had already called attention to the parallels between the two biracial societies during the post-Reconstruction years, but, as he said, their paths "diverged" after World War I, a change that surely would have been severely limited in a South free to pursue its own fate.[91] In this grim context, the Union dead, it seems, had not bled in vain.

Visionary and inward-looking to the very end, Henry Hughes whispered to his Methodist friend three deathbed words: "Nos sumus purificate." Perhaps as the Reverend W. D. Moore intoned from the pulpit, "A few moments after he was indeed purified forever from earthly sins and sorrows."[92] The same could not be said for the South he died to save. God Himself, it seemed, had deserted the cause. The Almighty wielded a mighty sword of destruction.

CHAPTER SEVEN

CHURCH, HONOR, AND DISUNIONISM

The right of secession . . . seems to me to be both immoral and absurd.
— *The Reverend Robert J. Breckinridge of Kentucky*

Anger and frustration were the root emotions that drove Southerners to secede, a visceral response to a collective sense of degradation and disgrace. Years of transatlantic criticism of slaveholding and growing Northern indifference to Southern interests had been a constant source of vexation. Contrary to some historical opinion, white Southerners were alarmed not simply because they feared what Abraham Lincoln and the Republicans might do once in power. Parties were soon moved in and out of office, prudent men advised. Have patience; conservatism would yet return. Much more disturbing was the election of an antislavery president. Southern politicians and editors had long threatened that such a political victory would mean national dissolution, but slave state grievances and claims to political parity were contemptuously swept aside by Northern balloting. It was bad enough to be insulted, but to have all warnings ignored was the final blow to Southern pride.[1]

Given the intensity of the humiliation, it is no wonder that the majority of clergy joined the practically universal political outcry for secession, particularly in the months leading to the election showdown. Scholars are almost unanimous in the opinion that the clergy as a whole were largely responsible for the rise of nationalistic spirit in the last decade before the Civil War and during the war itself.[2] The churches had been the first national institutions to split apart, setting an example for officeholders to follow some fifteen years later.[3] Moreover, nearly all recent scholars agree that religion exercised enormous power in the cultural and even political life of the United States, in the slave states no less than in the free ones. In the South, as Sidney Ahlstrom observed, the clergy rightfully claimed to be "the official custodians of the popular conscience."[4] Richard Carwardine likewise argues that evangelical clergy and laity, North and South, placed themselves in the thick of antebellum political discourse by forming a "special-interest" bloc. That term is misleading, however, with regard to the sectional crisis of 1860–61.

Indeed, though most clergymen followed their congregations into the ranks of secessionism, a significant minority failed to do so. We are concerned here with the holdouts, as it were, the leaders of the more conservative denominations who saw clearly the perils of disunion. The slave state clerical voice was more uncertain than one might have suspected. Far from endorsing slavery's positive goodness, Presbyterian and Episcopalian ministers in particular sounded various themes on the subject. None was hostile, but few called it holy. A good proportion of the South's ministers would rather have left the topic alone if they could have done so. "We have no right as a Church, to enjoin [slavery] as a duty, or to condemn it as a sin," proposed the Reverend James Henley Thornwell, the Presbyterian leader of South Carolina. "The social, civil, political problems connected with this great subject transcend our sphere, as God has not entrusted to his Church the organization of society, the construction of Government, nor the allotment of individuals to their various stations."[5] C. C. Goen observes that those who glorified slavery as biblically sanctioned revealed an inconsistency by simultaneously claiming that "it was strictly a civil institution beyond their concern." Perhaps by justifying slavery as a moral good, they could then claim to place the matter solely in the hands of civil government. Yet if such a strategy saved the Southern clergy from gross contradiction, they still had to conform in every respect to the dictates of the state as well as society, a loss of ecclesiastical and moral independence that few divines probably even dared to notice. Although a stalwart defender of a thoroughly Christianized slavery, Thornwell willingly rendered unto Caesar the things that were Caesar's. Methodists and Baptists generally deplored a mingling of religion and politics. Preachers considered politicians their rivals for public attention. In 1855 Daniel Witt, a Virginia Baptist clergyman, complained that "the hurricane of political excitement" turned people from God and incited "much asperity and bitterness and all manner of ill feeling in the masses of the people." Such earnest souls were less likely to applaud slavery as such, and some even boasted of their reticence on sectional controversies.[6]

Clergymen, of course, were citizens and held private opinions about politics that they readily suppressed in the pulpit. What concerns us are not informal pronouncements or private convictions but instead the public expression of clerical favor or disfavor on the regional decision of 1860–61. If, as Larry Tise demonstrates, over 60 percent of proslavery ministers with college degrees were Northern-trained and many Northern-bred, a cautious approach about secession was understandable. In a famous essay, "The Travail of Slavery," Charles Grier Sellers Jr. argued that slaveholding conservatives faced what he called "a paralysis of will." Inner conflicts, even a sense of guilt, engendered that response on the eve of war. Their confusion, Sellers contended, permitted the dominance of the fire-eaters. Sellers's interpretation, however, carries the matter too far. Guilt over bondage was very rare, apart from occasional deathbed contrition.[7] Nonetheless, great reluctance to promote radical political change did characterize at least a healthy number of the more urbane Southern clergy in 1860 and 1861.

Three major factors accounted for clerical foot-dragging as the political crisis grew increasingly ominous.[8] First, even though wedded to the practical exigencies of slaveholding, sophisticated church leaders recognized that they could not win polemical battles by upholding all the realities of slavery which abolitionist and antislavery critics constantly denounced. Second, they entertained a Whiggish and temperamental reluctance to disrupt the status quo. Finally, many of them held that regional honor required loyalty to the old Union with its compromises that neither endorsed nor repudiated human bondage. As a result, between Abraham Lincoln's election and the firing on Fort Sumter, the Southern clergy followed but seldom led the movement toward disunion. Some did so with heavy hearts and with premonitions of death and defeat. Even those who embraced the new Rebel order and sang the praises of slavery did so with a note of desperation. Being realists and conservatives, however, they lauded the new status quo with a vigor and dedication based less on Christian feeling than on the regional concept of honor.

With regard to a modulated rather than strident defense of slavery, some churchmen, chiefly in urban centers, were very much aware that the proslavery cause had its limitations. In 1851 Richard Fuller, the South Carolina Baptist leader, boldly criticized both abolitionists and proslavery zealots. Slavery, he intoned, "fosters indolence and luxury." Fuller even ventured to declare, "Slavery is not a good thing" and ought to be curtailed in the not so distant future. He preferred colonizing the freed people to Africa to the alternative of perpetual bondage.[9] And what was the devout clergyman to do with passages in scripture that exalted freedom? The Hebrew Year of Jubilee had once liberated many a slave. The writer of Deuteronomy commanded: "Thou shalt not deliver unto his master the servant which has escaped from his master unto thee" (Deut. 23:15). To devout Northern abolitionists such biblical sanctions justified the efforts to aid fugitives and the operation of state personal liberty laws. For Southern preachers and for the noted scholar Moses Stuart of Andover Theological Seminary in Massachusetts, the same passage had an opposite meaning. The scriptural writer, Stuart claimed, was referring to a slave belonging to a foreign enemy, not to a fellow Hebrew. Besides, the "thee" was not an individual who might harbor a slave but the entire nation of Israel, a matter of governmental policy. Therefore the Bible upheld the morality of the Fugitive Slave Law.[10]

With refutations of abolitionist rhetoric to support them, most Southern clergymen, as Drew Faust asserts, were "less troubled about *whether* slavery was right than precisely *why* it was right and how its justice could best be demonstrated."[11] But justifications not only had to satisfy Christian slaveholders at home but Southern sympathizers beyond the borders. In that process, churchmen could not entirely forget their denominations' antislavery past, however tentative had been their former criticism of bondage. Methodists were particularly embarrassed by early church pronouncements against the system. As a result, the latter-day followers of antislavery John Wesley themselves seldom meddled with the issue from their pulpits.

In the Methodist church, however, there were substantial exceptions. As one denominational journal put it, "to enforce the scriptural duties which grow out of the relation of master and servant" was also a civil duty. The same reversal occurred among the Baptists, as they drew in owners of bondspeople. Likewise, Presbyterians in 1818 declared at their General Assembly that slavery had to be condemned as "a gross violation of the most precious and sacred rights of human nature," a condition "utterly inconsistent with the law of God." They later fell away from such unpopular pronouncements but retained a degree of circumspection.[12] As late as 1861, Thornwell of South Carolina argued that the church had the right neither to require slave ownership "as a duty" nor "to condemn it as a sin." Slavery, he had also explained in 1850, "is a part of the curse which sin has introduced into the world, and stands in the same general relations to Christianity as poverty, sickness, disease or death. . . . It is not absolutely a good—a blessing" but rather "a natural evil which God has visited upon society." He did not argue, on this occasion at least, that slavery was an immutable and divine institution, blessed by God, but rather a circumstance with forlorn consequences—unless one were to welcome rather than simply endure with fortitude the visitations of illness and the other scourges in God's providence that he mentioned.

Admittedly, Thornwell's logic did not signify an abrupt conversion to immediate abolition, but his words did infer that "good and evil," as he continued, "are relative terms, and what may be good for one man may be evil for another." The point is not that Thornwell had abandoned the Southern cause. Rather, he had hedged any endorsement of slavery as a spotless instrument of God's design. According to Beth Barton Schweiger, "Few Virginia pastors believed that the presence of slavery in their society made it a righteous one. . . . If they argued that slavery was closer to the Biblical ideal of social organization than the Northern system, they saw signs everywhere that all was not well." Balance, prudence, sober objectivity—these were the watchwords of the proslavery argument—for the clear purpose, declared the intellectual George Frederick Holmes, of winning over those outside the South who "wished for argument instead of abuse."[13] Such an approach left room for more circumspection and even uncertainty about the issue, as churchmen saw it, than we have assumed.

By and large, the Southern clergy joined Thornwell in considering slavery a condition of life, like death and taxes—not to be celebrated but to be borne stoically and practiced humanely. Professor Nathaniel Beverley Tucker of William and Mary might exclaim to Southern slaveholders, "You have been chosen as the instrument in the hands of God, for accomplishing the great purpose of his benevolence." Such boasting, however, would make the thoughtful preacher wince. A solemn message of slavery as concomitant of all-too-human sin was perhaps theologically preferable—but not very inspirational, especially when compared with the Manichaean simplicity and self-confidence of abolitionist immediatism. Clerical defenders of slavery knew that few outside the South were shaken by their plodding justifications, despite alleged biblical foundations for Southern precedent. In most Northern churches, the spirit rather than the letter of the Old and New Dispensations served as answer to the literal analogies that proslavery clergy drew between Mosaic servitude and African American bondage. Like the Reverend Nehemiah Adams and a few other proslavery preachers in the North, Henry J. Van Dyke of Brooklyn, New York, reiterated the long-familiar arguments for a scriptural system in the South. While avoiding a strictly abolitionist rejoinder, a Professor Tayler Lewis, however, responded in rational style in the *New York World*: "The difference . . . between what was called servitude in the days of the patriarchs and slavery *as it exists* in the modern states of Mississippi and Texas, is so immense that no fair comparison can be made between them." Slavery in Middle Eastern antiquity was domestic, noncommercial, and nonracial, a total "absence of that feeling of caste, which is the curse of American slavery." No patriarch in Israel "ever *sold*, or thought of selling, for money, the humblest of his dependent vassals." Mercenary slavery was, by its soulless nature, brutal and self-serving, Lewis continued. "Have we been constantly improving it by giving it more of the social and less of the mercenary; more of the humanizing and less of the dehumanizing character; more of the fraternal and less of the caste aspect? Then may we quote the patriarchs—if not to the honor, at least not the shame of our Christianity." The dignity of man—a God-given sense of personality—could be achieved under bondage in which its subjects were by law and custom debased. With allusion to recent opinions from the bench of Thomas Ruffin of North Carolina, Lewis argued, "To be *owned* is degrading; to be *property*, and nothing more, is dehumanizing." These were sentiments, framed in Christian terms, that were not easily refuted by reference to a dry-as-dust scriptural literalism. As Lewis concluded, perhaps Southern Christians themselves felt that slavery induced in them "a hidden trouble of conscience" or "an obscure feeling, not allowed to come out in distinct thought, but which tells them there is, somewhere, something wrong about it." Even if he had not accurately read the Southern mind, Lewis struck a chord that even the most diffident Northerner was learning to appreciate.[14]

Part of the Southern clergy's polemical hesitancy might well have stemmed from the numerical weakness of the slave state church system. Powerful men—meaning most politicians—paid lip service to the Kingdom of Christ on Earth, but, by and large, most were absorbed in more worldly excitements than the pious emotions of the revival. In addition, there were over twice as many clergymen in New York than in all thirteen slave states put together, and the same number as preached in all the South served the single state of Pennsylvania. To put it another way, in the North, out of 187 inhabitants one was a minister, and in the South, the ratio was 1 to 329.[15]

Still more damaging to clerical self-esteem was the knowledge of how extensive and deep antislavery sentiment seemed to be growing throughout Christendom year by year. The skeptical reception of the proslavery argument in the greater world bears analogy with that of white South Africa in recent times. Southern apologists, lay or clerical, had to face the fact that few listened to their self-justifications unless to refute them. The theoretical and scriptural arguments for black bondage, scoffed Horace

Greeley of the *New York Tribune*, seemed the work of some "very curious maggots." They had overcome the "torpid stagnation" of their "planter brains" to bore the world with diatribes promoting slavery. Such views might be anticipated from a journalistic champion of the Republican Party, but Southern defenders of slavery did not find anywhere an attentive and receptive audience in the North or in Victorian Great Britain, which at the time was the moral and cultural arbiter of Western life.[16]

Unluckily for the conservative cause in those days, no spokesman as popular as Rush Limbaugh or Jerry Falwell rallied the Christian Right to defend slavery in all its facets. An exception, it might seem, was George Fitzhugh's visit to Yale College in 1855. There he proposed his special vision of the beauties of enslavement, not for blacks alone but as an institution suitable to deal with labor conditions the world over. After his presentation, the listeners, Fitzhugh wrote his friend George Frederick Holmes, fell to "thinking and talking. . . . Professor Silliman and many of the leading citizens paid me great attention." Academics are always intrigued with outrageous propositions, but the fun can last only so long. Fitzhugh might as well have offered himself as an exhibit for P. T. Barnum's collection of curiosities. In fact, most of the proslavery literature that Northerners were likely to read came to them in the form of printed colloquies, such as the reply of James Henry Hammond, former governor of South Carolina, to Thomas Clarkson, the venerable English antislavery leader, or that between the Reverend Francis Wayland of Brown University and Richard Fuller, Baptist leader of South Carolina. A work like E. N. Elliott's *Cotton Is King* surely found few buyers north of the Potomac.[17] Thomas Smyth, Presbyterian divine of South Carolina, sounded hurt to the quick when he declared that conservative Northern divines like Presbyterian Charles Hodge "profess to have lost confidence in our morality."[18]

Even Southerners did not read or comment on intellectual and theological productions with much interest. As the contemporary Southern humorist Roy Blount Jr. observed, "It is easier to enter into the kingdom of Heaven through the eye of an onion ring than it is to sell a book in the South."[19] After writing a major defense of slavery, South Carolinian Thornwell, of the Presbyterian persuasion, complained to a friend that he had found "hardly a notice of it in any of the papers."[20] The gloomy academician George Frederick Holmes, as Drew Faust points out, mourned that proslavery prophets, who, like himself, were ordained by God to warn a sinful world, had to expect nothing but "disbelief, dishonor, outrage, contempt, persecution." "I have long seen that you were not 'honored in your own country,'" James Henry Hammond commiserated with William Gilmore Simms.[21] To some degree clergymen felt the same sort of disrespect against which the secular leaders of intellect in the South murmured. When the boom of cannon announced the beginning of war, Holmes, embittered by debts and an unheeding, anti-intellectual Southern populace, echoed a sentiment that some of the Whiggish clergy may also have privately uttered. The horrors of war, the professor moaned, was God's punishment for the Southern people's "misplaced ambition . . . greed, rapacity, drinking, gambling, [and] dissipation."[22]

To be sure, the abolitionists had similarly difficult problems getting their message before an impervious public more preoccupied with mundane things than with church debates over slaveholding. Most Northern Christians mistrusted and resented the antislavery reformers in their midst. Nonetheless, church moderates and conservatives in the North heeded at least part of the abolitionist message and refused to embrace mindlessly an unadulterated proslavery doctrine. Particularly after the passage of the Fugitive Slave Law in 1850 and the Free-Soil struggle over the spoils of the Mexican War, what they chiefly sought was noncomplicity with slavery. No slave-catching, no support for bondage in the territories were the negatives of an antislavery position, as it were, but they were highly ominous signs of Northern opposition to the institution. For any Yankee to defend the Southern racial order would mean a repudiation of free labor capitalism along with the notion of steady progress toward personal liberty and Christian fulfillment, as Yankee churchmen understood it. Reflecting an almost universal Northern complacency on the topic, Horace Bushnell pointed out, "Why should I be contriving the abolition of slavery when the Almighty Himself has a silent campaign of inevitable doom against it, marching on the awful census tramp of South and North to push it away forever?"[23]

Exasperated by similar signs of Yankee condescension and self-righteousness, James Henley Thornwell of South Carolina pointed out that for years Northern friends of the plantation South had not been playing fairly. At best they treated the slaveholding region as if it were fit only for Christian charity. Thornwell complained that these so-called clerical allies continue to "pity the South as caught in the folds of a serpent, which is gradually squeezing out her life." What good was there in having such conservative supporters? When defending slaveholders from the abolitionist charge of sinful man-stealing, these Yankee brethren were ready with "so many distinctions" between slavery in the abstract and slavery in the concreteness of Southern laws and plantation practices that such a "defence would hardly avail to save us, if there were any power competent to hang and quarter us," Thornwell protested.[24] By the late 1850s Northern material and demographic power had grown so great, as Bushnell had observed, that Southern opinion made little or no intellectual difference. How galling it must have been to such productive theologians and thinkers as Thornwell to realize their own irrelevance in the world beyond the slave regime. "The North is the thinking power—the soul of the Government," he wrote in the *Southern Presbyterian Review.* "The life of the Government is Northern—not Southern. The North becomes the United States, and the South a subject province."[25]

Thornwell's sense of frustration was based on actual and not imagined slights. Another New Englander, Leonard Bacon of Connecticut, for instance, in 1854 charitably exonerated Southern proslavery ministers from loving slavery for the sake of "filthy lucre" but instead claimed their views had been perverted because they feared denunciation and even assassination if they professed the former antislavery credo of their denominations. Outside Bacon and Bushnell's New England, parts of the country that should have been staunchly favorable to the South did not rally to the proslavery cause. For instance, at Princeton, a major seat of Northern clerical conservatism, Charles Hodge and other Old School Presbyterians had gradually swung away from their Southern allies. Stately in appearance, sophisticated in manner, and affiliated with several leading families of the mid-Atlantic states, Hodge exercised great influence if only because he had trained more than two thousand clergymen, North and South, at the Princeton Seminary. Moreover, his *Biblical Repertory and Princeton Review* was one of the most prestigious church publications in the country. Outspoken in his opposition to the abolitionists, Hodge appealed to Yankee isolationism. "We do not expect to abolish despotism in Russia, by getting up indignation meetings in New York."[26] In like manner, Hodge continued, Northerners had neither the right nor the need to hurl epithets at slaveholders and expect them to repent. Yet even this archconservative limited his defense of his Southern brethren in Christ. As early as 1836, Hodge had observed in a widely disseminated essay that from a Christian perspective the power of masters was strictly circumscribed. The slave "can be used only as a rational, moral and immortal creature can, according to divine law." Moreover, he implied that a genuinely thorough movement to Christianize the South would provide "a peaceable and speedy extinction of slavery." Such a thought hardly seemed agreeable to slave state clergymen. They were inclined to think evangelization would mean improved slaveholding, not its swift disappearance. Such argumentation forced the Southern church leaders to tailor their own defenses in a similar fashion, an effort that took much of the spice and energy out of the enterprise.

Thus Thornwell, Richard Fuller, Thomas Smyth, and others agreed with Hodge that, in practice, masters ought not to exercise unlimited power over bondsmen but should confine themselves to exploitation of their labor and recognize only a right of slave proprietorship. Following the example that Hodge and other Northern conservatives were setting, the Southern churchmen preached that God was enjoining masters "to provide for the intellectual and moral education of the slave."[27] Moreover, marital and parental rights were to be respected, meaning that families ought never to be broken up. Once again, Southern clergy heeded their Northern conservative allies and proposed at church conventions and assemblies instruction in literacy and other ameliorations for slaves. They had little choice. To ignore Northern conservatives on these matters might snap crucial fraternal links. After all, even the *Saturday Evening Gazette,* a reactionary publication of New England, observed that "it needs no ghost from the grave to tell us that slavery is a great social and economical evil, and that every patriot and every Christian should be glad to see it removed."[28] To be sure, complete isolation from the rest of Christendom might inspire a martyr complex useful at home, but that state of affairs would shrink the moral and even political force of the proslavery argument beyond recovery. As a result, the Southern clergy had to show gratitude and even admit slavery's shortcomings that ought to be corrected. These endeavors could only be halfhearted, however, because neither the politicians nor the planters were about to surrender a slaveholder's untrammeled authority, least of all through the intervention of government. The Southern clergy might convert thousands of slaves through their earnest mission enterprise, but they could hardly boast of success in the state legislatures. For all the talk of an evangelical "special-interest" agenda, to borrow Carwardine's phrase, their lobbying, timid and sporadic, had produced not a single law that protected slave families, encouraged manumissions, or authorized even the most rudimentary forms of slave education. They felt much more at home complaining of tavern licensing, gambling, and other legal matters that posed little or no sectional peril. No wonder the clergy feared disunion; the prospect of still greater isolation from their Northern church allies was scarcely welcome.

Yet the policy of cooperation with sympathizers outside the South presented difficulties as well. Although the point might be conveniently overlooked, Northern conservative church fathers refused to sanctify slavery as an eternal condition appropriate solely to black-skinned descendants of Adam. Charles Hodge, for instance, carried his logic to a point that few Southern clergy dared to applaud. "Any laws inconsistent with these principles are unscriptural and unjust, and ought to be immediately abrogated." If Christian command were followed, Hodge continued, "the gradual elevation of the slaves to all the rights of free citizens" would proceed. "The feudal serf first became a tenant, then a proprietor invested with political power. This is the natural progress of political society, and it should be allowed freely to expand itself, or it will work its own destruction." [29]

Throughout the Northern states, most clergymen took a line similar to Hodge's. They failed to insist that slaveholding was inherently sinful, much to the relief of their Christian colleagues in the slave states. Yet they did object to what Charles Hodge criticized as the "slave system" of the South.[30] Southerners could take satisfaction that a general attack on the heretical position of the abolitionists accompanied these criticisms. Nevertheless, Southern slavery was still stigmatized as cruel and ungodly in practice—and this assessment came from the South's most loyal clerical allies in the North. The pronouncements that Northern conservatives made about slavery comforted the Southern leaders but hobbled any bolder defense of the institution—a more radical position that would inevitably have placed them at the forefront of secession.

The second factor restricting Southern clerical fervor for disunion was their relationship to the national and regional polity. Southern churchmen had always been much more circumspect about politics from the pulpit than their radical Northern opponents. The antebellum Southern clergy tiptoed around most controversial public issues. The *Southern Christian Advocate*, a Methodist paper, worried that the "preacher politician" would neglect the saving of souls, "say hard, and unkind, and uncharitable things" about adversaries, and rush after "worldly honor," a vice more "absorbing than avarice." [31] Even pulpit denunciations of duels were couched in terms of honor—true honor being defined as obedience to God and "false honor" a cowardly fear of disrepute.[32] Adversarial by temperament, Southern politicians were largely drawn from military and lawyerly ranks, but clergymen destined for city and town parishes were more likely to have pacific temperaments. For that reason, there was always a public suspicion that clergymen were too often effete and pusillanimous. More slaveholders failed to join a church than the number that did. Men outside the evangelical orbit thought them more comfortable in the parlor drinking tea with the ladies than attending political rallies or watching muster-ground parades. In fact, as Donald Mathews points out, 65 women filled the pews for every 35 men in the congregation, even though "men outnumbered women in the general population (51.5 : 48.5)."[33]

From the 1820s forward, moral reform in the North had largely emanated from politically minded clergy and lay evangelicals. Their approach was far from being sophisticated but instead divided the world between good and evil in the starkest terms imaginable. They did so perhaps because of a hidden uncertainty. As a friend of William Ellery Channing, a Unitarian from Boston, observed, they felt "less confident of being amongst the elect" because they had forsaken Calvinism and adopted doctrines of free will the better to serve their own salvation and their missionary purposes.[34] The first issue to arouse their concern had been federal desecration of the Sabbath. One remedy, they urged, was to close down the United States Postal Service one day a week. With some success the Democratic Party under Andrew Jackson stigmatized the movement as a fanatical effort of a "Christian party in politics" that endangered the republic. Such leaders of the Sabbatarian cause as the merchants Lewis and Arthur Tappan and Amos Phelps, however, then took up a new and much more politically troublesome crusade—the struggle against American slaveholding—applying the customary evangelical principles of Manichaean light and darkness.[35] The Southern clergy had reacted in horror to such mingling of moral and partisan matters. The New York abolitionists' postal campaign in the summer of 1835 opened their eyes to the dangers ahead.[36] As a Northern clerical sympathizer later wrote Virginia Presbyterian Moses Hoge, "the fierce demon of religious fanaticism breathes out threatening and slaughter."[37] Despite his comment, the Southern clergy's response to abolitionism was generally mild if compared with the hot words that Southern politicians customarily adopted.

Defending their slaveholding parishioners from the antislavery calumny of "men-stealing" was an easy task. A clerical outcry for changing allegiance from one government to another, however, was quite another matter. This hesitancy to enlist in the secession cause was particularly troubling for Old School Presbyterians in the South. As James O. Farmer has noted, of all Southern church fathers, they were the most likely to hold Whiggish convictions.[38] In 1859, Thornwell, leader of South Carolina Presbyterians, invoked the long-standing sanction against clerical politicking to back his Unionist sentiments. The church, he preached, was a "spiritual body, clothed only with spiritual powers," so that "intermeddling" with politics would be "foreign" to the church's "office and derogatory to its dignity."[39] Likewise, Unionist Robert L. Dabney, an influential Virginia Presbyterian, had long maintained that ministers ought never to plunge into partisanship, when acting "ministerially, publicly, or any way representatively of God's people as such." They risked squandering their "moral power" as "peacemakers and mediators." The people of the South, Dabney continued, were already "abundantly touchy" and needed no clergymen to prod them along the road to disunion. "There were plenty of politicians to make the fire burn hot enough, without my help to blow it," Dabney concluded.[40] One might suspect that since the church and the political party system sought to reach the same audience, rivalry for public attention induced clergymen to keep the distinctions between church activity and political partisanship as separate as possible.

. . . .

The third element inhibiting Southern clerical support for secession concerned the ambivalent role that the ethic and rhetoric of honor played in Southern life and discourse. Clergymen were unlikely to rattle sabers and glorify the chivalry in the manner of William Faulkner's Gail Hightower, but they were unlikely to defy public opinion for long. One reason for that concern to align themselves with the prevailing mood was the clergy's sense of propriety. They were sensitive to public sentiment, knowing that they were constantly under scrutiny—as intellectuals in a parochial environment. "Opposed to honor is shame, which is either the contempt of others manifested in some external expressions, or the fear, on our part, of doing that which justly shall expose us to disgrace." These words of James Henley Thornwell indicated that such men of God as he knew the society they inhabited very well. As the historian Brooks Hollifield notes, the sermons of the urban clergy expounded on the issue of guilt—"the transgression of prohibitions"—but they were largely wary of the more perilous stigma of shame. Philip Lindsley, a Nashville Presbyterian, warned his fellow divines never to betray themselves to the "contempt and derision of the intelligent and discerning."[41] Under such circumstances, the more refined ministers would gauge their politics and position on slavery by the criteria of community consensus.

As long as the political situation remained fluid and no Northern coercive action had been taken, the body of gentlemen theologians was content with the status quo. To them it seemed, in fact, a sectional disgrace to turn against the martial ardor that had produced the Revolution, the victory of New Orleans in 1815, the triumph over the Catholic Mexicans. Yet the church had also to confront the warlike character of Southern whites. They scarcely could encourage secession with clear

Christian consciences while the nation was still at peace and the existing order remained politically challenged. After reporting on local reaction to the secession crisis in January 1861, for instance, John Cowper Granbery, a young preacher of Charlottesville, Virginia, informed his fiancée: "I will check myself abruptly and violently so as not to pursue the path of political discussion which everybody travels these days. What have women and preachers to do with sucession [*sic*] and war?"[42]

The minister meant that he and members of the gentler sex had loftier duties. They had to fight "sin"—that is, those basic faults to which all mankind was subject. In addition, they confronted a system of rigid and sacralized customs that stressed masculinity over effeminacy and other formulations that separated what we might call Christian dominion from antique but still virulent male privilege. With regard to the age-old patriarchy to which the Southern father, brother, and husband were dedicated, biblical sanctification of tradition served the churchmen and the men of honor alike. Yet the aim for moral improvement was bound to require clergymen to stress the need for humility, penitence, and other signs of godly behavior in the face of human pride, hallmark of honor. They were aware that conceit, fear of shame, and hope for public acclaim affected all men, but most especially those used to the obedience of slaves and all other dependents. "It is a characteristic of our people that they are . . . vainglorious, to a degree that makes them ridiculous. They love to boast, and they love to sacrifice to their own drag and to burn incense in their own net," intoned James Thornwell. For that reason, along with his steadfast dedication to Whiggery, Thornwell long opposed secession. In 1850 he wrote a friend, "The prospect of disunion is one which I cannot contemplate without absolute horror." The consequent war, he foresaw, would be "the bloodiest, most ferocious, and cruel in the annals of history." Ten years later he steadfastly maintained that withdrawing from the Union would "bring 'defeat, and disaster, insecurity to slavery, oppression to ourselves, ruin to the State.'" In the opinion of Presbyterian Robert Dabney of Virginia, South Carolina "is as great a pest as the abolitionists." If he could have his way, Dabney proposed, the federal government "might whip her to their heart's content, so they would only do it by sea and not pester us."[43]

Fear of political change and a mistrust of what might be called the Hotspur mentality led other divines to deplore secessionism as well. Despite Lincoln's election in November 1860, James Otey, Episcopal bishop of Tennessee, for instance, thought principles of honor and patriotism demanded continued loyalty to the Union. Otey called South Carolina's preparations for separation "infamous. There is not a redeeming trait about the movement to save it from the just and deep condemnation of Posterity." Otey was dismayed enough to hope that President James Buchanan would be impeached for not having "throttled nullification" in the spirit of Otey's Tennessee compatriot, Andrew Jackson. In a subsequent appraisal, Otey, like some Northern politicians and reformers, expressed the view that, for at least twenty-five years, a party of unmanly and subterranean conspirators had sought a pretext for Southern separation. Like Thornwell, he predicted that the unplanned outcome of secession would be a "speedy inevitable extinction [of slavery], as certainly as the sun's rays fall upon the Earth."[44] The reason for slavery's demise, he shrewdly continued, was that the South would no longer have the moral support that a government with over thirty million people provided. If fugitive slaves were not likely to be returned in every case by a Lincoln government, the South had no chance of getting them back after separation. To think otherwise, he exclaimed, was "simply preposterous." The free states "will make no such treaty stipulations and we shall not have the color of law or pretext to demand them." Just look at the secessionists, Otey advised. They claim that "*they can whip all creation*—Cotton will make them 'princes and rulers in all lands'! Depend upon it, this is the pride that goes before a fall. . . . The day of vengeance I verily believe is near at hand."[45] Otey issued a pastoral letter in which he cautioned his Tennessee clergy to present themselves as men of "moderation" and "study to be quiet, and to mind their own business."[46] The fire-eater sensibility had no attractions for him but instead seemed a foolish as well as dishonorable, treacherous policy.

To be sure, Otey and other Whiggish clergy, particularly in the border states, scarcely spoke for all clergymen and pious laity. His version of honor was not universally accepted even in clerical ranks. In fact, his fellow bishop, Rt. Rev. Francis H. Rutledge of Florida, came out boldly for secession, backing his convictions with a five-hundred-dollar donation to the state legislature, payable upon news that an ordinance of secession had been passed. Originally from South Carolina, Rutledge "had himself already seceded with his native state, and in advance of Florida." Edmund Ruffin of Virginia, then in Florida, rejoiced in the bishop's decisiveness. An irascible fire-eater, Ruffin seldom had a good word for anyone, but on his visit to stir Florida to disunion he found that he "was very much pleased with the venerable old minister, & with his ardent & active patriotic sentiments."[47] Although many of the state politicians and militia leaders were Episcopalians with equally strong disunionist opinions, Bishop Rutledge, who was also rector of St. John's Church, Tallahassee, did not win over former Whig governor Richard Keith Call and founder of St. John's. Call worked tirelessly against Florida's departure. When a fire-eater exulted over the state's secessionist decision in Call's presence, the Unionist retorted, "Yes, you have opened the gates of Hell."[48]

Rutledge was by no means the only ecclesiastical figure to sport his disunionist colors openly. The honor of being the first clerical authority to propose disunion in 1860 went to the editor of the *Southern Presbyterian*, published in Columbia, South Carolina, capital of disunionism.[49] As early as the Nullification crisis of the early 1830s, Rev. Thomas Goulding at the Presbyterian Theological Seminary in Columbia, South Carolina, had announced that "unionism would be, in national politics, to prefer weakness to strength—degradation to honorable rank." Likewise, during the same episode, Richard P. Cater linked South Carolina's pride to exemplary Christian fervor and urged his congregation to "prefer the stillness and silence of the grave, to the heart chilling clangour [*sic*] of the chains of slavery."[50] After Lincoln's election, a minister of Jackson campaigned for secession throughout the state with Mississippi's attorney general. The Reverends James C. Furman and John Gill of South Carolina served as disunionist delegates to that state's secession convention.[51] By and large, however, press and pulpit throughout the South were scarcely uniform about following so violent and wrenching a policy.

As the crisis over the election of Lincoln developed, the mood gradually shifted, yet it did so against a firm resistance to change, particularly in the upper South. The *Central Presbyterian*, published in Richmond, warned in the September before Lincoln's election that secession would inevitably bring on "a horrible civil war." Also in the upper South, the Reverend Robert Breckinridge of the Presbyterian Church tirelessly spoke out for the Union. He lambasted the secessionists by warning his fellow Kentuckians, "If we desire to perish, all we have to do is to leap into this vortex of disunion." Like Bishop Otey of Tennessee, he thought the seceding slave states would destroy God's glorious plans for a united nation. Slavery was much better protected within the Union than it would be as a separate country. "So long as the union of the States survives," he advised, "the constitutional guaranty and the Federal power, which have proved adequate for more than seventy years, are that much added to whatever other force States or sections may possess to protect their rights."[52] Otey's widely disseminated views helped immeasurably to keep the border states in the Union.

In the lower South, however, Breckinridge's onetime friend Benjamin M. Palmer, a Presbyterian minister at New Orleans, adopted the secession cause, making rhetorical use of Southern adherence to the ancient ethic along with biblical passages he deemed supportive. The clergyman argued that fanaticism had sundered the Union by electing a purely sectional candidate. As a result, Southern statesmen were forming a government "to uphold and perpetuate what they cannot resign without dishonor and palpable ruin."[53] Palmer insisted that the Southern white people's "providential trust" required them "*to conserve and to perpetuate the institution of slavery as now existing.*" His widely distributed sermon had as much impact for secession in the lower South as Breckinridge's for Unionism in the border states. Yet even this fire-eating divine conceded that the relationship of master and slave was scarcely all that the church could hope for. "Still less," he admitted, "are we required dogmatically, to affirm that it will subsist through all time." Residual loyalty to the policy of a circumscribed defense of slavery induced him to express such sentiments.[54]

Palmer, however, provided the basis for the dramatic turn that soon overwhelmed the Whiggish clergy, even outside the lower South. He challenged Unionists like Breckinridge of Kentucky who contended that the federal executive was not the servant of the sovereign states but their master. "Had the Constitution been regarded as a compact whose bonds were mutual honor and good faith," Palmer concluded, "the apprehension of a rupture would have been the surest guaranty of its observance." The Northerners' "numerical majority" encouraged their aggression and imperialist ambitions, whereas a loose bond of states would have upheld "every consideration of honor and interest."[55] Such sentiments as these led the clergy of the lower South into the secessionist ranks as their states left the Union in the early months of 1861. In the upper South, Otey, Bishop William Meade of Virginia, and other Unionists remained loyal, but only until the firing on Fort Sumter in April. Soon thereafter most of them were echoing the demands for manhood and honor that once had been most closely identified with the disunionists of the 1850s.

The character of that discourse was well exemplified in the rhetoric of Jefferson Davis. At a state convention in 1851, the future Confederate president exclaimed that Mississippi's "honor was the first consideration"; before the citizens in the face of Northern perfidy, "her flag was hoisted to the mast and [he] for one" pledged to "cut away the halyards, and there let it float." The state's honor, Davis proclaimed, "was [his] honor." He called upon brave men to "transmit to their descendants the same heritage which had been given to themselves." Such expressions, which resounded through the length and breadth of the region, were bound to affect the clergy. They belonged to communities where the language of honor flourished; they could not escape its dictates. The idiom had long served as "the lingua franca" of Southern sectionalism.[56]

The clergy easily adjusted to the style because the rubrics of honor were part of the Hebraic and Christian traditions. Codification of the ethic could be located in Scripture. Middle Eastern cultures, then and now, have been partly based on rigid rules of honor and heightened fears of disgrace and humiliation. In Holy Scripture itself, the worship of God was conceptualized in terms of that code. The prophets' jeremiads denounced the wayward Israelites for the dishonoring offense of impugning the blamelessness of God. They took from God due honor and glory— two interconnected modes of praise, as explained earlier with reference to the concept of *kavod*.[57]

In sum, the Old—and even the New—Testament's rendering of honor endured among Southerners accustomed to face-to-face, small-scale, family-oriented usages that bore analogy with the pastoral society that produced the Holy Word.[58] As a result, biblical injunction seemed to supply the Southern clerical fire-eater and later Rebel with ample self-justifications. In March 1863, Rabbi M. J. Michelbacher informed the congregation of the German Hebrew Synagogue in Richmond: "*Thou dost call upon the people of the South in the words Thou gavest to Nehemiah: 'Fight for your brethren, your sons, and your daughters, your wives and your houses!'* "[59] The *Central Presbyterian* proudly boasted in May 1861, "Virginia's gallant sons . . . have sprung forward to the defense of their insulted Mother; assured that they are contending for the most sacred rights, and for the dearest interests for which patriot soldiers ever drew the sword."[60]

If biblical quotation did not fill the space reserved for honorable sentiment, the Confederate preacher could always turn to traditional sensibilities about manhood and glory. Warning that shame, the polar opposite of honor, was even a greater threat than death itself, a Presbyterian paper in 1862 preached that "*Defeat will be the death to us, and worse than death it will be* INFAMY."[61] Even the antipolitical Methodists took up the cry. The Georgia Methodist Conference in 1863 declared that giving up the fight would be "a disgrace to our manhood, a surrender of principles, a sin against our dependents and children."[62] In advocating secession in his impassioned address in New Orleans in November 1860, Benjamin Palmer pledged that "not till the last man has fallen behind the last rampart" shall the South yield its noble standard. If the new Confederacy were supinely to abandon the cause, she would transmit a shameful "curse as an heirloom to posterity."[63] Likewise, Thomas Smyth of South Carolina urged a martial boldness to protect "the undefiled purity and honor of our wives and daughters; unpillaged property; unravaged fields, uninjured harvests; uncontaminated servants; all—every thing that is sacred to honor and to happiness" were "involved in this contest."[64] Samuel Henderson, an Alabama Baptist editor, similarly argued that his state "owes it to her own honor . . . to secede from the Union."[65]

In other words, the Whig clerical elements made up for past doubts regarding disunion with a zeal typical of the recent convert. As James H. Moorhead has noted, "The almost joyous abandon with which the churches had thrown themselves into the business of war was in part an escape from ambiguities that had become too burdensome to sustain."[66] He was referring to the Northern churches, but the point was equally valid for the Southern ones. In clerical opinion, such sentiments advantageously united all white Southerners behind a single aim rather than perpetuating the divisions of political parties. Ministers generally believed that petty partisanship had no place in the Christian scheme. At the outset of the war Southern evangelicals had high hopes for a widespread spirit of cooperation behind Jefferson Davis and his colleagues in Richmond, a dream soon to vanish.[67]

In this Southern discourse, honor to God and honor to self were closely bound together. As a result, it was possible for churchgoers to reconcile the traditional ethic and evangelical belief. For instance, Sarah Dorsey, a wealthy plantation mistress of Louisiana, presented Confederate general Leonidas L. Polk, prewar Episcopal bishop of Louisiana, a battle flag on which she had emblazoned the "Labarum," that is, the Cross of Constantine. "We are fighting the Battle of the Cross against the Modern Barbarians who would rob a Christian people of Country, Liberty, and Life," she wrote him. As Dorsey's words suggest, romantic heroism and Christian zeal were congenially united.[68]

The abrupt transition to Confederate allegiance freed the new clerical loyalists from former deference to Northern conservative church opinion. In 1861 Southern Old School Presbyterians were horrified when such long-standing friends as Gardiner Spring of New York City backed resolutions at the General Assembly firmly supporting the Union. Yet such expressions of Union fealty freed the Rebel clergy from further national ties.[69] Later in the same year, Lewis Harvie pronounced, "We are hereafter to meet this question of slavery in a totally different spirit from that which controlled us" before. We must "become slavery propagandists."[70] The new freedom came at a price for some. Thomas Smyth of Charleston in 1863 sounded almost desperate when he proposed that God had decreed what amounted to a "divine right of slaveholding." Perhaps the ghost of the beheaded Charles I had risen to give a blessing to the new order. Smyth asked rhetorically, "What if God, by a positive divine enactment, ordained that throughout the history of the world, slavery should exist as a form of organized labor among certain races of man?" In his judgment, the North would be cursed forever for waging "a war of extermination against slavery." Yankee defiance was nothing short of blasphemy—a "rebellion against the Lord God omnipotent, who ruleth." The clergyman made these observations under the heading, "the divine right of secession."[71]

Even for churchmen less impassioned than Thomas Smyth, a sense arose that the issues of slavery and antislavery were happily no longer relevant. Lincoln's proclamation to begin military operations against the Rebel states freed them from the perplexing question of whether slavery was right or wrong. As a Virginia ecclesiastical biographer put it, "Henceforth, in the minds of her sober, Christian men, it was not a question of slavery, of secession, or of Union. It was a question of self-defence, self-government, and constitutional liberty." Warfare simplified decision making; emotions could take the place of rational thought.[72]

Such strongly Unionist clergy as Bishop Otey and Thornwell, however, continued to doubt a bright future. They had had little trouble swearing fidelity to the new government. Prudence, fear of lost reputation, dread of dwindling congregations—and above all their loyalty to Rebel kindred and neighbors—had shoved them into the secessionist parade. Thornwell, for instance, echoed the language of his honor-conscious compatriots in South Carolina when he concluded in late 1860 that "a free people can never consent to their own degradation."[73] Nonetheless, a note of sadness and expectation of ruin crept into his public utterances in favor of Confederate rule. In a fast-day sermon on the eve of South Carolinian secession, Thornwell declaimed, "We can make every pass a Thermopylae, every street a Salamis, and every plain a Marathon. If we are overrun, we can at least die."[74] In the language of honor, his tone was meant to be grimly determined, but it sounded almost suicidal. Rather than pray for victory, Thornwell made the disunion enterprise seem all too problematic when he declared, "Leaning upon the arm of everlasting strength, we shall achieve a name, whether we succeed or fall . . . posterity will not willingly let die." He ended the sermon on an uncomforting note by predicting that the state of South Carolina was bound to "suffer" and was doubtless "destined to fall." He repeated the word "suffer" four times in the closing paragraph, to drive home the upcoming perils about which Carolinian secessionists were so dismissive.[75] Even after South Carolina had seceded and hopes were running high for other states to join the movement, Thornwell had to observe that most men of his acquaintance could only pronounce "the word DISUNION, with sadness of heart."[76]

If ambiguity and pessimism were evident in Southern churchmen's reaction to disunion, matters did not wholly improve in the war itself. The Rebel government did not take very seriously the need for clergymen on the field of battle. Confederate army regulations never mentioned the role, duties, or even presence of chaplains in the ranks. Demonstrating their own indifference to religion—despite presidential appeals for fast days—Jefferson Davis and others in high places apparently thought paid chaplaincies a misallocation of scarce resources. Separation of church and state was carried to an extreme that could not have helped army esprit de corps in the long run. Eventually, the Confederate Congress grudgingly provided chaplains with a private's level of wage and rank. As a result, few clergymen took up the labor for long; even the pious Stonewall Jackson could supply but half of his regiments with chaplains. In the entire military establishment, only fifty ministers served through the duration.[77]

No wonder clerical morale during the war was not much better than that of the civilian population as a whole. Manfully, pastors, preaching to dwindling flocks, denounced the federals, abolitionists, and "Black Republicans" and swore that God was simply testing his chosen people before lavishing future glory and victories upon them.[78] Yet sustaining a buoyant outlook was not easy when churches were being turned into hospitals and military headquarters and the Yankee enemy was burning or vandalizing those that fell into their hands. As morale—and church alms—fell ever lower, James Thornwell tried to inspire his congregation's patriotic spirit, but even he alluded to the probability of defeat in set battles. He urged a continuation of the fighting in the form of "guerilla" warfare—to what godly purpose he failed to say.[79] Likewise, in her letter to Leonidas Polk, Sarah Dorsey phrased her Confederate convictions in unrecognized pessimism. "Never defeated, annihilated, never conquered," she boasted, but then ended: "When the land is conquered it will be time for us to die." Dorsey did not say, *if* the land is conquered but "when" that tragedy occurred, death would be welcome.[80] Unhappily these Whiggish Christians proved better prophets than they would have ever wished to be. Yet, at the start, hopes were high because the young men who were to fight and die thought their cause honorable, unconquerable, and sacred in the eyes of God.

PART THREE

WAR AND AFTERMATH

CHAPTER EIGHT
· · · · · · · · · · ·

SHAMEFUL SUBMISSION AND
HONORABLE SECESSION

If you attempt to force upon us sectional desolation
and — What to us is infinitely worse — sectional degradation,
we will resist you; and if in the conflict of resistance
the Union is dissolved, we are not responsible."
—Albert Gallatin Brown of Mississippi, 1850

In 1860–61, the lower South separated from the Union out of a sense of almost uncontrollable outrage.[1] To be sure, slavery was the root cause of sectional conflict. When the South Carolina secession convention met in November 1860, fire-eater congressman Lawrence Keitt insisted that the rationale should center solely on the issue of slavery. That was, he said, "the great central point from which we are now proceeding." Other fire-eaters sought to add a wider agenda. Robert Barnwell Rhett and Maxcey Gregg, two stalwart secessionists, protested that singling out just one grievance "dishonored the memory of South Carolinians" who had opposed the Tariff of Abominations, various internal improvement bills, and the second Bank of the United States. Keitt replied that these were no reasons for leaving the Union. Only slavery was. The dissenters were defeated.[2]

The defense of slavery, however, involved more than just the fact of its legitimacy in the midst of a free society. For both sides in the dispute, the "domestic institution" came to symbolize all that was right or wrong about Southern race relations, culture, politics, and livelihood. Albert Gallatin Brown of Mississippi declared on the floor of the Senate (cited in the epigraph) that it was not so much the prospect of a South devastated by slave insurrection as it was the stigma of submission to Northern tyranny.

In 1850 he reminded his colleagues that the Constitution had formed a union of "thirty sovereignties." Equality among them had to be observed. Without parity the slave states would be have no choice except disunion.[3] The threat to slavery's legitimacy in the Union prompted the sectional crisis, but it was Southern honor that pulled the trigger.

At the heart of the conflict was Southern fear of free state political and economic power and what that portended for the future of the peculiar institution. The phenomenal growth of an industrial and urban region threatened the long-standing parity of the free and slave sections that had existed under the constitutional compromises of 1787. Northerners, most especially those in New England, could no longer be trusted. Instead, criticism of the South—its slave system, morals, and culture—had so vastly expanded that Southern whites increasingly felt deeply insulted to the point of disunion and war. They reacted in the language they knew best—the rhetoric of honor—whose use provided the Southern cause with moral urgency and self-justification. Certainly that was the way its adherents saw it. Quite consciously, the secessionist newsmen and platform speakers drew analogies with their Revolutionary War forefathers. The language had not changed very much since that period. Yet the causes had greatly diverged.

Southern anger was scarcely a wonder. The relentlessness with which Northern politicians, preachers, and reformers had voiced their antislavery sentiments throughout the 1840s and 1850s was bound to prompt almost hysterical responses, particularly in the lower South. The density of its slave population, rural character, and relative isolation from Northern influences set the region apart, even from the other slave states closer to the Northern juggernaut. As an honor-guided people, the whites throughout the South took such pride in their Christianity, moral principles, and economic success that disunion seemed to growing numbers the only right course of action.[4] The irate Southerner was wont to assert that New England was "the birthplace of impurity of mind among men and of unchastity in women—the home of Free Love, of Fourierism [socialism], of Infidelity, of Abolitionism." Susan Keitt of Charleston improved the list: "a motley throng of Sans culottes and Dames des Halles, Infidels and Free Lovers, interspersed by Bloomer women, fugitive slaves and amalgamationists."[5] Added to this unflattering arraignment was the aspersions cast on Northern manhood. City-bred fops and limp-wristed reformers—and their fanatical congressional leaders—deserved Southern contempt. Senator Louis T. Wigfall of Texas crowed over the secession of the lower South before Lincoln took office. He told the free state senators, "Your flag has been insulted; redress it, if you will dare. You have submitted to it for two months, and you will submit to it forever."[6] That degree of arrogance proved disastrous for the South in the long run.

Meantime, the Southern press and pulpit were proclaiming undying loyalty to an institution that the outside world considered at least regressive if not downright immoral. Like Keitt in South Carolina, Alexander H. Stephens, Confederate vice-president, had no doubts about the centrality of slavery. He announced that the South's "corner-stone rests upon the great truth that the negro is not equal to the white man; that slavery— subordination to the superior race—is his natural and normal condition." Such differentiations, he continued, were "in conformity with the ordinance of the Creator."[7] When Mississippi seceded from the Union on 9 January 1861, the state convention asserted, "Our position is thoroughly identified with slavery—the greatest material interest of the world." The delegates complained that as early as the passage of the Northwest Ordinance of 1787, Northern antislavery hostility had jeopardized the slaveholders' rights to ownership. The Harpers Ferry insurrection plot, the Mississippi secession delegates complained, revealed that the Northern people were ready to invest "with honors of martyrdom the wretch whose purpose was to apply flames to our dwellings, and the weapons of destruction to our lives."[8] The object of Northern aggression was to obliterate three billion dollars worth of slave property, declared the Georgia state convention. Indeed, it was no small sum then or now.[9]

Yet paramount though slavery as a right of property was in the Southern ideology, the rationale for disunion was customarily presented in other terms—states' rights, Southern distinctiveness in culture and principled behavior, and the maintenance of honor. (Enough has been said about states' rights to require no elaboration here.) With regard to a sense of Southern uniqueness within the American framework, during the last years before the war, Southern spokesmen fashioned a curious myth that distorted their ethnic roots. A high proportion of Southern whites descended from Irish, Scots-Irish, Welsh, and Scottish settlers. Yet the small contingent of immigrants from England dominated the legend, as if the colony at Jamestown was the only seed from which the region had grown. The notion of a "cavalier" society that stemmed from seventeenth-century royalism became a reigning cliché in the ranks of the planter elite. In 1861, for instance, Samuel Phillips Day, an English newsman traveling through the Confederacy, reported, "This is no civil strife: no struggle of Guelph and Ghibelline; no contest between York and Lancaster." Instead, the contest involved "alien races, distinct nationalities, and antagonistic governments. Cavalier and Roundhead no longer designate parties, but nations, whose separate foundations . . . were laid on Plymouth Rock and the banks of the James River." The English journalist thought the "irreconcilable character of the Cavalier and Puritan" heightened the antipathies that ordinarily set commercial against agricultural interests and free against slave labor.[10]

Day's views mirrored the current discourse in upper-class secessionist circles. Readers of the *Richmond Messenger* in 1860 were doubtlessly enlightened by a screed on the editorial page outlining "The Difference of Race between Northern and Southern People."[11] In his first major political speech after the inauguration, Jefferson Davis harped on the same theme. The Northern Roundheads, "bred in the bogs and fens of Ireland and northern England," could never dominate the Southern people, who were "descendants of the bold and chivalrous cavaliers of old."[12]

Even as late as 1911, the notion of two separate cultures rooted in the English Civil War still animated the postwar defenders of slavery and the Old South. In that year Robert Cave claimed that the South, "led by the descendants of the Cavaliers," possessed "a manly contempt for moral littleness, a high sense of honor, a lofty regard for plighted faith, a strong tendency to conservatism." Against these paladins were arrayed the forces of a corrupted "Puritanism," Cave insisted. The New England political movement, shabbily disguised in religious raiment, "has ever been characterized by the pharisaism that worships itself." "Rebellion against constituted authority had always infatuated Yankees ever since the days of puritan witch-hunting. From the time of Oliver Cromwell to the time of Abraham Lincoln," New England "had never hesitated to trample on the rights of others in order to effect its own ends."[13] A contemporary critic rejoined that if only descendants of Cavaliers and heirs of Cromwellian Puritanism had materialized on the battlefields, "the Civil War could have been fought under a circus tent."[14]

However absurd such sentiments might appear to Northerners in 1911, the distinction between the followers of the Stuart crown and those in Cromwell's ranks also had its adherents in pre–Civil War New England, at least in antislavery circles. James Redpath, an English-born journalist with abolitionist connections, lumped together the Pilgrims at Plymouth Rock, Oliver Cromwell, and John Brown in Kansas. Brown, Redpath gushed, "was a great admirer of Oliver Cromwell." As happy coincidence or conscious decision would have it, the grizzled abolitionist warrior had planted his armed camp near a town "named Plymouth, in honour of the Puritans."[15] Thomas Carlyle, the English polemicist, had romanticized *Old*

Ironsides in a biography enormously popular on both sides of the Atlantic so that Redpath's readers had some acquaintance with the seventeenth-century English contest. (Ironically, Carlyle's defense of slavery, antidemocratic principles, hatred of industrialism, mistrust of reform, and Scottish contempt for England and its bourgeois culture earned him a special place in Southern intellectual life.)[16]

In contrast to the Southern fire-eating style for inspiring "matchless courage" and "deathless glory" to meet the sectional crisis, *honor* was a term not often used in Garrisonian company. To the abolitionist mind, it connoted aristocracy as well as slavocracy. Championing Yankee withdrawal from slaveholding sin and the United States Constitution which legalized it, Wendell Phillips in 1845 looked forward to the moment when "New England, cutting loose from a blood-stained Union, shall glory in being the house of refuge for the oppressed." The forming of a New England nation would "consecrate anew the soil of the Pilgrims as an asylum" for the African American sufferers of the land. The proclamation of free state independence from tyranny would "make the broken-hearted bondman leap up at the thought of old Massachusetts."[17] Given the racism of the North, the use of such rhetoric and symbols did not, however, reach very far into free state consciousness.

The Cavalier-Roundhead dichotomy of the Stuart era was not as powerful a symbol of sectional difference in the South, however, as a literary reliance on an earlier time. The basic theme was the same: a nostalgic harkening to a prior epoch in Western history, properly enveloped in romance and adventure. The ordinary white Southern farmer did not read Walter Scott's *Ivanhoe* and other historical novels, but the educated class avidly absorbed his work. In the same way that a film today gains a place in popular culture, language, and assumptions, antebellum steamboats, barges, stagecoaches, plantation houses, crossroads hamlets, slaves, and even children were named for characters and places to be found in one Scott tale or another. Southerners worshiped at the Abbotsford shrine because Scott's tales so well confirmed the ideals and virtues about manhood and valor that they already entertained.[18] For instance, Congressman Lawrence Keitt, friend of Preston Brooks, Sumner's assailant, adopted the language of Scott to described his warlike feelings. Keitt was ready, he remarked, to meet the Yankee enemy "with helmet on, with visor down, and lance couched." The war soon to come was for him to be fought on "the field" of honor.[19]

Thus the Scotian references and other romantic allusions did reflect in a fundamental way the moral distance between the two sections. Sometimes it was put in language stripped of historical romanticism but still carried the same message. Republican Justin S. Morrill of Vermont declared in the Senate chamber in December 1860 that we "must accept the truth that there is an 'irrepressible conflict'—between our systems of civilization." As a result, he could see "no compromise short of an entire surrender of our convictions of right and wrong, and I do not propose to make that surrender."[20]

Fantasies and pretentious impulses aside, the struggle for power over national destiny had become as lethal as the prelude to any major war could be. In his famous "Cornerstone Address," 24 March 1861, Alexander Stephens of Georgia sharpened the distinction not only between North and South but also between the Founding Fathers and the disunionist experiment. He argued that, despite guarantees for slavery, the Founding Fathers had erroneously based the Constitution upon "the assumption of the equality of races." Instead, he boasted, "Our New Government is founded upon exactly the opposite ideas; its foundations are laid, its cornerstone rests upon the great truth that the negro is not equal to the white man; that slavery subordination to the superior race, is his natural and moral condition."[21]

Northerners had long considered the federal Union theirs, and not the South's, to be defined and upheld. In 1860, at Leavenworth, Kansas, for instance, Abraham Lincoln applauded the execution of John Brown. The leader of the Harpers Ferry insurrection had been a traitor to his flag and country. Presidential candidate Lincoln vowed, "So, if constitutionally we elect a president, and therefore you undertake to destroy the Union, it will be our duty to deal with you as old John Brown was dealt with. We can only do our duty."[22] Shortly after Lincoln's election, the *Boston Advertiser* argued, "It rests with the Union-loving men of the South itself to hold their section to its duty."[23] Unfortunately, honor had swept the board of any alternatives in that region. Just as there were two interpretations of the Constitution, North and South, so there were different perceptions of these key words in the rhetorical sphere: honor and duty.

Just as slavery presided behind the rhetoric of honor and possible degradation in the South, so, too, was a resentment building in the North behind which was a concern for the growing misapportionment of national power. The Senate remained evenly divided between slave and free states until California's admission in 1850. Nevertheless, we must take the Northern suspicion of a great slave power conspiracy seriously. The North was politically segmented and therefore rendered powerless on key votes in national elections and legislative decisions. By contrast, Southern planters controlled all parties, regardless of their labels. By that means they thwarted Northern interests and forced on the nation unpalatable commitments to slavery and its advance across the country. Antislavery Whig congressman and former president John Quincy Adams had reason for bitterness about the three-fifths clause of Article 1 in the Constitution. The surrender of that point at the Constitutional Convention in 1787 enabled the slaveholders to increase their states' representation in the Congress and electoral college. Without the benefit of the misapportion, Thomas Jefferson would have lost the election of 1800 to John Quincy Adams's father the incumbent president, John Adams. Until Lincoln's success, Southern presidents held the White House for fifty of seventy-two years. The House Speakership belonged to a representative from a slaveholding state for over half the period. Nineteen members of the Supreme Court were Southerners, as opposed to fifteen Northerners—despite the ever-growing discrepancy in population between the two sections. Most sectionally divisive legislation had passed in the South's favor because the divided North had a large contingent of politicians—doughfaces, as they were called—willing to do the South's bidding for the sake of controlling key segments of national power.[24] Is it a wonder that free state resentment against the seeming injustice of the constitutional arrangement would excite notions of a conspiracy? [25]

Convinced that the South was the breeding ground of licentiousness, cruelty, and degeneracy, Northerners—and not abolitionists alone—concluded that the time had come for a different sort of honor to prevail. Carl Schurz, the leading German-American in the Republican camp, reasoned that the nineteenth century was the "age of conscience," not of honor and the restoration of aristocracy. Southerners had to learn how far out of touch with modernity they were.[26] Owen Lovejoy, whose brother had been killed by a proslavery mob, rejoiced that at last the hour had come "to wreak vengeance upon . . . 'the land of slavery.'" The notion of vengeance was not, however, so much a vindication of man over man in Lovejoy's eyes. Rather, the arm of God sanctioned an enforcement of His will "with fire and sword" to "desolate their land."[27] Destructiveness arrived at the same passionate and bloodthirsty destination, but the roads were different. It oversimplifies the complex interaction, but a major element was the exercise of Northern conscience, guilt, and righteousness and the promotion of Southern honor, dread of shame, and demand for vindication.

Feelings, expressed in high-flung hyperbole, thus ran high on both sides. Rhetoric about the valor and sense of manly independence that characterized their Revolutionary forefathers had to be invoked to meet the crisis. Fire-eaters often referred to that glorious past. The Reverend James Henley Thornwell announced, "We are upholding the great principles which our fathers bequeathed us." To perpetuate the liberty for which "Washington bled, and which the heroes of the Revolution achieved" was the standard about which all Carolinians should rally.[28] A popular song of the period put it this way:

> Rebels before,
> Our fathers of yore,
> Rebel's the righteous name
> Washington bore,
> Why, then, be ours the same.

Yankees had a different understanding of the same events. William Cullen Bryant, editor of the *New York Evening Post*, thought it libelous for Southerners to rationalize their treasonous conduct by claiming Revolutionary precedent from the moment when King George lost his American colonies. Instead, the first republicans stood for "rights of man . . . and principles of universal liberty." In February 1861, Abraham Lincoln interpreted the Revolution as a cause "that held out a great promise to all the people of the world for all time to come." It was not purely a national but a universal issue. In the course of their agitation since the 1830s, the abolitionists had often spoken of the hypocrisy of the Founding Fathers, who had permitted slavery under the Constitution. Yet they too found inspiration in recalling that earlier period of honor and valor. At a Boston meeting to celebrate John Brown's "martyrdom," William Lloyd Garrison, declared, "Give me, as a non-resistant, Bunker Hill and Lexington and Concord, rather than the cowardice and servility of a Southern slave plantation."[29]

Despite the various uses to which an understanding of a venerable revolutionary tradition could be put, one might ask if there were rationally sufficient cause for Southern departure. It was a drastic step. Many of the less reckless sort recognized just how dangerous the course was. Throughout the region prominent, exceedingly wealthy, and Whiggish planters and men of business questioned the wisdom of disunion. A Virginia paper prudently advised, "We have the Senate, the House of Representatives and the Supreme Court in our favor, either one of which would of itself be a sufficient protection of our rights." Moreover, presidential appointments were subject to the advice and consent of the Senate, the editor reasoned. As conservative leaders throughout the South recognized, most Yankees would much prefer peace and constitutional regularity to a confrontation over the election. As the fateful year 1860 closed, William Frierson Cooper, a Nashville attorney and later chief justice of the Tennessee Supreme Court (1876–86), wrote his father about his concerns. The president-elect better act quickly "in the right direction very soon." Otherwise, he "will find his realm diminished by the 4th of March nearly one half of its present extent." Like other border slave state Whigs, Cooper viewed the result of the election "as the direst calamity which could befall the human race, and were it not for the hope which I still entertain that we just again come together upon a different basis, should feel like selling out, and investing my means in the British national Debt. Alas for my democratic visions!"[30] Moreover, some politicians of the lower South still hoped that a peaceful settlement was still possible. Alexander Stephens, for instance, begged his fellow Georgians not to "yield to passion [and] take that step" which would only make everyone "demons" ready to cut each other's throats. Nor was the Georgia senator's a lone voice. The wealthy James Henry Hammond, formerly a leader of the South Carolina fire-eating faction, changed his mind. He argued that the best course would be a revival of the old cross-sectional conservative alliance that had held the Union together in the past.[31]

Of course, the upper South was most eager to see a reconciliation of the sections, and some leaders warned against precipitous action. Congressman Robert Hatton of Middle Tennessee, for instance, declared that some fanatics in the South were as unprincipled as those in the North. The "chivalry of the cotton States" offered unrequested "guardianship of both our interests and our honor; and, for the protection of one, and the vindication of the other, they counsel that we put in jeopardy our every material interest, and then—commit suicide!"[32] Under such circumstances, the leaders of the lower South would have had good reason not to plunge into the deep waters and embark on the experiment alone. Any observer with a measure of common sense could see, too, that the Republican administration had to be utterly foolhardy to tamper with property rights in the slave states. Southerners might have realized that the "Black Republican" hold on power was still very fragile. The newly elected president commanded no majority in the popular count. In addition, the Northern Democrats—the so-called doughfaces—were always prepared to serve as watchdogs. Although momentarily divided into quarreling Douglasite, Buchananite, and Southern Rights factions, the Jacksonian party had not abandoned the old principles of limited government, agrarian policies (in particular, low tariffs), and above all, white supremacy. Northern Democrats had little trouble including the slaveholding states in their sense of nationalistic unity.[33]

To understand more clearly the dynamic of Southern secessionism, consider the role that honor played in the initiation of another tragedy—a war that has been almost universally regarded as futile, avoidable, and irrational. Whereas the Civil War resulted in the expansion of freedom, the First World War had the very opposite effect. No leadership in the modern world was as concerned—even obsessed—with the principles of honor than Kaiser Wilhelm II, the German High Command, and the officer corps of the Wehrmacht. That heritage took a populistic and anti-Semitic turn under the Nazi regime. Before the Nazis' rise to power, the upper echelons of the Prussian monarchy had remained aristocratic even as Germany became a modern, industrial state. Even the Wilhelminian middle class enthusiastically took up the practice of dueling. In the armed services, the number of duels fought by members of the middle class was higher than that for aristocratic officers—4.7 for the former and 3.5 for the latter out of a total of 10,000. The bourgeois officers, chiefly in the lower ranks, had to be more sensitive to insult because they lacked social standing. Without lofty pedigrees, they were very likely to be passed over for promotion, and dueling helped to assuage their frustration.[34]

The dueling spirit was easily transformed into an obsession with the glories of battle. According to the German historian Ute Frevert, warmongering in the years before 1914 appealed to the German bourgeoisie because of long-standing discontent with "ever tighter social, political, and economic chains." A member of that social class recalled in 1920, "The war was bound to be a grand, powerful, solemn experience. It seemed to us to be a manly act."[35] Students and faculty members, reserve officers, most of them bourgeois, and the landed gentry applied Germanic thoroughness to the custom. In 1874, Wilhelm I had proclaimed to his military forces: "I expect the entire officer corps of my army that they will regard honor, henceforth as hitherto, as their greatest treasure; to keep it pure and unstained must be the holiest duty of the whole corps, as of the individual." Such a position found expression in the way foreign affairs were supposed to be conducted. Heinrich von Treitsche, the Prussian historian, put the matter clearly: "If the flag of the state is insulted, it is the duty of the State to demand satisfaction, and if satisfaction is not forthcoming, to declare war, however trivial the occasion may appear, for the State must strain every nerve to preserve for itself the respect which it enjoys in the state system."[36]

Southern attitudes were scarcely different from those of the German military class—and the masses who deferred to their judgment. To submit obsequiously to Lincoln's election would lead to untold disasters, a Mississippi newspaper declared. It would eventually mean the loss of self-rule, slave freedom, and, horror of horrors, "the grossest humiliation, to break down the stubborn pride and manliness native to the Southern breast."[37] J. A. Elmore wrote Governor A. B. Moore in November 1860 that he was sure that their fellow Alabamians "never will consent to remain degraded members" of the Union to which they had formerly been "loyal and true." Upon news of Lincoln's election, William S. Earnest from an Alabama mountain county recognized local divisions on the timing of disunion but insisted that "no line divides us on the point of duty and honor." When the hour of decision came, his fellow citizens "will pour like torrents into the army—the best and bravest of men."[38]

The truculent side of honor was not the only version to be voiced in the crisis of the 1860–61. Moderation, prudence, coolness under duress, and self-restraint were long admired and even idealized by the ancient Stoic tradition. The Whig element in the South was more likely than the Democratic to welcome such notions of honor as synonymous with Union loyalty. There were, however, exceptions, most notably Governor Sam Houston of Texas. He remained faithful to the Union until forced out of office in March 1861.[39] In November 1860, incumbent Democratic senator Thomas Clingman of North Carolina—barely renominated against secessionist opposition—argued that the Union could yet be saved. It would, however, be necessary, he told his Northern Senate colleagues, that "if proper guarantees can be obtained . . . sufficient to save our honor and insure our safety," the Southern people would reconsider and remain in the Union.[40]

In Alabama, a classic example of the contest between raw honor and Stoic precept arose when William L. Yancey, the always belligerent secessionist, strongly implied that those advising restraint were unfaithful to Southern interests. He labeled them Tories no less subject to the laws of treason than the Loyalists of the American Revolution had been. At once Robert Jemison of Tuscaloosa leaped to his feet. "Will the gentleman go into those sections of the State and hang all those who are opposed to Secession? Will he hang them by families, by neighborhoods, by counties, by Congressional Districts? Who, sir, will give the bloody order? Is this the spirit of Southern chivalry?" Convinced that the South's material interests and even the safety of slavery lay in preservation of the Union, Jemison appealed to the higher principles of honor, by which interpretation popular clamors should not deter the statesman from following the dictates of sound judgment. He put these concerns for public well-being and peaceful prosperity in terms of honor in order to meet secessionist objections that "principle" should overrule all other considerations, regardless of costs in blood, treasure, and risks to slavery itself. James S. Clarke seconded Jemison's caution. Jemison urged delay until Virginia and Tennessee acted. "Alabama's honor will not be compromised by the determined abandonment of a friend," he promised. Letting the more populous and powerful Southern states lead the way was just common sense, Clarke urged.[41] All the leaders favoring prudence over rash action hotly denied charges of timidity and submission. In reply to a direct attack from a Calhoun County delegate, a member from Tuscaloosa admitted that he belonged to the minority against immediate disunion, "but I do not associate with submissionists! There is not one in our company. We scorn the prospective Black Republican rule as much as the gentleman from Calhoun . . . or any of his friends."[42]

In like manner, Mississippi Unionists tried to show that genuine honor required a course quite different from the one secessionists proposed. A "fictitious chivalry," they said, offered only brave words but perversely claimed to be frightened of mannish Boston bluestockings and pious, effeminate abolitionists. Honor, the Mississippi Unionists explained, demanded that the Gulf states do nothing precipitous: if they seceded at once, they would, in effect, leave their upper South brethren in the clutches of hostile free state majorities.[43] Yet these shows of adherence to the conventions of honor could not outweigh the growing popularity of immediate retort to the free states.

· · · · · · · · ·

What drove the leaders of Southern extremism to their special madness — as the Conditional Unionists saw it? A factor that borders on the speculative is nonetheless worth some exploration. The anger that seemed to prompt a touchiness about the honor of the South and about their own community standing may well have had personal origins — a lifetime of depression and sense of worthlessssness. The most famous example was Edmund Ruffin of Virginia. He is best remembered as the first to fire a gun at the Union enemy in the besieged Fort Sumter to open the war. The honor on that occasion was owing to Ruffin's long antipathy to Northern politicians and abolitionist reformers. Among the very first to advocate secession, he also put his mark on the ending of the conflict when he killed himself, leaving a note attesting to his "unmitigated hatred to . . . the malignant and vile Yankee race."[44]

To explain his death as merely the result of Confederate defeat is to misunderstand the nature of suicide and the depressive mentality that incites it. More personal factors, including the unpredictability of death itself, were involved. Unanticipated and early death had always been a constant presence in the Ruffin clan of Virginia. Edmund Ruffin's father and grandfather were both the sole survivors in their respective families. His mother died in his infancy. None of Ruffin's kinfolk on his mother's side had survived to give the growing lad more information than her name. When his father remarried in 1799, he chose a wife from the Cocke family, whose record of early death matched the roster of his own. But then in 1810, when young Ruffin, sixteen, was attending William and Mary College, his father died.

Many in the phalanx of secessionism were cursed with parental losses. The resulting grief and turmoil in their young lives may well have unleashed a fury and sense of betrayal that found voice in partisan secessionism. At age four Nathaniel Beverley Tucker, Ruffin's comrade in arms in the struggle against the North, lost his mother and thereafter a succession of brothers and sisters before he was thirteen. Tucker published *The Partisan Leader* (1836) in the style of Walter Scott, a fiction predicting the coming of a civil war in 1849 and claiming honor and victory for the seceding Deep South states.

Many of the South's leading politicians were likewise figures of fury and melancholy (the two temperaments being psychologically connected). Jefferson Davis had bouts of severe depression, migraines, and other afflictions. Having lost his stern and distant father when a teenager, he never reconciled himself to the old man's death, about which he both grieved and took satisfaction. Thanks to his own haste in the summer of 1841 in installing his first wife, "Knoxie" Taylor, at Hurricane, his pestilent Mississippi plantation, she died from malaria within less than three months of their wedding. Davis knew that he was responsible. According to his most recent biographer, Davis repressed outward signs of unhappiness, "but the walls he erected to contain his grief in the first months and years after Sarah's death soon imprisoned other emotions as well." To observers he seemed thereafter much older than his years. Davis's reclusiveness during the Civil War in Richmond became notorious.[45] Alexander Stephens, George McDuffie, Robert Toombs, Louis T. Wigfall, William Lowndes Yancey, and Albert Gallatin Brown all had problems with episodic melancholy. William Gilmore Simms, the South Carolinian novelist and quondam politician, suffered from a deep sense of inadequacy and frustration that his outpouring of novels, poems, sketches, edited works, and correspondence seemed to belie. Left by an absconding widowered father in the hands of the boy's Charleston grandmother, Simms had reason for unreconciled mourning that he partly repressed in a workaholic frenzy. Like Wigfall and others of similar temperament, he immersed himself in secession politics. After the election Simms wrote his friend William Porcher Miles, "I am . . . like a bear with a sore head, & chained to the stake. I chafe, and roar and rage, but can do nothing. Do not be rash, but, do not let this old city forget her *prestige*. Charleston is worth all New England."[46]

Often personal distress combined with a hothouse environment to create a special wretchedness. Antebellum Southern society produced more men of sensitivity, intelligence, and education than positions of trust and honor for them to occupy. In antebellum Charleston, Michael O'Brien observes, for instance, that "estrangement" was unavoidable. There men "prized honor and male friendship but faced politically divisive, volatile, and whirling tensions, alienation that cut to the marrow was everywhere." Only a few like Ruffin killed themselves. Some—Wigfall, McDuffie, Prentiss, Yancey, and Hammond, for example—engaged in duels, which could be called a self-willed dalliance with mortality. Most others nursed their hurt feelings although presenting the public with outward self-possession in behalf of nullification, secession, or proslavery advocacy.[47]

The role of depression in the political maelstrom deserves more elaboration than can be offered here. The energy dispensed in forwarding any ideological goal in the Civil War period, however, may stem from psychological causes that must be considered part of the cultural climate. Certainly, Southern fire-eaters like Simms, the always seething James Henry Hammond, and the dueling, bibulous Wigfall, for instance, had no monopoly on chronic rather than just common periods of unhappiness. William T. Sherman, Ulysses Grant, Abraham Lincoln, and Charles Sumner, to name only a few, also had problems of this nature, but only for Sumner can it be said that his projection of internal despair approached the strains that John Brown had exhibited in his tempestuous life. About Lincoln it was said that "melancholy dripped from him as he walked." The problem began in his early life. No doubt the condition was both genetic and environmental—loss of his mother when he was very young.[48]

The parallel with some leaders on the German side of the Great War suggests that honor and pessimistic worry had some interconnection as the match to set afire the powder of war. General Helmuth von Moltke and the kaiser's war minister von Falkenhayn, Emperor Franz Josef, and his army chief of staff Conrad von Hotzendorff were all very doubtful of the outcome even before the first guns were fired. Conrad fretted that the war aims were unclear. For him as for Moltke, "the war was an expressive rather than an instrumental act, carried out against the odds in order to salvage a declining reputation," writes a perceptive German scholar. "We have to go for all or nothing," Conrad explained to a friend after the assassination of Prince Franz Ferdinand at Sarajevo. Had the war begun a few years earlier he thought it might have succeeded. Now, however, it was a "sheer gamble." Nonetheless, Conrad argued that hostilities had to begin even without good reason. "So ancient a monarchy and so glorious an army cannot be allowed to perish ignominiously," he rationalized. "I see the future black and the eve of my life in shadow." The emperor agreed with his chief of staff that the honor of the Hapsburgs was at stake. If the Austro-Hungarian Empire were "doomed" to die in the flames, "let it at least perish decorously." Later, Conrad mused, "It was the despairing resolve of an aged ruler driven to extremes by the enemies of his real interests."[49]

Honor trumped sober reflection. Its will had to be done. Just as in the Great War at the beginning of the twentieth century, the civil conflict in the United States had to be fought, regardless of the enormous costs in treasure and blood. The result could not be doubted, even the former Conditional Unionists maintained. Nonetheless, if God were to will Confederate defeat, wrote one Louisiana plantation mistress at the start of the conflict, "there will live defiance and resistance to those who would tread us beneath their feet." As mentioned before, she concluded in a depressive tone, "When the land is conquered it will be time for us to die."[50]

· · · · · · · ·

In contrast to the troubled thoughts of the more perceptive Southern leaders, the Northerners, apart from die-hard Peace Democrats, had no doubt about the ultimate outcome. Aware of the remarkable economic and demographic strength of the free states in the 1850s, some Republican Party leaders were led to be as materialistic as Southerners thought all Yankees were. Such individuals objected to the South less on moral than economic grounds—slaveholders' antipathy toward giving "Protection to domestic industry, Rivers and Harbors" and toward developing the nation's economy, as Hamilton Fish of New York put it. Another New York politician, E. Pershine Smith, wrote to a friend: "The first thing is to destroy the Southern domination" in the upcoming 1860 election. Once done, then "we shall begin to think of our bread and butter—and not before." But in final analysis, a principle not of capitalism but of power dominated Republican thinking, a conviction related to honor itself. To let the South depart without a fight would be an eternal disgrace, a supineness unworthy of a free people, at least as Republican propagandists insisted in the late 1850s. With other parties subservient to the great slave power, they said, "upon no organization, except the Republican party, can the country rely for successful resistance [to the] insolent and aggressive" demands of the South.[51]

Some of the most anti-Southern Unionists were Democrats who became associated, as members or allies, with the Republican cause. Unionist Democrats like Frank Blair and Montgomery Blair, border state politicians, and Gideon Welles of Connecticut (still a Democrat when he joined Lincoln's cabinet) worshiped at Jackson's shrine. They were the ones most concerned about national honor and sectional treason. Like Tennessee's Unionist senator Andrew Johnson, such politicians were scarcely racial egalitarians, but they were convinced that the slaveholders had insulted the Union flag and should be taught respect and submission. As one former Democrat from Illinois thundered, "There is not a man [in the state] who will not raise his hand and swear to eternal God" that the Union would be maintained, "if our arms can save it." Even the most conservative and Whiggish members of the new sectional party referred at times to the choice between glorious self-defense and base subservience to slave power demonism. For instance, an old-line Whig like Kentucky-born Orville H. Browning, a Quincy, Illinois, lawyer, could ring the changes on honor. At a Lincoln campaign rally in 1860, he pledged himself to stay in the Union and fight "for my right—if necessary with the sword. . . . Here I am within it, and here I mean to stand and die . . . defy[ing] all power on earth to expel me."[52]

Although the words and stylized presentation were the same as that which a prosecession politician might use in speaking of his own self-sacrifice, Browning's honor did not carry the moral freight that the Southern version did. Few Yankees would feel compelled to settle ideological differences on a dueling field. In a parallel to the description of Northern ideals of dignity, the free state citizen saw defense of honor as a last resort rather than a first consideration. Consequently, in Northern political discourse one finds less frequent use of such terms of honor as *fame, glory, shame, infamy,* and *insult* than in the South.

Behind these differences lay the bourgeois and highly institutionalized nature of Yankee culture. In the rapidly modernizing North, the strength of other institutions lessened personal dependency on family and community opinion, especially in the cities, which absorbed a large share of the Northern population. Even the few Southern cities that existed were more rural in culture and milieu than were their Yankee counterparts. As a result, a more parochial view of Unionism prevailed, one that reflected the primacy of race and rurality in Southern values. In contrast to Orville Browning's view of national allegiance, Alexander Stephens in 1845, for instance, offered a rather typical ranking of Southern fealties: "I have a patriotism that embraces, I trust, all parts of the Union." Yet, he continued, "The South is my home—my fatherland. . . . These are my hopes and prospects . . . her fate is my fate, and her destiny my destiny."[53]

The South was not without Northern friends, however, and the transsectional racism, which had also long held the Democratic Party together, involved a common understanding of honor. Of all the groups in the heterogeneous North, the party was by far the most comfortable with the Southern view of honor as a rationale for white supremacy, sectional parity, and anticentralism. The Douglas wing of the party, however, placed limits on its commitment to the Southern persuasion when Stephen Douglas broke with Buchanan over Kansas. Because of administration bungling and pro-Southern bias, and even the expedient of ballot fraud, the territory obtained a proslavery constitution. Douglas Democrats discovered that their honor no longer could permit further concessions to slavery's expansion. In December 1857, the Illinois Democrat said, "If this [Kansas proslavery] constitution is to be forced down our throats, in violation of the fundamental principle of free government, under a mode of submission that is a mockery and insult, I will resist it to the last."[54]

At the disastrous Democratic convention in Charleston in late April and early May 1860, the issue of honor figured in the controversy between the Douglas partisans and William L. Yancey and his followers. The fire-eaters demanded that free state Democrats repudiate "popular sovereignty," agree to Kansas statehood under the proslavery constitution, and submit to the expansion of slavery in the territories. According to Yancey, a soundness on the "goose question," as proslaveryites in Kansas called it, would cost the Northern party nothing—morally or politically. Outraged, George Pugh of Ohio replied, "You endeavor to bow us down into the dust. Gentlemen, you mistake us—you mistake us." He would not submit to dishonor. Pugh was not the only Northern delegate to appeal to the manly code: a Michigan Douglasite declared that if asked to "yield up a principle of honor," his retort would be "never, never, never." After the firing on Fort Sumter, Democrats of this persuasion preferred war to passivity. As Jean Baker has noted, they fought to "restore the object of their allegiance—the Union," an identification of honor with an all-embracing nationalism as they had always understood it but which so many of their Southern brethren had begun to repudiate in the 1850s.[55]

Within the Republican Party as the postelection crisis deepened, some were urging a toning down of the hot-eyed rhetoric. But others took a belligerent stand against the threat of secession. Even that old antiabolitionist and sometime duelist James Watson Webb, acerbic editor of the *New York Courier and Enquirer*, broke ranks from his increasingly moderate-minded patron, Senator William H. Seward. Webb vowed his readiness to swat any disunionist who came within range.[56]

Behind the rhetoric, particularly in the Deep South, was its grounding in the local political setting. Family heritage and local loyalties were exceedingly important components. According to Robert Kenzer, it was not "ideological differences between the two parties," Whig and Democrat, in Orange County, North Carolina, a representative mixed farming district, that accounted for the bitter partisanship. "Rather, the parties were shaped by the county's neighborhood structure and ties of kinship." In antebellum Georgia up-country politics, Steven Hahn has discovered, the same situation existed—a close-knit pattern of grocery store and family relationships. According to a new study of Mississippi secession politics, "Like hunting parties and other male rituals, politics was basically a neighborhood exercise, reflecting Mississippians' confidence in personal, rather than institutional relationships." Sons followed patriarchal patterns, perhaps without need for much consultation, in determining their partisan loyalties. One Mississippian recalled, "I found myself a democrat without being able to explain why. . . . My uncle was a staunch Jackson man and I adopted his preferences without examination."[57]

With just a few families and their relations dominating a local district's voting habits, pride of family and loyalty to friends helped to hold most voters to the same party, election after election. In addition, a process or secret balloting did not exist. In rural areas most especially, everyone *knew* each other's preferences. The powerful men influenced the votes of the common whites. The latter respected their leaders for their wealth, skills of command, and democratic manners. Certainly the yeomen did not intend their loyalty to be mistaken for meek obedience, but they did vote for men of wealth and education.

Obligations of blood, past favors, present indebtedness, and other commitments cemented political allegiances. Besides, just being neighbors was sufficient for all to vote the same way as a way of keeping alive a consensus on all matters, political and otherwise. In a neighboring, rival township, the competing party might have held the preference, again with few straying from the fold. Elections were hotly contested. The language used was highly volatile because personal and group honor, rather than simply a partisan policy, was often at stake. Fierce family and individual rivalries sometimes led to challenges and even duels. By the standards of this system, the Yankees had changed the rules, introducing ideological and moral questions, uncertainties, and fears into a family-based, honor-bound exercise.[58]

The employment of honor in its linguistic and political character helped immeasurably to reinforce the social order. The grandiloquent phrase, the references to manliness, bravery, nobility, and resolute action, for example, were scarcely reserved for politics alone. Yet political correspondence, public letters, editorials, and speeches all employed a tone that sounded bombastic and overblown to the unaccustomed, perhaps Northern ear. By and large, it was the rhetoric of gentlemen. Lesser folk often admired it. The oratorical flourish sanctified the existing social system. Of course, the Shakespearean and classical phrases were welcome at the campaign rally so long as they were familiar to the listeners. However exaggerated its character, the political vocabulary spoke to the most visceral feelings that Southerners possessed.

Given the character of Southern politics and its ethical framework, the road to secession does not seem so puzzling. In responding to Northern criticism and self-assertiveness, the South's defenders had to emphasize vindication and vengeance. As a result, the purpose of so much Southern rhetoric in the prewar period was to impugn the motives and policies of the abolitionists in and out of Congress. Any number of examples might be cited to show how Southern anguish at criticism reflected the psychological processes of injured pride. Abolitionists like Garrison thought that their sermons against slavery would force the slaveholder to listen to his conscience, but the effort was futile. Instead, antislavery polemics evoked feelings, not of guilt but of anger and indignation. As John S. Preston, a South Carolina proslavery advocate, declared, "There is not a Christian man, a slaveholder [in the South], who does not feel in his inmost heart as a Christian" that his fellow churchmen of the North have spilled "the last blood of sympathy [on the point of the] sword of the church. . . . They set the lamb of God between our seed and their seed."[59]

Preston Brooks's assault on Charles Sumner in May 1856 helps to illustrate the means for Southern vindication. What outraged Brooks and his accomplice Lawrence Keitt, the South Carolina congressman, was the Massachusetts senator's tasteless vilification of Senator Andrew Pickens Butler during the "Bleeding Kansas" speech. Butler was the first cousin of Brooks's father. Sumner had spoken of his kinsman in blatantly sexual terms. It was a breach of courtesy as well as of ordinary decency by the standards of an age in which reticence on sex was universally observed in educated circles. Butler, he announced, "had chosen a mistress to whom he has made his vows, and who, though ugly to others, is always lovely to him; though polluted in the sight of the world is chaste in his sight . . . the harlot Slavery." He also struck out at Stephen Douglas, calling him "the squire of Slavery, its very Sancho Panza." Douglas retorted under his breath, "That damn fool will get himself killed by some other damn fool." [60] On the second day of delivering his speech, Sumner again returned to the deficiencies of aged Senator Butler, a victim of a disabling stroke. The young Massachusetts senator accused his aging colleague from South Carolina of wandering from subjects on the floor, "with incoherent phrases" issuing from "the loose expectoration of his speech. . . . He cannot open his mouth, but out there flies a blunder." [61] In addition, Sumner had dwelled on the alleged ineffectualness, even cowardice, of South Carolina troops during the American Revolution. Finally, his speech was sprinkled with such epithets to describe the Kansas proslavery element as "Thugs," "Assassins," "murderous robbers," and "hirelings, picked from the drunken spew and vomit of an uneasy civilization." However accurate his characterization, the language was as raw as that of William Lloyd Garrison's equally graphic — and, to many, offensive — rhetoric in the abolitionist *Liberator*.[62]

By the rules of honor, Brooks was required to respond in an appropriately violent fashion. Hailing from the notoriously violent Ninety-Six District of South Carolina, the congressman was proud that a visitor "will read upon the tombstones epitaphs which would reproach him for [any] tame and ignominious submission to wrong and to insult." [63] Of course, he was under no obligation to call for a duel with Sumner because the field of honor was reserved solely for social and moral peers.

The two antagonists were almost caricatures of their sections' image of each other — Sumner, the self-righteous, priggish, intellectual Puritan zealot and Brooks the epitome of Southern savagery and violence. Indeed, Brooks was no stranger to riotous impulses. As a young student, he had been expelled from South Carolina College. Under the impression that his brother had been imprisoned and maltreated, he stormed the Columbia jailhouse, waving two pistols. The police subdued him, and the college authorities, fed up with his previous escapades, denied him his degree. His temper flared whenever he thought "a loved or cherished relative," as one newsman put it, was under attack.

Various duels and near duels in the 1840s involved the Edgefield families of Wigfalls, Brookses, Hammonds, and Richardsons—rivals for power in town affairs and South Carolina's gubernatorial politics. The Mexican War provided the young hothead with a grand chance to prove his mettle. At a farewell banquet, Edgefield's elite toasted "Capt. P. S. Brooks, in whose veins runs the blood of our revolutionary sires. We believe he will lead 'The 96 Boys' wherever duty, honor, or patriotism require." The typhoid he contracted almost upon arrival on Mexican soil so depressed him that he feared loss of face "in the eyes of his family, his community, his state, and his nation." Still worse, his brother Whitfield died in battle. Preston insisted on letters from companions to indicate that he had not feigned illness to escape the rigors and dangers of war. As soon as possible he returned and longed for a major engagement because, he said, "I know that to fight well is not always evidence of courage, still the reputation given by being in battle is valuable." William Gilmore Simms penned the appropriate sentiments to memorialize Preston's dead brother Whitfield:

> "Tell me," cried the youth when dying,
> "Tell me that I do not shame
> That dear land that gave me being,
> And my father's honored name;
> Say my General, that in falling,
> I was seeking still the strife.
> Through the tempest unappalling,
> For their honor staking life."

In the poem Whitfield dies believing that "my sire and country cherish / Proudest memories of their son."[64]

A mixture of honor and despair, hopes of glory and fears of anonymity or ridicule, and a deeply religious sensibility lay in the background of Brooks's assault. Before that event, Brooks was often on his knees praying to God to relieve him from his conviction of sin. "I hope yet to be known to the wicked of the world as an avowed and constant and humble Christian." But he recognized in his prayers that "the sinfulness of my nature and the villainy of humanity" would lead him into devilish temptations. Grace played its part in Brooks's life. He never saw any contradiction between his role in vindicating by assault "the insulting language used in reference to my State and absent relative." After all, Sumner had offended the sacredness of the Brooks's good name, as Congressman Keitt informed the House after the event.[65]

Thus the response to the Kansas speech took the form it did in keeping with the nature of the honor code itself. By Southern standards, Sumner fell considerably below the status of a peer in the gentlemanly class. A one-on-one horsewhipping was thought to be much more appropriate. The fire-eater Keitt, Brooks's closest adviser, explained the matter to the House after the event. By the ancient code, he said, "a churl was never touched with the knightly sword; his person was mulcted with the quarter-staff."[66]

The incident points to the sense of degradation that Yankees could feel when faced with Southern aggression. "We all or *nearly* all felt," a Bostonian wrote the wounded Sumner, "that we had been personally maltreated & insulted." According to William Gienapp, the attack on Sumner, perhaps more than the troubles in Kansas, aroused Northern opinion against the South. Even in conservative circles formerly hostile to the Massachusetts senator's course, concerns for Northern self-respect and for free speech were evident.[67] The Northern clergy in particular saw profound moral lessons in Brooks's barbarism and the South's applause for it. As the leader of the Massachusetts Congregational pastors, Henry Dexter, proclaimed, "We see an exhibition of the essentially corrupt and corrupting spirit of slavery, and a new necessity that we, as ministers of the Gospel and lovers of liberty, should gird ourselves to oppose its aggressions and secure its final overthrow."[68] As Sumner became the martyred prophet in the North, so Brooks was transformed into the grand knight of chivalry for which he longed to be known.

For both sides, Brooks's violence heightened an awareness of honor's demands. Sumner received from an admiring New England woman these hot words: "Thank Heaven that in our degenerate days of the Republic — when a decision between pure *right* and *wrong* must be darkened by fraud . . . we have yet one *hero martyr*, who following the footsteps of Christ, would have shed his blood for the truth."[69]

Antislavery attacks stained the reputation by which Southern whites judged their place and power in the world. Such, for instance, was the reason why slaveholders insisted on the right to carry their property into the free territories at will. It was not solely a matter of expanding slavery's boundaries, though that was of course important. No less significant, however, was Southern whites' resentment against any congressional measure that implied the moral inferiority of their region, labor system, or style of life.

Such reflections on Southern reputation were thought vile and humiliating. For example, in late 1846, Robert Toombs, senator from Georgia, took exception to the Wilmot Proviso, which would bar slaveholders from bringing slaves into lands seized from Mexico. Southern whites, he argued, "would be degraded, and unworthy of the name of American freemen, could they consent to remain, for a day or an hour, in a Union where they must stand on ground of inferiority, and be denied the rights and privileges which were extended to all others." Fear for personal losses from antislavery territorial laws did not matter half as much as the symbolism of such anti-Southern measures: its signification of still more dire consequences to come. As Toombs remarked in Congress during the sectional crisis of 1850, the right to enter any territory with slaves involved "political equality, [a status] worth a thousand such Unions as we have, even if they each were a thousand times more valuable than this." The issue was no small matter, in his opinion. He elevated the question of slaveholders' territorial prerogatives to the level of a casus belli, at least to his own satisfaction. "Deprive us of this right," he warned the Senate, and it becomes "your government, not mine. Then I am its enemy, and I will then, if I can, bring my children and my constituents to the altar of liberty, and like Hamilcar, I would swear them eternal hostility to your foul domination."[70] A telling example of Southern violent defensiveness came from a speech of William L. Yancey at the Democratic convention in Charleston in which he vindicated the Southern cause: "Ours is the property invaded; ours are the institutions which are at stake; ours is the peace that is to be destroyed; ours is the honor at stake—the honor of children, the honor of families, of the lives, perhaps, of all—all which rests upon what your course may ultimately make a great heaving volcano of passion and crime." Harboring sentiments like these, Southern leaders had no reason to question the use of violence as the best retort to obloquy. Thus in 1858, Jefferson Davis roused a Democratic rally in New York City against Republican "higher law" politicians such as William H. Seward. "The *traitors* [to the Constitution]," Davis exclaimed, as well as the "*preachers should be tarred and feathered, and whipped by those they have thus instigated.*"[71]

In the South, appeals to average citizens on the basis of community loyalty and honor could be made because "the sovereign people," as Southerners often liked to say, decided for themselves what was honorable and what was not. Racism, white freedom and equality, and honor were not discrete concerns in the Southern mind. They were all an inseparable part of personal and regional self-definition. To be sure, white supremacy, as Ulrich B. Phillips maintained long ago, was the "central theme" of Southern culture. Yet the language for expressing it was largely framed in terms of honor and shame. To put it another way, white liberty was sustainable, it was thought, only on the basis of black slavery. Black freedom, on the other hand, necessarily meant white disgrace because it placed the Southerner on a level with African Americans and Republicans.[72]

The power of popular coercion also intimidated the Unionist delegates to state secession conventions. Nonetheless, the submissionists, as they were dubbed, generally received the worst of this line of reasoning. James L. Alcorn, a Unionist politician and a delta planter with vast holdings, confided to a friend that the belligerence of the secession majority at the state convention had become almost intolerable. "Should we fail to commit ourselves [to secession], it will be charged that we intend to desert the South. . . . The epithet of coward and submissionist will be everywhere applied to us. We shall be scouted by the masses!" He and his Unionist colleagues signed the secession ordinance under duress. Yet they naturally had to claim that their action was as honorable and manly as their previous opposition had been. Both positions, they insisted, served the interests of the community and the glory of their state.[73]

While the lower South Unionists were thoroughly demoralized, the situation in the upper South before the firing on Fort Sumter was much more fluid. During the long secession meetings in Richmond even before the installation of the Republican president, commissioners from the seceded states lobbied and urged Virginia's departure. One and all, they complained of the constant stream of "insults" and "unconstitutional" aggressions emanating from Yankee quarters. The commissioners had to counter the Unionism of the "Northern yeoman" contingent from the counties west of the Blue Ridge, a vociferously anti-Tidewater faction that had many reasons for distrusting the eastern majority on questions of representation, allocation of state funds, and taxes. Hoping to divert attention from Virginia's complicated internal affairs, the commissioners focused on the common bonds of blood which all true Southerners were obliged to acknowledge. Reciting what had become a familiar litany, T. Fulton Anderson from Mississippi reminded the Virginia delegates on 18 February 1861 that the Southern people all shared the heroic heritage of the Revolutionary forefathers. A former Unionist himself, Anderson declared that "the hour has arrived when if the South would maintain her honor, she must take her destiny into her own hands." The people of Mississippi are "like you . . . the descendants of a revolutionary race [that] raised the banner of resistance. . . . They have decided . . . to trust for the safety of their honor and rights only to their own strong arms."[74]

Even more dedicated to the tenets of blood loyalty and honor was the speech of John S. Preston, a noted orator and South Carolina hothead. Perhaps more than any other Southern politician, Preston epitomized the rhetorical manner of ritual speech with its rolling cadences, repetitions, and reliance on the sonority of the long vowel. His purpose was not so much to convince as to confirm agreement on basic principles. Southern political oratory reminded listeners of the social and moral values that the region cherished. Familiar, even venerable ideas were put in forms just novel enough to please, and disturbingly innovative thoughts were seldom presented. For these reasons, Preston concentrated on achieving a cadence that resulted in some loss of coherence:

> Ah, gentlemen of Virginia, where[ever] outside the borders of Virginia the voice of a son of Virginia has spoken in this fight, it too has been renowned, because he spoke in the ancient tongue of his mother. . . . I, one of the humblest of her sons, told my countrymen, that before the spring grass grows long enough to weave one chaplet of victory, they will hear the resounding echo of that voice which has thundered into the hearts of your God-like sires—"give me liberty or give me death!" . . . We therefore believe, that although you centralize a coercing power at Washington, stronger than the Praetorian guard when the eagles of Rome made one coalition of the Gaul, the Briton, and the Ionian. No community of laws, no community of language, of religion, can amalgamate . . . people whose severance is proclaimed by the most rigid requisitions of universal necessity.

Inspired by such sentiments, delegate after delegate rose to announce that the honor of the Old Dominion, the honor of blood kinsmen and friends in the lower South, and their own personal honor demanded union with the departed slave states. Thomas Branch of Petersburg proclaimed, "If we are to be dragged either to the North or to the South, then in name of our ancient fame, by whom would we prefer to be dragged? Would you be dragged by the northern Confederacy, your known haters or would you prefer to be dragged by your brethren of kindred ties and similar interests? . . . I had rather be ruled by King Davis than by Autocrat Lincoln." Others felt the same way. The *Charlottesville Review* declared that Virginians "are humiliated" by not leaving with South Carolina and the rest of the cotton South. "We are conquered. We could not hold up our heads in that Union any more." Fear of being called womanish exerted a powerful force.[75] Yet a note of depression affected more than a few of the latecomers to the cause of disunion. As war clouds gathered, former Whig

Jonathan Worth sighed, "I think the South is committing suicide, but my lot is cast with the South and being unable to manage the ship, I intend to face the breakers manfully and go down with my companions."[76]

Despite these sentiments of defiance mingled with fatal resignation, the actual outbreak of armed hostilities and the new president's mobilization order stirred Virginia, North Carolina, Tennessee, and Arkansas to their fate. Thus, for instance, when Robert E. Lee, along with other former Unionists, swore allegiance to their kinfolk, their state, and their region, they were neither mouthing pieties nor cynically prettifying the rationale for slavery. Southern whites could not separate defense of slaveholding from defense of family and community. The common denominator for both the domestic and the labor institutions was the exigency of romanticized self-respect in both language and action. Ordinary citizens, not just politicians, felt obliged to close ranks behind the Stars and Bars on the fundamental principle of honor, family, and race supremacy, one and indivisible.[77]

CHAPTER NINE

· · · · · · · · · ·

INNOCENCE, WAR, AND HORROR

Forth from its scabbard, pure and bright

Flashed the sword of Lee!

Far in the front of the deadly fight,

High o'er the brave in the cause of Right.

Its stainless sheen, like a beacon light,

Led us to Victory.

—Father Abram J. Ryan, *"The Sword of Lee"*

More than any other human activity war requires the immediacy of aggression, valor, and comradeship. For Southern troops, as for an ancient poet of Crete, strength and courage resided in "my great spear and my sword." For an ability to wield such weapons, Hybrias declared, "I am called the master of slaves."[1] On that basis, determining why Southerners—indeed, soldiers on both sides—fought so hard was an easy matter to resolve. Display of manhood, will to survive, dedication to "cause and comrades," as a recent title puts it, dread of being thought cowardly, loyalty to flag, unit, and commanding officers—these have been the answers. Such an interpretation of mixed personal, collective, and ideological factors still applies. Yet there has been progress in probing the psychological character of men under arms. What had been so simple to explain from the days of the antique wars Hybrias of Crete described to the mid-twentieth century was no longer so. Since the end of the Second World War, battle psychologists have discovered a variety of reactions to warfare. Moreover, wartime—and also postwar—mental breakdowns have received much scientific investigation with impressive results.[2]

Despite these advances, military sociologists and historians overcompartmentalize their findings. Insofar as the Civil War is concerned, such scholars as Gerald Linderman, for instance, claim that Rebels and Yanks volunteered for and remained in service because of strictly personal impulses. He follows the conclusions that Bell Wiley, Bruce Catton, and David Donald had reached some years ago. Catton stressed that "the Civil War soldier usually identified himself first of all with his regiment." Pride in that unit and its record in combat (and not in his division's or brigade's) was uppermost in his thoughts.[3] Donald is even more emphatic: no matter what the Yanks claimed to be fighting for, the Rebel infantryman had "no very clear idea as to what caused the Civil War but very probably would have responded as did ninety-one percent of World War II soldiers who felt 'whatever our wishes in the matter, we have to fight now if we are to survive.'"[4]

In contrast, James M. McPherson and others maintain that ideology played a dominant role.[5] At the start of the conflict, some perhaps had not the vaguest idea of why they enlisted—except a fear of being left behind in a great adventure. Those who lived in states with divided allegiances— Tennessee, Kentucky, Missouri, Maryland, and even Virginia and North Carolina—might have had considerable trouble working out which army to join, which ideology or form of patriotism to follow—the Unionist or the states' rights cause. In recollection, Marcus Woodcock of the Ninth Kentucky Infantry (U.S.A.) remarked on the worries that vexed him in 1861: "Am I going to cast my fortunes with the party that are striving to maintain the true principle[s] of Self Government and National Sovereignty? Am I enlisting in the cause of the aggrieved or the aggressor?" He then recalled posing a question that afflicted most every new recruit: "And am I able to undergo the trials, hardships, privations, and dangers attendant upon the soldier's career?" Few realized ahead of time just how rigorous that testing would be.[6]

Doubtless, the historian could never supply a definitive answer about the foot soldiers' motivations. Besides, Civil War soldiers would have responded to any recorder of their sentiments according to the moment and circumstances of the inquiry. A second issue, no less important than the feelings about partisanship, patriotism, or personal survival, concerns a willingness to kill. It could be called the enigma of military psychology. The issue of whether the average soldier was ready to die in battle requires attention. Equally interesting is the matter of just how committed the common veteran may have been to the unpleasant, indeed tragic, duty of killing, even if the exploration fails to confirm the worst scenario of soldierly misconduct.

It is very likely that Southerners were more ideologically driven than their opposite numbers. One scholar concludes that "bravery and esprit" motivated the Union soldiers to reach victory, but he could detect "no great emotional outpouring" even at the end.[7] The Yanks could go home and resume the old life, but Johnny Reb, as one historian has put it, "was inclined to view defeat as a prelude to utter ruin."[8] The Confederate armies fought chiefly for three aims: first, to avenge Northern calumnies and political aggressions against their society—as these insults were thought to be. A sergeant in the Sixteenth Mississippi wrote his mother in 1862, "I joyfully embrace [war] as a means of repelling a dastardly, plundering, oppressive, and cowardly foe from our homes and borders."[9] Second, they sought to protect their "peculiar" dependence on slavery and, third, to sustain a new government that promised to achieve both the first and second purposes. To create a new nation primarily designed to preserve four billion dollars' worth of property—a hefty sum at that time—sounded crass, almost Yankee-like. Understandably, politicians, clergymen, and even common soldiers preferred to stress the cause of states' rights, liberty, and constitutional independence. "We only fought for our State rights," declared a Rebel veteran, "they for the Union and power."[10]

After Lincoln's order for mobilization in April 1861, residents of border slave states like Virginia coupled their determination for liberty—as white Southerners understood that term—with the imperative to aid their kinspeople in the lower slave states, which had already seceded. Mary Anne Custis, Robert E. Lee's wife, wrote a friend, "My husband has wept tears of blood over their terrible war, but as a man of honor and a Virginian, he must follow the destiny of his State." So far as gentlemen like Lee were concerned, the Commonwealth was synonymous with clan, tribe, family. Lee had written his sister Anne Marshall: "I have not been able to make up my mind to raise my hand against my relatives, my children, my home."[11]

To turn to a less defensive note, Rebels relished the possibility of eternal fame. James M. Williams of Prattville, Alabama, explained to his wife in June 1862, "What a pleasant thing to be a soldier! Rain, mud—want—sickness exposure—danger—death—and oblivion—are his portion! And Glory! Yes it is a glorious thing to be a soldier of the Confederacy—fighting and suffering all that I have named for the cause of liberty—What if he dies unknown and forgotten! Is he not the more surely recorded above in the Glorious Book of Noble Patriots!"[12] In the South, soldiers were likely to show an increased hatred for the enemy, especially when companions fell in the field. When a popular Texas colonel died in an engagement, a sergeant explained that "the men were too much exasperated after the death . . . to take prisoners—they were shot down."[13] Before the Battle of Gettysburg, so furious were the troops invading Chambersburg, Pennsylvania, that a soldier reported with pleasure how Rebels would come to a man's house and demand $500 not to burn it down. Another unit would come up with the same demand. Finally, the owner would run out of money, and his house would be set ablaze. "It was one of the best strokes we have ever inaugurated."[14] Such activities, however, were more common under reverse circumstances on the other side of the Mason-Dixon line.

On a less negative note, later in the war Southern soldiers also showed a greater reliance on religion than was true at the start. In light of Southern churchmanship today, it may seem surprising that the Confederacy did not even supply chaplains to the troops during the first year of the war. Once their presence was approved by the Congress in Richmond, the chaplains received a private's pay and food rations. By contrast, the Lincoln administration followed the policy of the pre–Civil War standing army: chaplains, though few in number, were considered part of the unit to which they were attached. By General Orders 15 and 16 (4 May 1861) colonels of regiments, both regular and volunteer, were commanded to appoint those chaplains selected by vote of the regimental officers. The appointees received the pay of captains of cavalry, about $1,700 a year, a very substantial sum that probably was more than most civilian preachers acquired.[15]

In the Army of Northern Virginia the first revival began in the fall of 1862 after the sobering experience of Antietam. As the fighting continued and the signs of Rebel victory became problematic, the solace of religion in the common ranks grew more significant.[16] The message of Southern evangelicalism stressed "sin, conversion, and salvation through the Atonement." That progression "suited the uncertain circumstances of the battlefield."[17] Officers discovered that religious conviction helped independent-minded fighters to understand the need for discipline and submission to higher authorities.[18]

As a result, the notion of male honor played its part in the religious conversion of the Southern soldier. Whereas women had dominated the antebellum Southern church, in the crucible of war, male virtues had to receive divine sanction. Given the range of biblical approaches to almost every situation, it was not hard to find sources for the masculinizing of the faith and the christianizing of the foot soldier. It was quickly discovered that Christ was the model warrior. Declared an editorial in the *Soldier's*

Visitor, "The old time idea that a good Christian cannot make a good soldier, had been thoroughly exploded." In fact, the better the Christian the more warlike the soldier, rhapsodized the religious editor. Pointing out that the most valorous soldiers in Western history were such devout worshipers as Oliver Cromwell, George Washington, and Stonewall Jackson, a popular article had a mother advise her soldier son, "Piety will not make you effeminate or cowardly." The Christian warrior "has less cause to love life or dread death than other men. In the path of duty he has nothing to fear." As the historian Kurt Berends points out, "For southern males, Christian characteristics often clashed with the old patriarchal honour they had created for themselves. They understood honour, with its emphasis on one's public presentation of self and the establishment of reputation, to be in conflict with the Church's message of spiritual equality, patience, humility and forgiveness."[19]

"There are no atheists in the foxholes" was a cliché some fifty years ago. So it was in the Civil War. A frequent comment in reminiscences and letters home was to this effect: "Death was staring us in the face all the time, a perpetual reminder of the final judgment in the presence of God."[20] The absence of women—most especially the effeminizing effects of that presence—helped men to express themselves openly in such religious terms that they might have avoided in civilian life. But of course, the notion of a divine providence to which the Christian had to submit well suited a land in which conservative principles cast suspicion on most sorts of public reform and moral innovation. Sixty years later, veteran Thomas Duncan of Mississippi had not fathomed why he had survived over fifty battles while his younger brother, a "boy by my side, found swift death in his first battle line. Only the Great Commander of all life knows the secret of this great disparity."[21] To some extent such thoughts could dissipate grief over loss of brothers, cousins, friends, and messmates.

Religious revivals swept through the Southern army. General John B. Gordon of Georgia commented on how they "prepared soldiers for more heroic endurance; lifted them, in a measure, above their sufferings; nerved them for the coming battles; exalted them to a high conception of duty," and "rendered them not insensible to danger, but superior to it." There was no way to separate that sort of inspiration from the traditional one of honor—the sense that defense of country offered the warrior an opportunity for unusual significance. Death in battle conferred an immortality in the eyes of the community just as the "divine blessing" of eternal life in the presence of God was thought to be the reward of religious faith. That dual linkage of grace and honor had always been a part of the warrior ethos, even in non-Christian as well as Christian societies.[22] The Reverend George L. Lee of the Baptist faith in Conecuh County, Alabama, preached to the Percy Walker Rangers before they left for war. "I want you to do noble deeds—deeds that will never be forgotten in time or eternity—deeds that will be published in history, and from the judgment seat of Christ—deeds that will bring glory to God, honor to Christ, happiness to man, confusion to devils, and to all of old Abe's fanatics, and eternal credit and honor to yourselves."[23] A more complete uniting of honor, grace, and vindication in war could scarcely be imagined.

Sometimes religion mingled with the adrenalin rush that often accompanied fierce engagements. At Fredericksburg, a Rebel chaplain reported that some of his mates felt heaven very close "and could hardly suppress their exultant religious shouts amid the loudest roar and din of the conflict."[24] The release of emotions in a revival where all participants were equally excited might well have accounted for the ecstasy the chaplain had noticed. Can the reader imagine that the famous, blood-curdling Rebel yell, pagan in origin and intent, included elements of the revival shout? Yet religious exercises did not always stir the blood to greater deeds. When, for instance, Jefferson Davis proclaimed a fast day for prayer in 1864, all soldiers were ordered to obey, with no work or duties to be carried out from dawn to sunset. At 4 P.M., though, they were at last allowed to eat all their rations for the day at once. "Of course, the 'Fasting' part," wrote Hiram Williams, an Alabama trooper, bitterly, "was the subject of much ridicule by the boys who *fast* every day . . . on Government rations." He added, "Now who has been the most power[ful] and who is the most readily obeyed—the Creator of the World or the President of the Confederacy?"[25] Another unconverted witness of campground piety complained to his wife, "Wherever I go I can never get rid of the Psalm-singers—they are in full blast with a Prayer meeting a few rods off."[26] Even so, the Southern soldiers were more dedicated to worship than their counterparts. President Lincoln himself mused that "rebel soldiers are praying with a great deal more earnestness . . . than our own troops."[27] "If a man ever needed God's help," wrote a Georgia private, "it is in time of battle."[28]

No less important than religion in the shaping of military ideology was that ancient code without which no army can survive: the ethic of honor. For Southerners the concept involved more than its ordinary principles or corollaries—valor, courtesy, duty, loyalty, virtue. It was, in fact, the very foundation of the slaveholding ethic. Writing in his diary, a Johnny Reb in Virginia was convinced that his side would win the war. "We are fighting for our property and homes," he explained, whereas "they, for the flimsy and abstract idea that a Negro is equal to an Anglo American."[29] Honor and racial domination were inseparable concepts. Like the notion of chastity, honor has practically dropped out of our discourse as a worthy ideal. It is occasionally invoked, but its full meaning as a social rather than individual force is seldom understood. As a reminder, it might be well to repeat what honor is. The ethic, writes the anthropologist Julian Pitt-Rivers, "is a sentiment, a manifestation of this sentiment in conduct, and the evaluation of this conduct by others, that is to say, reputation."[30] Honor may be felt within, but it must be presented outwardly, as earlier chapters explain.

For the Confederates, honor embodied the revolutionary heritage of freedom by which they meant the right of community self-governance. It also embraced *laisser asservir*—the white man's right to hold human property and dispose of it as he saw fit.[31] Liberty for the white male required all but absolute power over the dark-skinned races. Otherwise, it was not to be considered fully achieved. Abraham Lincoln had observed, "We all declare for liberty; but in using the same *word*, we do not all mean the same *thing*." For some it signifies a man's right to do as he sees fit with himself or his labor, the president continued, but others "mean for some men to do as they please with other men and the product of other men's labor."[32] Just as honor was posed against shame, so liberty's opposite was slavery, analogies with their own system of labor that Southerners of the eighteenth and nineteenth centuries constantly invoked. Racial bondage did not signify hypocrisy according to the values of white Southerners. Instead, it was the very underpinning of their concept of liberty.

In battle, where honor is the only "law" available, its mandate required fidelity to one's fellow soldiers. To let them down was tantamount to ostracism and contempt. For instance, a wounded color-bearer asked Private William A. Fletcher to take the Fifth Texas regimental flag. Fletcher promptly refused, saying, "I am too cowardly for a flag-bearer to risk myself; and I find the oftener I can load and shoot the better able am I to maintain my honor."[33] A foot soldier in the Twentieth Georgia Regiment spoke for many when he declared, "I had rather dye on the battle field than to disgrace my self & the hole [*sic*] family."[34] That sense of familial pride was an integral part of the ethic.

Whether the Civil War soldier measured courage by his own evaluation or that of others, he believed it to be the first dictum of honor. Cowardice was, of course, its contemptible opposite. These points are obvious, but there are corollaries. Honor could be invoked as a talisman of future triumph. Southerners were likely to say at the close of the war that all had been lost save honor. They meant that, because honor survived, success would yet be theirs. At a memorial service for the Confederate dead, the Reverend William Nelson Pendleton of Lexington, Virginia, in 1869 advised that his listeners should turn from the "gloom of political bondage" and await the moment when honor, "born of truth and baptized in the blood of our brothers, shall outlive the persecutions of a merciless enemy."[35] Cowardice, by contrast, could never be erased, even on grounds that forgiveness and peaceful intention were legitimate, Christian responses. To hide the other cheek is not to turn it, proponents of honor insisted. Less well grasped in our modern age, at least, was the notion that since honor traditionally was attached to blood—the blood of heroes that is inheritable—its shedding assumed a consecrated character. Until recent times, to die in war therefore did more than elicit the gratitude of nation, community, and kindred; it also became the warrior's mark of inextinguishable glory. It was assumed that God would honor that sacrifice. In 1879, the *Philadelphia Press* described a ceremony for a dead Civil War veteran as "a sacred, operatic drama . . . a solemn ritual of the grand Army, which is scarcely inferior to the services of the Church."[36]

Honor could sometimes lead, however, to apparent desertion. W. W. Heartsill of Texas and his companions in W. P. Lane's Rangers were incensed when, after Chickamauga, General Braxton Bragg refused to allow them to rejoin their unit from which they had been separated. As proud volunteers rather than mere conscripts, they felt that they had been "drag[g]ed and cuffed about like the meanest Negro that ever disgraced a southern plantation." Should a "man become a Dog" upon entering the army, Heartsill asked.[37] Such arbitrary action touched the men's honor and also their sense of interdependency and military cohesiveness. As a result, they simply left camp, marched seven hundred miles back to Texas, and then reenlisted in their original command. That undertaking required enormous effort. It also risked the appearance of desertion and thus still greater degradation. Luckily they were mistaken for Rebel prisoners who had recently escaped from a federal boat. Thus, Heartsill reported, they passed along as "perfect heroes."[38]

Heartsill and his fellows placed a high premium on the virtues of unit loyalty. Coupled with the positive hopes for distinction in the eyes of others, however, was the fear of dishonor. While Homeric wrath represented the height of honor in battle, fighters were also acquainted with its very opposite, dishonor. Soldiers witnessed in their campmates a state of lassitude, catatonic gloom, and paralyzed terror that we now call post-traumatic stress disorder. Prolonged exposure to danger, minimal shelter and clothing, poor diet, unclean drinking water, and other miseries might lead to a draining of norepinephrine and adrenalin and to chemical imbalances in the brain. But in ignorance of the medical and psychological causes, such behavior, in the absence of quick recovery, could appear to be chicken-heartedness. Many suffered recurrent nightmares in which whistling balls, booming cannon, and dying friends rekindled the anarchy of battle. Wounded men unable to move often thought of suicide if fire broke out in the meadows or woods. As one veteran recalled, "I saw one man, both whose legs were broken, lying on the ground with his cocked rifle by his side, and his ramrod in his hand . . . I knew he meant to kill himself in case of fire—knew it as surely as though I could read his thoughts."[39]

Dread of dishonor involved the soldiers' women folk. Private James Williams was an Ohioan who had thoroughly adapted himself to his new Alabama homeland in the 1850s. Writing his wife, Lizzie, in Mobile, he remarked, "I glory in war, and I know that you would rather have me now under the sod of Shiloh, than clasp me to your bosom a living coward—for you have told me so."[40] Young men who did not enlist speedily enough might find a petticoat draped ominously over a chair in their quarters. From the very start Southern ladies helped sustain the common principle of honor. For instance, in handing the troops a "talismanic flag," the virginal Sallie O. Smith of Marshall, Texas, addressed the W. P. Lane Rangers in April 1861. "Know that beneath these slender forms which ordinarily your gallantry 'suffers not the winds of Heaven to visit too roughly,'" she declaimed, "there slumbers no indifference to your fame your fortune or your achievements" as you prepare to challenge "menaces of madness and discomfited FANATICISM." Perhaps there was some validity in a propaganda tract that the Loyal Publications Society produced in 1863. The Union author contrasted the relatively calm and steadfast mood of Northern women with the unwomanly truculence of their Rebel counterparts. "The feelings of Northern women are rather deep than violent; their sense of duty is a quiet and constant rather than a headlong or impetuous impulse."[41] The Southern white women had more staying power, however, than that. When, as the war drew to a close, they confronted the ruin around them, they mourned, like Hecuba in Euripides' *Trojan Women,* "So pitiful, so pitiful your shame and lamentation. I shall look no more on the bodies of my sons. No more."[42]

Sometimes women could do little to prevent men from deserting ranks and disgracing themselves and their units. At a hard battle near Winchester, Virginia, in September 1864 General Jubal Early's army momentarily disintegrated. Regiments fell backward like dominoes into the town in complete panic. General Bryan Grimes reported, "The Ladies of Winchester came into the streets and begged them crying bitterly to make a stand for their sakes if not for their own honor." They failed to stop to listen.[43]

Basing his conclusion on such examples of soldierly indifference, Bell I. Wiley in the 1940s and 1950s argued that both Johnny Reb and Billy Yank were hardly at all "concerned with ideological issues." After reading the letters and diaries of 1,076 soldiers, 647 Union and 429 Confederate, James M. McPherson recently discovered a strong sense of ideology that his predecessor had missed entirely. Volunteers were not fighting blindly just to stay alive, McPherson asserts. Both sides understood very well why they were at war. In both warring sections, the Civil War historian explains, participants used the terms *duty* and *honor* freely and sometimes interchangeably. An Alabama cavalryman and former planter explained to his unhappy wife why he had to leave her: "My honor, my duty, your reputation & that of my darling little boy" left him no choice when "our bleeding country needs the services of every man." A Yankee soldier could have echoed these sentiments. Southerners, however, usually placed honor at the forefront of their reasons for repudiating the Union. Northerners were more likely to put their chief faith in duty. For the mid-nineteenth-century Yankee, the term wore Victorian broadcloth and had an institutional demeanor—the upholding of the Constitution and the suppression of disorder. A Union army physician declared, "I know no reason why I should not be subject to duty as any man, as I have had the protection of government all my life." Love of nation, hatred of its enemies, and the imperative to bear arms in defense of the homeland were all bound together. A bachelor farmer from Michigan solemnly advised his sister, "If the union is split up the goverment is distroid and we will be a Rewind [ruined] nation."[44]

Of course, the motives of volunteers ran higher than those of draftees. Throughout the South but especially in North Carolina, opposition to the conscription law of April 1862 was strong, particularly in the western and less slaveholding part of the state. When the law was under consideration, William Holden, editor of the *Raleigh Standard*, warned, "The heel of a domestic despot would bear heavily upon us as a foreign one. This is the people's war, and not a war to be waged by forced levies. If the people will not volunteer in sufficient numbers to carry it on, and to repel the invader, then let them bear the consequences." The honor of the state was about to be violated, Holden maintained, by the tyrannical exactions of the Richmond government.[45]

The application of the two principles of duty and honor changed over the years of war. Of course, so great a clash of arms was bound to change attitudes. According to McPherson, Northern opinions of the war evolved, however, more than those of the Southerners as the war progressed. Increasing contact with fleeing slaves and the system of slavery itself made the idea of abolishing the institution an ever stronger motivating factor in the Union army. At first, most Yankee soldiers sought to reknit the fractured Union. But early in 1862 War Democrats, whose party elevated racism to high principle, were already grumbling in the ranks that the struggle was fast becoming "an abolition war." Many of them delighted in using "insulting langige in regard to the same." From the outset, others were much more zealous to crush slavery. With the publication of the preliminary Emancipation Proclamation in September 1862, they were further encouraged. "Thank God," wrote a pious upstate New Yorker, "the contest is now between Slavery & freedom, & every honest man knows what he is fighting for."[46] Even those who had once despised abolitionism began to alter opinions if only for practical reasons. Almost from the start, "contrabands," as the fugitive slaves were called, spared Union troopers from washing clothes, chopping wood, watering overheated cannon, and other drudgery.

As the war lengthened, the soldiers grew accustomed to the presence and the usefulness of the freed people in their midst. Therefore, when the Lincoln government in 1863 authorized black recruitment, most white troops were reconciled to the addition of 186,000 black soldiers to shorten the war—and prolong, perhaps, their own lives. By that time even Democrats in the federal trenches had become disenchanted with the South's cherished institution. They were marching through a region they had once admired from a distance and, instead of a slaveholding paradise, had found white illiteracy, backwardness, and hostility. "There is scarcely a man in this county (Prince William) who can read and write," a Democratic brigade commander in Virginia wrote his wife in 1863, "another of the results of the peculiar and beautiful system."[47] Duty which had become linked with antislavery aims, McPherson contends, strengthened Union resolve.

In the South, these familiar terms—*duty* and *honor*—both had meanings somewhat different from Northern usage. In *The Structure of Complex Words* (1951), William Empson, the literary critic, points out that simple words like these require the greatest scrutiny. They are deeply embedded in the cultures in which they are used. Linguistic variations are often overlooked in historical accounts. It is an oversight that also signifies a misappreciation of the differences between the regional cultures. Instead, Northern understandings of duty and honor are generally the norms that one finds in scholarship and popular use. We are heirs of Northern victory and the resulting advancement of democracy and racial equity (however flawed it still may be). As a result, the concepts of duty and honor of a century and a half ago conform serviceably to our conventional reading of them. A normative comprehension, however, does not enlighten us about the Southern point of view and its departure from our familiar moral world.

To take *duty*, the less burdened word, first, Northern duty implied patriotism, loyalty to the Constitution, law, and order, defense of the Union, and later the advancement of human freedom. In contrast, Southerners could not endorse such principles. For white Southerners in revolt, duty instead meant self-sacrifice to family, community, race, and region against outside forces of evil and ruin. A Northern and normative reading would have made them traitors sowing disorder. In fact, to ward off that stigma, they often referred to the glory of their Revolutionary forefathers and their own resistance to the new tyrannies that the Republicans were supposed to be greedily imposing. Their position lacked elegance, simplicity, and even accuracy about constitutional law that supported the Union effort—at least as we see it now. Victory alone could justify the rebellion, but history was unkind to the cause.

With regard to *honor*, as James McPherson well points out, manliness in war was invariably linked to that ethic in the parlance of both sides, though in different ways. He observes that Northern recruits tended to internalize the sentiment—they worried how they might react in battle. Yet under grim battle conditions, men might become almost tender in their affections without loss of manliness. They could even risk an appearance of womanish sentimentality. According to Gerald F. Linderman, an admirer of Joshua Chamberlain's bravery and his care for his troops exclaimed, "General, you have the soul of a lion and the heart of a woman."[48]

In another Civil War study, Reid Mitchell points out that Union soldiers joined up with their friends, cousins, and brothers. They served together thereafter. As a result, news of a soldier's bravery or cowardice would soon reach home.[49] Awareness of that circumstance served as an additional reason to fight for comrades. Honor or perhaps dread of dishonor was a major factor in keeping soldiers at the front. The threat of ridicule and reprisal, if failing the unit or tent-mate, was a powerful incentive against straggling or desertion. One candid veteran of the 122d New York explained to his sister how he managed in 1864 to bear the savagery of the Wilderness, Spotsylvania, Cold Harbor, and Petersburg. "I myself am as big a coward as eny could be," but let me die, he swore, "before the coward when all my friends and companions are going forward."[50] Officers felt particularly obliged to live by the bond of comradeship. In Northern units one suspects that honor merged into duty less because of fears of blasted reputation than worry of losing self-respect. In February 1865 General Chamberlain, wounded, explained to solicitous female relatives that he could never turn his back to the battlefield "when other men are marching to the front." "Honor and manliness," he reasoned, required his services.[51]

Most important was the worry that one would lose face in the eyes of comrades. Sometimes even the bravest of men fell victim to fear and fled, if only momentarily. Stephen Crane's *Red Badge of Courage* revealed in a remarkable probing of military psychology just how easy it was to allow anxiety to overcome a sense of duty. Such a reaction was as common on one side of a battle as on the other.[52] Crane writes of his young soldier: "Since he had turned his back upon the fight his fears had been wondrously magnified. Death about to thrust him between the shoulder blades was far more dreadful than death about to smite him between the eyes. . . . The noises of the battlefield were like stones; he believed himself liable to be crushed."[53] And yet, like Crane's "youth," such alleged cowards often returned once again to honorable determination. As the historian Mark Weitz observes, combat prowess was often high on both sides, thanks to much drilling and training. "The Yankees," boasted Private Staughton Dent, C.S.A., "are decidedly afraid of us. They say they never saw such a fight in all their lives—and I do not believe such fighting was ever done before by any troops in the world." According to Weitz, "Obedience under fire signified a well-trained and disciplined army."[54]

If a renewed sense of esprit de corps were insufficient to stoke passions of determination, the threat of ridicule and possibility of reprisal were powerful incentives against straggling or desertion. The epithet "coward" had the sting of a whiplash. A typical example comes from the memoir of Private William Fletcher of Texas. He explained how during the Seven Days' Battle in Virginia, A. N. Vaughn, an old Texas friend, had a heel so sore that he could barely march. Fletcher recalled that he had urged him to report to the medics. Vaughn replied in words to this effect, "Bill, I have unfortunately been sick at each fight and the boys will soon take me to be a coward, and I would prefer death than to be looked upon in that light."[55] Fletcher himself, though, fell victim to a sudden attack of fright, he confessed. Demoralized by a sense of hopelessness at Gettysburg, he "felt we had gotten a good whipping . . . and I was considering which was preferable—disgrace or death." Hiding behind a rock, he fell asleep while still aware that "fear and disgrace" would be his "portion."[56] The respite, however, restored his courage, just as it had for Stephen Crane's young soldier.

Yet some of those who were exposed to severe danger did succumb to fright to the point of disgrace and punishment. Worst of all was defection to the enemy. Private Heartsill and his close friend Watson trekked over to another command after Chickamauga to see a deserter and turncoat executed. "He knelt by the side of his coffin, in front of his grave," and after a prayer by an aged clergyman, "Henry Roberts of the 26th Tennessee paid the penalty of the crime with his life."[57]

It could be said that honor had a very palpable physical or emotional aspect as well. Earlier I mentioned the adrenalin rush or "battle rage" that accompanied loud shouts that arose almost unbidden from the throat. "I always said, if ever I went into a charge, I wouldn't holler," remarked a Rebel private from Mississippi. "But the very first time I fired off my gun, I hollered as loud as I could."[58] The savage spirit bore the men forward, oblivious to the heat or cold, the earth-shaking thuds of shells, the stricken bodies, torn limbs, or groans of dying men around them. It could almost make the sick rise, the lame walk, and the blind see. Indeed, so powerful was the force of this chemical change under stress that wounds sometimes failed to generate pain or fear. Private Philip F. Brown, of Parham's Brigade in the Twelfth Virginia, wrote when the federals were a short distance away during the Antietam campaign, "I was shot in the left arm, about three inches below the elbow . . . but I felt no more pain than if a brush had hit me, but the blood trickling to finger tips and the . . . inability to move the arm, made me realize that it was broken." Brown was lucky. He stumbled into a shed where three federals were taking their ease in the midst of battle and drinking fresh cider. To revive their captive from a fainting spell, they offered him some of the brew.[59]

Likewise, battle excitement might even overcome grief for a comrade's death. Marcus Woodcock of the Kentucky First Infantry, a federal unit, remembered that he and James I. Tooley, who lay on the ground shot through the body, had been chatting only minutes beforehand. While watching Tooley's death throes, Woodcock reacted with the thought, thank God it was he, not I. Candidly he observed, "I felt *good*." Woodcock's feelings of relief, joy, and even a sense of power over fate had a very natural basis. Tooley and the other "suffering companions that were lying around" had helped to make possible the great victory in which the Kentuckian so manically was rejoicing.[60]

For the common soldiers like Woodcock, warfare was not an occupation but almost an obsession. A writer from his home state put it especially vividly in a Louisville newspaper in June 1864: "If the war continues four years longer, it seems to me those who escape death from bullets or pestilence must die of excitement, for there you see nothing but war. You eat war; you hear war; you talk nothing but war; and when you retire to your bed you dream of war. You wake tired of war but the despot has you by the throat, with a thousand bayonets bristling around you, and you must fight or do worse."[61]

Honor played its role on the field of battle, but it also shaped the Southern rationale for the war itself. According to the social scientists Richard Nisbett and Dov Cohen, the dishonor of an insult even today "is a much more serious matter to the southerner than to the northerner . . . because an insult makes the affronted southerner feel diminished." The result is a higher ratio of physical violence and even homicide in that region than elsewhere in the nation. White male Southerners, they find today, are nearly twice as likely to kill during an argument than white male non-Southerners are.[62] Such men knew how to hate. Private James Williams echoed a common sentiment when he announced after the battle of Shiloh, "I can't believe that Southern born men will ever submit to the degrading yoke of a hated abolition master."[63] General Francis Barlow, a New England Puritan of the old school, gazing at some Rebel prisoners at Cold Harbor, remarked on their "constancy, endurance, and discipline. . . . Their long grey lines . . . their lank, emaciated forms and pale, cadaverous faces made them seem like an army of phantoms. . . . They were terrible . . . and fearful from their fierce hate."[64] That bitterness and despair which Barlow detected in their dour faces had rendered men like these reckless of life and held them in ferocious bondage against the stigma of defeat.

One factor that cannot be ignored was the role of deep-seated racism in the Rebel sense of urgency to win national independence. With few exceptions the average white male Southerner could not imagine life without bondspeople fully under control—to give labor and deference to their owners and the prestige of the white skin to those without human property. Early in the hostilities Southerners often stressed the horror of white degradation if the Black Republicans had their way. "Better, far better! Endure all the horrors of civil war than to see the dusky sons of Ham leading the fair daughters of the South to the altar," fumed one of the soldiers at the front. In his own mind, the fighter was not exaggerating, so deep was the sense of possible stigmatization throughout the South. We are disturbed by the intensity of Southern white reaction to the prospect of what they called "mongrelization." At that time, however, the stain of black blood signified familial ruination and disgrace as well as blasted personal and group identity.

Confederates were particularly ruthless about Union black troops. They were convinced that Rebel honor was at jeopardy by their very use in warfare against a race of whites. In 1862 President Jefferson Davis signaled Southern indignation by having four captured black Union soldiers executed. General P. G. T. Beauregard was so incensed by Lincoln's official Emancipation Proclamation of 1 January 1863 that he urged the garroting of all Union prisoners, white or black, as abolitionist incendiaries. When the federal government refused to exchange prisoners until the Rebels returned captured black soldiers alive, a Rebel officer rejoiced. The army in Virginia, he wrote, "will not take negro prisoners." The policy was wholly justified because, "if we lose everything else," it would enable the Confederates to "preserve our honor." In April 1864 at Fort Pillow, a lieutenant tried to halt an indiscriminate slaughter of black prisoners, but General Nathan Bedford Forrest arrived and at once had the unarmed men "shot down like dogs and the carnage continued." Of course, Northern troops committed atrocities, too. On the whole, however, they did not consider the shooting of unarmed prisoners justifiable as a means to uphold the code of honor and racial superiority.

. . . .

For all the boastful tendencies, there was still the painful fact of a psychological downside to war. New findings about battle culture, as it were, cast some doubt on old assumptions and are worthy of consideration if not total acceptance. We should not blame the Confederate infantryman so much as the very nature of warfare with firearms. Hollywood and popular fiction tell us otherwise, but killing is a messy business. Contrarily, Grady McWhiney and others argue that "attack or die" was the Southern watchword. The almost disorganized mass assault, McWhiney proposed, was a vestige of the region's violent Celtic heritage. It included the famous blood-curdling Rebel yell inherited from Scotland. Men could be as easily outmaneuvered by chest-thumping bravado as by a canister explosion into the ranks. In the Wilderness campaign, both sides tried the histrionic tactic. "The yellers could not be seen," reports a military historian. "A company could make itself sound like a regiment if it shouted loud enough. Men spoke later of various units on both sides being 'yelled' out of their positions."[65]

Negotiating through the maze of contrary opinions and even verifiable but contradictory facts of warfare has complicated our understanding of battlefield psychology. The military historian Paddy Griffith, for instance, quarrels with the long-standing view that soldiers on both sides fought effectively in a consistent fashion. He reaches the conclusion that, as the war lengthened, troops in blue and gray became disillusioned with the use of shock tactics, by which he means a quick, open charge. The advancing troopers had to trust that even if the defenders had stout breastworks, they would be overcome by the surprise and break ranks. Posturing and loud bravado to scatter the enemy was much to be preferred over actually killing the adversary. That tactic, though, was bound to work best against fresh and untrained troops, not grizzled veterans. As a result, it was best to be prudent. Griffith argues that by 1865 soldiers were firing at greater distances than at the start. Neither side wasted much ammunition or time on practice firing, Griffith proposes. Target shooting was not encouraged because ammunition was too precious, especially on the Southern side. In fact, another historian finds that "it is far more common to read of massed inter-brigade snowball fights than of live firing" in unit competition.[66]

Civil War soldiers of North and South had been drilled as well as any citizen army was. They were not so well instructed, however, in the art of marksmanship. Because of this undertraining, it took stalwart leadership to convince the experienced foot soldier that he would better survive after ten minutes of fast firing and speedy advance than if he and his comrades moved cautiously forward for an hour or more. The latter tactic, which was the more likely in most engagements, was called the "firepower" technique. Nonetheless, Griffith asserts that "regardless of whether they favored the 'firepower' or the 'shock' theories of tactics," ranges of effective firing "meant something less than 150 yards, and sometimes as little as six feet." As a result, battles often ended indecisively. Both sides, Griffith contends, "had very definitely lost a taste for recklessness."[67] But aggravated prudence, as we might call it, was more damaging for the losing side — the Rebels.

In addition, there is the natural instinct not to kill even with the best means available because close proximity breeds a sense of familiarity. According to David Grossman, another historian to question soldierly competence, "The resistance to the close-range killing of one's own species is so great that it is often sufficient to overcome the cumulative influences of the instinct for self-preservation, the coercive forces of leadership, the expectancy of peers, and the obligation to preserve the lives of comrades."[68] To take another human being's life is, in a sense, a denial of one's own humanity. Thomas Hardy's poem "The Man He Killed" helps to explain—even though the outcome is lethal:

> Had he and I but met
> By some old ancient inn,
> We should have sat us down to wet
> Right many a nipperkin!
>
> But ranged as infantry,
> And staring face to face,
> I shot him as he at me,
> And killed him in his place.
>
> . . . .
>
> Yes; quaint and curious war is!
> You shoot a fellow down
> You'd treat if met where any bar is,
> Or help to half-a-crown.[69]

As Hardy's verses suggest, much campground instruction would have to be summoned to overcome the inhibition these historians insist on. A lack of thorough training in the Civil War on both sides, however, was evident in this fact: firing on command, according to Prussian discipline, was seldom seen in the Civil War. At Antietam Corporal Berry G. Benson of Gregg's Brigade of the First South Carolina noted an unusual maneuver. Finding a disordered Yankee group huddled in an exposed position, "we poured volley after volley, doubtless with terrible execution. I say volleys, and here was the only time in battle I now remember firing to be done by command. Maj. Alston many times gave the command, 'Right wing—ready—aim—fire—Load! Left wing—ready aim—fire!—Load!' with splendid effect, for the line obeyed as a drill."[70] By contrast, in European armies firing on signal was a standard tactic.

Throughout the Civil War the range of the musket was really at most no more than two hundred yards. Admittedly musketry was little advanced over the Napoleonic era, though effective ranges had increased a little. Veteran soldiers, firing at least one to five shots per minute, should have been able to kill hundreds of advancing troopers. They did not. If they fired at all, they aimed above the enemy's head.

Both sides had equally bad marksmen. At Antietam, Private Alexander

Hunter of Kemper's Brigade in the Seventeenth Virginia reported that the Rebel ranks were thinned by only three or four men because of the "fire of the enemy being too high."[71] Likewise, William Fletcher recalled that at Chickamauga at his part of the front, "I knew they were doing but little harm as their bullets were flying high."[72] Frank Wilkeson, a Union private, reported at the battle of the Wilderness that a soldier with an ugly gash on his forehead remarked on an unfamiliar phenomenon. The wounded Federal said, "The Confederates are shooting to kill this time. Few of their balls strike the trees higher than ten feet from the ground." As a result of their newfound accuracy, however, he concluded that nearly all the Union batteries had been silenced.[73]

At Petersburg, the Rebel lines, such as they were, were filled with new militiamen, untried in battle. The Union soldier Wilkeson remarked, "At sixty feet in front of the captured works I saw pine trees which had been struck with Confederate bullets thirty feet above the ground. This told, better than words, the nervous condition of the men who pretended to defend the line."[74] Pointing a barrel only a few inches upward is enough to assure that projectiles fly over the head of the enemy. To introduce a modern example of the same problem, in Vietnam it took fifty thousand rounds to kill one Viet Cong. Likewise, Brigadier General Samuel Lyman Marshall was astonished to discover from his men in the Second World War that out of one hundred men on a front line an average of only fifteen to twenty actually fired their guns. Civilized behavior interfered with the aggressions learned in basic training. "The fear of aggression has been expressed to [the ordinary foot soldier] so strongly and so deeply," Marshall contended, "that it is part of the normal man's emotional makeup. It stays his trigger finger even though he is hardly aware that it is a restraint upon him." The general argued that less than 1 percent of the American fighter pilots in the Second World War accounted for nearly 40 percent of all enemy aircraft shot down. Most generals of the Second World War and Vietnam declare his ideas utter nonsense.[75]

Indeed, like Paddy Griffith and Dave Grossman, Marshall represents an extreme position on the competence of the average soldier. By no means can the opinions of all three be taken at face value.[76] For one thing, the technology of military hardware—rifling of muskets and the use of minié-balls, for instance—had advanced dramatically by mid-century. New weaponry forced armies to lengthen their distance from each other, widening the spaces between soldiers in combat, and made more painful and doubtful the deployment of shock tactics.[77] Harold P. Leinbaugh, John D. Campbell, and Robert Spiller persuasively challenge Marshall's findings, and, like the general officers they interviewed, agree that the Marshall theory simply does not work. With bodies strewn over the disputed terrain, most everybody had to be doing something effectual or warfare would have been a bloodless game. Nor were the dead solely victims of an improved artillery capacity. Most died from musketry and not from bayonet up close or cannon from afar. Although potent against frontal assaults like General George Pickett's futile charge at Gettysburg, the big guns sometimes did little more than blow holes in the ground; the projectiles had crude and often defective detonators.[78]

A certain degree of reluctance to fire might be attributed to civilized man's inhibitions, as Marshall conjectured. After all, one of the most common impulses for effective fighting was not bravery as such but fear of lost esteem—dread of shame. The French infantry officer Ardant Du Picq put it this way at the close of the nineteenth century: "We animate with passion, a violent desire for independence, religious fanaticism, national pride, a love of glory. A madness for possession." Nonetheless, he continued, what mattered most was the surveillance of others over an individual soldier's behavior in combat.[79] When there is no place on the battlefield to hide, fear of what others close by might see, hear, or conjecture in one's conduct becomes a potent force for right action, especially when leadership is adequate. But such conditions did not invariably arise. Officers and men on both sides recognized that their mates did not always fight their hardest. Shirkers, as one historian has described them, were hooted down as "beats, or dead-beats, skulkers, sneaks, stragglers, or coffee-coolers." The most enthusiastic fighting units were those that endured the highest casualties. Whereas as high as 12 percent of all Confederates died in battle, nearly 30 percent lost their lives in the most aggressive regiments.[80]

Yet, should the official statistics about unfired weapons be dismissed altogether? To be sure, most battalions were fully engaged, but were there not exceptions? One option, it could be argued, was to enter the field and never shoot the firearm at all. At the Smithsonian Institution there is a display of Rebel guns with seven or more musket balls and powder jammed into the barrel. Even if the musket barrel was loaded to the very top with ten cartridges, ball, and powder, it might still fire, but, more likely, it would explode in the warrior's hands. So, it is unlikely that overexcitement in the rush of battle had prompted the multiple loadings. Instead, the soldier was simply pretending to load and fire amid the chaos of noise and explosions. Since he had to be standing up, he could be observed if he were not firing his gun: hence the constant loading without discharge. Of

27,574 weapons retrieved from the battlefield of Gettysburg, 24,000 or 90 percent were still loaded. Some 12,000 of them carried more than one wad of powder and ball. One musket had twenty-three loads jammed in. Of course, the weapons might have belonged to the mortally wounded or the incapacitated, but that might still have left unfired muskets in healthy soldiers' possession.[81]

To fire from too great a distance was also harmless but sometimes occurred. At Cold Harbor, one of the bloodiest engagements of the war, Ulysses S. Grant's troops moved steadily against Lee's formidable entrenchments on 3 June 1864. The lines separating the sides began at four hundred yards but over the hours the distance diminished to forty yards. Some seven thousand Federals were wounded or captured or died, but not in the eight minutes often attributed to the encounter. It actually took a whole day. In all that time the Army of the Potomac never retreated. But in this case, Lee's artillery, in a most favorable defensive position, inflicted the heavy damage—not Johnny Reb's musket.[82]

To kill without discrimination requires a detachment from the act itself and a sense that the enemy is not human at all. But despite the fact that the two sides belonged to the same country and shared many traditions and values, their similarity did not breed squeamishness about killing the enemy. As we are well aware from events in the Balkans most recently, men can slaughter each other when they look exactly alike and are, in many cases, neighbors of long acquaintance. It should be added, though, that neither side in the Civil War had a monopoly on brutish reaction to war. A Union army newspaper for the invading force in South Carolina in 1863 sought to stir up righteous indignation by dwelling on Southern habits of drunkenness and violence, the depravity of yeomen and poor whites, the arrogance of planters, "the recklessness of the young; the hardiness of the heart, and bitter ambition of the old." A coarsening of moral attitudes and the unleashing of passions that war usually promotes affected both sides. It influenced families divided by the war as well. An Iowa veteran promised that if his brother had joined the Rebel forces, he would seek him out for vengeance.[83]

In the border slave states, the passions and animosities aroused were even grimmer. Guerrilla warfare created a state of anarchy in western Virginia, the Tennessee and Kentucky hinterlands, and Missouri that belied the notion that the great conflict was purely a gentleman's war. Vengeance in the name of honor—retaliation for the enemy's alleged inhumanity— might seem to dictate such behavior, particularly when ill-disciplined, paramilitary units were involved as they have been in the atrocities of Kosovo.[84] "Retributive justice" was Sam Hildebrand's rationale for joining a guerrilla band in Missouri. The local Union vigilance committee had killed two of his brothers, the youngest in a fire that destroyed the homestead, had driven his mother out of the area, and had left him to die in a ditch with a bullet in his head. On recovery, he swore revenge. "To submit to further wrong from their hands would be an insult to the Being who gave me the power of resistance," he later reported. Hildebrand enjoyed picking off loyalist farmers as they went to work in the fields. The code of honor, as he understood it, however, restrained him from slaying women and children and burning houses. If he had done so, he said, "I would deserve the stigma cast upon my name."[85]

Guerrilla depredations in the backcountry brought war directly to the civilians on both sides and naturally aroused the kind of implacable feelings that Hildebrand's words expressed. At the same time, the well-trained, uniformed soldier, with high morale and undriven by some inner demon of fury, might at times find it harder than the infuriated irregular to kill someone who looked just like himself and stood only a few yards away. Sometimes that sense of oneness with the enemy came out in remarkably humane ways. After the Battle of Chattanooga a private in the W. P. Lane Rangers recorded in his diary, "I took a walk over a small portion of the battlefield, and it is enough to make the stoutest heart sicken, and I cannot but feel emotions of sorrow, pity and sympathy for our enemy, when I see him cold and stiff in death, or suffering from ghastly wounds."[86]

To be sure, empathy and distaste for violence were not invariably the response. Often enough, the enemy was the great beast to be exterminated. Nevertheless, relief from the obligation to kill, it turns out, can be documented as a common reaction in all wars, ancient or modern. Yet, it would be most unjust to denigrate the valor and dedication of soldiers on both sides.

Another factor in inhibiting the fighting spirit was the poor Confederate warrior's disgust with the upper classes, or in other words, mistrust of Rebel leadership. From the very start, there was trouble because Jefferson Davis permitted one-year enlistments for those furnishing their own gear. Whereas the rich planter, lawyer, or merchant could take advantage of that loophole, poor yeomen and day laborers were compelled to sign up for three years. In charge of recruitment, General Daniel Ruggles complained in August 1863, that "the spirit of volunteering has ceased to exist." A succession of draft laws failed to arouse much rejuvenation.[87] In March 1864, a south Georgia county paper protested, "It is strange to us that the Government allows its officers to conscript poor men who have the appearance of *dead men* while they turn loose rich ones who are *young, hale and hearty*." Colonel Carey W. Styles, a red-hot secessionist, was the local enrollment officer. He sold discharges from service for $1,000, a price that, even in inflated Confederate currency, few among the poor yeomen could meet. Complaints reached the Georgia governor, Joseph E. Brown, but Styles was never indicted for extortion and bribery. In violent reaction to court inaction, gangs of deserters roamed at will and subenrolling officers, fearful of assassination, hastily resigned. On his tour of the southwest to improve morale in 1862, Jefferson Davis had already encountered class resentments. He employed the customary rhetoric of the old ethic, earlier used by the Revolutionary Patriots, to rally support. The president declaimed, "Will you be free, or will you be the slaves of the most depraved and intolerant and tyrannical and hated people upon earth?"[88]

Class resentments arose from personal experiences as well. On furlough to heal a wound, William Fletcher stopped at a rich planter's house and asked for lodging and food. The gentleman replied that "he did not take in soldiers." The trooper exploded, saying that he was ready to lay down his arms, if that was all the Confederacy meant to his social betters. If Federals were plotting to blow up the planter's mansion, destroy his crops, and run off his slaves, he would give them directions on how to get there. "I guess you can stop at the overseer's," the suddenly patriotic slave owner relented.[89]

Such feelings in the common ranks arose on occasion, particularly if overbearing commanders appeared stupid or indifferent to the men. Why kill poor chaps like himself, a Rebel might ask, aiming high in the next battle. There must have been much resentment when officers belonging to the planter class had ready to hand a "servant" or two (slaves) to wash clothes, prepare meals, erect and dismantle tents, and perform other chores. They functioned much like the batmen in the English army, whose services continued well into the twentieth century. Yet there was, even in the not so egalitarian South, a democratic recourse. An enlisted foot soldier's sense of honor could be assuaged because the Southern military structure permitted voting on commanding officers. Those with political acuity flattered the men with promises of better behavior if they voted to remove their current commanders and replace them with those supposedly eager to improve the volunteers' sense of self-worth and their material well-being. A Mississippi soldier commented happily, "The new Lt. Col. celebrated his election by 'treating' the men of each company to a gallon or two of whiskey, consequently there is considerable noise in the air."[90] The honor of the individual combatant was as important to him as it was to the refined gentlemen who often led the troops. If an officer shrewdly asserted his social position without demeaning his inferiors in the ranks, he could capitalize on his virtuosity. George Cary Eggleston remarked, "The man of good family felt himself superior, as in most cases he unquestionably was, to his fellow-soldier of less excellent birth; and this distinction was sufficient, during the early years of the war, to override everything like military rank."[91] In fact, as David Donald observes, the roster of general officers resembles a list of the region's most ancient and prominent families. "The fathers" of the 425 generals in the Confederate army included a president, several senators, congressmen, and governors as well as a "French nobleman, ten officers of the regular United States army, eleven physicians, and six lawyers." Even later in the war, as this group was thinned out by death, incapacitation, and resignation, the South continued to draw its top military hierarchy from the socially eminent, college-educated elite.[92]

Of course, privates and sergeants might, with good reason, hold their officers to be their inferiors by the reigning standards of refinement. For instance, Henry St. John Dixon, an aristocratic North Carolina private, objected to serving under Bedford Forrest after "the death of the noble Van Dorn." He disliked "being commanded by a man having no pretension to gentility—a negro trader, gambler,—an ambitious man," who might be "the best cav[alry] officer in the West" but also "a tyrannical, hotheaded vulgarian."[93] Boisterous and bullying soldiers made sleeping difficult for one Mississippi gentleman, who griped that from dawn to dusk he heard nothing from the "blackguards" in the next tent but "one uninterrupted flow of the dirtiest talk I ever heard."[94]

Medical problems were much more serious deterrents than class resentments. Dysentery, diarrhea, and other stomach complaints from bad food and unbalanced diets destroyed morale as surely as poor leadership and the monotony of endless days idle in camp. William Clarke, a private from Cuthbert, Georgia, complained that he was reduced to ninety-five pounds from the lack of proper nourishment. "I have had chills more or less ever since I got started." Another soldier from the same area came down with measles, pneumonia, and typhoid all together. Private James K. Dowling was even more unlucky. After five months in service the measles took his life, and his mother nearly died, "giving up at the death of her precious boy."[95] The failure of Southern women to meet the medical needs of soldiers was also a problem affecting morale. Fear of losing respectability and lack of experience doing manual labor inhibited female members of the planter elite from emptying bedpans, dressing wounds, and assisting surgeons. Instead, slaves and men assumed such duties, not always well. A Danville, Virginia, physician called his military nurses no more than "rough country crackers," who were unable to show kindness or work efficiently. After being moved to a medical station at Gordonsville, Virginia, he protested against the "miserable nurses" he encountered there. They could not tell "castor from a gun rod nor laudanum from a hole in the ground." Although Union women were more likely to assume the difficult occupation, they too were in short supply. Marcus Woodcock in a loyal Kentucky regiment bitterly complained of their absence in the Union hospital where he was recovering from a nearly fatal attack of measles. "Your *presence* alone will do him good," he advised; "be with him in the first stroke of disease; in the awful hand of Death or in the doubtful state of convalescence."[96]

All these factors contributed to a problem not well recognized at the time: melancholia. The mental paralysis and dejection often affected the sleep-denied soldier. We now call the condition posttraumatic stress disorder, but it was known as battle fatigue in the Second World War, shell shock in the First World War, and "hypochondria" or the "blue devils" in the Civil War. James Williams, who was usually in high spirits, confessed to his wife, "I often get homesick, and the blue devils annoy me exceedingly, and the worst of it is, that I will always be sure to write [you] in the midst of such a state of mind."[97] Such symptoms of battle exhaustion were many. Sadly, they were often much worse than what Williams experienced: anxiety and depression, attention deficiency, arrhythmia, numbness, sleeplessness, night terrors, panic attacks, breathlessness, uncontrollable shaking, bed-wetting, loss of memory, impotence, nausea, eating disorders, complete or partial paralysis of mind and body, and survivor guilt.[98]

Finally, we have the modest but still significant issue of Rebel defection to the other side. East Tennessee, with a population greater than that of the states of Florida, Louisiana, Arkansas, Mississippi, and South Carolina, supplied thirty-six thousand troops to the North, nearly all of them poor non-slave-owning tenants and smallholders.[99] More surprising were the so-called galvanized Yankees, Confederates who joined Union ranks after capture and imprisonment. Formed into what were called volunteer regiments, six thousand of them were sent to the western frontier to police the Plains Indians. There they would not encounter old Rebel friends. Why they abandoned the Stars and Bars cannot be retrieved, of course. Even if interrogated by an experienced analyst—had such existed—they would have lied. But we can easily guess: the horrible encampment conditions were not much better than the notorious Andersonville on the Confederate side. It would have taken a "genius to beat the Chattanooga prison," declared William Fletcher, captured at Chickamauga.[100] Some deserted the Rebel cause out of complete despair, others because they were from Unionist districts at home; still others because they were poor illiterates who had no hope of owning a slave and resented those who did or simply lost faith in the Confederate cause. They turned out to be well-disciplined and, according to one admiring surgeon, "brave even to recklessness."[101]

. . . .

While negative attitudes must be recorded, we cannot take them as the full measure of Confederate foot soldiers as a whole. They did much better than anyone could expect, given the growing loss of hope that faced all free Southerners. They exceeded the enemy in determination but could not overcome the weaknesses, both military and economic, that had hobbled the cause from the start. Even if such TV documentaries as Ken Burns's series and novels like Charles Frazier's *Cold Mountain* present more realistic versions of what war is like, it is hard—perhaps even unwise—to shake the old concepts of individual heroism. Reading accounts of soldiers in battle leads one to the conclusion that the average trooper was "far from perfect, but his achievement against great odds," to borrow from Bell Wiley, "is an irrefutable evidence of his prowess and an eternal monument to his greatness as a fighting man."[102] Reactions to battle conditions were, as this exploration suggests, as varied as the individual personalities in the ranks. For most Johnny Rebs and Billy Yanks, the Civil War was the great, defining moment of their lives, never to be forgotten. Despite the questions that Paddy Griffith and others raise, there were simply too many engagements in which thousands died to make nonfiring, nonaction, and even desertion a plausible outcome of warfare. Out of the three million under arms, it is estimated that two hundred thousand soldiers died on the field and over twice as many suffered severe wounds.[103]

At the same time, we should not end on too positive a note. The horrors and wretchedness of the Civil War linger in the air we breathe even now. A private in the Fortieth Alabama tried his hand at poetry to express his bitter feelings against the Yanks and against the leaders of the Confederacy as well. One of his verses ran as follows:

I am weary of hearing shells burst in the air
With a shriek like a fiend in the depths of dispair [*sic*]
I am sick of hearing the balls whistle by
Saying so plainly, "I strike [and] you die."
I am weary of war, of powder [and] ball
I am weary [and] sick of the glory [and] all[.] [104]

CHAPTER TEN

· · · · · · · · ·

DEATH OF A NATION

Forth from its scabbard all in vain
Bright flashed the sword of Lee;
'Tis shrouded now in its sheath again,
It sleeps the sleep of our noble slain,
Defeated, yet without a stain,
Proudly and peacefully.
—Father Abram J. Ryan, "The Sword of Lee"

When the Civil War came to its bloody end, the white people of the Confederacy felt the shame of defeat, a sense of profound hopelessness, and a fear of the future in full measure. No one has provided a more evocative portrayal of the closing days than novelist Charles Frazier in *Cold Mountain*.[1] The hero of the story is a disillusioned deserter named Inman. After leaving a Confederate hospital, he undertakes a journey like that of Ulysses after the Trojan War. But one might also draw an analogy with Dante's travail of spirit in the *Divine Comedy*. In that sense, Inman's departure from the Raleigh infirmary is an ascent from the hell of war in the Virginia lowlands to the mountains of relative peace, rather than a journey into the depths of the Inferno.[2] Typical of his times and region, Inman is exasperatingly inarticulate about his feelings. Yet the way he responds to the fall of the Confederacy and the horrific experiences of his journey home to western North Carolina captures the mood of desolation that gripped so many Southern whites in 1865.

Was the return as harrowing as Frazier portrays it? After all, the Southern white people in fighting and then surrendering had it pretty easy by the unspeakable standards of modern warfare. In this civil conflict, unlike others now under way in the world, Federals carried out no genocide—

no Kosovos, no Rwandas occurred on American soil. A threatening moment did arise, however, when the news of Lincoln's assassination reached the Union troops. An Ohio artilleryman wrote home that the South Carolinians in Sherman's path were lucky that the tragedy had not occurred earlier. As it was, the troops were eager to "avenge the death of old Abe," but reliable guards were available to post around the Federal camps and prevent outrages. Two thousand infuriated soldiers in Sherman's army marched toward Raleigh, but Union general John Logan of the Fifteenth Corps prevented their mission to destroy the city. North Carolina's civilians were lucky that General Joseph E. Johnston surrendered before Sherman's troops started another march. "Every man would take it upon himself to do every thing he could to avenge the death of old Abe," an Ohio artilleryman explained, "and dearly he would have been avenged for the boys would have showed no mercy."[3] Cooler heads seemed to prevail in a most remarkable way.

Even by the standards of nineteenth-century warfare, the terms of surrender were unusually mild. General Grant set the stage by letting Lee's soldiers demob without penalty. Grant's model was not uniformly followed, but few were the official marks of Union victory for Rebels to witness as they lay down their arms. When Lee's army surrendered, the soldiers were placed in what they called the "Bull Pen," as a Rebel private, then eighteen, recalled. But the guards were not Yankees. "We could not have submitted to that if it had been attempted," he boasted.[4] Fellow Southerners assumed the task, and the victorious Federals were not even allowed to enter the bivouac. When artillery private Philip Stephenson of the Army of Tennessee surrendered at Meridian, Mississippi, his unit was treated with businesslike courtesy. "No excitement, no disorder," he remembered. "The Federal troops were kept well in hand, were not allowed to insult us, and they showed no disposition to do so. There was no marching out, lining us up opposite the Federal forces, and our general surrendering his sword to the victor, no pomp and parade of triumph." Even Sherman's troops, reported a surrendering Rebel, "show us a more liberal disposition than the most sanguine expected."[5] Blaming the war on the rich slaveholders, Sherman's troops had earlier vowed, "now let them suffer." With surrender, though, came softer words. "We can afford to be merciful," remarked a Wisconsin captain.[6]

Such magnanimity was welcome, but the element of condescension still grated. More humiliating than the rituals of surrender, though, was to see deserters emerge from hiding, clamoring to get their parole papers as if they had been loyal all along. Embarrassed, especially when the victors were watching, loyal Confederates beat the stragglers up, shaved half their heads and beards, and rode them about on rails in shivaree style. Private Stephenson recalled "a big fellow astride a rail held high up by a number of hands, yells of derision and contempt all around him."[7] The Yanks enjoyed the spectacle but did not participate.

To be sure, massive exhibitions of Union men in ranks did take place in the spring of 1865, most particularly in the nation's capital, but not in the Deep South itself.[8] If there were marching for display, the Rebels performed it but not with pressed trousers, polished boots, and bright brass. Joshua Chamberlain's ritual at Appomattox was exceptional. As if nature itself were collaborating with the Yankee victors, the Union banners, stirred by gusts of wind, revealed their full glory, Chamberlain remembered. Meantime, he added, "the ensigns of rebellion seem to shrink back and strain away from the fated farewell."[9] Not only were the Rebel infantrymen given unanticipated respect, but in the late spring of 1865, occupation forces for the most part did not impose themselves unduly on the population. Sometimes the Confederates could scarcely find them on the streets. In Tyler, Texas, Kate Stone reported in her diary that one "would not know there was an enemy in the Department. We all went to church today expecting to be outraged by a sight of the whole Yankee detachment but not a blue coat was in sight."[10]

Despite such signs of good faith, the sense of utter hopelessness that greeted the coming of peace—not only for Johnny Reb himself but for the whole white population—was much deeper and more complicated than legend would later have it. For instance, General Edward Porter Alexander, chief of artillery in James Longstreet's First Corps in the Army of Northern Virginia, witnessed the fall of Richmond from his mount on the south bank of the James River. He later recalled that bleak scene, knowing that the end had come. The city was enveloped in smoke and riven by erratic explosions. "I rode on with a distinctly heavy heart & with a peculiar sort of feeling of orphanage."[11] He had lost the land of his forefathers and knew it.

Frazier's *Cold Mountain* may have it right after all. Some years ago, David Donald observed, "It is hard for us today to realize how startling, how earth-shaking for most Southerners was the collapse of the Confederacy."[12] On a mission through the Gulf States to ascertain conditions for President Andrew Johnson, General Carl Schurz met a young Rebel on a steamer on 15 July 1865. His fellow passenger was on his way to Savannah and a plantation that included ninety slaves and four thousand acres. The handsome young officer "frankly 'accepted' the defeat of the South." Yet he could not fathom the consequences—emancipation. Despite Schurz's efforts to convince him otherwise, the planter could not imagine paying out wages to hire free black laborers. Over and over, he insisted, they would not work. Seated "in sad silence" for a while, he at last said, " 'No I can't sell my plantation. We must make the nigger work somehow.' " Schurz remarked that he heard in nearly all the voices and manners of those with whom he conversed the same sense of incredulity about the unfitness of the "nigger for freedom." Everywhere he was met with what he called "helpless stupefaction," as if the white Southerners' minds "were wholly incapable of grasping the fact that their former slaves were now free."[13] Katharine Du Pre Lumpkin explained in her memoir that "Nothing" provided the returning Rebels "so acute a sense of finality—this was true of the men of property among them—as the freedom of their slaves." Men in the streets watched their former property bargaining for better wages and showing other signs of independence. They muttered among themselves that "the heart of the South is beginning to sink in despair."[14] Contemporary opinion affirmed her impression. As early as September 1864 a Greenville citizen boldly informed Jefferson Davis that in a vote on "whether to continue the war or return to the union, a large majority" of his fellow Georgians "would vote for a return." Howell Cobb's wife learned from her husband that he had found Georgia civilians to be "depressed, disaffected, and too many of them disloyal." "Shall we indeed fight on against the decrees of God, to utter extermination!" a former secessionist editor wondered. Was it "the will of God . . . or the suggestion of the Demon of Pride" that kept the Confederate insanity afloat? "I say Peace!"[15]

Although the editor's remarks implied otherwise, the actuality of surrender was not just a matter of temporary dejection over getting whipped, stacking firearms, and leaving comrades to strike out for home. Rather, it concerned the general tone of Southern society for the next generation and even beyond, particularly with regard to the honor of the white and the attribution of shamelessness—and shiftlessness—assigned to the subordinated, stigmatized race. Reactions to defeat fell rather naturally into three categories. Just as there are various stages in battle motivation— from initial enthusiasm for glory to sober determination—so too are there levels of response to failure in war: first, the initial shock when confronting the hopelessness of further action; second, the discovery of home conditions upon return; and third, the long-term problems of readjustment. All these factors were to affect the cultural and civic life of the region for scores of years thereafter.

As if the Confederacy's demise meant an end to life itself, the shock seemed unbearable. General Josiah Gorgas, for instance, felt himself to be "walking in a dream, and expecting to awake."[16] Emotional denial was indeed a frequent response. For instance, throughout the South soldiers and civilians far from the Virginia battlefields could not admit that Lee had ordered a laying down of arms. Rumors to that effect were summarily dismissed. Edward Allston predicted that even if the armies surrendered, guerrilla warfare would ensue. "It will be a desperate game," he wrote his wife, Catherine, "but I think it will be eventually successful. If the Yankees attempt to drive us to the wall this is bound to be the result. There are too many men at home who know the use of arms ever to sit down quietly and submit." Fortunately, Lee and other general officers, many of them graduates of West Point, thought guerrilla operations an unprofessional, dishonorable, and counterproductive course of action.[17] Dr. Samuel Preston Moore called rumors that Lee had given up the fight a "moral impossibility." "No one is willing to believe it," declared one Mississippian as late as 20 April.[18]

When the facts did sink in, stunned Confederates, against their will, threw into question the original rationale for undertaking so long, bloody, and costly a struggle. At first the Reverend J. Henry Smith, minister of the Presbyterian church at Greensboro, North Carolina, had half-disbelieved rumors of Lee's capitulation. It had to be, he mused, the "*Saddest of days!*" Smith reported that on his way south "as a fugitive" Jefferson Davis had stopped briefly in town, his presence being an alarming sign of the Confederate collapse. News of these calamitous events so afflicted the clergyman that he "had to go to bed," and he made no entries for the next five days. Then, succinctly and mournfully, on 17 April 1865 he stated what so many Southerners must have felt: "One week ago Gen[era]l Lee surrendered himself & all his army. The doings & feelings, the disheartening, the gloom & burden & sorrow—no pen can describe. Oh is all gone? My bleeding, suffering country! Are all the prayers, the vows, the blood & lives & property of thousands & tears of many thousands in vain?" Henry Smith tried to rally his spirits, but for several days he had witnessed Joseph Johnston's army "drawing back" through the town. He knew that a final showdown could not be long delayed and yet hoped for the best.[19]

In a semiautobiographical novel, Claire Myers Owens reported that as a youngster she had observed how sad her grandfather had always looked. A Texas veteran, he had endured some of the most ferocious fighting from First Manassas to the bitter end. When the child asked for an explanation, her grandmother replied, "He never recovered from Lee's surrender, the whole war just seemed to break his heart forever."[20] No doubt his melancholy stemmed from emotional reactions to battle and not just the failure at arms.

Denial of the obvious was another way to handle defeat. It seemed to be a common Southern ailment in 1865. The journalist Whitelaw Reid ran into a major who had fought under James Longstreet. In the face of the South's utter ruin and the absolute Northern victory, the major warned the newspaperman that reconciliation with the South could be achieved only by reestablishing slavery, permitting the planters to use force to get their workers back in the fields, and helping the Southern farmer to get free white labor if the freedmen were to be colonized back to Africa. There he stood "battered, clad in worn-out Confederate gray, but with good army blue pantaloons," stolen from a dead Union soldier, no doubt. "Such waste and destruction all about us; and still these insatiable men—these handsome tigers—want more conciliation!"[21] Bill Arp, a Georgia newsman, wrote to the Northern humorist Artemus Ward that the South ought to be treated deferentially because "We made a bully fite, and the whole American nation ought to feel proud of it." Still burying their own dead and treating the wounded, the Federals were not in a forgiving frame of mind to meet that demand.

The underlying principle of honor that had helped to justify polemical defenses of slavery and the cause of secession years before still assisted such attitudes of defiance and pride. Some of Lee's surrendered soldiers were reported to have felt that they had " 'left no blot on their name' and can 'look proudly to heaven from the death-bed of fame.' " Civilians, however, might pretend that they had been against the war all along. Ethelred Philips of Marianna, Florida, reported in August 1865 that the Union captain of the local garrison wondered how the state had seceded with Union men observed at every turn. "An original *secesh* is now hard to find," Philips agreed.[22]

At first, old customs of personal combat did not disappear despite the ubiquity of feats of arms in battle. General Nathan Forrest challenged a Northerner to a duel for having charged the Rebel general with the crime of slaughtering black troops at Fort Pillow after they had surrendered and were disarmed. As a rule, though, Northern offenders, like Forrest's accuser, disregarded the demand for satisfaction.[23] Henry Watkins Allen, wartime governor of Louisiana, likewise had challenged a Union officer to a duel, an invitation the recipient of the demand had duly ignored.

Allen's biographer and friend, Sarah Dorsey, scornfully remarked, "The federal did not understand *Sir Lancelot, redivivus!*" Allen was "a Representative Man—his virtues and his faults were entirely Southern."[24]

Regardless of the inevitability of defeat, truculence in the name of honor also appeared in collective form. As the fires of resistance were sputtering out in late April 1865, David Pierson wrote his father about the dying cause in Shreveport. General Hays and others had gathered a mass meeting to "start a patriotic party," Pierson bitterly explained. Their effort was designed "to give confidence to the doubting and despondent." But Pierson was skeptical that "plausible reasonings and sweet words" could "bind up the wounds of the mangled Confederacy." The organizers themselves, he complained, had all quit the army already or never had faced the enemy at all.[25] After surrendering his army to General Sherman, Joe Johnston encountered an unreconstructed secessionist blowhard on a Chesapeake Bay steamboat. The passenger confidently told the general: "The South was conquered but not subdued!" The general quietly responded by asking, "What was your command, sir?" The fire-eater replied, "Unfortunately, circumstances made it impossible for me to—" Johnson interrupted. "Well, sir, I was. You may not be subdued, but I am."[26] As late as 1871, Horace Greeley, on a tour of the lower South, found that "here and there a hot-head may talk of renewing, at some auspicious season the struggle for an independent Confederacy; but a great majority have had enough of war." Greeley noted, however, that whereas "a bitter spirit is cherished by many," most were disposed to "renew the fight" not with "gun and saber" but with political action. But actually political revival did not engage as many in 1865 as he thought. There was too much despair and concern about how to survive for an immediate return to antebellum zeal for partisan contest.[27]

On their return from the war, the footsore veterans found that honor and disaster made strange companions. Samuel French, a graduate of West Point in 1843, returned to his Mississippi home stricken by what greeted him there. "Where were the laurels that were to crown my brow?" he mourned. "Fences burned, bridges destroyed; the plantation a forest of tall weeds; horses, mules, cattle, sheep, poultry, provisions, wagons, implements of every kind—all gone; wealth, servants, comforts—all means of support for my family gone; all lost save honor."[28] Honor could not produce a meal or saddle a mount, but it could salve the painful reality of defeat.

At the other end of the spectrum, dogged determination to continue the fight was another but perhaps less common reaction. Mrs. Giraud

Wright in Montgomery, Alabama, saw her brother, a Confederate officer, approaching her after years of absence. "He walked slowly, unlike the brisk step I knew of old; absolute dejection was in his mien, and he had no joyous greeting to give me. . . . Somehow I had no words to say. We stood and looked at each other." Finally, she asked what to do. He replied, head west and join Kirby Smith. " 'Have you not heard,' I said, 'Kirby Smith has surrendered.' " Like Mrs. Wright's brother, a captured Rebel sergeant had been ready to fight on but only in deference to "a sentiment of honor," as he put it. While many others had quit, he and the loyal few still in uniform "did not wish to disgrace themselves by deserting their flag" even though they "had given up all hope of . . . [triumph] long since." [29] That justification was repeated countless times and prevented efforts at negotiation. Surrender itself was preferable. David Carter declared that such a course of action "would at least save us our honor." [30] At the turn of the nineteenth century, Senator John Sharp Williams of Mississippi asked an old-timer why he and his fellow soldiers had battled so valiantly and so desperately, even though they had no hope of victory. "We were afraid to stop." "Afraid of what?" asked the politician. "Afraid of the women at home, John. They would have been ashamed of us." [31]

The old soldier spoke perhaps for a minority, however. Many others had long since given up and deserted by the thousands—a total of at least 103,400.[32] At first it was a matter of individual disappearances from the front lines, usually because the soldier missed his home or received word of dire conditions there. "Albert," wrote Grace Brown Elmore, "has come home, deserted rather than surrender." He justified himself on the grounds that hundreds of Joe Johnston's troops had done the same, in hopes of escaping parole and possible imprisonment in a Union stockade.[33] At the end of 1864, one woman wrote her husband that the children lacked blankets, shoes, and clothing, and she had run out of firewood. If he did not hurry back, she warned, "we'll all . . . of us be out there in the garden in the old grave yard with your ma and mine." He took off.[34]

As morale further deteriorated, men fled from the ranks in groups. According to the historian Tracy Power, if Lee were to have had his full complement of troops instead of just a few loyal infantrymen in early April 1865 he might possibly have broken out of the Petersburg-Richmond siege and joined up with Joseph Johnston a hundred miles away in North Carolina. As it was, however, desertions had reached such proportions that it was impossible to hold the miles of defense lines in front of the two cities.[35]

Out West, matters were no better. Fiery General Edmund Kirby Smith, who still commanded the Trans-Mississippi Department, was eager to carry on until the Day of Judgment if need be. The men in the ranks, though, had much less exalted plans in mind. In Kirby Smith's army, Captain Elijah Petty reported in May 1865 that the Texas troops of his command "consider the contest a hopeless one, and will lay down their arms at the first appearance of the enemy." General Kirby Smith himself had to escape from a mob of soldiers out of control at Huntsville, Texas. In his final, bitter message to the fast vanishing troops, the soldierless general declared, "You have volunteerly destroyed your organizations, and thrown away all means of resistance. . . . May God, in his mercy, direct you aright, and heal the wounds of our distracted country."[36] Like Kirby Smith, some of the other officers also felt that it had been highly dishonorable to surrender by simply breaking up. "I reached my home," said one, "a down-spirited man." He confessed to laying arms aside "with no foe near us."[37] For others, losing the war made its horrors still worse because of the futility and failure of it all. Harriet Palmer of South Carolina voiced a familiar reaction to news of troops surrendering. On 3 May 1865 she wrote in her diary, "Never! Never! It can't be so. Why so much bloodshed? Why so many valuable lives lost? Oh, God grant it may not be so!"[38]

Women of Harriet Palmer's class were generally very outspoken in their anger over the outcome after so much sacrifice. Deprived of serving in an active way, they tended to be more belligerent in their reflections—and sometimes their behavior toward the conquerors—than were their husbands, fathers, and brothers. Mary Chesnut came away from one of Dr. Benjamin Palmer's fiery sermons filled with defiance and indignation. "My very flesh crept and tingled. A red-hot glow of patriotism passed over me," she recorded in her diary. "There was more exhortation to fight and die à la Joshua than meek Christianity, however."[39] The once wealthy Amanda Worthington of the delta region in Mississippi grieved for a lost plantation world. "As long as I thought we would conquer in our just cause, I cared nothing for the loss of property for I felt as if we would still be rich if we had *our rights* & *our country* left us—but now they are lost too, & *we have* suffered *in vain*. In vain! There is where the bitterness lies!"[40] Men were less articulate. Mary Chesnut received a note from Quentin Washington: "I have given up. The bitterness is over. I will write you no more—I have not the heart."[41]

Some historians claim that the women's loss of faith in the cause prompted Confederate defeat. There may be some grounds to support that reading, but generally women's feelings had been much too volatile and at times confused for a determination to end the war at any cost to have prevailed, even in the closing months. Throughout the conflict, there had been moments of elation and times of deep melancholy. In 1863, for instance, Harriott Middleton of South Carolina had written a cousin. The war, she confessed, "seems to stretch on interminably before us, carrying off all the youths and worth of the country, I can see nothing but desolated homes, and broken hopes. We seem to make so little impression on the North, the men we kill are foreigners, and there are hundreds of thousands more to take their places." But premonitions of defeat might well be followed by a mood of complete defiance. Upon hearing of anti-draft rioting in the North and momentary Confederate advances, Harriott Middleton again wrote her cousin a few weeks later, "How delightful all this fluttering is in the northern cities. Oh! Susan I feel so bloodthirsty. . . . I long to hear of burning and destruction and wading in [Yankee] militia blood!!!"[42]

In addition, women, desperate, alone, and distracted by uncertainties on the home front, had beseeched Confederate authorities to discharge their husbands, fathers, and brothers. They expressed no wish, of course, to bring the war to a close. Rather they insisted on their heartfelt loyalty. But conditions at home required, the petitioners pled, the restoration of a male presence. "I am now about to do what at the commencement of this war I should have blushed to have thought of but am now reduced by necessity of doing," Sallie Robertson of Albemarle explained to the Confederate secretary of war. Her mother had died, her father was ill with cancer, a brother had been killed. That left four daughters at home to fend for the family unless a surviving brother could be discharged. A woman of Whitman County, Georgia, also proclaimed her devotion to the Confederacy. She pointed out, however, that she had already sacrificed five dead sons to the cause. Could she not retrieve the sole remaining son, she asked President Davis. "Will you bee my friend?" One might argue that petitioners were compelled to claim a wholehearted allegiance to the government that they did not feel. But by and large these and thousands of other women were not insincere. They accepted and largely embraced the Rebel cause.[43]

In fact, when the end came, plantation women throughout the South felt the crush of defeat no less than the men on their way home. For the most part, they had supported the effort at least as fervently as the troops in the field. Catherine Rowland of Georgia, for instance, wrote as late as January 1865 that members of her sex had "suffered too much to think of giving up now & it is a sacrilege to the dead to speak of such a thing." Having lost a brother, she, like many other women, was certain that his spirit "cries out in vengeance & we ought to fight on as long as we have a man left."[44] But even the stoutest feminine hearts had to admit that carrying on the war until the last infantryman had fallen would gain nothing. Instead, for mothers, sisters, and wives, there was the prospective joy—and sometimes pain—of greeting the survivors on their homeward journey. In early May 1865, Sarah Morgan of Baton Rouge, Louisiana, for example, reported in her diary that she looked forward to the arrival of "those who fought so nobly for us." Yet, she mourned, "how I have dreaded their first days at home!" George and Gibbes Morgan, her two brothers, dead in Virginia battles, would not be among them. How hard it will be, she lamented, to have other families reunited when her own could never meet together, "save in heaven." Sarah Morgan noted that 750 Louisianian parolees had arrived on 29 April 1865. These remnants from Robert E. Lee's army consisted of the "sole survivors of ten regiments who left four years ago so full of hope and determination."[45]

Lee's capitulation was one of the heaviest blows to morale, both civilian and military. "Father came in suddenly pale and grave," reported young Lucy Buck of Virginia, and moaned, " 'Well, I fear the die is cast—Lee has surrendered'—almost torn from his lips." Lucy Buck felt the news could not be true, "—the one thought—subjugation—all staked, all lost. Our dearest hopes dashed— . . . slaves to such a tyrant. God only knows how nearly mad I must have been." She mourned, too, for Lee. "Poor fellow! What a trial to his noble heart."[46]

As Lucy Buck guessed, Lee himself was deeply stricken. When A. P. Hill was killed after the Petersburg breakthrough on 2 April, Lee himself wept. A week later he told his staff, "How easily I could be rid of this, and be at rest. I have only to ride along the line and all will be over."[47] And on that cold but sunny spring day at a farmer's house near Appomattox Court House, it was. Even men of an optimistic turn of mind felt the loss deeply. Sergeant James E. Whitehorne, for instance, remarked as he trudged toward home a week after Appomattox, "The memory hurts like an open wound."[48] On the day of the surrender, one of Lee's commanders, General Bryan Grimes, did not know exactly how to give his troops the bad news, but he proved no actor. Observing Grimes's agonized expression, a soldier asked him whether the rumors were true. Grimes had to say yes. In fury, grief, and frustration, the soldier threw down his weapon, and "it bounced on the spring grass." Raising his arms to the sky, he cried, " 'Blow, Gabriel, blow! My God, let him blow, I am ready to die!' "[49]

Whether the infantryman meant this in a religious spirit or not, Christians under arms had their faith sorely tested. Had not the preachers insisted that God was committed to their cause? William Faulkner caught the suspicion of a divine abandonment. He has Quentin Compson in *Absalom, Absalom!* imagine how Charles Bon in the Rebel army retreating before Sherman voices a frequently heard sentiment. Bon muses that "*evidently we have done without Him for four years, only He just didn't think to notify us.*" As a result, Bon argues to himself, "*if you dont have God and you dont need food or clothes and shelter, there isn't anything for honor and pride to climb on and hold to and flourish. And if you haven't honor and pride, then nothing matters.*"[50]

In actuality, the clergy fought against a cynicism that was bound to creep into the stoutest hearts as the conditions gradually deteriorated. For instance, as early as May 1862, the Presbyterian clergyman J. W. Tucker of Tennessee warned his congregation, "Look not to fortune nor to accidents for help in this hour of our country's peril, but to the God of battles and of nations." Luck did not exist; all was foreordained as part of the Almighty's plan, Tucker preached. Every act was designed "for the advancement of [God's] glory and the well being of his people."[51] The influential Presbyterian Benjamin Palmer also insisted, "The language of true prayer is never the cry of supine imbecility, nor the wail of craven despondency. It is always the language of hope and expectation." God could turn his favor on the beleaguered Southern republic at any moment. "I thank God that, in the darkest hour, I have never despaired of the republic," Palmer prayed. The Battle of Gettysburg was to be fought only a few weeks after he delivered his sermon in South Carolina. Presumably even that event failed to undermine his faith.[52] After all, Psalm 88 offered scriptural validation for laying current woes before an apparently indifferent God: "O Lord God of my salvation, I have cried day and night before thee. . . . Free among the dead, like the slain that lieth in the grave, whom thou rememberest no more: and they are cut off from thy hand. . . . Lover and friend hast thou put far from me, and mine acquaintance into darkness" (Psa. 88:1, 5, 18).

Despite such fervent reassurances, the doubtful began to ask why the Almighty was so seemingly reluctant to lend His arm in the struggle. Why the misery, loss, and prospect of defeat for his faithful Southern believers? "It seems like the Lord has turned his face from us," a soldier in Georgia wrote home.[53] "I fear the subjugation of the South will make an infidel of me," declared another. "A just God," he insisted, simply could not "allow people who have battled so heroically for their rights to be overthrown."[54] According to George Eggleston, superstitions, born out of fear of dying, helped to account for the religious revivals that swept the Confederate ranks during the war. A "gloomy fatalism took possession of many minds," certain that God had already planned when they should leave this earth, Eggleston recalled. One soldier insisted, against Eggleston's protests, that his time was drawing nigh. " 'I don't care. A few days more or less don't signify much,' " the soldier had remarked. "An hour later the poor fellow's head was blown from his shoulders as he stood by my side."[55]

Similar sentiments were echoed by some in the civilian population. Some, however, tried to strengthen their religious convictions. Ellen House, for instance, undertook to curb her bitterness over the defeat and desolation. "We have depended too much on Gen. Lee too little on God."[56] But many others felt too stunned to rekindle their faith. Lizzie Hardin, a young Rebel Kentuckian, declared, "Sometimes I fear I am becoming an infidel. I feel how wrong . . . such thoughts are, I try to force myself to believe that 'whatever is, is right'; but oh! To live in this land of sorrow and humiliation; to breathe this air of oppression," and yet "to remember that God is omnipotent." What good were all the prayers and national fast days that Jefferson Davis had appointed, she wondered. "I feel like one groping in darkness."[57] As the end drew near, even pious General Josiah Gorgas mourned, "What have we done that the Almighty should scourge us with such a war—so relentless and so repugnant?"[58]

Indeed, what had been the gain?—a devastated country, a humiliating present, an uncertain future. Defeat also drained patriotic feelings that had long animated the troops. Around the battle site they saw burned houses, slaughtered pigs and cattle, broken fences, and half-starving women and children. Such scenes persisted in the weeks after the fighting stopped. Yet with comrades vanishing and hope fleeing with them, there was no means to wreak vengeance on the foe.

In addition, physical chemistry played a part. With the laying down of arms came the loss of adrenaline that had formerly sustained the soldier in battle. The letdown, whatever the cause, was devastating, at least for some. One-legged and one-armed, General Richard Ewell surrendered at Sailor's Creek, finding his troops surrounded on all sides. Almost immediately he fell into a deep despondency and "stared at the ground, as if trying to avoid attention," observed a soldier. Another Confederate noted that " 'Fighting Dick Ewell' looked like an old eagle with one of his wings clipped."[59] Traveling through Georgia just after the fighting had ceased, journalist Whitelaw Reid observed, "Aimless young men in gray, ragged and filthy, seemed, with the downfall of the rebellion . . . to have lost their object in life, and stared stupidly at the clothes and comfortable air of officers and strangers from the North." Marks of emotional depletion could be seen in the eyes of so many. Another Northern correspondent remarked on "the 'careworn and anxious look, a played-out manner' among the Rebel soldiers on their wearisome route toward home.[60]

Reaction to surrender might well have brought on insomnia, night terrors, even temporary mental paralysis. According to a Mobile newspaper, some men became so withdrawn that they hid from society and lived like hermits in a desert. In a report to President Andrew Johnson, Union general Carl Schurz observed that he saw former soldiers "cross their arms in gloomy despondency, incapable of rising to manly resolution. Others, who still possess means, are at a loss how to use them. Others are still trying to go on in the old way."[61]

But rejecting guilty feelings for their own inadequacies in the emergency did not always lead to violence. Rather, many indulged in the easy habit of assailing scapegoats. Some had good reason for bitterness. On a day in March 1870, General George Pickett, by accident, ran into General Lee in the lobby of a Richmond hotel. General John Mosby observed the stiffness of their greeting. Formidable as always, Lee was not above "freezing out a man he did not like," Mosby reported. Both no doubt tacitly recalled their fateful exchange on 3 July 1863 at Gettysburg, when Lee offered Pickett his highest expression of praise for the valor shown on the field earlier that day: "You have covered yourself with glory." As he later recollected, the division commander had replied, "Alas, what will ever repay Virginia for her best & noblest blood poured out for naught[?]." Lee's subordinate had cast doubt on his leadership, and the two men never healed the breach. Turning to Mosby after Lee had left the hotel lobby, Pickett muttered, "He had my division massacred," but Mosby retorted, "Well, it made you immortal."[62]

With some justice, however, Lee himself found reason to complain about the poor response in some civilian quarters to wartime exigencies. At the close of February 1865 he had written Zebulon Vance, governor of North Carolina, "The state of despondency that now prevails among our people is producing a bad effect upon the troops. . . . Their friends at home," he continued, were leading "hundreds to desert."[63] North Carolina loyalists thought the peace-demanding editorials that William Woods Holden of the *Raleigh Standard* composed had prompted low morale and desertion in the ranks. "I think N[orth] C[arolina] Soldiers passing through Raleigh," protested one private, "ought to stop and hang the old son of a bitch."[64] Holden's peace maneuvers came close to sedition. Privately he called Davis and his allies "the Destructives."[65] In North Carolina, the war had never been popular with many even at the start. Governor Zebulon Vance voiced a sentiment quite common in the Old North State as well as other parts of the upper South. In the fall of 1864 he confided to his friend David Swain, "The great *popular heart* is not now & never has been in this war. . . . The beginning was bad & I had no hand in it." But he had fought the good fight in spite of early misgivings. His conscience, he liked to think, was clear, and "if the end be bad I shall with Gods help be equally blameless." [66]

Most of the angry recriminations for defeat were less justified than Pickett's sense of betrayal and Lee's worries about the effects of homefront morale. A few, though, blamed the Southern whites as a whole for their individual and collective failure. Catholic bishop Augustin Verot of Florida pointed out that perhaps God intended Southern defeat to free the slaves and chastise the whites for their sins against the race. During the war the theologian John Leadley Dagg worried, "The failure of our laws to recognize and protect marriages among slaves has attracted the attention of our religious bodies, but this failure is only part of a general evil." [67] God could well be punishing an unrepentant South. Renowned for his soaring Presbyterian oratory, the Reverend Benjamin Palmer delivered in Richmond a very mournful sermon as early as September 1864. Mary Chesnut reported a chilling experience: "I did not know before how utterly hopeless was our situation. This man is so eloquent. It was hard to listen and not give way. Despair was his word—and martyrdom. He offered us nothing more in this world than the martyr's crown." Palmer, she was surprised to learn, no longer favored slavery and its defense. Rather, she reported, "He is for freedom—and the freedom to govern our own country as we see fit." That was the only issue at stake because, Palmer announced, "slavery is doomed the world over. For that he thanked God." The divine then concluded, almost sobbing, "Help us, oh God. Vain is the help of man." Mary Chesnut added, "And so we came away—shaken to the depths." [68] As one of the earliest prosecession ministers, Palmer had certainly lost his former zeal and seemed to attribute the hopeless situation to God's condemnation of slaveholding. On most occasions, however, the clergy throughout the South blamed defeat on the conventional sins of pride, arrogance, greed, and failure to pray at home and honor God in his holy temple on Sundays.

In fact, the greed of some Southerners aroused the indignation of many more. Black marketeers, smugglers, and speculators grew fat on the misery and loyalty of the civilians and undermined morale. The Rhett Butlers, as it were, were heartily despised, but no one could do much about it.[69] One Confederate commissary officer named Harrow used to requisition supplies and blatantly cheat the local farmers in Chancellorsville, Virginia. He was said to have poured the money he made "down his own throat." A soldier had protested, and the commissary officer had him arrested. "That ground into his feelin's," a neighbor reported to a traveling postwar journalist, "and he deserted fo' no other purpose than to shoot him. He shot Harrow in that house you see burnt to the ground."[70]

The women at home also became a convenient target. According to rumor, when Richmond fell, the dead-letter bags were opened and the contents revealed that "nearly all" the common soldiers' wives throughout the South were "were begging the men to desert!" The Reverend John Paris, a Methodist chaplain, visited twenty-two soldiers about to be executed by hanging for desertion in February 1864. He offered a stern homily on the justice of the sentences yet observed that these were decent men who had become the victims of antiwar feeling at home. All of them, he declared, had heard from their wives and kinspeople on the home front who treasonously urged, "We are whipt!" "We might as well give up!" "It is useless to fight any longer!" The "poisonous contagion" had insidiously invaded the army, Paris exclaimed.[71]

The pleas from the home front for loved ones to return were not the sole reason for leaving the ranks. Nonslaveholding soldiers were likely to desert sooner than slaveholding veterans, but not necessarily because their womenfolk urged them to betray their Rebel loyalties. Rather, it was because they might never have heard from their dependents at all and returned to find out how bad conditions were. Moreover, as several scholars have concluded, the South was itself so internally divided, especially in the hill regions, that allegiance to the Confederacy was hardly a matter of fierce conviction even at the start of hostilities. As the war drew to its close, some Rebels continued to lambast the rich as many had during the war itself. A Georgian asked candidates for public office to consider placing taxes on slaves. "Is it right that the poor man should be taxed for the support of the war, when the war was brought about on the slave question, and the slave at home accumulating for the benefit of his master, and the poor man's farm left uncultivated, and a chance for his wife to be a widow, and his children orphans?"[72] Dissent was especially strong in North Carolina, where the yeomanry protested against fighting to protect the low country planters' property. "A wide chasm," writes a recent scholar, "separated the champions of secession from much of the army and civilian population" throughout the South. A Columbus, Georgia, shoemaker spoke for many poor whites when he wrote after a Rebel victory in 1862, "What is gained anyway? It is a rich man's war and a poor man's fight, at best."[73]

The members of the slaveholding elite complained less about the loyalty of their white inferiors than they did about the leaders of the cause, most of whom belonged to the gentry class. In Camden, South Carolina, Mary Chesnut listened while gentlemen explained the disaster to each other. "It was the mere audacity of despair," she sighed as they singled out one general to lambast after another. General James Chesnut, her husband, and the rest settled on P. G. T. Beauregard for his supposed "inefficiency," "blunders," and "dense stupidity."[74] In pursuit of the various architects of disaster, disgruntled losers often found politicians who had led the cause of secession as the most vulnerable creatures deserving censure. Captain McBlair told Lizinka Ewell that many in Richmond had come to "dislike or despise Jeff. Davis." They complained, the veteran told her, that if someone proved successful, the Confederate president turned "jealous of him and hated him." Shortly after his capture, General Richard Ewell, Lizinka's husband, confided to Union commander Orlando B. Willcox that the Richmond crowd, including Jefferson Davis and his cronies, had criminally mismanaged the war effort. Amused, Willcox wrote his wife, "I think U S Grant had something to do with the matter!"[75]

. . . .

With reference to the second phase—reaction to conditions at home—the returning veterans faced the problems of readjustment and losses of loved ones, news of whom they had not learned in the chaos of the final days. Even the return itself was scarcely easy for a variety of reasons. The members of a Texas cavalry unit remembered how at the beginning of the war the crowds had cheered and waved, but in 1865 "the soldiers were regarded at best with indifference, sadness, and perhaps a little embarrassment." In Waxahachie, soldiers drifting through on their way homeward served "merely as an unpleasant reminder of the hardships of war and the humiliation of defeat."[76] Washington, Georgia, had escaped the ravages of General William T. Sherman's March to the Sea. In May 1865 the townspeople warmly greeted the first Confederate soldiers returning to their homes. As further hordes of veterans passed through, however, the town served hospitality to less welcome visitors—an infestation of lice that "crawled thickly on grass, sidewalks, and houses."[77] This was not the time to organize veterans clubs, plan war memorials, or write solemn hymns about the fallen. It would be some years before the Lost Cause movement became a major force in Southern culture and politics.

In fact, returning soldiers were not necessarily greeted as heroes at all. Sometimes civilians had reason to be circumspect if not suspicious, contrary to later legend. The countryside was overridden with hostile forces — uncontrolled Federal units, wandering freedmen, marauding bands. It was said that Wheeler's Rebel men were a greater threat to chicken coops and pigpens than Sherman's army had been. Bedraggled veterans were easily mistaken for thieving bushwhackers, who pretended to be Rebels or Yanks as circumstances suited.[78] Throughout the South, the closing days of the war and early months of peace were marked in many places by sheer anarchy. Feeling that their honor and manhood were in doubt, veterans sometimes showered their fury on civilians. They looted homes and abandoned Confederate storehouses, and they smote those suspected of Unionism. In 1865 the governor of Texas remarked that "human life" in his state "is not to day worth as much, so far as law or protection can give value to it, as that of domestic cattle."[79] From random pillaging, it was only a step to join a vigilance committee to terrorize freedmen as a way to assuage the sense of remorse for their failure to win Southern independence.

Not all Southerners were ready to honor the defeated — either because they thought the veterans had not fought hard enough or because they had opposed the conflict from start to finish. One unpatriotic planter greeted half-starved Private Carlton McCarthy and his brother, both from Lee's army, by providing them a breakfast consisting of "a platter of cleanly picked fishbones."[80] Even a handful of downcast, ragged, homeward-bound veterans were easily typed as dangerous brigands to be shunned or driven away. Alone on the farm, Emily Harris in the piedmont of South Carolina took in a cavalry officer, who had begged for shelter, but she pledged not to repeat the hospitality to other uniformed strangers. "I have heard things about my lodger since dark which will cause me a sleepless night."[81]

In the South's hill country, matters were far worse. There Union sentiment had always been very strong. Some returning veterans encountered horrors that only the battlefield itself could match. In fact, the war continued well into the summer of 1865 in parts of East Tennessee. Unionists, who had been thoroughly intimidated by the Rebels in prior years, were in a position to wreak vengeance on defeated enemies. Three veterans in the Union forces wrote their father to warn the former secesh enthusiasts in Carter and Washington Counties that they would not be forgotten in peace. "They was for separation and we a posed it all we cold they said when they got thear independence that the Union famelyes cold not stay hear no how now we expect to come hear shortly and we have concluded that separation is Best and they must leave before we come." One soldier from Blount County, Tennessee, was greeted by neighbors and "given 34 licks with a two-handed brush." In some beats, returning Rebels had to leave at once or be beaten and even killed. Unionists also executed or whipped civilian secessionist advocates. In Knoxville, a female resident reported, "Dr. Massengill was terribly cowhided—Bob West had his skull broken—Epps was beaten all most to a death—and a good many more— a man by the name of Beard was severely beaten by Shade Harris." A resident of Morristown, Tennessee, lamented "that not a day passes but what some 'rebel' receives his 400 lashes or its equivalent—the contents of a minnie rifle—Even persons whose names have not been associated with the armies of this or any adjacent department share the same brutal fate."[82] Unionist employers refused to hire the Rebel veteran, who was already strapped for U.S. dollars.

Not surprisingly under such circumstances, some soldiers discovered that the Yankee enemy could prove a better friend than fellow Rebels or irate neighbors who had fought on the other side. As he prepared to leave for home, Private Philip Stevenson found some Northern soldiers nearby especially helpful. He managed to secure clothing and even a flashy "cravat" from the victors. His own rags had become too lice-ridden to wear any longer. But he dared not return to guerrilla-ravaged Missouri until June, some weeks later. He recalled, "The feeling was too fierce there." A zealous Rebel, Stephenson worried that life under an "intolerant and infamous" Union regime in St. Louis would be more galling than any man of honor could endure. Moreover, there was the danger of physical assault, expulsion, or death in that tumultuous city and state.[83]

Veterans who were not immediately sent off to Union stockades as prisoners of war had to fend for themselves, bearing parole papers. Those in prisons or sent to them after surrender endured hardships equal to the conditions at the front. "Today [I] saw a man with a bullet hole in his head over an inch deep," reported Alabama private John Ransom in a Union prisoner-of-war compound. The POW was mindlessly roaming the grounds, "and you could look down in it and see maggots squirming about in the bottom."[84] Health conditions were sometimes not much better than the notorious Confederate Andersonville in Georgia. The food was scarcely edible. But provisions were short everywhere in the South. One small detachment from Lee's army found a young ox that had grazed too close to the famished soldiers as they staggered down the road. The soldiers feverishly devoured it raw.[85] Luckily, some units on the way home received the charity of their victors whom they met on the way. To restore a semblance of order, the Federals often furnished railroad and steamboat tickets, clothing, shoes, and provisions.

Despite such help, the numbers leaving a battle site together could not be too large. Members of a sizable contingent would be forced into competition with each other when the land had already been subjected to earlier foraging. Nor could the Southern civilians always be trusted: they feared the ragged, armed intruders or were robbers themselves. To travel alone, however, was to invite death. Stragglers and deserters infested the hinterlands hunting for loot, as Frazier's *Cold Mountain* relates. Those with severe war wounds or amputations were wise to postpone departure until conditions of peace and order improved. They could not have kept pace with their healthy companions. Joseph McClure in a Texas unit had to spend a year convalescing, then on crutches he started from Atlanta in mid-July. Riding a mule on the last leg, he reached home, Mount Prairie, Texas, a month later.

Veteran McClure recalled that a company of perhaps fifty men might leave the site of surrender, if paroled, but soon broke off into groups of three or four.[86] According to Private William Fletcher in a Texas regiment, the men with whom he traveled would peel off, "dropping out to visit relatives or friends." By the time they reached Alabama, out of fifty who started the trek, only three remained on their "westerly course."[87] The pattern illustrated the trail of kinspeople who had long kept in touch with their brethren throughout the South. As a result, soldiers could stop for days or even weeks to visit a married sister, a third cousin, or an in-law as they made their way south and west to their native locale.

Homecoming had other risks. Some boys in gray brought back contagions to family members—tuberculosis and other transmissible maladies. Worse were the carriers of venereal diseases. The historian Margaret Wolfe observes that, by one estimate, a third of the men who died in Union and Confederate veterans' homes were victims of advanced sexual diseases. Some of their wives "went to their graves, rotted and ravaged by the pox that their men brought home, or how many veterans' children were blinded by gonorrhea or stunted by syphilis."[88] Part of the problem was the demoralizing effects of defeat and the strains of battle. Men took their pleasure where they could find it. At least one occasion caused outrage in the ranks. In a Virginia artillery unit in 1865, a private informed his sister, "The boys . . . rode one of our company on a rail last night for . . . going to sleep with Captain Lowry's black man."[89]

Added to the problems of health was the still more serious question of starvation. In the mountainous parts of the South, most especially, shortages were alarming. Mrs. John Harris, a Yankee doing relief work among Southern Unionist refugees, found them a demoralized group: "It is a very dark picture, made up of miserable looking and old men, with naked children of all ages. Many come here to die, no provision being made for them other than the food and shelter provided by the government." She was especially struck by the women's "vacant, listless expression seeming to say, 'We are only poor white trash.'"[90] In early 1866, Governor Robert Patton of Alabama received the following communication from Coosa County: the people were "out of Corn and Cant Git it . . . what is best to doo it was too late for us to Make a Crop when we got home last year Wee maid Nothin and wee haint [made] Nothin yet." Some spoke of conditions in the mountains equal to the famine years in Ireland—"the sickening wail of a perishing people is hourly heard crying for bread."[91]

The returning soldier might not even be wholly recognizable—with an arm or leg missing and a changed expression in his face, a distracted look in his eyes. In some parts of the South, a third of the veterans had lost a limb or were otherwise maimed. As late as 1879, the government of Georgia was spending $35,000 a year on artificial legs and arms. South Carolina spent $20,000 for that purpose.[92] Some took their disability as well as could be imagined. Lieutenant Richard Lewis of Bratton's Brigade in Longstreet's Corps was captured, had to have his left leg amputated, and convalesced in a Federal hospital. Remarkably, he kept up his spirits—at least so far as his letters to his mother reveal. But he did sound a plaintive note in his last communication at the close of the war: "You need not fret and worry about me, for I cannot be of any use or service to my country or at home, and I am going to take it easy. . . . Tell Ella Sloan that I don't reckon we will ever run any more horse races."[93]

At a gathering of women, Mary Chesnut, the famous diarist, heard them debate the dubious merits of marrying men with a missing limb or two. But one dissented: "Don't waste your delicacy. Sally H. is going to marry a man who has lost an arm . . . and she is proud of it. The cause glorifies such wounds." In reply, Chesnut recorded, "Annie said meekly, 'I fear it will be my fate to marry one who has lost his head.'"[94] On the other hand, men at home joked that one-armed veterans had a better chance with the ladies than those fully equipped. "Sorry about that ugly wound, Captain," exclaimed one convivial soul in Georgia. "A hand is a bad thing to lose, but it won't hurt you among the ladies of Savannah. There are plenty that you can persuade to give you one. What'll you drink?"[95] Lizinka Brown Ewell, wife of General Richard Ewell of Lee's army, reported the reactions of several amputees to their plight. Among them was a Colonel Holladay in Virginia who had to have an arm removed. The pain, she reported, was so great that he declared "death would be a relief." Both he and a General Trimble had undergone additional amputations of their limbs, owing to the progress of infections. An amputee from Georgia showed monumental grit. Returning home armless, he "made his wife hitch him to a plow which she drove; they made a crop."[96]

For most returning soldiers conditions were not so grim. In fact, some even missed the war almost from the start. Philip Stephenson remarked that he suddenly felt "a constraint" upon leaving his comrades in arms on the wharf at St. Louis. He recognized that "the veneer of civilization" returning was the cause of that new coldness of spirit. "Army life is congenial only to the brief period of youth," he sighed, "the freeness of it, the comradeship of it, the simple honor, fidelity of it."[97] A nostalgia for the drama of battle and bonding of men in the ranks would become paramount at the reunions of the veterans years later. Returning soldiers, of course, delighted in the prospect of peace, home, and drink. In late July 1865, two Kentucky regiments on their way back by train were "as boisterous in their delight as boys." They cleared Burkesville Junction, Virginia, of all "eatables and drinkables," remarked a Yankee reporter.[98] There was, however, often a note of malaise in the merrymaking. "An epidemic of drunkenness, gambling, and fighting prevailed while we were waiting for our final orders," one Confederate recalled. The absence of military orders and discipline unleashed passions and pent-up frustrations. Gambling with worthless Rebel dollars led to free-for-all battles among the unofficered ranks.[99]

Demobbed from a Kentucky unit, Sergeant Major Johnny Green reached his father and home after fending off bushwhackers and thieving Union soldiers. "Of course it was a great joy to both of us to be together again." But, he quickly added, "being out of money I had to get to work at once."[100] The Palmers of South Santee were delighted when Thomas Palmer III and cousin Philip Palmer arrived unexpectedly on May 3. Thomas explained that Joe Johnston's army had been ready to surrender when they decided to desert. By that means they could avoid parole and the loyalty oath and be ready to fight again. "I must admit," wrote Thomas's sister Harriet, "they were right" to do so.[101]

The Palmer boys in good health and with all their limbs had come back to households sometimes despoiled by the Yankees and freed people. Yet the home folks had survived and remained physically and mentally vigorous. Other veterans and their civilian kinfolk were not so lucky. Josia

Reams of McNairy County, Tennessee, arrived to find an empty household. He had lost his father, his stepmother, and a brother, killed in battle. A half-brother who had fought for the Union was dead as well. Reams explained, "So our home was broken up and I was penniless."[102]

When most Confederates started for home, Confederate bills were useful only for gambling as if with play money. The contrast with Billy Yank was pronounced. He carried "a 'real 'wad,'" as the historian Carl Fish put it. Mustering-out pay for the Union soldier came to a hefty $250. Some walked away with as much as $550, from bounty payments and back pay.[103] Southerners by and large were, like Josia Reams, "penniless." Thus the business of beginning over from scratch could be a cause of severe anxiety. George Collins, awaiting parole from Joe Johnston's army, wrote his wife, "I feel more down cast with the prospect of attempting to start anew than I had thought possible."[104] Jobs were scarce, and even general officers, formerly wealthy planters with slaves to do their bidding, found themselves unemployed or taking menial positions.

Plantations not only were in ruins, but the occupants scattered—both masters and slaves—as Union armies pressed toward triumph. The Dabney family in Mississippi had fled to Louisiana and on return found Burleigh, their Mississippi home, vandalized and the livestock gone. Adding to the problem was an unexpected woe. Shortly after order was restored in the neighborhood, the aristocratic (and once snobbish) Thomas Dabney of Hinds County entered the upstairs children's room with an ashen face and some dire words. "My children," his daughter recalled the aging planter say, "I am a ruined man. The sheriff is downstairs. He has served this writ on me. It is for a security debt."[105] A prewar friend, whom he had considered a man of unimpeachable honor, had asked for his signature on a promissory note for thousands of U.S. dollars. Through years of war, Dabney had given the matter little thought, but at this point he had no choice except to meet the bankrupt friend's obligation. The sheriff's auction sale took place shortly thereafter. Years of penury followed. With Dabney's daughters performing duties once assigned to domestic slaves, the family managed to repay old obligations and take barrels of vegetables to the New Orleans market. Himself scarcely used to hand labor, Dabney personally sawed firewood for the household's cooking and heating.[106]

Those in the path of Sherman's army were, of course, much worse off than the Dabney family. In April 1865, from Chesterville, South Carolina, Mrs. Robert Smith wrote to her daughter-in-law, Eliza Carolina Middleton Huger Smith. She described the misery of the civilians while the Yankees swarmed into Columbia. "God's judgments," she moaned, "are pressing heavily upon us & we almost despair of ever being cheered by the light of his countenance." So many of her women friends had witnessed their homes afire. In the frantic chaos, others, trapped while trying to flee, had hastily packed trunks and valuables stolen from them. One friend, Sue Pringle, had lost her mansion on the Ashley River, Mrs. Smith reported. The house was "now smouldering in ashes; her beautiful trees the work & culture of years cut down; lands & negroes all in the hands of the Yankees; the house at Darlington robbed." [107]

Mrs. Stuart, a boardinghouse landlady who had been in Sherman's way, could not hide her bitterness from the newly arrived occupying forces. A young Unionist soldier had heard the embittered woman glumly rejoice at the news of Abraham Lincoln's assassination. He was a "wretch," she snapped, who "has gotten his just deserts." The childless widow had lost both her husband, at Antietam, and her only son, a fifteen-year-old drummer-boy killed while serving under Stonewall Jackson. Ransacking the house and finding Mrs. Stuart's severe, black widow's veil, the federals ordered that she display it on the front veranda as a signal of contrition and submission to Unionist rule. "She stared at them for a few seconds with eyes in which hate, horror, and revenge strove for mastery," a female lodger recalled. Grimly Mrs. Stuart nodded assent. To spare her pride, the lodger, setting the example, managed to move the soldiers across the street. After a little while, they saw the widow walk outside in full black mourning weeds. She mounted a chair ostensibly to place the veil on a hook. Then she tossed it angrily from herself—"the badge of her stricken life." She put something else over the spot—they could not see what— and suddenly kicked the chair out from under her. To the horror of all those watching, they saw her body abruptly convulse. The soldiers rushed forward, but it was too late to save her. "Under the crape veil floating out upon the April-kissed breezes, with a strong cord firmly knotted about her neck," the witness declared, "hung all that was mortal of that once proud southern woman." [108]

Women of rank were not the only Rebels who might pitch into the dark of hatred. We have no idea of the number of suicides that took place in the early days after the defeat. Yet oddly enough, it would seem that male civilians may have been more likely to take their own lives than the war veterans were. Or at least a couple of prominent figures did so. Governor John Milton of Florida, a once ardent secessionist, vigorously denied that he had ever turned against the Union. In the summer of 1865, however, a veil of melancholy enveloped him. At his middle Florida plantation, Sylvania, in Jackson County, the wartime governor pointed a musket at his eyes. With his toe, he reached the trigger and "sprinkled his brains over the ceiling of his room." Ethelred Philips, a dyed-in-the-wool Unionist throughout the war, exclaimed that it was "by far the best act of his bad life." The weapon, Philips observed wryly, had been used thirty years before in Columbus, South Carolina, to "assassinate a brave man" whom Milton had been "afraid of." The irascible Virginia secessionist Edmund Ruffin's suicide by similar means is well known.[109]

Most white Southerners found their world shattered. Some would never recover. Many lost hope and even faith. The Reverend Dr. William Brown declared in the last year of the war, "You have been called upon to pass through deep water, you have sorrow upon sorrow. It was the path your Savior trod and He will grant you the comfort of His love and the fellowship of His spirit."[110] Redemption was to come, many preachers promised, but the world of Southern whites was never the same again. In the years that followed Appomattox, the demons of despair were to howl and nip at the heels of many former Rebels.

CHAPTER ELEVEN

HONOR CHASTENED

Wherefore hidest thou thy face, and forgettest our affliction
and our oppression? For our soul is bowed down to the dust:
our belly cleaveth unto the earth.

—Psalm 44:24–25

The years following the apocalyptic end to the Confederacy left many
former Rebels in a state of sullen resignation and, for some, permanent
dejection. "I have no country, no flag, no emblems, no public spirit,"
mourned one veteran.[1] The historian Jackson Lears notes that a sense of
doubt was not confined to the post–Civil War Southerner alone. "Despite
the Promethean optimism of the official culture" in the reunited America,
he writes, "a sense of human finitude persisted among the more comfortably situated as well as those on the margins of society." He attributes
the melancholy mood in part to the Civil War itself. The sense of a dark-
ening future stemmed from the sight of the ubiquitous veterans "—not
just heroes but hollow-eyed men who had merely survived, maimed at
Antietam, gone mad at Chickamauga, reminders of the tragic limits on
all human aspirations."[2]

If such were the thoughts that the victors entertained, how much more
profound was the gloom abroad in a region struggling to recover from
the war's devastations. With worries about livelihood, physical health, and
political uncertainties, the former soldiers and their families at first had
little time or inclination for celebrating battlefield heroism, a movement
that had to await the revival of a little confidence and sense of regional
autonomy. That did not develop fully until the 1880s. Instead of reciting
happy memories of days in the ranks, some veterans sank into lethargy
and a few into numb terror. How galling it must have been to take the
loyalty oath, no matter how reluctantly or cynically, to see former slaves

going to the polls or asserting newly acquired rights, and to read in Northern papers about the sins of the South and God's vengeance for the holding of a race in bonds. A Federal surgeon, who married into a Winchester, Virginia, family, astonished his wife's friend, Lizinka Ewell. He arrogantly told her circle that "we must make all the friends we can from the North — we will need them in the coming trials."[3] The time was too soon after the conflict to arouse anything else than deep resentment. Of all white Americans throughout national history, only the Southern members of the race had to drink the bitter cup of psychological ruin. The sense of unrelenting humiliation was bound to be turned into anger, racial hatred, and revenge, despite the economic and moral costs.

The long-lasting consequences of the Confederate defeat were first and foremost a crisis of confidence in the leadership ranks of the fallen South. Many had lost not only their property but also their once prestigious vocations. Even general officers, formerly wealthy planters with slaves to do their bidding, found themselves unemployed or taking menial positions. It was said that General Pendleton had to plow his Kentucky farm in clothes so threadbare that he was mistaken for a hired man. General Elliott, a Charleston blueblood, hawked fish and oysters that he had caught himself in the bay. Another Charlestonian, Colonel Cary, sold baked goods prepared by his wife. According to historian Dixon Wecter, "Officers of 'good social position' went to work as hodcarriers in Richmond and Columbia, harnessing horses they had ridden home from the battlefield to hacks and wagons serving Union commissaries and quartermasters, or wound up as clerks or mechanics for the government they had fought four years, or sold tea and molasses to their former slaves."[4]

According to diarist Emma Holmes, Randolph Withers, son of a distinguished South Carolina judge, had to cut and carry wood to his widowed mother, after being so long "accustomed to live in the greatest luxury." Randolph's sister was so humiliated by the Witherses' fall in fortune that she seldom left the house after 1864, "even to go to church & most of the time has been spent in her chamber."[5] Likewise, Mrs. Motte of South Carolina reported that her once wealthy family could only provide corn bread and occasionally molasses on the table. "Mr. Motte quit going to church because he owned no decent clothes to wear." His despair was palpable: "I can't push him up to even try and help us in any way." Owing to his fatal procrastination he failed to land a buyer for some property the family needed to sell.[6] At Marianna, in middle Florida, Ethelred Philips, a physician, gossiped to his brother that "many of our wisest and best and

strongest men . . . have, like a reed bent to the blast . . . snapped asunder."
In Mississippi, planter Henry Garrett worried, "I am constantly stricken
with fatigue." According to the historian Dan Carter, that state of lassitude was often called in the South at this time "paralysis," "apathy," and
"moral catalepsy."[7]

Military men grievously missed the predictable army routines, the moments of battle excitement, and the opportunity of command which Confederate service had afforded them. After General George Pickett returned from an escape into Canada to avoid arrest for alleged war crimes
in North Carolina, he tried farming and failed in part because swords, not
plowshares, had marked his life. Attempts at business were equally disastrous. Pickett tried selling insurance for a New York firm. Never did he
overcome his bitterness for the foolish charge at Gettysburg which Lee
had ordered. But financial worries, the problematic health of his beloved
wife, LaSalle, the sad death of his young son Campbell, and a sense of futility left the West Point graduate dreading the future. It was "a thousand
times" more perilous than "any battle I have ever been in," he sighed. A
cousin sympathized. He remarked, "The[se] infernal hard time[s] are bad
enough to make a man mad without having family afflictions to to[r]ment
his feelings." In 1875, Pickett died of a "gastric fever" when only fifty years
old.[8]

Families of distinguished lineage suffered, too, from the social and economic woes that unconditional Union victory had wrought. The Palmers
of South Santee, South Carolina, for instance, fell from great heights to
poverty. Family holdings had once consisted of twenty-five thousand acres.
High land taxes (now that revenues from slave evaluations no longer applied), labor shortages, and poor prices reduced the clan to the yeomanry
class in one generation. The fall from social eminence prompted well-
educated Palmer daughters to marry bricklayers and small farmers of limited education.[9] Day labor was cheap but capital scarce for anyone starting
up a small factory or business. A brickmaker in Richmond named Stickler
and his Yankee partner managed to hire the necessary workers, and they
obtained the financing. But, it was reported, "the people have no money
to buy the bricks after they are made."[10]

A few veterans discovered that sisters, wives, or mothers had broken
under the strain of their absence, the war, and the deprivations they
had endured. According to insane asylum records in Georgia, Mrs. Elizabeth W. Warner "had an attack of mental disorder . . . resulting from
fright by Sherman's soldiers." Years later a breakdown recurred: "Her

most prominent delusion appears to be the idea that it is her duty to burn and break up everything that she can."[11] Lucinda C. Ozburn, age twenty-one and single, was another war casualty: her insanity was attributed to "Menstrual derangements and the excitement resulting from the arrival of the Federal Army at Jonesboro battle &c." Emily Johnson was also literally scared out of her wits, the asylum records disclosed, during "the burning of Columbia and the sacking of the City by Sherman's Army." The house the family was living in had burned to the ground. According to her asylum record, she had barely escaped death by fire. The patient, a caregiver wrote, "is usually quiet but occasionally becomes angry, when urged to do what she is averse from and uses harsh language, but has only once struck any one." Still worse, the unmarried twenty-five-year-old woman had a stillborn child, and she was afflicted with childbed fever. She was not "known to have had convulsions previous to the burning of Columbia. They are induced by any undue excitement but usually occur at night."[12]

Those women with a tendency toward depression found themselves even more aggravated by the wartime conditions that added so much gloom and care in their lives. One South Carolina planter's wife noted, "I sometimes have days of misry [sic] for which I cannot give, even to myself, a cause. These spells are periodical and today for the first time I thought perhaps they were the premonitory symptoms of insanity. It is a dark doom to dread . . . Oh! The war, the war!"[13]

Although evangelical revivals developed in the 1880s, the churches fell for a time into the maw of despondency. For so long confident that God favored people as righteous as themselves, churchgoers felt mortified and apathetic. The Eufala Alabama Association complained in 1868 that the Baptist churches under its ecclesiastical jurisdiction had become "cold and indifferent." The departure of discouraged farmers for points west depleted church resources and lowered the spirits of those remaining. The neglect and destruction of church property scarcely aroused a new spirit of renewal when funds were so short, manpower to rebuild so diminished, and congregants fully occupied with mere survival—or the politics of Reconstruction. Ministers were not easy to find when salaries could not meet the standards of subsistence living. Moreover, the exodus of the black members to form their own churches not only showed an independence not at all welcome but also revealed that the old scheme of white paternalism and slave deference no longer obtained. Whereas in antebellum times in Georgia, 35 to 40 percent of Baptists consisted of slaves, by 1890, they constituted 54 percent of the Baptist total throughout the nation, nearly all in their own churches.[14]

. . . .

The plight of churches and the women—the widows and the fatherless most especially—paled in comparison with the difficulties that the veterans themselves had to face. The chaos of war and poor record-keeping hid the extent of mental suffering among the Rebels. But it was there and in greater numbers than ever can be found in the archives. Southern culture permitted little disclosure of psychological breakdown or suicide because such signs of alleged weakness stained the esteem in which family members held themselves.

Thanks to the historian Eric Dean's research, the records of the state asylum in central Georgia provide some clues. For instance, Abner Burks had collapsed during and after the siege of Vicksburg in 1864. The report on his health noted: "Has a disposition to assault members of his own family under the idea that they are plotting against him. He is also in the habit of seeking to do mischief with fire. . . . Sleeps irregularly." [15] Samuel Ware of Marion County, Georgia, a thirty-year-old bachelor, had left the Confederate army "in a state of mental derangement," and the illness persisted as late as 1872. The report suggested "hereditary predisposition; his mother was insane for several years." James Taylor, a former soldier from Taliaferro County, suffered literally from shell shock, according to the asylum authorities. He had received a concussion from "the bursting of a shell near him, his mind became so much worse, that he was sent home." For years he had been quiet, but then, more recently in 1872, he tried to slit his brother's throat. Joseph Henderson from Hamilton County, the Chattanooga area of Tennessee, was supposed to have gone insane from "masturbation." That was a commonly held opinion, but the record also mentions that "his mind was discovered to be affected" while serving in General Sterling Price's army in Missouri where he had undergone "many fatigues." About every three days or so he would grow excitable and uncontrollable, threatening to hang himself but never attempted it. A nurse or physician noted that he "is very lecherous. His sole desire is to gratify the animal appetite." Albinus Snelson had showed signs of battle fatigue in 1864 but grew steadily worse. In 1866, the records show that the twenty-two-year-old had tried to burn himself to death. Once he had to be restrained from flinging himself from an upstairs window. Like most acute depressives, he could not sleep, haunted perhaps by night terrors from his war experiences. Captain William J. Dixon, a bachelor of twenty-five, had served in the Sixty-third Georgia Regiment, "but at the close of the War came home deeply chagrined and depressed by the issue. And for the first time in his life became the subject of habits of intemperance." The alcohol, the officials thought, had affected his mind; he mumbled incoherently to himself and experienced periodic bouts of overstimulation. William R. MacRae's disordered mind was attributed to "religious excitement" after his service in the Confederate army, but his mental health was apparently a matter of concern during the war as well.[16]

At first, politics offered no remedies to assuage the sense of loss and disaster. Veterans did not necessarily win local or state offices when elections were held in 1865 and 1866. Indifferent after losing their heady wartime idealism, former Rebels failed to vote for their own kind, and civilians looked for leadership, not glorious exploit on the battlefield, as recommendation. "I am sick of everything connected with political offices," declared a Virginia planter. Another from Georgia pledged to "vote no more; let them squabble to their hearts content; I want no further share in it."[17]

In contrast to the liveliness and attentiveness of the campaigns in the 1850s, the privilege of suffrage attracted less than half the prewar numbers in 1865. It is estimated that only one of three veterans went to the polls.[18] That would sharply change as confidence and apathy turned to anger later in the effort to overthrow "Negro rule." At first, however, confusion in Washington over Reconstruction policies led to perplexity and inanition at home. Andrew Johnson had offered the South terms that seemed almost reasonable, but after acting as they thought in a "manly and honorable fashion," the Black Republicans in Congress once more had "tricked and betrayed" them, a Georgia paper protested, as they had in 1861. How discouraging it must have seemed to the soldiers once more home that their most "conciliatory leaders"—men of high Confederate standing but willing to cooperate with the national government—were greeted with Yankee contempt. These elected officials were rejected at the very "doors of the National Temple" in Washington and were "scorned and insulted," as the Georgia editor put it.

The dictates of expediency and of surrender to allegedly outrageous demands about how to conduct their once compliant labor force were too much for many to bear. Rumors of confiscation of land and possessions to benefit the freedmen abounded. Doing his best to reconcile congressional demands with Southern white opposition, Benjamin Perry of South Carolina and a handful of others could find few supporters. The die-hard former Rebels moaned about the impending loss of their properties, but, as a friend of Perry told him, " 'we have only got two dollars and a half a piece,' and why should we sacrifice our honor to save that."[19]

Despite the difficult political situation, most of those who returned to civilian life had to comply with the requirement of swearing loyalty to the victorious foe. Even that gesture aroused much passion and soul-searching. David Golightly Harris, a North Carolina farmer and veteran, reported in his diary that, while some fifteen Yankees were aiding the freedmen and "administering the oath of allegeance [sic] to the United States," he refused to swear his loyalty "until circumstances compel me." Harris did not mention how long he held out. In June 1865, for the sake of his family's well-being, John Holmes of Louisiana went before Captain C. W. Ferguson and took the oath. Yet his cousin Emma Holmes recorded that "he felt so ashamed of himself he did not wait to find out the others" who did the same. Some remained adamant. Catherine Edmonston of North Carolina smoldered, "We feel a deep & abiding resentment towards a nation who thus debases our sense of personal honour & weakens the heretofore sacred obligation of an oath taken in the name of the Almighty God." No one should not take the legal rite seriously, she argued, and warned the enemy: "You have sullied the purity of our integrity. You have us promise what we will not pay, & for all this we hate you!"[20]

An inability to meet the daily challenges of life in a poverty-ridden environment was by no means a rare reaction. We might call this the Ashley Wilkes Syndrome—as it applied to the planter class as well as to less fortunate whites in the Southern social hierarchy. For planters—whether veterans or not—the loss of slave labor was a blow to the pocketbook and also to the sense of who they were. It may have struck hard those soldiers who had heard how labor relations had changed on the home front during their absence. Some found the reality quite unnerving. A Virginia planter observed, "I must have niggers work for me. I can't do nothin' on my place without 'em. If they send all the niggers to Africa, I'll have to go thar, too." The same sentiment was expressed by a South Carolina landholder. He declared, "If I had to work my land with whites, I'd quit, I couldn't manage or depend on them."[21] General Josiah Gorgas, the former chief of Confederate ordnance, complained in January 1867, "For the most part I have lived in a state of profound depression, which has made life a burden to me." His management of the Briarfield Iron Works had failed. In 1868, he accepted the appointment of vice-chancellor of the University of the South. The experience was not a happy one. He and the trustees quarreled for years and finally he resigned in 1878.[22]

A more poignant example of maladjustment to postwar conditions was J. D. P. Wilkinson, a veteran, planter, and businessman of Pleasant Ridge, Greene County, Alabama. He lost all his slaves during the war and then his lands in 1867, owing to unpaid debts. His wife left him, and his daughter, a country schoolteacher, was his sole support until he drifted off to Little Rock, Arkansas. There he failed as an insurance salesman, worked in a shoe shop in Memphis, and then sold newspaper subscriptions for some months. Finally, he found some peace in 1874 by "pasting papers" for a Shaker community in South Union, Kentucky. "For this unhappy itinerant," as the historian Robert Gilmour observes, "migration became a hopeless way of life." There were others like him—wandering from state to state in search of some security.[23]

Addiction to alcohol was a common reaction to defeat in war and failure in peace.[24] No less unexceptional was the fate of some who simply could not end prewar habits of high living and fast spending. Such matters may not appear in official records. The historian must depend instead on the written remarks of friends and relatives of despondent veterans. Thomas Watson, the Populist leader of Georgia, recalled that his father, John, returned home an emotional cripple. Blessed in 1860 with an estate worth $55,000 and lands that some forty-five slaves had worked, the former army private returned home wounded and penniless. He failed at farming. The economic uncertainties of the postwar period and the need to support a family of a wife and seven children added to his misery. "My father," Watson reported, "used to be virtually paralyzed for weeks by what he called 'the blues.'" The popular term was short for the "blue devils" of depression. Hard liquor was at best a doubtful remedy for the ailment because ethanol is a depressive ingredient. As if these circumstances were not sufficiently wretched, John Smith Watson, who had been twice wounded in the war, tried to make up by gambling the losses from growing cotton. He sank further toward ruin and lost on one occasion as much as $1,500. He had hoped to re-create a dream not realized even before the great disaster of war. In the late 1860s he tried to build a pillared mansion in front of the old log cabin that he had inhabited before going off to war. Under such delusions, Watson went bankrupt in the crash of 1873 and, according to C. Vann Woodward, his son Tom Watson's biographer, he became "more prone than ever to the 'blues' and the indulgence of his weaknesses." Watson had to move his family to an Augusta boardinghouse and bar that he managed. For weeks at a time he lay abed, sunk in hopeless torpor, turning his blank stare toward the wall. Even before "he had lost a single child," a very understandable source of grief, Tom Watson reported, "this depression would come upon" his father.[25]

The Rebel veteran John Smith Watson was intemperate, hard-fisted, taking out his inner pain on his son Thomas. Years later, Tom ruminated that "had I been firmly governed and not with fitful harshness: had I not been abused, ridiculed, mocked and scorned there would be sunshine where now there is shadow."[26] Perhaps the son exaggerated, but he blamed his father while remaining devoted to his mother. He confessed his own tendency toward a "very despondent" temperament. The mood resembled, he confessed, "a shadow that follows like a hungry wolf." It was "a presence that poisons every joy, stains every beauty, checks every impulse."[27] Years later he recalled that in 1877, when a young lawyer, he had been struck down with melancholia. "For months I lay in my office on a big sofa perfectly benumbed. My mind was chained to one subject and it was utterly impossible for me to think of anything else. I became morose, wordy and well nigh desperate." The unease developed into a sense of complete frustration that found an outlet in accosting "a noted fighting cock," named Skip Wright. He had cursed Wright for striking his brother in an earlier altercation. When Wright tried to run him down on his horse, Watson pulled out his pistol. Reflecting on his intemperate conduct, he later remarked, "Well, what was all this grieving about?"[28] Scarcely introspective, Watson had no clue. His sense of honor was as much a part of his character as it was in the heart of any fiery gentleman of the old school. "Prompt as a hornet to resent affront," a reporter noted, Watson nonetheless "will never insult others any more than he'll brook outrage from them." The *New York Journal* reported that, as an advocate for the code duello, Watson once shot "very satisfactory holes in a fellow attorney" named W. D. Tutt. His antagonist had, Watson thought, "invaded his sensibilities" during a law case.[29] A "shooting scrape" as he dismissed it, hindered his first attempt to win a state legislative seat.[30]

Such a temperament had its origins early in Watson's life. Undoubtedly a home environment so marred by a father's depression was bound to affect the growing child and even young adult. Tom Watson learned how to hate and throw out his own despair in a truculent way. That approach prepared him for his later role as a Populist leader and race-baiter. Even in his most radical pronouncements—when the Populists sought to unite workers, poor whites, and African American sharecroppers—Watson sounded both defiant and depressed. Politicians and journalists in the pay of the big corporations were claiming that he would fail, Watson said of himself. "But I will fight on. The tired hands grow discouraged, & the weary feet long for rest. But Duty unveils her starlike face & says 'Weary hands—fight on—Tired feet—march on.'"[31] Watson could sound poetic in his public expression of the gloom within when he spoke of "Stagnation since the war—Dead Sea of Politics—wandering among the ruins of our homes, seeking to lead out the green battalions of corn in the wasted fields."[32]

Few others in that period after the Civil War had Watson's witty iconoclasm, oratorical skill, and indomitable drive. Singular though he was, many other former soldiers and their troubled offspring shared his sense of outrage for wrongs and persecutions they could not wholly define but partially were the consequences of Confederate defeat. Such an unhappy frame of mind crops up in so many postwar diaries and collections of letters. Ella Thomas of Georgia noted that her husband, a former officer, was acting as if "utterly in spirit broken." Indeed, his disposition grew worse as the years passed. Always emotionally fragile, he felt overwhelmed by mounting debts, crop failures, and deteriorating health, made worse from overdrinking.[33] Ella Thomas reflected, "Men go out into the world & endeavour to retrieve their loss & come home depressed dejected and irritable, glad of a safety valve for the annoyance of the day. They come to wifes [sic] who have been fretted with careless servants and crying children, fretted by little worries while the ever present thought of debt is pressing like an iron weight upon them." The men, she continued, expect soothing words and calm reassurances. She claimed to do her best, but "seating himself in an attitude of abject dejection his head aching if a child touches his chair & so nervous that the least thing annoys him, Mr Thomas presents an appearance well calculated to try my nerves."[34] Her restraint of expression was an exercise in courageous reticence in itself.

Although Ella Thomas never expected her thoughts would become public knowledge, she was more outspoken about her troubles than Mary Chesnut. Similarly reduced in circumstances and yoked to a failed husband, Mrs. Chesnut made no complaints in her famous diary about her husband's postwar behavior. The Chesnuts' neighbor, Colonel William Johnson, however, wrote his brother that South Carolina's former U.S. senator was outwardly "the same elegant Gentleman he always was." Yet he had become "of not much account, he gets pretty comfortably drunk *about every* evening." In fact, despite the growing genuflections before the altar of the Lost Cause in the 1880s, gentlemen like "the Chesnuts, Mannings, Boykins," as veteran Johnson asserted, would never again "come to the front" of the social phalanx. Johnson speculated that Carolinians had grown tired of that sort of leadership out of a now-dead tradition. A friend of the aging general foolishly placed his name in nomination for the state legislature. He had to withdraw it, Johnson gossiped, as "there was no chance" for Chesnut to win the office. The voters, Johnson concluded, could no longer trust Chesnut's judgment.[35]

Behind these unpleasantries over the value of chivalric ardor was a deep sense of psychic injury. The hair of the relatively young Gorm Shannon, once a valorous soldier, had turned completely white during his war experiences. Colonel William Johnson, a neighbor, commented that Shannon's conduct had been "remarkable, for a man with the fine brain he was known to have. He shut himself in his house and yard." Hiding from the public, the unhappy Shannon declared that he "would 'die and go to Hell' before he would work," Colonel Johnson explained. For a time, Shannon's friends arranged for him to keep the books of a store, but he soon quit. "After another period of idleness money was raised with much difficulty to send him to Washington," Johnson gossiped. General Butler, a prominent member of Governor Wade Hampton's Democratic "fusion" allies, had no chance to place him in a government office before Shannon went off to New York. There he "was so in debauch" that he had to be shipped back to Charleston by steamer. Many others in Colonel Johnson's circle of Camden acquaintances seemed almost caricatures of feckless planters unable to recover from the experience of war. Veteran Dr. Boykin of distinguished Carolinian breeding sought appointment as professor of belles lettres at the university in Columbia. He needed the salary of $2,500 to keep up his enormous white elephant of a pillared mansion in Camden. When a more qualified candidate won the job, Boykin had blamed his defeat on local enemies—most especially Colonel William Shannon, Gorm Shannon's brother, who sat on the Board of Trustees. Colonel Johnson concluded, however, that the college authorities had been wise for there was no reason why they should fill professorial chairs "with used up and superannuated Doctors & Planters." The colonel moved his lengthy account of local failure to Jack Cantey, who lived nearby. Cantey "does nothing except work his garden," Johnson observed. Although notably intelligent, Sam Shannon, another in the hapless clan, "has proven to be entirely worthless," Johnson remarked. The informative Johnson was himself often depressed. He found that "my only real enjoyment" was deer hunting "when I can get out in the fields" with a "pleasant companion," yapping dogs, and careening birds overhead. Such moments enabled him to "bid farewell for 12 hours, to my debts, and other troubles." [36]

Living with men of this character was a hardship for their families and marked for life both young and old. If an illustration from fiction is permitted, William Faulkner's Quentin Compson and Miss Rosa Coldfield in *Absalom, Absalom!* may represent the aftereffects that war, death, and economic ruin visited upon families in the postwar years. The twenty-year-old Quentin, just about to leave for Harvard, considers himself a tragic heir of the Lost Cause. In reference to Quentin's forebears—the veterans and their women, victims on the home front—Faulkner writes: "His childhood was full of them; his very body was an empty hall echoing sonorous defeated names. He was not a being, an entity, he was a . . . barracks filled with stubborn back-looking ghosts." Likewise, Miss Rosa Coldfield is portrayed as a ghost. Quentin's father explains, "Years ago we in the South made our women into ladies. Then the War came and made the ladies into ghosts."[37] Embittered, angry ones, one might add. For instance, in actual life, Colonel Shannon's relative, a Miss Matthew, could not reside with her relations because her temper grew so "unreasonable." She had some justification. Worth some $40,000 before the war, she had patriotically put it all into Confederate bonds on the advice of all around her. She blamed William personally for allegedly cheating her. Neighborhood opinion had it that Miss Matthew had actually lost her mind from her frustration and fury at him and other kinspeople.[38]

Most of the women associated with the veterans were resigned to their plight and sympathized with the woes their men were suffering. For instance, Sarah Dorsey, a wealthy landowner and novelist of Louisiana, was depressed to "see on every side of you those near & dear to you by ties of blood & kinship struggling so hard & so ineffectually in this hard hard Battle of Life." Sarah Dorsey's first cousin John Knox Routh, once a planter worth half a million dollars, was barely managing to survive. A credit reporter for a Northern agency came to the blunt conclusion that he was worth not "a cent" of credit, having lost all his slaves and gained only an enormous load of debts. Besides, he said, Routh was "too indolent & stupid ever to work out."[39]

More common than the dejection that Colonel Thomas Routh, various Shannons, and other "Ashley Wilkeses" represented was the dispirited but not altogether hopeless mood of Caleb Forshey. Writing to another Louisiana veteran in 1867, Colonel Forshey declared, "There seemed to be little to live for after the death & burial of our country, the slaughter of the flower of our land, in defense of Civil liberty; and but for our family ties, neither you nor I would have given much for life. Certainly I had a thousand wishes that we could have all *sunk* together."[40] Likewise, Mary Pegram, the niece of a Colonel Johnson from a prominent Virginia family, called her uncle "the most miserable man she ever saw. He says if there were no hereafter he would blow his brains out." He had the prospect of becoming chancellor of the University of Virginia, but Mary Pegram worried that his mood would kill his chances. Aside from Johnson's war experiences, she added, he "never did anything in his life & that is the reason he is so queer & hypochondriacal." With fifty-five applicants equally desperate for so comfortable a post, his niece feared the worst.[41]

Some men, however, showed unusual pluck and made fortunes after the war—some honestly. A few chose riskier means. General Samuel Wragg Ferguson of Mississippi, for instance, reestablished his prewar fortune in cotton with a large plantation near Greenville. A high-living politician, he was treasurer of the local Levee Board until 1894, when some $39,000 was found missing from the ill-kept books. At a meeting of irate taxpayers at which Ferguson failed to show up, one of his friends, Judge Wynn, appealed to the old code of chivalry. "Do you, fellow men, want to see an old man, bowed with age, in delicate health—those of you especially who wore the gray in times of distress, see the man who led you in the thick of battle, he whom you honored and loved—wear the stripes of a felon?"[42] It was never clear whether the general stole the money outright, but Ferguson took no chances and left the community. He was next found in Ecuador, working on railroad construction.[43] A tried and true Redeemer of the Democratic persuasion, Samuel Ferguson was one of several Southern state financial officers and former soldiers, from Virginia to Louisiana, who absconded in the late 1880s or early 1890s. Their conduct made a mockery of Southern complaints about corrupt scalawags and carpetbaggers of the previous era.[44]

Others rose without stains to their honor, most particularly in the railroad business—the growth industry of the age. General Nathan Bedford Forrest was elected president of the Memphis, Okolona, and Selma Railroad in 1868. Alfred M. Shook, a private in the war, joined the Tennessee Coal and Iron Company. By the 1880s he was one of the leaders of industry in Birmingham, Alabama. General Joseph Johnston tried his hand at running railroads, but the work was boring, and he was relieved when the company failed. He took up insurance and, trading on his fame and the loyalty of former soldiers, he did exceedingly well. Others, though, tried as hard as possible to succeed, but lack of capital wore them down, and their companies foundered in debt. So it was with the Selma and Meridian Railroad that General William J. Hardee tried to resurrect from utter chaos. Despite his monumental efforts to rebuild it, loans came due, and the line was still unprofitable in 1868. Hardee had to relinquish control and turn to something else. Likewise, General Braxton Bragg, chief engineer for the Gulf, Colorado, and Santa Fe line, embroiled himself in a controversy like the ones that marked his less than glorious military career. He was fired. He then gained a post as a railroad inspector but died a few months later in 1876.[45] According to Lizinka Ewell, wife of General Ewell, some "96 physicians and 120 lawyers from the South" settled in Baltimore in 1865 and 1866. Unsurprisingly, their practices foundered under the weight of so much competition. Staying home was no answer either. A Dr. Tyler of Gloucester County, Virginia, she reported to her son Campbell Brown, had plenty of patients, but in the past four months of 1866 he had collected only $4 "because the people have no money." [46]

In a study of over five hundred former Confederate officers, William B. Hesseltine found that, along with railroad management, corporation law was a preferred occupation. Almost one out of eight in his biographical survey, though, fared poorly, "folded their hands and passed into oblivion." They died of "heartbreak, wounds, and disease within a few months of Appomattox." Thoroughly pro-Confederate himself, Hesseltine rejoiced in the contributions of the successful former Rebel generals, colonels, and majors. Much to the historian's satisfaction, they rebuilt the economy of the New South and restored white power under the Democratic banner.[47]

Some Confederate leaders went north or abroad to recoup their fortunes. In New York City, the remarkably resilient Burton Harrison, once Jefferson Davis's private secretary, who had spent nine months in a federal prison, established himself as a prosperous attorney before the New York City bar. There was also a Confederate "set" in France. In London, Judah P. Benjamin, another member of Davis's inner circle, rose to the prominence of queen's counsel. By 1870 if not sooner, most exiles returned home, including some of those who migrated with the idea of cash-crop planting with slave labor in Brazil.[48]

Farmers and planters who stayed on the land had to meet severe agricultural problems. Failing in their agrarian pursuits as prices declined, lands eroded, and capital grew ever scarcer, some of them turned to radical politics. Throughout the 1880s they railed against the factory, banking, and railroad interests. These leaders were not small farmers and sharecroppers. Instead, angered by the monopoly of officeholding positions that ruling factions enjoyed, men of short tempers like Ellerbe Cash and Tom Watson tried to develop alternative parties and arouse the ordinary farmers to their worsening economic prospects. Yet, ironically, in the politically turbulent year 1882, Ellerbe Cash ran on the radical Greenback ticket for the governor's chair with the help of both white and black poor farmers. He hated the smug, established New South businessmen and lawyers. With considerable boldness he repudiated the Democratic Party's resort to lynch law and the "assassination" of freedmen who had dared to voice their "political opinions."[49] Cash, however, lost by a wide but respectable margin.

The pattern of defeat that war had begun continued for the ordinary farmer and the disgruntled planter. P. D. Hyler, one of Cash's Greenback supporters, for instance, wrote him in 1881 that "the broken promises and mismanagement of the Democratic party" had set ablaze a sense of "national indignation" because of the corruption and fraud that marked the state's elections. Resorting to the antique rhetorical flourishes of the honor code, Hyler exclaimed in reference to the Palmetto State, "Her name which used to be the proud ensign of all that was honorable, nobler, grand, has been debased into a 'by-word and a reproach' among nations by the political vampires which prey upon her." Cash and his friends were outraged that Democrats thought their rule "too sacred" to be challenged, as Hyler put it. The brave soul, he fumed, who dissented from the reigning party was instantly "branded a political heretic" and was singled out as "a fit subject for the stake, the gibbet or the guillotine." Yet he warned Cash that the organizers of the new party had to avoid any sign of plans to subject the state to "negro rule." Hyler established his credentials for his candid remarks on the basis of some strong claims "to the lofty instruments of chivalry" even though reared outside "the limits of Charleston's refinement." He further established his legitimacy by referring to other bluebloods, former Confederate colonels, and distinguished legislators whom he called his friends.[50] The marks of the antebellum South's political traditions, with their stress on honor and lineage, were still in evidence. The coming Populist era would erode some of those vestiges of the old order but more gradually than one might have expected.

It is worth recalling what the late C. Vann Woodward wrote some years ago. He pointed out how the South throughout the later part of its history had "known the bitter taste of defeat and humiliation." In his famous essay "The Irony of Southern History," the Southern historian noted that, in common with most nations of the world, the victorious North excepted, the South "had repeatedly met with failure and frustration."[51] The unresolved mourning that the South displayed in its statues for the glorious dead, its legends of heroism and self-sacrifice, helped to perpetuate a collective sense of sullen anger. It is not too fanciful to suggest that losers are seldom magnanimous and show less charity toward the weak than victors.

. . . .

CHAPTER TWELVE

HONOR REDEEMED IN BLOOD

Gallant nation, foiled by numbers,
Say not that your hopes are fled;
Keep that glorious flag that slumbers,
One day to avenge your dead.
—Thomas E. Watson of Georgia,
"A Reply to the 'Conquered Banner'"

By the 1880s, honor, it might be said, was no longer chastened but was in the process of being redeemed. The means used was violence in the name of a holy vengeance. This time, though, the instrument of vindication was not civil war but two other modes of violence. The first involved white against white in personal encounters. The second and more tragic set whites against the lately freed people in mob actions as if the black race collectively bore total responsibility for the failure of Rebel arms. Southern murder rates had always been high, a circumstance often attributed to its frontier state, its heritage of herdspeople from the rough British borderlands, and its slaveholding traditions.[1] These factors, along with the honor code, certainly played a role, but in the postwar years, after four years of bloody war, one might have expected a decline in resort to arms and mayhem. Such was not the case. A major factor was the use of coercion and murder to overturn the Reconstruction governments by means of paramilitary organizations including the Ku Klux Klan. That subject has been treated sufficiently that it need not be explored here.

With regard to the first, personal combat took a different form in the postwar era, at least among gentlemen. Dueling took place fairly spottily for a variety of reasons, including the rise of evangelical religion among the upper classes and the obliteration of slaveholding wealth that undermined the antebellum principles of noblesse oblige. The absence of a two-party system also played a role. Until 1852 Democrats and Whigs had paired off over partisan matters, sometimes petty in nature, but the parties were thought to be equal in moral and social standing. Post–Civil War white Republicans—stigmatized as carpetbaggers and scalawags—did not meet that standard. Assassination, cart-whippings, and intimidation better suited the needs of the hour as Democratic "straight-outs" saw it. Redeemers of a less bloodthirsty character preferred to employ bribery, economic arm-twisting, and temptations of minor officeholding emoluments. In addition, evangelical preachings induced churchgoing gentlemen to forswear the pleasures of the dueling field. That trend had begun even before the Civil War. Finally, New South enthusiasts condemned the duel as an outworn, barbarous method of vindication, an obsolete tradition that frightened off Northern capital and subverted the new commercial values that the agrarian South required to meet the exigencies of the modern world. Although dueling enjoyed popularity among the military and possessing classes on the European continent, in the American South the practice gave way to less ritualistic forms of conflict—murder by ambush or simple encounter.

In one of the last duels in the nineteenth-century South, one can discern the relation of military defeat and the psychology of personal violence. The duel was a symbol of the old order. In the summer of 1880, Chesnut, Johnson, and other members of the Camden, South Carolina, elite were appalled by the prospect of a seemingly pointless encounter between Colonel James Shannon, a Camden attorney, and Colonel Ellerbe B. C. Cash, a hotheaded planter. After the victory at First Manassas, Colonel Cash tried to shoot an unarmed U.S. congressman, shouting, "You infernal s. of a b.! You came to see the fun did you? God damn your dirty soul I'll show you." Luckily, a sober-headed sergeant major and General Edward Porter Alexander, Cash's superior, who had just appeared, prevented the murder of this civilian prisoner. Thwarted, Cash then galloped off to hunt down Senator Lafayette Sabine Foster of Connecticut, who was supposed to be hiding in the woods.[2]

For all the petty truculence of Colonel Cash, the dispute in 1880 shed significant light on the dismal, even demoralized psychological state of the Carolinian community. General Chesnut threw up his hands and worried plaintively about "what could he do to stop it."[3] He belonged to the antebellum past, when such affairs between gentlemen had moral meaning for the participants and onlookers. But in these times, he retreated into bibulous silence. Never once did he speak to Shannon about the pending affair or try to intervene in any way. Yet their law offices faced each other on the street. (Mary Chesnut, it was rumored, had warned her husband to stay clear of the mess.)[4] Curiously, as often had happened when duels were still popular, attorneys like Shannon, representing the "gown law" that police and courts administered, resorted to "the law of reputation"—the code duello—to settle personal disputes.[5]

In an extraordinarily dramatic way, Colonel Shannon was perhaps himself a victim of the horrors of war that could still have lingered in his mind. Likewise, his opponent Cash's disposition since 1865 had become notorious. He quarreled endlessly with his neighbors. Behind the duel was a tangle of local quarrels and confused affairs that so often appeared in the annals of the Southern duel. To simplify: the circumstances that brought about the confrontation arose from a lawsuit in which Robert Ellerbe, the insolvent brother-in-law of Colonel Cash, was involved. Finding that the defendant had no available money, Shannon's law firm sought to attach his property only to discover that most of it was held in the name of Colonel Cash's wife, the defendant's sister. The attorneys tried to demonstrate that the mortgage arrangement between the pair was fraudulent. Cash's wife died before the case was settled, and in his grief the colonel decided to vindicate what he thought had been a slur on her honor. Ellerbe agreed that his sister's name had been outrageously maligned, issued a challenge to "the old gentleman," as Shannon was called, while Cash drew up one against Captain J. W. DePass, Shannon's law partner.[6]

DePass, however, had probably been the more insulting in his remarks but lacked the social and political stature that the senior partner enjoyed. Under the plea that a press of "professional engagements" explained his departure, DePass went off to North Carolina. The junior partner had himself accepted Ellerbe's challenge. The local antidueling society, however, prevented any encounter by having them arrested, not once but twice, and restrained. As for the other contest that ended in tragedy, DePass disclaimed any foreknowledge about it. For his seeming "lack of manhood," shady legal maneuvers, and unwillingness to prevent Shannon from entering the controversy, Colonel Johnson declared, DePass had been "utterly damned by all good people here."[7] In vain DePass pleaded, "All I ask, in God's name, from the citizens of my native State, for whose honour I have more than once shed my blood" is the good opinion of the public.[8]

William Bogan Cash, the colonel's son, had denounced Shannon as a "poltroon and coward," the requisite words for the upper-class deadly ritual. Stung by an offensive poem under Bogan's hand and by a column in a local paper that Cash had penned, the Shannon boys were outraged. At first their father had refused to fight on the grounds that duels violated state law and affronted his Christian principles. He was drawn into the affair because of their involvement. Horrified, he learned that one of his own sons had already issued a challenge and was to duel William Bogan Cash, the colonel's son, that very evening. A friend reported that Colonel Shannon had "turned pale and the perspiration showed itself on his face." "My God has it come to this," Shannon was said to exclaim, "that my sons should have to fight for me & me in full health . . . I will be disgraced and a ruined man."[9] He was determined not to allow any of his sons take his place on the mark.

The ins and outs of close kin and friends and the entanglements of various parties made this affair resemble the duels of the pre–Civil War era in the South. Shannon then issued a challenge against Colonel Cash if only to prevent the principals' sons from deadly encounters. Shannon claimed little knowledge about either the case, which his partner had chiefly handled, or the controversy arising from it. Nonetheless, he sought satisfaction for the honor of the firm and his reputation for military valor. Cash readily accepted the invitation to fight.[10]

Shannon's motives may not have been totally pure. They almost suggested a suicidal state of mind that could have been partly an outgrowth of his war experiences. Taking out three different policies, over the previous year he had insured himself for a sum of $6,500, a large amount in that period. Although a major figure in local politics and civic life, Shannon was burdened with debts and had a wife and fourteen children to support. Perhaps practicing law in the dusty town was insufficient for keeping up the old style of life. Colonel Johnson reported that "Col. Shannon was very much distressed for the want of money, and although he kept up appearances and a cheerful countenance, yet I know there was no one more paralis'd than he was."[11] Admittedly it is purely speculative to suggest that Shannon might have had emotional problems stemming from the war which he never outwardly betrayed. Johnson suspected, however, that there were emotional as well as financial worries on the attorney's mind. He acknowledged Shannon's own explanation—a sense of "religeous [sic] duty" to protect his name and the lives of his sons.[12] The contentiousness of the parties and their misrepresentation of each other seemed to some members of the elite as a violation of the politer engagements which they nostalgically remembered (or, more accurately, misremembered) from the allegedly glorious past. General Matthew Butler mourned to a newsman, "In former days the most punctilious decorum and chivalric courtesy distinguished the conduct of gentlemen in 'affairs of honor,' and coarse ribaldry and gasconade in correspondence was as odious as the brand of cowardice; but now the 'swashbuckler style' seems to be fashionable."[13]

The dueling party—principals, seconds, two surgeons (one for each duelist), and six observers, three for each side—stepped across the boundary from Kershaw County to Darlington County at DuBose's (sometimes spelled DuBois's) Bridge. At fifteen yards distance (instead of the usual ten or twelve paces), the pair squared off at two-thirty on the sultry afternoon of 5 July 1880. About a hundred spectators gathered a further distance to witness the affair. Their presence signaled that dueling was no longer as private as it had been in the more hierarchical antebellum period. The signal was the firing of Colonel Johnson's pistol. The unusual choice was a concession to Colonel Cash, who was partially deaf from his war experiences. Shannon shot first, but his ball merely struck the ground, though it threw sand in Cash's face. Thinking it was powder from Shannon's gun, Cash quickly returned fire "without taking aim," it was erroneously claimed by his supporters. Actually, however, he waited a second or two for the smoke from Shannon's position to clear before aiming accurately. The ball found its mark two inches above Shannon's right-breast nipple. Exclaiming "Oh, God," Shannon staggered into the arms of his second and died within a minute or so. It was all that the seconds could do to restrain the Shannon boys, Charlie and Willie, from issuing an immediate challenge against their father's killer.[14]

The insurance companies were suspicious. One of Shannon's policies was held by a company called the Knights of Honor. That firm had a special appeal to Confederate veterans and combined the insurance benefits with Masonic-like passwords, rituals, and regalia.[15] Gossip had it that Shannon's insurers would pay only out of sympathy for the widow and her brood. Shannon, though, was so in debt that the widow obtained only about half the total. But there was more to the insurers' quick acknowledgment of the obligation. It would not do for one of the companies, registered under so chivalrous a name, to refuse the claim on the grounds of the colonel's cowardice and deception in arranging his own death. In fact, William Johnson reported that the company seldom if ever barred "loss of life in a duel" in meeting obligations. Besides, witnesses to the event would have strenuously testified to Shannon's integrity on the field of honor as well as off it.[16]

According to Colonel Johnson, Shannon's second, it had been "a fair fight." Known to be a crack shot against a mediocre one, Cash did not enjoy the vindication he felt was his due. Instead, he became a social pariah in some circles. Perhaps out of sympathy, General John B. Gordon, a political figure of note in Georgia and a successful executive of an insurance company, urged Colonel Cash to join his firm. Cash, however, felt that a gentleman of honor could not stoop so low as to wheedle neighbors and friends into buying policies.[17] Tales circulated that Chesnut and other gentlemen could easily have prevented the action if only they had made "half an effort."[18] Throughout the state editors rivaled each other in denunciations of duels in general and the Camden affair in particular. "The code of Honour (so called) is a disgrace and blot upon our civilization, and must be wiped out," preached the Sumter (S.C.) True Southron.[19] Two duels recently preceding the Cash-Shannon tragedy had stirred the formation of the Camden and Kershaw Anti-Dueling Association. Neighboring Darlingtonians were vexed that the duelists in all three cases had stepped into their county for the opportunity to blaze away in the name of personal vindication.

For his part, Cash found the outcry against him maddening, outrageous, and insulting to his family and himself. In reply to General Butler, who had labeled him either a "lunatic" or a blackguard, Cash exploded. His supposed "lunacy," he declared, might be judged by others, not himself. But " 'Blackguard' is an epithet indigenous to the lips of cowards . . . it is the war whoop of the Poltroon as he skirmishes *to the rear*, and it is croaked from the throat of the cackling craven as he wings his flights to the arks of safety."[20] (Had he wished, Butler could then have challenged Cash, and the feud among Carolinian gentlemen would have spread.)

As part of his defense, Cash did make one logical point. Previous challenges and duels before the war, he correctly observed, had caused no popular outcry. In those times, a few Protestant clergy and the Baptist denomination came out solidly against the duel, but it had not then aroused mass indignation. In his opinion, the impotent protests of a few pious hypocrites and busybodies had gained no following in those happier days. Yet, he fumed, "up pops" an antidueling society in the county, "with a reformed drunkard, the tail end of the State bench, as president, and I suppose every bully in the town as members." In his opinion, the club was a veritable "god-send for all the liars, slanderers and cowards of the place" who could malign fellow citizens without fear of retribution.[21] C. G. Simmons of Walhalla, Oconee County, wrote a South Carolina paper in support of the dueling tradition. Cash's vituperative ravings, Simmons contended, undermined support for the duel itself. Nonetheless, the code duello was still needed as a means to defend Southern ladyhood, declared the correspondent. "At present if the duel be abolished, sensitive and refined ladyhood is a misfortune, for the more damnable the insult, or wrong, the more 'scott free must it go.'" Remember, Simmons argued, Cash's wife had been grossly maligned, and the antiduelists would not permit her the benefit of vindication—"a woman, and she dead and in her grave!"[22] The same argument for the necessity of dueling was, of course, used with equal sanctimoniousness to justify lynchings of "impudent" and "lascivious" freedmen. Walter Hines Page, a Northern-based journalist with unimpeachable Virginia credentials, applauded the "old-fashioned gallantry" and the "knightly" impulses that drove Southern males to employ lynch law as the means to avenge a white woman's loss of honor.[23]

Although indicted for murder, Ellerbe Cash enjoyed substantial support from local veterans of the war and upholders of the ancient litany: "*ab ira odio et omni mala voluntate, libera nos Domine*," as Simmons grandly put it. (From anger, hatred and malice, deliver us O Lord.)[24] Many of the dueling advocates were then challenging the regular Democratic regime under Governor Wade Hampton. The "straight-outs," as they were called, disputed Hampton's Redeemer alliance with compliant African American politicians. Shannon was associated with the "fusionists" in Hampton's camp. As a result, truculent white supremacists were drawn to Cash's part in the dispute. General Martin W. Gary, leader of the "straight-outs," boisterously joined Cash's cause. The general reported to have overheard a stranger in Greenville, South Carolina, remark "'that if any jury dared to convict Col. Cash & he was sentenced for murder that he would form one of a party to tear down every jail in the State in which he was held.'" Nobody who heard the statement challenged it, Gary was gratified to report.[25] Indeed, he wrote, "I have always been of the opinion that you have been most outrageously treated, in all sides, between the Press, the Bench, Pulpit, and the Politicians." Gary praised him for acting "in accordance with the rule of action that was of force amongst 'men of honor' in this State" and for repudiating the clamor against dueling "in which every one seems to join." Their commotion appeared to Gary no less worrisome than an "advance courier of Yankee civilization" that threatened to overwhelm the South. To defend the practice of dueling was, some thought, to honor the Confederate dead.[26] In a colloquy with one of the prosecutors against Cash, Gary urged him to drop the indictment of murder. The attorney, however, claimed that his hands were tied: the legislature and Governor Hampton were demanding a trial. Gary reported to Cash that he had then declared, "I did not care a straw for the sentiment of the legislature, that the sentiment of the Community was more important than a dozen Legislatures."[27]

The most damaging editorials for Cash's side were those appearing in the *Charleston News and Courier* because Gary Martin made it his task to denounce Henry W. Dawson, the paper's editor. They had already clashed over politics in the state, and a duel between them would have been fought if Dawson had not scoffed at the practice.[28] Dawson was by no means a coward, despite the taunts of his enemies. He had fought in both the Confederate navy and the Army of Northern Virginia under Lee.[29] Gary stigmatized him as "a bastard, a liar, a bribe-taker, a coward and a blackguard"—the ritual words to initiate a duel. If Dawson had sought vindication, Gary's "mentita"—giving the lie—provided the occasion. In his harangue that Dawson had published in his own newspaper, Gary defended Cash's right to protect his wife's reputation: "in God's name what do" the antiduelists "regard as sacred and worthy of fighting for?"[30] In response, Dawson, who was himself a fiery-spirited gentleman, took a satirical line, trying to shame the participants into a recognition of their pretentiousness. In a duel, he noted in the *News and Courier*, "there is much correspondence and little bloodshed, and it is the ridiculous character of the common encounters on the 'field of honor'" to which sensible men would "look for the gradual diminution of a foolish as well as illogical practice. The mere 'mention of a 'meeting' provokes" nothing more than "a titter and—'a languid interest.'"[31]

The state newspapers took up Dawson's persistent theme because most were connected with the local business community. Merchants, lawyers, and bankers were eager to impress the world with Southern strides toward modernity and profit. A bourgeois South was timidly emerging. Dawson pointed out, "The State and city need Northern capital for the development of mines, for the promotion of manufacturers, for the restoration and extension of railroad and steamship lines."[32] Dueling would not add a penny to industrial purpose, protested the English-born editor. Gentlemen like Cash, Shannon, and their veteran friends were not properly attuned to the emerging commercial order that editors like Dawson deemed the promise of the future.

The situation, however, was complicated and ambiguous. The code of honor that upheld the actions of duelists had its very outspoken defenders and even men like Dawson himself were not immune to the requirements of manly display. For instance, just as the Republican administration of Daniel Chamberlain was about to collapse in 1876, Charles H. Moise of

Sumter, one of Dawson's friends, praised Dawson's refusal to fight a duel. Robert Barnwell Rhett Jr. was the editor of a rival newspaper but an important figure in the rising Democratic Party under General Hampton. "Surely with your war record known, no man, not even Mr. Rhett, can doubt your manhood—and while I believe 'the Code' is (in extreme cases) a proper mode of settling difficulties, I can admire the independence which repudiates 'the Code' when inconsistent with convictions of conscience." After some further reflections, Moise concluded that reconciliation with opponents like Rhett was a better course than the trading of personal insults leading to the implementation of "the Code." "We cannot afford to have dissensions among ourselves," Moise advised.[33]

On another occasion Dawson went to the courts to protect his name, but even his closest allies thought he should have simply ignored the insults.[34] Similar counsel came from C. W. Dudley of Bennettsville, South Carolina, who urged Dawson not to harass his opponent with a lawsuit, which would "place you in a position of unenviable publicity, not at all pleasant to one of proper sensibilities." After all, "to be gazed at in a Court House by an onion eating crowd, & furnish food for their curiosity is a predicament not to be sought but to be avoided."[35] A right-thinking gentleman did not wish to be the object of public gossip. A reason for the duel as a means of settling disputes was its relative distance from general scrutiny.

The members of the tiny Redeemer elite that ousted the Republican party in 1876 recognized the necessity for solidarity. The Republicans were capable of making a comeback if the arrival of federal guns enabled black voters to exercise their rights without fear of reprisal and death from Hampton's "Red Shirts" and other paramilitary vigilantes. One way to prevent such a catastrophe was to make some gestures toward the African American voter and politician—the fusion, as it was called, of white and black under the rule of the paternalistic planter class whom General Hampton represented. Assigning African Americans a few spots on the ballot, permitting them to serve on juries, and even allowing them to have some constabulary posts were moves designed to keep the Yankees at bay. But the policy also sought to weaken black loyalty to the Republican Party without, it was hoped, fracturing white unity over issues of class and economic disparities.

Even General Gary, who sought much greater repressions against Republican African Americans in the name of white supremacy, had recognized the need to keep the Democratic ranks united. In 1877, before the later squabble over the Cash-Shannon duel, he had agreed to end a simmering controversy with Henry Dawson and "let bygones be bygones."[36] Dudley in his advice to Dawson echoed the refrain: "The Democratic party must suffer" when its leaders fall upon each other and resort to extreme measures.[37]

Perhaps it was ironic that the antiduelist Dawson should have died a few years later in the cause of honor—a matter of old-fashioned chivalry indeed. Impetuous and fiery-tempered, he had strode down the street on 12 March 1889 to confront Dr. Thomas McDow in his Charleston house. A boozy ne'er-do-well, McDow had been stalking Hellene Burdaron, the Dawsons' handsome Swiss governess. The encounter was fatal to the indignant editor. The killer tried to bury his victim in the cellar but was caught and arrested the same day.

According to his obituary in a provincial paper, Dawson was known for his "chivalrous nature. From the day he first unsheathed his stainless sword" in the four-year cause of Confederate freedom, he had always proved himself "a very perfect, gentle knight," especially when, at the end, he "offered his life as a sacrifice on the alter [sic] of woman's honor, the stamp of true knighthood."[38] According to another pro-Dawson editor, the unwashed of the city had long resented Dawson's editorials against Cash's success on the dueling field. As in Cash's case, the jury found McDow not guilty on grounds of self-defense. The seven African Americans on the twelve-panel jury had their own grievances against Dawson. Recent editorials in the *News and Courier* had criticized the race in very haughty and demeaning terms.[39] Loud cheers from whites and from members of the black community greeted the verdict. The whites, it seemed, resented the lofty, holier-than-thou tone of Dawson's daily. Ironically, Pope Leo XIII had earlier conferred upon Dawson a singular honor. In 1883, he had knighted him a Chevalier in the Order of St. Gregory the Great for his antidueling editorials.[40] Such recognition did not benefit his widow. Sarah Morgan Dawson, his outspoken wife and collaborator in running the newspaper, found herself ostracized from Charleston society, as if McDow were the hero and her husband the villain.[41] She wrote indignantly to an old family friend that South Carolinians "alone believe in the fiction of their law, justice or decency," but in truth "they are an unprincipled, mongrel, ungrateful race, playing at 'honor' and 'chivalry.'" A writer of some note, she later published a short story in *Cosmopolitan* magazine. In it she flayed the precepts of honor to which Carolinians adhered.[42]

Like the Rebel heroes Dawson and Cash, Gary had also found in war-fare—and in the kind of politics it stimulated—a means to vent his inner furies. Long before the sectional conflict began, he had shown a touchy disposition. In 1852, the authorities of South Carolina College had expelled him for rebelliousness. A leader of the secession contingent in the South Carolina legislature, Gary had taken up arms in 1861, and he ascended from captain to brigadier general in Carolinian units. He was one of the last Confederates to surrender. Having broken through Federal lines surrounding Lee, he galloped from Virginia to join Jefferson Davis's vain flight into South Carolina.[43]

When former general and senator Butler, the Hampton supporter, denounced the Cash family and backed editor Dawson, Martin Gary grew thoroughly incensed. Described by a South Carolina historian as "an embittered, disappointed old man," Gary, "the Bald Eagle of Oakley Park," sought swift vengeance. The Democratic Party faction under the popular Hampton had failed, he thought, to recognize his talents and reputation.[44] Had he lived for a few more years, Gary would probably have preceded his protégé, Benjamin Tillman, as a red-eyed fanatic to open a populistic revolt against the freedmen and their paternalistic, corporation-minded, and wealthy protectors—the "fusion" contingent to which Shannon had belonged.

While the forces of white insurgency were gathering, the old code of the dueling, with its aristocratic pretensions, was fading. Although its truculent adherents fought a stout rear-guard action, resort to the field of honor was no longer an unchallenged part of Carolinian culture. The Cash-Shannon affair was one of the last duels of significance on South Carolinian soil. There had been enough bloodshed fifteen years before in a much more significant duel with a powerful challenger from the puritan North. The social basis—the exclusivity of the gentlemanly class—had been another casualty of the Confederacy's demise.

Yet the language of honor persisted in the South in a way that must have sounded amusingly antique to the Northern intelligentsia. For instance, the poet and literary critic Paul A. Hayne of Charleston in 1877 congratulated Henry Dawson for his manly way of handling the confrontation with Gary as it appeared in a "gallant" and stirring narrative in the *News and Courier*. Having thought him merely a "*practical* person," Hayne rejoiced to see that Dawson had risen to "chivalric" heights. "As Sydney used to remark of the war ballads of *his* time," Hayne gushed, "it stirred my heart as with the sound of a Trumpet!" Sir, I "*salute you,*" as a worthy son of my *Mother land, that England* from which *all* my ancestors . . . originally came;

that England a thousand times dearer to my soul, now than these dis-United States with their massive vulgarity and the half-veiled despotism lurking under the name — Republic!"[45]

Some years ago, David Donald offered an imaginative explanation for this postwar phenomenon. He proposed that the real reason for the rise of Jim Crowism was as much psychological as it was political and economic. Borrowing from "generational theory," he argued that the movement for disfranchisement and segregation in the 1890s marked "the final public acts, the last bequests, of the Southern Civil War generation." War, he pointed out, coarsens men's manners, chills hearts, and stimulates anger, violence. Donald shrewdly borrows from Thomas Wolfe's rendition of a North Carolina veteran, reminiscing about how war had changed him. "Lord, when I think of hit!" recalls Wolfe's veteran. He had once been an ignorant and tenderhearted country boy, but "when I came back after the war was over I could a-stood by and seed a man murdered right before my eyes with no more feelin' than I'd have had for . . . the life of a sparrer . . . I'd seed so much . . . killin' that I didn't care for nothin'. I just felt dead and numb like all the brains had been shot out of me."[46]

In addition, there is the sense of having been morally degraded by the overwhelming character of the loss. It was a point which few openly expressed because even to raise the issue was to confess its truth. Some years later, Lillian Smith was one of the few in her generation of Southern whites to recognize the ugly depth of that response. She recalled "the bitterness on the faces of my father's and grandfather's friends and other men on Main Street." They "clung to their white culture as a cripple clings to his crutches." Perceptively she saw the relationship between Confederate defeat and the heritage of bigoted despair it bequeathed. Their "passions and memories," Smith speculated, "had been deeply repressed," and they "had forbidden themselves ever to trespass them."[47]

Donald speculated that in those postwar years Southern whites sought to restore the glories that they had valorously garnered on the battlefield, in defeat or victory, in the great conflict and joined in the clamor to put down the blacks. His insight deserves exploration. To be sure, the increased tension between the races had many causes in the late nineteenth century, particularly as freed people grew more assertive and prosperous and whites more threatened economically, socially, and politically. The state of the Southern economy, the sluggishness of industrial development, the periodic collapse of commodity prices, especially in cotton, the high rates for transporting crops to market, and the lack of capital all were important ingredients in the volatility of race relations. At one time, the paternal order over slave subordination had provided an unchallenged notion of white superiority. War casualties and Union occupation had helped to alter that assumption.

Out of the weakness that military and racial overthrow had created in 1865, Southern whites gradually constructed a fabric of nostalgia for the Lost Cause. When coupled with the notion of "Redemption" from allegedly evil Republican and black rule, this means of interpreting the late war offered the concept of victimization, not abject military defeat. Like the Japanese in the years since the fall of their empire in 1945, white Southerners accepted no blame for oppression against weaker people. In fact, denial was uppermost as it had been for the first generation of Germans in acknowledging culpability for the Nazi Holocaust.[48] For most whites, slavery may have been economically deficient, but, most everyone agreed, owners had largely been magnanimous, scrupulous, loving, and responsible in their rule. Yankee skulduggery, not Southern impulsiveness, had brought on the great conflict.

Denial of blame joined hands with a passionate veneration of the fallen. For some, participation in veterans' day parades, barbeques, and the like was a way to compensate for the meager livelihood and low prestige of the jobs they had to take. Katharine Lumpkin's father was representative of the type. A railroad employee during the week, he was "ever at the beck and call" of his fellow veterans in the Third Georgia Regiment whenever he could free himself from selling tickets. A gifted speaker, William Lumpkin, his daughter wrote, "was an inveterate reunion-goer and planner. So were literally hundreds of his kind, men who were also of the Old South's disinherited, who had lost so much and regained so little. . . . Where but in the past lay their real glory?" Lumpkin's anger, though, was not directed so much against the complacent victors up North as upon a victim closer to home. Young Katharine was horrified to witness her father's savage thrashing of their cook, who kept screaming vainly for mercy, for some supposed offense.[49]

Ceremonies to unveil statues in the public square or cemetery, as Lumpkin and his cohorts arranged, helped to heal the festering wounds of humiliation and unresolved mourning. No rigorous analysis of the factors contributing to Confederate failure could emerge from the postwar exercise in nostalgia. "Blame for defeat and the consequences of war fell to a greater purpose," writes a historian, "that validated the noble struggles and losses of the participants." The enormous effort invested in the mourning enterprise survives even today in the Civil War reenactment movement, the commercialization of things Confederate, and the disputes over hoisting the Stars and Bars atop state capitols. But Southern adherence to honor and to dread of shame could not be wholly satisfied in that relatively benign way. The Lost Cause movement offered no program for "eventual triumph," writes one historian, while "the promise of vindication remained vague and distant." As Peter Novick comments, that "memory may continue to resonate in a society . . . when it is the framework for continuing conflict."[50] And certainly conflict also continues between whites and blacks, "straight-outs," and the fast disappearing Republican leaders.

Was it mere coincidence that the movement to honor the Confederate heroes and the onslaught of antiblack lynchings arose simultaneously throughout the South? Of course there had been lynchings of slaves and freedmen in the antebellum period. According to a local paper, at Marshall, Saline County, Missouri, a "negro," either free or slave, had been caught in 1859 after he had allegedly slain a white "gentleman." Before he could be hanged, however, a mob seized him and piled dry wood around the stake to which he was tied. As the fire caught and grew hotter, he desperately tried to "move his feet." Then the flames began to eat at his flesh and he cried out in agony, begging to be killed. His pleas only excited the crowd still more. "He seized his chains — they were hot, and burnt his flesh off his hands. He would drop them and catch at them again and again." One of the other blacks charged with the murder "exhibited no remorse. One of them simply remarked, 'that he hoped before they hurt him they would let him see the other boy burnt!' "[51]

Of course, lynchings of whites also took place, but usually a simple hanging was deemed adequate. In 1882 in Tampa, Florida, for instance, militia general Joseph Wall, once a surgeon in the Confederate service, led a mob that lynched Charles Owens, a white transient, about to stand trial for murder. At a similar scene in 1920, a Kentucky witness remarked with approval that "the old-time chivalry, deference and honor, reverence and protection, which the Southern gentleman threw about woman has decayed lamentably."[52]

After the Civil War such sickening brutalities became much more common. Certainly the ties between a Confederate ideology of state sovereignty and racial repression encouraged the atrocities. Joan Cashin, for instance, recounts the lynching of a slave, Saxe Joiner, in Union County, South Carolina. It took place on 15 March 1865. The lynchers attired themselves in Rebel uniforms even though not one of the rioters was actively in service. The offense of the slave had been to send a note offering to protect an unmarried teenage girl if and when the Federals arrived.

That so-called impudence cost him his life. Cashin relates that Joiner's body was left to hang from a tree on the lawn of a prominent resident as "a gruesome symbol of white supremacy," even as the Confederacy was collapsing.[53] The adoption of Confederate insignia and attire in the rites of lynching was fairly common throughout the post–Civil War South.

It can be argued that as the duel dropped out of favor, it was replaced with hangings, burnings, and mutilations. The collective behavior of lynch mobs, Neil J. Smelser argues, was a mobilization around a common set of beliefs which were "akin" in character to "magical beliefs."[54] Both lynch law and the code duello were steeped in the traditions of Southern conventions of honor. Each had its sacred if different stylizations.[55] One was to effect the removal of an allegedly insulting stain, the other to return the local community to its unblemished state of racial order. Like the charivari or tar-and-feather traditions of the Old South, the lynching of selected freedmen ritualistically washed clean the local moral life and rid it of a subversive devil, as the victim was thought to be.[56]

The purification rites by burning did not first emerge in the post–Civil War South. In fact, at one time they were part of the judicial system itself. In 1740 a South Carolina court ordered that a slave convicted of burning down a white man's house be burned alive. There was no such authorization provided in the province's slave code, but justice in slaveholding regions had always been rough and ready. A South Carolinian historian of the late nineteenth century justified the penalty on the grounds that "the ancient laws of England" permitted such a punishment "as a kind of *lex talionis* under the statute of Edward I."[57] Disembowelment, castration, branding, and other torturous modes of death had once been part of the legal systems of Europe. They reappeared with extraordinary virulence in the era of the New South.

The duel and the extralegal mob action were alike in the rationales employed to justify them. The honor of family and community was involved in both, and to shy away from either form of violence was to show a cowardly spirit. Both were supposed to have a vindicating and cleansing effect so that community members could return to their usual pursuits, happy in the thought that somehow a balance of nature had been restored. Photographs of white crowds stolidly and unashamedly facing the camera with a black body dangling from a nearby tree limb reveal their collective sense of having done a righteous and honorable deed.

Dueling and lynching presented the outside world with complementary images of the South—the brutality of race antagonism and the absurdity of lethal quarreling. In the 1880s Mark Twain satirized both forms of Southern violence in *Huckleberry Finn*, highlighting the cowardliness of the lynch mob, contrary to public understanding. Dueling, of course, was the easier tradition to relinquish. Yet the principle of a white society's notion of honor, upon which justification for the duel rested, continued to inspire fierce repression of the underrace—not in lynching alone but in whippings, threats, and other signals of antipathy. Of course, differences between mob executions of blacks and stately encounters on the proverbial field of honor are obvious. For one thing, the clergy were never invited to participate in the duel, given the church's long-standing disapproval of the practice. Sometimes, though, preachers attended the degradation ceremonies of black punishment.

Southern vigilantes assured themselves that they were upholding traditional values of honor, the sacredness of white womanhood, and community ethics. They acted with a religious energy analogous to the rush that many of them, as former common soldiers, had experienced on the battlefield. Their actions were sanctioned by nearly all the inhabitants. In South Carolina, as late as 1916, Anthony Crawford, an African American farmer too prosperous for his physical well-being, fell victim to an angry mob and was beaten, mutilated, hanged, and shot. The Abbeville newspaper proclaimed, "The 'best people' of South Carolina know that when white men cease to whip, or kill negroes who become obnoxious, that they will take advantage of the laxity, and soon make this state untenable for whites of ALL kinds, and that under such conditions the 'best' will be 'like the worst, and the worst like the best.'" The entire community, the editor insisted, bore "the responsibility for his death," which was occasioned by "his own reckless course, due to chest inflation from wealth." Therefore his assassination was "RACIALLY JUSTIFIABLE." Crawford had had the temerity to accumulate over $20,000, a sum that few white farmers could even come close to reaching. Nonetheless, the president of the Abbeville Bank fully approved the ritual slaying. He contended that Crawford had been "insolent to a white man and he deserved a thrashing."[58] Thus, as in the executions of alleged slave insurrectionists of antebellum times, social distinctions among the white participants temporarily abated in the name of group solidarity. A churchman or member of the elite seldom could have prevented a lynching of a postwar freedman just as his father or grandfather was likely to fail in halting the killing of a slave thought guilty of insurgency.[59]

Unlike the lynching parties, duels had been restricted to the upper ranks of society—although within a democratic setting in which the definition of gentility varied from locale to locale. The unwashed, however, were not entitled to attend the lethal rites. The decline of the duel signaled a shift in the exercise of political power in the postwar period. Patron-client relations had lost their military underpinnings: clients no longer were obliged to fight for patrons and vice versa as they had in the Jacksonian era. Yet the principle of honor remained in the rationale of lynchings. The connection between lynchings and the continued rule of honor in another form from dueling was complex. Whites, it must be remembered, were not only confused but also humiliated to find their former slaves in charge of their own lives after the Civil War. They felt a need to seek new means of coercion or their world would be utterly devoid of meaning and potency. As Stephen Kantrowitz observes, the restoration of white rule in the late 1870s meant the triumph of white supremacy but had no prescriptions to lift up the poverty of the white farmer. In South Carolina, paternalistic conservatives of the Wade Hampton and Marion Butler school were obedient to corporate interests and sought a new prosperity in industrialization, commercial exchange, and Northern capital investment. They stressed the need for stability, law, and order by which lynching would be regarded as primitive, savage, and even dishonorable. Governor Benjamin R. Tillman, their triumphant nemesis, however, took a different and more grassroots approach that won him great popularity. He proposed not indiscriminate lynchings of blacks but rather a more open-ended interaction between law and vigilantism. As Kantrowitz puts it, "In practice," the whites were to decide "among themselves which infractions could wait for the law to run its course and which challenged their authority, manhood, and independence, and thus their honor."[60]

In the late nineteenth century economic pressures mounted year by year not just in South Carolina but throughout the former slave states. White Southerners recovered political power, to be sure, but it seemed as if the ritual aspects of the duel had been channeled into degradation ceremonies designed to repress the freed people. For instance, the post–Civil War Ku Klux Klan was thought to be a thoroughly Christian institution—by the standards of those joining in its demonic activities. Much recent work on lynching offers persuasive evidence about the interrelationship of economic, demographic, and institutional reasons for the rise of the practice.[61] A study that takes seriously the role of collective psychological factors found that ritual filled a vacuum for whites.[62] That need, it can be argued, included a sense of collective self-esteem growing out of losing a war against fellow whites. The apparent need to ritualize and sanctify the process of black lynching and assassination in the post–Civil War era is baffling in its horror. As Leon Litwack observes, "The ordinary modes of execution and punishment were deemed insufficient. They no longer satisfied the appetite of the crowd." Capital punishments by vigilantes were fashioned into "a public ritual, a collective experience, and the victim needed to be subjected to extraordinary torture and mutilation," Litwack explains.[63] Burning at the stake was not uncommon. In Kirvin, Texas, for instance, three African Americans, "Shap" Curry, Moses Jones, and John Cornish, were seized by a mob. They worked at the King Ranch. Their boss John King's granddaughter, age seventeen, had been found dead from thirty stab wounds. Until their final, agonized death, the three insisted on their innocence. To extract confessions, the members of the crowd horribly mutilated them. "Ears, toes, and fingers were snipped off," reported a journalist. "Eyes were gouged out, no organ of the negroes was allowed to remain protruding," he noted delicately. Then "preachers from two churches which flank the square came forward and prayed for the salvation of the blacks' souls." Doused in oil and set aflame, Curry chanted over and over " 'O, Lord, I'm comin.' " The others were similarly treated, and all were dead within a few minutes of their burning.[64]

The religious character of lynching activities took a variety of forms, some directly intermingled with memories of the late war. The confluence of Confederate mythmaking and religious devoutness came together in a most peculiar way in the lynching of blacks on bridges. The sociologist Orlando Patterson observes that the site was often chosen not simply to terrorize the black passerby but to memorialize Stonewall Jackson. The general's expiring exclamation after the Battle of Chancellorsville was to whisper the words of the hymn, "Let us cross over the river / And rest under the shade of the trees."[65] Hanging victims from trees bore analogy with Christ's death on the treelike cross. Just as there were once saints' relics, white lynchers seized the victims' knuckles, bones, skull, or some other part of the body and treated them as icons to be treasured and proudly displayed.

When a Newnan, Georgia, black was burned in 1895 for the alleged murder of a farmer and rape of his wife, the lynchers eagerly carved bits of his flesh to save as relics of the occasion. In Cuthbert, Georgia, a sixteen-year-old admitted his guilt before the mob's noose was placed around his neck. An Episcopal minister watched the scene to the tragic end and found redeeming comfort in the thought that "the Almighty is a God of love and mercy as well as Justice."[66] In Morganton, North Carolina, in 1889 prayers preceded the work of a lynch mob. Ministers felt obliged to keep silent about the practice because their parishioners might take exception to the admonitions and turn on the clergymen themselves. When a Georgia minister expelled a member of his congregation for participating in an extralegal hanging, twenty-five members walked out.[67] By and large, however, ministers in the backlands were more likely to approve silently. They could turn to Numbers:6–9 and there discover, a newspaperman reported in 1897, "an account of the first great lynching, see the Bible condemnation for the gratification of lust, and God's condemnation of the lyncher."[68]

No less appropriate to the connection of religious belief and lynch law was an event in Blount County, Alabama, in 1870. A local white preacher had continued to speak boldly against the rampaging violence of the Klan despite undergoing the agony of two whippings. When his wife gave birth to a deformed child, his enemies brought the dead infant to his revival service and showed it to those gathered about. They claimed "it was a perfect representation and facsimile of a disguised Ku Klux." The forehead was square and flat and much larger than that of a normal infant. Two horns, it was said, projected from the sides of the head as if in imitation of Klan headgear. Then, "around the neck was a scarlet red band; and from the point of the shoulder, extending down each side to about the center of the abdomen, was all scarlet red." At that time, Klansmen wore costumes of red and black, not white. To the faithful, God had clearly given them a special sign: a blessing for the Klan, a punishment for its foes.[69] Grace and violence were thus united in the manner that Flannery O'Connor many years later would treat in her short stories.

In addition to the religious overtones of lynching and retribution against African Americans, the Southerners' emotional state about the great Confederate loss continued to inspire the horrors well into the 1890s. An example came from North Carolina, where white Southerners conducted what could almost be called a pogrom because the attack aroused no more official or public outrage than an anti-Semitic atrocity in contemporary czarist Russia. Perhaps as many as three hundred African Americans were killed in the Wilmington race riot of 1898. The exact number, however, will never be known.[70]

The leader of the vicious assault was Alfred Moore Waddell, a former Confederate lieutenant colonel of the North Carolina Third Cavalry Regiment. He had fought at Cold Harbor, Hanover Court House, and other battles. Although subject to undefined "ill health" during much of his life, he had served in Congress from 1871 to 1877 for Wilmington, North Carolina. In the early 1890s he ran unsuccessfully for the U.S. Senate.[71] After the war, he had accepted defeat and, as he put it, "would treat that lamentable chapter in American history as Noah's sons had done in the hour of their father's humiliation—they would avert their looks, and, with back-ward step, cast the mantle of oblivion over it." [72] Such sentiments won him praise in Northern Unionist papers. He had appeared to reflect an appro-priate sense of regional humility that the Northern victors vainly hoped applied throughout the South. Thus Waddell showed a moderate course on race and sectional divisions and earlier had even endorsed limited suf-frage for "qualified" freedmen.

As a good Democrat, Waddell was encouraged, however, by his party's victory in North Carolina, which had routed the Republicans on the state level in 1876 by means of intimidation, assassination, and terror.[73] A some-time editor, he penned a poem titled "There's Music in the Air" to cele-brate a reviving sense of Southern nationhood. The first verse read in part: "Lift up your head, oh! Southern Land / Long bowed by dark de-spair." A new age was dawning, the poet predicted: "Look up! Rejoice! Stretch forth thy hand! / Pour out the grateful prayer / From mountain-top to ocean-strand / 'There's music in the air.'" No longer should South-erners wallow in "voiceless agony" because the Northern "foe" has been "shamed" into repentance by "the proud humility" of the South. The enemy offered words of "promise fair," and because the chords of tyranny were unloosening, whites could exult: "There's music in the air." [74]

Waddell did not marry until late in life. His wife, Gabrielle, had long suffered in spinsterhood. To support herself, she had served as a govern-ess in New England for a time. She returned to Wilmington because her grandfather needed a nurse, since cancer was eating away his face. Finally, he died, but she suffered a nervous breakdown. At thirty-three, an old maid by the standards of the day, she then married "old man" Waddell, as he was known. Bonded in not the most loving of marital ties, she always called her sixty-two-year-old husband "Colonel," not Alfred. He then took up the cause of white supremacy as if it were a newfound creed as power-ful as the Christian message. Waddell belonged to a group of determined white supremicists under the leadership of North Carolina attorney gen-eral and later governor Charles Brantley Aycock. They sought a military overthrow of the existing political system in which African Americans were allowed to vote and sometimes elect a few major offices, state and local. In Wilmington Waddell intended to combine a military determina-tion to triumph by violence with an equally military sense of discipline and orderliness. Some show of restraint, however superficial, was needed if only to disarm any possibility of Yankee intervention as in the days of Reconstruction.[75]

Along with others fearful of black advance and their own stagnation,

Waddell charged the underclass with heinous crimes, most especially against white women. In a speech at the Opera House, an observer recalled that "he used some rather violent language about choking the Cape Fear River with the bodies of negroes."[76] During the city election of 1898 Waddell exhorted a crowd, "You are Anglo-Saxons. You are armed and prepared, and you will do your duty. . . . Go to the polls tomorrow, and if you find the negro out voting, tell him to leave the polls, and if he refuses, kill him." His call for violence, however, was at this point overruled. On election day, 8 November, Waddell and his followers prevented blacks from voting and claimed a victory that installed him as the new mayor.

That coup d'état, as it were, was insufficient to satisfy the racial bloodlust. The following day, incited by Waddell's furious exhortations, mob action, arson, and random killing and maiming began. Justifying the action, Thomas W. Clawson, editor of the *Wilmington Messenger*, recalled how the paramilitary leaders organized their forces by "sections and blocks." At the head of each of these units were "certain men with military titles." As "Commander in Chief," Colonel Roger B. Moore, who had proved himself "a brave and gallant veteran of the Southern Confederacy" directed operations. According to Clawson, the object, after the whites' victory at the polls, was "to settle scores with a weekly paper" run by two mulatto brothers, the Manlys. They had allegedly defamed "white women" in some fashion in an editorial.[77] An ultimatum requiring their immediate departure from the city received no response, and so the onslaught, carefully planned, began. White citizens hunted down prominent black spokesmen in Wilmington and shot them dead in the streets. The blacks were poorly armed and unready for the planned assault on their section of town. A militia unit, the Wilmington Light Rifles, the Red Shirts, and other paramilitary groups assembled. The troops headed for the Brooklyn section of Wilmington, center of black residence.

A Gatling gun, seated in a wagon, was the chief weapon of destruction. Colonel Moore, a prominent veteran of both the war itself and the postwar Ku Klux Klan, flashed his old sword about until the firebell sounded ominously to announce the start of the campaign. Then Moore and his subordinate Captain William Rand Kenan manned the gun. It was mounted on a "large truck, drawn by two fine horses." Clawson had watched in awe as the Rebel pair and a "brave gun crew of Naval Reserves" fired at panic-stricken African Americans in "a dramatic and thrilling spectacle." Truly, Clawson rhapsodized, these warriors gloriously represented "the magnificent soldiery of the Southern Confederacy." Firing with a precision and discipline learned in the late sectional war, the whites quickly reduced all resistance except for some sporadic sniping.

Meantime, Colonel Waddell led a party that destroyed the newspaper plant whose independence of spirit had so outraged the white suprema- cists. Republican municipal leaders, white and black, were seized and placed in jail cells. Moore and Captain Walter G. MacRae, another "gal- lant Confederate veteran," stood guard at the jail entrance that evening. They sought to prevent a lynching that would discredit the resort to armed violence that lacked military discipline. Mob control would have spoiled an old-fashioned chivalry that was supposed to create order and not disorder. On the following morning, Waddell and his allies had the captives escorted to the train station and "banished from the city."[78] George Rountree, a white conservative leader, helped to save the resign- ing aldermen from a fate worse than forced exile. Like nearly all whites, whether straight-outs or former fusionists, however, his conscience was scarcely pricked by the end result.[79]

Chilled by the cold night and by fright, women and children from the black neighborhoods hid in the woods. Soon thereafter an exodus of com- munity leaders to Northern parts depleted the ranks of Wilmington's once thriving black middle class.[80] Despite these tragic results, Mayor Waddell and the others jubilantly congratulated themselves as men of honor and integrity. "There was not a flaw in the legality of our government," he pro- claimed. "It was the result of revolution, but the forms of law were strictly complied with."[81] Clawson echoed these sentiments in 1944, when he re- called the events: "The election of 1898 was portentous for the civilization of North Carolina. Fusion had set up negroism again." Clawson was grati- fied that "fusion, confusions and negroism" had been expelled from the state along with the demoralized black leaders.[82]

The famous article in the Manly brothers' Wilmington paper, dated 18 August 1898, had replied editorially to a Georgia white woman who claimed that black rapes of white women justified the large number of lynchings. The editor had declared that she, "like so many other so called Christians, loses sight of the basic principle of the religion of Christ in her plea for one class of Religion as against another." The editor noted that the morals of poor whites were about "on a par" with those of their equally destitute black neighbors. He urged that "the whole lump . . . be leavened those who profess so much Religion." Quite sensibly the author argued that often enough those lynched were mulattoes whose fathers had been white. He suggested that devout white women should "teach your women purity. Let virtue be something more than an example for them to intimidate and torture a helpless people."[83] To the white racist, such frankness was an impudence and a shameful insult to white ladyhood that could not be tolerated by men of honor.

In the few remaining outposts of Republican strength in North Carolina, the Wilmington riot was roundly condemned. Throughout the nation African Americans expressed their indignation; some urged an eye for an eye. But among whites across the nation either silence or justification prevailed.[84] The Confederate veteran and his sons could finally claim a victory: black manhood had been brought almost as low as it had been in the days of Ibrahima, the African slave in Mississippi. The freedmen of North Carolina—as elsewhere too—were soon eliminated from the political scene, not to regain the franchise until more than half a century had passed.

The years since Appomattox were slipping by. Yet memories and feelings arising from those earlier scenes of horror and humiliation still excited aging Rebel souls and the next generation of whites. At Wilmington and elsewhere they visited all manner of horrors on those beneath them. In the bleakness of despair some Confederate veterans leaped at the chance to avenge the great disaster of 1865 in racial vindictiveness. In the subsequent years, Johnny Reb denied that he and his dead companions had sacrificed themselves in vain and insisted that their failed cause had been worth four years of pain, death, and destruction. In fact, as late as 1912, the Reverend James McNeilly offered a stalwart defense of slavery, secession, and warfare against the North. During the struggle, he had served as chaplain of Quarles's Brigade. The clergyman argued that the vast majority of white Southerners still believed that "those sacrifices and those grand heroisms were endured and wrought for the sake of a false and ruinous theory which was contrary to God's law and to human rights." As far as he and many others were concerned, however, Confederate defeat had been nothing short of "a calamity." Although God's "hand holds every human event," McNeilly insisted, He does not afflict a people with death and destruction as "punishments for special sins," such as the holding of slaves. After all, had not the Israelites of the Old Testament suffered at the hands of "heathen conquerors" and yet were they not the chosen people? McNeilly asserted his conviction that emancipation had benefited the race not at all. White people "of high Christian character" had so ameliorated the harshness of bondage that any honest observer would see the justice of the Southern cause. As it was, "ignorant negroes" became easy prey to "the demagogue and the corruptionist" with heavy consequences for the maintenance of civilization. Jim Crow and disfranchisement had solved that supposed curse, he noted with satisfaction.[85]

McNeilly's sentiments were hardly exceptional. Nor was his amnesia about the wartime reliance on God a singular lapse. During the war his fellow clergymen had promised that God would crown the Confederacy with victory if the people's Christian faith were wholly enlisted. Their message had vanished years before.

The cause of honor would remain alive for many years after the Civil War but largely in the language of a belligerent racism and an assertion of manhood over effeminacy and even over women in general. Lost were some of the ancient foundations of the ethic—notably its roots in ascriptive hierarchy. In the slave South, the rule of a landed aristocracy had never attained more than a foothold, even in the early colonial era. Instead, a "timocracy" of white men—the equality of all with the proper color of skin that Andrew Jackson had espoused—replaced that European structure of social order. The legacy of honor and virility, righteous adherence to biblical inerrancy, lingered, however, much longer than the victorious Union forces would ever have imagined in 1865.

In 1907 Edward Ward Carmack, a noted Tennessee editor, politician, and Confederate Veterans Day orator, put the matter in a way that left no doubt how white Southerners felt regarding their region's defeat. When unveiling a statue of Jefferson Davis in Richmond, he declared: "Whether for chieftain or private, we make no confession of wrong, we plead no forgiveness of error, we ask no tenderness of the future historian, no charity from the enlightened judgement of mankind." Some mindlessly might be shocked and have insisted that, in "pledge" of loyalty to the United States, white Southerners ought to "give the memory of our heroes to oblivion and their graves to the wilderness." "Never," Carmack thundered, would that disgrace occur. No fidelity to the American flag could require a repudiation of those "noblest sentiments" that had animated the Confederate armies in the field. Pealing out the familiar changes on a theme that never seemed to grow threadbare to the white Southern listener, he continued, "I say that the valor of our Southern soldiers, the fortitude of our Southern women, and an inextinguishable allegiance to the memory of their brave deeds symbolized the honor of this reunited nation no less than 'the flag that floats over it from the lakes to the gulf and from sea to sea.'"[86] Repeated in thousands of speeches and newspaper columns, such words bespoke a people with the longest of memories.

On one level, spokesmen like Carmack may have cynically echoed the familiar voice of rhetorical honor for the sake of party advantage, New

South boosterism, or ritual community gratification. Nonetheless, words, as much as deeds of violence, could be far more dangerous than even those who spoke or wrote them may have wished to convey. Carmack himself might serve as a tragic example. The gifted but intemperate editor loved to engage in partisan battles. In 1908 he produced a scathing editorial in the *Tennessean* against Duncan Cooper, a prominent Democrat in the state capital. Shortly after the newsboys began hawking the paper, Cooper spied his journalistic assailant walking with a woman down a Nashville street. "You dastardly coward, you cowardly scoundrel, hiding behind that woman, are you?" he shouted. Carmack pulled back, fumbled for his gun, and managed to fire two shots that struck Cooper's son Robin, who had moved to protect his father. Only superficially wounded, Robin managed to draw his pistol and fire three shots in this brief exchange. Carmack fell into the gutter dead.[87] It had been no duel; that form had disappeared but not an exchange of gunfire among gentlemen of prominence. The forms of ritualized means to preserve reputation may have died out but not the reasons for taking vengeance.

Perhaps it stretches credulity to claim that Confederate defeat bore a direct relationship to racial tragedies and the level of personal violence among whites a quarter-century later. Yet recent controversies over the waving of the Rebel flag attest to the continuation of deep feelings in some whites about the meaning of that shattering, devastating loss. In 1880, Father Abram Ryan, poet laureate of the Lost Cause, tried to lay that emblem to rest in a reverential way. It almost seems as if Father Ryan had it wrong when he wrote "The Conquered Banner" in 1880:

> Furl that Banner, softly, slowly!
> Treat it gently—it is holy—
> For it droops above the dead.
> Touch it not—unfold it never,
> Let it droop there, furled forever,
> For its people's hopes are dead!

Tom Watson's "reply" to Ryan's poem, cited in the epigraph for this chapter, was closer to the mark. At the time of this writing, the Rebel flag still flies over the statehouse in Columbia, South Carolina. Eventually the flag will be lowered never to be returned to the flagstaff. At that point, Southern honor, particularly in its racist aspect, will have been chastened once again. But those who claim that the Stars and Bars represent a gallant tradition, a reverence for local governance, and a strict interpretation of the Constitution should read what their post–Civil War ancestors thought that flag symbolized. To Martin Gary, Waddell, Tillman, Watson, Carmack, and many thousands of others, the Rebel banner was the emblem of a sacralized determination to keep African Americans underfoot. Any means to do so were deemed honorable. The ethic that so long has sustained the racial prescriptions of the white South required no respect or humanity toward those outside its moral boundaries. As Julian Pitt-Rivers remarks in the opening epigraph to this study, "Honor has caused more deaths than the plague."[88]

RECENT HISTORIOGRAPHY ON HONOR

In a truly analytical way, the concept of honor has entered the historians' vocabulary only recently. When gathering material for a study of the subject in the late 1970s, I discovered that the subject catalog at Case Western Reserve University's Freiberger Library contained almost no entries for historical approaches to the ethic. Only those related to the Shakespearean and German literary past appeared.[1] If mentioned at all, historians, with the exception of Clement Eaton, Dickson Bruce, and a few others, treated the ethic of honor in the South as no more than a mischievous hypocrisy.[2] It was not examined as a complicated impulse, one that involved the interaction of the claimant and the public arena in which badges of gentility or sheer virility were conferred or withheld. The rituals and rhetoric of honor have likewise failed to reach the American historian's consciousness.

Still, the concepts of honor and shame—the latter being generally treated in a residual way—possess explanatory power. It must be admitted, though, that some anthropologists have questioned the value or even validity of the twin conceptualizations.[3] Such typologies as honor and shame tend to exaggerate stasis, as if no evolutionary factors or abrupt changes were possible within the scheme itself. We must be prepared to face the complexities and contradictions of social systems, conventions, and beliefs. Honor and shame are convenient labels that cover a very wide range of conduct and moral judgment. Ambiguity, even murky distortion in the way people, most of whom considered themselves honorable, behaved in the past, cannot be wholly removed.

Despite these problems, which can never be fully resolved, few paradigms for dealing with broad social and moral conventions have paid higher dividends than the formulation of honor and shame. For generations in Western society, the only fundamental basis for treating historical events and individuals in terms of moral assessment was the polarity of conscience and guilt. Honor and shame—and indeed shamelessness as a rejection of both positions—are concepts that help us to reach the minds and actions of those who by their time and culture could not anticipate and act upon our liberating but wholly alien standards. Honor is, however, a restricted code of conduct. It thrives in the absence of law but can exist as an alternative to law. As the encounter between Major Generals Gordon and Chamberlain reveals, it glorifies the warrior spirit. Sometimes honor mistakes gentleness for weakness, kindness for effeminacy. Its grip on the Southern mentality was great enough, as the historians Christine Heyrman and Ted Ownby point out, to hobble the advancement of Christian conversions, most especially in the Christianizing of early antebellum slaveholders. "Many masters," Heyrman writes, "were willing to discuss, some even to debate, theology. But when preachers tried to probe their souls or to insist on the truth of evangelical creeds, most drew back." In the early years of the nineteenth century, dread of self-exposure and fear of being seen as womanlike had left churchgoing chiefly to the opposite sex.[4] Even Sir Walter Scott himself recognized the threat that chivalry posed to good order and Christian practice. As for the morality of dueling, Scott declared that its "usage, at once so ridiculous, and so detrimental to the peace and happiness of society, must give way in proportion to the progress of common sense."[5]

With disciples of the code like Scott showing signs of ambivalence so many epochs ago, it is curious that the ramifications of honor have only lately come to the historian's attention. Such has not been the case with writers in other disciplines. Over the last twenty years, social scientists—sociologists, political scientists, anthropologists, and investigative journalists—quickly recognized the concept as it applied in the contemporary world. For instance, the journalist Suzanne Ruggi discloses how Palestinian women of the West Bank and Gaza are murdered by their male kin to avenge alleged sexual violations to family honor. Such cases require no legal consequences and are still unnumbered and underreported. By Jordanian law, "the act of killing another" requires no indictment of the murderer when "committed as an act in defense of his life, or his honor, or somebody else's life or honor."[6] In this country, Fox Butterfield of the *New York Times* gave nationally syndicated coverage to what the *Atlanta Journal-Constitution* headlined as "Deadly Code of Honor: Warrior Ethic, Slavery behind South's Comparatively High Murder Rate."[7] Two political scientists have also ventured into the intellectual territory of U.S. Southern history. Richard E. Nisbett and Dov Cohen explain in *Culture of Honor* (1996) just how the South today remains so close to the ancient ethic. They have in mind the persistence of a regional dedication to the possession of lethal weapons, a sense of male possessiveness over women (though not so powerful as in the Middle East), and a tradition of personal truculence in the face of supposed insult.[8]

American historians have not kept pace with the advances made by their colleagues in other branches of the discipline. Incorporating the interpretive framework of the social sciences, they began in the 1980s to investigate the role of honor in the ancient, medieval, early modern, and modern European, Asiatic, and Canadian pasts.[9] Natalie Zemon Davis has been the leader of this interpretive school with brilliant social analyses of early modern French culture.[10] A special concentration has also developed on the custom of dueling abroad. Robert Nye and Kevin McAleer, in particular, have shown the relationship between duels and class exclusivities.[11] Just how powerful a force honor still was in early twentieth-century Central Europe is evident in the persuasive article by Avner Offer, "Going to War in 1914: A Matter of Honor?" Likewise, John Keegan observes that all prior crises over the Balkans and African colonial disputes had been settled through diplomacy and "touched matters of national interest only, not matters of national honor or prestige." [12]

When the young Serb Gavrilo Princip shot the heir to the Austro-Hungarian throne, the Serbs had answered the insult of Franz Ferdinand's presence in Sarajevo on the Serbian National Day. His death was at once taken as an unforgivable affront to the monarchy. Like a personal duel, the resulting declaration of war against Serbia was designed to vindicate the honor of the empire. Kaiser Wilhelm and Emperor Franz Josef embarked on a course of action almost as suicidal as a duel itself. In particular, the German emperor had long insisted that he would tolerate no officers in his army unwilling to accept a challenge. Years before, Southern secessionists had responded in like fashion to the Northern "insult" of electing a Black Republican to the presidency of the United States. To emphasize Keegan's point, sectional interest resided in the maintenance of peace, for the sake of union—and the continuance of slavery, too. But defense of self-esteem seemed to dictate the decision for Southern secession and, in reaction, for Northern determination to restore the Union by armed force.

To draw on more recent events, the war in Vietnam clearly invoked matters of honor—a concept with limited appeal in parts of the country. The war was least favored in the old New England–settled states, from Massachusetts to the northern West Coast. In the South and Southwest, however, the ethno-regional approach that David Hackett Fischer outlined in *Albion's Seed* demonstrates that the war was highly popular in that honor-drenched sector of the republic, a sentiment disclosed in the polls of the day. As representative of that frontier spirit, Lyndon Johnson, the war's most intense defender, put the matter succinctly almost exactly a century after Appomattox: "If America's commitment is dishonored in South Vietnam, it is dishonored in forty other alliances or more . . . *we do what we must*" regardless of consequences. By his perspective, honor had its own logic. Practical considerations and prudence drew out no imperative to cast it aside. "We love peace. We hate war. But our course," Johnson announced in 1965, "is charted always by the compass of honor."[13] It was the pathway to death, but any other option apparently would have betrayed America's "word of honor." These political and military signs of a continuing spirit of honor deserve a greater hearing and investigation than they have so far received.

· · · · · · · ·

So far I have painted too stark a picture. Progress, albeit confined to a handful of scholars, has been made in using anthropological findings in American history, most especially with regard to the Southern states. Edward L. Ayers, Steven M. Stowe, and Kenneth S. Greenberg have added enormously to a comprehension of honor in that region. They have revealed the pervasiveness of honor and shame in family settings, criminal justice, personal encounters, and race relations to such a degree that any historian writing on Southern culture cannot dismiss or neglect their findings, most especially with regard to the emotionally volatile character of the regional mind.

Indeed, the subject of Southern violence has gradually drawn scholarly investigation after years of unaccountable neglect. Important work has been done on lynching in particular in both book and article forms.[14] Yet much of it finds demographic, gender, and economic explanations for the horrors. There are exceptions: Elliot Gorn treats backwoods fighting as an honor-shame phenomenon. William F. Holmes has found evidence of the old rites of mob action called the charivari, in Georgia, in 1890. Laura Edwards discloses interracial factors in a "shivaree" in North Carolina, and, using the theme of honor, David Courtwright on a broader canvas has depicted the persistence of personal, male violence from early American history to the anarchy of inner-city life.[15] Even the popular media have discovered the topic of Southern violence, honor, and shame with the airing of television documentaries on tar and feathers and on the duel. In the national press, the almost ludicrous affair between the young and overly ambitious attorney Abraham Lincoln and James Shields in 1842 has received attention. (As the party challenged, Lincoln chose the broadsword over the customary pistol. The decision was decidedly to his advantage, given the extraordinary length of his arms and the shortness of his opponent's.)[16] Yet no book-length interpretation of American dueling has so far emerged.

Surprisingly little has appeared on Northern honor and politics as well —apart from Joanne Freeman's recent work. Despite the outstanding quality of Richard Bushman's *The Refinement of America*, there is much more yet to be learned about the free-state upper classes and the role of gentility, that is, honor at its most refined.[17] Furthermore, historians of the colonial and constitutional periods have had almost nothing to say on the subject. In fact, colonial and backcountry historians in general stoutly reject David Hackett Fischer's *Albion's Seed*, a work that proposes a cultural interpretation similar to that offered in these pages.[18]

Instead of delving into the relationship of the honor ethic to Northern business and social life, attention has focused on the role of racism in Northern society. Some years ago, a group of historians revealed the depth of antiblack prejudice throughout the Northern states.[19] No doubt their findings will bear the test of further study. Nonetheless, we ought never to forget the forces that promoted Northern antislavery tendencies. Most important were the rise of the evangelical revival movement and the ever-deepening concern in the free states for sectional equity in politics (as opposed to slave state demands for continued parity) as the Civil War was approaching. In a paper as yet unpublished, Leonard Richards discloses how the Constitution's three-fifths rule gave the South disproportionate strength not only in representation in the electoral college and the Congress but also in the passage of key legislation averse to Northern interests. As a result, Yankee resentment grew as the disparity over the years between the demographic and economic power became ever more egregious in a so-called democracy. The Jacksonians in the North willingly supported the Southern position on the basis of common racist principles, but Southern truculence and threats of secession awakened growing numbers to the high price that slaveholding power was exacting. For instance, Richards notes, "Thanks to the three-fifths rule and party discipline, complained John Quincy Adams in 1843, northern members of the House had been 'reduced to the condition of auxiliaries to the rival candidates of the South.' Having 'no common centre of attraction to rally their forces,' they were 'never admitted to even propose a candidate of their own,' but were only 'magnanimously permitted' to choose the slaveholder whom they believed would be 'the most complacent master.'"[20] Abolitionism and Northern political self-consciousness merged in the struggle over free soil and other issues in the 1850s. These two forces threatened the South on both the moral and the political fronts and prompted the fiery assertions of honor to overcome such insults to the slaveholding regime.

Despite these missing elements and turns in other historiographical directions, the appearance of new studies both here and abroad has naturally led me to reconsider points that were reached in *Southern Honor: Ethics and Behavior in the Old South* (1982). The most significant of these was my proposition in that study that honor had been constantly operative throughout American and European history, though gradually succumbing to market attitudes and evangelical strictures. To some degree, this initial proposition was influenced by European historians' notion of *la longue durée.* Instead, it might well have been a downward projection less smooth and predictable, with hills and valleys of intensity in different locales that depended on historical circumstances still not entirely clear. James Kelly writing on Ireland, Kevin McAleer on Germany, and Robert Nye on France, and others, for instance, have convinced me that the custom of ritualized personal combat in the upper echelons of Western societies, including the United States, had a broken, not a steady history.[21] Like religion with its revivals and declensions, honor, or at least its most mortal, most formal ritual, seems to have had a more problematic and discontinuous past everywhere on the European continent than once might have been assumed. Yet whatever the trajectory may have been, undoubtedly the ethic of honor was powerful enough in slaveholding, Southern hearts to generate the secession crisis and the cause of Confederate chivalry against Yankee imperialism, as Southerners deemed their struggle.

This book explores fresh aspects of honor that could not be treated very thoroughly in a book as long as *Southern Honor* already was. The roles of rhetoric and ritual are stressed because demonstrations of honorable behavior required stylized performance in speech acts and in gesture and demeanor. Then, as now, the ethic depends on public display. By that means, men and women articulated who they thought themselves to be and how they judged others, whether strangers, decided foes, neighbors, kinfolk, or fellow churchgoers. Known for their punctilious manners, Southern whites of refinement found in the formulae of social discourse a sense of order and memory. In a society in which oral constructions carried more weight than the written word, ritual prevented the possibility of a rupture with the past, loss of identity and place "through the human act of forgetfulness," as Jonathan Z. Smith argues.[22] In a more positive vein, the use of familiar phrases, gestures, and other articulations established an atmosphere of elegance, something that wealthy Southerners found as aesthetically pleasing as the acquisition of oil paintings, porcelains, and Oriental rugs.

Mentioning the issue of class structure in the explication of honor at once requires modification. Important as property holding and educational experience were in determining who mattered and who did not on the social ladder, honor is not entirely restricted to those with inherited wealth and social prominence. Certainly honor has been long associated with the traditions of hierarchy in the Western world. In 1602, Sir William Segar declared, "The Principall markes whereat euery mans endeauour in the life aimeth, are either Profit, or Honour; Th'one proper to vulgar people, and men of inferior Fortune; The other due to persons of better birth, and generous disposition." The vulgar must work to gather wealth, but the gentlemen of honor achieve their goal of "Honor, and humane glory . . . by Military skil, or knowledge in Ciuill gouverment."[23] Even today we say "poor but honest," as if it were a contradiction to be both at the same time.

As the anthropologist Frank Henderson Stewart notes in *Honor*, however, peasants in Europe developed a sense of honor. Basing his conclusions on work among the Bedouins of Arabia, Stewart persuades us that human equality and claim for respect are not incompatible. The Old South's yeomanry and poor were hardly immune to the dictates of honor. Nor did they hesitate to shame alleged offenders with punishments when personal or collective honor had been violated. Thus honor was by no means a monopoly of the planter class. As explorations of Andrew Jackson's sense of honor have shown, we can see how honor could operate in what I call in another study "timocratic" white democracy. Jackson managed to link the two concepts: *vox populi, vox honoris,* to coin a phrase. Likewise, an analysis of the antimission Baptists has revealed how honor and shame had played a part in the life of a sect that appealed most strongly to hardhanded mountain and backcountry Southern folk.

White egalitarian honorableness is another way of explaining the phenomenon that George Fredrickson labeled "*herrenvolk* democracy."[24] The difference between the two terms is that timocratic honor establishes a distinction from the genteel ideals of the upper classes. The gentry of the South developed refined and polished, "grammatical" ways, as it were, to express their gentility and adherence to the code. From the Revolution to the Civil War, white Southern commoners retained a strong sense of primal honor. In the years after the great conflict, the ordinary white grew increasingly vocal, especially on means to assure the continuation of white rule over African Americans. As one chapter explained, however, African Americans could not be wholly denied their own standards of behavior and their practices among themselves in the realm of honor.

Under such circumstances of shifting power relations within and around racial and class hierarchies, it might appear impossible to locate an all-embracing definition for honor and shame. The Primitive Baptists, for instance, were shown to have combined honor with their own egalitarian conventions. A more familiar usage has always linked honor with social standing. Another form suggests that slaves, too, had not only their own sense of honor but also, like the other groups, a recognition of shame and shamelessness. In addition, a fourth adaptation of the virtue is identifiable, one that animated ordinary whites before, during, and after Civil War, to commit mob violence, almost religious in character, upon supposed violators of racial and moral rules of behavior. What logic could possibly draw these disparate reactions together to be placed under a single rubric?

The answer exposes the tragic flaws of honor itself. The conventions governing the code were essentially the stratified ascriptions of human inheritance: male over female, white over black (in the whites' world), age over youth—and the powerful over the helpless. The powerful in some cases were the wealthy arbiters of social, economic, and civic life. In other cases, a crowd of ordinary folk derived strength from sheer numbers and general community support. The gruesome activities of the Ku Klux Klan, in both its Reconstruction and post–First World War phases, were rituals of honor, conducted by the common people and by the supposedly enlightened gentry. The historian Christopher Waldrep observes, "Feelings of community solidarity make law seem more or less necessary in a way that can incite or discourage the extralegal imposition of order. Communities that imagine themselves as snug and unified feel a reduced need for law."[25] What they did imagine as well was an imperative to defend a strongly held, collective ideal of honor. That purpose required bloody vengeance upon those identified as shameless, sometimes white but more often black. *Blut und Ehre*, the German faith in blood and honor, had its devastating American equivalent.

The antebellum policing of social and racial order by popular, extralegal action seldom met much repression in the courts which the gentry class controlled. In the Redeemer period after the Civil War, however, the former planter class, by this time composed of corporation lawyers, bankers, and landholders, gradually weakened as a political force under the insurgency of Populism and economic disruptions in the 1890s. The old concept of noblesse oblige or paternalistic protectiveness, about which the Christian slaveholding class had prided itself, also waned. More often than not, the lynch mobs of the 1880s had leaders drawn from small farmer and small town ranks. That democratic or populistic pattern continued in the makeup of the Ku Kluxers of the 1920s.[26] (Some historians, however, dispute that point.)

With regard to race and antebellum slavery, the rituals that denoted honor on the one hand and submission on the other had been a common means to establish predictability in race relations. When one or the other party broke the rules of ritual interchange, masters resorted to the brute power of the lash. Savage reaction supplanted the assumptions of authority and deference that the tipping of a slave's hat or bow and smiled greeting signified. How gratifying it was for slave owners, male and female, to presume a bondsman's sincerity. The thought flattered their sense of place in God's natural hierarchy, as they believed. Pleasant exchanges across the racial divide proved to the large-scale planters that their system of labor worked with the smoothness of a well-oiled coach on hard pavement. Even the communications preceding a duel were designed to assure a tidiness in an otherwise messy, even chaotic situation. The performance or drama of the duel at once suggests that the objective in the contest could not be the killing of an opponent. A hired assassin would be a much less risky way to remove an enemy. Instead, it was a means to prove one's masculinity and right to claim respect, possibly leadership. In other words, dueling helped the participant to establish a special identity that included one's kin as well as one's self. Ritual also worked along similar lines in the transactions of rich and poor whites. The courtesies had best be observed. Otherwise the haughty planter would find his barn on fire, a favorite nag made lame, a cotton crop ablaze. Even the poor had honor although they had no access to the punctilious staging of a duel.[27]

Under the rubrics of honor, ritual and rhetoric also had a function allied to the sacred in social estimation. Certainly the relationship of religion and the code must figure greatly in any understanding of the slave South. The region was becoming ever more Christianized as the era of a devastating sectional war approached. How could one be both a devout Christian, whose guiding principle must be the rule of love, and yet a man of honor who relied on a code demanding vengeance against slights? The American South was much less tied to the code of honor than southern Italy, where the code of revenge was much more intensely obeyed. Yet the duality of honor and grace resided in the heart of Dixie.[28]

NOTES

ABBREVIATIONS

ADAH	Alabama State Department of Archives and History
ASSU	American Sunday School Union Archives, Presbyterian Historical Society, Philadelphia
CSH, GDAH	Central State Hospital, Georgia Department of Archives and History
MDAH	Maryland Department of Archives and History
MHS	Maine Historical Society, Portland
NCDAH	North Carolina Department of Archives and History
SCDAH	South Carolina Department of Archives and History
SCL, USC	South Caroliniana Library, University of South Carolina
SHC	Southern Historical Collection, University of North Carolina, Wilson Library
TSA	Tennessee State Archives

PREFACE

1. Joshua Lawrence Chamberlain, *"Bayonet Forward": My Civil War Reminiscences* (Gettysburg: Stan Clark Military Books, 1994), 236; Alice Rains Trulock, *In the Hands of Providence: Joshua L. Chamberlain and the American Civil War* (Chapel Hill: University of North Carolina Press, 1992), 302.

2. Chamberlain, *"Bayonet Forward,"* 236.

3. Quoted in Trulock, *In the Hands of Providence,* 303.

4. James Oakes, *The Ruling Race: A History of American Slaveholders* (New York: Norton, 1982), 227. For a fine historiographical treatment of slavery as the sole distinction of Southern culture, see Peter Kolchin, "American Historians and Antebellum Southern Slavery, 1959–1984," in *A Master's Due: Essays in Honor of David Herbert Donald* (Baton Rouge: Louisiana State University Press, 1985), 87–111.

5. The literature on American manhood, particularly with regard to mid- and late nineteenth century, worries about reinvigorating manly behavior to counteract allegedly effete tendencies in the urban and bourgeois world of Northern business and intellect. Yet the connection of that so-called "crisis" with issues of honor, which cover more than just virility alone, has been largely ignored. See Gail Bederman, *Manliness and Civilization: A Cultural History of Gender and Race in the United States, 1880–1917* (Chicago: University of Chicago Press, 1995), esp. 16–20; E. Anthony

Rotundo, *American Manhood: Transformations in Masculinity from the Revolution to the Modern Era* (New York: Basic Books, 1993), which identifies New England habits as national; David Leverenz, *Manhood and the American Renaissance* (Ithaca, N.Y.: Cornell University Press, 1989); J. A. Mangan and James Walvin, eds., *Manliness and Morality: Middle-Class Masculinity in Britain and America, 1800–1940* (New York: St. Martin's Press, 1987); Paula Baker, "The Domestication of Politics: Women and American Political Society, 1780–1920," *American Historical Review* 89 (June 1984): 620–47; and Baker, *The Moral Framework of Public Life: Gender, Politics, and the State in Rural New York, 1870–1930* (New York: Oxford University Press, 1991).

6. Julian Pitt-Rivers, "Honor and Social Status," in *Honour and Shame: The Values of Mediterranean Society*, ed. Jean Georges Péristiany (Chicago: University of Chicago Press, 1966), 19–77; and Pierre Bourdieu, "The Sentiment of Honour in Kabyle Society,"191–241; see also *Contributions to Mediterranean Sociology; Mediterranean Rural Communities and Social Change: Acts of the Mediterranean Sociological Conference, Athens, July 1963*, ed. Jean Georges Péristiany (Paris, The Hague: Mouton, 1968).

7. See Stephen R. Haynes, "The Genesis of Race: Noah's Curse and the Biblical Imagination," a work soon to appear. I am indebted to the author for allowing me to refer to his fascinating text.

8. Leon Litwack, *Trouble in Mind: Black Southerners in the Age of Jim Crow* (New York: Vintage, 1999), 297.

9. See René Girard, *Violence and the Sacred*, trans. Patrick Gregory (Baltimore: Johns Hopkins University Press, 1972).

10. Meantime, the women took on the purifying duty of promoting the Lost Cause Legend, a topic which is given in the last pages less play than it perhaps deserves. Some of the ideas in this paragraph were inspired by the work of Alice Freifeld, *Nationalism and the Crowd in Liberal Hungary, 1848–1914* (Baltimore: Johns Hopkins University Press, 2000), pp. 379–80 in MS.

11. Thomas W. Gallant, " 'We're All Whores Here': Women, Slander, and the Courts in a Nineteenth-Century Greek Town," a chapter from his forthcoming *Experiencing Dominion*, kindly lent by the author.

12. See the appendix for a review of the literature on the subject of honor.

CHAPTER ONE

1. The Royal African Company returned to Africa a Muslim slave named Ayuba b. Sulayman, or Job Ben Solomon, in 1733 from colonial Maryland. See Michael A. Gomez, *Exchanging Our Country Marks: The Transformation of African Identities in the Colonial and Antebellum South* (Chapel Hill: University of North Carolina, 1998), 71. See also Gomez, "Muslims in Early America," *Journal of Southern History* 60 (November 1994): 671–710.

2. Benjamin Drew, *The Refugee: A North-Side View of Slavery* (1855; reprint, Reading, Pa.: Addison-Wesley, 1969), 4. This account is based on Terry Alford, *Prince among Slaves* (New York: Harcourt Brace Jovanovich, 1977), esp. 3–38. See Philip D.

Curtin, *The Image of Africa: British Ideas and Action, 1780–1850* (Madison: University of Wisconsin Press, 1964), 1:144, 2:308; Allan G. B. Fisher and Humphrey J. Fisher, *Slavery and Muslim Society in Africa: The Institution in Saharan and Sudanic Africa and the Trans-Saharan Trade* (New York: Doubleday, 1971), 30; Paul Lovejoy, *Transformation in Slavery: A History of Slavery in West Africa* (Cambridge, Eng.: Cambridge University Press, 1983), 114–15; Bruce L. Mousser, "Accommodation and Assimilation in the Landlord-Stranger Relationship," in *West African Culture Dynamics: Archeological and Historical Perspectives,* ed. B. K. Schwartz Jr. and Raymond E. Dumett (The Hague: Mouton, 1980), 499; Thomas H. Gallaudet, *A Statement with Regard to the Moorish Prince, Abduhl Rahhahman* (New York: Daniel Fanshaw, 1828), 3–4. Entries for 9–12 March 1794 in "Journal of James Watt in his expedition to and from Teembo in 1794 copied from the author's own hand," MSS Afr. 22, Rhodes House, Oxford University.

3. Alford, *Prince among Slaves,* 21, 44; Gomez, *Exchanging Our Country Marks,* 71–73.

4. Alford, *Prince among Slaves,* 45–47; and Major Steve Power, *The Memento: Old and New Natchez, 1700 to 1897* (Natchez, Miss: S. Power, 1897), 13–14.

5. See Joseph Boskin, *Sambo: The Rise and Demise of an American Jester* (New York: Oxford University Press, 1986), 17–41; Boskin, however, stresses only the white role in shaping and reshaping the Sambo stereotype.

6. Erik H. Erikson, *Insight and Responsibility: Lectures on the Ethical Implications of Psychoanalytic Insight* (New York: Norton, 1964), 96.

7. Stanley Elkins, *Slavery: An Intellectual and Institutional Problem* (Chicago: University of Chicago Press, 1956).

8. Elkins's critics claimed to detect a "reminstrelizing," one might say, of the dancing Sambo. An uproar ensued in 1969 with the publication of William Styron's best-selling gothic romance *The Confessions of Nat Turner,* in which the major fiction characters reflected Elkins's influence on the novelist.

9. Herbert George Gutman, *The Black Family in Slavery and Freedom, 1750–1925* (New York: Pantheon Books, 1976). Cf. Bertram Wyatt-Brown, "The New Consensus," *Commentary* 63 (January 1971): 76–78.

10. See the selections in Ann J. Lane, ed., *The Debate over Slavery: Stanley Elkins and His Critics* (Urbana: University of Illinois Press, 1971), and Kenneth M. Stampp, "Rebels and Sambos: The Search for the Negro's Personality in Slavery," *Journal of Southern History* 37 (August 1971): 367–92.

11. The pioneering analytic work on First World War "shell-shock" veterans at Craiglockhart under W. H. R. Rivers was not at all well known even in the late 1950s. Battle disorders in the Second World War might have been helpful to Elkins had there been a substantial body of publications on the topic. See J. M. W. Binneveld, *From Shell Shock to Combat Stress: A Comparative History of Military Psychiatry,* trans. John O'Keane (Amsterdam: Amsterdam University Press, 1997); William F. Page, *The Health of Former Prisoners of War: Results from the Medical Examination Survey of Former POWs of World War II and the Korean Conflict: A Report for the Medical Follow-Up Agency,*

Institute of Medicine (Washington, D.C.: National Academy Press, 1992); John Rawlings Rees, *The Shaping of Psychiatry by War* (New York: Norton, 1945); Paul Fussell, *The Great War and Modern Memory* (New York: Oxford University Press, 1975). On camp resistance, I cite only one work of many, one that Elkins might have used to considerable advantage: Olga Lengyel, *Five Chimneys: A Woman Survivor's True Story of Auschwitz* (1947; reprint; Chicago: Academy Chicago Publishers, 1995).

12. Quoted in Mary Lowenthal Felstiner, *To Paint Her Life: Charlotte Solomon in the Nazi Era* (1994; reprint; Berkeley: University of California Press, 1997), 112–33.

13. Martin Gilbert, *The Holocaust: A History of the Jews of Europe during the Second World War* (New York: Henry Holt, 1985), 389–90, 539. For other examples, see Gilbert's lengthy index entry on suicides.

14. See, for instance, Philip D. Curtin, *Africa Remembered* (Madison: University of Wisconsin Press, 1967), 85–92, 297–98.

15. See Christopher Browning, *The Path to Genocide: Essays on Launching the Final Solution* (Cambridge, Eng.: Cambridge University Press, 1992), ix–x; Richard B. Speed III, *Prisoners, Diplomats, and the Great War: A Study in the Diplomacy of Captivity* (New York: Greenwood, 1990), 2, 79; Robert-Jan Van Pelt, "A Site in Search of a Mission," in *Anatomy of the Auschwitz Death Camp*, ed. Yisrael Gutman and Michael Berenbaum (Bloomington: Indiana University Press, 1998), 104–17. I thank Peter Bergman for these references.

16. Lawrence L. Langer, *Holocaust Testimonies: The Ruins of Memory* (New Haven: Yale University Press, 1991), 164. But it also sprang from recognition of powerlessness. Any act of resistance meant reprisals against countless others as well as against oneself.

17. Quotations from Gomez, *Exchanging Our Country Marks*, 163–64.

18. Kenneth M. Stampp, *The Peculiar Institution: Slavery in the Ante-Bellum South* (New York: Knopf, 1961), 128–29; Ulrich Bonnell Phillips, ed., *Plantation and Frontier, 1649–1863*, 2 vols. (New York: Franklin, 1969), 2:31, 94; Pierson, "White Cannibals, Black Martyrs," 150, 151, 152.

19. Inga Clendinnen, *Reading the Holocaust* (New York: Cambridge University Press, 1999), 72.

20. Primo Levi, *Survival in Auschwitz: The Nazi Assault on Humanity*, trans. Stuart Woolf (1958; reprint; New York: Simon and Schuster, 1996), 26–27; Gizella Abramson, lecture to the "Constructing America" Jessie Ball DuPont Seminar, 22 June 2000, National Humanities Center, Research Triangle Park, N.C.; entry for 24 August 1938, in Victor Klemperer, I *Will Bear Witness: A Diary of the Nazi Years, 1933–1941*, trans. Martin Chalmers (New York: Random House, 1998), 264–65.

21. Gomez, *Exchanging Our Country Marks*, 159.

22. Gilbert, *Holocaust*, 540, 572.

23. Orlando Patterson, *Rituals of Blood: Consequences of Slavery in Two American Centuries* (Washington, D.C.: Civitas/Counterpoint, 1998), 211. The value of comparing the Nazi atrocities with terrorism and genocide in other places and times has to be challenged because such comparisons by German scholarly apologists

are intended to reduce the singular effort systematically to destroy whole categories of people that stirred considerable controversy among European scholars. See Charles S. Maier, *The Unmasterable Past: History, Holocaust, and German Nationality* (Cambridge, Mass.: Harvard University Press, 1988), 31–33, 66–99. Likewise, historians in America are scarcely agreed about whether the concentration camp–African slavery comparison is legitimate, but the purpose here is different. It is to show the unjustifiable and corruptive nature of all forms of oppression.

24. Orlando Patterson, *Slavery and Social Death: A Comparative Study* (New York: Oxford University Press, 1982).

25. Hosea Easton, *To Heal the Scourge of Prejudice: The Life and Writings of Hosea Easton*, ed. George R. Price and James Brewer Stewart (Amherst: University of Massachusetts Press, 1999), 100–111.

26. Aharon Appelfeld, *Beyond Despair: Three Lectures and a Conversation with Philip Roth* (New York: Fromm, 1994), 11–15.

27. Wilma King, *Stolen Childhood: Slave Youth in Nineteenth-Century America* (Bloomington: Indiana University Press,1995), 93.

28. Paul Riesman, *Freedom in Fulani Social Life: An Introspective Ethnography* (Chicago: University of Chicago Press, 1977), 117, 135. Slavery was practiced by many tribes—Wolofs and Yorubas among others—from which transatlantic slaves were drawn, but there were great variations in household incorporation and intermarriage. Even in Fulani areas (Hausa of Nigeria), according to M. G. Smith, generals were sometimes slaves "as much through fear of internal revolt as for defense against invaders" (M. G. Smith, *Government in Zazzau* [New York: Oxford University Press, 1960], 242).

29. See Ann-Mari Sellerberg, review of William Ian Miller, *Humiliation and Other Essays on Honor, Social Discomfort, and Violence* in *Society* 32 (September–October 1995): 89; and William Ian Miller, *Humiliation and Other Essays on Honor, Social Discomfort, and Violence* (Ithaca, N.Y.: Cornell University Press, 1993), 133, 165–67.

30. Bernd Baldus, "Responses to Dependence in a Servile Group: The Machube of Northern Benin," in *Slavery in Africa: Historical and Anthropological Perspectives*, ed. Suzanne Miers and Igor Kopytoff (Madison: University of Wisconsin Press, 1977), 435–58, (quotation, 446).

31. Anna Freud, *The Ego and the Mechanisms of Defense*, trans. Cecil Baines (New York: International Universities Press, 1946).

32. Ibid., 446–58 (quotation, 447). The machube were Islamic in conviction as were their masters, a common identification of faith as Max Weber first theorized regarding the nature of slave religious belief. So too does Weber's hypothesis apply in North American slavery. See Weber as discussed in John C. Gager, *Kingdom and Community: The Social World of Early Christianity* (Englewood Cliffs, N.J.: Prentice-Hall, 1975), 105–6.

33. Ariela Gross, "Pandora's Box: Slave Character on Trial in the Antebellum Deep South," in *Slavery and the Law*, ed. Paul Finkelman (Madison, Wisc.: Madison House, 1997), 300 (quotation) and 304.

34. Baldus, "Responses to Dependence," 448–56 (quotation, 448).

35. John J. Grace, "Slavery and Emancipation among the Mende in Sierra Leone, 1896–1928," in *Slavery in Africa*, ed. Miers and Kopytoff, 419–20; Alford, *Prince among Slaves*, 61. The newly arrived slave could have brought Prince news from Futa Jallon, says Alford (61).

36. Henry Louis Gates Jr., *The Signifying Monkey: A Theory of African-American Literary Criticism* (New York: Oxford University Press, 1988), 66.

37. Ibid., 53.

38. Sylvia R. Frey, *Water from the Rock: Black Resistance in a Revolutionary Age* (Princeton, N.J.: Princeton University Press, 1991), 45–80. Frey deals astutely with the complexity of African modes of slavery—from the semiautonomous soldier-slave to the abject servant who must be sacrificed to wait on his dead master. See also James Sidbury, "Saint Domingue in Virginia: Ideology, Local Meanings, and Resistance to Slavery, 1790–1800," *Journal of Southern History* 63 (August 1997): 531–52.

39. Philip D. Morgan, *Slave Counterpoint: Black Culture in the Eighteenth Century Chesapeake and Lowcountry* (Chapel Hill: University of North Carolina Press, 1998), 443.

40. Shane White and Graham White, *Stylin': African American Expressive Culture from Its Beginnings to the Zoot Suit* (Ithaca, N.Y.: Cornell University Press, 1998), 5–6, 9.

41. Alford, *Prince among Slaves*, 49, but see also 208 (note for p. 8); John Grace, *Domestic Slavery in West Africa with Particular Reference to the Sierra Leone Protectorate, 1896–1927* (New York: Harpers, 1975), 1–19 (quotation, 10). The introduction to *Slavery in Africa*, ed. Miers and Kopytoff, 3–81, shows the diversity of African slavery but stresses the marginality of the slaves' status. Watson, "Slavery as an Institution: Open and Closed Systems," 3–15, criticizes Miers and Kopytoff for overlooking the "closed" types and for underplaying the "property" aspect of slavery in all societies. See Frederick Cooper, *Plantation Slavery on the East Coast of Africa* (New Haven: Yale University Press, 1977). On Nigerian slavery, see Cohen, *The Kanuri of Bornu*; Hoben, "Social Stratification in Traditional Amhara Society," 197–98; M. G. Smith, "Slavery and Emancipation in Two Societies," *Social and Economic Studies* 3 (December 1954): 243; see also Lovejoy, "Plantations in the Nineteenth-Century Sokoto Caliphate," 1290.

42. Frederick Douglass, *My Bondage and My Freedom*, ed. William L. Andrews (1855; reprint, Urbana: University of Illinois Press, 1987), 111. See also Josiah Henson, *Father Henson's Story of His Own Life* (1858; reprint, Williamstown, Mass.: Corner House, 1973), 48, 51.

43. Entry for 10 April 1866, *The Private Journal of Henry William Ravenel, 1859–1887*, ed. Arney Robinson Childs (Columbia: University of South Carolina Press, 1947), 278; Leon Litwack, *Been in the Storm So Long: The Aftermath of Slavery* (New York: Knopf, 1979), 253.

44. Sylvia R. Frey and Betty Wood, *Come Shouting to Zion: African American Protestantism in the American South and British Caribbean to 1830* (Chapel Hill: University of

North Carolina Press, 1998); Robert Olwell, *Masters, Slaves, and Subjects: The Culture of Power in the South Carolina Low Country, 1740–1790* (Ithaca, N.Y.: Cornell University Press, 1998); Jon F. Sensbach, *A Separate Canaan: The Making of an Afro-Moravian World in North Carolina, 1763–1840* (Chapel Hill: University of North Carolina Press for the Omohundro Institute of Early American History and Culture, 1998).

45. Alford, *Prince among Slaves*, 17, 48 (quotation), 79–81; for corroboration on Prince's character, see "Letter from a Gentleman of Natchez to a Lady of Cincinnati . . . April 7th, 1828," *Washington National Intelligencer*, 8 May 1828 (quoted from *Cincinnati Republican*). See also *African Repository* 3 (February 1828): 364–67, and 4 (May 1828): 77, 243, 379; Gomez, *Exchanging Our Country Marks*, 74. See also John W. Blassingame, ed., *Slave Testimony: Two Centuries of Letters, Speeches, Interviews, and Autobiographies* (Baton Rouge: Louisiana State University Press, 1977), 682–86. Omar Ibn Said, another formerly highly placed Fullah, enslaved in North Carolina, refused inquiries about returning to his homeland; he also submitted to Christian convictions after years of serving Allah in America (ibid., 470–74).

46. In 1828, Prince claimed to be a loyal Muslim but "anxious" to have a Bible in Arabic. See *Washington National Intelligencer*, 8 May 1828; Alford, *Prince among Slaves*, 57. Thomas H. Gallaudet, *A Statement with Regard to the Moorish Prince, Abduhl Rahhahman* (New York: Daniel Fanshaw, 1828), 3, asserted that Abd al-Rahman, "wife, and eldest son have been baptized, and are in connexion with the Baptist Church" (Patterson, *Slavery and Social Death*, 84 n. 12, citing Riesman). For other less exotic examples of dignified, loyal slaves, see entry for 22 July 1861, Nimrod Porter Diary, TSA; A. B. Cooper to Charles Tait, 24 January 1835, Daniel McLeod (overseer) to Tait, 24 May 1835 (both concerning Tait's accomplished and literate manservant Harford), and Harford to Tait, 10 January and 6 November 1827, Charles Tait Papers, ADAH; and Charles and Tess Hoffmann, "The Limits of Paternalism: Driver-Master Relations on a Bryan County Plantation," *Georgia Historical Quarterly* 67 (Fall 1983): 321–35.

47. Kathleen M. Brown, *Good Wives, Nasty Wenches, and Anxious Patriarchs: Gender, Race, and Power in Colonial Virginia* (Chapel Hill: University of North Carolina Press, 1996), 184.

48. Entry for 4 June 1865, *The Private Mary Chesnut: The Unpublished Civil War Diaries*, ed. C. Vann Woodward and Elizabeth Muhlenfeld (New York: Oxford University Press, 1984), 25. See also Elizabeth Robinson, in Charles L. Perdue Jr., Thomas E. Barden, and Robert K. Phillips, eds., *Weevils in the Wheat: Interviews with Virginia Ex-Slaves* (Bloomington: Indiana University Press, 1980), 238.

49. Nerys W. Patterson, "Honour and Shame in Medieval Welsh Society: A Study of the Role of Burlesque in the Welsh Laws," *Studia Celtica* 14–17 (1981–82): 73–103, esp. 91–93; Joseph Vogt, *Ancient Slavery and the Ideal of Man*, trans. Thomas Wiedemann (Cambridge, Mass.: Harvard University Press, 1975). In fact, as Keith Hopkins says, "the character of slaves in Roman comedy has a lot in common with the American stereotypical slave Sambo: impudent, gossiping, lazy, deceitful, lightfingered, unscrupulous" (*Conquerors and Slaves* [Cambridge, Eng.: Cambridge Uni-

versity Press, 1978], 121). On ancient stereotypes based on observed behavior, see W. Thomas MacCary, "Menander's Slaves: The Names, Roles, and Masks," *Proceedings of the American Philological Association* 100 (1969): 277–94; Philip Whaley Harsh, "The Intriguing Slave in Greek Comedy," *Transactions and Proceedings of the American Philological Association* 86 (1955): 135–42; George E. Duckworth, *The Nature of Roman Comedy* (Princeton: Princeton University Press, 1952), 249–50. On Muscovy, see Richard Hellie, *Slavery in Russia, 1400–1725* (Chicago: University of Chicago Press, 1982), 313–17. On Asia, see James H. Vaughan, "Mafakur: A Limbie Institution of the Margi (Nigeria)," in *Slavery in Africa: Historical and Anthropological Perspectives*, ed. Miers and Kopytoff, 85–102. The essay on this isolated highland people, the Margi, indicates that the "mafa," loosely translated as slave or a person of liminal status, accepted the situation as legitimate in *some instances*, depending on the circumstances by which this unhappy fate came about. Diversity of response is the author's theme. Among the mafa, however, one ("K.") was "servile and obsequious, completely unlike W. It was the general consensus that K.'s demeanor was more typical of mafa, whereas W., who was both dignified and respected, was exceptional" (95). See also Carol P. MacCormack, "Wono: Institutionalized Dependency in Sherbro Descent Groups (Sierra Leone)," ibid., 197, which shows how slave children were assumed to be unrighteous, while free ones were lashed and advised: " 'Don't act like a slave.' "

50. Ebenezer Hazard, a New Englander visiting Georgia in 1778, remarked: "The *Country Gentlemen* are . . . accustomed to tyrannize from their Infancy, they carry with them a Disposition to treat all Mankind in the same manner they have been used to treat their Negroes. If a man has not as many Slaves as they, he is esteemed by them their Inferior, even though he vastly exceeds them in every other Respect" (Entry for 25 February 1778, in "The Journal of Ebenezer Hazard in Georgia, 1778," ed. Fred Shelley, *Georgia Historical Quarterly* 41 [September 1957]: 318–19, citation kindly supplied by George Crawford). Though harsher than many observers, Hazard was only echoing the perceptions of men like Thomas Jefferson, who thought slavery inflated the owners' ego, a posture learned in childhood and continually exercised impulsively throughout life. See also Solomon Northup, in Gilbert Osofsky, ed., *Puttin' on Ole Massa* (New York: Harper & Row, 1969), 338.

51. Patterson, *Slavery and Social Death*, 79, quoting from Julian Pitt-Rivers. See Pitt-Rivers, "Honour and Social Status," in J. G. Péristiany, ed., *Honour and Shame: The Values of Mediterranean Society* (Chicago: University of Chicago Press, 1966), 19–78.

52. James Sidbury, *Ploughshares into Swords: Race, Rebellion, and Identity in Gabriel's Virginia, 1730–1810* (New York: Cambridge University Press, 1997), 219; Stanislaw Taubenschlag (Stanley Townsend), *To Be a Jew in Occupied Poland*, trans. David Herman Oświęcim [Auschwitz], Poland: Parol and Panstwowe Muzeum Oświęcim-Brezinka, 1998), 82–84).

53. See Harry G. LeFever, " 'Playing the Dozens': A Mechanism for Social Control," *Phylon* 42 (Spring 1981): 73–85 (quotation, 77); Lawrence Levine, *Black Culture and Black Consciousness* (New York: Pantheon Books, 1977), 358.

54. Riesman, *Freedom in Fulani Social Life*, 76–79, 124 (quotation), 198. Riesman

does not suggest the connection between ideal self-control and the insult test as I have sketched it, but his description does not conflict with that reading. See also John Dollard, "The Dozens: The Dialect of Insult," *American Imago* 1 (November 1939): 3–25; Roger Abrahams, "Playing the Dozens," *Journal of American Folklore* 75 (July–September 1962): 213; William Labov, "Rules for Ritual Insults," in *Rappin' and Stylin' Out*, ed. Thomas Kochman (Urbana: University of Illinois Press, 1972), 314; Amuzie Chimezie, "The Dozens: An African Heritage Theory," *Journal of Black Studies* 6 (June 1976): 401–20; Donald Simmons, "Possible West African Sources for the American Negro Dozens," *Journal of American Folklore* 76 (October–December 1963): 337–41; Walter F. Edwards, "Speech Acts in Guyana: Communicating Ritual and Personal Insults," *Journal of Black Studies* 10 (September 1979): 20–39; Millicent R. Ayoub and Stephen A. Barnett, "Ritualized Verbal Insult in White High School Culture," *Journal of American Folklore* 78 (October–December 1965): 337–44.

55. South Carolina Sessional Papers, Minutes of Council, December 1748–December 1749, Journal 17, Part 1, Public Record Office British Manuscripts Project, Reel 34, I.C.O. 5/457, microfilm, January 27, 1749, pp. 55–120, SCDAH, hereafter cited as Minutes of Council.

56. Ibid., 64. Sambo, a witness, declared that they had collected no arms, at once a hint that no plot was under way. The head of the conspiracy was supposedly an overseer named James Springer, who had left for a Northern colony long before the hearings and therefore could not be made a material witness. See ibid., 73, 85. Lawrence Kelley, an Irishman, formerly of Pennsylvania, was also accused along with several others (99–106). See also Philip D. Morgan and George D. Terry, "Slavery in Microcosm: A Conspiracy Scare in Colonial South Carolina," *Southern Studies* 21 (Summer 1982): 122 and passim.

57. See, for example, the "Samboism" of a thoroughly frightened slave whose master was a murderer and sadist: Frank Bell, in Norman R. Yetman, ed., *Life under the "Peculiar Institution": Selections from the Slave Narrative Collection* (New York: Holt, Rinehart and Winston, 1970), 21–23: "You know, the nigger was wild till the white man made what he has of the nigger," was, ironically, Bell's conclusion (23). See also Josiah Henson, *Father Henson's Story of His Own Life*, 12th ed. (Boston: J. P. Jewett, 1858); and Solomon Northup, *Twelve Years a Slave*, ed. Sue Eakin and Joseph Logsdon (Baton Rouge: Louisiana State University Press, 1968).

58. Katharine Du Pre Lumpkin, *The Making of a Southerner* (1948; reprint, Athens, Ga.: University of Georgia Press, 1974), 32, 80.

59. Constantin Stanislavski, *Building a Character*, trans. Elizabeth Reynolds Hapgood (New York: Theatre Arts Books, 1949), 167; Erik H. Erikson, *Childhood and Society* (1950; reprint, New York: Norton, 1963), 252–53. Whereas guilt is concerned with the transgression of one's own moral sense, shame deals with loss of pride, fear of or experience with ridicule, and anxiety of failure to achieve one's goals, usually higher than one could manage. Under the rubric of shame, fear of others' contempt is greater than fear of others' hatred. See Helen B. Lewis, *Shame and Guilt in Neurosis* (New York: International Universities Press, 1971), 18–23, and Gerhart Piers and

Milton B. Singer, *Shame and Guilt: A Psychoanalytic and Cultural Study*, cited in Fred Weinstein and Gerald M. Platt, *Psychoanalytic Sociology: An Essay on the Interpretation of Historical Data and the Phenomena of Collective Behavior* (Baltimore: Johns Hopkins University Press, 1973), 8 n. 13. See also Richard Wright, *Black Boy: A Record of Childhood and Youth* (1945; reprint, New York: Harper & Row, 1966), 250.

60. Erikson, *Childhood and Society*, 253. Charles Ball, *Fifty Years in Chains* (1837; reprint, New York: Dover, 1970), 19–23 (quotation, 19). Ball's grandfather Ben "expressed great contempt for his fellow slaves, they being, as he said, a mean and vulgar race, quite beneath his rank, and the dignity of his former station." Undoubtedly it was this "significant other" who gave Ball his sense of specialness. See Ralph Ellison, *Invisible Man* (New York: Random House, 1947); Wright, *Black Boy*, and his characterization of Bigger Thomas in *Native Son* (New York: Harper & Row, 1940); Alice Walker, *The Third Life of Grange Copeland* (New York: Harcourt Brace Jovanovich, 1970), and *The Color Purple* (New York: Harcourt Brace Jovanovich, 1982); Ernest J. Gaines, *Bloodline* (New York: Norton, 1964), among other works.

61. See esp. Ronald L. Braithwaite, "Interpersonal Relations between Black Males and Black Females," in *Black Men*, ed. Lawrence E. Gary (Beverly Hills: Sage, 1981), 83–97, noting "low self-disclosure" tendencies and sex-role ambiguity among black males; David Wilkerson and Ronald Taylor, eds., *The Black Male* (Chicago: Nelson-Hall, 1977). Thomas L. Webber, *Deep Like the Rivers: Education in the Slave Quarter Community, 1831–1865* (New York: Norton, 1978), 32–42, explains methods of enforcing internalization of deferential habits but denies the tactics were effective (91–110). But see Charles S. Johnson, *Shadow of the Plantation* (1934; reprint, Chicago: University of Chicago Press, 1966), 27–31; Floyd J. Miller, introduction to *Blake or the Huts of America*, by Martin R. Delaney (1861–62; reprint, Boston: Beacon Press, 1970), xxiv-xxv (Delaney substantiating internalized dependence in the novel itself). "The nigger during slavery was like the sheep," one former slave recalled in the 1930s. "We have always had to follow the white folks and do what we saw them do, and that's all there is to it" (B. A. Botkin, ed., *Lay My Burden Down: A Folk History of Slavery* [Chicago: University of Chicago Press, 1945], 14–15).

62. Karen Horney, *Neurosis and Human Growth: The Struggle toward Self-Realization* (New York: Norton, 1950).

63. Frederick Marryat, *Peter Simple* (New York: Munro's Sons, 1896), 39.

64. Charles Wiltse, ed., *David Walker's Appeal to the Colored Citizens of the World* (1829; reprint, New York: Hill and Wang, 1965), 22; Blyden, quoted in Wilson Jeremiah Moses, *Black Messiahs and Uncle Toms: Social and Literary Manipulations of a Religious Myth* (University Park: Pennsylvania State University Press, 1982), 51. For an example of wife-beating, desertion, and male sense of inadequacy and rage, see Jane White, affidavit, 29 January 1867, in Selected Records of the Freedmen's Bureau, 1865–72, Reports, Affidavits, Oaths, Appointments and Letters Rec'd by Ass't Commissioner, 1866–68, microfilm #39, TSA. William Styron, *The Confessions of Nat Turner* (New York: Random House, 1967); James R. Huffman, "A Psychological Re-

definition of William Styron's *Confessions of Nat Turner*," *Literary Review* 24 (Winter 1981): 279–307; Douglass, *Narrative of the Life of an American Slave*, 36.

65. James B. Stewart, "The Psychic Duality of Afro-Americans in the Novels of W. E. B. Du Bois," *Phylon* 44 (June 1983): 99 (quotation), 101. Du Bois expanded on this theme in *Dark Princess*, explaining that "the white always felt a Negro was watching him and he acted his assumed part . . . of strutting walk, loud talk, and swagger . . . accordingly. And the Negroes did watch from behind another veil. This was the veil of amusement or feigned, impudent humility" (Stewart, "Psychic Duality," 102). Du Bois, says Stewart, concluded that the psychic damage of slavery was "an intense self-hatred" that made "racial solidarity an alien concept" so that "a pathological, Fanon-type consciousness emerged" (101). See also Dickson D. Bruce Jr., "W. E. B. Du Bois and the Idea of Double Consciousness," *American Literature* 64 (June 1992): 299–309. For a penetrating study of an analogous situation under colonial rule and the subtle and overt modes for overcoming it, see Leroy Vail and Landeg White, "Forms of Resistance: Songs and Perceptions of Power in Colonial Mozambique," *American Historical Review* 88 (October 1983): 883–919.

66. David Brion Davis, "White Wives and Slave Mothers," review of Brenda Stevenson, *Life in Black and White, New York Review of Books* 44 (20 February 1997): 38.

67. Walter L. Williams, "The 'Sambo' Deception: The Experience of John McElroy in Andersonville Prison," *Phylon* 39 (Fall 1978): 261–63 (quotation, 262). See Gutman, *Black Family in Slavery and Freedom*, and Herbert J. Foster, "African Patterns in the Afro-American Family," *Journal of Black Studies* 14 (December 1983): 201–31, which challenges Gutman's emphasis on the nuclear family. Daniel E. Sutherland, "A Special Kind of Problem: The Response of Household Servants and Their Masters to Freedom," *Southern Studies* 20 (Summer 1981): 151–66, makes a useful distinction between house and field hands and casts doubt on the unity of reactions and perspectives that sometimes is asserted for the slave community. It did exist but not as uniformly and consistently as we would like to imagine. Also, Orlando Patterson in *Rituals of Blood* assails the limitations of the Gutman school of revisionists and points to the regional variations and diverse slave groupings on small farms and medium and large plantations. According to Patterson, these and other factors affected (often adversely) the formation of ties beyond simple reproductive functions. He carries the argument much too far, however. See Patterson, *Rituals of Blood*, 31–34.

68. Peter Kolchin, "Reevaluating the Antebellum Slave Community: A Comparative Perspective," *Journal of American History* 70 (December 1983): 584; Douglass, *Narrative of the Life of an American Slave*, 92; W. E. B. Du Bois, *The Souls of Black Folk* (New York: Fawcett, 1961), 16–17. On the internalization of the deferential mode, see John Dollard, *Caste and Class in a Southern Town* (1937; reprint, New York: Harper & Brothers, 1949), 175–87, 286–313, which notes that some Southern blacks were deferential as a matter of second nature, others were less able to hide hostility but performed the rituals with obvious internal reservations, and still others (a few)

were openly aggrieved and aggressive toward whites. See also Allison Davis, Burleigh B. Gardner, and Mary Gardner, *Deep South: A Social Anthropological Study of Caste and Class* (1941; reprint, Chicago: University of Chicago Press, 1948), 2–24, and 230–34, on black quarter class differentiations that disunited the community. As Bernard Meltzer reminds us, "The mind is social in both origin and function. It arises in the social process of communication. Through association with the members of his groups, the individual comes to internalize the definitions transmitted to him." Du Bois's double consciousness then makes psychological sense: for survival's sake. See Bernard N. Meltzer, "Mead's Social Psychology," in *Symbolic Interaction: A Reader in Social Psychology*, ed. Jerome G. Main and Bernard N. Meltzer (Boston: Allyn and Bacon, 1972), 13. If there is no valid communication, but only threats of torture or death, institutional rules, as Elkins logically pointed out, simply do not matter. The individual is thrust back upon the most primitive of resources: the imitation of childhood dependency or some other less than adult demeanor, with mental depression a result. Yet resilience of mind does permit a fast recovery when that condition ends, though dreams and nightmares might linger. See fugitive accounts in Drew, *Refugee*, 20, 26–27, 29, 30, 34, 35, 53–54, 58, 79–80, 125.

69. Herbert G. Gutman, *Slavery and the Numbers Game: A Critique of "Time on the Cross"* (Urbana: University of Illinois Press, 1975).

70. Entry for 23 July 1858, Corydon Fuller Diary, William L. Clements Library, University of Michigan, Ann Arbor.

71. Douglass, quoted in John W. Blassingame, ed., *The Frederick Douglass Papers. Series One: Speeches, Debates, and Interviews*, Vol. 1, *1841–1846* (New Haven: Yale University Press, 1979), 41–42, 357.

72. Peter Kolchin, *Unfree Labor: American Slavery and Russian Serfdom* (Cambridge, Mass.: Harvard University Press, 1987), 330–31.

73. Entry for 24 December 1839, *Plantation Life in the Florida Parishes of Louisiana, 1836–1846, as Reflected in the Diary of Bennet H. Barrow*, ed. Edwin Adams Davis (New York: Columbia University Press, 1945), 175; pumpkin story told in Botkin, ed., *Lay My Burden Down*, 6. For a similar acceptance of white perceptions in labeling of deviant slaves, see Bessie Hough Williams, "Memoir of the King Family," William Rufus King Family Papers, ADAH.

74. See John W. Cell, *The Highest Stage of White Supremacy: The Origins of Segregation in South Africa and the American South* (Cambridge, Eng.: Cambridge University Press, 1982), 241–43. Some planters insisted on maintaining their slaves' dependence on them for food and prohibited garden plots for fear of encouraging self-reliance, confidence, and laxness when working for the master instead of themselves. See "Governor [James H.] Hammond's Instructions to His Overseer," in *A Documentary History of Slavery in North America*, ed. Willie Lee Rose (New York: Oxford University Press, 1976), 348. Dependence *was* a habit—less widespread and certainly more quickly overcome than the Rebels ever thought possible, but it was real enough. See Botkin, ed., *Lay My Burden Down*, 25, 35, 93. W. J. Cash, *The Mind of the South* (New York: Random House, 1941), 326–27.

75. Brenda E. Stevenson, *Life in Black and White: Family and Community in the Slave South* (New York: Oxford University Press, 1996), 255. The sheer physical problems facing the slave couple, many of them living on separate and not always adjacent plantations, appears vividly in Larry E. Hudson Jr., *To Have and to Hold: Slave Work and Family Life in Antebellum South Carolina* (Athens: University of Georgia Press, 1997), 141–70.

76. For excellent work on this topic, see Christopher Morris, "Within the Slave Cabin: Violence in Mississippi Slave Families," in *Over the Threshold: Intimate Violence in Early America*, ed. Christine Daniels and Michael V. Kennedy (New York: Routledge, 1999), 268–86; Brenda Stevenson, "Distress and Discord in Virginia Slave Families, 1830–1860," in *In Joy and Sorrow: Women, Family, and Marriage in the Victorian South, 1830–1900*, ed. Carol Bleser (New York: Oxford University Press, 1988), 113–17; Wilma King, *Stolen Childhood: Slave Youth in Nineteenth Century America* (Bloomington: Indiana University Press, 1995), 97; and Hudson, *To Have and to Hold*, 177–84.

77. Henry Bibb, in Osofsky, ed., *Puttin' on Ole Massa*, 132; Douglass, *Narrative of the Life of an American Slave*, 109–27.

78. Sidbury, *Ploughshares into Swords*, 115–16; Douglas R. Egerton, *Gabriel's Rebellion: The Virginia Slave Conspiracies of 1800 and 1802* (Chapel Hill: University of North Carolina Press, 1993), 69–71; Egerton, *He Shall Go Out Free: The Lives of Denmark Vesey* (Madison, Wisc.: Madison House, 1999), 156–57; Ferdinando Camon, *Conversations with Primo Levi*, trans. John Shepley (1987 reprint; Marlboro, Vt.: Marlboro Press, 1989), 46.

79. Morgan, *Slave Counterpoint*, 205.

80. Lorena S. Walsh, *From Calabar to Carter's Grove: The History of a Virginia Slave Community* (Charlottesville: University Press of Virginia, 1997), 37.

81. Michael Agar, "The Yucatan's Flooded Basement," *Smithsonian* 29 (April 1998): 94.

82. See Egerton, *He Shall Go Out Free*.

83. William Faulkner, *Intruder in the Dust* (New York: Random House, 1948); "The Bear" in Faulkner, *Go Down, Moses, and Other Stories* (New York, Random House, 1942).

84. See also, for another example of self-contained professionalism at work, John Drayton in Botkin, ed., *Lay My Burden Down*, 11–12; May in Louis D. Rubin Jr., *William Elliott Shoots a Bear: Essays on the Southern Literary Tradition* (Baton Rouge: Louisiana State University Press, 1975), 1–27, esp. 3.

85. Quoted in Curtis D. Johnson, *Redeeming America: Evangelicals and the Road to Civil War* (Chicago: Ivan R. Dee, 1993), 44–45.

86. Mechal Sobel, *Trabelin' On: The Slave Journey to an Afro-Baptist Faith* (Princeton: Princeton University Press, 1988), 207, 236–37.

87. Alford, *Prince among Slaves*, 180–83. Abd al-Rahman did not wish very much to return to Africa sooner than he did (late 1820s) because he learned, through other slaves imported from Futa Jallon, that his brother had been assassinated on the throne and contests over the succession were unceasing between Sori's descen-

dants. See Winston McGowan, "Fula Resistance to French Expansion into Futa Jallon, 1889–1896," *Journal of African History* 22 (1981): 245–61, esp. 254–55, and genealogical table for Abd al-Rahman, in Alford, *Prince among Slaves*, after 187, and also 239n.

To be sure, slaves did not always passively submit to punishment. A few took direct and such unequivocal action as slave June did when she burned down her master and mistress's house and outbuildings in 1863. The court record offered no motivational clues, only that "her *Old Mistress* had made her *mad*." See State v. June, [Aaron G. Smith's], 27 April 1863, Magistrates and Freeholders Court, Anderson District, SCDAH. Some ran away; some ran and bargained for leniency or sale elsewhere; some fought back. See, for instance, B. G. L. Simms to George A. Washington, 22 June 1840, Washington Family Papers, TSA. An overseer boasted that on his plantation in Louisiana the driver "can whip all the fellows but fore," who, he continued, "wont let them whip them without a fite." The others, though, were compliant enough and they "holds their[selves] strate" and "come at onst." Judging from the satisfaction that planters and overseers expressed about the results of floggings, the practice worked all too effectively. See Henry A. Thigpen to John Jackson, 19 April 1862, in Harvey H. Jackson, ed., "The Calm before the Storm: A Louisiana Overseer's World on the Eve of the Civil War," *Southern Studies* 18 (Summer 1979): 245.

CHAPTER TWO

1. Josiah Quincy, quoted in Peter Shaw, *American Patriots and the Rituals of Revolution* (Cambridge, Mass.: Harvard University Press, 1981), 160. See also Philip Davidson, *Propaganda and the American Revolution, 1763–1783* (1941; reprint, New York: Norton, 1965), 144; Ebenezer Baldwin in Appendix to Samuel Sherwood, *A Sermon, Containing Scriptural Instructions to Civil Rulers, and All Free-Born Subjects . . .* (New Haven: T. S. Green, 1774), 74–75.

2. Gordon S. Wood, "Rhetoric and Reality in the American Revolution," *William and Mary Quarterly* 3d ser., 23 (January 1966): 3–32. The literature on Republicanism and its origins includes Robert E. Shalhope, "Toward a Republican Synthesis: The Emergence of an Understanding of Republicanism in American Historiography," *William and Mary Quarterly* 3d ser., 29 (January 1972): 49–80; Joyce Appleby, "Republicanism in Old and New Contexts," *William and Mary Quarterly* 3d ser., 43 (January 1986): 20–34, and *Capitalism and a New Social Order: The Republican Vision of the 1790s* (New York: New York University Press, 1984); Bernard Bailyn, *The Ideological Origins of the American Revolution* (Cambridge, Mass.: Harvard University Press, 1967), and "The Central Themes of the American Revolution: An Interpretation," in *Essays on the American Revolution*, ed. Stephen G. Kurtz and James H. Hutson (Chapel Hill: University of North Carolina Press, 1973), 3–33. See also Douglass Adair, "The Tenth Federalist Revisited," *William and Mary Quarterly* 3d ser., 8 (January 1951): 48–67; J. G. A. Pocock, *The Machiavellian Moment: Florentine*

Political Thought and the Atlantic Republican Tradition (Princeton: Princeton University Press, 1975), and *Virtue, Commerce, and History* (Cambridge, Eng.: Cambridge University Press, 1985); Gordon S. Wood, *The Creation of the American Republic, 1776–1787* (Chapel Hill: University of North Carolina Press, 1969), and "*The Creation of the American Republic, 1776–1787*: A Symposium of Views and Reviews," *William and Mary Quarterly* 3d ser., 44 (July 1987): 549–640.

3. Wood, *Creation of the American Republic*, 4.

4. Albert O. Hirschman, *The Passions and the Interests: Political Arguments for Capitalism before Its Triumph* (Princeton: Princeton University Press, 1972), 9–12.

5. Ibid., 108.

6. Melvin Richter, "Montesquieu and the Politics of Language," *History of Political Thought* 10 (Spring 1989): 71.

7. Pierre Bourdieu, *Outline of a Theory of Practice* (New York: Cambridge University Press, 1977), 21.

8. Murray Edelman, *Politics as Symbolic Action: Mass Arousal and Quiescence* (Chicago: Markham, 1971), 65.

9. Rev. Abraham Williams, "An Election Sermon, Boston, 1762," in *American Political Writing during the Founding Era, 1760–1805*, ed. Charles S. Hyneman and Donald S. Lutz, 2 vols. (Indianapolis: Liberty Press, 1983), 1:9.

10. Quoted in John E. Godfrey, "Captain Mowatt," March 1877, Collection 110, Maine Historical Society, Portland.

11. Thomas Bradford Chandler, *What Think Ye of Congress Now? Or, An Enquiry How Far the Americans Are Bound to Abide by, and Execute the Decisions of, the Late Congress?* (New York: James Rivington, 1775), 47. Serle's quotation is in the entry for 8 August 1776, contained in Edward H. Tatum Jr., ed., *The American Journal of Ambrose Serle, Secretary to Lord Howe, 1776–1778* (San Marino: Huntington Library, 1940), 60. His reaction to the Declaration of Independence used the same language. "A more impudent, false and atrocious Proclamation was never fabricated by the Hands of Man," he wrote. "Hitherto, they had thrown all the Blame and Insult upon the Parliament and ministry: Now, they have the Audacity to calumniate the King and People of Great Britain. . . . Surely Providence will honor its own Truth and Justice upon this Occasion, and, as they have made an appeal to it for Success, reward them after their own Deservings" (Entry for 13 July 1776, ibid., 31).

12. Quoted in Janice Potter, *The Liberty We Seek: Loyalist Ideology in Colonial New York and Massachusetts* (Cambridge, Mass.: Harvard University Press, 1983), 137.

13. Quoted in Hirschman, *The Passions and the Interests*, 10.

14. Montesquieu, quoted in Richter, "Montesquieu and the Politics of Language," 20.

15. Aedanus Burke [Cassius], *An Address to the Freemen of the State of South-Carolina* . . . (Philadelphia: Robert Bell, 1783), 8.

16. James T. Kloppenberg, "The Virtues of Liberalism: Christianity, Republicanism, and Ethics in Early American Political Discourse," *Journal of American History* 74 (June 1987): 9–33.

17. James Britton et al., *The Development of Writing Abilities (11–18)* (London: Macmillan, 1975), 98–100.

18. *An Address of the Legislature to the Inhabitants of the Commonwealth of Massachusetts* (Boston: Benjamin Edes, 1781), 21; John McKenzie, *Letters of Freemen*, 23, 61, 64, quoted in Jack P. Greene, "'Slavery or Independence': Some Reflections on the Relationship among Liberty, Black Bondage, and Equality in Revolutionary South Carolina," in Greene, *Imperatives, Behaviors, and Identities: Essays in Early American Cultural History* (Charlottesville: University Press of Virginia, 1992), 268–89.

19. Thomas Paine, *Common Sense* in *Common Sense and The Crisis* (New York: Freethought Press, 1946), 26–27.

20. See J. G. Péristiany, ed., *Honor and Shame: The Values of Mediterranean Society* (London: Weidenfeld & Nicolson, 1965), and Michael Herzfeld, "Honour and Shame: Problems in Comparative Analyses of Moral Systems," *Man* n.s., 15 (June 1980): 339–51. On New England and secular honor, see Evarts B. Greene, "The Code of Honor in Colonial and Revolutionary Times with Special Reference to New England," in *Publications of the Colonial Society of Massachusetts* 26 (Boston: Colonial Society of Massachusetts, 1927), 367–88.

21. John Allen ["A British Bostonian"], *An Oration, Upon the Beauties of Liberty, Or the Essential Rights of the Americans. Delivered at the Second Baptist-Church in Boston. Upon the Last Annual Thanksgiving. Humbly Dedicated to the Right-Honourable the Earl of Dartmouth* (Boston: D. Kneeland and N. Davis, 1773), 27–28.

22. Thacher, quoted in Harry S. Stout, *The New England Soul: Preaching and Religious Culture in Colonial New England* (New York: Oxford University Press, 1986), 306.

23. John Hancock, *An Oration Delivered March 5, 1774, at the Request of the Inhabitants of the Town of Boston: To Commemorate the Bloody Tragedy of the Fifth of March 1770* (Boston: Edes and Gill, 1774), 18.

24. Warren, quoted in Howard Mumford Jones, *O Strange New World, American Culture: The Formative Years* (New York: Viking Press, 1964), 286.

25. Quotations from Melvin Yazawa, *From Colonies to Commonwealth: Familial Ideology and the Beginnings of the American Republic* (Baltimore: Johns Hopkins University Press, 1985), 94–95.

26. Hutchinson, quoted in Shaw, *American Patriots and the Rituals of Revolution*, 161.

27. James Otis, *The Rights of the British Colonies Asserted and Proved*, in Bernard Bailyn, ed., *Pamphlets of the American Revolution, 1750–1776*, Vol. 1, *1750–1765* (Cambridge, Mass.: Harvard University Press, 1965), 437.

28. Robert R. Palmer, *Revolution in the Democratic Age: A Political History of Europe and America, 1760–1800* (Princeton: Princeton University Press, 1959), 1:155. The rates were in 1765: Great Britain, 26s; Ireland 6s 8d; Massachusetts 1s; Connecticut 7d; Virginia 5d. Palmer does not, however, make clear what his figures mean. Do they include county, parish, and provincial taxes or merely the sums garnered for the central authority? The subject of pre-Revolutionary taxation on all levels of government has not received the historical scrutiny the topic warrants.

29. Thomas Jefferson, "Virginia Resolutions on Lord North's Conciliatory Proposal [June 10, 1775]," in *The Papers of Thomas Jefferson*, ed. Julian Parks Boyd, 22 vols. (Princeton: Princeton University Press, 1950), 1:172–73, 231. For an anthropological approach, see F. G. Bailey, *Gifts and Poison* (Oxford: Blackwell, 1971).

30. Niccolò Machiavelli, "The Prince," in *The Prince and the Discourses* (New York: Modern Library, 1940), 62; see also 57–58.

31. Bailyn, *Ideological Origins*, 162ff. See also Conrad Russell, *Parliaments and English Politics, 1621–1629* (New York: Oxford University Press, 1979), 49–53, 56–57, and 376, on subsidy issues. On Irish taxation, see *Four Letters on Interesting Subjects*, quoted in Bailyn, ed., *Pamphlets of the American Revolution*, 1:78.

32. Otis, *Rights of the British Colonies*, 452.

33. William Gordon, *The Separation of the Jewish Tribes after the Death of Solomon, Accounted for, and Applied to the Present Day, in a Sermon before the General Court, on Friday, July the 4th, 1777, Being the Anniversary of the Declaration of Independency* (Boston: J. Gill, 1777), 11.

34. Quoted in Davidson, *Propaganda and the American Revolution*, 140–41. Men of more temperate dispositions also spoke in passionate language.

35. J. G. A. Pocock, *The Ancient Constitution and the Feudal Law: A Study of English Historical Thought in the Seventeenth Century* (1957; reprint, Cambridge, Eng.: Cambridge University Press, 1987), 331–32. See also Lois G. Schwoerer, *"No Standing Armies!": The Antiarmy Ideology in Seventeenth-Century England* (Baltimore: Johns Hopkins University Press, 1974); J. G. A. Pocock, "Machiavelli, Harrington, and English Political Ideologies in the Eighteenth Century," *William and Mary Quarterly* 3d ser., 22 (October 1965): 549–83, esp. 558–64; Lewis D. Cress, *Citizens in Arms: The Army and the Militia in American Society to the War of 1812* (Chapel Hill: University of North Carolina Press, 1982), 15–33; Jerrilyn Greene Marston, *King and Congress: The Transfer of Political Legitimacy, 1774–1776* (Princeton: Princeton University Press, 1987), 134–45.

36. Caroline Robbins, *The Eighteenth-Century Commonwealthman: Studies in the Transmission and Circumstances of English Liberal Thought from the Restoration of Charles II until the War with the Thirteen Colonies* (Cambridge, Mass.: Harvard University Press, 1959), 339; Bernard Bailyn, introduction to *Pamphlets of the American Revolution, 1750–1765*, 1:41–44, esp. 42 n. 7, in which he points out that J. G. A. Pocock dates the issue only as far back as 1675, but there was a nostalgia in Commonwealthman writings for feudal times when "the 'nobility' secured 'the people against the insults of the prince and the prince against the popularity of the commons.'" See Robbins, *Eighteenth-Century Commonwealthman*, 104.

37. Quoted in Walter H. Conser Jr., "The Stamp Act Resistance," in *Resistance, Politics, and the American Struggle for Independence, 1765–1775*, ed. Walter H. Conser Jr., Ronald M. McCarthy, David J. Toscano, and Gene Sharp (Boulder: Lynne Rienner, 1986), 26.

38. See Frank W. C. Hersey, "Tar and Feathers: The Adventures of Captain John

Malcolm," *Publications of the Colonial Society of Massachusetts* 34 (April 1941): 450–51; Shaw, *American Patriots and the Rituals of Revolution,* passim; Jones, *O Strange New World,* 281–93.

39. Paul A. Gilje, *The Road to Mobocracy: Popular Disorder in New York City, 1763–1834* (Chapel Hill: University of North Carolina Press, 1987), vii, 66.

40. Conser, "Stamp Act Resistance," 42.

41. Blackstone, quoted in Marston, *King and Congress,* 18.

42. See Andrew Swatland, *The House of Lords in the Reign of Charles II* (Cambridge, Eng.: Cambridge University Press, 1996), 187–88, 193, 239.

43. Julian Pitt-Rivers, "Honor," in *International Encyclopedia of the Social Sciences,* ed. David L. Sills, 17 vols. (New York: Macmillan, 1968), 6:506.

44. Michael Kammen, "The American Revolution as a *Crise de Conscience*: The Case of New York," in *Society, Freedom, and Conscience: The American Revolution in Virginia, Massachusetts, and New York,* ed. Richard M. Jellison (New York: Norton, 1976), 125.

45. Quoted in Christopher Hill, "From Oaths to Interest," in *Society and Puritanism in Pre-Revolutionary England* (New York: Schocken, 1964), 382.

46. Kammen, "The American Revolution as a *Crise de Conscience,*" 144–89.

47. Cf. Jack P. Greene, *Interpreting Early America: Historiographical Essays* (Charlottesville: University Press of Virginia, 1996), and *Imperatives, Behaviors, and Identities: Essays in Early American Cultural History* (Charlottesville: University Press of Virginia, 1992). No reference in the index to the code of honor can be found in these and other books on colonial history that I have checked.

48. See Holly Brewer, "Entailing Aristocracy in Colonial Virginia: 'Ancient Feudal Restraints' and Revolutionary Reform," *William and Mary Quarterly* 3d ser., 54 (April 1997): 308.

49. Thomas Jefferson, *The Autobiography, 1743–1790,* in *Thomas Jefferson: Writings,* ed. Merrill D. Peterson (New York: Library of America, 1984), 38.

50. I am greatly indebted to Professor Holly Brewer of North Carolina State University and the North Carolina Seminar for Early American History, where a version of this chapter was presented, 19 March 1999, for pointing out this important aspect of the Revolution and how historians have underrated the vitality of Virginia aristocracy until Revolutionary reform. See Brewer, "Entailing Aristocracy in Colonial Virginia," 307, 341.

51. Frederic M. Litto, "Addison's *Cato* in the Colonies," *William and Mary Quarterly* 3d ser., 23 (July 1966): 431–49.

52. Louis B. Wright, *The First Gentlemen of Virginia: Intellectual Qualities of the Early Colonial Ruling Class* (San Marino: Huntington Library, 1940), esp. 283; Moses Coit Tyler, *The Literary History of the American Revolution, 1763–1783,* 2 vols. (New York: G. P. Putnam's Sons, 1897), 1:210 and 213 ff. "Give me liberty or give me death," Patrick Henry's famous exclamation, bears resemblance to Addison's lines in *Cato*: "It is not now a time to talk of aught / But chains, or conquest; liberty, or death" (Litto, "Addison's *Cato,*" 445).

53. Elliot J. Gorn, " 'Gouge, Bite, Pull Hair and Scratch': The Social Significance of Fighting in the Southern Backcountry," *American Historical Review* 90 (February 1985): 18–43. See also Carl Bridenbaugh, "Violence and Virtue in Virginia, 1766; Or, the Importance of the Trivial," in *Early Americans* (New York: Oxford University Press, 1981), 188–212. Court-martial order remanded by General George Washington: General Orders, 18 January 1778, *The Writings of George Washington from the Original Manuscript Sources, 1745–1799*, ed. John C. Fitzpatrick, 39 vols. (Washington, D.C.: U.S. Government Printing Office, 1933), 10:312; 3 August 1778, ibid., 12:272–73.

54. Bertram Wyatt-Brown, *Southern Honor: Ethics and Behavior in the Old South* (New York: Oxford University Press, 1982), 352–53.

55. Hezekiah Hayden to "Honor'd Father & Mother," 4 July 1776, quoted in Davidson, *Propaganda and the American Revolution, 1763–1783*, 341.

56. James Kirby Martin and Mark Edward Lender, *A Respectable Army: The Military Origins of the Republic, 1763–1789* (Arlington Heights, Ill.: Harlan Davidson, 1982), 103.

57. Robert Howe to Henry Laurens, 9 June 1777, quoted in Richard Walsh, ed., *The Writings of Christopher Gadsden, 1764–1805* (Columbia: University of South Carolina Press, 1966), xxiv.

58. Nathanael Greene to Joseph Reed, 9 March 1778, *The Papers of Nathanael Greene*, Vol. 2, *1 January 1777–16 October 1778*, ed. Richard K. Showman (Chapel Hill: University of North Carolina Press, 1980), 307; see also Greene to Alexander McDougall, 28 March 1778, ibid., 326.

59. Quoted in Charles Royster, *A Revolutionary People at War: The Continental Army and American Character, 1775–1783* (Chapel Hill: University of North Carolina Press, 1979), 199.

60. Robert M. Calhoon, review in *William and Mary Quarterly* 3rd ser., 56 (January 1999): 218–19; Charles Royster, " 'The Nature of Treason': Revolutionary Virtue and American Reactions to Benedict Arnold," *William and Mary Quarterly* 3rd ser., 36 (April 1979): 163–93, esp. 188–89.

61. Martin and Lender, *A Respectable Army*, 104–6.

62. I am indebted to Robert Calhoon for bringing Benedict Arnold to my attention by means of his review of James Kirby Martin's biography in the *William and Mary Quarterly* 3rd ser., 56 (January 1999): 218–20. The quotations from the biography and from Royster's article on Arnold are contained in Calhoon's review.

63. Royster, *Revolutionary People*, 58–96, quotation, 88.

64. John Trumbull to John Hancock, 22 February 1777, and John Trumbull to James Lovell, 30 March 1777, *The Autobiography of Colonel John Trumbull: Patriot-Artist, 1756–1843*, ed. Theodore Sizer (New Haven: Yale University Press, 1953), 39, 46. See also Royster, *Revolutionary People*, 85–91, 200, and Charles P. Whittemore, *A General of the Revolution: John Sullivan of New Hampshire* (New York: Columbia University Press, 1961), 24–25, 227–29, and James Thomas Flexner, *The Young Hamilton: A Biography* (Boston: Little, Brown, 1978), 262–63.

65. Nathanael Greene to George Washington, 21 May 1776, *The Papers of General Nathanael Greene*, Vol. 1, *December 1766–December 1776*, ed. Richard K. Showman (Chapel Hill: University of North Carolina Press, 1976), 216–17.

66. H. Trevor Colbourn, ed., *Fame and the Founding Fathers: Essays by Douglass Adair* (New York: Norton, 1974), 3–26.

67. Christopher Grasso, *A Speaking Aristocracy: Transforming Public Discourse in Eighteenth Century Connecticut* (Chapel Hill: University of North Carolina Press, 1999), 417–18.

68. George Washington to Alexander Hamilton, 28 August 1788, *The Words of Washington*, ed. James Parton (Boston: Joseph Knight, 1871), 133.

69. George Washington, "To the People of the United States," 19 September 1796, *The Washington Papers: Basic Selections from the Public and Private Writings of George Washington*, ed. Saul K. Padover (New York: Grosset & Dunlap, 1955), 309–10.

70. Shirley Robin Letwin, *The Gentleman in Anthony Trollope: Individuality and Moral Conduct* (Cambridge, Mass.: Harvard University Press, 1982), 7–9.

71. Quoted ibid., 3–13.

72. Quoted by Trevor Colbourn, headnote, before Douglass Adair, "Fame and the Founding Fathers," in *Fame and the Founding Fathers: Essays by Douglass Adair*, ed. H. Trevor Colbourn (New York: Norton, 1974), 3.

73. Israel Evans, *An Oration Delivered at Hackinsack, on the Tenth of September, 1780. At the Interment of the Honorable Brigadier Enoch Poor, General of the New-Hampshire Brigade* (Newburyport, Mass.: J. Mycall, 1781), 8 (emphasis added) (available in RW No. 14). Parenthetically, the distinction he drew between honor as moral principle guiding the conscience and honor as reputation for civic excellence touched upon an inherent ambiguity in the ethic, one long recognized since the time of Aristotle.

74. Samuel Sherwood, *A Sermon, Containing Scriptural Instructions to Civil Rulers, and All Free-Born Subjects . . . Also an Appendix . . . by the Rev. Ebenezer Baldwin* (New Haven: T. and S. Green, 1774), vi.

75. See Plutarch, *The Life of Timoleon*, noted in Douglass Adair, "Fame and the Founding Fathers," 13 n. 9. See also Niccolò Machiavelli, *The Discourses*, in *The Prince and the Discourses*, 141–45.

76. Adair, "Fame and the Founding Fathers," 7.

77. Joseph Addison, as quoted in Forrest McDonald, *Novus Ordo Secolorum: The Intellectual Origins of the Constitution* (Lawrence: University Press of Kansas, 1985), 198.

78. Although McDonald does not see this formulation as part of a larger concern over gentility and honor as such, I have paraphrased his words here and owe much to his insights. See McDonald, *Novus Ordo Secolorum*, 198–99. See also Robert M. Weir, " 'The Harmony We Were Famous For': An Interpretation of Pre-Revolutionary South Carolina Politics," *William and Mary Quarterly* 3d ser., 26 (October 1969): 473–501, esp. 496.

79. McDonald, *Novus Ordo Secolorum*, 192. A graceful horseman, always in com-

mand of his mount, and a favorite among women, Washington also fulfilled the parlor graces and the athletic requirements of the country gentleman. See Paul Leicester Ford, *Washington and the Theatre* (New York: Dunlap Society, 1899), 50; Forrest McDonald, *The Presidency of George Washington* (Lawrence: University Press of Kansas, 1974), 26.

80. Adams, quoted in McDonald, *Novus Ordo Secolorum*, 191 n. 10. "Inspired with public virtue, touched with the wrongs and indignant at the insults offered his country, the high-spirited Cassius exhibits an heroic example: — 'Resolved as we are,' (replied the hero to his friend) 'resolved as we are, let us march against the enemy, for tho' we should not conquer, we have nothing to fear' " (Josiah Quincy Jr., *Observations on the Act of Parliament Commonly Called the Boston Port-Bill; With Thoughts on Civil Society and Standing Armies* [Philadelphia: Printed for John Sparhawk, 1774], 60). Such sentiments were common: they show how the classical past served very immediate circumstances.

81. William Smith, *An Oration in Memory of General Montgomery, and of the Officers and Soldiers Who Fell With Him* . . . (Newport, R.I.: Reprinted by Solomon Southwick, 1776), 4 [RW 36].

82. Douglass Adair, " 'Experience Must Be Our Only Guide,' History, Democratic Theory, and the United States Constitution," in *Fame and the Founding Fathers*, ed. Colbourn, 107–23.

83. Wood, *Creation of the American Republic*, 48–53, devotes attention to "the appeal of antiquity" but does not seem to recognize its connection with the ethics of gentility and honor.

84. Howard Miller, *The Revolutionary College: American Presbyterian Higher Education, 1707–1837* (New York: New York University Press, 1976), 180. See also Susan Ford Wiltshire, ed., *The Usefulness of Classical Learning in the Eighteenth Century: Papers Presented at the 107th Annual Meeting of the American Philological Association* (New York: American Philological Association, 1977).

85. Phyllis Vine, "The Social Function of Eighteenth-Century Higher Education," *History of Education Quarterly* 16, no. 4 (1976): 409–24.

86. James Emerson, *A Thanksgiving Sermon* . . . (Boston: Edes and Gill, 1766), 7.

87. Quoted in David Hackett Fischer, *Albion's Seed: Four British Folkways in America* (New York: Oxford University Press, 1989), 410.

88. Quincy, *Observations on the Act of Parliament*, 69–70.

89. Caroline Robbins, "Algernon Sidney's *Discourses Concerning Government*: Textbook of Revolution," *William and Mary Quarterly* 3d ser., 4 (July 1947): 267–96, and *The Eighteenth-Century Commonwealthman*.

90. F. Nwabueze Okoye, "Chattel Slavery as the Nightmare of the American Revolutionaries," *William and Mary Quarterly* 3d ser., 37 (January 1980): 5. This scholar has accused Bernard Bailyn and other leading historians of Revolutionary America with a gross and "fallacious" misrepresentation of the question when they note that the existence of chattel bondage had no major part in the struggle for American

independence. But he himself has misunderstood the problem as explained in the text.

91. Thomas Gordon, letter of 21 April 1722, from *Cato's Letters*, quoted in John Philip Reid, *The Concept of Liberty in the Age of the American Revolution* (Chicago: University of Chicago Press, 1988), 38.

92. Duncan J. McLeod did not put the matter in these terms, but his statement that "John Dickinson could think of no 'idea of slavery more *complete*, more *miserable*, more *disgraceful*, than that of a people, *where justice is administered, government exercised*, and a *standing army maintained* AT THE EXPENCE OF THE PEOPLE and yet WITHOUT THE LEAST Dependence UPON THEM,' " makes sense only when the rubrics of honor are considered as the foundation of the protest. See Duncan J. McLeod, *Slavery, Race, and the American Revolution* (New York: Cambridge University Press, 1974), 16; cf. Okoye, "Chattel Slavery as the Nightmare," 8.

93. Jonathan Mayhew, quoted in Reid, *Concept of Liberty*, 45.

94. John Adams, "Thoughts on Government, 1776," in *American Political Writing during the Founding Era, 1760–1805*, ed. Charles S. Hyneman and Donald S. Lutz, 2 vols. (Indianapolis: Liberty Press, 1983), 1:402–3.

95. Sarah A. Dorsey, *Recollections of Henry Watkins Allen* (New Orleans: M. Doolady, 1866), 10. Dorsey's three principles are a quotation from Jean Paul F. Richter.

96. Timothy Ford [Americanus], *The Constitutionalist: Or, An Inquiry How Far It Is Expedient and Proper to Alter the Constitution of South Carolina* (Charleston: Markland, M'Kiver, 1794), 39–40, quoted in Greene, " 'Slavery or Independence,' " 205.

97. Wyatt-Brown, *Southern Honor*, 104; Edward McCrady, "Slavery in the Province of South Carolina, 1670–1770," in *Annual Report, American Historical Association for the Year 1895* (Washington, D.C.: U.S. Government Printing Office, 1896), 659.

98. Christopher Gadsden to Henry Laurens, 5 June 1774, *The Writings of Christopher Gadsden, 1746–1805*, ed. Richard Walsh (Columbia: University of South Carolina Press, 1966), 95. See also Kenneth S. Greenberg, "Revolutionary Ideology and the Proslavery Argument: The Abolition of Slavery in Antebellum South Carolina," *Journal of Southern History* 42 (August 1976): 365–84; and Donald L. Robinson, *Slavery in the Structure of American Politics, 1765–1820* (New York: Norton 1971), 60–61, 463 n. 23; Paul K. Conkin, *Self-Evident Truths* (Bloomington: Indiana University Press, 1974), 109–10.

99. George Washington to Bryan Fairfax, 24 August 1774, *Writings of George Washington*, ed. Sparks, 3:242.

100. Thomas Paine, *Letter Addressed to the Abbe Raynal on the Affairs of North-America. In which The Mistakes of the Abbe's Account of the Revolution of America Are Corrected and Cleared Up* (Philadelphia: Melchior Steiner, 1782), 13 (available in RW 1). Needless to say, the British pamphleteers also worried that national honor would be stained if the Americans were successful. See *Considerations on the Measures Carrying on with Respect to the British Colonies in North America* (London: R. Baldwin, 1774), 48–49, 84–85, 157–58.

101. *Observations on the American Revolution Published According to a Resolution of Congress by Their Committee for the Consideration of Those Who Are Desirous of Comparing the Conduct of the Opposed Parties and the Several Consequences Which Have Flowed from It* (Philadelphia: Styner and Cist, 1779), 34 (available in RW 6).

102. *An Address of the Legislature to the Inhabitants of the Commonwealth of Massachusetts* (Boston: Benjamin Edes, 1781), 21.

103. Joanne B. Freeman, "The Election of 1800: A Study in the Logic of Political Change," *Yale Law Journal* 108 (June 1999): 1959–94, quotations, 1983–85.

CHAPTER THREE

1. John G. Péristiany and Julian Pitt-Rivers, eds., *Honor and Grace in Anthropology* (New York: Cambridge University Press, 1992), 2.

2. Quoted in Charles Fenwick Jones, *Honor in German Literature* (1959; reprint, New York: AMS Press, 1966), 40.

3. See Joanne B. Freeman, "Dueling as Politics: Reinterpreting the Hamilton-Burr Duel," *William and Mary Quarterly* 3d ser., 53 (April 1996): 289–318.

4. Jackson, however, should not be accused of any violation of honor when he took an oath of allegiance to the king of Spain early in his commercial career. He only followed the example of other Americans trading or living in Spanish Mississippi because failure to do so would have meant expulsion or arrest. Oath-taking under a Catholic monarchy meant nothing to such as he. The same reaction was prevalent in the post–Civil War era when some former Rebels did struggle with their consciences over taking the oath of loyalty to the Union, but most found the obligation a matter of coercion not to mention convenience; oaths under such circumstances scarcely signified. Robert V. Remini explores the matter thoroughly in "Andrew Jackson Takes an Oath of Allegiance to Spain," *Tennessee Historical Quarterly* 54 (Spring 1995): 2–15.

5. Pedro Calderón de la Barca, *The Painter of Dishonour*, trans. and ed. David Johnston and Laurence Boswell (Bath, Eng.: Absolute Classics, 1995), 106; see also B. W. Ife, "More Than a Show of Respect: Locating the Seat of Honour in Spanish Golden Age Drama," *Times Literary Supplement*, 11 August 1995, 16–17.

6. See David Chaney, "The Spectacle of Honour: The Changing Dramatization of Status," *Theory, Culture, and Society* 12 (1995): 147–67.

7. Ronald P. Formisano, *The Transformation of Political Culture: Massachusetts Politics, 1790s–1840s* (New York: Oxford University Press, 1983), 18.

8. Andrew Jackson and John William Ward, quoted in Gregory H. Nobles, *American Frontiers: Cultural Encounters and Continental Conquest* (New York: Hill and Wang, 1996), 120, and also 124–25; Robert Remini, *The Battle of New Orleans* (New York: Hill and Wang, 1999).

9. Louis Filler, *The Crusade against Slavery, 1830–1860* (New York: Harper, 1960), 98; Leonard L. Richards, *"Gentlemen of Property and Standing": Anti-Abolition Mobs*

in Jacksonian America (New York: Oxford University Press, 1970), 50–51; Bertram Wyatt-Brown, "The Abolitionists' Postal Campaign of 1835," *Journal of Negro History* 50 (October 1965): 227–38.

10. See Mervyn James, *Society, Politics and Culture: Studies in Early Modern England* (Cambridge, Eng.: Cambridge University Press, 1986), 339–40.

11. On Southern horse racing, see Timothy H. Breen, *Puritans and Adventurers: Change and Persistence in Early America* (New York: Oxford University Press, 1980), 148–63. The classic essay on the utility of gaming is Clifford Geertz, "Deep Play: Notes on the Balinese Cockfight," in *The Interpretation of Cultures: Selected Essays* (New York: Basic Books, 1973), 412–56, and the classic study is Johann Huizinga, *Homo Ludens: A Study of the Play-Element in Culture* (Boston: Beacon Press, 1955). On the origins of the dispute and a good narrative of the sequence leading toward the duel, see Harold D. Moser and Sharon MacPherson, eds., *The Papers of Andrew Jackson*, Vol. 2, *1804–1813* (Knoxville: University of Tennessee Press, 1984), 77–78.

12. See Memorandum of Agreement with John Verell for the Purchase of Truxton, *Papers of Andrew Jackson*, 2:57–58.

13. John Hutchings to editor, *Impartial Review*, 10 February 1806, *Correspondence of Andrew Jackson*, ed. John Spencer Bassett, 7 vols. (Washington, D.C.: Carnegie Institution, 1926), 1:127–28; Charles S. Carson to Jackson, 10 February 1806, ibid., ·135; Announcement of Race between Truxton and Ploughboy, 1 March 1806, *Papers of Andrew Jackson*, 2:90 (a second race after Ploughboy's recovery).

14. Jackson to Thomas Swann, 7 January 1806, *Correspondence of Andrew Jackson*, 1:124.

15. John Coffee, statement, 5 February 1806, ibid., 130; Thomas Swann to Jackson, 3 January 1806, *Papers of Andrew Jackson*, 2:78, and 12 January 1806, ibid., 82.

16. Coffee, statement, 5 February 1806, *Correspondence of Andrew Jackson*, 1:130. Among other failings that discredited "this valiant squire," Swann, Jackson sarcastically noted, had once in a duel fired before the word was given and claimed the violation an accident. Nathaniel McNairy proposed that a "court of honor" should decide whether his friend Swann was a gentleman, but Coffee, as Jackson's spokesman, observed, "I thought that gentleman's honor and feelings was too delicate, to arbitrate, that under the existing circumstances" the general had made sufficient answer (ibid., 131). On Jackson's opinion of Swann, see statement, *Impartial Review*, 1 March 1806, ibid., 137.

17. Ibid., 1:131–32.

18. See John Brahan to John Overton, 8 March 1806, *Papers of Andrew Jackson*, 2:90–91.

19. Robert V. Remini, *Andrew Jackson and the Course of American Empire, 1767–1821* (New York: Harper & Row, 1977), 138–39; James Kelly, *That Damn'd Thing Called Honour: Duelling in Ireland, 1570–1860* (Cork, Ireland: Cork University Press, 1995).

20. James Parton, quoted in Paul F. Boller Jr., *Presidential Anecdotes* (New York: Oxford University Press, 1996), 68; Jackson to Thomas Swann, 7 January 1806, *Correspondence of Andrew Jackson*, 1:124.

21. Charles Dickinson card, *Impartial Review*, 24 May 1806, *Correspondence of Andrew Jackson*, 1:142–43.

22. Jackson to Dickinson, 23 May 1806, *Correspondence of Andrew Jackson*, 1:143–44.

23. For information on the duel and the prior exchanges, see ibid., 122–49; Remini, *Andrew Jackson and the Course of American Empire*, 142; James Parton, *Life of Andrew Jackson*, 3 vols. (New York: Mason Brothers, 1861), 1:297–300.

24. The matter of Jackson's right to fire again is in some dispute. Parton does not record a conference of seconds, but see *Correspondence of Andrew Jackson*, 1:145 n. 2. Bassett reported that, according to tradition, the seconds conferred before Jackson could take aim again, and that, according to the rules of the code, seems a most likely event. Surely the seconds would have done so.

25. Parton, *Jackson*, 1:300. Jackson told Parton, that since "Dickinson considered himself the best shot in the world, and was certain of killing him at the first fire, *he did not want him to have the gratification even of knowing that he had touched him*" (1:301).

26. Ibid., 304–5.

27. Jackson, quoted ibid., 297.

28. Ibid., 303–4; Jackson to Thomas Gassaway Watkins, 15 June 1806, *Papers of Andrew Jackson*, 2:102–3, Jackson to Thomas Eastin, ca. June 1806, ibid., 106–7; Jackson to Randall McGavock, 23 August 1806, ibid., 107–8 and 109 n. 1.

29. Parton, *Jackson*, 1:305; Remini, *Andrew Jackson and the Course of American Empire*, 143; Freeman, "Dueling as Politics," 289–318.

30. Quoted in Boller, *Presidential Anecdotes*, 67.

31. On patron-client relations, see Eric R. Wolf, "Kinship, Friendship, and Patron-Client Relations in Complex Societies," in *The Anthropology of Complex Societies*, ed. Michael Banton (New York: Praeger, 1966), 1–22; Sharon Kettering, "The Historical Development of Political Clientelism," *Journal of Interdisciplinary History* 18 (Winter 1988): 419–47; Saul N. Eisenstadt and Louis Roniger, "Patron-Client Relations as a Model of Structuring Social Exchanges," *Comparative Studies in Society and History* 22 (January 1980): 42–77; Carl H. Landé, "The Dyad Basis of Clientelism," in *Friends, Followers and Factions: A Reader in Political Clientelism*, ed. Steffen W. Schmidt et al. (Berkeley: University of California Press, 1977); Kenneth Brown, "Changing Forms of Patronage in a Moroccan City," in *Patrons and Clients in Mediterranean Societies*, ed. Ernest Gellner and John Waterbury (London: Duckworth, 1977), 309–27; René Lemarchand and Keith Legg, "Political Clientelism and Development: A Preliminary Analysis," *Comparative Politics* 4 (January 1972): 68–90; René Lemarchand, "Political Clientelism and Ethnicity in Tropical Africa: Competing Solidarities in Nation-Building," *American Political Science Review* 66 (March 1972): 68–90; Luigi Graziano, "Patron-Client Relationships in Southern Italy," *European Journal of Political Research* 1 (April 1973): 3–34, and "A Conceptual Framework for the Study of Clientelistic Behavior," *European Journal of Political Research* 4 (June 1976): 149–74; Sharon Kettering, *Patrons, Brokers, and Clients in Seventeenth Century France* (New York: Oxford University Press, 1986).

32. Julian A. Pitt-Rivers, *The People of the Sierra* (New York: Criterion, 1954), 140.

33. J. Russell Major, the early modern French scholar, is quoted in Kristen Brooke Neuschel, *Word of Honor: Interpreting Noble Culture in Sixteenth-Century France* (Ithaca, N.Y.: Cornell University Press, 1989), 7.

34. Jackson to George W. Campbell, 28 April 1804, *Correspondence of Andrew Jackson*, 1:90–91.

35. Jackson to Major Samuel Swartwout, 4 March 1824, in "Some Letters of Andrew Jackson," ed. Henry F. DePuy, *Proceedings of the American Antiquarian Society Proceedings* 31 (April 1921): 76.

36. Wolf, "Kinship, Friendship, and Patron-Client Relations," 11–13.

37. Jackson, quoted in Charles Sellers, *The Market Revolution: Jacksonian America, 1815–1846* (New York: Oxford University Press, 1991), 302.

38. Freeman, "Dueling as Politics," 306.

39. See Steven Hughes, "Men of Steel: Dueling, Honor, and Politics in Liberal Italy," in *Men and Violence: Gender, Honor, and Rituals in Modern Europe and America*, ed. Pieter Spierenburg (Columbus: Ohio State University Press, 1998), 64–81.

40. Entry for 9 December 1846, *Secret and Sacred: The Diaries of James Henry Hammond, a Southern Slaveholder*, ed. Carol Bleser (New York: Oxford University Press, 1988), 174; Andrew Jackson to Thomas Hart Benton, 4 August 1813, *Papers of Andrew Jackson*, 2:418; Julian Pitt-Rivers, "The Stranger, the Guest, and the Hostile Host: Introduction to the Study of the Laws of Hospitality," in *Contributions to Mediterranean Sociology: Mediterranean Rural Communities and Social Change*, ed. John G. Péristiany (Paris: Mouton, 1967), 13–30.

41. Sharon Kettering, "Forum: Patronage, Language, and Political Culture: Patronage in Early Modern France," *French Historical Studies* 17 (Fall 1992): 839–62, offers a very thorough examination of the complications of courtesies and ideals on one side and actual power realities on the other that were conveyed through action and language in patron-client relations.

42. See, for instance, J. William Harris, *Plain Folk and Gentry in a Slave Society: White Liberty and Black Slavery in Augusta's Hinterlands* (Middletown, Conn.: Wesleyan University Press, 1985), 97–100, and Ralph Mann, "Mountains, Land, and Kin Networks: Burkes Garden, Virginia, in the 1840s and 1850s," *Journal of Southern History* 58 (August 1992): 411–34.

43. J. Mills Thornton III, *Politics and Power in a Slave Society: Alabama, 1800–1860* (Baton Rouge: Louisiana State University Press, 1978), 20.

44. Robert Remini, *Andrew Jackson and the Course of American Democracy, 1833–1845* (New York: Harper & Row, 1984), 118, 123; Robert V. Remini, *The Election of Andrew Jackson* (Philadelphia: J. B. Lippincott, 1963), 156–57; William B. Lewis to John Coffee, 27 July 1828, John Coffee Papers, TSA. The figures on the 1828 election are presented in the brilliant but regrettably unpublished essay of Leonard L. Richards, "The Question of Slaveholder Domination," 26.

45. Antony E. Simpson, "Dandelions on the Field of Honor: Dueling, the Middle

Classes and the Law in Nineteenth-Century England," *Criminal Justice History* 9 (1988): 107.

46. Charles M. Wiltse, *John C. Calhoun*, Vol. 1, *Nationalist, 1782–1828* (Indianapolis: Bobbs-Merrill, 1944), 49–50, 213, 252, 254–55. "Never have my feelings undergone so great a change [to happiness] in so short a time," Calhoun exulted upon learning of his protégé's survival (255). See also Michael O'Brien, *A Character of Hugh Legare* (Knoxville: University of Tennessee Press, 1985), 41–42; William W. Freehling, *Prelude to Civil War: The Nullification Controversy in South Carolina, 1816–1836* (New York: Harper & Row, 1965), 145–46.

47. Jackson to Waightsill Avery, 12 August 1788, *The Papers of Andrew Jackson*, Vol. 1, *1770–1803*, ed. Sam B. Smith and Harriet Chappell Owsley (Knoxville: University of Tennessee Press, 1980), 12; Remini, *Andrew Jackson and the Course of American Empire*, 28–39.

48. One-half of the duelists in Upper Canada in the early nineteenth century were lawyers by one estimation: Cecilia Morgan, " 'In Search of the Phantom Misnamed Honour': Duelling in Upper Canada," *Canadian Historical Review* 76 (December 1995): 545 n. 53. I have been unable to locate the origin for this stated estimate of lawyer participation in duels, but Jack Kenny Williams, *Vogues in Villainy: Crime and Retribution in Ante-Bellum South Carolina* (Columbia: University of South Carolina Press, 1959), 98–99 offers supporting conclusions.

49. Jack Kenny Williams, *Dueling in the Old South* (University Station: Texas A & M Press, 1980), 27; Bertram Wyatt-Brown, *Southern Honor: Ethics and Behavior in the Old South* (New York: Oxford University Press, 1982), 355.

50. Ronald P. Formisano, "Deferential-Participant Politics: The Early Republic's Political Culture, 1789–1840," *American Political Science Review* 68 (June 1974): 473–87, was the first major challenge to the older historiographical assumptions of early party solidity, professionalism, and organizational discipline. With reference to land speculation and politics, Jackson himself had difficulties, but they were not as incriminating as the manipulations of William Blount, the early Tennessee leader who sponsored Jackson's rise in politics. See Buckner F. Melton Jr., *The First Impeachment: The Constitution's Framers and the Case of Senator William Blount* (Macon, Ga.: Mercer University Press, 1998), and *Proceedings on the Impeachment of William Blount, a Senator of the United States from the State of Tennessee, for High Crimes and Misdemeanors* (Philadelphia: Joseph Gales, 1799); William H. Masterson, *William Blount* (Baton Rouge: Louisiana State University Press, 1954), 300–301; Remini, *Andrew Jackson and the Course of American Empire*, 86–90, 103–6. Jackson's troubles with land deals are covered ibid., 87–90.

51. Jackson quoted in John Hope Franklin, *The Militant South, 1800–1861* (Boston: Beacon Press, 1956), 61.

52. Agreements with John Overton, 12 May 1794, *Papers of Andrew Jackson*, 1:46–47; also other business transactions, 54–60; John H. Eaton to John Overton, 7 January 1826, *Dear Judge: Selected Letters of John Overton of Traveller's Rest*, ed. Fletch Coke (Nashville: Traveller's Rest Historic Museum House, 1989), 70–72. On supporters

and leaders outside the slave states who dueled on behalf of each other, see Freeman, "Dueling as Politics," 307.

53. Jackson himself, having been a client at the service of Senator William Blount, would have dueled on Blount's behalf just as Coffee had on Jackson's account.

54. Remini, *Andrew Jackson and the Course of American Empire*, 8.

55. For an example of typical toasts of the day, see *Papers of Andrew Jackson*, 2:63–64.

56. Robert Baldick, *The Duel: A History of Dueling* (London: Chapman and Hall, 1965), 33. Dueling is avoidable, he notes, except for the "lie direct." Reference supplied by Kenneth S. Greenberg, *Honor and Slavery* (Princeton: Princeton University Press, 1996), 149 n. 20.

57. Remini, *Election of Andrew Jackson*, 26–27. The late Edward Pessen wrongly claims that Jackson and his party misrepresented what had happened. They had it right, and everyone understood the matter quite well. Even Clay recognized that he had erred, as Pessen admits. See Edward Pessen, *Jacksonian America: Society, Personality, and Politics* (Urbana: University of Illinois Press, 1985), 163.

58. Wolf, "Kinship, Friendship, and Patron-Client Relations," 12–13, differentiates between emotional and instrumental friendships, but both can end in quick ruptures.

59. The best brief examination of the Eaton controversy is Richard B. Latner, "The Eaton Affair Revisited," *Tennessee Historical Quarterly* 36 (Fall 1977): 330–51, esp. 340–41; also, Jackson to Coffee, 22 March 1829, *Correspondence of Andrew Jackson*, 4:15. See also John F. Marszalek, *The Petticoat Affair* (New York: Free Press, 1997). A severe criticism of Jackson's handling of the affair can be found in Edward Pessen, *Jacksonian America: Society, Personality, and Politics*, rev. ed. (Urbana: University of Illinois Press, 1985), 288–91.

60. Robert V. Remini, *Andrew Jackson and the Course of American Freedom, 1822–1832* (New York: Harper & Row, 1981), 292.

61. See Jackson to Calhoun, 30 May 1830, *Correspondence of Andrew Jackson*, 4:141.

62. Jackson and Calhoun, quoted in Irving H. Bartlett, *John C. Calhoun: A Biography* (New York: Norton, 1993), 175.

63. See Rule 14, "The Irish Code of Honor," appended to John Lyde Wilson, *The Code of Honor; or, Rules for the Government of Principals and Seconds in Duelling* (Charleston, S.C.: T. J. Eccles, 1838), 15.

64. Remini, *Andrew Jackson and the Course of American Freedom*, 293–314.

65. Remini, *Andrew Jackson and the Course of American Empire*, 15.

66. John Henry Eaton, *The Life of Andrew Jackson, Major-General in the Service of the United States: Comprising a History of the War in the South, from the Commencement of the Creek Campaign to the Termination of Hostilities before New Orleans* (Philadelphia: Samuel F. Bradford, 1824), 13.

67. Remini, *Andrew Jackson and the Course of American Empire*, 25; Frances Tomlinson Gardner, "The Gentleman from Tennessee," *Surgery, Gynecology, and Obstetrics* 88 (March 1949): 404.

68. James C. Curtis, *Andrew Jackson and the Search for Vindication* (Boston: Little, Brown, 1976), 12; John Trotwood Moore, quoted in "Andrew Jackson's Duel in a New Light: Lately Found Documents Reveal Details of Dramatic Episode in the President's Life," *New York Times*, 15 March 1925, clipping, Andrew Jackson MSS, TSA.

69. E. James Anthony, "Psychoanalysis and Environment," in *The Course of Life*, Vol. 6, *Late Adulthood*, ed. George H. Pollock and Stanley I. Greenspan (Madison, Conn.: International Universities Press, 1993), 261–310 (quotation, 304). I owe this citation to Anne Wyatt-Brown, who called my attention to its relevance.

70. Remini, *Andrew Jackson and the Course of American Empire*, 10–12.

71. Gardner, "Gentleman from Tennessee," 404.

72. Curtis, *Andrew Jackson and the Search for Vindication*, 11–12. I am much indebted to Curtis's sensitive biography.

73. An example of Jackson's conformity to the rules of honor was evident in his handling of the duel between two very young men, Thomas J. Overton, a friend, and John Dickinson, in 1805. Jackson insisted that his principal had the right to choose the distance—seven feet from the point of back-to-back positions—but Dickinson refused to fight at less than twenty-four feet. Jackson argued, "If [Dickinson] did not come forward on these terms [of fourteen feet] he would be exposed to the world and that Mr. T[homas] O[verton] would Kain him for the expression used in the note aforesaid." Such were the rules, even governing boys. The duel took place; Dickinson, in a second volley of firing, shot his adversary from a distance of six inches, Overton having missed a second time. Overton survived the wound. See Jackson, deposition on the duel, July 1805, *Correspondence of Andrew Jackson*, 1:117–19.

74. Jackson to Rachel Jackson, 9 May 1796, *Papers of Andrew Jackson*, 1:91.

75. Marriage License, 18 January 1794, ibid., 44.

76. Appointment as Mero District Attorney for the Southwest Territory, 15 February 1791, ibid., 26; Commission as Judge Advocate, 10 September 1792, ibid., 37–38; William Blount to James Robertson, 2 January 1792, in "The Correspondence of Gen. James Robertson," *American Historical Magazine* 1 (July 1896): 280; Masterson, *William Blount*, 292; Gen. Marcus J. Wright, *Some Account of the Life and Services of William Blount* (Washington, D.C.: E. J. Gray, [ca. 1884]), 9.

77. Curtis, *Jackson*, 40. Sevier and Jackson skirted a duel earlier in 1797. John Sevier to Andrew Jackson, 8 May 1797, *Correspondence of Andrew Jackson*, 1:31. Like other men of honor, Sevier readily declared, "My reputation Mr. Jackson is to me my only treasure" (32). But after word play by further correspondence, Sevier offered the olive branch using the language appropriate to the occasion: "A man of merit will always find me his friend, and I am a foe only to such who in private and public life continue to act dishonorable and disgraceful. The objects of us both seem to be an honorable reconciliation. When men act cooly and dispassionately this may be easily effected; and if language of sincerity be used, that reconciliation may be durable" (Sevier to Jackson, 11 May 1797, ibid., 36). But on the 1803 episode, see Jackson to Sevier, 2, 3, 9 October 1803, ibid., 71–76. See also Sevier to Jackson,

10 October 1803, *Papers of Andrew Jackson*, 1:380–81; Jackson to Sevier, 11 October 1803, ibid., 384–85.

78. Curtis, *Jackson*, 40.

79. Remini, *Andrew Jackson and the Course of American Freedom*, 2–3; Remini, *Andrew Jackson and the Course of American Empire*, 224–25, 364–65.

80. On his duel with Benton, see Jackson to Benton, 4 August 1813, *Papers of Andrew Jackson*, 2:418–22.

81. Remini, *Andrew Jackson and the Course of American Freedom*, 2–3; "Gentleman from Tennessee," 404–11.

82. Remini, *Andrew Jackson and the Course of American Empire*, 378–79.

83. Marquis James, *Andrew Jackson, the Border Captain* (Indianapolis: Bobbs-Merrill, 1933), 139; Jackson to Rachel Jackson, 29 December 1813, as quoted in Remini, *Andrew Jackson and the Course of American Empire*, 194.

84. Marszalek, *Petticoat Affair*, 16.

85. Remini, *Andrew Jackson and the Course of American Democracy*, 152–55.

86. Andrew Jackson to William Rabun, 7 May 1818, *The Papers of Andrew Jackson*, Vol. 4, *1816–1820*, ed. Harold D. Moser, David R. Hoth, and George H. Hoemann (Knoxville: University of Tennessee Press, 1994), 202.

87. This account is gratefully taken from Greenberg, *Honor and Slavery*, 20–22.

88. Robert V. Remini, *The Battle of New Orleans: Andrew Jackson and America's First Military Victory* (New York: Viking, 1999), 41.

89. Peter Gay, *The Cultivation of Hatred, the Bourgeois Experience, Victoria to Freud*, Vol. 3 (New York: Norton, 1993), 113.

90. Bertram Wyatt-Brown, *Yankee Saints and Southern Sinners* (Baton Rouge: Louisiana State University Press, 1985), 187.

91. Quoted in Remini, *The Battle of New Orleans*, 42.

CHAPTER FOUR

1. Christine Heyrman, *Southern Cross: The Beginnings of the Bible Belt* (New York: Knopf, 1997), and Ted Ownby, *Subduing Satan: Religion, Recreation, and Manhood in the Rural South, 1865–1890* (Chapel Hill: University of North Carolina Press, 1990). See also Jon Butler, "Magic, Astrology, and the Early American Religious Heritage, 1600–1760," *American Historical Review* 84 (April 1979): 318. The major reexamination of Southern religious development, which is still under way, is traceable to Samuel S. Hill Jr., *The South and the North in American Religion* (Athens: University of Georgia Press, 1980); Hill, *Religion and the South* (Nashville: Abingdon Press, 1972); Donald G. Mathews, *Slavery and Methodism: A Chapter in American Morality, 1780–1845* (Princeton: Princeton University Press, 1965); and Mathews, *Religion in the Old South* (Chicago: University of Chicago Press, 1977).

2. The Rt. Rev. Stephen Elliott, "Ezra's Dilemma, August 21, 1863," in *"God Ordained This War": Sermons on the Sectional Crisis, 1830–1865*, ed. David B. Chesebrough (Columbia: University of South Carolina Press, 1991), 246–47.

3. Louis Isaac Rabinowitz, "Honor," in *Encyclopaedia Judaica*, 16 vols. (Jerusalem: Keeter, 1972), 8:966.

4. Evertt W. Huffard, "Biblical Word Study KABOD: 'Honor,'" *Exegete* 3 (1983): 1–5, esp. 3; Johannes Pedersen, *Israel: Its Life and Culture*, 4 vols. (London: Oxford University Press, 1926–40); Rabinowitz, "Honor," 966 (quotation).

5. See Bruce J. Malina, *The New Testament World: Insights from Cultural Anthropology* (Louisville, Ky.: Westminster/John Knox Press, 1993), 67–71, 86–88.

6. See Frank Henderson Stewart, *Honor* (Chicago: University of Chicago Press, 1994), 121–23.

7. See David Arthur deSilva, "'Worthy of His Kingdom': Honor Discourse and Social Engineering in 1 Thessalonians," *Journal for the Study of the New Testament*, no. 64 (1996): 49–71, esp. 66; see also deSilva, *Despising Shame: Honor Discourse and Community Maintenance in Hebrews* (Atlanta: Scholars Press, 1995); Bruce Malina and J. H. Neyrey, "Honor and Shame in Luke-Acts: Pivotal Values in the Mediterranean World," in *The Social World of Luke-Acts*, ed. J. H. Neyrey (Peabody, Mass.: Hendrickson, 1991), 25–65.

8. Donald G. Mathews, *Religion in the Old South* (Chicago: University of Chicago Press, 1977), 62.

9. See deSilva, *Despising Shame*, 209–12.

10. Kurt Berends of Calvin College, in an absorbing dissertation in process of publication, has supplied this valuable information. See "'Thus Saith the Lord,' The Use of the Bible by Southern Evangelicals in the Era of the American Civil War" (Ph.D. diss., Oxford University, 1997), 193.

11. Thomas Miles Garrett, Diary, Southern Historical Collection, University of North Carolina, Wilson Library, as cited by Berends, "'Thus Saith the Lord,'" 191. I am indebted to Berends for this citation and the interpretation in this paragraph; see ibid., 191 n. 33, and Heyrman, *Southern Cross*, 306–32.

12. Quoted in Mitchell Snay, *The Gospel of Disunion: Religion and Separation in the Antebellum South* (1993; reprint, Chapel Hill: University of North Carolina Press, 1997), 178.

13. Quoted ibid., 146, 157.

14. deSilva, *Despising Shame*, 304, 112.

15. Paul Friedrich, "Sanity and the Myth of Honor: The Problem of Achilles," *Ethos* 5 (Fall 1977): 285.

16. Edward L. Ayers, *Vengeance and Justice: Crime and Punishment in the Nineteenth-Century American South* (New York: Oxford University Press, 1984), 33.

17. See Rina Palumbo, "Religious Declension, Psychic Discontinuity and Guilt: Perspectives in Nineteenth-Century American Revivalism," seminar paper, Department of History, Queen's University, Kingston, Canada, kindly lent by the author. See deSilva, *Despising Shame*; Halvor Moxnes, "Honor and Shame," *Biblical Theology Bulletin* 23 (1993): 167–76, "Honour and Righteousness in Romans," *Journal for the Study of the New Testament* 32 (Summer 1988): 61–77, and "Honor, Shame and the Outside World in Paul's Letter to the Romans," in *The Social World of Formative Chris-*

tianity and Judaism, ed. J. Neusner, P. Borgen, E. S. Frerichs, and R. Horsely (Philadelphia: Fortress, 1988), 207–18; John H. Elliott, "Disgraced Yet Graced: The Gospel According to 1 Peter in the Key of Honor and Shame," *Biblical Theology Bulletin* 25 (1995): 166–78.

18. Sir Benjamin Rudyerd (1628), quoted in Mervyn James, *Family, Lineage, and Civil Society: A Study of Society, Politics, and Mentality in the Durham Region, 1500–1640* (Oxford: Clarendon Press, 1974), 125 (first quotation). Second quotation from Darrett B. Rutman, "The Evolution of Religious Life in Early Virginia," *Lex et Scientia: The International Journal of Law and Science* 14 (October–December 1978): 192, 196; Butler, "Magic, Astrology, and the Early American Religious Heritage," 317–46.

19. On witchcraft and witch trials, see Richard Beale Davis, "The Devil in Virginia in the Seventeenth Century," *Virginia Magazine of History and Biography* 65 (April 1957), 131–49; Raphael Semmes, *Crime and Punishment in Early Maryland* (Baltimore: Johns Hopkins University Press, 1938), 167–69; Samuel Kercheval, *History of the Valley of Virginia* (1833; reprint, Strasburg, Va.: Shenandoah, 1925), 280–83; Rutman, "Evolution of Religious Life in Early Virginia," 193–94, 196; Keith Thomas, *Religion and the Decline of Magic* (New York: Charles Scribner's Sons, 1971), 535–83.

20. Cf. Patricia Bonomi, *Under the Cope of Heaven: Religion, Society, and Politics in Colonial America* (New York: Oxford University Press, 1986), esp. 91–102; Patricia U. Bonomi and Peter R. Eisenstadt, "Church Adherence in the Eighteenth-Century British American Colonies," *William and Mary Quarterly* 3d ser., 39 (April 1982): 245–86, should be judged in light of Rodney Stark and Roger Finke, "American Religion in 1776: A Statistical Portrait," *Sociological Analysis* 49 (Spring 1988): 39–51. Stark and Finke found that Southern churchmanship averaged less than 7 percent of the population when a national average came to 10 percent (partly because slaves were yet to be converted in great numbers).

21. See Darrett B. Rutman and Anita H. Rutman, *A Place in Time: Middlesex County, Virginia, 1650–1750* (New York: Norton, 1984), 125; Jon Butler, "Enlarging the Bonds of Christ: Slavery, Evangelism, and the Christianization of the White South, 1690–1790," in *The Evangelical Tradition in America,* ed. Leonard I. Sweet (Macon, Ga.: Mercer University Press, 1984), 96; Ralph Emmett Fall, ed., *The Diary of Robert Rose: A View of Virginia by a Scottish Colonial Parson, 1746–1751* (Verona, Va.: McClure Press, 1977).

22. *Staunton Vindicator,* 22 January 1859, and *Staunton Spectator,* 22 March 1859, in http://jefferson.village.virginia...w2/Browser1/aubrowser/rvjan59.html.

23. Rutman, "Evolution of Religious Life in Early Virginia," 198, 204.

24. Rutman and Rutman, *Place in Time,* 143; Philip Alexander Bruce, *Social Life in Old Virginia: From the Institutional History of Virginia in the Seventeenth Century* (1910; reprint, New York: Capricorn Books, 1965), 65–72.

25. Winton U. Solberg, *Redeem the Time: The Puritan Sabbath in Early America* (Cambridge, Mass.: Harvard University Press, 1977), 85–106 (quotation, 103).

26. William Gooch to Edmund Gibson, 20 September 1735, in "The Virginia

Clergy: Governor Gooch's Letters to the Bishop of London, 1727–1749 from the Fulham Manuscripts," ed. Rev. G. McLaren Bryden, *Virginia Magazine of History and Biography* 32 (October 1924): 333; Kercheval, *History of the Valley of Virginia*, 284, 290.

27. Norbert Elias, *The Civilizing Process: The Development of Manners, Changes in the Code of Conduct and Feeling in Early Modern Times*, trans. Edmund Jephcott (1939; reprint, New York: Urizen Books, 1978); Patrick H. Hutton, "The History of Mentalities: The New Map of Cultural History," *History and Theory* 20 (1981): 237–59. See also Georges Duby, ed., *A History of Private Life*, Vol. 2, *Revelations of the Medieval World*, trans. Arthur Goldhammer (Cambridge, Mass.: Harvard University Press, 1988), esp. Phillippe Braunstein, "Towards Intimacy," 535–630.

28. Elias, *Civilizing Process*, 163–68.

29. See David Hackett Fischer, *Albion's Seed: British Folkways in North America* (New York: Oxford University Press, 1990), on origins of Virginians; see Cleanth Brooks, *The Language of the American South* (Athens: University of Georgia Press, 1985), 8–15, and *The Relation of the Alabama-Georgia Dialect to the Provincial Dialects of Great Britain* (Baton Rouge: Louisiana State University Press, 1935).

30. Rhys Isaac, *The Transformation of Virginia, 1740–1790* (Chapel Hill: University of North Carolina Press, 1982), 72.

31. Rutman and Rutman, *Place in Time*, 235–36; Harold Robert Shurtleff, *The Log Cabin Myth: A Study of the Early Dwellings of the English Colonists in North America* (1939; reprint, Cambridge, Mass.: Harvard University Press, 1967), 127–62; Lois Green Carr and Lorena S. Walsh, "Inventories and the Analysis of Wealth and Consumption Patterns in St. Mary's County, Maryland, 1658–1777," *Historical Methods* 13 (Spring 1980): 81–104, and "The Standard of Living in the Colonial Chesapeake," *William and Mary Quarterly* 3d ser., 45 (January 1988): 135–59; and Billy G. Smith, "Comment," ibid., 163–66.

32. Isaac, *Transformation of Virginia*, 72–73. The blanket as partition is discussed in David H. Flaherty, *Privacy in Colonial New England* (Charlottesville: University Press of Virginia, 1967), 36 (although a reference only to New England, such an obvious expediency must have been used in Virginia); entry for 12 August 1776, the *Journal and Letters*, ed. Elmer T. Clark, J. Manning Potts, and Jacob S. Payton, 3 vols. (Nashville: Abingdon Press, 1958), 1:197. See also A. A. Parker, *Trip to the West and Texas . . . in the Autumn and Winter of 1834–35* (Concord, N.H.: White & Fisher, 1835), 112–15.

33. See Erik H. Erikson, *Identity and the Life Cycle* (New York: Norton, 1959), 65–74; Helen M. Lynd, *On Shame and the Search for Identity* (New York: Harcourt, Brace, 1958); Malina, *New Testament World*, 84.

34. Jon Butler, *Awash in a Sea of Faith: Christianizing the American People* (Cambridge, Mass.: Harvard University Press, 1990), 141–42.

35. Ibid., 145–46.

36. See Frances Trollope, *Domestic Manners of Americans*, ed. Donald Smalley (New

York: Random House, 1960), 249–50; Sarah Hicks Williams to Sarah and Samuel Hicks, 10 October 1853, in "Plantation Experiences of a New York Woman," ed. James C. Bonner, *North Carolina Historical Review* 33 (July 1956): 389.

37. Entry for 22 June 1781, "Military Journal of Lt. William Feltman, May 26, 1781 to April 25, 1782," in *Collections of the Historical Society of Pennsylvania,* (1853), 1:305; for quotation, see Winthrop Jordan, *White over Black: American Attitudes toward the Negro, 1550–1812* (Chapel Hill: University of North Carolina Press, 1968), 159. (Passage deleted in published version of diary.)

38. See Keith Thomas, *Man and the Natural World: A History of the Modern Sensibility* (New York: Pantheon Books, 1983), 44–46; Jordan, *White over Black,* 161–62; Benjamin West to Rev. Samuel West, 23 July 1778, *Life in the South, 1778–1779: The Letters of Dr. Benjamin West,* ed. James S. Schoff (Ann Arbor: University of Michigan Press, 1963), 32–33.

39. Rutman and Rutman, *Place in Time,* 171.

40. Quoted in Robert Olwell, *Masters, Slaves, and Subjects: The Culture of Power in the South Carolina Low Country, 1740–1840* (Ithaca, N.Y.: Cornell University Press, 1998), 128.

41. Quoted in Sylvia R. Frey and Betty Wood, *Come Shouting to Zion: African American Protestantism in the American South and British Caribbean to 1830* (Chapel Hill: University of North Carolina Press, 1998), 66.

42. Butler, *Awash in a Sea of Faith,* 133; Jon F. Sensbach, *A Separate Canaan: The Making of an Afro-Moravian World in North Carolina, 1763–1840* (Chapel Hill: University of North Carolina Press for the Omohundro Institute of Early American History and Culture, 1998).

43. The differences and interconnections of honor and shame, conscience and guilt are discussed in Bertram Wyatt-Brown, *Southern Honor: Ethics and Behavior in the Old South* (New York: Oxford University Press, 1982), 145–55 and passim.

44. Ibid., 15. See also 3–87.

45. Eliott J. Gorn, " 'Gouge and Bite, Pull Hair and Scratch': The Social Significance of Fighting in the Southern Backcountry," *American Historical Review* 90 (February 1985): 18–43; Tom Parramore, "Gouging in Early North Carolina," *North Carolina Folklore Journal* 22 (May 1974): 55–62; Jennie Holliman, *American Sports (1785–1835)* (Durham: Seeman Press, 1931), 138–39; Jane Carson, *Colonial Virginians at Play* (Williamsburg, Va.: Colonial Williamsburg, 1965), 164–66; Henry Benjamin Whipple, *Bishop Whipple's Southern Diary, 1843–1844,* ed. Lester Burrell Shippee (Minneapolis: University of Minnesota Press, 1937), 26–27; Merrill E. Gaddis, "Religious Ideas and Attitudes in the Early Frontier," *Church History* 2 (September 1933): 152–70, a surprisingly realistic exposition.

46. Heyrman, *Southern Cross,* 19.

47. Ibid., 5.

48. Robert Fogel and Stanley L. Engerman, *Time on the Cross: The Economics of American Slavery* (Boston: Little, Brown, 1974); Stanley L. Engerman, "A Reconsid-

eration of Southern Economic Growth, 1770–1860," *Agricultural History* 49 (April 1975): 343–61.

49. See, for instance, on slavery's corruptibility, William Byrd II, in *The Correspondence of the Three William Byrds*, ed. Marion Tinling, 2 vols. (Charlottesville: Virginia Historical Society, 1977), 2:487–88.

50. Quoted in Garnett Ryland, *The Baptists of Virginia, 1699–1926* (Richmond: Baptist Board of Missions and Education, 1955), 24.

51. Entry for 6 March 1774, *Journal and Letters of Philip Vickers Fithian, 1773–1774: A Plantation Tutor of the Old Dominion*, ed. Hunter Dickinson Farish (Williamsburg, Va.: Colonial Williamsburg, 1957), 72.

52. Heyrman, *Southern Cross*, 55.

53. See Nancy L. Struna, *The Cultural Significance of Sport in the Colonial Chesapeake and Massachusetts* (Ph.D. diss., University of Maryland, 1979; Eugene, Ore.: Microform Publications, College of Health, Physical Education and Recreation, University of Oregon, 1981), 155.

54. As F. G. Bailey (*Stratagems and Spoils: A Social Anthropology of Politics* [New York: Schocken Books, 1969]) points out: "Honour has meaning only when some people are without honour; power and wealth are got at the expense of other people. People compete only because the prizes are in short supply" (21).

55. See Christopher Waldrep, "'So Much Sin': The Decline of Religious Discipline and the 'Tidal Wave of Crime,'" *Journal of Social History* 23 (Spring 1990): 535–52; Richard R. Beeman, *The Evolution of the Southern Backcountry: A Case Study of Lunenburg County, Virginia, 1746–1832* (Philadelphia: University of Pennsylvania Press, 1984), 108; W. D. Blanks, "Corrective Church Discipline in the Presbyterian Churches of the Nineteenth Century South," *Journal of Presbyterian History* 44 (June 1966): 89–105.

56. Heyrman, *Southern Cross*, 20–21.

57. W. J. Rorabaugh, *The Alcoholic Republic: An American Tradition* (New York: Oxford University Press, 1979), 8, 9 (charts 1.1 and 1.2).

58. Samuel Gaillard Stoney, ed., "The Autobiography of William John Grayson," *South Carolina Historical and Genealogical Magazine* 49 (1948): 25–26.

59. John B. Boles, "Evangelical Protestantism in the Old South: From Religious Dissent to Cultural Dominance," in *Religion in the South*, ed. Charles Reagan Wilson (Jackson: University Press of Mississippi, 1985), 13–34. See also Jon Butler, "Enthusiasm Described and Decried: The Great Awakening as Interpretive Fiction," *Journal of American History* 69 (September 1982): 305–25.

60. Ann Douglas, *The Feminization of American Culture* (New York: Knopf, 1977); Rev. Walter C. Whitaker, "Bishop Richard Hooker Wilmer," *Transactions of the Alabama Historical Society*, 5 vols. (Montgomery, Ala.: Alabama Historical Society, 1904), 4:23; Sarah McCulloh Lemmon, *Parson Pettigrew of the 'Old Church,' 1744–1807* (Chapel Hill: University of North Carolina Press, 1970), 23; entry for 14 September 1851, Lida Bestor Robertson Diary, ADAH.

61. Steven M. Stowe, *Intimacy and Power in the Old South: Ritual in the Lives of the Planters* (Baltimore: Johns Hopkins University Press, 1987), 151.

62. Johann Huizinga, *Homo Ludens: A Study of the Play-Element in Culture* (1949; reprint, Boston: Little, Brown, 1955), 25. For instance, take the gamester William Byrd III; see David Meade, recollections, in "Letters of William Byrd III," *Virginia Magazine of History and Biography* 37 (October 1929): 310–11.

63. Lester B. Shippee, ed., *Bishop Whipple's Southern Diary, 1843–1844* (Minneapolis: University of Minnesota Press, 1937), 101.

64. Ted Ownby, "Evangelicalism and Male Culture: Recreation and Religion in the Rural South, 1865–1920" (Ph.D. diss., Johns Hopkins University, 1986), 20–21. There were, of course, conversions of tavern-keepers, gamesters, and horsemen. See, for instance, "The Autobiography of Rev. Robertson Gannaway," *Virginia Magazine of History and Biography* 37 (October 1929): 316–20.

65. George Washington Paschal, *History of the North Carolina Baptists*, 2 vols. (Raleigh: General Board of the North Carolina Baptist State Convention, 1930–55), 2:238.

66. Quoted in Deborah Vansau McCauley, *Appalachian Mountain Religion: A History* (Urbana: University of Illinois Press, 1995), 27–28.

67. Ibid., 26.

68. William Lynwood Montell, *Killings: Folk Justice in the Upper South* (Lexington: University Press of Kentucky, 1986), 36–37; Rev. Charles Woodmason, *The Carolina Backcountry on the Eve of the Revolution*, ed. Richard J. Hooker (Chapel Hill: University of North Carolina Press, 1953). On the church and violence, see, however, Rt. Rev. B. B. Smith, bishop of the Episcopal Diocese of Kentucky, as quoted in Theodore Dwight Weld, *American Slavery as It Is: Testimony of a Thousand Witnesses* (New York: American Anti-Slavery Society, 1839), 204–5.

69. See esp. Waldrep, " 'So Much Sin,' " 535–52.

70. John G. Crowley, *Primitive Baptists of the Wiregrass South: 1815 to the Present* (Gainesville: University Press of Florida, 1998), 47.

71. Anne C. Loveland, *Southern Evangelicals and the Social Order, 1800–1860* (Baton Rouge: Louisiana State University Press, 1980), 52–64. One minister in thirteen hundred in the slave states and one minister in nine hundred in the free states were estimates of the Southern Aid Society. See Frederick Law Olmsted, *The Cotton Kingdom*, ed. Arthur M. Schlesinger Sr. (New York: Random House, 1984), 203.

72. "Conditions of American Baptists" (reprint from *Baptist Repository*), *Baptist Weekly Journal of the Mississippi Valley* (Cincinnati), 15 March 1832; Christopher MacRae et al. to Frederick Porter, 16 March 1827, ASSU. See David Edwin Harrell Jr., "The Evolution of Plain-Folk Religion in the South, 1835–1920," in *Varieties of Southern Religious Experience*, ed. Samuel S. Hill (Baton Rouge: Louisiana State University Press, 1988), 24–51.

73. Quoted from Ralph R. Smith, " 'In Every Destitute Place': The Mission Program of the America Sunday School Union, 1817–1834" (Ph.D. diss., University of

Southern California, 1973), 94 n. 33; see also Samuel P. Barton to Porter, 28 June 1835, and James W. Douglass to Porter, 27 June 1836, ASSU.

74. Richard Hooker to Porter, 19 May, 19 June 1830, W. A. N. Campbell to Porter, 18 January 1828, and John Endith to Porter, 20 February 1828, ASSU.

75. Norton, quoted by Smith, in "'In Every Destitute Place,'" 163; see also Hooker to Porter, 31 May 1830, ASSU; Joseph Mitchell, "Traveling Preacher and Settled Farmer," *Methodist History* 5 (July 1967): 3–14.

76. Don H. Doyle, "The Social Functions of Voluntary Associations in a Nineteenth-Century American Town," *Social Science History* 1 (Spring 1977): 333–55; Richard D. Brown, *Modernization: The Transformation of American Life, 1600–1865* (New York: Hill and Wang, 1976), 147.

77. Mathews, *Religion in the Old South*, 88; Suzanne Lebsock, *The Free Women of Petersburg: Status and Culture in a Southern Town, 1784–1860* (New York: Norton, 1984), 216–25. Opposition to women's activism hindered female voluntary work in the South. See Jean Friedman, *The Enclosed Garden: Women and Community in the Evangelical South, 1830–1900* (Chapel Hill: University of North Carolina Press, 1985), 19–20. On Southern weakness of organization, see "Cassandra Warnings," *The Diary of Edmund Ruffin*, ed. William Scarborough, 3 vols. (Chapel Hill: University of North Carolina Press, 1972–89), 1:630 (Appendix D).

78. See Friedman, *Enclosed Garden*, 9–11; Gwen Kennedy Neville, *Kinship and Pilgrimage: Rituals of Reunion in American Protestant Culture* (New York: Oxford University Press, 1987), 94–104.

79. Clanton W. Williams, "Early Ante-Bellum Montgomery: A Black Belt Constituency," *Journal of Southern History* 7 (November 1941): 502; *State* v. *Mary DuBois*, Citizens of Warren County to H. G. Runnels, Governors Papers (RG 27), n.d. [1833], MDAH.

80. See Donald G. Mathews, "North Carolina Methodists in the Nineteenth Century: Church and Society," in *Methodism Alive in North Carolina*, ed. O. Kelly Ingram (Durham: Divinity School of Duke University, 1976), 59–74.

81. Goulding and Cater, quoted from Mitchell Snay, "Gospel of Disunion: Religion and the Rise of Southern Separatism, 1830–1861" (Ph.D. diss., Brandeis University, 1984), 14, 19. See also, for instance, Saranne E. Crabtree, "*South Western Baptist*, 1850–1860: Defender of Southern Rights" (M.A. thesis, Auburn University, 1973), 82 (on Charles Sumner's caning).

82. See Snay, "Gospel of Disunion," 44–45.

83. Miller, "Traveling Preacher and Settled Farmer," 3; Samuel S. Hill Jr., *The South and the North in American Religion* (Athens: University of Georgia Press, 1980), 73–74.

84. C. C. Pearson and J. Edwin Hendricks, *Liquor and Anti-Liquor in Virginia, 1619–1919* (Durham: Duke University Press, 1967), 147; Clement Eaton, *The Freedom-of-Thought Struggle in the Old South* (New York: Harper & Row, 1964), 300–301.

85. See, for an example of common talk about religion among men, Olmsted, *Cotton Kingdom*, 204–5; William Warren Sweet, "The Churches as Moral Courts of the Frontier," *Church History* 2 (March 1933): 4.

86. Loveland, *Southern Evangelicals and the Social Order*, 210–12; Reuben Edward Alley, *A History of Baptists in Virginia* (Richmond: Virginia Baptist General Board, 1973), 230–32; Mathews, *Slavery and Methodism*; and "Charles Colcock Jones and the Southern Evangelical Crusade to Form a Bi-Racial Community," *Journal of Southern History* 41 (August 1975): 299–320; Eugene D. Genovese and Elizabeth Fox-Genovese, "The Divine Sanction of Social Order: Religious Foundations of the Southern Slaveholders' World View," *Journal of the American Academy of Religion* 55 (Summer 1987): 211–33, and "The Religious Ideals of Southern Slave Society," *Georgia Historical Quarterly* 70 (Spring 1986): 1–16; Larry E. Tise, *Proslavery: A History of the Defense of Slavery in America, 1701–1840* (Athens: University of Georgia Press, 1987), 308–46.

87. Mary P. Ryan, *Cradle of the Middle Class: The Family in Oneida County, New York, 1790–1865* (Cambridge, Eng.: Cambridge University Press, 1981), 147 (quotation), see also 48–49.

88. Anne Newport Royall, "Letter L," 8 June 1822, *Letters from Alabama, 1817–1822*, ed. Lucille Griffith (University: University of Alabama Press, 1969), 248–49.

89. Daniel Jay Whitener, *Prohibition in North Carolina, 1715–1945* (Chapel Hill: University of North Carolina Press, 1946), 17; Loveland, *Southern Evangelicals and the Social Order*, 142–58; Sweet, "The Church as Moral Courts of the Frontier," 14.

90. Bertram Wyatt-Brown, "The Anti-Mission Movement in the Jacksonian South: A Study in Folk Culture," *Journal of Southern History* 36 (November 1970): 501–29; Harrell, "Evolution of Plain-Folk Religion in the South," 24–31.

91. Dale A. Somers, *The Rise of Sports in New Orleans, 1850–1900* (Baton Rouge: Louisiana State University Press, 1972), 12 (quotation), 13–14; and [Joseph Holt Ingraham], *The South-West. By a Yankee . . .*, 2 vols. (New York: Harper Bros., 1835), 1:219; Whipple, *Southern Diary*, 117–20.

92. Ted Ownby, *Subduing Satan: Religion, Recreation, and Manhood in the Rural South, 1865–1920* (Chapel Hill: University of North Carolina Press, 1990), 54.

93. John Hartwell Cocke to Joseph C. Cabell, [?] June 1852, John Hartwell Cocke MSS, Alderman Library, University of Virginia, as quoted in Pearson and Hendricks, *Liquor and Anti-Liquor in Virginia*, 130 n. 64; see also, on states'-rights reactions to temperance, Whitener, *Prohibition in North Carolina*, 43.

94. John Lee Eighmy, *Churches in Cultural Captivity: A History of the Social Attitudes of Southern Baptists* (Knoxville: University of Tennessee Press, 1972), 52; Loveland, *Southern Evangelicals and the Social Order*, 145–58.

95. John H. Caldwell, *Slavery and Southern Methodism: Two Sermons Preached in Newnan, Georgia* (N.p.: Printed for the author, 1865), 20–21. See also Daniel W. Stowell, " 'We Have Sinned, and God Has Smitten Us!': John H. Caldwell and the Religious Meaning of Confederate Defeat," *Georgia Historical Quarterly* 78 (Spring 1994): 1–38. "Who among us has ever lifted up a true, manly, martyr-like remonstrance against the crying evils of slavery. There has not been one martyr to the principles of true conservatism," he told his congregation (Caldwell, *Slavery and Southern Methodism*, 69).

96. See particularly, Grady McWhiney, *Cracker Culture: Celtic Ways in the Old South* (Tuscaloosa: University of Alabama Press, 1988), 171–92.

97. Ownby, "Evangelicalism and Male Culture," 20–21.

98. Jon G. Appleton, "Samuel Henderson: Southern Minister, Editor, and Crusader, 1853–1866" (M.A. thesis, Auburn University, 1968), 8.

99. William Faulkner, *Light in August* (1932; reprint, New York: Modern Library, 1950), 426.

CHAPTER FIVE

1. Quoted in Randy J. Sparks, " 'To Rend the Body of Christ': Proslavery Ideology and Religious Schism from a Mississippi Perspective," in *Religion and the Antebellum Debate over Slavery*, ed. John R. McKivigan and Mitchell Snay (Athens: University of Georgia Press, 1998), 279–80.

2. Following the form used by Randy Sparks, " 'To Rend the Body of Christ,' " I adopt the term *traditionalist* to describe this sectarian movement. See Deborah V. McCauley, "Grace and the Heart of Appalachian Mountain Religion," in *Appalachia: Social Context Past and Present*, ed. Bruce Ergood and Bruce E. Kuhre (Dubuque, Ia.: Kendall/Hunt, 1991), 357.

3. Frank Henderson Stewart, *Honor* (Chicago: University of Chicago Press, 1994), 132. Julian Pitt-Rivers and others take the position that wealth is a major determinant of status in the honor hierarchy, but Stewart's point is well taken. Cf. Julian Pitt-Rivers, "Honour and Social Status," in *Honour and Shame: The Values of Mediterranean Society*, ed. J. G. Péristiany (Chicago: University of Chicago Press, 1966), 507.

4. Bertram Wyatt-Brown, *Southern Honor: Ethics and Behavior in the Old South* (New York: Oxford University Press, 1982), 46, 66–68, 298–99, "The Typology of Southern Culture," *Societas* 5 (Winter 1975): 1–29, and "The Old South: A 'Culture of Courage,' " *Southern Studies* 20 (Fall 1981): 213–46.

5. Edward Pessen, *Riches, Class, and Power before the Civil War* (Lexington, Mass.: D. C. Heath, 1973); Edward Pessen, *Jacksonian America: Society, Personality, and Politics* (Homewood, Ill.: Dorsey Press, 1978).

6. Rhys Isaac, *The Transformation of Virginia, 1740–1790* (1982; reprint, New York: Norton, 1988), 162–64.

7. John W. Quist, *Restless Visionaries: The Social Roots of Antebellum Reform in Alabama and Michigan* (Baton Rouge: Louisiana State University Press, 1998).

8. Gordon A. Cotton, *Of Primitive Faith and Order: A History of the Mississippi Primitive Baptist Church, 1780–1974* (Raymond, Miss.: Keith Press, 1974), 1–2.

9. Ibid., 3; James R. Mathis, " 'Can Two Walk Together Unless They Be Agreed?': The Origins of the Primitive Baptists, 1800–1840" (Ph.D. diss., University of Florida, 1997), 23.

10. James L. Peacock and Ruel W. Tyson Jr., *Pilgrims of Paradox: Calvinism and Experience among the Primitive Baptists of the Blue Ridge* (Washington, D.C.: Smithsonian Institution, 1989), 33.

11. John Taylor, *A History of Ten Baptist Churches* (1823; 2d ed., Bloomfield, Ky.: W. H. Holmes, 1827), 17.

12. John Taylor, *The Baptists on the American Frontier: A History of Ten Baptist Churches of Which the Author Has Been Alternately a Member*, ed. Chester Raymond Young (Macon, Ga.: Mercer University Press, 1995), 85.

13. See John Boles, *The Great Revival* (Lexington: University of Kentucky Press, 1972); Nathan O. Hatch, *The Democratization of American Christianity* (New Haven: Yale University Press, 1989).

14. Peacock and Tyson, *Pilgrims of Paradox*, 3, 16, 115–17; Christine Heyrman, *Southern Cross: The Beginnings of the Bible Belt* (Chapel Hill: University of North Carolina Press, 1997), 21; Dickson D. Bruce, *And They All Sang Hallelujah: Plain-Folk Camp-Meeting Religion, 1800–1845* (Knoxville: University of Tennessee Press, 1974); Beverly Bush Patterson, *The Sound of the Dove: Singing in Appalachian Primitive Baptist Churches* (Urbana: University of Illinois Press, 1995).

15. Quoted in Robert A. Baker, *The Southern Baptist Convention and Its People, 1607–1972* (Nashville: Broadman Press, 1974), 96; see also Robert T. Handy, "Biblical Primitivism in the American Baptist Tradition," in *The American Quest for the Primitive Church*, ed. Richard T. Hughes (Urbana: University of Illinois Press, 1988), 143–52.

16. Randy J. Sparks, *On Jordan's Stormy Banks: Evangelicalism in Mississippi, 1773–1876* (Athens: University of Georgia Press, 1994), 50, 51; Peacock and Tyson, *Pilgrims of Paradox*, 16, 196. When asked what women do, "Elder Lyle" told the anthropologists, "They cook!" (196).

17. Deborah Vansau McCauley, *Appalachian Mountain Religion: A History* (Urbana: University of Illinois Press, 1995), 87, also see 219, 223–24.

18. Ibid., 388.

19. Mathis, " 'Can Two Walk Together?' "

20. McCauley, *Appalachian Mountain Religion*, 169; Howard Dorgan, *Giving Glory to God in Appalachia: Worship Practices of Six Baptist Subdenominations* (Knoxville: University of Tennessee Press, 1987), 128; quotation from Melanie L. Sovine, "Traditionalism, Antimissionism, and the Primitive Baptist Religion," in *Reshaping the Image of Appalachia*, ed. Loyal Jones (Berea, Ky.: Berea College Appalachian Center, 1986), 56, 57.

21. See, for instance, John W. Quist, *Restless Visionaries: The Social Roots of Antebellum Reform in Alabama and Michigan* (Baton Rouge: Louisiana State University Press, 1998), 97–101.

22. James G. Crowley, *Primitive Baptists of the Wiregrass South: 1815 to the Present* (Gainesville: University Press of Florida, 1998), 68.

23. Beth Barton Schweiger, "Slavery, Denominations, and the Clerical Profession in Virginia," in *Religion and the Antebellum Debate over Slavery*, ed. McKivigan and Snay, 296.

24. Benjamin Franklin Riley, *A History of the Baptists in the Southern States East of the Mississippi* (Philadelphia: American Baptist Publication Society, 1898), 170, 173; on

Arkansas, see James Sterling Rogers, *History of Arkansas Baptists* (Little Rock, Ark.: Executive Board of the Arkansas Baptist State Convention, 1948), 423–26; on Delaware, Maryland, and New Jersey, see David Benedict, *A General History of the Baptist Denomination in America and Other Parts of the World* (New York: Lewis Colby, 1848), 630, 637, 638; and Norman H. Maring, *Baptists in New Jersey: A Study in Transition* (Valley Forge, Pa.: Judson Press, 1964), 129–40; on Florida, see John L. Rosser, *A History of Florida Baptists* (Nashville: Broadman Press, 1949), 22, 51; on Georgia, see *History of the Baptist Denomination in Georgia: With Biographical Compendium and Portrait Gallery of Baptist Ministers and Other Georgia Baptists Compiled for the Christian Index* (Atlanta, Ga.: J. P. Harrison, 1881), 174; on Missouri, see H. F. Tong, *Historical Sketches of the Baptists of Southeast Missouri* (St. Louis: National Baptist Pub. Co., 1888), 41–42; on North Carolina, see James W. Douglass to Frederick W. Porter, 27 June 1838, ASSU); and George Washington Paschal, *History of North Carolina Baptists*, 2 vols. (Raleigh: General Board, North Carolina Baptist State Convention, 1930–55), 2:273–80. On cities mentioned, see Richard Briscoe Cook, *The Early and Later Delaware Baptists* (Philadelphia: American Baptist Publication Society, 1880), 77–96; and Benedict, *General History*, 634, 638.

25. John F. Cady, *The Origin and Development of the Missionary Baptist Church in Indiana* (Franklin, Ind.: Franklin College, 1942), 31–75. On the Universalist connections with Baptist antimissionism, see Elmo A. Robinson, "Universalism in Indiana," *Indiana Magazine of History* 13 (March 1917): 1–19 and (June 1917): 157–88. Some scholars argue that a "Celtic" tradition explains the persistence of agrarian ways in the American hinterland. It is estimated that close to 70 percent of all the Texas Methodists, Baptists, and Presbyterians traced their heritage to the wild, often violent, but religious borderlands of Great Britain—Ireland, Wales, and Scotland. The Welsh "hywl" or oratorical gift could be found in the style of extemporaneous preachers active in the mountain fastnesses of the South. See J. Wayne Flynt, *Alabama Baptists: Southern Baptists in the Heart of Dixie* (Tuscaloosa: University of Alabama Press, 1998), 35; Grady McWhinney, *Cracker Culture: Celtic Ways in the Old South* (Tuscaloosa: University of Alabama Press, 1988), 6–7, 188, 189, 191; David Hackett Fischer, *Albion's Seed: Four British Folkways in America* (New York: Oxford University Press, 1989), 617–18; Loyal Jones, "A Preliminary Look at the Welsh Component of Celtic Influence in Appalachia," in *The Appalachian Experience: Proceedings of the Sixth Annual Appalachian Studies Conference*, ed. Barry M. Buxton et al. (Boone, N.C.: Appalachian State University Press, 1983), 31.

26. William W. Freehling, "Why Secession, Why Defeat? How Southern Divisions Helped Generate, Then Doom, a Revolution," paper presented at the British American Nineteenth Century Historians Conference, Myrtle Beach, S.C., March 1999. The paper is an exciting foretaste of Freehling's succeeding volume to *The Road to Disunion: Secession at Bay, 1776–1854* (New York: Oxford University Press, 1990).

27. Howard Dorgan, *The Old Regular Baptists of Central Appalachia: Brothers and Sisters in Hope* (Knoxville: University of Tennessee Press, 1989), 120–21.

28. Gregory A. Wills, *Democratic Religion: Freedom, Authority, and Church Discipline in the Baptist South, 1785–1900* (New York: Oxford University Press, 1996), 17, 35, 43, 55–56.

29. Stephanie McCurry, *Masters of Small Worlds: Yeomen Households, Gender Relations, and the Political Culture of the Antebellum South Carolina Low Country* (New York: Oxford University Press, 1995), 132.

30. Ibid., 133 (quotation), 131–35.

31. Peacock and Tyson, *Pilgrims of Paradox*, 100; Cotton, *Of Primitive Faith and Order*, vii.

32. Peacock and Tyson, *Pilgrims of Paradox*, 75–76.

33. Quoted in Loyal Jones, *Faith and Meaning in the Southern Uplands* (Urbana: University of Illinois Press, 1999), 141; see also Jones, "Mountain Religion: An Overview," in *Christianity in Appalachia: Profiles in Regional Pluralism*, ed. Bill J. Leonard (Knoxville: University of Tennessee Press, 1999), 91–92.

34. Quoted in Anne M. Boylan, *Sunday School: The Formation of an American Institution, 1790–1880* (New Haven: Yale University Press, 1988), 83.

35. Isaac, *Transformation of Virginia*, 164.

36. Garnett Ryland, *The Baptists of Virginia, 1699–1926* (Richmond: Baptist Board of Missions and Education, 1955), 1–36; C. C. Goen, *Revivalism and Separatism in New England, 1740–1800: Strict Congregationalists and Separate Baptists in the Great Awakening* (Middletown, Conn.: Wesleyan University Press, 1987), 298–99; William Staughton, ed., *Gill's Complete Body of Practical and Doctrinal Divinity: Being a System of Evangelical Truths Deduced from the Sacred Scriptures* (Philadelphia: Delaplaine and Hellings, 1810), 119–33; Peter Toon, *The Emergence of Hyper-Calvinism in English Nonconformity, 1689–1765* (London: Olive Tree, 1967), 80, 143–50. On other topics of dispute between Regulars and Separates, see Benedict, *General History*, 650–52, 689, 940n; Ryland, *Baptists of Virginia*, 41.

37. Albert Henry Newman, *A History of the Baptist Churches in the United States* (New York: Christian Literature, 1894), 55. Rigid predestinarians were sometimes ardent revivalists, but there was a tension in their position that predisposed many to depend on the movements of the Holy Spirit rather than on pulpit enthusiasm. For a discussion of the intellectual basis for the antimissionists, see Mathis, " 'Can Two Walk Together?' "

38. Nathan O. Hatch, *The Democratization of American Christianity* (New Haven: Yale University Press, 1989).

39. Robert A. Baker, *Relations between Northern and Southern Baptists* ([Fort Worth]: N.p., 1954), 13, 15–16; Whitney R. Cross, *The Burned-Over District: The Social and Intellectual History of Enthusiastic Religion in Western New York, 1800–1850* (Ithaca, N.Y.: Cornell University Press, 1950), 23–24. Francis Wayland tried to interest Baptists in centralized "conventional" operations with only limited success: see Robert A. Baker, ed., *A Baptist Source Book with Particular Reference to Southern Baptists* (Nashville: Broadman Press, 1966), 68–71, 73–74. On interdenominational agencies, see Charles I. Foster, *An Errand of Mercy: The Evangelical United Front, 1790–1837* (Chapel

Hill: University of North Carolina Press, 1960), and Clifford S. Griffin, *Their Brothers' Keepers: Moral Stewardship in the United States, 1800–1865* (New Brunswick, N.J.: Rutgers University Press, 1960).

40. Taylor quoted in John W. Kuykendall, *Southern Enterprise: The Work of National Evangelical Societies in the Antebellum South* (Westport, Conn.: Greenwood, 1982), 45. See also F. Wilbur Helmbold, "The Initial Missionary Dispute in North Alabama," *Alabama Baptist Historian* 1 (June 1965): 11–13.

41. Luther Rice and Adoniram Judson were from Massachusetts, Going was from Vermont. Wayland, a New Yorker, attended Andover Seminary in Massachusetts and became president of Brown University. Consult *Dictionary of American Biography* for their biographies. Francis Scott Key of Georgetown and Benjamin H. Latrobe of Baltimore were prominent in the colonization movement. John H. Cocke of Virginia and John B. O'Neall of South Carolina promoted the temperance and tract causes, for example. Yet Southern ranks in Yankee-led religious causes were thin.

42. *Baptist Tract and Youth's Magazine* (Philadelphia) 5 (June 1832): 134.

43. Baker, *Relations*, 36, 252n; Cross, *Burned-Over District*, 22–23; Foster, *Errand of Mercy*, 199–204.

44. Quotation from "Wants of Pennsylvania," *Spectator* (Pittsburgh) 1 (20 March 1828): 83; *Regular Baptist Miscellany* (Zanesville) 1 (August 1830): 174–75; *Cincinnati Baptist Weekly Journal*, 22 July 1831; and "Sabbath-Schools & Bible Classes Demanded by Patriotism," ibid., 16 September 1831. See Page Smith, *As a City upon a Hill: The Town in American History* (New York: Knopf, 1966), 52–54, on frontier conservatism. See "The Autobiography of Flavel Bascom, 1833–40," in *Religion on the American Frontier: A Collection of Source Materials*, Vol. 3, *The Congregationalists, 1783–1850*, ed. William W. Sweet (Chicago: University of Chicago Press, 1939), 257–58, 261.

45. There was a painful shortage of trained talent of every kind, not just of Southern and western volunteers. When Ohio Baptists set up a seminary in Covington, Kentucky, across the river from Cincinnati, they were not only unable to hire an eastern fund-raiser at inflated wages, but they could find few students to attend. See Western Baptist Education Society, Minutes, 1832–44, Western Reserve Historical Society, Cleveland; Cincinnati *Baptist Weekly Journal*, 18 January 1833; and Elder William Chafee to editor, ibid., 9 November 1832; Baker, *Relations*, 37–39.

46. Benevolent society leaders claimed "Colonel Crockett" as a devout participant at New Jersey senator Theodore Frelinghuysen's boardinghouse prayer meetings in Washington, but the stigma of ecclesiastical ties with business interests was not so easily erased. See *New York Observer*, quoted in *(Ravenna, Ohio) Watchman*, 24 December 1836. See also John Marshall to Committee of Arrangements of the Richmond Sabbath School Union, *New York Observer*, 26 July 1828.

47. Mark S. Schantz, "Religious Tracts, Evangelical Reform, and the Market Revolution in Antebellum America," *Journal of the Early Republic* 17 (Fall 1997): 425–66; Lewis Tappan, *Is It Right to Be Rich?* (New York: Anson D. F. Randolph, 1869). Quotation in Bertram Wyatt-Brown, *Lewis Tappan and the Evangelical War against Slavery* (1969; reprint, Baton Rouge: Louisiana State University Press, 1997), 341. The lit-

erature on evangelical motivations is extensive; see Schantz's article above for a thorough bibliography and discussion of the matter.

48. Young, introduction to Taylor, *History of Ten Baptist Churches*, 12–17, 33–34.

49. John Henderson Spencer, *A History of Kentucky Baptists, from 1769 to 1885, Including More Than 800 Biographical Sketches*, 2 vols. (Cincinnati: J. R. Baumes, 1886), 1:108; Dorothy B. Thompson, "John Taylor of the Ten Churches," *Kentucky Historical Society Register* 46 (July 1948): 541–72, and "John Taylor and the Day of Controversy," ibid., 53 (July 1955): 197–233; *Plain Truth* (Canandaigua, N.Y.) 1 (1 November 1822): 124.

50. Taylor, quoted in Baker, ed., *Baptist Source Book*, 79–81.

51. Taylor, cited by Oury Wilburn Taylor, *Early Tennessee Baptists, 1769–1832* (Nashville: Executive Board, Tennessee Baptist Convention, 1957), 180–82. Baker, *Relations*, 9–17, and William W. Barnes, *The Southern Baptist Convention, 1845–1953* (Nashville: Broadman Press, 1954), 9–10, 98–99, maintain that the societal arrangement represented individualistic and decentralizing tendencies. See also Stanley M. Elkins, *Slavery: A Problem in American Institutional and Intellectual Life* (Chicago: University of Chicago Press, 1959), 28–29. Nevertheless, institutional fragmentation paradoxically coexisted with nationalistic, communal trends. The societies sought to reach the individual, it is true, but for purposes of binding him to a centralized, national cause at the expense of his local loyalties and obligations.

52. *History of the Baptist Denomination in Georgia*, 166; Hosea Holcombe, *A History of the Rise and Progress of the Baptists in Alabama* (Philadelphia: King and Baird, 1840), 90, 97–98; Ryland, *Baptists of Virginia*, 258. See also Ted Ownby, *Subduing Satan: Religion, Recreation, and Manhood in the Rural South, 1865–1920* (Chapel Hill: University of North Carolina Press, 1990), 172.

53. Holcombe, *History of the Rise and Progress*, 38.

54. Ownby, *Subduing Satan*, 135.

55. Hooker to Porter, 19 June 1830, ASSU Archives; see also Hooker to Porter, 19, 31 May 1830, ibid.

56. Christopher H. Owen, *The Sacred Flame of Love: Methodism and Society in Nineteenth-Century Georgia* (Athens: University of Georgia Press, 1998), 39–40, 80–81; Donald G. Mathews, "Charles Colcock Jones and the Southern Evangelical Crusade to Form a Biracial Community," *Journal of Southern History* 41 (August 1975): 299–320, and *Slavery and Methodism: A Chapter in American Morality, 1785–1845* (Princeton: Princeton University Press, 1965).

57. Entry for 13 April 1843, James Mallory, *Fear God and Walk Humbly: The Agricultural Journal of James Mallory, 1843–1877*, ed. Grady McWhiney, Warner O. Moore Jr., and Robert F. Pace (Tuscaloosa: University of Alabama Press, 1997), 33.

58. Welch to Porter, 20 November 1828; Campbell to Porter, 18 January 1828; Christopher MacRae et al. to Porter, 16 March 1827; Charles P. Grosvener to Porter, 17 May 1830, ASSU Archives; *Calvinistic Magazine* (Rogersville, Tenn.) 3 (March 1829): 66. See Boylan, *Sunday School*.

59. Quoted in Cotton, *Of Primitive Faith and Order*, 26.

60. Scott, quoted by Cook, *Early and Later Delaware Baptists*, 93; *Holston Messenger*, quoted in *Gospel Advocate and Impartial Investigator* (Auburn, N.Y.) 5 (8 December 1827): 390–91; see also letter to editor, *Cincinnati Baptist Weekly Journal*, 28 December 1832.

61. See James Oakes, *The Ruling Race: A History of American Slaveholders* (New York: Knopf, 1983).

62. David T. Bailey, *Shadow on the Church: Southwestern Evangelical Religion and the Issue of Slavery, 1783–1860* (Ithaca, N.Y.: Cornell University Press, 1985), 126; see also Tetsuo Scott Miyakawa, *Protestants and Pioneers: Individualism and Conformity on the American Frontier* (Chicago: University of Chicago Press, 1964), 155–58; Michael A. Lebowitz, "The Jacksonians: Paradox Lost?" in *Towards a New Past: Dissenting Essays in American History*, ed. Barton J. Bernstein (New York: Pantheon, 1968), 65–89.

63. Benedict, *General History*, 935; Bailey, *Shadow on the Church*, 124–27.

64. "The Black Rock Declaration," quoted in Baker, ed., *Baptist Source Book*, 83, and by Joseph Thomas Watts, *The Rise and Progress of Maryland Baptists* (Baltimore: State Mission Board of the Maryland Baptist Union Association, [195?]), 28–29.

65. Illinois Baptist Association, quoted in *The Reformer* (Philadelphia) 10 (January 1829): 45. *The Reformer* was the organ of Theophilus Gates, an acerbic antimission millennialist. See Hatch, *Democratization of American Christianity*, 176–79.

66. Quoted in Crowley, *Primitive Baptists in the Wiregrass South*, 73.

67. John Gill, *The Doctrine of Imputed Righteousness without Works Asserted and Proved* ([London]: N.p., 1784).

68. Sovine, "Traditionalism, Antimissionism, and the Primitive Baptist Religion," 38.

69. Malcolm Barber, "The Decline of the Cathars," paper presented to the Lilly Collegium on Religion and the Humanities, National Humanities Center, Research Triangle Park, N.C., March 1999; Cotton, *Of Primitive Faith and Order*, 4.

70. Peacock and Tyson, *Pilgrims of Paradox*; Crowley, *Primitive Baptists of the Wiregrass South*, 119.

71. Mathis, " 'Can Two Walk Together?,' " 144.

72. Quoted in Beverly Bush Patterson, *The Sound of the Dove: Singing in Appalachian Primitive Baptist Churches* (Urbana: University of Illinois Press, 1995), 70. On acedia, see Siegfried Wenzel, *The Sin of Sloth: Acedia in Medieval Thought and Literature* (Chapel Hill: University of North Carolina Press, 1960).

73. "Autobiography of Jacob Bower," in *Religion on the American Frontier: A Collection of Source Materials*, Vol. 1, *The Baptists, 1783–1830*, ed. William W. Sweet (Chicago: University of Chicago Press, 1931), 188.

74. Melanie L. Sovine, "Studying Religious Belief Systems in Their Social Historical Context," in *Appalachia and America: Autonomy and Regional Dependence*, ed. Allen Batteau (Lexington: University of Kentucky Press, 1983), 52.

75. Joshua Lawrence quoted in Mathis, " 'Can Two Walk Together?,' " 179, 181, 184, 185. See, on the gyrations of conversion and backsliding, Anne Hunsaker

Hawkins, *Archetypes of Conversion: The Autobiography of Augustine, Bunyan, and Merton* (Lewisburg, Pa.: Bucknell University Press, 1985), 13.

76. Vaughan, quoted in *Non-Slaveholder* (Philadelphia) 3 (January 1848): 18–19; see also "Poor White Folks," ibid. 2 (March 1847): 69–70. Lawrence, quoted by Elder D. Bryant in *Regular Baptist Miscellany* 2 (April 1831): 106, and by *Ravenna Ohio Watchman*, 28 November 1835. The Black Rock proclamation of 1832, which set the Primitive Baptists apart, denounced the Missionary Baptists, who "claim the honor of converting their tens of thousands; of leading the tender minds of children to the knowledge of Jesus. . . . Such arrogant pretensions we feel bound to oppose." See Loyal Jones, "Old-Time Baptists and Mainline Christians," in *An Appalachian Symposium: Essays in Honor of Cratis D. Williams*, ed. J. W. Williamson (Boone, N.C.: Appalachian State University Press, 1977), 123.

77. Peck to Porter, 9 July 1830, ASSU Archives; Sweet, ed., *Religion on the American Frontier*, Vol 1., *The Baptists, 1783–1830*, 73–74. See also Paul M. Harrison, introduction to *Forty Years of Pioneer Life: Memoir of John Mason Peck, D.D.*, ed. Rufus Babcock (Carbondale: University of Southern Illinois Press, 1965), 1iii–1xv.

78. Caleb Mills to Porter, 24 June 1830, ASSU Archives; "Journal 'R. D. Hall,' Essay #14, Part 2," 65ff., a transcription prepared for Kenneth S. LaTourette, American Bible Society Library, New York City. Judging from this journal and others, the Bible Society agents were particularly eager to obtain support from the local gentry. See also John W. Quist, "Slaveholding Operatives of the Benevolent Empire: Bible, Tract, and Sunday School Societies in Antebellum Tuscaloosa, County, Alabama," *Journal of Southern History* 52 (August 1996): 481–526.

79. Endith to Porter, 18 February 1828, ASSU Archives; Barbara Bellows, *Benevolence among Slaveholders: Assisting the Poor in Charleston, 1670–1860* (Baton Rouge: Louisiana State University Press, 1993), 32–33.

80. Ebenezer Carter Tracy, *Memoir of the Life of Jeremiah Evarts* (Boston: Crocker and Brewster, 1845), 196; Richard Hooker to Porter, 19, 31 May, 19 June, 1830; W. A. N. Campbell to Porter, 18 January 1830, ASSU Archives.

81. McCauley, *Appalachian Mountain Religion*, 26.

82. Basil Manly to Basil Manly Jr., 23 September 1844, in Quist, *Restless Visionaries*, 99–100 n. 138.

83. Patterson, *Sound of the Dove*, 71.

84. See Marion Pearsall, *Little Smoky Ridge: The Natural History of a Southern Appalachian Neighborhood* (University: University of Alabama Press, 1959); Elmora Messer Matthews, *Neighbor and Kin: Life in a Tennessee Ridge Community* (Nashville: Vanderbilt University Press, 1965).

85. See Bertram Wyatt-Brown, *Southern Honor: Ethics and Behavior in the Old South* (New York: Oxford University Press, 1982), chap. 16; Christopher S. Waldrep, " 'So Much Sin': The Decline of Religious Discipline and the 'Tidal Wave of Crime,' " *Journal of Social History* 23 (Spring 1990): 535–52; also a communication by e-mail from Christopher Waldrep, 24 March 1999. I am indebted to Professor Waldrep for his insights.

86. Robert A. Baker, *The Southern Baptist Convention and Its People, 1607–1972* (Nashville: Broadman Press, 1974), 150.

87. Owen, *Sacred Flame of Love*, 36–37.

88. *History of the Baptist Denomination in Georgia*, 337–43; Wilson Lumpkin, *The Removal of the Cherokee Indians from Georgia, Including His Speeches in the United States Congress on the Indian Question*, 2 vols. (New York: Dodd, Mead, 1907), 1:68–69; Leland Winfield Meyer, *The Life and Times of Colonel Richard M. Johnson of Kentucky* (New York: Columbia University Press, 1932), 256–63, 379–86; and Bertram Wyatt-Brown, "Prelude to Abolitionism: Sabbatarian Politics and the Rise of the Second Party System," *Journal of American History* 58 (September 1971): 316–41.

89. Holcombe, *History of the Rise and Progress of Baptists in Alabama*, 62. Mathews, *Slavery and Methodism*, pursues this question well; see esp. 170–73. See also Winthrop D. Jordan, *White over Black: American Attitudes toward the Negro, 1550–1812* (Chapel Hill: University of North Carolina Press, 1968), 365–74; *History of the Baptist Denomination in Georgia*, 171.

90. Crowley, *Primitive Baptists of the Wiregrass South*, 51–52.

91. McCauley, *Appalachian Mountain Religion*, 6.

CHAPTER SIX

1. I have in mind Eugene D. Genovese, *"Slavery Ordained of God": The Southern Slaveholders' View of Biblical History and Modern Politics* (Gettysburg, Pa.: Gettysburg College, 1985); Genovese, "Religious and Economic Thought in the Proslavery Argument," *Essays in Economic and Business History* 15 (1997): 1–9; Genovese, "Religion and the Collapse of the American Union," in *Religion and the American Civil War*, ed. Randall Miller and Charles Reagan Wilson (New York: Oxford University Press, 1997), 1–10; Kenneth M. Stampp, *The Root of All Evil: The Protestant Clergy and the Economic Mind of the Old South* (Athens: University of Georgia Press, 1997); Mitchell Snay, *The Gospel of Disunion: Religion and Separatism in the Antebellum South* (New York: Cambridge University Press, 1993), among other works.

2. Quoted in Virgil S. Davis, "Stephen Elliott: A Southern Bishop in Peace and War" (Ph.D. diss., University of Georgia, 1964), 218.

3. Samuel S. Hill, *Southern Churches in Crisis Revisited* (University: University of Alabama Press, 1999), 30.

4. Beth Barton Schweiger, *The Gospel Working Up: Progress and the Pulpit in Nineteenth-Century Virginia* (New York: Oxford University Press, 2000), 84.

5. In addition to the works already cited, other examples of Eugene D. Genovese's thinking on this matter include *A Consuming Fire: The Fall of the Confederacy in the Mind of the White Christian South* (Athens: University of Georgia Press, 1998), *The Southern Tradition: The Achievement and Limitations of an American Conservatism* (Cambridge, Mass.: Harvard University Press, 1994), and *The Slaveholder's Dilemma: Freedom and Progress in Southern Conservative Thought, 1820–1860* (Columbia: University of South Carolina Press, 1992).

6. Rev. Richard Fuller and Rev. Francis Wayland, *Domestic Slavery Considered as a Scriptural Institution* (New York: Lewis Colby, 1845).

7. There were, of course, some Southerners opposed to slavery, and the major denominations had at one time considered it a moral evil; declensions from Revolutionary zeal and Enlightenment principles, however, were at least partly a result of an appearance of evangelical practice in slave management, not just crass expediency. On Southern antislavery, see Carl N. Degler, *The Other South: Southern Dissenters in the Nineteenth Century* (New York: Harper & Row, 1974), and *Memoirs of Samuel M. Janney* (Philadelphia: Friends' Book Association, 1881), 28–29, 92. Admissions of "guilt" sometimes appeared in proslavery writings, but usually as a rhetorical device; see, for instance, Albert T. Bledsoe, *An Essay on Liberty and Slavery* (Philadelphia: Lippincott, 1856), 12. This issue is well explored in two works: Eugene D. Genovese, *The World the Slaveholders Made: Two Essays in Interpretation* (New York: Harper & Row, 1988), 144–50, and Dickson D. Bruce Jr., *Violence and Culture in the Antebellum South* (Austin: University of Texas Press, 1979), 114–36.

8. Henry Hughes, "New Duties of the South," *Port Gibson* (Miss.) *Southern Reveille*, 18 November 1854, clipping, Henry Hughes Scrapbook, MDAH. Ideological instruction of young people was a universal concern in the Victorian era; see also William A. Smith, *Lectures on the Philosophy and Practice of Slavery* (Nashville, Tenn.: Stevenson and Evans, 1856), 15, 17, 18, 26. The best summary, though largely uninterpretive, is William Sumner Jenkins, *Pro-Slavery Thought in the Old South* (Chapel Hill: University of North Carolina Press, 1935).

9. A very suggestive analysis of Alabama's ambivalent response to institutional modernization is found in J. Mills Thornton III, *Politics and Power in a Slave Society: Alabama, 1800–1860* (Baton Rouge: Louisiana State University Press, 1978); also see the persuasive reinterpretation of Jacksonian politics in William J. Cooper Jr., *The South and the Politics of Slavery, 1828–1856* (Baton Rouge: Louisiana State University Press, 1978).

10. Quotation from Robin Mayhead, *Walter Scott* (Cambridge, Eng.: Cambridge University Press, 1973), 43; see also David Daiches, "Scott's Achievement as a Novelist," in *Walter Scott*, ed. D. D. Devlin (Nashville, Tenn.: Aurora, 1970), 37; Grace W. Landtrim, "Sir Walter Scott and His Literary Rivals in the Old South," *American Literature* 2 (November 1930): 256–76; David Daiches, "Scott and Scotland," in *Scott Bicentenary Essays: Selected Papers Read at the Sir Walter Scott Bicentenary Conference*, ed. Alan Bell (Edinburgh: Scottish Academic Press, 1973), 38–60. On Scots-Irish ethnicity, see George Tucker, *The Valley of Shenandoah; Or, Memoirs of the Graysons* (1824; reprint, Chapel Hill: University of North Carolina Press, 1970), 47–58. Marcus Cunliffe, *Chattel Slavery and Wage Slavery: The Anglo-American Context, 1830–1860* (Athens: University of Georgia Press, 1979).

11. George Fitzhugh, "Southern Thoughts," *De Bow's Review* 23 (October 1857): 337. See William Harper, "Harper on Slavery," in *The Pro-Slavery Argument, as Maintained by the Most Distinguished Writers of the Southern States . . .* (Charleston: Walker, Richards, 1852), 1–2, passim; see also James H. Hammond, "Slavery in the Light

of Political Science," in *Cotton Is King, and Pro-Slavery Arguments* . . . , ed. E. N. Elliott (Augusta, Ga.: Pritchard, Abbott & Loomis, 1860), 647; cf. Genovese, *World the Slaveholders Made*, 158. Genovese claims that proslavery writers had to justify the system against "the whole social, ethical, political, and economic philosophy of the day." Victorian philosophies were very wide-ranging, and one could argue that authoritarianism and conservatism were as much a part of intellectual baggage as democracy and liberalism. After all, the South did not lack for defenders, who admired the policing, curfew, antiliquor regulations, and other suppressions of Southern blacks that contrasted with the "chaos" and degradation of the urban poor elsewhere. See Nehemiah Adams, D.D., *A South-side View of Slavery; Or Three Months at the South, in 1854* (Boston: T. R. Marvin, 1854), and consider, too, the observations of British travelers like Sir Charles Lyell and others, conveniently summarized in J. D. B. De Bow, *The Industrial Resources, Etc. of the Southern and Western States* . . . , (3 vols. (New Orleans: Office of *De Bow's Review*, 1852–53), 3:62–70.

12. Edward J. Pringle of South Carolina put the matter in these words: "One object in this [essay] has been not so much to answer the objections of the opponents of slavery, as to prove for the slaveholder that his dependent laborer is capable of better things than the world would have him believe, and especially to remind him that whatever arguments he urges in favor of the slave's position are all of necessity so many pledges for the faithful discharge of his own duties" (Edward J. Pringle, *Slavery in the Southern States*, 3d ed. [Cambridge: J. Bartlett, 1853], 43).

13. For example, David M. Erskine, an English visitor, reported that in Norfolk in 1798, "it is not at all uncommon for a white to keep blacks to let out as horses are in England." Quoted in Robert McColley, *Slavery and Jeffersonian Virginia* (Charlottesville: University Press of Virginia, 1964), 58.

14. Gerald W. Mullin, *Flight and Rebellion: Slave Resistance in Eighteenth-Century Virginia* (New York: Oxford University Press, 1972); Peter H. Wood, *Black Majority: Negroes in Colonial South Carolina from 1670 through the Stono Rebellion* (New York: Knopf, 1974); Richard B. Sheridan, *Sugar and Slavery: An Economic History of the British West Indies, 1623–1775* (Baltimore: Johns Hopkins University Press, 1974); and Winthrop D. Jordan, *White over Black: American Attitudes toward the Negro, 1550–1812* (Chapel Hill: published for the Institute of Early American History and Culture at Williamsburg, Va., by the University of North Carolina Press, 1968). For a historiographical overview of early black history, see Peter H. Wood, " 'I Did the Best I Could for My Day': The Study of Early Black History during the Second Reconstruction, 1960 to 1976," *William and Mary Quarterly* 3d ser., 35 (April 1978): 185–225, and Allan Kulikoff, "The Origins of Afro-American Society in Tidewater Maryland and Virginia, 1700 to 1790," ibid., 226–59.

15. The negative reference approach to self-identity is evident in the Christian slaveholder as well as in the teetotaler: Charles C. Jones Jr., for instance, wrote his pious father of a decision not to settle his blacks in Bryan County, owing to "the character of the region, the semi-barbaric tone in morals and religion, the charac-

ter of the treatment to which Negroes are there subjected, the esteem in which they are held" (Jones to Charles Colcock Jones, 26 December 1859, *The Children of Pride: A True Story of Georgia and the Civil War*, ed. Robert Manson Myers [New Haven: Yale University Press, 1972], 551).

16. Professor Rose kindly lent me a draft of her paper, "The Domestication of Domestic Slavery," delivered at the Charles Warren Center, Harvard University, Spring 1974; this interesting essay clarifies the issue of slavery's evolution.

17. The Reverend R. G. Grundy, "Thoughts for the People—No. 9," *Memphis Bulletin*, 19 October 1862, a reference given to me by John Cimprich.

18. James L. Petigru to his daughter, Jane North, 14 December 1835, transcription, James L. Petigru MSS, Library of Congress. Like Harriet Beecher Stowe's Shelby family in *Uncle Tom's Cabin*, however, Petigru was classically improvident, which circumstance led to the breakup of slave families, a situation Southern pietists invariably lamented as a fall from God's grace. See William R. Taylor, *Cavalier and Yankee: The Old South and American National Character* (New York: Braziller, 1961), 285–94.

19. Emmet F. Horine, ed., *Dr. Daniel Drake's Letters on Slavery to Dr. John C. Warren, of Boston . . .* (1851; reprint, New York: Schuman, 1940), 7; Robert William Fogel and Stanley L. Engerman, *Time on the Cross: The Economics of American Negro Slavery* (Boston: Little, Brown, 1974). "Practicality" was a key word in the proslavery vocabulary; see Smith, *Lectures*, 26.

20. John C. Hurd, *The Law of Freedom and Bondage in the United States*, 2 vols. (Boston: Little, Brown, 1862), 2:94, 98, 107. See also Edward R. Laurens, *A Letter to the Hon. Whitemarsh Seabrook, of St. John's Colleton: In Explanation and Defence of an Act to Amend the Law in Relation to Slaves and Free Persons of Color* (Charleston: Observer Office Press, 1835), 9–10; Rosser H. Taylor, "Humanizing the Slave Code of North Carolina," *North Carolina Historical Review* 2 (July 1925): 323–31.

21. Dale A. Somers, "Black and White in New Orleans: A Study in Urban Race Relations, 1865–1900," *Journal of Southern History* 40 (February 1974): 19–42; Richard C. Wade, *Slavery in the Cities: The South, 1820–1860* (New York: Oxford University Press, 1964), 97–110.

22. For examples, see Hurd, *Law of Freedom and Bondage*, 2:85, 91, 104, 106–7; Ivan E. McDougle, *Slavery in Kentucky, 1792–1865* (Lancaster, Pa.: Press of the New Era Printing Co., 1918), 36; Eugene D. Genovese, *Roll, Jordan, Roll: The World the Slaves Made* (New York: Pantheon Books, 1974), 37–39, 42.

23. Daniel J. Flanigan, "Criminal Procedure in Slave Trials in the Antebellum South," *Journal of Southern History* 40 (November 1974): 537–64, and "The Criminal Law of Slavery and Freedom, 1800–1868" (Ph.D. diss., Rice University, 1973). The author points out in "Criminal Procedure," 546 n. 26, that slaves had better rights of appeal than an Englishman convicted of a felony (until 1907). The legal situation in the total context of Southern justice was much more complex than Genovese indicates in his otherwise remarkable work, *Roll, Jordan, Roll* (see esp. 43–49). On the professionalizing of Southern legal life, see Daniel H. Calhoun, *Professional Lives in*

America: Structure and Aspiration, 1750–1850 (Cambridge, Mass.: Harvard University Press, 1965), 59–87.

24. Charles C. Jones to Charles C. Jones Jr., 10 December 1859, *Children of Pride,* 545; Jones to Jones Sr., 12 December 1859, ibid., 546.

25. Genovese, *World the Slaveholders Made,* 228–34.

26. See Bertram Wyatt-Brown, *Southern Honor: Ethics and Behavior in the Old South* (New York: Oxford University Press, 1982), and "The Ideal Typology and Ante-Bellum Southern History: A Testing of a New Approach," *Societas* 5 (Winter 1975): 16–22.

27. The closing of the foreign slave trade on 1 January 1808, by the act of 1807, granted a boon to the defense of slavery by removing an indefensible, inhuman aspect of the system.

28. Frank E. Vandiver, "The Southerner as Extremist," in *The Idea of the South: Pursuit of a Central Theme,* ed. Vandiver (Chicago: Published for William Marsh Rice University by the University of Chicago Press, 1964), 45.

29. A good summary, despite the obvious bias, is found in the Reverend James H. McNeilly, D.D., *Religion and Slavery: A Vindication of the Southern Churches* (Nashville: Smith and Lamar, 1911), 12–14. For a contemporary summary, see *Natchez* (Miss.) *Courier,* 3 September 1835, and Albert G. Seal, ed., "Notes and Documents: Letters from the South, A Mississippian's Defense of Slavery," *Journal of Mississippi History* 2 (October 1940): 212–31.

30. Jeremiah Jeter, quoted in Anne C. Loveland, *Southern Evangelicals and the Social Order, 1800–1860* (Baton Rouge: Louisiana State University Press, 1980), 186.

31. James McBride Dabney, *Who Speaks for the South?* (New York: Funk and Wagnalls, 1964), 225–26.

32. Benjamin M. Palmer, as quoted in Jenkins, *Pro-Slavery Thought,* 216; David Ewart, *A Scriptural View of the Moral Relations of African Slavery* (Charleston: Walker, Evans, 1859), 9, 11; Rev. W. T. Hamilton, D.D., *The Duties of Masters and Slaves Respectively, or, Domestic Servitude as Sanctioned by the Bible: A Discourse Delivered in the Government Street Church, Mobile, Ala.* (Mobile, Ala.: F. H. Brooks, 1845), 14; Rev. J. H. Thornwell, D.D., *The Rights and the Duties of Masters: A Sermon Preached at the Dedication of a Church Erected in Charleston, S.C., for the Benefit and Instruction of the Coloured Population* (Charleston: Walker & James, 1850), 31. See Larry E. Tise, *Proslavery: A History of the Defense of Slavery in America, 1701–1840* (Athens: University of Georgia Press, 1987). Tise argues that most spokesmen for slavery were Yankee or Yankee-trained clergymen. The point demonstrates that slavery was so ingrained in white mores that it required little rationalization until the more literate culture of the North influenced Southern styles of thinking and argumentation. Yale and other schools trained students in rhetoric; that such techniques would be applied in such conservative causes as proslavery polemics is not as surprising as it might appear.

33. Charles C. Jones, *The Religious Instruction of the Negroes in the United States* (Savannah, Ga.: T. Purse, 1842), 227: "The churches are composed of households: parents and children, masters and servants."

34. Lucy Kenny ["A Lady of Fredericksburg, Virginia"], *A Death Blow to the Principles of Abolition* (183–[?]; reprint, Washington, D.C.: Lost Cause Press, 19—[?]), 4; see also Nathaniel Bowen, D.D., *A Pastoral Letter, on the Religious Instruction of the Slaves of Members of the Protestant Episcopal Church in the State of South-Carolina* (Charleston: A. E. Miller, 1835), 4, 6–7; Jones, *Religious Instruction*, 110.

35. Pringle, *Slavery in the Southern States*, 17.

36. Patricia Hickin, " 'Situation Ethics' and Antislavery Attitudes in the Virginia Churches," in *America, The Middle Period: Essays in Honor of Bernard Mayo*, ed. John B. Boles (Charlottesville: University Press of Virginia, 1973), 188–215.

37. Grundy, *Memphis Bulletin*, 19 October 1862.

38. C. G. Memminger, *Lecture Delivered before the Young Men's Library Association, of Augusta, April 10th, 1851* (Augusta, Ga.: Printed by W. S. Jones, 1851), 14.

39. Philip J. Greven Jr., comp., *Child-Rearing Concepts, 1628–1861: Historical Sources* (Itasca, Ill.: F. E. Peacock, 1973); Ronald G. Walters, *Primers for Prudery: Sexual Advice to Victorian America* (Englewood Cliffs, N.J.: Prentice-Hall, 1973); Bernard Wishy, *The Child and the Republic: The Dawn of Modern American Child Nurture* (Philadelphia: University of Pennsylvania Press, 1972).

40. Of course, this advice was not confined to pietists: see Charles D. Lowery, "James Barbour, a Progressive Farmer of Antebellum Virginia," in *America*, ed. Boles, 178–79, for example.

41. Jones, *Religious Instruction*, 241–42.

42. Legal and social changes in attitudes about corporal penalties were much slower in the South than in the North, but the disciplinary transition was under way before 1861.

43. William Gilmore Simms, "The Morals of Slavery," in *The Pro-Slavery Argument, as Maintained by the Most Distinguished Writers of the Southern States . . .* (Charleston: Walker, Richards, 1852), 275; Thomas S. Clay, *Detail of a Plan for the Moral Improvement of Negroes on Plantations. Read before the Georgia Presbytery* (N.p., 1833), 10–21; Calvin H. Wiley, "The Art of Governing," a chapter in "The Christian Duty of Masters," Calvin H. Wiley MSS, SHC, UNC; Horine, ed., *Drake's Letters*, 17; Eugene D. Genovese, *A Consuming Fire: The Fall of the Confederacy in the Mind of the White Christian South* (Athens: University of Georgia Press, 1998), 5.

44. Quoted in Robert B. Forbes, "Slavery and the Evangelical Enlightenment," in John R. McKivigan and Mitchell Snay, eds., *Religion and the Antebellum Debate over Slavery* (Athens: University of Georgia Press, 1998), 70.

45. Marcus J. Borg, *Conflict, Holiness, and Politics in the Teachings of Jesus* (New York: Edward Mellen, 1984); Jerome Neyrey, "The Idea of Purity in Mark," *Semeia* 35 (February 1986): 91–128; William Countryman, *Dirt, Greed and Sex* (Minneapolis: Fortress Press, 1989); Mary Douglas, *Purity and Danger* (London: Routledge and Kegan Paul, 1966).

46. George Bourne, *The Book and Slavery Irreconcilable* (Philadelphia: J. M. Sanderson, 1816), 25.

47. Katherine L. Dvorak, "After Apocalypse, Moses," in *Masters and Slaves in the*

House of the Lord: Race and Religion in the American South, 1740–1870, ed. John B. Boles (Lexington: University Press of Kentucky, 1988), 175.

48. Fuller and Wayland, *Domestic Slavery as a Scriptural Institution*, 175–76.

49. Albert Barnes, *An Inquiry into the Scriptural Views of Slavery* (Philadelphia: Parry & McMillan, 1855), 61, 71.

50. Barnes, *An Inquiry*, 358, 359.

51. Albert Taylor Bledsoe, *An Essay on Liberty and Slavery* (Philadelphia: Lippincott, 1856), 198–216.

52. Jon Butler, *Awash in a Sea of Faith: Christianizing the American People* (Cambridge, Mass.: Harvard University Press, 1990), 274–77; Donald G. Mathews, *Religion in the Old South* (Chicago: University of Chicago Press, 1974), 158.

53. See Ralph T. Parkinson, "The Religious Instruction of Slaves, 1820–1860" (M.A. thesis, University of North Carolina, 1948), 13–15; Fuller and Wayland, *Domestic Slavery*, 143.

54. Quotation in David T. Bailey, *Shadow on the Church: Southwestern Evangelical Religion and the Issue of Slavery, 1783–1860* (Ithaca, N.Y.: Cornell University Press, 1985), 129. See Donald G. Mathews, "Reform in the Old South: Charles Colcock Jones and the Southern Evangelical Crusade to Form a Biracial Community," *Journal of Southern History* 41 (August 1975): 299–320; see also Mathews's classic work *Religion in the Old South* (Chicago: University of Chicago Press, 1977), 137–50. Charles Colcock Jones, *The Religious Instruction of the Negroes in the United States* (1842; reprint, New York: Negro Universities Press, 1969); David Christy, *Pulpit Politics; Or, Ecclesiastical Legislation on Slavery, in Its Disturbing Influences on the American Union* (1862; reprint, New York: Negro Universities Press, 1969).

55. Calvin H. Wiley, "Christian Duty of Masters," Wiley MSS, SHC, UNC; the Reverend Thornton Stringfellow, "The Bible Argument," in *Cotton Is King, and Pro-Slavery Arguments . . .* , ed. E. N. Elliott (Augusta, Ga.: Pritchard, Abbott & Loomis, 1860), 522; George F. Holmes, "A Key to *Uncle Tom's Cabin*," *Southern Literary Messenger* 19 (June 1853): 321–30, esp. 324; [Edwin C. Holland], *A Refutation of the Calumnies Circulated against the Southern and Western States, Respecting the Institution and Existence of Slavery among Them* (Charleston: A. E. Miller, 1822), 46.

56. Jones, *Religious Instruction*, 175–205; Frances A. Cabaniss and James A. Cabaniss, "Religion in Ante-Bellum Mississippi," *Journal of Mississippi History* 6 (October 1944): 191–224; Clay, *Detail of a Plan*, 20; C. F. Sturgis, *Melville Letters, or, The Duties of Masters to Their Servants* (Charleston: Southern Baptist Publication Society, 1851), 54.

57. Hamilton, *Duties of Masters and Slaves*, 22, 23; the Reverend James A. Lyon, quoted in James Pilar, "Religious and Cultural Life, 1817–1860," in *A History of Mississippi*, ed. Richard A. McLemore (Jackson: University Press of Mississippi, 1973), 409. See also Pringle, *Slavery in the Southern States*, 34.

58. See James H. Otey, "The Duty of Ministers of the Gospel to Their People, Considered in Their Civil Relations, Primary Charge to the Clergy, October 11, 1837, Nashville Diocesan Convention," in appendix of Rt. Rev. William Mercer

Green, *Memoir of Rt. Rev. James Hervey Otey, D.D., LL.D., the First Bishop of Tennessee* (New York: J. Pott, 1885), 194–210; see also Jenkins, *Pro-Slavery Thought*, 208–10.

59. Hammond in Elliott, ed., *Cotton Is King*, 651.

60. George F. Simmons, *Two Sermons on the Kind Treatment and on the Emancipation of Slaves. Preached at Mobile, on Sunday the 10th, and Sunday the 17th of May, 1840* (Boston: W. Crosby, 1840), 23.

61. Thornwell, *Rights and Duties of Masters*, 12. Freehling, *Prelude to Civil War*, 80–81, suggests that in the 1820s there was hesitation at calling slavery a "positive good," a posture that died out in South Carolina, he says, later on. But Presbyterians, particularly, had to be careful to avoid labeling any human institution perfect; otherwise the doctrine of Adamic sin would be lost. Thus one continues to find qualifications. Wiley, in his lengthy essay on Christian slaveholding, devoted a chapter to the origins of slavery in "sin" (Wiley MSS, SHC, UNC). See Theodore D. Bozeman, "Science, Nature and Society: A New Approach to James Henley Thornwell," *Journal of Presbyterian History* 50 (Winter 1972): 307–25; also Drew G. Faust, "Evangelicalism and the Meaning of the Proslavery Argument: The Reverend Thornton Stringfellow of Virginia," *Virginia Magazine of History and Biography* 85 (January 1977): 3–17; William B. Gravely, "Methodist Preachers, Slavery and Caste: Types of Social Concern in Antebellum America," *Duke Divinity School Review* 34 (Autumn 1969): 209–29; Anne C. Loveland, "Richard Furman's 'Questions on Slavery,'" *Baptist History and Heritage* 10 (July 1975): 177–81; Jack Maddex, "Proslavery Millennialism: Social Eschatology in Antebellum Southern Calvinism," *American Quarterly* 31 (Spring 1979): 46–62; and Thomas Virgil Peterson, *Ham and Japheth: The Mythic World of Whites in the Antebellum South* (Metuchen, N.J.: Scarecrow Press, 1978), 111–14. Wilson is quoted in Robert Bober, "The Young Woodrow Wilson, A Study of the Formative Years" (Ph.D. diss., Case Western Reserve University, 1980).

62. See Donald G. Mathews, *Slavery and Methodism: A Chapter in American Morality, 1780–1845* (Princeton: Princeton University Press, 1965), 67–87, and "Reform in the Old South," 299–320; McNeilly, *Religion and Slavery*, 34–37; Jones, *Religious Instruction*, 1–110. H. Shelton Smith, *In His Image, but Racism in Religion, 1780–1910* (Durham, N.C.: Duke University Press, 1972), 153–54, wrongly, I think, causally connects the mission to slaves with the tightening of controls, whereas the religious effort reflected a growing institutionalization of Southern life, a transformation that was under way in many other areas of regional experience.

63. Douglas Ambrose, *Henry Hughes and Proslavery Thought in the Old South* (Baton Rouge: Louisiana State University Press, 1996), 1–37.

64. Ibid., 51–52.

65. Entry for Henry Hughes, *Dictionary of American Biography*, ed. Allen Johnson et al. (New York: Scribner, 1932), 9:350; Henry Hughes, *Treatise on Sociology, Theoretical and Practical* (1854; reprint, New York: Negro Universities Press, 1968).

66. Entry for 28 January 1849, Henry Hughes Diary (transcription), 56, MDAH. Except for this early diary, 1 January 1848–1 May 1853, and a scrapbook, all of Hughes's papers have disappeared.

67. Ibid., 24 October 1852 (220). Hughes apparently studied architecture, sculpture, painting, social science, anatomy, chemistry, ancient and modern languages and literature, and moral philosophy, in France and Italy, as well as law, in New Orleans.

68. See Bertram Wyatt-Brown, "Conscience and Career: Young Abolitionists and Missionaries," in *Religion, Reform, and Anti-Slavery: Essays in Memory of Roger Anstey*, ed. Seymour Drescher and Christine Bolt (Folkstone, Eng.: Archon, 1980), 183–203, and "John Brown and Weathermen: The Antinomian Impulse in American Radicalism," *Soundings* 58 (Spring 1975): 417–40; Michael Fellman, *The Unbounded Frame: Freedom and Community in Nineteenth Century American Utopianism* (Westport, Conn.: Greenwood Press, 1973), 42–61.

69. Kraditor, "American Radical Historians," 136–52.

70. Hughes, "New Duties of the South," *Port Gibson* (Miss.) *Southern Reveille*, 18 November 1854, Henry Hughes Scrapbook, MDAH.

71. *Southern Commercial Convention, Vicksburg, Miss. A Report on the African Apprenticeship System, Read at the Southern Commercial Convention by Henry Hughes. Held at Vicksburg, May 10th, 1859* (Vicksburg, Miss.: Whig, 1859), 2.

72. Ibid., 2–3, 12.

73. Hughes, *Treatise on Sociology*, 91.

74. Rev. W. D. Moore, *The Life and Works of Col. Henry Hughes: A Funeral Sermon, Preached in the Methodist Episcopal Church, Port Gibson, Miss., October 26th, 1862* (Mobile, Ala.: Farrow & Dennett, 1863), 28–31. Josiah Nott of Mobile, exponent of "scientific" explanations for black inferiority, also opposed revealed religion. See William Stanton, *The Leopard's Spots: Scientific Attitudes toward Race in America, 1815–59* (Chicago: University of Chicago Press, 1960), 120–21; Ronald T. Takaki, *A Pro-Slavery Crusade: The Agitation to Reopen the African Slave Trade* (New York: Free Press, 1971).

75. Hughes, *Treatise on Sociology*, 110, 113, 256. See also Genovese, *World the Slaveholders Made*, 167.

76. An example of his Positivist style, much resembling the French tradition of epigrammatic abstractionism, is, "Subordination is not slavery; ethical segregation is not ethical degradation. For the duties coupled to the relation of races, must be actualized. Purity of race, is right" (Hughes, *Treatise on Sociology*, 243).

77. Ibid., 350–55.

78. Hughes, in *Port Gibson* (Miss.) *Southern Reveille*, 30 July 1859, clipping, Henry Hughes Scrapbook, MDAH; Hughes, *Treatise on Sociology*, 69, 73, 258.

79. Otto H. Olsen, "Historians and the Extent of Slave Ownership in the Southern United States," *Civil War History* 18 (June 1972): 101–17; Gavin Wright, *The Political Economy of the Cotton South: Households, Markets, and Wealth in the Nineteenth Century* (New York: Norton, 1978), 83–84.

80. Hughes, "Warranteeism and Free Labor," *Jackson* (Miss.) *Eagle of the South*, 28 March 1859, and "Re-Opening of the Slave Trade," *Port Gibson* (Miss.) *Southern Reveille*, 30 July 1859, Henry Hughes Scrapbook, MDAH.

81. William L. Yancey of Alabama and John A. Quitman of Mississippi were two other leaders in the African scheme. Hughes admired them both. See Hughes, "Letter from Montgomery," *New Orleans Delta*, 19 May 1858, and "Eulogy of Quitman . . . August 26, 1858," [*Port Gibson* (Miss.) *Southern Reveille*, n.d.], Henry Hughes Scrapbook, MDAH.

82. Hughes, "A Quartette of Objections to African Labor Immigration," 9 March 1858, Henry Hughes Scrapbook, MDAH. See also Stella Herron, "The African Apprentice Bill," in *Proceedings of the Mississippi Valley Historical Association, for the Year 1914–15* (Cedar Rapids, Iowa: Torch Press, 1916), 135–45.

83. Hughes, "Negro Mechanics," *Jackson* (Miss.) *Eagle of the South*, 16 October 1858, Henry Hughes Scrapbook, MDAH; *Treatise on Sociology*, 112; *Southern Commercial Convention*, 14; "Large Slaveholders and the African Immigration Scheme," *New Orleans Delta*, 14 February 1858, Henry Hughes Scrapbook, MDAH.

84. Hughes, *Treatise on Sociology*, 199–200, 253–54: under his scheme, slaves would have been "warranted" a sufficiency of household utensils, furniture, medicines, medical services, religious and educational opportunities, entertainments and recreational activity, as well as the additional legal right to sue for damages. Quotation from *Southern Commercial Convention*, 12.

85. Hughes, "Compensation for Executed Slaves," *Port Gibson* (Miss.) *Herald*, 18 June 1856, Henry Hughes Scrapbook, MDAH.

86. See De Bow, *Industrial Resources*, 11, 233; Hughes, "Re-Opening of the Slave Trade."

87. Moore, *Life and Works*, 9, 10, 17.

88. Ibid., 30–31.

89. Ibid., 13–14.

90. Genovese, *World the Slaveholders Made*, 227–29, draws an interesting analogy between the Prussian state and the South, but South Africa may be a closer parallel. See George M. Fredrickson, *White Supremacy: A Comparative Study in American and South African History* (New York: Oxford University Press, 1981).

91. C. Vann Woodward, *The Strange Career of Jim Crow*, 2d rev. ed. (New York: Oxford University Press, 1966), 111–12, 121–22.

92. Moore, *Life and Works*, 35.

CHAPTER SEVEN

1. See Bertram Wyatt-Brown, *Yankee Saints and Southern Sinners* (Baton Rouge: Louisiana State University Press, 1985), 183–213.

2. See Mitchell Snay, *Gospel of Disunion: Religion and Separatism in the Antebellum South* (New York: Cambridge University Press, 1993); Drew Gilpin Faust, *The Creation of Confederate Nationalism: Ideology and Identity in the Civil War South* (Baton Rouge: Louisiana State University Press, 1988); James W. Silver, *Confederate Morale and Church Propaganda* (New York: Norton, 1957).

3. Donald G. Mathews, *Slavery and Methodism: A Chapter in American Morality, 1780–*

1845 (Princeton: Princeton University Press, 1965); Robert M. Calhoon, *Evangelicals and Conservatives in the Early South, 1740–1861* (Columbia: University of South Carolina Press, 1988); C. C. Goen, *Broken Churches, Broken Nation: Denominational Schisms and the Coming of the Civil War* (Macon, Ga.: Mercer University Press, 1985); John McKivigan, *The War against Proslavery Religion: Abolitionism and the Northern Churches, 1830–1865* (Ithaca, N.Y.: Cornell University Press, 1984).

4. Sydney Ahlstrom, *Religious History of the American People* (New Haven: Yale University Press, 1972), 672.

5. James Henley Thornwell, quoted in David B. Chesebrough, ed., *"God Ordained This War": Sermons on the Sectional Crisis, 1830–1865* (Columbia: University of South Carolina Press, 1991), 144.

6. Witt quoted in Beth Barton Schweiger, *The Gospel Working Up: Progress and the Pulpit in Nineteenth-Century Virginia* (New York: Oxford University Press, 2000), 88; Goen, *Broken Churches*, 169.

7. See Larry Edward Tise, *Proslavery: A History of the Defense of Slavery in America, 1701–1840* (Athens: University of Georgia Press, 1987), 143; Charles G. Sellers, "The Travail of Slavery," in *The Southerner as American*, by John Hope Franklin et al., ed. Charles G. Sellers (Chapel Hill: University of North Carolina Press, 1960), 40–71. For an elegant review of this aspect of the proslavery debate in historiography, see Gaines M. Foster, "Guilt over Slavery: A Historiographical Analysis," *Journal of Southern History* 56 (November 1990): 665–94. See also Orlando Patterson, *Slavery as Social Death: A Comparative Study* (Cambridge, Mass.: Harvard University Press, 1982), 262–96, on the meaning or lack of meaning of Southern manumissions.

8. Cf. C. C. Goen, "Broken Churches, Broken Nation: Regional Religion and North-South Alienation in Antebellum America," *Church History* 52 (March 1983): 21–35. Goen argues that "southern church leaders could easily think of themselves as the first line of defense for the South and its way of life" (22). Perhaps so, but on the whole politicians were much more eager to engage the issue than they were.

9. Richard Fuller, quoted in Chesebrough, *"God Ordained This War,"* 144–45.

10. See Laura L. Mitchell, " 'Matters of Justice between Man and Man': Northern Divines, the Bible, and the Fugitive Slave Act of 1850," in *Religion and the Antebellum Debate over Slavery*, ed. John R. McKivigan and Mitchell Snay (Athens: University of Georgia Press, 1998), 134–65, esp. 141–42.

11. Drew Gilpin Faust, "Introduction: The Proslavery Argument in History," in *The Ideology of Slavery: Proslavery Thought in the Antebellum South, 1830–1860*, ed. Faust (Baton Rouge: Louisiana State University Press, 1981), 5–6.

12. Lewis M. Purifoy, "The Southern Methodist Church and the Proslavery Argument," *Journal of Southern History* 32 (August 1966): 325–41; James David Essig, "A Very Wintry Season: Virginia Baptists and Slavery, 1785–1797," *Virginia Magazine of History and Biography* 88 (April 1980): 181; Presbyterian General Assembly, quoted in McKivigan, *War against Proslavery Religion*, 26.

13. James Henley Thornwell, quoted in Goen, *Broken Churches*, 165; second quota-

tion, Thornwell, *The Rights and Duties of Master: A Sermon Preached at the Dedication of a Church, Erected in Charleston, S.C. for the Benefit and Instruction of the Coloured Population* (Charleston: Walker and James, 1850), 31, 32. See also Beth Barton Schweiger, "The Transformation of Southern Religion: Clergy and Congregations in Virginia, 1830–1895" (Ph.D. diss., University of Virginia, 1994), 182; George F. Holmes, quoted in Faust, "Introduction," 10.

14. Nathaniel Beverley Tucker, quoted in Faust, "Introduction," 13; Prof. Tayler Lewis, "Patriarchal and Jewish Servitude No Argument for American Slavery: Published in 'The World' in Reply to the Preceding Sermon of Rev. Henry J. Van Dyke," in *Fast-Day Sermons, Or The Pulpit on the State of the Country* (New York: Rudd & Carleton, 1861), 181–83.

15. Figures derived by Andrew Frank of the University of Florida from the Eighth U.S. Census, 1860. New York clergy numbered 49,597, Pennsylvania 19,208, and in the states of Alabama, Arkansas, Florida, Georgia, Kentucky, Louisiana, Maryland, Mississippi, North Carolina, South Carolina, Tennessee, Texas, and Virginia, a total of 19,803. See also James O. Farmer, *The Metaphysical Confederacy: James Henley Thornwell and the Synthesis of Southern Values* (Macon, Ga.: Mercer University Press, 1986), 12. One must remember, however, that part-time ministries were more common in the Southern and other rural and western states than in the more urbanized North. Nevertheless, the sectional divergences are notable.

16. From the *New York Tribune*, quoted in Bertram Wyatt-Brown, "Proslavery and Antislavery Intellectuals: Class Concepts and Polemical Struggle," in *Antislavery Reconsidered: New Perspectives on the Abolitionists*, ed. Lewis Perry and Michael Fellman (Baton Rouge: Louisiana State University Press, 1979), 310.

17. George Fitzhugh to George Frederick Holmes, 27 March 1855, George Frederick Holmes copybook, Duke University Library, Durham, N.C.; James Henry Hammond, *Gov. Hammond's Letters on Southern Slavery: Addressed to Thomas Clarkson, the English Abolitionist* (Charleston: Walter V. Burke, 1845); Richard Fuller and Francis Wayland, *Domestic Slavery Considered as a Scriptural Institution: In a Correspondence between the Rev. Richard Fuller, of Beaufort, S.C., and the Rev. Francis Wayland, of Providence, R.I.*, rev. ed. (New York, L. Colby: 1845); E. N. Elliott, ed., *Cotton Is King, and Pro-Slavery Arguments: Comprising the Writings of Hammond, Harper, Christy, Stringfellow, Hodge, Bledsoe, and Cartwright* (Augusta, Ga.: Pritchard, Abbott & Loomis, 1860).

18. Rev. Thomas Smyth, D.D., "The War against the South Vindicated," *Southern Presbyterian Review* 15 (April 1863): 481, see also 497, 499.

19. Roy Blount Jr., poster from Atlantic Monthly Press/Little, Brown, available at the Southeast Booksellers' Association meeting, Kissimmee, Florida, 28 September 1994.

20. James Henry Thornwell to Matthew Williams, 26 August 1850, in Benjamin Morgan Palmer, *Life and Letters of James Henley Thornwell, D.D., LL.D.* (Richmond: Whittet & Shepperson, 1875), 344.

21. George Frederick Holmes and James Henry Hammond, quoted in Drew Gil-

pin Faust, *The Sacred Circle: The Dilemma of the Intellectual in the Old South, 1840–1860* (Baltimore: Johns Hopkins University Press, 1977), 48.

22. Faust, *Sacred Circle*, 140.

23. Horace Bushnell, quoted in James H. Moorhead, *American Apocalypse: Yankee Protestants and the Civil War, 1860–1869* (New Haven: Yale University Press, 1978), 93; McKivigan, *War against Proslavery Religion*, 154.

24. J. H. Thornwell, *The State of the Country: An Article Republished from the Southern Presbyterian Review* (Columbia, S.C.: Southern Guardian Steam-Power Press, 1861), 21–22.

25. Ibid., 22.

26. Leonard Bacon, quoted in Jack P. Maddex Jr., " 'The Southern Apostasy' Revisited: The Significance of Proslavery Christianity," *Marxist Perspectives* 2 (Fall 1979): 133; Charles Hodge, "The Bible Argument on Slavery," in *Cotton Is King*, ed. Elliott, 843.

27. Alexander Archibald Hodge, *The Life of Charles Hodge, D.D. LL.D.* (1881; reprint, New York: Arno Press, 1969), 335–36; *Princeton Review* article, quoted in Moorhead, *American Apocalypse*, 89.

28. From the *Boston Courier*, quoted in David Christy, *Pulpit Politics; Or, Ecclesiastical Legislation on Slavery in Its Disturbing Influences on the American Union* (1862; reprint, New York: Negro Universities Press, 1969), 613.

29. Quoted in Hodge, *Charles Hodge*, 334–35. See Goen, *Broken Churches*, 146–47.

30. Hodge, *Charles Hodge*, 333; Lewis G. Vander Velde, *The Presbyterian Churches and the Federal Union, 1861–1869* (Cambridge, Mass.: Harvard University Press, 1932), 34–36.

31. From the *Southern Christian Advocate*, quoted in Anne C. Loveland, *Southern Evangelicals and the Social Order, 1800–1860* (Baton Rouge: Louisiana State University Press, 1980), 117.

32. Loveland, *Southern Evangelicals*, 181.

33. Bertram Wyatt-Brown, *Southern Honor: Ethics and Behavior in the Old South* (New York: Oxford University Press, 1982), 410, and "Religion and the 'Civilizing Process,' in the Early American South, 1600–1860," in *Religion and American Politics: From the Colonial Period to the 1980s*, ed. Mark A. Noll (New York: Oxford University Press, 1990), 172–98; Donald G. Mathews, *Religion in the Old South* (Chicago: University of Chicago Press, 1977), 47 (quotation), 245. See also Suzanne Lebsock, *The Free Women of Petersburg: Status and Culture in a Southern Town, 1784–1860* (New York: Norton, 1984), 226–27.

34. Quoted in Bertram Wyatt-Brown, *Lewis Tappan and the Evangelical War against Slavery* (Cleveland: Case Western Reserve University Press, 1969), 60.

35. George M. Marsden, *The Evangelical Mind and the New School Presbyterian Experience: A Case Study of Thought and Theology in Nineteenth-Century America* (New Haven: Yale University Press, 1970), 26–27.

36. Bertram Wyatt-Brown, "The Abolitionists' Postal Campaign of 1835," *Journal of Negro History* 50 (October 1965): 227–38.

37. Peyton H. Hoge, *Moses Drury Hoge: Life and Letters* (Richmond: Presbyterian Publication Committee, 1899), 143.

38. Farmer, *Metaphysical Confederacy*, 245.

39. James H. Thornwell, quoted in "The Princeton Review on the State of the Country and of the Church," *Biblical Repertory and Princeton Review* 37 (October 1865): 645.

40. Robert L. Dabney, quoted in Hoge, *Moses Drury Hoge*, 139. Virginia Episcopalians reacted in a similar fashion. See Leonard I. Sweet, "The Reaction of the Protestant Episcopal Church in Virginia to the Secession Crisis: October, 1859 to May, 1861," *Historical Magazine of the Protestant Episcopal Church* 4 (June 1972): 137–51.

41. Brooks Hollifield, *The Gentlemen Theologians: American Theology in Southern Culture, 1795–1860* (Durham, N.C.: Duke University Press, 1978), 37.

42. John Cowper Granbery, quoted in Schweiger, "Transformation of Southern Religion," 204–5.

43. James Henley Thornwell to Rev. Dr. Hooper, 8 March 1850, *Life and Letters of James Henley Thornwell*, 477–78; James Henley Thornwell, "Our National Sins: A Sermon Preached in the Presbyterian Church, Columbia, S.C. on the Day of the State Fast, Nov. 21, 1860," in *Fast-Day Sermons; Or, The Pulpit on the State of the Country* (New York: Rudd & Carleton, 1861), 44. Also, Thornwell, quoted in Margaret Burr DesChamps, "Union or Division? South Atlantic Presbyterians and Southern Nationalism, 1820–1861," *Journal of Southern History* 20 (November 1954): 494; Robert L. Dabney, quoted in W. Harrison Daniel, "Southern Presbyterians in the Confederacy," *North Carolina Historical Review* 44 (Summer 1967): 234.

44. James H. Otey to Edward Calohill Burks, 23 November 1860, in James E. Walmsley, ed., "Documents: The Change of Secession Sentiment in Virginia in 1861 [Part II: Letters of James H. Otey to E. C. Burks]," *American Historical Review* 31 (October 1925): 98–99.

45. James H. Otey to Edward Calohill Burks, 23 November 1860, ibid., 98–100.

46. Joseph Blount Cheshire, *The Church in the Confederate States* (New York: Longmans Green, 1912), 11.

47. Joseph D. Cushman, *A Goodly Heritage: The Episcopal Church in Florida, 1821–1892* (Gainesville: University of Florida Press, 1965), 42–44; entry for 4 January 1861, *The Diary of Edmund Ruffin*, Vol. 1, *Toward Independence, October 1856–April 1861*, ed. William Kauffman Scarborough (Baton Rouge: Louisiana State University Press, 1972), 524.

48. Quoted in Cushman, *Goodly Heritage*, 45.

49. See Daniel, "Southern Presbyterians," 232; from the *Central Presbyterian*, quoted in Loveland, *Southern Evangelicals*, 259–60.

50. Rev. Thomas Goulding and Richard P. Cater, quoted in Mitchell Snay, "Gospel of Disunion: Religion and the Rise of Southern Separatism, 1830–1861" (Ph.D. diss., Brandeis University, 1984), 14, 19.

51. "Introduction," McKivigan and Snay, eds., *Religion and the Antebellum Debate over Slavery*, 19.

52. *Central Presbyterian*, quoted in Daniel, "Southern Presbyterians," 231; Rev. Robert Breckinridge, quoted in James C. Klotter, *The Breckinridges of Kentucky, 1760–1981* (Lexington: University Press of Kentucky, 1986), 80; second quotation, Robert J. Breckinridge, "The Union to Be Preserved: A Discourse Delivered at Lexington, Ky., on the Day of the National Fast, Jan. 4, 1861," in *Fast-Day Sermons*, 112.

53. Benjamin M. Palmer, "Slavery a Divine Trust, Duty of the South to Preserve and Perpetuate It: A Sermon Preached in the First Presbyterian Church of New Orleans, La., Nov. 29, 1860," in *Fast-Day Sermons*, 77.

54. Historians will be reminded of the stress on "conditional termination" of slavery that William W. Freehling proposes in *The Road to Disunion: Secessionists at Bay, 1776–1854* (New York: Oxford University Press, 1990), 121–32.

55. Palmer, quoted in *Quarterly Review of the Methodist Episcopal Church—South* 13 (July 1861): 460–61.

56. Jefferson Davis, "Speech at Fayette," 11 July 1851, in *The Papers of Jefferson Davis*, Vol. 4, *1849–1852*, ed. Lynda Lasswell Crist (Baton Rouge: Louisiana State University Press, 1983), 209, 213; Christopher Olsen, "Community, Honor, and Secession in the Deep South: Mississippi's Political Culture, 1840s–1861" (Ph.D. diss., University of Florida, 1997), chap. 2, p. 1; Wyatt-Brown, *Yankee Saints*, 183–213.

57. Evertt W. Huffard, "Biblical Word Study KABOD: 'Honor,' " *Exegete*, 3 (October 1983), 1–5, esp. 3; Johannes Pedersen, *Israel: Its Life and Culture*, 4 vols. (London: Oxford University Press, 1926–40).

58. Paul Friedrich, "Sanity and the Myth of Honor: The Problem of Achilles," *Ethos* 5 (Fall 1977): 285.

59. Quoted by James W. Silver, "The Confederate Preacher Goes to War," *North Carolina Historical Review* 33 (October 1956): 503.

60. Quoted in Goen, *Broken Churches*, 173.

61. Quoted in Silver, "The Confederate Preacher Goes to War," 506.

62. Quoted in Willard E. Wright, "The Churches and the Confederate Cause," *Civil War History* 6 (December 1960): 368.

63. Palmer, "Slavery a Divine Trust," 77, 79.

64. Smyth, "The War against the South Vindicated," 513.

65. Jon G. Appleton, "Samuel Henderson: Southern Minister, Editor, and Crusader, 1853–1866" (M.A. thesis, Auburn University, 1968), 8.

66. Moorhead, *American Apocalypse*, 82.

67. See Schweiger, "Transformation of Southern Religion," chap. 7.

68. Sarah A. Dorsey to Leonidas L. Polk, 20 February 1862, Leonidas L. Polk Papers, Jessie Ball DuPont Memorial Library, University of the South, Sewanee, Tenn.

69. J. Treadwell Davis, "The Presbyterians and the Sectional Conflict," *Southern Quarterly* 8 (January 1970): 124–25.

70. Lewis Harvie, quoted in Drew Gilpin Faust, *The Creation of Confederate Nationalism: Ideology and Identity in the Civil War South* (Baton Rouge: Louisiana State University Press, 1988), 61; see also ibid., 61–62.

71. Smyth, "The War of the South Vindicated," 497–98; see also John William Flinn, ed., *Complete Works of Reverend Thomas Smyth*, 10 vols. (Columbia, S.C.: R. L. Bryan, 1908–12), 7:724–25.

72. Anonymous to Moses D. Hoge, 16 April 1861, in Hoge, *Moses Drury Hoge*, 145.

73. James H. Otey to Edward Calohill Burks, 17 July 1861, in Walmsley, ed., "Documents," 100; Thornwell, quoted in David B. Chesebrough, *"God Ordained This War,"* 196.

74. Thornwell, quoted in Silver, "The Confederate Preacher Goes to War," 504.

75. Thornwell, "Our National Sins," 56.

76. Thornwell, *State of the Country*, 24. See also Mary Jones to the Hon. Charles C. Jones, 3 January 1861, *The Children of Pride: A True Story of Georgia and the Civil War*, ed. Robert Manson Myers (New Haven: Yale University Press, 1972), 641, and Haskell Monroe, "Southern Presbyterians and the Secession Crisis," *Civil War History* 6 (December 1960): 353.

77. Schweiger, "Transformation of Southern Religion," 219–20.

78. See Daniel, "Southern Presbyterians," 236–55.

79. James Henley Thornwell, "Our Danger and Our Duty," in Benjamin Morgan Palmer, *Life and Letters of James Henley Thornwell, D.D., LL.D.* (Richmond: Whittet & Shepperson, 1875), 586 (Appendix II).

80. Sarah A. Dorsey to Leonidas L. Polk, 20 February 1862, Leonidas L. Polk Papers, Jessie Ball DuPont Memorial Library, University of the South, Sewanee, Tenn.

CHAPTER EIGHT

1. The dates of state secessions are as follows: South Carolina, 20 December 1860, Mississippi, 9 January, Florida, 10 January, Alabama, 11 January, Georgia, 19 January Louisiana, 26 January, Texas, 1 February 1861.

2. Quoted in John H. Marchant, "Lawrence M. Keitt, South Carolina Fire-Eater" (Ph.D. diss., University of Virginia, 1976), 343.

3. Albert Gallatin Brown, "The Slave Question," in *Speeches, Messages, and Other Writings of the Hon. Albert G. Brown, A Senator in Congress from the State of Mississippi*, ed. M. W. Cluskey (Philadelphia: Jas. B. Smith & Co., 1859), 164, 168.

4. Cf. Phillip S. Paludan, "The American Civil War Considered a Crisis in Law and Order," *American Historical Review* 77 (October 1972): 1013; William J. Cooper Jr., *The South and the Politics of Slavery, 1828–1856* (Baton Rouge: Louisiana State University Press, 1978), and *Liberty and Slavery: Southern Politics to 1860* (New York: Knopf, 1983).

5. Susan Keitt quoted in Marchant, "Keitt," 348; see also William Howard Russell, *Pictures of Southern Life: Social, Political, and Military* (New York: James G. Gregory, 1861), 5.

6. Quoted in Eric H. Walther, *The Fire-Eaters* (Baton Rouge: Louisiana Sate University Press, 1992), 188.

7. Alexander H. Stephens, "Speech Delivered on the 21st March, 1861, in Savannah, Known as, 'the Corner Stone Speech,'" in Henry Cleveland, *Alexander H. Stephens in Public and Private with Letters and Speeches, before, during and since the War* (Philadelphia: National Publishing Co., 1866), 721.

8. "A Declaration of the Immediate Causes Which Induce and Justify the Secession of the State of Mississippi from the Federal Union," *Journal of the State Convention* copied by Justin Sanders (Jackson, Miss.: E. Barksdale, 1861), 86.

9. State of Georgia, 29 January 1861, U.S. War Department, *The War of the Rebellion: A Compilation of the Official Records of the Union and Confederate Armies*, 128 vols. (Washington, D.C.: U.S. Government Printing Office, 1880–1901), ser. 4, 1:85.

10. Samuel Phillips Day, *Down South; or, An Englishman's Experience at the Seat of the American War* (London: Hurst and Blackett, 1862), 208.

11. Cited in Rollin Gustav Osterweis, *Romanticism and Nationalism in the Old South* (Baton Rouge: Louisiana State University Press, 1967), 123.

12. See William C. Davis, *Jefferson Davis: The Man and His Hour, a Biography* (New York: HarperCollins, 1991), 486.

13. Robert Catlett Cave, *The Men in Gray* (Nashville: Confederate Veteran, 1911), 96.

14. Ibid., 98.

15. Quoted in John Seelye, *Memory's Nation: The Place of Plymouth Rock* (Chapel Hill: University of North Carolina Press, 1998), 334.

16. Drew Gilpin Faust, *A Sacred Circle: The Dilemma of the Intellectual in the Old South, 1840–1860* (Baltimore: Johns Hopkins University Press, 1977), 88, 130; Gerald Straka, "The Influence of Thomas Carlyle in the Old South" (M.A. thesis, University of Virginia, 1953).

17. Quoted in Seelye, *Memory's Nation*, 321.

18. Osterweis, *Romanticism and Nationalism in the Old South*, 203; G. Harrison Orians, "Walter Scott, Mark Twain and the Civil War," *South Atlantic Quarterly* 40 (1941): 351; Orians, "The Romance Ferment after Waverley," *American Literature* 3 (1932), 408–31.

19. Keitt is quoted in Walther, *Fire-Eaters*, 186.

20. Quoted in Maury Klein, *Days of Defiance: Sumter, Secession, and the Coming of the Civil War* (New York: Random House, 1997), 130.

21. "Appendix B. Alexander H. Stephens, 'Cornerstone Address,'" in Jon L. Wakelyn, ed., *Southern Pamphlets on Secession: November 1860–April 1861* (Chapel Hill: University of North Carolina Press, 1996), 406.

22. Lincoln quoted in Kenneth M. Stampp, *And the War Came: The North and the Secession Crisis, 1860–1861* (Baton Rouge: Louisiana State University Press, 1950), 6.

23. *Boston Advertiser* quoted in Stampp, *And the War Came*, 17.

24. See Leonard L. Richards, "The Question of Slaveholder Domination," unpublished paper. I am indebted to Professor Richards for lending this insightful essay.

25. David Brion Davis, *The Slave Power Conspiracy and the Paranoid Style* (Baton Rouge: Louisiana State University Press, 1970).

26. Quoted in Carl Schurz, *Intimate Letters of Carl Schurz*, ed. Joseph Schafer (Madison: University of Wisconsin Press, 1928), 239–41.

27. Stampp, *And the War Came*, 252.

28. Quoted in Lacy K. Ford Jr., *Origins of Southern Radicalism: The South Carolina Upcountry, 1800–1860* (New York: Oxford University Press, 1988), 368.

29. Poem, Bryant, and Lincoln quoted in James M. McPherson, *Abraham Lincoln and the Second American Revolution* (New York: Oxford University Press, 1991), 26–27, 176; Garrison quoted in Truman Nelson, ed., *Documents of Upheaval: Selections from William Lloyd Garrison's The Liberator, 1831–1865* (New York: Hill and Wang, 1966), 267.

30. William Frierson Cooper to William L. Cooper, 28 December 1860, Cooper Family Papers, TSA.

31. Alexander Stephens, "Speech Against Secession [November 14, 1860]," in Cleveland, *Alexander Stephens in Public and Private*, 704–8; Drew Gilpin Faust, *James Henry Hammond and the Old South: A Design for Mastery* (Baton Rouge: Louisiana State University Press, 1982), 331–59; Ralph A. Wooster, "The Secession of the Lower South: An Examination of Changing Interpretations," *Civil War History* 7 (June 1961): 117–27.

32. Hatton quoted in Daniel W. Crofts, *Reluctant Confederates: Upper South Unionists in the Secession Crisis* (Chapel Hill: University of North Carolina Press, 1989), 105.

33. Jean H. Baker, *Affairs of Party: The Political Culture of Northern Democrats in the Mid-Nineteenth Century* (Ithaca, N.Y.: Cornell University Press, 1983), 317–54; *Spectator* (Staunton, Va.), 13 November 1860.

34. Ute Frevert, *Men of Honour: A Social and Cultural History of the Duel*, trans. Anthony Williams (1991; Cambridge, Eng.: Polity Press, 1995), 82–83.

35. Ibid., 201.

36. Quoted in Avner Offer, "Going to War in 1914: A Matter of Honor?," *Politics and Society* 23 (June 1995): 216.

37. Quoted in Larry M. Logue, *To Appomattox and Beyond: The Civil War Soldier in War and Peace* (Chicago: Ivan Dee, 1996), 23.

38. William S. Earnest of Jefferson County, Alabama, quoted in William Russell Smith, *The History and Debates of the Convention of the People of Alabama, Begun and Held in the City of Montgomery, on the Seventh Day of January, 1861 . . .* (Montgomery: White, Pfister, & Co., 1861), 63.

39. Dale Baum, *The Shattering of Texas Unionism: Politics in the Lone Star State during the Civil War* (Baton Rouge: Louisiana State University Press, 1998), 42–43, 59.

40. Thomas E. Jeffrey, *Thomas Lanier Clingman: Fire Eater of the Carolina Mountains* (Athens: University of Georgia Press, 1998), 157.

41. *History and Debates of the Convention of the People of Alabama*, 82.

42. Quoted in Dwight L. Dumond, *The Secession Movement, 1860–1861* (New York: Macmillan, 1931), 201–2.

43. Jemison quoted in Smith, *History and Debates, Alabama,* 68–70; Donald B. Dodd, "Unionism in Northwest Alabama through 1865" (M.A. thesis, Auburn University, 1966); Hugh C. Bailey, "Disloyalty in Early Confederate Alabama," *Journal of Southern History,* 23 (November 1957): 522–28; Perry Lee Rainwater, *Mississippi: Storm Center of Secession, 1856–1861* (Baton Rouge: O. Claitor, 1938), 182–83.

44. Martin Abbott, "The First Shot at Fort Sumter," *Civil War History* 3 (March 1957): 41–45.

45. Davis, *Jefferson Davis,* 74–75, 84–85 (quotation).

46. Mack Buckley Swearingen, *The Early Years of George Poindexter: A Story of the First Southwest* (Chicago: University of Chicago Press, 1934), 3–21; Dallas C. Dickey, *Seargent S. Prentiss: Whig Orator of the Old South* (Baton Rouge: Louisiana State University Press, 1945); Thomas E. Schott, *Alexander H. Stephens: A Biography* (Baton Rouge: Louisiana State University Press, 1988), 1–17; Alvey L. King, *Louis T. Wigfall: Southern Fire-Eater* (Baton Rouge: Louisiana State University Press, 1970), 1–12; William C. Davis, *Jefferson Davis: The Man and His Hour* (New York: Harper-Collins, 1991), 4–24, 692–93; John Witherspoon DuBose, *The Life and Times of William Lowndes Yancey: A History of Political Parties in the United States from 1834 to 1864; Especially as to the Origin of the Confederate States,* 2 vols. (1892; reprint, New York: Peter Smith, 1942): 1:1–406; Ralph B. Draughon Jr., "The Young Manhood of William L. Yancey," *Alabama Review* 19 (January 1966): 28–40; William Gilmore Simms to William Porcher Miles, 14 November 1860, in Mary C. Simms Oliphant, Alfred Odell, and T. C. Duncan Eaves, eds., *The Letters of William Gilmore Simms,* 6 vols. (Columbia: University of South Carolina Press, 1982), 4:315.

47. Drew Gilpin Faust, *A Sacred Circle: The Dilemma of the Intellectual in the Old South, 1840–1860* (Baltimore: Johns Hopkins University Press, 1977).

48. See Michael Burlingame, *The Inner World of Abraham Lincoln* (Urbana: University of Illinois Press, 1994), esp. 92–122.

49. Quoted in Offer, "Going to War in 1914," 213.

50. Sarah A. Dorsey to Rt. Rev. Leonidas L. Polk, 20 February 1862, Leonidas L. Polk MSS, Jessie Ball Dupont Library, University of the South, Sewanee, Tennessee.

51. Fish and Smith quoted in Eric Foner, *Free Soil, Free Labor, Free Men: The Ideology of the Republican Party before the Civil War* (New York: Oxford University Press, 1970), 192–93; Michael F. Holt, *The Political Crisis of the 1850s* (New York: Wiley, 1978), 209.

52. Bissell of Illinois quoted in Foner, *Free Soil,* 179; Browning quoted in Halbert E. Gulley, "Springfield Lincoln Rally, 1860," in *Antislavery and Disunion, 1858–1861: Studies in the Rhetoric of Compromise and Conflict,* ed. J. Jeffrey Auer (New York: Harper & Row, 1963), 220.

53. David R. Goldfield, *Cotton Fields and Skyscrapers: Southern City and Region, 1607–1980* (Baton Rouge: Louisiana State University Press, 1982). Stephens quoted in Gladys F. Williams, "The Divided Mind of an Antebellum Statesman: Alexander Stephens, the South and the Nation" (M.A. thesis, University of Alabama in Huntsville, 1982), 52–53.

54. Douglas quoted in Richard H. Sewell, *Ballots for Freedom: Antislavery Politics in the United States, 1837–1860* (New York: Oxford University Press, 1976), 344.

55. Pugh quoted in *Charleston Courier*, April 30, 1860 [quotation differs slightly from Murat Halstead, *Three against Lincoln: Murat Halstead Reports the Caucuses of 1860* (Baton Rouge: Louisiana State University, 1960), 48; Stuart of Michigan in *Charleston Courier*, May 2, 1860; Baker, *Affairs of Party*, 319. Southerners rejected the Douglas Democrats' version of nationalism, but secession did not represent a fully developed Southern nationalism. Traditional honor encouraged too parochial a view, so that slavery, states' rights, and kinship ties, not abstract nationalism, held the South together—imperfectly and only for a while. Compare John M. McCardell, *The Idea of Southern Nation: Southern Nationalists and Southern Nationalism, 1830–1860* (New York: Norton, 1979).

56. Stampp, *And the War Came*, 26.

57. Christopher Olsen, "The Secession Crisis and the Political Culture of Mississippi" (Ph.D. diss., University of Florida, 1997), 152–53, 158. I am grateful for the permission of the author, whose book will be published by Oxford University Press, to make use of this draft.

58. Robert Charles Kenzer, "Portrait of a Southern Community, 1849–1881: Family, Kinship, and Neighborhood in Orange County, North Carolina" (Ph.D. diss., Harvard University, 1982), 74–83; Steven H. Hahn, *The Roots of Southern Populism: Yeoman Farmer and the Transformation of the Georgia Upcountry, 1850–1890* (New York: Oxford University Press, 1983), and "The Yeomanry of the Nonplantation South: Upper Piedmont Georgia, 1850–1860," in *Class, Conflict, and Consensus: Antebellum Southern Community Studies*, ed. Orville V. Burton and Robert C. McMath (Westport, Conn.: Greenwood Press, 1982), 38–39; Paul F. Bourke and Donald A. DeBats, "Identifiable Voting in Nineteenth-Century America: Toward a Comparison of Britain and the United States before the Secret Ballot," *Perspectives in American History* 11 (1977–78), 285; Harry L. Watson, *Jacksonian Politics and Community Conflict: The Emergence of the Second American Party System in Cumberland County, North Carolina* (Baton Rouge: Louisiana State University Press, 1981), 311; Whitman Ridgway, *Community Leadership in Maryland, 1790–1840* (Chapel Hill: University of North Carolina Press, 1979), 130–35. Olsen's new findings also support this interpretation of Southern politics.

59. See Bertram Wyatt-Brown, *Southern Honor: Ethics and Behavior in the Old South* (New York: Oxford University Press, 1982); Preston quoted in George H. Reese, ed., *Proceedings of the Virginia State Convention of 1861, February 13–May 1*, 4 vols. (Richmond: Richmond State Library [Historical Publications Divisions], 1965), 1:90.

60. Quoted in David Donald, *Charles Sumner and the Coming of the Civil War* (New York: Knopf, 1960), 285–86.

61. Quoted in Kenneth S. Greenberg, "Honor and Sectional Conflict in Antebellum America: 'Something' Happened on May 22, 1856," 3, paper presented at the Two South Commonwealth Fund Conference, University College, London, January 29, 1999.

62. Quoted ibid., 5.

63. Kenneth S. Greenberg, "Honor and Sectional Conflict in Antebellum America: 'Something Happened on May 22, 1856,'" in press, kindly lent by the author, 7.

64. I am indebted to Harlan Joel Gradin, "Losing Control: The Caning of Charles Sumner and the Breakdown of Antebellum Political Culture" (Ph.D. diss., University of North Carolina, Chapel Hill, 1991), 155–64, for this account.

65. Quoted in Gradin, "Losing Control," 172–73.

66. Keitt quoted in Marchant, "Keitt," 120.

67. Ibid., Donald, *Charles Sumner and the Coming of the Civil War*, 290–95; William E. Gienapp, "The Crime against Sumner: The Caning of Charles Sumner and the Rise of the Republican Party," *Civil War History* 25 (September 1979): 218–45, 224 (quotation).

68. Quoted in Gradin, "Losing Control," 246.

69. Ibid., 247.

70. Toombs quoted in William Y. Thompson, *Robert Toombs of Georgia* (Baton Rouge: Louisiana State University Press, 1966), 42, 65.

71. Yancey quoted in Dickson D. Bruce, Jr., *Violence and Culture in the Antebellum South* (Austin: University of Texas Press, 1979), 192; Davis quoted in Dunbar Rowland, ed., *Jefferson Davis, Constitutionalist: His Letters, Papers and Speeches*, 10 vols. (New York: J. J. Ives, 1923), 3:337–38.

72. Ulrich B. Phillips, "The Central Theme of Southern History," *American Historical Review* 34 (October 1928): 30–43.

73. Alcorn quoted in William L. Barney, *The Secessionist Impulse: Alabama and Mississippi in 1860* (Princeton: Princeton University Press, 1974), 309.

74. Crofts, "The Union Party of 1861 and the Secession Crisis," 327–76; Marc W. Kruman, *Parties and Politics in North Carolina, 1836–1865* (Baton Rouge: Louisiana State University Press, 1983), 200–202; William H. Freehling, "The Editorial Revolution, Virginia and the Coming of the Civil War: A Review Essay," *Civil War History* 16 (March 1970): 64–72, esp. 67; Anderson quoted in Reese, ed., *Proceedings of the Virginia State Convention of 1861*, 1:56, 59.

75. Preston and Branch quoted in Reese, ed., *Proceedings of the Virginia State Convention of 1861*, 1:87,113; *Charlottesville Review* quoted in William J. Cooper Jr., "The Politics of Slavery Affirmed: The South and the Secession Crisis," in *The Southern Enigma: Essays on Race, Class, and Folk Culture*, ed. Walter J. Fraser Jr. and Winfred B. Moore Jr. (Westport, Conn.: Greenwood Press, 1983), 212.

76. Richard Zuber, *Jonathan Worth: A Biography of a Southern Unionist* (Chapel Hill: University of North Carolina Press, 1965), 123.

77. William M. E. Rachal, ed., "'Secession Is Nothing but Revolution': A Letter of R. E. Lee to his Son 'Rooney,'" *Virginia Magazine of History and Biography* (January 1961): 3–6; Captain Robert E. Lee, *Recollection and Letters of General Robert E. Lee* (New York: Doubleday, Page, 1904), 25.

CHAPTER NINE

1. The poet Hybrias quoted by Paul Rahe, *Republics Ancient and Modern: Classical Republicanism and the American Revolution* (Chapel Hill: University of North Carolina Press, 1992), 32–33.

2. Eric T. Dean Jr., *Shook over Hell: Post-Traumatic Stress, Vietnam, and the Civil War* (Cambridge, Mass.: Harvard University Press, 1997); Richard Holmes, *Acts of War: The Behavior of Men in Battle* (New York: Free Press, 1985), 254–69.

3. Bruce Catton, "Billy Yank and the Army of the Potomac," *Military Affairs* 18 (Winter 1954): 169–75 (quotation, 170).

4. Quotation, David Donald, "The Confederate as a Fighting Man," *Journal of Southern History* 25 (May 1959): 178; see also Gerald F. Linderman, *Embattled Courage: The Experience of Combat in the American Civil War* (New York: Free Press, 1987); Bell Irvin Wiley, *The Life of Johnny Reb: The Common Soldier of the Confederacy* (1943; reprint, Baton Rouge: Louisiana State University Press, 1978); Bell Irvin Wiley, *The Life of Billy Yank: The Common Soldier of the Union* (Indianapolis: Bobbs-Merrill, 1952); Samuel A. Stouffer et al., *The American Soldier: Studies in Social Psychology in World War II* (Princeton: Princeton University Press, 1949); S. L. A. Marshall, *Men against Fire: The Problem of Battle Command in Future War* (1947; reprint, New York: Morrow, 1964). Pete Maslowski, "A Study of Morale in Civil War Soldiers," *Military Affairs* 34 (December 1970): 122–26, disputed the distinctions that Wiley drew that gave the Southern foot soldier the better ideological reading, but his article supports the interpretation that ideology counted less than personal motives.

5. See James M. McPherson, *What They Fought For, 1861–1865* (Baton Rouge: Louisiana State University Press, 1994), and *For Cause and Comrades: Why Men Fought in the Civil War* (New York: Oxford University Press, 1997).

6. Marcus Woodcock, *A Southern Boy in Blue: The Memoir of Marcus Woodcock, 9th Kentucky Infantry (U.S.A.)*, ed. Kenneth W. Noe (Knoxville: University of Tennessee Press, 1996), 15.

7. Marvin R. Cain, "A 'Face of Battle' Needed: An Assessment of Motives and Men in Civil War Historiography," *Civil War History* 28 (March 1982): 25.

8. Wiley, *Life of Billy Yank*, 360.

9. Quoted in McPherson, *What They Fought For*, 21.

10. Quoted in Maslowski, "Study of Morale," 123.

11. General Robert E. Lee to Anne Marshall, 10 April 1861, in Captain Robert E. Lee, *Recollections and Letters of General Robert E. Lee* (Garden City, N.Y.: Doubleday, Page, 1904), 25; Burton J. Hendrick, *The Lees of Virginia* (Boston: Little, Brown, 1935), 435.

12. Private James M. Williams to Eliza Jane Rennison Williams, 2 June 1862, *From That Terrible Field: Civil War Letters of James M. Williams, Twenty-First Alabama Infantry Volunteers*, ed. John Kent Folmar (University: University of Alabama Press, 1981), 81.

13. McPherson, *What They Fought For*, 21.

14. Ibid., 23.

15. The pay was later reduced by act of Congress to $1,200. See Gardiner H. Shattuck Jr., *A Shield and Hiding Place: The Religious Life of the Civil War Armies* (Macon, Ga.: Mercer University Press, 1987), 52–53.

16. Drew Gilpin Faust, "Christian Soldiers: The Meaning of Revivalism in the Confederate Army," *Journal of Southern History* 53 (February 1987): 63–90.

17. Samuel J. Watson, "Religion and Combat Motivation in the Confederate Armies," *Journal of Military History* 58 (January 1994): 29–55 (quotation, 30).

18. Faust, "Christian Soldiers," 76.

19. Kurt H. Berends, " 'Thus Saith the Lord': The Use of the Bible by Southern Evangelicals in the Era of the American Civil War" (Ph.D. diss., Oxford University, 1997), 190, 193. I am much in debt to Berends's splendid exposition of religion in the Southern army.

20. Albert Theodore Goodloe, *Confederate Echoes: A Soldier's Personal Story of Life in the Confederate Army from Mississippi to the Carolinas* (1897; reprint, Washington, D.C.: Zenger, 1983), 236.

21. Thomas D. Duncan, *Recollections of Thomas D. Duncan, a Confederate Soldier* (Nashville: McQuiddy, 1922), 137, as quoted in Watson, "Religion and Combat Motivation," 42.

22. General John B. Gordon, quoted in Watson, "Religion and Combat Motivation," 42; Raymond Jamous, "From the Death of Men to the Peace of God: Violence and Peace-Making in the Rif," in John G. Péristiany and Julian Pitt-Rivers, *Honor and Grace in Anthropology* (New York: Dutton, 1995), 167–91.

23. Quoted in Wayne Flynt, *Alabama Baptists: Southern Baptists in the Heart of Dixie* (Tuscaloosa: University of Alabama Press, 1998), 114.

24. J. William Jones, *Christ in the Camp or Religion in the Confederate Army* (Atlanta: Matin and Hoyt, 1887), 274–75.

25. Entry for 10 April 1864, *This War So Horrible: The Civil War Diary of Hiram Smith Williams*, ed. Lewis N. Wynne and Robert A. Taylor (Tuscaloosa: University of Alabama Press, 1993), 46.

26. Quoted in Faust, "Christian Soldiers," 65.

27. Abraham Lincoln, quoted ibid., 67.

28. Quoted in McPherson, *For Cause and Comrades*, 63.

29. Quoted in McPherson, *What They Fought For*, 56.

30. Julian Pitt-Rivers, "Honor," in *International Encyclopedia of the Social Sciences*, ed. David L. Sills, 17 vols. (New York: Macmillan, 1968), 6:503.

31. David H. Fisher, *Albion's Seed: Four British Folkways in America* (New York: Oxford University Press, 1989), 412.

32. James M. McPherson, *Abraham Lincoln and the Second American Revolution* (New York: Oxford University Press, 1991), 43–44.

33. William A. Fletcher, *Rebel Private, Front and Rear: Memoirs of a Confederate Soldier* (Austin: University of Texas Press, 1951), 57.

34. Quoted in McPherson, *For Cause and Comrades*, 80.

35. William Nelson Pendleton, quoted in Gaines M. Foster, *Ghosts of the Confeder-*

acy: *Defeat, the Lost Cause, and the Emergence of the New South, 1865 to 1913* (New York: Oxford University Press, 1987), 42.

36. *Philadelphia Press,* quoted in Stuart McConnell, *Glorious Contentment: The Grand Army of the Republic, 1865–1900* (Chapel Hill: University of North Carolina Press, 1992), 125.

37. W. W. Heartsill, *Fourteen Hundred and 91 Days in the Confederate Army,* ed. Bell Irvin Wiley (Jackson, Tenn.: McCowat-Mercer Press, 1953), 166.

38. Ibid., 183.

39. Frank Wilkeson, *Turned Inside Out: Recollections of a Private Soldier in the Army of the Potomac* (Lincoln: University of Nebraska Press, 1997), 67.

40. Private James M. Williams to Eliza Williams, 28 June 1862, in *From That Terrible Field,* 93.

41. Quoted in Reid Mitchell, *The Vacant Chair: The Northern Soldier Leaves Home* (New York: Oxford University Press, 1993), 94.

42. Euripides, *The Trojan Women,* in *Euripides III,* ed. David Green and Richard Lattimore (Chicago: University of Chicago Press, 1958), 144.

43. Wiley, *Life of Johnny Reb,* 86.

44. Quotations from McPherson, *For Cause and Comrades,* 18, 23, 24.

45. Quoted in William C. Harris, *William Woods Holden: Firebrand of North Carolina Politics* (Baton Rouge: Louisiana State University Press, 1987), 113.

46. Ibid., 24.

47. Ibid., 118–19.

48. Quoted in Linderman, *Embattled Courage,* 27.

49. Mitchell, *Vacant Chair.*

50. McPherson, *For Cause and Comrades,* 87.

51. Ibid., 170.

52. Mark A. Weitz, "Drill, Training, and the Combat Performance of the Civil War Soldier: Dispelling the Myth of the Poor Soldier, Great Fighter," *Journal of Military History* 62 (April 1999): 269–70.

53. Stephen Crane, *Red Badge of Courage* (New York: Library of America, 1984), 120.

54. Staughton Dent, quoted in Weitz, "Drill, Training, and the Combat Performance of the Civil War Soldier," 282; second quotation, 283.

55. Fletcher, *Rebel Private,* 22.

56. Ibid., 82.

57. Heartsill, *Fourteen Hundred and 91 Days,* 163.

58. Quoted in McPherson, *For Cause and Comrades,* 38.

59. Private Philip F. Brown, quoted in *Voices of the Civil War: Antietam* (New York: Time-Life Books, 1996), 40.

60. Woodcock, *Southern Boy in Blue,* 137. I gratefully acknowledge Joan Cashin for giving me this reference.

61. *Louisville Press and Times,* 28 June 1864, quoted in Robert S. Davis Jr., "Selec-

tive Memories of Civil War Atlanta: The Memoir of Sallie Clayton," *Georgia Historical Quarterly* 82 (Winter 1998): 742–43.

62. Richard E. Nisbett and Dov Cohen, *Culture of Honor: The Psychology of Violence in the South* (Boulder: Westview Press, 1996), 21 (Fig. 2.3) (in cities of less than 200,000), and 53 (quotation).

63. Private James Williams to Lizzie Williams, 22 June 1862, *From That Terrible Field*, 90.

64. Thomas B. Buell, *The Warrior Generals: Combat Leadership in the Civil War* (New York: Random House, 1997), 335.

65. Dave Grossman, *On Killing: The Psychological Cost of Learning to Kill in War and Society* (Boston: Little, Brown, 1995), 7.

66. Paddy Griffith, *Battle Tactics of the Civil War* (New Haven: Yale University Press, 1987), 51, 87 (quotation).

67. Ibid., 51 (quotation), 137–50.

68. Grossman, *On Killing*, 87.

69. Thomas Hardy, *The Complete Poems*, ed. James Gibson (London: Macmillan, 1976), 287.

70. Corporal Berry G. Benson, in *Voices of the Civil War*, 130.

71. Private Alexander Hunter, ibid., 126.

72. Fletcher, *Rebel Private*, 99.

73. Wilkeson, *Turned Inside Out*, 57–58.

74. Ibid., 164.

75. General Samuel Lyman Marshall, quoted in Fredric Smolar, "The Secret of the Soldier Who Didn't Shoot," *American Heritage* 40 (March 1989): 37–45; Marshall, *Men against Fire*; L. Van Loan Naisawald, *Grape and Canister: The Story of the Field Artillery of the Army of the Potomac* (New York: Oxford University Press, 1960); Gary W. Gallagher, ed., *Fighting for the Confederacy: The Personal Recollections of General Edward Porter Alexander* (Chapel Hill: University of North Carolina Press, 1989).

76. For an excellent review of this topic of soldierly effectiveness and the historians' debate, see Joseph T. Glatthaar, "Battlefield Tactics," in *Writing the Civil War: The Quest to Understand*, ed. James M. McPherson and William J. Cooper Jr. (Columbia: University of South Carolina Press, 1998), 60–80, esp. 69. I thank Gary Gallagher for suggesting this source.

77. Ibid., 67.

78. Marshall, quoted in Smolar, "The Secret of the Soldier Who Didn't Shoot," 37–45; Grossman, *On Killing*, 29–31. The premature firing of Confederate artillery shells was a major problem, General Edward Porter Alexander pointed out in his memoir: Gallagher, ed., *Fighting for the Confederacy*, 62. Naisawald observes that "No less than twelve Yankee battery commanders complained bitterly over one type of shell or another exploding prematurely, failing to take the rifling, or failing to detonate" (*Grape and Canister*, 243).

79. Rahe, *Republics Ancient and Modern*, 120.

80. McPherson, *What They Fought For*, 17.

81. Grossman, *On Killing*, 21–22.

82. Ibid., 4, 25–27.

83. Joseph Allan Frank, *With Ballot and Bayonet: The Political Socialization of American Civil War Soldiers* (Athens: University of Georgia Press, 1998), 156 (quotation), 156–57.

84. I thank Mark Schantz for pointing out to me this inhuman side of the psychological situation.

85. Quoted in Michael Fellman, *Inside War: The Guerrilla Conflict in Missouri during the American Civil War* (New York: Oxford University Press, 1989), 252–53.

86. Heartsill, *Fourteen Hundred and 91 Days*, 159.

87. Wiley, *Life of Johnny Reb*, 124–25.

88. David Carlson, " 'The Distemper of the Time': Conscription, the Courts, and Planter Privilege in Civil War South Georgia," *Journal of Southwest Georgia History* 14 (Fall 1999): 9 (quotation) and 11. Davis quoted in Paul D. Escott, *After Secession: Jefferson Davis and the Failure of Confederate Nationalism* (Baton Rouge: Louisiana State University Press, 1978), 186.

89. Fletcher, *Rebel Private*, 59.

90. William Pitt Chambers, "My Journal: The Story of a Soldier's Life," *Mississippi Historical Society Publications*, Centenary Series (1925), 5:234.

91. George Cary Eggleston, *A Rebel's Recollections* (Indianapolis: Bobbs-Merrill, 1959), 69.

92. Donald, "Confederate as a Fighting Man," 189–90. Donald reaches the conclusion that there was a paradox in the Southern common man's devotion to democracy and his deference to hierarchical leadership. That tension, to which the ethic of honor and shame is by nature subjected, however, existed within the framework of the ethic itself. See Bertram Wyatt-Brown, *Southern Honor: Ethics and Behavior in the Old South* (New York: Oxford University Press, 1982), 67–74.

93. Private Harry St. John Dixon, quoted in Wiley, *Life of Johnny Reb*, 338.

94. Quoted in Faust, "Christian Soldiers," 77.

95. Soldiers cited in David Williams, *Rich Man's War: Class, Caste, and Confederate Defeat in the Lower Chattahoochie Valley* (Athens: University of Georgia Press, 1998), 121–22.

96. Woodcock, *Southern Boy in Blue*, 37; H. H. Cunningham, *Doctors in Gray: The Confederate Medical Service* (1958; reprint, Baton Rouge: Louisiana State University Press, 1986), 72–73, 76–78.

97. Private James Williams to Lizzie Williams, 18 April 1862, *From That Terrible Field*, 70.

98. See Dean, *Shook over Hell*, passim.

99. Peter Wallenstein, "Which Side Are You On?: The Social Origins of White Union Troops from Civil War Tennessee," *Journal of East Tennessee History* 63 (Spring 1992): 72–103. See also Richard N. Current, *Lincoln's Loyalists: Union Soldiers from the Confederacy* (Boston: Northeastern University Press, 1992).

100. Fletcher, *Rebel Private*, 153.

101. D. Alexander Brown, *The Galvanized Yankees* (Urbana: University of Illinois, 1963), 6.

102. Wiley, *Life of Johnny Reb*, 347.

103. See Glatthaar, "Battlefield Tactics," 62.

104. Entry for 4 April 1864, Williams, *This War So Horrible*, 44.

CHAPTER TEN

1. Charles Frazier, *Cold Mountain* (New York: Atlantic Monthly Press, 1997).

2. I owe this insight to Jason Parker of the University of Florida Graduate History Program.

3. Quotations from Joseph T. Glatthaar, *The March to the Sea and Beyond: Sherman's Troops in the Savannah and Carolina Campaigns* (New York: New York University Press, 1986), 176–77.

4. Frank M. Mixson, *Reminiscences of a Private* (1910; reprint, Camden, S.C.: J. J. Fox, n.d.), 119.

5. Philip Daingerfield Stephenson, *The Civil War Memoir of Philip Daingerfield Stephenson, D.D., Private, Company K, 13th Arkansas Volunteer Infantry and Loader, Piece No. 4, 5th Company, Washington Artillery, Army of Tennessee, C.S.A.*, ed. Nathaniel Cheairs Hughes, Jr. (Conway, Ark.: USA Press, 1995), 371; Glatthaar, *March to the Sea*, 177.

6. Glatthaar, *March to the Sea*, 78, 178.

7. Stephenson, *Civil War Memoir*, 371.

8. James Reston Jr., *Sherman's March and Vietnam* (New York: Macmillan, 1984), 193; Glatthaar, *March to the Sea*, 180–81.

9. Joshua Lawrence Chamberlain, *"Bayonet Forward": My Civil War Reminiscences* (Gettysburg, Pa.: Stan Clark Military Books, 1994), 228; Thomas B. Buell, *The Warrior Generals: Combat Leadership in the Civil War* (New York: Crown, 1997), 420.

10. Entry for 12 June 1865, *Brokenburn: The Journal of Kate Stone, 1861–1865*, ed. John Q. Anderson (1955; reprint, Baton Rouge: Louisiana State University Press, 1995), 351.

11. Quoted in Gary W. Gallagher, ed., *Fighting for the Confederacy: The Personal Recollections of General Edward Porter Alexander* (Chapel Hill: University of North Carolina Press, 1989), xiii.

12. David Donald, "A Generation of Defeat," in *From the Old South to the New: Essays on the Transitional South*, ed. Walter J. Fraser Jr. and Winfred B. Moore Jr. (Westport, Conn.: Greenwood Press, 1981), 9.

13. Carl Schurz, *The Reminiscences of Carl Schurz*, 3 vols. (New York: McClure, 1908), 3:160, 161, 169.

14. Katharine Du Pre Lumpkin, *The Making of a Southerner* (1946; reprint, Athens: University of Georgia Press, 1991), 57.

15. These Georgians are cited in David Williams, *Rich Man's War: Class, Caste,*

and Confederate Defeat in the Lower Chattahoochie Valley (Athens: University of Georgia Press, 1998), 173.

16. Entry for 4 May 1865, *The Civil War Diary of General Josiah Gorgas*, ed. Frank Everson Vandiver (University: University of Alabama Press, 1947), 167.

17. Edward Francis Allston to Catherine Palmer Allston, 27 April 1865, in *A World Turned Upside Down: The Palmers of South Santee, 1818–1881*, ed. Louis P. Towles (Columbia: University of South Carolina Press, 1996), 473.

18. Entries for 11, 14, 20 April 1865, Samuel A. Agnew Diary, SHC; Dr. Samuel Preston Moore, quoted in entry for 17 April 1865, *Kate: The Journal of a Confederate Nurse*, ed. Richard Barksdale Harwell (Baton Rouge: Louisiana State University Press, 1987), 271.

19. See entries for 11 and 17 April 1865 in "The Civil War Decade in Greensboro, N.C. as Recorded in the Diary of Rev. Mr. J. Henry Smith, Pastor of the Presbyterian Church of Greensboro," transcript, 118, 119, in the possession of O. Norris Smith, M.D., of Greensboro, North Carolina. I am indebted to Dr. Smith for the use of this valuable diary, written by his grandfather.

20. Miriam Kalmań Harris, *Rivers of Light: The Life of Claire Myers Owens, 1896–1983* (Baton Rouge: Louisiana State University Press, forthcoming), MS p. 9. I thank the author for permitting the use of the quotation.

21. Whitelaw Reid, *After the War: A Tour of the Southern States, 1865–1866* (1866; reprint, New York: Random House, 1965), 361.

22. Entry for 1 May 1865, *Kate*, ed. Harwell, 276; Ethelred Philips to James Jones Philips, 2 August 1865, James Jones Philips Papers, SHC.

23. Bill Arp, quoted in Gaines M. Foster, *Ghosts of the Confederacy: Defeat, the Lost Cause, and the Emergence of the New South* (New York: Oxford University Press, 1987), 34; for Forrest incident, see ibid., 25.

24. Quotations from Sarah A. Dorsey, *Recollections of Henry Watkins Allen* (New Orleans: M. Doolady, 1866), 56, 61.

25. See David Pierson to William H. Pierson, 27 April 1865, *Brothers in Gray: The Civil War Letters of the Pierson Family*, ed. Thomas W. Cutrer and T. Michael Parrish (Baton Rouge: Louisiana State University Press, 1997), 256.

26. Quoted in Dixon Wecter, *When Johnny Comes Marching Home* (Cambridge, Mass.: Houghton Mifflin, 1944), 116.

27. Horace Greeley, *Mr. Greeley's Letters from Texas and the Lower Mississippi to Which Are Added His Address to the Farmers of Texas and His Speech on His Return to New York, June 12, 1871* (New York: Tribune Office, 1871), 41.

28. Samuel G. French, *Two Wars: An Autobiography of Gen. Samuel G. French* (Nashville, Tenn.: Confederate Veteran, 1901), 320.

29. Quoted in Ella Lonn, *Desertion during the Civil War* (New York: Century, 1928), 18.

30. David M. Carter to William A. Graham, 16 March 1864, in William Alexander Graham, *Papers*, ed. J. G. Roulhac Hamilton, 8 vols. (Raleigh, N.C.: Publications of the State Department of Archives and History, 1957–84), 6:46; see also George

Cary Eggleston, *A Rebel's Recollections*, ed. David Donald (Bloomington: Indiana University Press, 1959), 176–79.

31. See Bertram Wyatt-Brown, *Southern Honor: Ethics and Behavior of the Old South* (New York: Oxford University Press, 1982), 172.

32. Wecter, *When Johnny Comes Marching Home*, 121.

33. Entry for 1 May 1865, *A Heritage of Woe: The Civil War Diary of Grace Brown Elmore, 1861–1868*, ed. Marli F. Weiner (Athens: University of Georgia Press, 1997), 118.

34. Quoted in Randall C. Jimerson, *The Private Civil War: Popular Thought during the Sectional Conflict* (Baton Rouge: Louisiana State University Press, 1988), 234.

35. J. Tracy Power, *Lee's Miserables: Life in the Army of Northern Virginia from the Wildernesses to Appomattox* (Chapel Hill: University of North Carolina Press, 1998), 319.

36. Elijah P. Petty, *Journey to Pleasant Hill: The Civil War Letters of Captain Elijah P. Petty, Walker's Texas Division, C.S.A.*, ed. Norman Brown (San Antonio, Tex.: Institute of Texas Cultures, 1982), 444, 447.

37. Petty, *Journey to Pleasant Hill*, 448.

38. Entry for 3 May 1865, Harriet R. Palmer Diary, in *World Turned Upside Down*, ed. Towles, 475.

39. Entry for 17 November 1864 in *Mary Chesnut's Civil War*, ed. C. Vann Woodward (New Haven: Yale University Press, 1981), 671.

40. Amanda Worthington, quoted in George C. Rable, *Civil Wars: Women and the Crisis of Southern Nationalism* (Urbana: University of Illinois Press, 1989), 240.

41. Entries for 5 March and 12 June 1865, *Mary Chesnut's Civil War*, ed. Woodward, 747, 826.

42. Harriott Middleton quoted in John Hammond Moore, *Southern Homefront, 1861–1865* (Columbia, S.C.: Summerhouse Press, 1998), 210–11.

43. Quoted in Amy E. Murrell, "'Of Necessity and Public Benefit': Southern Families and Appeals for Protection," in *Families at War: Loyalty and Conflict in the Civil War South*, ed. Catherine Clinton (New York: Oxford University Press, forthcoming), 4–5, typescript. I am grateful to Professor Clinton and the author for permission to use this material.

44. Rowland quoted in Lee Ann Whites, *The Civil War as a Crisis in Gender: Augusta, Georgia, 1860–1890* (Athens: University of Georgia Press, 1995), 105–6.

45. Entry for 2 May 1865 in Sarah Morgan, *The Civil War Diary of Sarah Morgan*, ed. Charles East (Athens: University of Georgia Press, 1991), 610.

46. Entry for 13 April 1865, *Shadows on My Heart: The Civil War Diary of Lucy Rebecca Buck of Virginia*, ed. Elizabeth R. Blair (Athens: University of Georgia Press, 1997), 319.

47. Marshall W. Fishwick, *Lee after the War* (New York: Dodd, Mead, 1963), 15.

48. Sergeant James E. Whitehorne, quoted in Power, *Lee's Miserables*, 320.

49. Manly Wade Wellman, *Rebel Boast: First at Bethel—Last at Appomattox* (Westport, Conn.: Greenwood Press, 1956), 245.

50. William Faulkner, *Absalom, Absalom!* (New York: Penguin Library of America, 1990), 287.

51. J. W. Tucker, "God's Providence in War, May 16, 1862," in *"God Ordained This War": Sermons on the Sectional Crisis, 1830–1865*, ed. David B. Chesebrough (Columbia: University of South Carolina Press, 1991), 230.

52. Benjamin Morgan Palmer, *A Discourse before the General Assembly of South Carolina* (Columbia, S.C.: Charles P. Pelham, 1864), as quoted in Richard E. Beringer, Herman Hattaway, Archer Jones, and William N. Still Jr., *Why the South Lost the Civil War* (Athens: University of Georgia Press, 1986), 101.

53. Quoted in Reid Mitchell, *Civil War Soldiers* (New York: Viking, 1988), 173.

54. Quoted in Samuel J. Watson, "Religion and Combat Motivation in the Confederate Armies," *Journal of Military History* 58 (January 1994): 49. For pious Rebel women's reactions to defeat, see Drew Gilpin Faust, *Mothers of Invention: Women of the Slaveholding South in the American Civil War* (Chapel Hill: University of North Carolina Press, 1996), and Rable, *Civil Wars*.

55. Eggleston, *Rebel's Recollections*, ed. Donald, 177.

56. Ellen House, quoted in Eugene D. Genovese, *The Consuming Fire: The Fall of the Confederacy in the Mind of the White Christian South* (Athens: University of Georgia Press, 1998), 66.

57. Lizzie Hardin, *The Private War of Lizzie Hardin: A Kentucky Confederate Girl's Diary of the Civil War in Kentucky, Virginia, Tennessee, Alabama, and Georgia*, ed. G. Glenn Clift (Frankfort: Kentucky Historical Society, 1963), 280–81.

58. Entry for 6 January 1865, *Civil War Diary of General Josiah Gorgas*, ed. Vandiver, 164.

59. Quotations from Donald C. Pfanz, *Richard S. Ewell: A Soldier's Life* (Chapel Hill: University of North Carolina Press, 1998), 442. See for quotation, Westwood A. Todd, "Reminiscences of the War between the States, From April '61 to July '65," SHC.

60. See Reid, *After the War*, 360.

61. Carl Schurz, quoted in Wecter, *When Johnny Comes Marching Home*, 118.

62. Lesley J. Gordon, *General George E. Pickett in Life and Legend* (Chapel Hill: University of North Carolina Press, 1998), 163; Gary W. Gallagher, *Lee and His Generals in War and Memory* (Baton Rouge: Louisiana State University Press, 1998), 55–56.

63. Robert E. Lee to Zebulon Vance, 24 February 1865, Papers of Zebulon Baird Vance, NCDAH, and entry for 29 May 1865, *Kate*, ed. Harwell, 296.

64. C. F. Mills to Harrison Mills, 6 September 1863, Amanda E. Mills MSS, Duke University, Durham, N.C.

65. See William C. Harris, *William Woods Holden: Firebrand of North Carolina Politics* (Baton Rouge: Louisiana State University Press, 1987), 52.

66. Zebulon Vance to David L. Swain, 22 September 1864, copy, Vance Papers, NCDAH.

67. John Leadley Dagg, quoted in Genovese, *Consuming Fire*, 67.

68. Entry for 21 September 1864 in *Mary Chesnut's Civil War*, ed. Woodward, 644.

69. See Charles W. Ramsdell, *Behind the Lines in the Southern Confederacy* (Baton Rouge: Louisiana State University Press, 1944), 83–122.

70. John T. Trowbridge, *The Desolate South, 1865–1866: A Picture of the Battlefields and of the Devastated Confederacy*, ed. Gordon Carroll (Freeport, N.Y.: Books for Libraries Press, 1956), 69.

71. Entry for 29 May 1865, *Kate*, ed. Harwell, 294; John Paris, quoted in David B. Chesebrough, *Clergy Dissent in the Old South, 1830–1865* (Carbondale: Southern Illinois University Press, 1996), 28.

72. Quoted in Paul Escott, *After Secession: Jefferson Davis and the Failure of Confederate Nationalism* (Baton Rouge: Louisiana State University Press, 1978), 95.

73. Samuel C. Hyde, Jr., introduction to *Plain Folk of the South Revisited*, ed. Samuel C. Hyde Jr. (Baton Rouge: Louisiana State University Press, 1997), 12–13; shoemaker quoted in Williams, *Rich Man's War*, 195.

74. Entry for 12 June 1865, *Mary Chesnut's Civil War*, ed. Woodward, 826.

75. First quotation, Lizinka Brown Ewell to Campbell Brown, 28 July 1866, Brown-Ewell Papers, TSA; second quotation, Pfanz, *Richard S. Ewell*, 444.

76. B. P. Gallaway, *The Ragged Rebel: A Common Soldier in W. H. Parsons' Texas Cavalry, 1861–1865* (Austin: University of Texas Press, 1988), 131.

77. Michael B. Ballard, *The Long Shadow: Jefferson Davis and the Final Days of the Confederacy* (Jackson: University Press of Mississippi, 1986), 129.

78. John Green, *Johnny Green of the Orphan Brigade: The Journal of a Confederate Soldier*, ed. A. D. Kirwan (Lexington: University of Kentucky Press, 1956), 202–3.

79. Quoted in Larry M. Logue, *To Appomattox and Beyond: The Civil War Soldier in War and Peace* (Chicago: Ivan Dee, 1996), 105.

80. Wecter, *When Johnny Comes Marching Home*, 122.

81. Emily Liles Harris, entry for 2 March 1865, *Piedmont Farmer: The Journals of David Golightly Harris, 1855–1870*, ed. Philip N. Racine (Knoxville: University of Tennessee Press, 1990), 366.

82. Quoted in Noel C. Fisher, *War at Every Door: Partisan Politics and Guerrilla Violence in East Tennessee, 1860–1869* (Chapel Hill: University of North Carolina Press, 1997), 157, 158.

83. Stephenson, *Civil War Memoir*, 372, 378.

84. Private John Ransom, quoted in Lonnie R. Speer, *Portals to Hell: Military Prisons of the Civil War* (Mechanicsburg, Pa.: Stackpole Books, 1997), 284.

85. See Pfanz, *Richard S. Ewell*, 435.

86. James M. McCaffrey, *This Band of Heroes: Granbury's Texas Brigade, C.S.A.* (College Station: Texas A & M University Press, 1996), 156–57.

87. William A. Fletcher, *Rebel Private, Front and Rear: Memoirs of a Confederate Soldier* (1908; reprint, New York: Dutton, 1995), 200.

88. Margaret Wolfe, "When Johnny Reb Came Marching Home: A Feminine Perspective," paper presented at the meeting of the Southern Historical Association,

Birmingham, Alabama, November 1998. See also Thomas P. Lowry, *The Story the Soldiers Wouldn't Tell: Sex in the Civil War* (Mechanicsburg, Pa.: Stackpole Books, 1994).

89. Lowry, *The Story the Soldiers Wouldn't Tell,* 112.

90. Frank Moore, *Women of the War: Their Heroism and Self-Sacrifice* (Hartford, Conn.: S. S. Scranton, 1866), 206–7.

91. R. S. Green and others to Robert M. Patton, 4 February 1866, quoted in Robert Arthur Gilmour, "The Other Emancipation: Studies in the Society and Economy of Alabama Whites during Reconstruction" (Ph.D. diss., Johns Hopkins University, 1972), 67.

92. E. Merton Coulter, *The South during Reconstruction, 1865–1877* (Baton Rouge: Louisiana State University Press, 1947), 14.

93. Richard Lewis, *Camp Life of a Confederate Boy, of Bratton's Brigade, Longstreet's Corps, C.S.A.: Letters Written by Lieut. Richard Lewis, of Walker's Regiment, to His Mother, during the War* (Charleston: News and Courier Press, 1883), 102.

94. Entry for 18 March 1864, *Mary Chesnut's Civil War,* ed. Woodward, 588–89.

95. Reid, *After the War,* 138.

96. Lizinka Brown Ewell to Campbell Brown, 28 July 1866, Brown-Ewell Papers, TSA; second quotation from William W. White, *The Confederate Veteran* (Tuscaloosa, Ala.: Confederate, 1962), 51.

97. Stephenson, *Civil War Memoir,* 382.

98. John Richard Dennett, *The South as It Is, 1865–1866,* ed. Henry M. Christman (Athens: University of Georgia, 1987), 36.

99. Wecter, *When Johnny Comes Marching Home,* 110.

100. Green, *Johnny Green,* 207.

101. Entry for 3 May 1865, Harriet R. Palmer Diary, in *World Turned Upside Down,* ed. Towles, 475.

102. Josia Reams, quoted in James I. Robertson Jr., *Soldiers Blue and Gray* (Columbia: University of South Carolina Press, 1988), 227.

103. Carl R. Fish, "Back to Peace in 1865," *American Historical Review* 24 (April 1919): 435–43 (quotation, 436).

104. George Collins, quoted in Donald, "Generation of Defeat," 13.

105. Susan Dabney Smedes, *Memorials of a Southern Planter,* ed. Fletcher M. Green (New York: Knopf, 1965), xliv, 221–22.

106. Smedes, *Memorials of a Southern Planter,* 221.

107. Mrs. Robert Smith to Mrs. William Mason Smith, 11 April 1865, in Daniel E. Huger Smith, Alice R. Huger Smith, and Arney R. Childs, eds., *Mason Smith Family Letters, 1860–1868* (Columbia: University of South Carolina Press, 1950), 195.

108. Mrs. Alexander H. Major, "A Crape Veil," in *Reminiscences of the Women of Missouri during the Sixties* (N.p.: United Daughters of the Confederacy, Missouri Division, n.d.), 294–98 (quotations, 297–98).

109. Philips to a friend, 2 August 1865, Philips Papers, SHC.

110. Brown quoted in Genovese, *Consuming Fire,* 65.

CHAPTER ELEVEN

1. Clement H. Eaton, *The Waning of the Old South Civilization, 1860–1880's* (Athens: University of Georgia Press, 1968), 113.

2. T. J. Jackson Lears, *No Place of Grace: Antimodernism and the Transformation of American Culture, 1880–1920* (New York: Pantheon, 1981), 4.

3. Lizinka Ewell to Campbell Brown, 28 July 1866, Brown-Ewell papers, TSA.

4. Dixon Wecter, *When Johnny Comes Marching Home* (Cambridge: Houghton Mifflin, 1994), 123.

5. Entry for 10 November 1865, *The Diary of Miss Emma Holmes, 1861–1886*, ed. John F. Marszalek (Baton Rouge: Louisiana State University Press, 1979), 479.

6. W. Martin Hope and Jason H. Silverman, *Relief and Recovery in Post–Civil War South Carolina: A Death by Inches* (Lewiston, N.Y.: Edwin Mellen Press, 1997), 3.

7. All quotations from Dan T. Carter, *When the War Was Over: The Failure of Self-Reconstruction in the South, 1865–1867* (Baton Rouge: Louisiana State University Press, 1985), 271.

8. Lesley J. Gordon, *General George E. Pickett in Life and Legend* (Chapel Hill: University of North Carolina Press, 1998), 156–67.

9. *A World Turned Upside Down: The Palmers of South Santee, 1818–1881*, ed. Louis P. Towles (Columbia: University of South Carolina Press, 1996), 7–10.

10. Lizinka Brown Ewell to Campbell Brown, 28 July 1866, Brown-Ewell Papers, TSA.

11. This material was kindly lent to this author by Dr. Eric T. Dean, whose meticulous notes are invaluable: Mrs. Elizabeth W. Warner, 28 July 1877, Medical Case Histories, CSH, GDAH.

12. Lucinda Ozburn, 9 August 1865, Emily Johnson, 10 January 1866, vol. 3 (9 October 1860–31 July 1873), CSH, GDAH.

13. Emily Harris, entry for 17 February 1865, in David Golightly Harris, *Piedmont Farmer: The Journals of David Golightly Harris, 1855–1870*, ed. Philip N. Racine (Knoxville: University of Tennessee Press, 1990), 364.

14. Wayne Flynt, *Alabama Baptists: Southern Baptists in the Heart of Dixie* (Tuscaloosa: University of Alabama Press, 1998), 144; Paul Harvey, *Redeeming the South: Religious Cultures and Racial Identities among Southern Baptists, 1865–1925* (Chapel Hill: University of North Carolina Press, 1997), 46.

15. Abner Burks, 20 February 1864, vol. 3, CSH, GDAH. Eric Dean supplied me with copies from the records of the Georgia asylum, for which generosity I am highly grateful.

16. Joseph Henderson, 3 April 1862, Albinus N. Snelson, 25 March 1866, James Taylor, 9 December 1872, Captain William J. Dixon, 4 May 1869, William R. McRae, 20 June 1873, vol. 3, CSH, GDAH.

17. Quoted in Carter, *When the War Was Over*, 270.

18. See Larry M. Logue, *To Appomattox and Beyond: The Civil War Soldier in War and Peace* (Chicago: I. R. Dee, 1996), 106.

19. Georgia editor and Perry quoted in Carter, *When the War Was Over,* 262–63.

20. Entry for 15 June 1865, *Diary of Miss Emma Holmes,* ed. Marszalek, 456; entry for 4 September 1865, Harris, *Piedmont Farmer,* 391; entry for 28 July 1865 in Catherine Anne Devereux Edmonston, *"Journal of a Secesh Lady": The Diary of Catherine Anne Devereux Edmonston, 1860–1866,* ed. Beth G. Crabtree and James W. Patton (Raleigh: North Carolina Department of Archives and History, 1979), 716.

21. Quoted in Leon F. Litwack, *Trouble in Mind: Black Southerners in the Age of Jim Crow* (New York: Knopf, 1968), 118.

22. Entry for 6 January 1867, *The Journals of Josiah Gorgas, 1857–1878,* ed. Sarah Woollfolk Wiggins (Tuscaloosa: University of Alabama Press, 1995), 203, and introduction.

23. Robert Arthur Gilmour, "The Other Emancipation: Studies in the Society and Economy of Alabama Whites during Reconstruction" (Ph.D. diss., Johns Hopkins University, 1972), 60.

24. Certainly the problem arose in the Federal homes for aging veterans. See W. Andrew Achenbaum, Joel D. Howell, and Major Michael Parker, "Patterns of Alcohol Use and Abuse among Aging Civil War Veterans, 1865–1920," *Bulletin of the Medical Academy of New York* 69 (January–February 1993): 69–85.

25. C. Vann Woodward, *Tom Watson: Agrarian Rebel* (1938; reprint, Savannah, Ga.: Beehive Press, 1973), 3, 27.

26. Ibid., 3, 11, 13; Thomas E. Watson to William W. Brewton, n.d., quoted in William W. Brewton, *The Life of Thomas E. Watson* (Atlanta: Privately printed, 1926), 367.

27. Watson to Brewton, n.d., in Brewton, *Life of Watson,* 367; Woodward, *Tom Watson,* 15.

28. Box 24, vol. 5, p. 194, Watson Papers, SHC.

29. Clipping from *New York Journal,* n.d., Box 29, vol. 26, ibid.

30. "The Legislative Race," Box 25, vol. 5, ibid.

31. Speech at Athens, Georgia, 25 July 1893, Box 29, vol. 25, ibid.

32. South Georgia Campaign, Murray's Cross-Roads Speech, n.d., ibid.

33. Entry for 8 May 1865, *The Secret Eye: The Journal of Ella Gertrude Clanton Thomas, 1848–1889,* ed. Virginia Ingraham Burr (Chapel Hill: University of North Carolina Press, 1990), 265.

34. Entry for 10 January 1870, ibid., 326–27.

35. William E. Johnson to his brother, 25 August 1880, William Johnson MSS, SCL, USC.

36. Ibid.

37. William Faulkner, *Absalom, Absalom!* (1936; reprint, New York: Library of America, 1990), 9.

38. Johnson to his brother, 25 August 1880, William Johnson MSS, SCL, USC.

39. Sarah Dorsey to Lyulph Stanley, 5 November 1871 (quotation), 1094, Stanley Family MSS, Rylands Library, University of Manchester; John K. Routh, St. Joseph,

25 May, 31 July 1869 (quotation), Tensas Parish, Louisiana, vol. 22, R. G. Dun & Company Archives, Baker Library, Harvard University.

40. Caleb Forshey to St. John Richardson Liddell, 14 March 1869, St. John Richardson Liddell Family MSS, Louisiana State University Library, Baton Rouge.

41. Lizinka Ewell to Campbell Brown, 28 July 1886, Brown-Ewell Family Papers, TSA.

42. *Greenville* (Miss.) *Times*, 18 August 1894.

43. See Bertram Wyatt-Brown, *The Literary Percys: Family History, Gender, and the Southern Imagination* (Athens: University of Georgia Press, 1994), 44–50.

44. See C. Vann Woodward, *Origins of the New South, 1877–1913* (Baton Rouge: Louisiana State University Press, 1951), 72–74.

45. Craig L. Symonds, *Joseph E. Johnston: A Civil War Biography* (New York: Norton, 1992), 326; Nathaniel Cheairs Hughes Jr., *General William J. Hardee: Old Reliable* (Baton Rouge: Louisiana State University Press, 1965), 307–9; Judith Lee Hallock, *Braxton Bragg and Confederate Defeat*, 2 vols. (Tuscaloosa: University of Alabama Press, 1991), 2:263–65.

46. Lizinka Ewell to Campbell Brown, 28 July 1866, Brown-Ewell Family Papers, TSA.

47. William B. Hesseltine, *Confederate Leaders in the New South* (Baton Rouge: Louisiana State University Press, 1950), 16 (quotations).

48. See Daniel E. Sutherland, *The Confederate Carpetbaggers* (Baton Rouge: Louisiana State University Press, 1988), 12, 28, 31–37.

49. Quoted in Kantrowitz, "Shotgun Wedding," 160. At the time of this preparation, Professor Stephen Kantrowitz's valuable published edition of his dissertation work had not yet appeared, but it is entitled *Ben Tillman and the Reconstruction of White Supremacy*, in press at the University of North Carolina Press, 2000.

50. P. D. Hyler to Ellerbe B. C. Cash, 28 September 1881, Cash MSS, SCL, USC.

51. C. Vann Woodward, *The Burden of Southern History*, 3d ed. (1960; reprint, Baton Rouge: Louisiana State University Press, 1993), 190.

CHAPTER TWELVE

1. See Bertram Wyatt-Brown, "Honor," in Ronald Gottesman, ed., *Violence in America: An Encyclopedia*, 3 vols. (New York: Charles Scribner's Sons, 1999), 3:133–38; David T. Courtwright, "Frontier," ibid., 594–600; Richard E. Nisbett and Dov Cohen, *Culture of Honor: The Psychology of Violence in the South* (New York: Westview, 1996).

2. The incident is mentioned in Gary W. Gallagher, ed., *Fighting for the Confederacy: The Personal Recollections of General Edward Porter Alexander* (Chapel Hill: University of North Carolina Press, 1989), 55.

3. William E. Johnson to his brother, 25 August 1880, William Johnson MSS, SCL, USC.

4. Ibid.

5. See *Charleston News and Courier*, 4 August 1880.

6. Ibid., 8 July 1880; *Bishopsville* (S.C.) *Messenger*, 2 July 1964, single issue, Ellerbe B. C. Cash Papers, SCL, USC.

7. Johnson to his brother, 12 July 1880, William Johnson MSS, SCL, USC.

8. *Charleston News and Courier*, 10, 14 July 1880; *Bishopsville Messenger*, 2 July 1964; William Bogan Cash to Colonel John M. Cantry, 26 July 1880, William Johnson MSS, SCL, USC.

9. Johnson to his brother, 12 July 1880, William Johnson MSS, SCL, USC.

10. *Charleston News and Courier*, 7, 8, 9 July 1880.

11. Johnson to his brother, 25 August 1880, William Johnson MSS, SCL, USC.

12. Johnson to his brother 12 July 1880, William Johnson MSS, SCL, USC.

13. Matthew C. Butler to B. R. Riordan and Henry Warrington Dawson, 13 July 1880, letter to the *Charleston News and Courier* reprinted in Ellerbe Bogan Crawford Cash, *The Cash-Shannon Duel* (Greenville, S.C.: Daily News Job Printing Office, 1881), 15–16.

14. *Charleston News and Courier*, 8, 10 July 1880; *Bishopsville Messenger*, 2 July 1880; Johnson to his brother, 12 July 1880, William Johnson MSS, SCL, USC; Cash, *Cash-Shannon Duel*, 14.

15. Knights of Honor, Marlboro Records, 1879–1900, SCL, USC; William Johnson to his brother, 25 August 1880, Johnson MSS, SCL, USC.

16. Johnson to his brother, 25 August 1880, William Johnson MSS, SCL, USC.

17. Johnson, quoted in *Charleston News and Courier*, 13 July 1880.

18. Ibid.

19. *Sumter* (S.C.) *True Southron*, quoted in *Charleston News and Courier*, 15 July 1880.

20. Cash, *Cash-Shannon Duel*, 17.

21. Colonel Ellerbe B. C. Cash, quoted in *Charleston News and Courier*, 7 July 1880.

22. C. G. Simmons to editor of the *Greenville Daily News*, 15 July 1880, in Cash, *Cash-Shannon Duel*, 18.

23. Quoted in Nina Silber, *The Romance of Reunion: Northerners and the South, 1865–1900* (Chapel Hill: University of North Carolina Press, 1993), 154.

24. Ibid. Simmons's rendering of the verse from the litany has a number of misspellings that have been corrected in the text.

25. See Steven Kantrowitz, "The Shotgun Wedding of White Supremacy and Reform in South Carolina," draft dissertation, chapter 3, p. 144, kindly lent by the author.

26. Martin W. Gary to Ellerbe B. C. Cash, 16 December 1880, 28 January 1881, Ellerbe B. C. Cash Papers, SCL, USC.

27. Martin W. Gary to Cash, 12 July 1881, ibid.

28. See N. A. Patterson to Dawson, 3 August 1876, Dawson MSS, SCL, USC; Culpeper Clark, *Francis Warrington Dawson and the Politics of Restoration, South Carolina, 1874–1889* (University: University of Alabama Press, 1980), 63–67.

29. Francis Warrington Dawson, *Reminiscences of Confederate Services, 1861–1865*, ed. Bell I. Wiley (1882; reprint, Baton Rouge: Louisiana State University Press, 1980).

30. Quoted in Kantrowitz, "Shotgun Wedding," from *Charleston News and Courier* as reprinted in *Keowee Courier*, 13 July 1880.

31. *Charleston News and Courier*, 2 July 1880.

32. Clark, *Francis Warrington Dawson*, 115–25; *Charleston News and Courier*, 27 July 1880.

33. Charles H. Moise to Henry Dawson, 11 August 1876, Henry Dawson MSS, SCL, USC.

34. Clark, *Francis Warrington Dawson*, 76. Dawson was himself sued for libeling a Charleston Republican Sheriff: see *The Great Libel Case: Report of the Criminal Prosecution of the News and Courier for Libeling Sheriff and Ex-Congressman C. C. Bowen, The State vs. F. W. Dawson* (Charleston: N.p., 1875) and Clark, *Francis Warrington Dawson*, 41–45.

35. C. W. Dudley to Dawson, 28 November 1877, Dawson MSS, SCL, USC.

36. Martin W. Gary to Dawson, 8 December 1877, Dawson MSS, SCL, USC. See also, W. D. Clancy to Dawson, 8 December, 1877, ibid.

37. Dudley to Dawson, 28 November 1877, ibid.

38. Quoted in Mary Katherine Davis, "Sarah Morgan Dawson: A Renunciation of Southern Society" (M.A. thesis, University of North Carolina, 1970), 68, from *Greenville* (S.C.) *News*, 13 March 1889.

39. *Charleston Sun*, 1 July 1889.

40. S. Frank Logan, "Francis W. Dawson, 1840–1889: South Carolina Editor" (M.A. thesis, Duke University, 1947), 211.

41. Davis, "Sarah Morgan Dawson," 54–77.

42. Ibid., 89.

43. "Gary, Martin Witherspoon," *Dictionary of American Biography*, ed. William Johnson (CD-ROM version; New York: Charles Scribner's Sons, 1931), 4, 177.

44. Logan, "Dawson," 201, 202.

45. Paul A. Hayne to Dawson, 30 December 1877, Dawson MSS, SCL, USC.

46. Thomas Wolfe, quoted in David Donald, "A Generation of Defeat," in *From the Old South to the New*, ed. Walter J. Fraser Jr. and Winfred B. Moore Jr. (Westport, Conn.: Greenwood Press, 1981), 8.

47. Lillian Eugenia Smith, *Killers of the Dream* (New York: Norton, 1949), 133.

48. See Ian Buruma, *The Wages of Guilt: Memories of War in Germany and Japan* (New York: Farrar, Straus and Giroux, 1994); Franziska Seraphim, "Japan's 'Postwar' as Memory Project: World War II, Special Interests, Changing Publics" (Ph.D. diss., Columbia University, 2000), introduction; Peter Novick, *The Holocaust in American Life* (New York: Houghton Mifflin, 1999).

49. Katharine Du Pre Lumpkin, *The Making of a Southerner* (1946; reprint, Athens: University of Georgia Press, 1991), 112, 131–32.

50. Gaines M. Foster, *Ghosts of the Confederacy: Defeat, The Lost Cause, and the Emergence of the New South* (New York: Oxford University Press, 1987), 46; Davis, "Selective Memories of Civil War Atlanta," 750; Novick, *Holocaust*, 278.

51. *Staunton* (Va.) *Spectator* 2 August 1859, in http://jefferson.village.virginia....w2/Browser/aubrowser/ssaug59.html.

52. Robert P. Ingalls, *Urban Vigilantes in the New South: Tampa, 1882–1936* (Knoxville: University of Tennessee Press,1988), 1–5, 20–25, 209 (quotation).

53. Joan E. Cashin, "A Lynching in Wartime Carolina: The Death of Saxe Joiner," in *Sentence of Death: Lynching in the South*, ed. W. Fitzhugh Brundage (Chapel Hill: University of North Carolina Press, 1997), 109 (quotation), 109–31.

54. Neil J. Smelser, *Theory of Collective Behavior* (New York: Free Press, 1962), 8.

55. See Orlando Patterson, *Rituals of Blood: Consequences of Slavery in Two American Centuries* (Washington, D.C.: Civitas, 1999), 171–232.

56. Bertram Wyatt-Brown, *Southern Honor: Ethics and Behavior in the Old South* (New York: Oxford University Press, 1982), 453–61; Fitzhugh Brundage, in Gottesman, ed, *Violence in America*: 3:297–303.

57. Edward McCrady, "Slavery in the Province of South Carolina, 1670–1770," in *Annual Report, American Historical Association for the Year 1895* (Washington, D.C.: U.S. Government Printing Office, 1896), 659.

58. Leon F. Litwack, *Trouble in Mind: Black Southerners in the Age of Jim Crow* (New York: Knopf, 1998), 309–11.

59. Wyatt-Brown, *Southern Honor*, 402–34.

60. Stephen Kantrowitz, "White Supremicist Justice and the Rule of Law," in *Men and Violence: Gender, Honor, and Rituals in Modern Europe and America*, ed. Pieter Spierenburg (Columbus: Ohio State University Press, 1998), 217.

61. For the economic, gender, and other factors, the following studies are highly recommended: Stewart E. Tolnay and E. M. Beck, *A Festival of Violence: An Analysis of Southern Lynchings, 1882–1930* (Urbana: University of Illinois Press, 1995); W. Fitzhugh Brundage, *Lynching in the New South: Georgia and Virginia, 1880–1930* (Urbana: University of Illinois Press, 1993); Nancy MacLean, "The Leo Frank Case Reconsidered: Gender and Sexual Politics in the Making of Reactionary Populism," *Journal of American History* 78 (December 1991): 917–48.

62. Trudier Harris, *Exorcizing Blackness: Historical and Literary Lynching and Burning Rituals* (Bloomington: Indiana University Press, 1984), 19.

63. Litwack, *Trouble in Mind*, 285.

64. *Brooklyn Citizen*, 6 May 1922, in Ralph Ginzberg, *100 Years of Lynchings* (Baltimore: Black Class Press, 1962), 162–63.

65. Patterson, *Rituals of Blood*, 210.

66. *Kissimmee Valley* (Florida) *Gazette*, 28 April 1899, in Ginzberg, *100 Years of Lynching*, 10–11; Litwack, *Trouble in Mind*, 287–93, quotation, 291.

67. Litwack, *Trouble in Mind*, 297.

68. Ibid., 297–98.

69. Joint Select Committee, *The Condition of Affairs in the Late Insurrectionary States:*

Alabama. House Reports, No. 22, pt. 8 (Washington, D.C.: U.S. Government Printing Office, 1872), 1:118–19, 2:757–58.

70. Leon Prather Sr., "We Have Taken a City," in *Democracy Betrayed: The Wilmington Race Riot of 1898 and Its Legacy*, ed. David S. Cecelski and Timothy B. Tyson (Chapel Hill: University of North Carolina Press, 1998), 35–36.

71. See undated newspaper clippings, Scrapbook, vol. 6, pp. 1–17, Alfred Moore Waddell MSS, SHC.

72. Speech reported in 187?, *Philadelphia Day*, 19 January 187?, p. 31, Scrapbook, ibid.

73. Helen G. Edmonds, *The Negro and Fusion Politics in North Carolina, 1894–1901* (Chapel Hill: University of North Carolina Press, 1966), 11–14.

74. Scrapbook, p. 1, Waddell MSS, SHC.

75. See Prather, "We Have Taken a City," 21–22.

76. Quoted in Joel Williamson, *The Crucible of Race: Black-White Relations in the American South since Emancipation* (New York: Oxford University Press, 1984), 199.

77. Thomas W. Clawson, "The Wilmington Race Riot in 1898: Recollections and Memories," ca. 1944, Thomas W. Clawson MSS, SHC.

78. Ibid.

79. Williamson, *Crucible of Race*, 196–201, gives an excellent account of the riot and Rountree's part.

80. Glenda Elizabeth Gilmore, *Gender and Jim Crow: Women and the Politics of White Supremacy in North Carolina, 1896–1920* (Chapel Hill: University of North Carolina Press, 1996), 108–11; Prather, "We Have Taken a City," 15–39, esp. 33. The definitive work on the riot is Leon Prather, Sr., *We Have Taken a City: Wilmington Racial Massacre and Coup of 1898* (Cranbury, N.J.: Associated University Presses, 1984).

81. Waddell quoted in John Haley, "Race, Rhetoric, and Revolution," in *Democracy Betrayed*, ed. Cecelski and Tyson, 208.

82. Clawson, "Wilmington Riot," Clawson MSS, SHC.

83. Appendix to Clawson, "Wilmington Riot," with an affidavit certifying that the copy was accurate in all respects.

84. Haley, "Race, Rhetoric, and Revolution," 208–22.

85. James H. McNeilly, *The Failure of the Confederacy—Was It a Blessing?* (Nashville, Tenn.: Sons of the Confederate Veterans, 1912), 4, 8, 9, 12, 13.

86. Quoted in William R. Majors, *Editorial Wild Oats: Edward Ward Carmack and Tennessee Politics* (Macon, Ga.: Mercer University Press, 1984), 101.

87. Ibid., 146.

88. Julian Pitt-Rivers, front matter, in *Honor and Grace in Anthropology*, ed. John G. Péristiany and Julian Pitt-Rivers (New York: Cambridge University Press, 1992).

APPENDIX

1. George Fenwick Jones, *Honor in German Literature* (Chapel Hill: University of North Carolina Press, 1959). See also George Fenwick Jones, *Honor Bright* (Savan-

nah, Ga.: Frederic C. Beil, 2000), a reexamination of honor in ancient, medieval, and modern Western literature. Curtis Brown Watson, *Shakespeare and the Renaissance Concept of Honor* (Princeton: Princeton University Press, 1960); Edwin Honig, *Calderón and the Seizures of Honor* (Cambridge, Mass.: Harvard University Press, 1972); Frederick R. Bryson, *The Sixteenth-Century Italian Duel: A Study in Renaissance Social History* (Chicago: University of Chicago Press, 1938).

2. Dickson D. Bruce Jr., *Violence and Culture in the Antebellum South* (Austin: University of Texas Press, 1979), and Clement Eaton, "The Role of Honor in Southern Society," *Southern Humanities Review* 10 (supplement 1976): 47–58. I should mention, however, that, without always employing the word *honor* as such, W. J. Cash, *The Mind of the South* (New York: Knopf, 1941), Rollin Gustav Osterweis, *Romanticism and Nationalism in the Old South* (New Haven: Yale University Press, 1949), and John Hope Franklin, *The Militant South, 1800–1861* (Cambridge, Mass.: Harvard University Press, 1956), pioneered studies of the Southern psyche along traditional but not anthropological lines of inquiry.

3. See, for instance, A. Lever, "Honour as Red Herring," *Critique of Anthropology* 6, no. 3 (1985): 333–49; J. R. Llobera, "Fieldwork in Southwestern Europe," *Critique of Anthropology* 6, no. 2 (1986): 502–23; M. Herzfeld, " 'As in Your Own House': Hospitality, Ethnography, and the Stereotype of Mediterranean Society," in *Honor and Shame and the Unity of the Mediterranean*, ed. David Gilmore (Washington, D.C.: American Anthropological Association, 1987), 75–89; Maria Pia Di Bella, "Name, Blood, and Miracles: The Claims to Renown in Traditional Sicily," in *Honor and Grace in Anthropology*, ed. John G. Péristiany and Julian Pitt-Rivers (New York: Cambridge University Press, 1992), 151–65.

4. Christine Heyrman, *Southern Cross: The Beginnings of the Bible Belt* (New York: Knopf, 1997), 216, see also 206–60, and Ted Ownby, *Subduing Satan: Religion, Recreation, and Manhood in the Rural South, 1865–1890* (Chapel Hill: University of North Carolina Press, 1990).

5. Sir Walter Scott, *Essays on Chivalry, Romance, and the Drama: Miscellaneous Prose Works* (Edinburgh: R. Cadell, 1834), 6:48. I am indebted to John Seelye for pointing out Scott's essay and for exploring its ramifications in his as yet unpublished paper, "Ivan Who? Being a Second Look at the Other Book That Is Supposed to Have Started the Civil War."

6. Suzanne Ruggi, "Commodifying Honor in Female Sexuality: Honor Killings in Palestine," *Middle East Report* 28 (Spring 1998): 12–15. Even those raped are executed by family members, while the rapist goes free. A four-year-old child, raped by a twenty-five-year-old, was allowed by her family to bleed to death because she had "dishonored" her family (15).

7. *Atlanta Journal-Constitution*, 25 October 1998, sec. G2.

8. Richard E. Nisbett and Dov Cohen, *Culture of Honor: The Psychology of Violence in the South* (New York: Westview Press, 1996). A sample of social science studies of honor also includes J. G. Péristiany, ed., *Honour and Shame: The Values of Mediterranean Society* (Chicago: University of Chicago Press, 1970); J. K. Campbell, *Hon-*

our, Family, and Patronage: A Study of Institutions and Moral Values in a Greek Mountain Community (New York: Oxford University Press, 1964); David Gilmore, Aggression and Community: Paradoxes of Andalusian Culture (New Haven: Yale University Press, 1987); Ruth Horowitz, Honor and Culture and the American Dream: Culture and Identity in a Chicano Community (New Brunswick, N.J.: Rutgers University Press, 1983); Ruth Horowitz and Gary Schwartz, "Honor, Normative Ambiguity and Gang Violence," American Sociological Review 39 (April 1974): 238–51; Julian Pitt-Rivers, "Honor," International Encyclopedia of the Social Sciences, ed. David L. Sills, 17 vols. (New York: Collier and Macmillan, 1968), 6:503–10; Julian Pitt-Rivers, The Fate of Sechem or the Politics of Sex (Cambridge, Eng.: Cambridge University Press, 1977); Michael Emmison, "Victors and Vanquished," Language and Communications 7, no. 2 (1987): 93–110; Phil Manning, "Ritual Talk," Sociology 23 (August 1989): 365–85. Frank Henderson Stewart, Honor (Chicago: University of Chicago Press, 1994), surveys the field. See also Lila Abu-Lughod, Veiled Sentiments: Honor and Poetry in a Bedouin Society (Berkeley: University of California Press, 1986), 86–87; William Ian Miller, Bloodtaking and Peacemaking: Feud, Law, and Society in Saga Iceland (Chicago: University of Chicago Press, 1996).

9. For examples, see C. Andrew Gerstle, "Heroic Honor: Chikamatsu and the Samurai Ideal," Harvard Journal of Asiatic Studies 57 (December 1997): 307–81, a study of Japanese "honor violence," the playwright Chikamatsu Monzaemon (1653–1725), and the "democratization," as it were, of the ancient ethic; Eiko Ikegami, The Taming of the Samurai: Honorific Individualism and the Making of Modern Japan (Cambridge, Mass.: Harvard University Press, 1995); E. Albanis, "Arthur Schnitzler and the Discourse of Honor and Dueling," Journal of Jewish Studies 49 (Spring 1998): 184–85; Thomas W. Gallant, "Honor, Masculinity, and Ritual Knife Fighting in Nineteenth-Century Greece," paper kindly lent by author and to be published by the American Historical Review; Michael Herzfeld, The Poetics of Manhood: Contest and Identity in a Cretan Mountain Village (Princeton: Princeton University Press, 1985); Elvin Hatch, "Theories of Social Honor," American Anthropologist 91 (June 1989): 341–54; Daniel Boschi, "Homicide and Knife Fighting in Rome during the Nineteenth and Twentieth Centuries," in Men and Violence: Gender, Honor, and Rituals in Modern Europe and America, ed. Pieter Spierenburg (Columbus: Ohio State University Press, 1998), 64–81; Victoria A. Goddard, "From Mediterranean to Europe: Honour, Kinship and Gender," in The Anthropology of Europe: Identity and Boundaries in Conflict, ed. Victoria A. Goddard, Josep R. Llobera, and Cris Shore (Providence, R.I.: Berg, 1994), 52–92.

10. Natalie Zemon Davis, Society and Culture in Early Modern France: Eight Essays (Stanford: Stanford University Press, 1975); Barbara B. Diefendorf and Carla Hesse, eds., Culture and Identity in Early Modern Europe (1500–1800): Essays in Honor of Natalie Zemon Davis (Ann Arbor: University of Michigan Press, 1993).

11. A most useful collection of essays on dueling is Spierenburg, ed., Men and Violence, with essays by Ute Frevert (Germany), Steven Hughes (Italy), and Robert Nye (France). They all show how dueling began in various European countries

among the nobility, then throve in the army officer corps, and, finally, flourished by the nineteenth century in the ranks of the bourgeoisie. See also James Kelly, *That Damn'd Thing Called Honour: Duelling in Ireland, 1570–1860* (Cork, Ireland: Cork University Press, 1995); Robert A. Nye, *Masculinity and Male Codes of Honor in Modern France* (New York: Oxford University Press, 1993); Kevin McAleer, *Dueling: The Cult of Honor in Fin-de-Siècle Germany* (Princeton: Princeton University Press, 1994); Ute Frevert, *Men of Honour: A Social and Cultural History of the Duel*, trans. Anthony Williams (1991; Cambridge, Eng.: Polity Press, 1995); Kirsten Brooke Neuschel, *Word of Honor: Interpreting Noble Culture in Sixteenth-Century France* (Ithaca, N.Y.: Cornell University Press, 1989); David Warren Sabean, *Power in the Blood: Popular Culture and Village Discourse in Early Modern Germany* (New York: Cambridge University Press, 1984); Eul-Soo Pang, *In Pursuit of Honor and Power: Noblemen of the Southern Cross in Nineteenth-Century Brazil* (Tuscaloosa: University of Alabama Press, 1988); Lyman L. Johnson and Sonya Lipsett-Rivera, eds., *The Faces of Honor: Sex, Shame, and Violence* (Albuquerque: University of New Mexico Press, 1998); Ellery Schalk, *From Valor to Pedigree: Ideas of Nobility in France in the Sixteenth and Seventeenth Centuries* (Princeton: Princeton University Press, 1986); Cecilia Morgan, " 'In Search of the Phantom Misnamed Honour': Duelling in Upper Canada," *Canadian Historical Review* 76 (December 1995): 529–62; V. G. Kiernan, *The Duel in European History: Honour and the Reign of Aristocracy* (New York: Oxford University Press, 1988); Antony E. Simpson, "Dandelions on the Field of Honor: Dueling, the Middle Classes, and the Law in Nineteenth-Century England," *Criminal Justice History* 9 (1988): 99–155; Stephen Wilson, "Infanticide, Child Abandonment and Female Honour in Nineteenth Century Corsica," *Comparative Studies in Society and History* 30 (October 1988): 762–83; François Billaois, *The Duel: Its Rise and Fall in Early Modern France* (New Haven: Yale University Press, 1990); Lauro Martines, ed., *Violence and Civil Disorder in Italian Cities* (Berkeley: University of California Press, 1972); Mervyn James, *Family, Lineage, and Civil Society* (Oxford: Oxford University Press, 1986); E. P. Thompson, *Customs in Common: Studies in Traditional Popular Culture* (New York: New Press, 1994); Pieter Spierenburg, "Faces of Violence: Homicide Trends and Cultural Meanings: Amsterdam, 1431–1816," *Journal of Social History* 24 (Summer 1994): 701–16. Orlando Patterson, *Slavery and Social Death: A Sociological Study* (Cambridge, Mass.: Harvard University Press, 1982), explains the ethic of honor as an underpinning of slave societies.

12. Avner Offer, "Going to War in 1914: A Matter of Honor?" *Politics and Society* 23 (June 1995): 213–41; John Keegan, *The First World War* (New York: Knopf, 1999), 48.

13. David Hackett Fischer, *Albion's Seed: Four British Folkways in America* (New York: Oxford University Press, 1989), 866; Michael Lind, *Vietnam, the Necessary War: A Reinterpretation of America's Most Disastrous Military Conflict* (New York: Free Press, 1999); quotations in Ronnie Dugger, *The Politician, the Life and Times of Lyndon Johnson: The Drive for Power, from the Frontier to Master of the Senate* (New York: Norton, 1982), 146, 147.

14. This list could be extended, but these are significant contributions: W. Fitz-

hugh Brundage, *Lynching in the New South: Georgia and Virginia, 1880–1930* (Urbana: University of Illinois Press, 1993); W. Fitzhugh Brundage, ed., *Under Sentence of Death: Lynching in the New South* (Chapel Hill: University of North Carolina Press, 1997). Journal articles of exceptional quality include W. Fitzhugh Brundage, " 'To Howl Loudly': John Mitchell, Jr., and His Campaign against Lynching in Virginia," *Canadian Review of American Studies* 22 (Winter 1991): 325–42; Nancy McLean, "The Leo Frank Case Reconsidered: Gender and Sexual Politics in the Making of Revolutionary Populism," *Journal of American History* 78 (December 1991): 917–48.

15. Elliott J. Gorn, " 'Gouge and Bite, Pull Hair and Scratch': The Social Significance of Fighting in the Southern Backcountry," *American Historical Review* 90 (February 1985): 18–43; Marvin Wolfgang, *The Subculture of Violence* (London: Tavistock, 1967); Elliott J. Gorn, *The Manly Art: Bare-Knuckle Prize Fighting in America* (Ithaca, N.Y.: Cornell University Press, 1986); Laura F. Edwards, "Sexual Violence, Gender, Reconstruction, and the Extension of Patriarchy in Granville County, North Carolina," *North Carolina Historical Review* 68 (July 1991): 249–51; David T. Courtwright, *Violent Land: Single Men and Social Disorder from the Frontier to the Inner City* (Cambridge, Mass.: Harvard University Press, 1996), 27–30. See also Orlando Patterson, *Rituals of Blood: Consequences of Slavery in Two American Centuries* (Washington, D.C.: Civitas, 1998).

16. Edward L. Ayers, *Vengeance and Justice: Crime and Punishment in the Nineteenth-Century American South* (New York: Oxford University Press, 1984); Steven M. Stowe, *Intimacy and Power in the Old South: Ritual in the Lives of the Planters* (Baltimore: Johns Hopkins University Press, 1987), and "The 'Touchiness' of the Gentleman Planter: The Sense of Esteem and Continuity in the Antebellum South," *Psychohistory Review* 8 (Winter 1979): 6–17; Gorn, " 'Gouge and Bite, Pull Hair and Scratch,' " 18–43; Kenneth S. Greenberg, *Masters and Statesmen: The Political Culture of American Slavery* (Baltimore: Johns Hopkins University Press, 1985), and *Honor and Slavery* (Princeton: Princeton University Press, 1996); Douglas L. Wilson, "Lincoln's Affair of Honor," *Atlantic Monthly* 281 (February 1998): 64–71. We should not overlook these classic studies: Sheldon Hackney, "Southern Violence," *American Historical Review* 74 (February 1969): 906–25; Richard M. Brown, *Strain of Violence: Historical Studies of American Violence and Vigilantism* (New York: Oxford University Press, 1975); and Bruce, *Violence and Culture in the Antebellum South.*

17. See Joanne B. Freeman, "Aristocratic Murder and Democratic Fury: Honor and Politics in Early National New England," paper presented at the seventeenth annual meeting of the Society for Historians of the Early American Republic, Vanderbilt University, Nashville, Tenn., July 1996, "Dueling as Politics: Reinterpreting the Hamilton-Burr Duel," *William and Mary Quarterly* 3d ser., 53 (April 1996): 289–318, and a forthcoming monograph, "Affairs of Honor." Cf. Evarts B. Greene, "The Code of Honor in Colonial and Revolutionary Times, with Special Reference to New England," *Publications of the Colonial Society of Massachusetts* 26 (Boston: Colonial Society, 1927): 367–88; Richard L. Bushman, *The Refinement of America: Persons, Houses, Cities* (New York: Knopf, 1992).

18. David Hackett Fischer et al., "*Albion* and the Critics: Further Evidence and Reflection," *William and Mary Quarterly* 3d ser., 48 (April 1991): 260–308, and "Rejoinder," ibid. (October 1991): 608–11.

19. David Roediger and Martin H. Blatt, eds., *The Meaning of Slavery in the North* (New York: Garland, 1998); David R. Roediger, *The Wages of Whiteness: Race and the Making of the American Working Class* (New York: Verso, 1991); Larry E. Tise, *Proslavery: A History of the Defense of Slavery in America, 1701–1840* (Athens: University of Georgia Press, 1987); Gary B. Nash, *Forging Freedom: The Formation of Philadelphia's Black Community, 1720–1840* (Cambridge, Mass.: Harvard University Press, 1988); Gary B. Nash and Jean R. Soderlund, *Freedom by Degrees: Emancipation in Pennsylvania and Its Aftermath* (New York: Oxford University Press, 1991); Leon F. Litwack, *North of Slavery: The Negro in the Free States, 1790–1860* (Chicago: University of Chicago Press, 1961).

20. Leonard L. Richards, "The Question of Slaveholder Domination," kindly lent by the author.

21. Kelly, *That Damn'd Thing Called Honour*; Nye, *Masculinity and Male Codes of Honor in Modern France*; McAleer, *Dueling*; Bertram Wyatt-Brown, *Southern Honor: Ethics and Behavior in the Old South* (New York: Oxford University Press, 1982); Bruce C. Baird, "Dueling and the Origins of the Old South," paper presented at the seventeenth annual meeting of the Society for Historians of the Early American Republic, Vanderbilt University, Nashville, Tenn., July 1996, a prospectus, as it were, of a more thorough work in progress on this topic.

22. Jonathan Z. Smith, *To Take Place: Toward Theory in Ritual* (Chicago: University of Chicago Press, 1987), 13.

23. Charles Laurence Barber, *The Theme of Honour's Tongue: A Study of the Social Attitudes in the English Drama from Shakespeare to Dryden*, Gothenburg Studies in English, vol. 58 (Gothenburg, Germany: Acta Universitatis Gothoburgensis, 1985), 7.

24. Stewart, *Honor*, 130–33; Charles L. Barber entry for "Honor," in *Encyclopedia of Violence* (New York: Scribner, 2000), in press; George Fredrickson, *The Black Image in the White Mind: The Debate on Afro-American Character and Destiny, 1817–1914* (New York: Harper & Row, 1971).

25. Christopher Waldrep, *Roots of Disorder: Race and Criminal Justice in the American South, 1817–80* (Urbana: University of Illinois Press, 1998), 2.

26. Brundage, *Lynching in the New South*; Waldrep, *Roots of Disorder*, 1–2, 25, 29–30, 169. Based on an examination of KKK records in Athens, Georgia, Nancy MacLean, *Behind the Mask of Chivalry: The Making of the Second Ku Klux Klan* (New York: Oxford University Press, 1994), concludes that the upper classes were more involved in Klan activities than previously thought. Studies of the Klan in Mississippi, Texas, and Louisiana would sustain that argument only with modification. Small communities generally shared a common set of values, from the top of the social order to the bottom. Thus a community involvement, in which elements of all classes participated, was often likely. Yet it should be recalled that such wealthy and well-connected individuals as Governor John Parker of Louisiana and the Percys of Greenville, Mis-

sissippi, defied the Klan at considerable personal risk. Moreover, the Klan in Birmingham did not enjoy much upper-class support despite the brief membership of Hugo Black, a young labor lawyer and later a liberal Supreme Court justice. On these states, see Bertram Wyatt-Brown, *The House of Percy: Honor, Melancholy, and Imagination in a Southern Family* (New York: Oxford University Press, 1994), 226–46.

27. See esp. Roy A. Rappaport, *Ecology, Meaning, and Religion* (Richmond, Calif.: North Atlantic Books, 1979), 173–221; David Chaney, "The Spectacle of Honour: The Changing Dramatization of Status," *Theory, Culture and Society* 12 (1995): 147, 152–53; Bertram Wyatt-Brown, "Barnburning and Other Snopesian Crimes: Class and Justice in the Old South," in *Class, Conflict, and Consensus: Antebellum Southern Community Studies*, ed. Orville Vernon Burton and Robert C. McMath Jr. (Westport, Conn.: Greenwood Press, 1981), 173–206; Bertram Wyatt-Brown, "The Old South: A 'Culture of Courage,'" *Southern Studies* 20 (Fall 1981): 213–46.

28. One might find no paradox if the proposition were applied to a Mafia capo in Sicily. In that part of the nineteenth- and twentieth-century world, the conventions and coercions of honor pervaded every aspect of economic and social life, most especially by the alliance of the Cosa Nostra with the landed aristocracy over the peasantry. Religious custom and institutional life also fell under its sway. See Raimondo Catanzaro, *Men of Respect: A Social History of the Sicilian Mafia*, trans. Raymond Rosenthal (New York: Free Press, 1992); Lewis Norman, *The Honoured Society: The Sicilian Mafia Observed* (New York: Verso, 1996); Joseph Farrell, ed., *Understanding the Mafia* (New York: St. Martin's Press, 1997); Anton Blok, *The Mafia of a Sicilian Village, 1860–1960: A Study of Violent Peasant Entrepreneurs* (Oxford: Blackwell, 1974); and Giovanna Fiume, ed., *Onore e Storia nelle Società Mediterranee* (Palermo: La Luna, 1984), which unfortunately has not been translated into English as yet. See esp. Paul Henri Stahl, "L'Onore e il Sacro: Strutture Sociali e Spazi Sacri," ibid., 23–47, also, Paolo Pezzino, "Per una critica dell'onore mafioso: Mafia e codici culturali dal sicilianismo agli scienziati sociali," ibid., 229–48.

ACKNOWLEDGMENTS

I acknowledge with much gratitude those individuals, scholarly institutions, and presses that have made this work possible. The material for the preface passed through several drafts, but I am especially indebted to Jane H. Pease and William H. Pease for their keen eyes and sharp insights into the problems that it engendered. Chapter 1, "Dignity, Deception, and Identity in the Male Slave Experience" has also been thoroughly revised and updated, so much so that its origins in "The Mask of Obedience: Male Slave Psychology in the Old South," *American Historical Review* 93 (December 1988): 1228–55, might only appear largely in the African parts of it. I thank Robert Forbes and David Brion Davis for permitting me the chance to present the more recent material under the title "The Complexities of Male Slave Identity" to the Gilder Lehrman Center for the Study of Slavery, Resistance, and Abolition at Yale University, 11 January 2000. In 1989, the second chapter was first presented at the Conference of Irish Historians, Trinity College, Dublin, under the title "Honor and Republicanism in American Politics, a Neglected Corollary." I am grateful for the permission of Professor Ciaran Brady to make use of the text. He edited *Ideology and the Historians*, Historical Studies 17 (Dublin, Ireland: Lilliput Press, 1991), where it appeared, pp. 49–65. American readers, however, probably are unacquainted with that volume. It drew no comment or criticism from Revolutionary War specialists. The revised and expanded version benefited greatly from the critical readings of Holly Brewer of North Carolina State University and other faculty members and graduate students who participated in a session devoted to it at the North Carolina Early American History Seminar in February 1999.

"Andrew Jackson's Honor," Chapter 3, was originally the presidential address of the Society for Historians of the Early American Republic, July 1996, at Vanderbilt University, Nashville. It was published in the *Journal of the Early Republic* 17 (Spring 1997): 1–36, and permission was obtained for republication. Chapter 4, "Religion and the Unchurched in the Old South," appeared first as "Religion and the 'Civilizing Process' in the Early American South, 1600–1860," in Mark Noll and Joel Carpenter, eds., *Evangelicalism and American Politics* (New York: Oxford University

Press, 1990), 172–95. Oxford University Press is acknowledged for agreeing to an incorporation of material from that piece for this volume. Perhaps no part of the previously published portions of this book, however, has been so thoroughly recast as Chapter 5, "Paradox, Shame, and Grace in the Backcountry." After thirty years, the original article, "The Antimission Movement in the Jacksonian South: A Study in Regional Folk Culture," *Journal of Southern History* 36 (November 1970): 501–29, showed its age and required massive overhaul. I am very much indebted to Beth Barton Schweiger, editor of the *Journal of Southern Religion*, Mark Schantz of Hendrix College, and James L. Peacock of the Anthropology Department of the University of North Carolina. All three gave superb advice and criticism in this lengthier treatment. Mark Schantz in particular opened a number of doors for a better understanding of New Testament scholarship. John Boles, editor of the *Journal of Southern History*, allowed me to use parts of the original essay.

Chapter 6 has been updated in light of new interpretations of the proslavery argument. Its resemblance, however, to "Modernizing Southern Slavery: The Proslavery Argument Reinterpreted," in J. Morgan Kousser and James M. McPherson, eds., *Region, Race, and Reconstruction: Essays in Honor of C. Vann Woodward* (New York: Oxford University Press, 1982), 27–50, is not coincidental. Chapter 7, "Church, Honor, and Disunionism," is the most recently published of them all. Yet I have rethought some of the points raised in the earlier version and have taken advantage of the work of such scholars as Eugene D. Genovese. It was published as "Church, Honor, and Secession," in Randall M. Miller, Harry S. Stout, and Charles R. Wilson, eds., *Religion and the American Civil War* (New York: Oxford University Press, 1998), 89–109. I am grateful to Oxford University Press for permitting much of the text to appear herein. Chapter 8, "Shameful Submission and Honorable Secession," is based in part on my last chapter, "Honor and Secession," in *Yankee Saints and Southern Sinners*, published by Louisiana State University Press in 1985.

Chapters 9, 10, 11, and 12 are the result of recent investigations. They have not appeared in print before. Susan Lewis, Judith Hunt, and Lisa Tendrich, all of the University of Florida History Ph.D. program, as well as Ben Justesen of Alexandria, Virginia, Stephen Kantrowitz, author of the forthcoming *Ben Tillman and the Reconstruction of White Supremacy* (University of North Carolina Press), and James Michael Denham of Florida Southern College aided with materials or criticism to the great improvement of the drafts. I am indebted to Gary Gallagher and Eric Dean, the distinguished Civil War historians, for their considerable assistance with documents and corrections of errors on the military aspects of the Civil War.

I must also acknowledge the generous help of the National Humanities Center, and in particular from W. Robert Connor and Kent Mullikin, director and deputy director. Both have been most encouraging and helpful. I acknowledge with much gratitude the Henry Luce Foundation for having me serve as its Fellow of the year. The administrative staff of the National Humanities Center, including particularly Corbett Capps, Pat Schreiber, Richard Schramm, Crystal Waters, and Sarah Woodard helped greatly to make the year there an inspiration and an unforgettable joy.

With regard to the preparation of the text itself, I am particularly aware of how much Karen Carroll, as the center's resident editor, has contributed to the text. Her careful checking of notes and texts was enormously helpful. Also, I mention Linda Morgan for her computer expertise. Special thanks are given to that indispensable and conscientious library staff —Alan Tuttle, Eliza Robertson, and Jean Houston—for their remarkably imaginative, consistent, and invaluable help. To be selected to join the ranks of fellows at the center is a privilege that I wish could be spread to include every worthy applicant, but that would be physically impossible. In any event, I benefited greatly from the lively transactions in the Biography Seminar, which included Anthony LaVopa, Rochelle Gurstein, Suzanne Raitt, Edward Friedman, Elizabeth McHenry, Marilynn Richtarik, Wilfred Prest, Anne Wyatt-Brown, and Ashraf Rushdy. Quite apart from these colleagues at the center for the year 1998–99, I must mention the assistance on points of information, bibliography, and exchange of ideas that I received from Malcolm Barber of the University of Reading, England, John Watanabe, Dartmouth College, and Robert Bireley, Chicago Loyola. At the University of North Carolina Press, I thank Lewis Bateman, Pam Upton, and Trudie Calvert, whose copyediting revealed a splendid expertise.

My sister-in-law Susan Marbury should have been an editor of academic works; she has a keen eye for structure and logic; she was especially useful in the reorganizing of the two last chapters. With much gratitude I note the contribution of Jack Kirby of Miami University. He read the manuscript with thoroughness and dispatch, offering some invaluable advice. Without his favorable recommendation for its publication, however, the work might not have appeared. Sam S. Hill, professor of religion emeritus, University of Florida, read the chapters that dealt with his specialty and saved me from theological heresy, errors in terminology, and other sins. The late C. Vann Woodward must be mentioned as a constant inspiration in all my work. In his later years, the Sterling Professor Emeritus of History was a model of aging productively and gracefully. It was a distinct honor and source of gratification to have his advice and friendship.

Finally, I mention my wife, Anne, who is always a source of rigorous and well-framed editorial advice and intellectual vigor. More than anyone else, she can discover the larger meanings of materials of which I was only half-consciously aware. I would not be half the scholar I would like to be without her participation in the intellectual conversations in which we seem to be forever happily engaged. This work is dedicated to all the Lauras in the Wyatt-Brown clan, my sister, living in Barnes, London, my mother, and our daughter, whom we continue to remember so fondly after nearly thirty years since her death in 1971 at age seven.

Bertram Wyatt-Brown
Gainesville, Florida
July 2000

INDEX

Abolitionism, 87, 116, 142, 143, 145, 146, 150, 184, 161, 165, 173, 174, 178, 180, 181, 188, 195, 209, 300. *See also* Antislavery

Abstinence, 103

Acedia, 127–28

Adair, Douglas, 48

Adams, John, 39, 49, 52, 53, 325 (n. 80)

Adams, John Quincy, 62, 69, 70, 183, 300

Adams, Nehemiah, 158

Adams, Samuel, 36

Addison, Joseph, 43, 322 (n. 52)

African Americans: and family, 6, 314 (n. 64), 315 (n. 67), 317 (n. 75); killed in response to Emancipation Proclamation, 218; religion of, 93, 94, 258; and Wilmington race riot, 288–91. *See also* Slavery; Slaves

Age of Ambivalence, 101

Age of Custom, 88–89

Age of Fervor, 89, 94

Ahlstrom, Sydney, 154–55

Akin, James, 20–21

Alcohol, 98–99, 102, 104, 122–23, 262–64, 384 (n. 24)

Alcorn, James L., 200

Alexander, Edward Porter, 375 (n. 78)

Allen, Ethan, 44

Allen, Henry Watkins, 235

Allen, John, 36, 53

Alston, Catherine, 234

Alston, Edward, 234

American Bible Society, 119, 350 (n. 78)

American Sunday School Union, 116, 123–24, 129

American Tract Society, 119, 121

Anderson, T. Fuller, 200

Antimodernism, 138

Antislavery, 157, 159, 160, 165, 173, 198; Southern, 352 (n. 7)

Appelfeld, Aharon, 11

Arnold, Benedict, 44–45

Asbury, Francis, 92

Aycock, Charles Brantley, 289

Ayers, Edward, 88, 299

Backus, Isaac, 117

Bacon, Leonard, 162

Bacon's Rebellion, 91

Bailey, F. G., 339 (n. 54)

Bailey, T., 125

Bailyn, Bernard, 321 (n. 36), 325 (n. 90)

Baker, Jean, 193

Baldwin, James, 23

Ball, Charles, 25, 314 (n. 16)

Baptist Home Missionary Society, 119–20

Baptists, 92, 94, 95, 96, 102, 106, 108, 118, 120, 258; and baptism, 96; and family, 110, 114–15; and politics, 155–57; and "right hand of fellowship," 96; and seminary education, 125, 347 (n. 45)

—Primitive, 98, 102, 103, 106–15, 126, 130, 131, 133–34, 346 (n. 37), 347 (n. 46), 350 (n. 76); and church discipline, 113–15, 131; and foot washing, 96, 111–12; geographical distribution of, 112–13; and Jacksonianism, 106–7; oppose secret secular organizations, 134; and religious conversion of women, 110–11; rituals of, 110, 131; secede from Southern Baptists, 134; and Westminister Covenant, 109, 117

Barlow, Francis, 217

Barnes, Albert, 145, 146

Barrow, Bennet, 25

Beauregard, P. G. T., 246

Benjamin, Judah, 268

Benton, Thomas Hart, 75

Berends, Kurt, 207

Bibb, Henry, 27

Bible, xiii, xiv, xv, xviii, 28–29, 53, 84, 85, 87, 88, 92, 108–9, 110, 148, 171, 288; antislavery in, 145, 146; jeremiads in, 84; Paul's teachings in, 85–86, 109, 110, 111, 113, 125, 145, 146; Peter's teachings in, 143

Biddle, Nicholas, 69, 79

Black, Hugo, 395 (n. 26)

"Black Rock Address," 125, 350 (n. 76)

Blair, Frank, 192

Blair, Montgomery, 192

Bledsoe, Albert Taylor, 146

Blount, Roy, Jr., 160

Blount, William, 75, 331 (n. 50), 332 (n. 53)

Blyden, Edward Wilmot, 23

Boles, John, 145

Bourdieux, Pierre, 32

Bourne, George, 145

Bragg, Braxton, 267

Branch, Thomas, 201

Breckinridge, Robert, 169, 170

Brewer, Holly, 42, 322 (n. 50)

Brewster, William, 46

Brooks, Preston, 181, 195–98

Brooks, Whitfield, 197

Brown, Albert Gallatin, 177, 182

Brown, John, xiv, 78, 179, 184, 191

Browning, Orville H, 191, 192

Bruce, Dickson, 296

Bryant, William Cullen, 184

Buchanan, James, 168, 193

Buck, Lucy, 240

Burr, Aaron, 54, 62

Bushman, Richard, 300

Bushnell, Horace, 161–62

Butler, Andrew Pickens, 196

Butler, Jon, 93

Butler, Matthew, 273, 275, 280

Butterfield, Fox, 297

Calderón de la Barca, Pedro, 57

Caldwell, John H., 104

Calhoon, Robert, 45, 323 (n. 61)

Calhoun, John C., xi, 66, 71, 72, 79

Call, Robert Keith, 169

Calvinism, 108, 109, 115, 125–26, 127

Campbell, George W., 63

Caning, 195–97, 333 (n. 73)

Cantey, Jack, 265

Carlyle, Thomas, 138, 180–81

Carmack, Edward Ward, 293, 294, 295

Cartwright, Samuel, 13

Carwardine, Richard, 155, 163

Cash, Ellerbe B. C., 268, 269, 271–79

Cash, William Bogan, 272–73

Cash, W. J., 26

Cashin, Joan, 283–84

Cater, Richard P., 101, 169

Catton, Bruce, 204

"Cavalier," myth of, 179–80, 198, 280–81

Cave, Robert, 180

Celts, traditions of in South, 139, 179–80, 218, 345 (n. 25)

Chamberlain, Daniel H., 277, 278

Chamberlain, Joshua L., ix–xi, 214, 215, 232, 297

Chandler, Thomas, 33

Channing, William Ellery, 165

Chaplains, 174, 206, 208

Charivari, 40, 100, 131–32, 299

Chesnut, James, 246, 275

Chesnut, Mary Boykin, 18, 238, 244, 246, 250, 264

Churches: membership in, 89–90, 94, 95, 101, 120, 132, 134; and politics, 167; and Sunday schools, 116, 123–24, 129, 130. *See also* Religion; *specific denominations*

Cilley, John, 62

Civil War: chaplains in, 174, 206, 208; as cultural factor, xv; dishonor in, 222; effectiveness of troops in, 218–24; end of, 230–54; guerrilla warfare in, 224; medical conditions in, 226–27, 248–50; motivations in, 204–29; and Northern ideology, 213, 214, 215; occupational declension after, 256, 261–62, 265–66; occupational success after, 267–69; and religion, 238, 239, 342 (n. 95), 206–8, 240–42, 253–54; and Southern civilian devastation, 236–37, 242, 245, 246–49, 255; Southern dissent against, 246, 247–48; and Southern ideology, 212; Union treatment of Confederate soldiers in, 231–32. *See also* Confederate Army

Clarke, James S., 188

Clarkson, Thomas, 160

Clawson, Thomas W., 290

Clay, Henry, 69–70, 332 (n. 57)

Clay, Thomas, 144

Cleaver, Eldridge, 23

Clergy, Southern shortage of, 99, 258, 340 (n. 71), 347 (n. 45), 362 (n. 15)

Clingman, Thomas, 187

Cobb, Howell, 233

Cocke, John Hartwell, 103, 347 (n. 41)

Coffee, John, 59, 66, 68, 328 (n. 16)

Cohen, Dov, 217, 297–98

Conditional Unionists, 188, 191, 200

Confederacy: and honor, 89, 237

—defeat of, 191, 230–54; accommodation to, 256; denial of and incredulity over, 235, 236, 240; and disillusionment with politics, 260, 263; as God's condemnation of slavery, 244–45, 293. *See also* Women: and Confederate defeat

Confederate Army: artillery of, 375 (n. 78); and desertion, 211–13, 227–28, 231–32, 237, 245, 251

Conscience. *See* Guilt

"Contrabands," 213

Cooper, Duncan, 294

Cooper, William Frierson, 185

Courtwright, David, 299

Crane, Stephen, 215

Crawford, Anthony, 285

Crockett, David, 347 (n. 46)

Cumming, William, 66

Cunliffe, Marcus, 138

Curtis, James, 74

Dabney, James McBride, 142

Dabney, Robert L., 165, 167

Dabney, Thomas, 252

Davis, David Brion, 24

Davis, Jefferson, 170–71, 172, 174, 180, 189, 199, 201, 208, 218, 224, 233, 234, 242, 246, 268, 293

Davis, Natalie Zemon, 298

Davis, Sarah "Knoxie" Taylor, 189

Dawson, Henry Warrington, 277, 278, 279, 280

Dawson, Sarah Morgan, 240, 279

Day, Samuel Phillips, 179–80

Dean, Eric T., 259

Declaration of Independence, 319 (n. 11)

Defoe, Daniel, 47

DePass, J. W., 272

Depression, 7, 8, 217; and Confederate defeat, 233–54 passim, 255–67; and

Civil War, 173–74, 188–91, 201–2, 203, 240–43, 266, 272
deSilva, David Arthur, 87
Dew, T. R., 152
Dexter, Henry, 198
Dickinson, Charles Henry, 58, 59–61, 67, 68, 329 (n. 25)
Dickinson, John, 326 (n. 92)
Donald, David H., 204, 226, 281–82, 376 (n. 92)
Dorsey, Sarah, 172, 174, 236, 266
Doughfaces, 185
Douglas, Stephen, 185, 193, 196, 370 (n. 55)
Douglass, Frederick, 16, 23–24, 25
Doyle, Don, 100
Du Bois, W. E. B., 24, 315 (n. 65)
Dudley, C. W., 278
Dueling, 43, 56, 57, 59–62, 64, 66–69, 72, 75, 164, 186–87, 190, 195, 197, 235–36, 271–77, 284, 299–300, 331 (nn. 48, 52), 332 (n. 56), 333 (n. 73)
Du Picq, Ardent, 222
Duty, 212, 213–14, 263
Dwight, Timothy, 127

Early, Jubal, 212
Earnest, William S., 187
Easton, Hosea, 10
Eaton, Clement, 296
Eaton, John H., 66, 71
Eaton, Peggy Timberlake, 71
Edwards, Jonathan, 117, 126
Edwards, Laura, 299
Edwards, Linda, 299
Eggleston, George Cary, 226, 241–42
Elias, Norbert, 91
Elkins, Stanley, xvi, 5, 6, 7, 8, 17, 21, 25, 307 (n. 11), 316 (n. 68)
Ellerbe, Robert, 272
Elliott, E. N., 160
Elliott, Stephen, 84, 136

Ellison, Ralph, 23
Elmore, J. A., 187
Elyot, Thomas, 48
Emancipation Proclamation, 213, 218; white reaction to, 233, 260, 261
Emerson, James, 50
Empson, William, 213–14
Endith, John, 129
Engerman, Stanley, 140
Entail, 41–42
Episcopalians, Southern (Anglicans), 84, 89–90, 92, 168, 170, 364 (n. 40); and honor, 90–91
Erikson, Erik, 5
Ervin, Joseph, 59, 61, 70
Evangelicals, 85, 96, 99, 100, 107, 116, 118, 119, 120, 120, 126, 130, 133; and politics, 156–64; Southern, 104
Evans, Israel, 48
Evarts, Jeremiah, 130
Ewell, Lizinka Brown, 246, 251, 256, 267–68
Ewell, Richard, 242–43, 246, 251, 267–68

Farmer, James O., 165
Faulkner, William, 28, 104–5, 241, 265–66
Faust, Drew Gilpin, 157, 160
Feltman, William, 93
Ferguson, Samuel Wragg, 267
Finney, Charles Grandison, 107
Fire-eaters, 104, 181, 184, 190, 247
Fischer, David Hackett, 298, 300
Fish, Carl, 252
Fish, Hamilton, 191
Fithian, Philip, 95
Fitzhugh, George, 139, 143, 160
Fletcher, William, 209, 215–16, 221, 225, 228, 249
Fogel, Robert, 140
Ford, Timothy, 52

Formisano, Ronald P., 331 (n. 50)
Forrest, Nathan Bedford, 226, 235, 267
Forshey, Caleb, 266
Fort Pillow, 235
Fort Sumter, 156, 188, 193, 200
Foster, Gaines M., 361 (n. 7)
Foster, Thomas, 4, 21, 29
Franz Ferdinand (prince of Austro-Hungary), 191, 298
Franz Josef (emperor of Austro-Hungary), 190, 298
Frazier, Charles, 228, 230, 232, 249
Fredrickson, George M., 302, 360 (n. 90)
Freedmen: and politics, 268–69
Freehling, William W., 113, 345 (n. 26), 358 (n. 61), 365 (n. 54)
Freeman, Joanne, 54, 300
Free-Soil, 161
French, Samuel, 236
Freud, Anna, 12
Frevert, Uta, 186
Frey, Sylvia, 15, 310 (n. 38)
Friedrich, Paul, 87
Fugitive Slave Law, 157, 161
Fuller, Andrew, 117
Fuller, Richard, 145, 146, 156, 160, 163
Furman, James C., 169

Gadsden, Christopher, 52
Gaines, Ernest J., 23
Gallant, Thomas W., xviii–xix
Garrett, Thomas Miles, 86
Garrison, William Lloyd, 116, 150, 184, 195, 196
Gary, Martin W., 276, 278, 280, 295
Gates, Henry Louis, 14–15
Gates, Horatio, 44
Gay, Peter, 79
Genovese, Eugene D., 23, 143, 144, 353 (n. 11), 354 (n. 23), 360 (n. 90)

Gienapp, William, 198
Gilbert, Martin, 9
Gilje, Paul, 40
Gill, John (of England), 117, 126
Gill, John (of South Carolina), 169
Goen, C. C., 155, 361 (n. 8)
Going, Jonathan, 119, 347 (n. 41)
Gomez, Michael, 9
Gooch, William, 91
Gordon, John B., ix–x, 207, 297
Gordon, Thomas, 43, 51
Gordon, William, 39
Gorgas, Josiah, 234, 242
Gorn, Elliott, 299
Goulding, Thomas, 169
Grace, 126, 197, 304; defined, xii–xv, 116. See also Religion
Granbery, John Cowper, 167
Grant, Ulysses S., ix, 190, 223, 231, 246
Graves, William J., 62
Grayson, William J., 96
Greeley, Horace, 159–60, 236
Greenback Party, 268–69
Greenberg, Kenneth S., 299
Greene, Nathanael, 45, 46
Gregg, Maxcey, 177
Griffith, Paddy, 219, 228
Grimes, Bryant, 212, 240
Grimké, Thomas S., 128
Grossman, David, 219–20
Guilt, 128, 137, 142, 146, 159, 296–97, 313 (n. 59)
Gutman, Herbert G., 5, 315 (n. 67)

Hahn, Stephen, 194
Hall, Robert, 117, 126
Hamilton, Alexander, 46, 49, 62
Hamilton, W. T., 147
Hammond, James Henry, 65, 147, 160–61, 185, 190
Hampton, Wade, 276, 278, 286
Hancock, John, 36, 51

Hardee, William J., 267

Hardy, Thomas, 220

Harrington, James, 39

Harrison, Burton, 268

Harvie, Lewis, 172

Hatton, Robert, 185

Hawthorne, Nathaniel, 138

Hayne, Paul A., 280

Haynes, Stephen R., xiii, 306 (n. 7)

Hazard, Ebenezer, 312 (n. 50)

Heartsill, William, 210–11, 216

Henderson, Samuel, 104, 172

Henry, Patrick, 322 (n. 52)

"*Herrenvolk* democracy," 302

Hesseltine, William B., 268

Heyrman, Christine, 94, 95, 111, 297

Hill, Samuel S., 101, 137

Hirschman, Albert, 32

Hodge, Charles, 160, 162, 164

Hoge, Moses, 165

Holcombe, Hosea, 134

Holden, William W., 212–13, 243

Holmes, Emma, 256

Holmes, George Frederick, 158, 160

Holmes, William F., 299

Holocaust. *See* Nazism

Honor: and African American identity, 3–4, 11, 14–17, 21, 26–28, 314 (n. 60); American, 212; and American Revolution, 31–55, 183–84, 187, 200, 322 (n. 47); and anti-honor, 88, 95; and classical learning, 38, 48, 49, 50, 88, 195, 325 (n. 80); as commodity, 339 (n. 54); and Confederacy, 89, 237; and defeat, 172, 174, 211, 230–31, 234–36, 239–40, 242, 249, 260, 282; defined, xii–xv, 303; and democracy, 79, 103, 107, 376 (n. 92); and fame, 48, 56, 103, 173, 302, 343, 324 (n. 73), 333 (n. 73); German, 186–87, 297; and historical neglect, 31, 41, 296; and Andrew Jackson, 78–80; and kinship, 201,

202, 205, 284; and manliness, xviii, 5, 35–38, 40, 48, 103–4, 178, 209, 211, 212, 214, 215, 217, 280, 293, 305 (n. 5); and military, ix–xi, 41, 43, 44, 45, 209–12, 299; and nation-state, 32, 33, 289; Near Eastern, 297, 302; Northern, 191–92; and political patriarchy, 34, 35, 46, 47, 50, 51, 64, 66, 194; and religion, 53, 56, 83–88, 89, 96, 104, 119, 133, 167, 171, 172–73, 345 (n. 25); and republicanism, 32, 35, 50; royal, 191; and secession, 154, 166, 177–78, 183–88, 370 (n. 55); and slavery, 326 (n. 92); and taxation, 37–38, 40, 245, 320 (n. 28); and violence, 52, 94, 270–95, 303; and white supremacy, 52, 103, 278–95, 304; and women, 75, 77, 79, 103, 211, 245, 250

Hooker, Richard, 123

Hopkins, Keith, 311 (n. 49)

Hopkins, Samuel, 127

Horney, Karen, 23

Horseshoe Bend, battle of, 57

Hotspur, Harry, 44, 167

Hotzendorff, Conrad von, 190–91

Houston, Sam, 187

Howe, Robert, 44

Howison, Robert R., 42

Hughes, Henry, 138, 148–53, 359 (nn. 67, 76), 360 (nn. 81, 84)

Hughes, Steven, 64

Huizinga, Johann, 97

Huntington, Enoch, 39

Hutchinson, Thomas, 37

Hyler, P. D., 269

Ibrahima, Abd al-Rahman, 3–5, 9, 11, 13, 14, 15–17, 18, 21, 29, 317–18 (n. 87)

"Invulnerable child," 73

Isaacs, Rhys, 108, 117

Islam, 309 (n. 32), 311 (nn. 45, 46)

Jackson, Andrew, xiv, xvi, 54–55, 56–
    80, 106, 119, 122, 125, 132, 137,
    293; childhood of, 74; duels with
    C. Dickinson, 58–61, 329 (n. 24);
    duels with Sevier, 75; health of,
    74–76; and honor, 56–80; and Jack-
    sonianism, 107, 300, 302; and Native
    Americans, 57–58, 75–76; and reli-
    gion, 79–80, 165, 168, 240–42;
    and Spanish oath of allegiance, 327
    (n. 4)
Jackson, Andrew, Jr. (Lyncoya), 76
Jackson, Elizabeth, 73–74, 78–79
Jackson, Hugh, 72–73
Jackson, Rachel Donelson, 56, 60,
    74–76
Jackson, Robert, 73
Jackson, Thomas H. "Stonewall," 174,
    207, 287
Jefferson, Thomas, 38, 42, 47, 54, 63,
    147, 150, 312 (n. 50)
Jemison, Robert, 187–88
Jeremiads, 84
Jeter, Jeremiah, 142
Jim Crow, 153
Johnson, Andrew, 192, 243, 258, 260
Johnson, Frank, xiii
Johnson, Lyndon B., 299
Johnson, Richard Mentor, 132
Johnson, Samuel, 50
Johnson, William, 264, 265, 266, 273
Johnston, Joseph E., 231, 236, 237,
    251, 252, 267
Joiner, Saxe, 283
Jones, Charles Colcock, 141, 143–44
Judson, Adoniram, 119, 347 (n. 41)

Kammen, Michael, 41
Kantrowitz, Stephen, 286
Keegan, John, 298
Keitt, Lawrence, 177, 179, 181, 195,
    197–98
Keitt, Susan, 178

Kelly, James, 301
Kenny, Lucy, 142
Kenzer, Robert, 194
Kercheval, Samuel, 91
Kettering, Sharon, 330 (n. 41)
Key, Francis Scott, 120, 347 (n. 41)
King, John, 287
King, Martin Luther, Jr., xiii
King, Wilma, 11
Kingsley, Charles, 138
Kirby Smith, Edmund, 237–38
Knott, Josiah, 143
Knox, Henry, 45
Kolchin, Peter, 25
Ku Klux Klan, 134, 270, 271, 286–87,
    288, 290, 303, 304, 394 (n. 26)

Landsberg, Paul Louis, 7
Langdon, Samuel, 37
Langer, Lawrence L., 7
Latner, Richard B., 332 (n. 59)
Latrobe, Benjamin, 67, 347 (n. 41)
Laurens, Henry, 44
Lawrence, Joshua, 128, 129
Lears, Jackson, 255
Lee, Mary Anne Custis, 205
Lee, Robert E., ix, xiv, 202, 223, 242,
    243, 247, 251, 257; allegiance to,
    202, 205; surrender of, 234, 235,
    240
Leinbaugh, Harold P., 221
LeJau, Francis, 92, 94
Leo XIII (pope), 279
Levi, Primo, 8, 27
Lewis, Taylor, 158–59
Lewis, William B., 66
Lincoln, Abraham, xiv, 78, 112, 156,
    167, 168, 173, 178, 180, 182, 183,
    184, 187, 190, 201, 205, 208, 209,
    213; assassination of, 231; duels with
    Shields, 299–300
Linderman, Gerald F., 204, 214
Litwack, Leon F., 29, 286–87

Logan, John, 231
Longstreet, James, 235, 250
Lost Cause, 246, 264, 265, 282, 294,
    306 (n. 10)
Lumpkin, Katherine Du Pre, 21, 233,
    282
Lumpkin, William, 282
Lumpkin, Wilson, 132
Lynching, 268, 270–71, 283, 284, 285,
    286, 287, 291–92
Lyon, James, 147

McAleer, Kevin, 298, 301
McCauley, Deborah, 98, 111, 115, 130,
    135
McCurry, Stephanie, 114
McDonald, Forrest, 43, 49, 324 (n. 78)
McDow, Thomas, 279
McDuffie, George, 66, 189, 190
Machiavelli, Niccolò, 38, 50
McKenzie, John, 35
MacLean, Nancy, 394 (n. 26)
McLeod, Duncan J., 326 (n. 92)
McNairy, Nathaniel, 60, 68, 328 (n. 16)
McNeilly, James, 292
McPherson, James M., 204, 212, 213,
    214
MacRae, Walter G., 291
McWhiney, Grady, 218–19
Madison, James, 54
Mafia, 395 (n. 28)
Manliness, xviii, 5, 35–38, 40, 48,
    102, 103–4, 178, 209, 211, 212, 214,
    215, 217, 280, 293, 304, 305 (n. 5);
    and wounded Confederate soldiers,
    250–51
Manly, Basil, 130–31
Manly, Basil, Jr., 131
Marryat, Frederick, 23
Marshall, Anne Lee, 205
Marshall, John, 120
Marshall, Samuel Lynn, 221–22
Martin, James Kirby, 44

Martyn, Charles, 93
Mathews, Donald H., 85
Mayhew, Jonathan, 51
Meltzer, Bernard N., 316 (n. 68)
Melville, Herman, 138
Memminger, Christopher, 143
Methodists, 87, 94, 95, 96, 100, 102,
    104, 118, 119, 120, 124, 130, 155,
    157, 164, 171
Mexican War, 161, 197, 199
Michelbacher, M. J., 171
Middleton, Harriott, 239
Miles, William Porcher, 190
Mills, Samuel J., 121
Milton, John, 253–54
Mitchell, Reid, 214
Moise, Charles H., 277–78
Moltke, Helmuth von, 190
Monroe, James, 71
Montesquieu, Charles Louis de
    Secondat, baron de, 34, 35, 53
Montgomery, Richard, 49
Moore, A. B., 187
Moore, Roger B., 290
Moore, Samuel Preston, 234
Moore, W. D., 152, 153
Moorhead, James, 172
Moravians, 94
Morgan, Philip, 15, 27
Morgan, Sarah, 240, 279
Morrill, Justin S., 182
Morris, Christopher, 317 (n. 76)
Mosby, John, 243
Mowat, Henry, 33
Moxnes, Halvor, 88
Moynihan, Daniel Patrick, 5

Nazism, xvi, 5, 6, 7, 8, 9, 16, 18, 19, 27,
    303, 308–9 (n. 33)
New South, boosterism for, 277–78,
    286
Nisbett, Richard, 217, 297–98
Norbert, Elias, 91

Nose-pulling, 78
Nott, Josiah, 359 (n. 74)
Novick, Peter, 283
Nullification, 79, 100–101, 125
Nye, Robert, 298, 301

Oakes, James, xi
Oath-taking, 40, 41, 79, 261, 327 (n. 4)
O'Brien, Michael, 190
Occupational declension, postbellum, 256, 261–62, 265–66
Occupational success, postbellum, 267–69
Offer, Avner, 298
Okoye, F. Nwabueze, 325–26 (n. 90)
O'Neall, John Belton, 13, 347 (n. 41)
Otey, James, 167–69, 173
Otis, James, 38
Overton, John, 60–61, 66, 68, 333 (n. 73)
Owens, Claire Myers, 234–35
Ownby, Ted, 97, 103, 123, 133, 297

Page, Walter Hines, 276
Paine, Thomas, 36
Palmer, Benjamin, 87, 103, 169–70, 171, 238, 241, 244
Palmer, Harriet, 238, 251
Palmer, Philip, 251, 257
Palmer, Robert R., 169–70, 171, 320 (n. 28)
Palmer, Thomas, III, 251, 257
Paris, John, 245
Parker, Daniel, 112, 127
Parker, John, 394–95 (n. 26)
Parton, James, 60, 62, 328 (n. 24)
Patriarchy, 34, 35, 46, 47, 50, 51, 64, 66, 167, 194
Patron-client relations, 62–72, 75, 195, 331 (n. 50), 332 (n. 53)
Patterson, Beverly Bush, 131
Patterson, Orlando, 10, 18, 50, 287, 315 (n. 67), 361 (n. 7)

Patton, Robert, 250
Peacock, James, 115, 123, 127
Peck, John M., 129
Pegram, Mary, 266
Pendleton, Edmund, 42
"People's timocracy," 79
Percy, Leroy, 394–95 (n. 26)
Perry, Benjamin, 260
Pessen, Edward, 332 (n. 57)
Petigru, James L., 140
Phelps, Amos A., 165
Philadelphia Association, 116–17
Philips, Ethelred, 235, 254, 256–57
Phillips, Ulrich B., 199–200
Phillips, Wendell, 181
Pickett, George, 222, 243
Pinckney, Charles, 54
Pitt-Rivers, Julian, 37, 63, 209, 295, 343 (n. 3)
Polk, Leonidas L., 172, 174
Poor, Enoch, 48
Populists, 263
Porter, R. K., 87
Post-traumatic stress disorder, 6, 203, 227, 255–56, 257–58, 259, 307 (n. 11)
Power, Tracy, 237
Prentiss, S. S., 190
Presbyterians, 87, 94, 98, 103, 119, 120, 133, 147, 157, 165–66, 169–70, 358 (n. 61)
Preston, John S., 195, 201
Price, Sterling, 259
Pringle, Edward J., 353 (n. 12)
Privacy, lack of, 91, 101–2; and slavery, 93
Proslavery argument, 101, 136–53, 292–93, 353 (n. 11, 12, 15), 355 (n. 32), 358 (n. 61), 361 (n. 7, 8); and evangelicalism, 140, 143, 144, 146, 147, 156–57, 161–62, 170; and improvements in slavery, 139–40, 158, 163; as modernist rationale,

146–47; as scientific racism, 143; secular, 138, 139, 141, 148–53

Prosser, Gabriel, 27, 28
Pugh, George, 193

Quincy, Josiah, 31, 36, 50
Quitman, John A., 360 (n. 81)

Rabun, William, 77
Racism, 3–31, 217–18, 282–84; and Confederate defeat, 247–48; and Redeemers, 269, 270–71, 276, 278, 280, 286
Randolph, Robert Beverly, 77–78
Ravenel, Henry William, 16
Ray, Nicholas, 37
Redeemers, 269, 278, 303
Redpath, James, 180, 181
Reid, Whitelaw, 235, 242
Reisman, Paul, 11
Religion: and democracy, 118; and slave conversions, 123, 134, 136–37, 143, 145; and slave rebellion, 95; and slave rights, 101; and white violence, 89–91, 92–93, 94, 97, 98, 99, 103, 110–11, 287–88, 291–92. See also Churches
Remini, Robert V., 62, 73, 75–76, 101, 327 (n. 4)
Republicans, 174, 185, 187, 191–93, 200, 218, 260, 271, 278, 298
Revivals, 96–97, 116–17, 258; Confederate, 206–8, 345 (n. 25), 346 (n. 37)
Rhett, Robert Barnwell, Jr., 177, 278
Rice, Luther, 119, 121, 347 (n. 41)
Richards, Leonard L., 300–301, 330 (n. 44)
Richter, Melvin, 32
Rivers, W. H. R., 307 (n. 11)
Robards, Lewis, 75
Robato, Rosa, 28
Rose, Willie Lee, 140, 142

Routh, John Knox, 266
Royall, Anne, 102
Royster, Charles, 44
Rudyerd, Benjamin, 89
Ruffin, Edmund, 168, 188–89, 190, 254
Ruffin, Thomas, 159
Ruggi, Susan, 297
Ruggles, Daniel, 224
Runnels, Hiram G., 100
Rutledge, Francis H., 168–69
Rutman, Anita, 92
Rutman, Darrett, 89, 92
Ryan, Abram, 294
Ryan, Mary, 101

Sabbatarianism, 133, 165
Sambo, stereotype of: ancient, 311–12 (n. 49); docility of, 5, 10, 13, 14, 16–26; psychology of, 141–42, 313 (n. 57), 314 (n. 61), 315 (n. 68), 316 (n. 68); submission, 143, 146
Schantz, Mark S., 347–48 (n. 47), 376 (n. 84)
Schermerhorn, John F., 121
Schurz, Carl, 232–33, 243
Schweiger, Beth Barton, 137, 158
Scott, Sir Walter, 138, 139, 181–82, 189, 297
Secession, 155–56, 167–73, 177–202, 370 (n. 55)
Second Great Awakening, 96–97, 116
Seger, William, 302
Sellers, Charles Grier, Jr., 156
Servility. See Sambo, stereotype of
Sevier, John, 75, 333–34 (n. 77)
Seward, William H., 199
Shakespeare, William, xvii, 44
Shame, 313 (n. 59); African American, 22, 23, 25, 26; and Christianity, 85–86, 88, 128; and Confederate defeat, xvii, 233–35, 240, 249, 283; and secession, 177–78

Shamelessness, 296–97, 304; African American, 19, 20–24, 26, 27
Shannon, Gorm, 265
Shannon, William, 265, 266, 271–77
Sherman, William Tecumseh, 190, 231, 236, 246, 247
Shields, James, 299
Shook, Alfred M., 267
Sidbury, James, 18
Sidney, Algernon, 50–51
Simmons, C. G., 275
Simmons, George F., 147, 148
Simms, William Gilmore, 161, 189–90, 197
Slavery, 3–30, 92–94; African, 309 (n. 28), 312 (n. 49); as cause for secession, 177–79; dehumanizing aspects of, 93; as God-sanctioned, 138, 145–46, 176–77; justification for, 139–42; and legal rights, 141, 354 (n. 23); and misapportionment of national power, 182–84; as psychological control, 143–44, 316 (n. 74). *See also* Slaves
Slaves: families of broken up, 354 (nn. 18, 19); punishments of, 3–30, 92–93, 143–44; trade in, 9, 10, 11, 12, 25, 151–53, 355 (n. 27); as tricksters, 15, 18–21; whippings of, 24–25
—oppression of, xviii, 6–9, 10, 11, 12, 21–23, 26–27, 309 (n. 23), 312 (n. 50); resistance to, 7, 17, 316 (n. 68), 318 (n. 87). *See also* Slavery
Smelser, Neil J., 284
Smith, F. Pershine, 191
Smith, H. Shelton, 358 (n. 62)
Smith, Jonathan Z., 301
Smith, Lillian, 281
Smyth, Thomas, 160, 163, 171, 172–73
Society for the Propagation of the Christian Gospel, 90, 92
Southern Honor, 301
Sovine, Melanie, 126

Sparks, Randy, 343 (n. 2)
Staël, Madame Anne-Louise-Germaine de, 48
Stamp Act, 33, 39
Stanislavski, Constantin, 22, 24
States' rights, 179–80
Steele, Richard, 48
Stephens, Alexander H., 179, 182, 185, 193
Stephenson, Philip, 248, 251
Stevenson, Brenda, 26
Stewart, Frank Henderson, 107, 302, 343 (n. 3)
Stoll, Daniel W., 342 (n. 95)
Stout, Harry, 100
Stowe, Steven M., 299
Styles, Carey W., 225
Styron, William, 23
Suicide, 7, 8, 189–90, 252–53, 273–74
Sullivan, John, 45
Sumner, Charles, 190, 195–98
Sutherland, Daniel E., 315 (n. 67)
Swann, Thomas, 59, 60, 328 (n. 16)

Tappan, Arthur, 165
Tappan, Lewis, 121, 165
Taubenschlag, Stanislaw, 18, 19
Taylor, John (of Caroline), 122
Taylor, John (of Kentucky), 109, 119, 121, 122, 123–24
Thacher, Peter, 36
Thomas, Ella, 264
Thoreau, Henry David, 138
Thornton, J. Mills, 65, 352 (n. 9)
Thornwell, James Henley, 103, 148, 150, 155, 157–58, 160, 161, 162, 165, 167, 173, 174, 184
Tillman, Benjamin R., 280, 286, 295
Tise, Larry E., 156, 355 (n. 32)
Toombs, Robert, 189, 198–99
Tories, 319 (n. 11)
Trenchard, John, 39
Trollope, Frances, 93

12

Trumbull, John, 45
Tucker, Nathaniel Beverly, 158, 189
Turner, Nat, 23, 28
Twain, Mark, 284–85
Tyson, Ruel, 115, 123, 127

Van Buren, Martin, 71–72, 132
Vance, Zebulon, 243–44
Vandiver, Frank, 142
Van Dyke, Henry J., 158
Vaughn, John C., 128, 129
Verot, Augustin, 244
Vesey, Denmark, 27, 28
Vietnam War, 299

Waddell, Alfred Moore, 288–91
Waldrep, Christopher, 303
Walker, Alice, 23
Wall, Joseph, 283
Ward, Artemus, 235
Warren, Joseph, 37
Washington, George, 40, 45, 46, 47,
    49, 53, 150, 207, 324–25 (n. 79)
Watson, John Smith, 262–63
Watson, Thomas, 262–63, 294, 295
Wayland, Francis, 145, 160, 346 (n. 39)
Webb, James Watson, 195
Webber, Thomas L., 314 (n. 61)
Wecter, Dixon, 256
Weitz, Mark, 215
Wells, Richard, 37
West, Benjamin, 93
Westminister Covenant, 109, 117
White, Graham, 15
White, Shane, 15
Wigfall, Louis T., 178, 189, 190
Wiley, Bell I., 204, 212, 228, 372 (n. 4)
Wiley, Calvin, 144, 147, 358 (n. 61)
Wilhelm I (emperor of Germany), 186,
    190–91
Wilhelm II (emperor of Germany),
    186, 298

Willcox, Orlando B., 246
Williams, Abraham, 33
Williams, John Sharp, 237
Wills, Gregory, 113–14
Wilmington, N.C.: race riot in, 288–91
Wilmot Proviso, 199
Wilson, Joseph, 148
Witchcraft, 89
Witt, Daniel, 155
Wolf, Eric, 63
Wolfe, Margaret Ripley, 249
Wolfe, Thomas, 281
Women, xviii–xix; and alcohol, 99;
    anti-Northern, 239–40; blamed for
    war loss, 238–39, 245; and Confed-
    erate defeat, 238, 252–53, 257–58,
    266; and Confederate desertion,
    211–12, 237; and Lost Cause, 292,
    306 (n. 10); men fear, 237; and
    petitions for discharges, 239, 245;
    pro-war, 239, 240; and religion, 97,
    134, 207, 238; slave, xviii; and vol-
    untarism, 341 (n. 77); and war, 207,
    211, 226–27; and wounded veterans,
    250–51
Wood, Forrest G., 144
Wood, Gordon, 31, 275, 325 (n. 83)
Woodmason, Charles, 98
Woodward, C. Vann, 153, 262, 269
World War II, 221–22
Worth, Jonathan, 202
Worthington, Amanda, 238
Wright, Obed, 77
Wright, Richard, 22, 23

Yancey, William L., 187, 189, 190, 193,
    199, 360 (n. 81)
Yazawa, Melvin, 37
Yeomanry, 195, 224–25, 227, 245, 247,
    263, 285